THE ONS

TIM PARKS

ITALIAN NEIGHBOURS

AND

AN ITALIAN EDUCATION

VINTAGE

Other authors in the series

STEPHEN FRY
CHARLES HANDY
ROBERT HARRIS
JAMES HAWES
ANNE TYLER

By Tim Parks

Fiction

Tongues of Flame
Loving Roger
Home Thoughts
Family Planning
Goodness
Cara Massimina
Shear
Mimi's Ghost
Europa

Non-fiction

Italian Neighbours
An Italian Education
Adultery & Other Diversions

Tim Parks is the author of seven novels and has been awarded the John Llewellyn Rhys Prize, the Somerset Maugham Award and the Betty Trask Award. His most recent novel, *Europa*, was shortlisted for the 1997 Booker Prize. He is also the author of two bestselling works of non-fiction, *Italian Neighbours* and *An Italian Education*. He has lived in Italy since 1981.

ITALIAN NEIGHBOURS

An Englishman in Verona

TIM PARKS

VINTAGE

Published by Vintage 1999

2 4 6 8 10 9 7 5 3 1

First published in Great Britain in 1992 by
William Heinemann Limited

Vintage
Random House, 20 Vauxhall Bridge Road,
London SW1V 2SA

Random House Australia (Pty) Limited
20 Alfred Street, Milsons Point, Sydney
New South Wales 2061, Australia

Random House New Zealand Limited
18 Poland Road, Glenfield, Auckland 10, New Zealand

Random House South Africa (Pty) Limited
Endulini, 5A Jubilee Road, Parktown 2193, South Africa

Random House, UK Limited Reg. No. 954009

A CIP catalogue record for this book
is available from the British Library

ISBN 0 7493 1102 9

Papers used by Random House UK Limited are natural, recyclable products made from wood grown in sustainable forests. The manufacturing processes conform to the environmental regulations of the country of origin

Printed and bound in Great Britain by
Mackays of Chatham plc, Chatham, Kent

Author's Note

I often find it useful, or at least amusing, to think of a book in terms of a gesture, a mood, a posture. In which case the gesture of this book might be that of a busy but inexpert fellow dashing about the narrow confines of his territory waving a net on the end of a long stick. It's not a butterfly net, by the looks of it. It's altogether too big for that, huge in fact. But it might be a will-o'-the-wisp net. Which would explain the extremely fine silk mesh, the random way it is being waved. And if we were to ask this frantic fellow what particular species of will-o'-the-wisp he is after? He stops, out of breath, surprised at our interest. Well, some of the most common, he pants: national character, a sense of place, the feeling people, place and weather generate. And how is he getting on? He shrugs, pouts, as if to say, this is a mug's game if ever there was one. Will-o'-the-wisps – you know – the thing is, even when you do catch one for a moment you have a terrible job recognising them, and then when you pin them on the pages of your book they immediately lose all colour and shape. Anyway, he is spending most of his time picking truisms, clichés and caricatures out of his net. Not to mention the mere grit and chaff the air is full of. You leave him to get on with it. He rushes off, apparently at random. And it seems that in his desperation he's beginning to wield his net quite wildly, and perhaps in not altogether legitimate fashion, sweeping backwards in time when he ought to go forwards, allowing the fine fabric to fill with all kinds of things from moments years apart, and places, even dimensions, far from contiguous. You shake your head. Whatever it is that finally gets catalogued in his book, obviously this is not a man you'll be able to trust on such imponderables as documentary authenticity.

1
Afa

How to forget the day we arrived in Montecchio? How even to begin to describe the weather to someone who has not been in the Veneto in July? For the weather must surely have played its part in how things went.

We're not talking about heat really. Or that's only part of the problem. The temperature is maybe only 31°C or 32, which is not impossibly hot. One has managed with 35 and more on beaches down south or in the mountains. But there is no sunshine with this heat today, no blue sky, no colour, no air. Above you – and it doesn't seem very far above you either – is a uniform, oppressive, at once damp and gritty greyness, the sun only a suspicion somewhere, a blond thumbprint, a smudge. Nor is there the slightest inkling that this strange, simmering, spongy atmosphere is going to roll itself up into some kind of raincloud or liberating storm. There's not a breath, not a whisper of wind.

You don't notice it perhaps in the town, but as you leave Verona, heading east, you suddenly become aware how miserable visibility is. The hills immediately to the north whose cherry blossom you enjoyed so much in spring, the toothy peaks of the Alps beyond which were so dramatic in sharp and slanting winter light, have all disappeared. Perhaps you're not seeing more than a couple of kilometres. And if – and God forbid – you were to turn south into the *bassa padana* itself, Po-bound across the open plain, you might well find, beyond Nogarole Rocca towards Mantua, a sort of brilliant grey heat fog, so dense the world will seem a haze and the other cars ghosts, and the vines and fruit trees and towering maize and tobacco plants one vast steaming minestrone of a landscape . . .

But we are going to Montecchio, which, like Verona itself, lies at the foot of those first now invisible hills that mark the beginning of the long climb up to the Alps. And, curiously, it is the Alps, you are always told, which are one of the guilty parties as far as this weather is concerned. But only in this sense: that they shut out the merciful winds that might otherwise blow away everything that makes the atmosphere in the plain so unpleasant: the slow accumulation of exhaust fumes, the exhalations of a thousand pig- and chicken-factories, and the abundant insecticides that hover and mingle in the stale air over what otherwise, or in other weather, would be scenes of exquisite beauty.

The local name for the whole phenomenon is *afa* – or *lo smog* (pronounced zzzmog). You pick your shirt away from armpits and feel uncomfortable about the crotch. The only thing close to it in British terms perhaps is a packed Friday afternoon rush hour on bus or tube when the *Standard* has taken up half its front page to tell you WHAT A SIZZLER!

But, just at the moment, we are travelling behind the rusty white Fiat 127 of our future landlady, our *padrona di casa*. We are going to see and hopefully move into a 110-square-metre flat in the outlying village of Montecchio. Hence our own car, an ageing tangerine Passat, is loaded to the stops with all our worldly belongings; the boot is held down by shotcord over piles of boxes, the handlebar of one of our bicycles is creeping down the windscreen.

Across the toneless, almost invisible countryside, the narrow road is flanked by low cement walls, deep flood-emergency dikes, dusty poplars, cypresses, vines. We pass an occasional peasant figure, broad-butted on his puttering *motorino*, helmetless, cigarette in the corner of his mouth. Or it might be a woman, shopping-bag between fat knees, kerchief tight on grey hair, monumental somehow despite precarious movement, the face so grimly set. Other vehicles our cautious guide chooses to overtake are a tractor with an ageing dog balancing on the mudguard and a three-wheeled *furgoncino*, a sort of motorised wheel-barrow with tiny cabin, handlebar drive and a pile of scrap metal rattling perilously behind. Meanwhile, we ourselves are overtaken by bikes so white and fast my wing mirror doesn't appear to register them, space-suited riders flashing into the distance, and then, of course, the usual chase of black or metallic Mercedes, Alfas, Lancias, BMWs. It was a traffic mix, a social mix, with which we were to become familiar.

Perhaps ten minutes out of town, without any noticeable change of speed, we find we are in a built-up area again;

first a loose alignment of stuccoed houses, then the broad open space of Montecchio's main, Montecchio's only real piazza: small shops, tall cedars in two patches of scrubby green, a petrol pump with a weigh-in for trucks, a war memorial. All at once, the buildings close in, the road narrows drastically, the pavement on each side rises to a metre above ground level. Stout legs and slim are barely a foot from the passenger window. And still the traffic doesn't change speed. We emerge, cross a bridge, wind left past the glaring heterogeneity of a huge new red-brick church, then more bridges, ditches and streams, until, just before the road climbs out of the village and into the hills, our would-be *padrona* indicates left and we are in Via Colombare.

Narrow, perhaps two hundred metres long, and straight as straight, Via Colombare achieves an exquisite confusion of invading suburbia and peasant tradition. It is where *furgoncino* and Mercedes both come home to lunch. Closely packed along either side, the houses are all different: two, three or four storeys, one facing this way, one that, some centuries old, handsome or poverty-stricken, others new, crude or lavish; one pink-stuccoed, one blue, one green, many with just bare, pitted cement the same grim colour as today's unpromising sky. There may be a new Alfa 75 drawn up outside one door, and a decrepit straw-hatted grandfather on rickety chair parked outside the next. To add to the sense of emblematic collision, from the far end of the street a painted Madonna gazes from her shrine in the wall of a cherry orchard, right along the flat ribbon of patchy tarmac to where a derelict bottling factory is due for redevelopment opposite.

There is no pavement in Via Colombare. The front doors

of most of the older, poorer houses thus open directly on to the hot asphalt. Their owners have to remember to keep their window shutters tied back in case a truck (presumably lost) should carry them away (one day it was an old stone balcony that went). And where the newer houses of urban arrivals or peasant farmers made good are set back from the road, or perhaps there is a garden, the welcome breathing space that might result is lost because of the obsession with tall and elaborate iron railings as an indicator of wealth. Likewise, gates must be tall and iron and complicated and, where possible, rendered all the more impressive by the addition of little brick and stucco shelters with terracotta-tile roofs.

It was by these gates, as we parked the car, and by the humbler doorways with their fly curtains, as we climbed out, that the street's inhabitants had begun, if not quite to gather, then at least to appear: a heavy woman with the alibi of a broom, a man not quite intent on forcing his dog into the boot of his car, others with no more excuse than the walls or railings they were leaning on. And it was impossible not to get the feeling that they were there to watch us. Not in any way suspiciously, nor with hostility. But with curiosity, yes. With definite and considerable interest.

Well, we felt uncomfortable enough with the heat, the humidity. It was possible we looked out of sorts. And, of course, we were aware by now that Italians don't drive bright orange cars (or bright yellow or green cars for that matter) and that the owners of such cars are looked upon with a certain amount of condescension and immediately understood to be Germans, an epithet more or less synonymous with bad taste. Then despite our new Verona plates we still had that old GB sticker on the back, and so could be, what, from *Gibilterra* it has often been suggested. Yes, we were used to all this; in a mild, light-hearted kind of way perhaps we even cultivated it, for it is fun to be foreign, at least for a year or two. But however far out in the country we were, an orange car and an air of disorientation and discomfort were not usually enough to get ten or fifteen people hanging around their doors in the glaring heat to watch us. And so soon after lunch, too. Did they know something we didn't? Were they expecting a show?

Our future *padrona* was nervous, clumsily pushing the wrong key into the gate of what was certainly the most modern building on the street: newish lime-green stucco with a rough, *graffiato* finish, huge, broad, quite superfluous Californian eaves, double-glazed glass front door, large terrace balconies to each of the four flats. She made no comment on the watching faces around us; they did not surprise her. Was it safe to assume that what they knew, she knew too? And why had she insisted, so uncharacteristically for an Italian, on arranging our meeting at a time when most people were resting, shutters half drawn, dazed by the combination of heavy lunch and humid heat?

Quite unprompted now, and in a nervous attempt to be offhand, this dry, thin-faced, intelligent woman with her small bright brown eyes was telling us about some gynaecological problem she had. She'd been to the clinic again this morning. All the tests doctors made one do nowadays. The time, the expense. Especially when one more or less had to go privately if one was to get any decent service. But who could afford to risk the unnameable diseases? You know how it is? Her hand was shaking. She was having terrible trouble with her bunch of keys, forcing quite improbable versions into the lock on the gate.

My wife and I exchanged glances, looked about us. The sun did not so much lie along the street like a white-hot poker, as it would do later in August and September; it was more that the whole scene, the scarred asphalt, the flaking stone or cement of the walls, the gardens, the vines, the dusty ivies, were fizzing with light. Everything glared.

'*Eccoci!*' the gate snapped open. And at that precise moment Lucilla appeared on a balcony above us and began to shout, or rather to yell, to shriek, to scream.

Lucilla was, is, a short, squat woman, big-breasted, fat, more than round-faced, tinted hair thinning almost to baldness, teeth with the quality of bones, set apart from each other and slightly protruding. Certainly the general impression she gave us that first day in Montecchio was not improved by the fact that every feature was contorted with rage.

This, then, was what the inhabitants of Via Colombare had been waiting for. The tubby woman danced and screamed on her balcony. Her voice filled the air in the narrow street. She pointed down at us, waving her arm as if to hurl anathema and excommunication.

I had been in Italy just over a year at the time. I lay no claims to being a linguist, but I think I had reached the point where I understood perhaps 80 per cent of what was spoken directly to me, and say 50 per cent (far more than enough) of what was merely said in my presence. But that afternoon I could identify not one syllable of what Signora Lucilla was so urgently bawling.

I turned to Rita for help. She understood very little more than me. This was not apparently the local dialect. Which was reassuring. On the balcony above us the little woman continued to be galvanised by rage. A quite extraordinary energy. As if determined to spit out her teeth at us by dint of shrieking.

'*Pazza*', Signora Marta said firmly. 'Crazy.' She was refusing to look up and acknowledge the tirade. '*Completamente pazza*. It's the *afa*.' By great good luck she got the key to the glass front door first time and we were inside; there were creamy marble stairs, a feeling akin to coolness, tropical plants, a reduction in the noise level, but absolutely no time to lose. Up we panted past the two ground-floor flats on the first landing with their funereal, polished-wood doors and round, brass knobs; on we rushed to the second landing where an identical pair of doors again faced each other like diametrically opposed choices in some masonic trial. Our *padrona* knew to go left. Out came the keys again amidst growing nervousness. Ah, *finalmente*! But no, there was still the security lock. And Lucilla simply exploded from the door opposite.

Later I came to think of Lucilla's story as something that in England would be exclusively the stuff of nineteenth-century novels – child labour and deprivation, uncertain inheritance, deathbed fawning, wills burnt or buried and others with forged signatures or clauses added under duress with the complicity of generously bribed physicians – a world where money was not sensibly regulated by the likes of pension funds and insurance policies. I remember planning a novel around Lucilla, but then thought nobody would believe it, they'd think I'd been reading too much Dickens, was stealing passages from *Middlemarch*. Hence, in describing now the scene that followed, it seems natural to use expressions like, 'her bosom heaved', for heave it did, and greatly; or, 'eyes and cheeks were blown out with apoplexy', for blown out they most certainly were. Smaller even than I had imagined, and bigger breasted, Lucilla stamped a high-heeled foot as if to strike sparks from the marble. Her heavy jowls quivered. The blue print dress stretched and strained about her. Tears of rage rolled down her cheeks. And now we began to understand something. Her shouting had resolved itself into a simple chant of, '*è mio, è mio, l'appartamento è mio*! The flat is mine! Mine, mine, mine!' She grabbed the other woman and shook her. She spat. As for ourselves, it was as if we hadn't existed. Which was just as well . . .

Still fumbling with her keys – I wished she would give them to me – Signora Marta at last lost her nerve. So far she had been playing cool city woman to this ill-bred, peasant savagery. Now she too began to shout. 'You need a doctor, *signora*, a *psichiatra*!' And in her eagerness to get away from the unpleasant scene, she yanked quite viciously at the key in the security lock and it snapped in her hands.

Silence. Surprise. Then Lucilla was saying, '*Grazie Gesù, grazie*!' Behind her back, after swiftly making the sign of the cross, her hands seemed to be trying to loosen off some girdle or brassiere. Her face was purple: '*Maria Santissima, grazie*!' The key had broken. We couldn't get in. It was a sign from God. It was proof of her claim to ownership. She was weeping for joy. Signora Marta led us in a hasty retreat down the stairs. As we drove away the onlookers were already converging on the house for news of how the battle had gone.

2
Iella

Over *espresso* in a bar back in Verona, Signora Marta endeavoured to reassure us. That ignorant old witch had run the cleaning company for which Marta's uncle – Patuzzi – had done the accounts. When the company was sold off, Lucilla, her brother Giosuè and sister-in-law Vittorina had built the *palazzina* in Via Colombare together with Patuzzi so that they could all retire happily together. Lucilla's daughter had been supposed to move into the fourth flat but hadn't wanted to be near her mother. Signora Marta pouted thin lips and tapped a city nose, as if to say, 'and we know why, don't we?' In any event, Lucilla had somehow got it into her head that the whole *palazzina* had been built with her money, that is the company's money, and that all flats would revert to her or her heirs on the death of the occupant. 'Can you imagine anything so crazy?' Uncle Patuzzi had died a year ago. His wife, Anna Rosa, Marta's aunt, had hung on in the flat a year longer, but was ill, infirm and constantly harangued by an ever more threatening Lucilla with whom she had never *andata d'accordo*, being herself from an altogether different social class. Now the old lady, *poveretta*, had gone into a home, mainly to escape Lucilla, and she, Signora Marta, as future heir and present administrator, needed to make some money out of the place, if only, as we would surely appreciate, to pay the various bills and taxes. No sooner were we actually in the flat than Lucilla would accept the situation, this afternoon's outburst being anyway mainly due to this abysmal weather which could play havoc with anyone's nerves.

Well, Rita and I had spent most of our life together looking for rented accommodation. We had searched twice in Boston, three times in London, and this was our second time in Italy. We knew that finding a place is tough and that the more generous and idealistic the tenancy laws are, the tougher it becomes. Italy's laws are idealistic in the extreme, with a sort of permanent freeze on evictions, since no political party seems ready to face the flak of unfreezing the situation (the same might be said of almost every area of Italian politics). What's more, we had no place to stay. So it was agreed that no sooner had the locksmith done his job – and Signora Marta had a friend who had another friend who knew something about locks – than we would try again under cover of darkness.

Thus it was. Poor Lucilla must have been in bed, or deafened by her television. Signora Marta had her keys carefully labelled. Barely a minute after the cars had been parked, their doors clicked quietly shut, we were already tiptoeing into the flat. Under a 40-watt bulb, Marta made us sign something on the kitchen table; to the effect that we promised to leave in exactly one year's time or at any moment thereafter when she should so desire. Of course, such a contract could have no legal validity since wise Signora Marta had no intention of declaring us as tenants and getting caught for tax on her rent. But as you discover after a while, Italians lay great store by the signing of pieces of paper, '*documenti*' they insist on calling them. There is a certain ritual attached to the practice, a warding off of evil spirits, and an appeal to the notion of honour which, people feel, should take precedence over legal quibbling, if only because it is generally more convenient to keep the government out of things.

Satisfied, but still nervous, Signora Marta gathered up her piece of paper. Here was the bank account number to pay the rent to: at the Banca Popolare di Verona in Piazza Nogara. Three hundred thousand Lire. Apparently, she didn't have time to show us the place. If we had any problems finding anything we could call her on the phone. The furnishings, she could guarantee – and she made the gesture of someone in a hurry – were excellent. Her uncle and aunt had been people of considerable culture, well educated, much travelled. We would find books and art works that were *estremamente interessanti*. If there was anything left in the drawers or cupboards we could store it in the *solaio*, the loft, upstairs. The key was on the bunch. '*Va bene*?' This thin, nervous woman took more than a cursory look through the Judas hole in the door, drew a deep breath, whispered *arrivederci* and scuttled off down the stairs.

So far we had barely looked about us. Now we explored. And discovered that none of the light bulbs in the flat were any more than 40 watts, so that even the grotesque five-armed chandelier in the *salotto* dripping with globules of smoky glass cast only a dim glow of sad pomp. For such a cultured man Uncle Patuzzi had been doing remarkably little reading of an evening.

Still, minor shortcomings of this variety could easily be remedied, we thought. Likewise the array of department store Madonnas, Sacred Hearts, Sant'Antonios and clumsy bric-à-brac crucifixions that stared down from every wall could be removed and stored away with minimum effort. And the orange-and-green floor tiles did have a smooth, clean, cool feel to them; the window fittingswere, by London standards, quite luxurious, while the bathroom, with walls tiled almost to the ceiling, hardwood loo seat and handsome creamy beige bidet and bath, was palatial. Certainly, when one remembered the bedsits and miniflats of Acton and Willesden, this was a very well-appointed place indeed.

But the furniture . . . Well, we had seen it elsewhere, so it was not entirely unexpected. But depressing all the same. So many Italians, even young Italians, will move into the most modern buildings, light and airy with attractive ceramics and fittings, only to clutter the space with heavy coffin-quality furniture which affects the antique and noble but achieves only the cumbersome and uncleanable, casting sad shadows into the bargain. Thus, a dark-stained console with twisting candlestick legs was shedding neat piles of sawdust to let us know the woodworm were at work. Veneer was blistering on a mammoth bookcase with surely anachronous frosted glass doors, while above the sofa a teak-framed mirror with cracked silvering found 40-watt reflections of a darkly noble dinner-table opposite. Venturing as far as the bedroom, and rather disconcerted now, we found great, square, black-varnished head– and footboards supporting a sagging boat shape between, reminiscent of the bed in a school-of-Veronese *Death of the Virgin* I had recently seen in a local church. On opening dusty chests, dark wardrobes, deep drawers, we discovered that all without exception were full to overflowing with the worn-out possessions of thirty years ago.

In need of air, we rolled up plastic slat shutters and walked out on to the main terrace balcony into the luminous, breathless heat of the evening. Across the street, in front of an older peasant house with fine pink stucco, a group of people our own age were laughing, drinking, smoking and playing table tennis under a fluorescent tube whirring with moths, strung up between two tall cypresses. In the street, despite the hour, their numerous children kicked a football amongst the cars, including our own, bicycles still on top, strips of chrome hanging off the sides. We sat on the arms of an old armchair that Uncle or Aunty Patuzzi had abandoned out here to make a home for spiders and provide the stuff of birds' nests. The sharp tock-tocking of the ping-pong ball, the laughter of adults and children, the background whirring of crickets, was not unpleasant. And would have been pleasanter still with a glass of chilled white wine in our hands. That was something to look forward to. Walking to the far end of the balcony, we saw a young man manoeuvring his sober blue Lancia into a makeshift garage of corrugated iron and breeze block. Then came the strains of the news programme from perhaps three or four open windows. What time was it, eleven o'clock? At midnight we could expect the first fresh stirring of the air. And we intended to be naked on the bed for that.

This has always been one of the pleasures of high summer here. You have been uncomfortably sticky all day. Maybe you've showered twice, tried shorts, long cotton trousers, T-shirts, tank tops, exchanged shoes for tennis shoes, tennis shoes for sandals, sandals for bare feet, had the fan on top speed blowing your papers about while you're typing, sucked ice cubes, put your legs in a bucket of cold water, etc., etc., and nothing has worked. The heat seems to come from inside you. Comfort is unimaginable.

Naturally, you feel irritable. Towards evening, you look at the sky, listen to distant thunder, watch the heat lightning playing over low hills, and you know that it won't rain; so often the elements put on this show just to tease. Going to bed you must decide: the open windows and the *zanzare*, the mosquitoes, or the closed windows and the heat. Inevitably, you opt for the mosquitoes, because in the end, at least around Verona, there aren't that many.

You lie there naked. The idea of any superfluous contact with your body in the form of a sheet or pyjamas is unthinkable. Through a kind of breathy intimacy the summer darkness has, you listen to chatter, facetious variety shows, card games and music from other open windows; because nobody in the entire neighbourhood is asleep, nobody would dream of installing air-conditioning so as to be able to turn in at the normal time (and even mosquito nets are rare). Everybody is waiting for it to happen. Until at last, around midnight or shortly afterwards, like some good spirit suddenly moving across the face of the earth, or the touch of a lover's finger dipped in cool water, the air stirs, it shifts, it breathes, and the notion of freshness becomes imaginable again. Almost immediately the sounds fade, the TVs snap off, the children cease to shriek and chatter, Via Colombare is falling asleep.

It was an hour or so later on this particular night that Vega began to bark. I am not exaggerating when I say of Vega that I have never heard another dog sound so deeply disturbed, so much an *anima in pena*, a tormented soul. She bayed, wailed, was at once furious and desperate. I remember asking Rita which circle of the *Inferno* we might be in.

The third or fourth time the beast woke up, I went out on to the tiny balcony of our bedroom at the back of the house away from the street. On a raised terrace not five yards away, the other side of a narrow canyon of garden between, a big golden labrador strained a long chain to paw at flaking shutters barring the back door of an old peasant house. It howled rather than barked, perhaps moaned rather than howled. And as I watched, enjoying the now cool night air on my skin, somebody threw something at the creature from an upper window, food perhaps, for the dog was immediately scrabbling excitedly among the terrace sweepings between a Cinquecento and an Alfetta.

Back in bed, the apparent relief of silence was shortlived. The insidious whine of a *zanzara* hovered just above our pillows. Up in a flash, light on, a dusty accountancy magazine of Patuzzi's grabbed from the bedside table, within a minute I'd reduced the thing to a bright red spot of blood on the greying tempera wall. 'Can AIDS be passed on by mosquitoes?' the local paper had recently been alarming us.

'I wonder, you know,' I asked, coming back to bed, 'I wonder if the yups and artsy guys and retired professors checking through estate agents' lists of farmhouses in Tuscany have been adequately filled in on these details.' My wife, who always seems ready for questions of this kind, remarked that first the weather was never this unpleasantly sultry in Tuscany, second that local dialects there were all more or less comprehensible, since they formed the basis of modern Italian, and third, and most convincingly, that anybody who could afford to buy a farmhouse in Tuscany need not have somebody else's hunting dog breathing down their necks, and would doubtless have screen windows fitted before moving in. As far as we were concerned, however, she continued, there was just the small problem that we were not so fortunately placed *vis-à-vis* our bank accounts and, furthermore, that there were so many Brits in Tuscany that our linguistic skills would not be in the kind of demand that might allow us to pay a hefty rent.

'Plus the fact', she added, '*che tu porti iella*. You bring bad luck.'

Only months later, when I took the liberty of saying the same thing to a business acquaintance, did I appreciate that such an accusation is one of the worst things an Italian can say to somebody. Had I known, we would doubtless have argued long into the night.

3
Pasticceria Maggia

Am I giving the impression that I don't like the Veneto? It's not true. I love it. I'm going to tell you some wonderful things about it. When I've finished, I hope you'll be wishing you'd been here too, at least for a little while. But like any place that's become home, I hate it too. And, of course, you can't separate the things you love and hate: you can't say, let's move to so and so where they have the *cappuccini*, the wines, the *lasagna*, the marvellous peaches, the handsome people in handsome clothes, the fine buildings, the close-knit, friendly secretiveness of village life, but not, please, the howling maltreated hunting dogs, the spoilt adolescents on their *motorini*, the hopeless postal service, the *afa*. You can't do it. It's a package deal.

In any event, the morning after our unnerving arrival,

we set off to find the village bar/*pasticceria* and console ourselves with the pleasanter side of the arrangement, make ourselves known, see the lie of the land. And for anyone moving to Italy, this is a habit I really can't recommend too warmly: frequent your local bar, and if possible bar/*pasticceria*; frequent it assiduously, decorously, even religiously.

Timing is important. In general, if you want to order a *cappuccino* with *brioche* you should try to arrive before ten-thirty. Of course, you could still order the same things later, but this would be a declaration of your foreignness. And while Italians usually seem to like foreigners, the foreigners they like most are the ones who know the score, the ones who have caved in and agreed that the Italian way of doing things is the best. For this is a proud and profoundly conservative people, as careful observation of ordering at the bar will confirm. And a tightly knit one too. How is it that they all instinctively sense, without even glancing at stylish watches, that such and such a time is the moment to switch to their *aperitivi*? How they chuckle and grin when a German orders a *cappuccino* rather than an *espresso* after lunch, pouring that milk on to an already full stomach. And here's a curious detail: *espresso* is always OK, twenty-four hours a day, even *corretto* (i.e., with *grappa*), but *cappuccino* has a very definite time slot: 8–10.30 a.m. Trivia? No, good training. When the full complexity of these nuances becomes apparent – because the *digestivo*, the *gingerino*, the *prosecco* all have their right times and contexts too – you will be less surprised by the labyrinthine process of, say, switching your driving licence to an Italian one or sorting out your position *vis-à-vis* the health system. There is an order to all things; follow it, even when it borders on the superstitious and ritualistic.

Warning. If the first sip of your *cappuccino* tells you that long-life milk is being used, change bar before you have invested too much time there. Use of UHT milk (all too frequent alas) indicates that either you are far far out in the sticks where the urbane delights of the *cappuccino* have never really been understood, or that this is a bar where most people (men) are ordering *grappa* or wine, or if they are ordering coffee are putting *grappa* and wine in it, not milk. A typical confirmation that you are in this variety of bar might be that the *barista* replies to your Italian, whether competent or hesitant, in defiantly incomprehensible dialect, quite probably revealing that dental work and oral hygiene are not high on the list of personal priorities. No matter how characteristic you may find this UHT bar, how picturesque its old wooden chairs, dusty pergola, sports trophies, sentimental paintings hung askew, and weather-beaten old characters arguing volubly over games of *briscola*, the fact is that, ultimately, you have no business here, you will never be accepted however many times you come. You are only making these doubtless very wholesome people feel slightly uncomfortable.

Another scene which is definitely to be avoided is the bar where you are invited first to pay at the till, then present your receipt to the, in this case smartly dressed, even uniformed *barista* behind his polished pink granite bar under a row of fashionable halogen lights. Reasons? First because this is probably a bar where if you want to sit down you will have to pay for waiter service, and hence, having picked up your coffee and taken it to your seat, you will be scolded, perhaps quite severely, and invited to pay a surcharge. Payment for seating is of course perfectly understandable in the busy city centre, but not really on if you plan to be in that bar as frequently as I'm suggesting. But the second and more important reason is because this is not the sort of bar where the same people come and relax every day and can thus, as weeks and months pass by, be placed and identified and become part of your life. No, this is a busy bar. A business bar. A tourist bar. And we are not interested in any of those.

I cannot claim to being widely travelled, but I have lived in London, Cambridge, Boston, spent fairly long periods in Switzerland, in New York, holidayed in most of Western Europe. You can draw your own conclusions. In any event, I'm now going to stick my neck out and say that I honestly know of nowhere, nowhere, where the whole experience of ordering and consuming coffee and a pastry is, *or could be,* more pleasant than in Pasticceria Maggia, Piazza Buccari, Montecchio. And we selected it from five or six other candidates that very first Sunday. Obviously, we had a nose for these things by now.

You enter through a glass door polished only seconds before you arrived, display windows to either side frothing with colourful goodies, since Italians will always favour the most extravagant packages, however miserly the contents, and are always ready to renew their long love affair with crinkly Cellophane and foil, ribbons, bows and tinsel flourishes of every kind. Opposite you, as you adjust to a pleasant but not excessive dimming of light, is a long bar with attractive curved corner, polished wood to the front and yellow travertine on top. Behind and above is the typical array of bottles, mainly *amari*, *digestivi*, distillations of this and that (artichokes, rhubarb), things you have never heard of and most probably will never learn to like; to the left is the seating area, just a handful of tables, to the right a great glass counter with four tiers of small and dainty biscuits, cakes and pastries.

Needless to say, the whole arrangement has a cleanliness, smoothness of line, sureness of touch unthinkable in England, but without the antiseptic feel of the same thing in Switzerland, the self-consciousness of anything that is not a fast-food chain in the States. Tense as you may well be after negotiating that main street where the zebra faded years ago, depressed perhaps by a broken fountain full of litter, you can hardly help wondering, as you push in through the door, at the way this same people so infallibly reproduces these two starkly contrasting environments: anarchy without, ceremony within.

But, now we're here, by all means let the ceremony begin. You close the door on the busy, dangerous world outside, glance around. The girl serving is small, dark, pixily attractive, and loves to be looked at. So look. And take a seat. The first times we went to Pasticceria Maggia I remember experiencing a sniff of anxiety over the question of seating: was there space for us? Later one realises that part of the civilisation, the magic of the place is that there always seems to be just enough space for everyone who wants to sit. Good. You settle into a comfortably cushioned chair. The simple red tablecloths are pleasant without creating the impression that you must be paying for them in some way or other. The *cappuccino* (and this is so important) is absolutely right: dark strong coffee at the bottom, thick creamy foam above, with, on request, the *cappuccio*, or hat of bitter cocoa sprinkled on top. Add just a dusting of sugar, use your spoon to draw up a little coffee and mix it with the foam. Now spoon up the frothy sweetened milk between bites of *brioche* and relax.

To spin things out, it's a good idea to try and get hold of one of the newspapers the bar is legally obliged to buy for its customers. Don't worry if the thick pink *Gazzetta dello Sport*, by far the most widely sold daily in Italy, seems a little daunting at first. Sports writing is almost the only journalism with any verve to it here (and in lots of other places for that matter) and the Sunday edition will have the first division results from England even if it never quite stretches to cricket. After a while you learn not to be ashamed of a residual interest in the home country.

On another table – wait until somebody kindly passes it to you – is *L'Arena*, Verona's local newspaper. Since they are talking about the agricultural fair, a headline proudly announces that the city is *L'ombelico verde d'Europa* – the Green Belly Button of the EC. Well, there are the two scrubby patches of green outside the window in Piazza Buccari . . . The fact that a member of the local government is under investigation for corruption barely gets ten column centimetres, for this is his party's newspaper. Turning a page, yesterday's dead stare at you from identity-card photographs – you can look for the features of some hated employer – while advertisements opposite offer tickets for tonight's *Aida* at the Arena, Shakespeare at the Teatro Romano, ten or twelve channels of TV viewing.

Why am I advising you to do all this? Because, quite apart from its simply seeming the height of relaxation and civilisation, it is impossible to be a regular customer here at Pasticceria Maggia, to soak up the chit-chat around you, to be sweetly served and smiled at by that pretty *barista*, to browse through the local scandals in the paper, watch bicycle races passing by amidst honking and cheers across the street, without gradually beginning to feel that you are getting into the spirit of things.

People begin to nod to you, beginning disconcertingly with the child-size village idiot in his deerstalker cap. But you will gain respect by putting up with his badgering. Smile, show no embarrassment. Say: *Salve, Moreno, tutto bene*? He's a nice boy in the end. And here's an invitation to teach your doctor's struggling daughter English; a request that can be politely turned down having discussed at length the inadequacies of the education system (the *Arena* will keep you informed). On weekday mornings around ten you can score points by greeting the post-office workers coming in for their long coffee break. These are not your favourite people when they refuse to look up at you from behind their murky little windows and then start weighing your postcards and forgetting whether Britain is part of the EC. Now you can enjoy perhaps glancing at your watch and smiling too brightly as they lean on the bar and discuss what shopping they have to do. Frustratingly, they are unperturbed. They even seem friendly, as if the bar were a place of truce. Perhaps they will serve you faster if they see you here a lot. Or, when those British football oo-lee-gans commit one of their regular atrocities, you can agree with local youngsters poring over the strident *Gazzetta* that your fellow countrymen are a degenerate lot, although pointing out in their defence that the performance of the national team, at least until Gazza came, has often been almost an incitement to insurrection (nothing more welcome to Italians than gently running down *la perfida Albione*, they feel extraordinarily competitive in our regard).

As the months pass and you continue to sit and sup, you

will doubtless be approached by the ex-priest, Lorenzo, now converted to ecology and admirably determined to save Montecchio's famous ditches. He will ask you to sign something and you will sign it. In the corner, old men are muttering over Verona's relegation prospects; soon you will be able to talk about that too. After Mass on Sunday mornings (did I mention the tiny crucifix on the wall above the liquor?) it will be the eight widows who put two tables together and confabulate in low voices, forming, in winter, a wall of fur coats. Even they will begin to smile at you after a year or so, perhaps wondering how long your own wife will outlast you.

Maybe you spot your butcher, your greengrocer, your dentist. Somebody asks you if you can do a translation for them. They run a picture-frame company. No invoice required. For heaven's sake. Somebody walks over to mention a friend who has failed his exam at the university a couple of times and needs a helping hand. 'Perhaps you'll remember the name if it's you doing his oral.' 'Well, I'm afraid I shouldn't really . . .' 'Virgilio, he's called. Virgilio Gandini.' Somebody else is having trouble with the American instruction manual to the sprinkler system for his lawn. And that somebody knows another somebody who could fix the wobbly bearings on your car . . .

It would be a foolish resident of Montecchio who did not at least occasionally pop into Pasticceria Maggia, a short-sighted newcomer who did not invest in at least a couple of years' worth of *cappuccini* . . .

Coming out on that first occasion, the morning after the evening before, I remember we almost ran into two grinning young *carabinieri* sauntering in in their beautiful uniforms with the scarlet-striped trousers and white breast straps. Something that might have been an elongated black beer-can swung from a handsome belt, complete with trigger. A tall, dark girl appeared from the kitchen holding high two trays of *cannoli* and various other pastries; there were smiles, some relaxed flirtation. The *barista* minced. They ordered their *cappuccini*. Cigarettes were lit. One crouched down to chat to a little child, asked predictably: What is your name, where do you live? Nobody seemed at all concerned by the submachine-gun the other was fingering as he spooned sugar over his foam.

Outside, we found their small, dark blue 850cc Fiat van parked in the middle of the small road, blocking anyone who wanted to get by. A radio could be heard calling them with some urgency. Should we go back in to tell them? But no. They are having their *cappuccino*. They only have a few minutes before it's *aperitivo* time. They wouldn't want to be disturbed.

4
Laghetto Squarà

With all that unpleasant unpacking and sorting out awaiting us back at the flat, we might well have chosen to make a detour before returning to Via Colombare that morning. Anything to stave off the evil day. We would thus have discovered how, following the line of the hills coming down from the north, the village of Montecchio, grey-green with dust and heat, is crossed, crisscrossed, by perhaps a score of small, lively streams bubbling swiftly through stone and grass and following a complex system of sluices which divert the water to feed neglected sheep dips, duckponds, irrigation ditches and great flat scouring slabs at the bottom of broken steps where the occasional older woman can still be seen scrubbing her husband's underwear with a soapstick. The through road from

Verona thus corners sharply left, right and left again, as it gropes for the two key bridges that will allow it to continue on its way to the outlying village of Olivè. With all the dips and curves it takes in the process, the sudden widenings and narrowings, the canyon-high kerbs followed by treacherous gutters and unexpected cambers, this chameleon strip of tarmac confers upon the village a splendid sense of the haphazard *ad hoc*, as if the asphalt had been put down in thick fog to reach the scene of some emergency, or, more likely, festival.

Geography, we discovered, is immediately mystified in Montecchio. Paths cut this way and that. One watercourse flows over, beside, under another. House, factory, farm, supermarket, all stand next to each other, although higgledy-piggledy, or are even built one inside the shell of another. The most obvious routes are blocked by dikes or long stone walls. Apparently parallel streets mysteriously lose all contact with each other. So that for the first few weeks one feels a sense of admiration, even bewilderment at seeing how confidently and, above all, how fast, cars shoot through streets where, due to the lack of pavements, so many corners are blind. Such things as bollards are unknown of course, and certainly undesired. Only a memory of a white line haunts the thoroughfares like some sermon heard and ignored long before; with the result that the sharp bends and corners of the main street are viciously cut by motorists and cyclists alike, especially during siesta time when it is not generally supposed that anybody could be coming the other way.

Tyres screech between the narrow walls of a bridge and into the tight bend immediately afterwards. A Vespa swerves: the little boy sitting in front of his father has grabbed the handlebars. Wrists precariously interlocked, a fourteen-year-old on his *motorino* pulls a younger girl on her bicycle up the slope of a dike, finding time to rev and buzz his buzzer as he does so. Somehow, beneath it all, the sleepy, underlying, village serenity persists, is always there, but there to be constantly violated by this indomitable Dionysiac principle on wheels. Here comes a moped reared up for fifty metres on its back wheel, overtaken by a Porsche in second at forty, roaring past the new church straight into the vicious turn by the chemist's. So that if Via Olivè was not in fact laid in a fog or a drunken stupor, one can only presume that it was conceived as a practice track for apprentice race drivers, stunt artists and other would-be suicides. All of which inevitably takes its toll of those heedless elderly cyclists in trilby and shirtsleeves, head-scarf and blouse, who wind and wobble about one-handed as they clutch walking-stick, fishing-rod or shopping-bag. As so often in Italy, the picturesque is combined with a sharp edge of danger.

The first bridge, around which cars will be loosely parked for butcher, barber and cobbler, takes you over a dry flood-overflow ditch. Perhaps five metres deep, seven wide, and straight as a die for miles, this unfortunately necessary piece of engineering slices the village in half with a ribbon of brambly scrub, Coke-cans, bottles and other discarded trophies of summer nights. As we were to discover later, the fact that such a considerable obstacle has still only been bridged to one end of the village, is a matter of smouldering political recrimination in Montecchio. For us, that first morning, it merely meant that the bar was perhaps five minutes further away than it need have been.

Having crossed the ditch, you follow the road past the

new church, past a single AGIP petrol pump, perfectly at home beside a handsome stone arch, and arrive at the second bridge. More attractive than the first, this spans a tiny river, the Fibbio, which flows beneath windows and balconies, linking ponds where men stand fishing under NO FISHING signs, taking the mountain rains southwards toward the Adige, the Po, the Adriatic.

Returning from the bar that morning, we doubtless turned left here to follow the stream a little way to its source, since this was also the direction for Via Colombare. And so would have made our second delightful discovery of the morning: at the bottom of a little dead-end, not two hundred yards from our new flat, a great battered water-wheel was thrashing away in magnificent dereliction. The discovery was all the more welcome when we found that, standing on a little bridge a few yards downstream of the wheel, the air was mercifully cooler, sparkling with bright droplets, damp and breezy.

Did we go on to the Laghetto Squarà that morning? I imagine we did. The little path behind the wheel would have been too inviting to ignore with anything more than an hour before lunch. It's stony underfoot. There are tall, sagging fences to protect an extravaganza of peppers, aubergines, young tomato plants. Water is everywhere: tiny streams gurgling through the vegetable patches, the small river rushing at the millwheel, and to the right, through a Roman arch framing rusty silos, a stagnant pond with stone surrounds which presumably once had some industrial purpose. There are big blue dragonflies and livid green surface weeds. A scooter buzzes urgently at a blind corner, forcing one to step smartly aside, and then the path emerges into the open space of Laghetto Squarà.

What happens here is that spring water rising beneath an abandoned seventeenth-century church flows out under its rotting door and bubbles across the path into a small square lake, the *laghetto*. There are tall plane and poplar trees around it, a stone embankment this side, and grassy banks the other, with three or four sluice gates. Moving to the edge, the glass clearness of the water allows you to look down two or three metres on to abandoned Roman building stones, pollution-fed weeds and that characteristic assortment of junk that people all over the world feel obliged to throw into attractive expanses of water: old tyres, a shoe, electrical appliances.

It's sad. Despite the obvious attraction of Laghetto Squarà, nothing has been composed or finished, nothing appears to be tended or even cleaned. For this is the public sector, not the private commercial world of the bar. Indeed, it's difficult to imagine the *comune*, the local government, having spent anything on the place in the last ten years, aside from paying someone to prune the surrounding trees with extraordinary ruthlessness (because paid, we later discovered, in the form of firewood procured).

Yet precisely because of this neglect, the *laghetto* hangs on to a quality it might lose with transformation into some modern notion of the recreational picturesque; it retains its weathered, rather haphazard air of simply, naturally being there. You sit by the waterside on a big square stone fished out from the bottom some years ago; there are faded Roman inscriptions on its bumpy surface, a date, a few letters suggesting the name of an emperor. Spring water chuckles over the shale path to your left; the hills are behind you; the lake, the busy village and the plain in front. 'So,' you think, 'this is the water table, I am at the foot of the Alps.' Kids throw themselves into the lake in their underwear. Girls scream, protesting they don't want to be pushed. And maybe they don't. It's a little more comfortable here than back in the dusty streets. A lizard basks just a few inches from your foot, reminding you how long you've been sitting still. Montecchio, you feel, may turn out to be OK.

5
Fantasmi

It took us two long, hot days. We made friends at Brandoli, the local supermarket, where three trips were required to accumulate the necessary boxes, and we moved a whole culture from Flat 3 up into the suffocating *solaio* below the roof.

Should we have paid more attention to what we were moving? Would I know more about Italy if I had read all the various diaries and letters with attention? Perhaps so. But old bric-à-brac, old clothes, old medicines, old shoes, old files, accounts, newspapers, rags, toiletries, shopping lists, votive items, paperbacks, military hats, jewellery boxes, camp cooking equipment and tins upon tins of assorted nuts, bolts and nails, have a very bad effect on my morale. Where another might find each item numinous with meaning, I feel overwhelmed by a sense of insignificance. I think of mountains and mountains of such relics multiplied by every household in every corner of the world – varying, of course, from country to country, each with its own cultural matrix, its own peculiar make-up, implying this value and that, but in the end just debris, life's parings waiting to be thrown out – and all I want to do is to see the back of it all as fast as possible. I'd never make it in archaeology or anthropology. Thus, what I did save from our supermarket boxes for a moment's examination, and what my memory and my wife's now offer me in the way of details of that marathon clean-up, can only be scraps, clues, hints to the character, life and times of Umberto Patuzzi – or '*il professore*' as we were later to come to think of him – and of his still vegetating wife, Maria Rosa. Had we known how intriguing these people were to become for us, we might have paid more attention.

Signora Marta had said her aunt and uncle were well travelled and, indeed, the gigantic frosted glass and peeling veneer cupboard in the *salotto* was stacked with sufficient tourist brochures to keep an agency going for a couple of months in high season: except that these brochures dated back ten, twenty, even forty years. The oldest, in alphabetically ordered piles, for the most part extolled cheap hotels in the local mountains or on the nearby Adriatic coast, with fragile brown-and-white photographs giving ample evidence of the fifties building spree. Tuscany, Elba, the Abruzzi, Rome and Sicily followed close behind, like pieces in a rapidly expanding and now colourful jigsaw – Technicolor seas and gaudy local delicacies – until, with the sixties boom, mass prosperity and the Italians' love affair with the *automobile*, here came the first price lists for hotels in Austria, Switzerland, Yugoslavia. Pile after pile of them. The most recent and lavishly seductive exhibits featured the Azores, the Bahamas, pensioners' package trips to Florida.

Clearly there was material for a couple of Ph.D.s in this cupboard but, nevertheless, straight into our Brandoli boxes it all went. We were in a hurry. An essay on holiday destinations as an expression of Italian economic development over the last three decades was not what we had in mind. Except that here, beneath the brochures, was a photograph album. Well, who can resist at least glancing at photographs?

Such was Patuzzi's love of the road and his motor car, he must have had the habit of getting someone, presumably Maria Rosa, to snap him by exotic road signs (as others might want to record their presence at the top of mountains). So here he is, in black and white, full head of virile hair brushed back, thin aquiline, intelligent nose, arriving in Trento with stout climbing boots round his neck and a knapsack on his shoulders; he has the confident, satisfied look on his face of someone who has just been admired for making an intelligent remark, or at the very least has eaten a good lunch. Nineteen thirty-seven, says the spidery hand. And here he is again, in colour now, balding, but still sporty, in wool trousers and green anorak, by a sign that tells us 'Wien'. We flick through page after page of these things: mountain villages, hotel billboards, *autostrada* exits; until finally, most recently and most extraordinarily, here is a much older, weathered, bent Patuzzi, leaning on a stick, by black lettering on a white road sign announcing 'Praha', with, beside him, and even more extraordinarily, a very recognisable Lucilla.

That does put a new slant on things. More a ménage than a condominium perhaps? Could she even be right about ownership of the flat? Or am I jumping the gun?

Further back in the cupboard are some collectors' items from the war days: an army hat, a school textbook ('Describe your feelings – of admiration and gratitude – on contemplating a photograph of *il Duce*'), and a stack of the macabre *Signal* magazines: tabloid-size, in German with Italian translations, these offer comic-strip propaganda, mainly directed against – well, against *us*. '*Bombe sull'Inghilterra!*' one enthusiastic piece is entitled. Is this, I sometimes wonder, why the young men in the bar still feel such rivalry? And what had friend Patuzzi done in the war apart from reading such heady stuff (later we learned that Lucilla had been begging for bread on the streets of Vicenza).

Further back still (I said the cupboard was huge) was a rather more harmless (and more numerous) collection of magazines going under the enigmatic title of *NAT*. A moment's close attention to the inside cover revealed that these letters stood for *NUOVA ALTA TENSIONE*, and it took only a few seconds' leafing through them to appreciate that such tension was presumably meant to be created in the lower abdominal area by late fifties and early sixties pin-ups of Brigitte Bardot, Jane Fonda, Sophia Loren and a host of lesser names, photos of such breathtaking touched-up tameness you wondered how people managed after all the bomb-toggling excitement of wartime. Was Patuzzi slipping them in between his accountancy journals as he walked out of the *tabaccheria*? Did he read harmless gossip about bathing beauties between toiling over accounts on the great ugly desk in the second bedroom which clearly had a longer history than this house? At what point had Lucilla come in, if she had? Beneath a photo of a tiny, delicate-featured girl from the south, a caption was still telling us twenty-five years later that Mariangela Rainaldi, a devout Catholic, presently worked as a party hostess but was eager to become a film star.

In the drawer of Patuzzi's bedside table we found a long shoehorn, a catechism, an *Alpini* hat (the famous Italian mountain regiment), a long expired tube of haemorrhoid cream, an oval, silver-framed photo of a solemn Maria Rosa, and a long piece of thick leather with a handgrip at one end and a heavy ball of lead tied to the other. What on earth for?

But there was a problem with rubbish now. Not that we felt we could throw away anything precious, like the diaries full of additions and subtractions in figures of eight and nine digits, the replies to letters Maria Rosa's brother must have sent to a number of marriage bureaux in Paris – no, everything that should be preserved for prying eyes more patient than our own would be preserved. All the same, there was much in the way of old toothbrushes and toiletries from the early seventies that would be missed by no one. Who needed to know that *il professore* had cleaned his teeth with *Pasta del capitano*?

Unable to locate anything inside or outside the flat that remotely resembled a dustbin, we eventually tiptoed downstairs to make ourselves known to the Visentini in the flat below Lucilla's (the one that had been meant for her daughter). Presumably they would be able to tell us what the score was.

We knocked lightly on the door. A voice asked who we might be, for nobody will ever open in Italy until identity is declared. Security, even in the remotest villages, is at New York standards. We explained. Came the sound of a heavy lock turning over once, twice, three times, and the door opened. A wispy, attractive little woman in a pink tracksuit stood before us and immediately insisted we come in.

Well, we were in the same country, the same village, the same building even, in a flat that in structural terms was a straight mirror image of our own, and yet on stepping into *casa Visentini* we were immediately in a different world. Everything here was modern, pleasantly styled, clean as a pin, with a light touch to the ornaments, the lithographs on the walls, the low, modern, comfortable sofa. If there was, perhaps, just one thing in common with our own accommodation, and with so many other homes I have been into in the Veneto, it was in the desire for a certain formality, a certain achieved composition in every room, ritualistic and ceremonial. Cosy is not a word one would normally apply to an Italian interior, nor would the owners be proud to hear their furnishings thus described. The briefest glance at the Visentini's flat showed that the whole domestic environment had been most painstakingly arranged, nothing left to chance, nothing haphazard. Everywhere lines met and diverged in clean, carefully calculated, stylish angles. The exact opposite of the world outside.

And at first Orietta and Giampaolo were as guarded and rigidly polite as their furniture was attractive and composed. Yes, we were invited in, and with kindness. Indeed they insisted we come in. For this was the right thing. But it was not clear what we were to talk about. They did not want to be drawn immediately on the – for us – burning issues of a hostile Lucilla and a howling dog. Giampaolo in particular was poker-faced. The rubbish, he explained, was usually placed in a large, shared, plastic dustbin which was then put outside the gate for collection every morning. However, Lucilla had removed this bin on our arrival, making it abundantly clear she did not want us to enjoy the use of it.

The Visentini offered no comment on this state of affairs. Presumably, we must procure a bin of our own.

I then asked about the garage which Signora Marta had mentioned. Tall and serious, but handsome too, and with something boyish about him somewhere, Giampaolo led me downstairs to a semi-basement where, turning right at the bottom of the stairs, a very big area the size of a whole flat served as the shared condominium garage. I was immediately impressed by the positively licked cleanness of the smoothly finished red-brick tiles that had been chosen for the flooring: no oil stains, barely visible tyre marks. Attractive as it was, this simply didn't seem necessary for a garage.

Four parking spaces had been marked out between cement pillars. To the far side was Giampaolo's gleaming white twin-carburettor Giulietta, just in front of us a minuscule Fiat 126, again white. The other two places were empty.

I asked which was my space. Giampaolo said this one on our right was Flat 1's and so Vittorina's (Lucilla's sister-in-law), and the space to the left of the Giulietta at the far end was Flat 3's, our own. *Però*, he warned, neither space had been used since the death of the male members of those households: Umberto Patuzzi and Giosuè Zambon. This was a question of respect. He showed me the small crucifixes on the pillars beside the spaces. Lucilla, he said, was a superstitious person, but not ultimately an unpleasant one. It was merely a question of time.

I remarked that if using the garage meant war with Lucilla, forget it, it didn't matter, my car had little bodywork worth saving. This did not bring a smile, and in retrospect it occurs to me how foolish such jokiness is amidst a nation of car worshippers. A man who has spent six months of his *stipendio* buying an Alfa Romeo twin-carburettor Giulietta which he hardly ever uses, does not want to hear that others are quite happy to get by with a ten-year-old rusting Passat. And bright orange at that.

Before returning to the women upstairs, Giampaolo made a point of showing me the communal *taverna*.

A *taverna* is a large basement or semi-basement room situated beneath a modern *villetta*, *palazzina*, or small condominium of central or northern Italy, and it is dedicated to partying. It must have a large, preferably enormous fireplace, suitable for barbecuing; a selection of strictly labelless wines, alpine-style pine furniture, one long banqueting table, an area with sink for washing dishes, and perhaps a stereo. On the walls, as was the case in Via Colombare, decorations should include old posters showing views of the mountains or the country, some hunting trophies (here, remarkably, a surely fake cheetah) and such things as old swords or shot-guns. In Via Colombare there were Patuzzi's wooden skis from perhaps forty years ago.

It should be said that old houses do not have *taverne*. Only new ones. For the *taverna* is the contemporary Italian's dream of the past, an exercise in urban adaptation and nostalgia. That is to say, this big below-ground party room attempts to recreate, for the modern flat-dweller in his cramped condominium, the feeling of those huge old country kitchens with their abundance of game, *polenta* and local wine which still take up such a large space in the national consciousness. Thus, in many a *taverna*, often beneath the most uninspiring prefabricated structures, you will find that the occupants have bought an authentic old *pietra serena* fireplace to install in the wall, or, if they cannot afford the real thing, then at least a decent imitation, with an impressive array of black iron fire-tending implements. Tables likewise tend to be old or to look old and you must have at least one ornate high-backed hard wooden chair which no one ever sits on.

When a couple of condominium families get together to invite their friends to eat here, on the Bank-holiday evening of *ferragosto* perhaps (15 August), or on 25 April, *la festa della Liberazione*, they expect these furnishings, particularly the splintery pine benches and fake oil-lamp light fittings, to induce a mood at once of merriment and traditional wholesomeness, the rightness of family and friends enjoying the fruits of their labours around the common hearth. As if for the space of an evening, the office worker, or shopkeeper, or pharmaceutical salesman could enjoy the healthy repose of the *contadino* after the grape harvest; as if, like some Jungian subconscious, the *taverna* could be used to store away a primitive past and all its richness.

My own experience is that, like so many dreams, the *taverna* is better in the dreamer's imagination than in the realisation. Happier the Veronese choosing his fireplace and barbecuing instruments, than the same irritated fellow trying to enjoy them. You go to a *taverna* party in a damp basement, unheated and un-aired since the last binge, and quite possibly you will catch your death despite the most stifling weather above ground. The chimney doesn't draw properly because it is rarely used. You eat off a miscellany of plates, survivors of other dinner services once used upstairs; you drink from dusty glasses that no amount of rinsing will clean, perhaps because there is no hot water in the basement sink. Items of cutlery are found to be missing. Your knife doesn't cut very well. Conversation booms about the bare cement walls. After about an hour or so, just when the wine and barbecuing are beginning to take the chill off the place, the condominium dog-in-the-manger comes downstairs to complain that the noise is making it impossible for him to follow the latest episode of some favourite *telenovela*, i.e., a recycling of *Dallas*, *Dynasty* or whatever. He is reassured, amidst much contrition and invitation to join in (for this is by definition a wholesome party), then promptly forgotten, though remaining perhaps as a nagging subconscious irritation.

The food begins to arrive. You eat the flesh and sometimes it seems the bones and feathers too of blackbirds and small pigeons, crushing, as instructed, Malteser-sized heads between your molars so as to suck out the brains inside. Which are indeed toothsome. But pitifully small. While all around the table people are trying too hard to be jolly.

Out come the *carabinieri* jokes (right angles boiling at 90° and so on), the shaggy dog stories of bureaucratic odysseys ('so when I went back for the third time he says that since my birth certificate was from another province and dated prior to 1959, the whole procedure should have been done by post with the office in Rimini . . .'). There is much loud guffawing, head shaking, glass filling. 'No, you must have another *uccellino*. You must. They're *squisiti* and I've already cooked it now.' The thing falls on your plate with a definite resemblance to those hapless little corpses one finds on wet pavements in spring. Accordion music strikes out from the stereo. Six couples launch themselves into traditional dances in six square metres. Loud giggles. Somebody burns themself on a hot poker left sticking out of the hearth, etc. etc.

The *taverna* seems to induce this behaviour, this determination to be festive at all costs. Indeed, almost any *taverna* party has the flavour of those New Year's Eves when you simply can't feel there is anything to celebrate and wish you had stayed at home. But then my wife constantly tells me I'm a *gufo*, an owl, a spoilsport. She thoroughly enjoys these occasions. In my defence, I would merely say that, whatever the surroundings, I always love the wine, I can even tell with my eyes closed more or less which of the local varieties I'm drinking, and if only we could be having it in well-ventilated accommodation upstairs with some tortellini *al dente*, followed perhaps by a plate of finely sliced rare horsemeat and a *tiramisù* straight from the fridge, I would be in heaven.

Throwing open the iron door, drawing me to the threshold to gaze inside, Giampaolo Visentini was obviously a *taverna* fan. Perhaps for him the *taverna* represented some unthinkable loosening up, or an occasion when the more difficult social skills could be replaced by simple prowess with the barbecuing fork. In any event, showing me the gloomy place (I remember antlers and crossed ski poles on thin whitewash) he began to betray the first signs of life and enthusiasm. Did I like barbecuing? Did I like grilled aubergine? And *bruschetta* (toasted bread with olive oil and garlic)? I said, yes, yes I did. And was I interested in bottling my own wine? The people in his company always clubbed together to bring a truck-load of casks from a particularly good vineyard in Friuli. If I would like to split a cask of Cabernet or *prosecco* with him I should let him know in good time. We could buy in October and bottle next spring. The price was low and the quality excellent. I said to count me in at once, I was always ready to give something a try. By the time we were climbing the stairs again there was a feeling we might just make it as neighbours.

Then, running the gauntlet of Lucilla's door to get back through our own, we heard our phone ringing for the first time. Signora Marta, perhaps, having forgotten to tell us where the serious books and spare light bulbs were kept. Or one of the numerous schools and agencies we had immediately passed the number on to.

'*C'è il dottor Patuzzi?*' a confident older man's voice asked.

I froze.

'*Parla Giordano. Una questione di documenti.*'

'But Patuzzi's dead. He's been dead two years and more.'

'But his name's in the phone book,' this voice objected.

'He's dead,' I said.

'*Ah. In quel caso non insisto.*' And the phone went, well, dead.

Rita said: 'It's if they say, "Patuzzi speaking", you should start worrying.'

But somehow it seemed that when you had just cleaned all of a man's junk out and read a few of his letters and seen his well-thumbed girly magazines and his boyhood skis and a crucifix by his parking space, then *fantasmi* were not an unreasonable proposition.

6
Residenza

It would have been some weeks later we tried to change that entry in the phone book. We phoned SIP, the telephone company and were told that in order to have our names in the phone book with that number we would need a recent certificate of *residenza in bollo* (that is with a few thousand Lire's worth of special stamps on it) and signed renunciation of the number by Patuzzi, or his heir. The *contratto* for the phone would then be shifted, for a small charge, into our name and the bills would be addressed to us.

By the standards I have grown used to, this seemed something of a breeze. A check at our local *comune*, a pleasant enough little office with the inevitable crucifix, an impressive collection of rubberstamps and a large computer on line to the city registry, provided the information that for certificates of residency we would need either proof of ownership of the said flat as first home, or a written statement from the owner that we were tenants there. This should be on *carta bollata* – legal paper with, again, a few thousand Lire's worth of stamps on it.

So we rang Singora Marta. She was very polite but unable to understand why we wanted to change the name, 'referring to the number in the phone book'. Couldn't we simply tell everybody we wanted to phone us what our number was? We explained that there might be people who wanted to track us down for work. We were *liberi professionisti*. But if, she objected, they knew of our names, then they could ask the people they'd heard of us from. *Non è vero*? People who would surely have our telephone number or know someone who had it. Telephone directories were thus demonstrated to be entirely useless.

No, she added, the point was, it would be extravagant if we were only staying for a year. Because when we were gone we would of course renounce the number, so as not to be listed under it any more and have bills for it in our names, at which point she could if she chose have the line disconnected, but then God knew how long it might take to get it reconnected and how much that would cost. The result being that she would most probably have to take the number on in her own name (rather than Patuzzi's). And since she already had a phone number, this number (Via Colombare's) would be registered as a second home phone, meaning much higher basic bills even if she made no calls.

So many conversations in Italy follow these serpentine paths, with new laws and regulations constantly raising their ugly heads to turn the most obvious ways forward into dead ends. With the creeping sense of paranoia that results, you occasionally find that people have been imagining rules that don't actually exist, simply because they seem to be the kind of thing the government would invent to make life more difficult and hence probably has. Was it really true, for example, that Marta would be obliged to register the number in her name. Couldn't she register it in a child's or grandmother's? Or was it that if she did that they would then have to switch their *residenza* to Via Colombare with all the problems that entailed?

I proceeded cautiously: when we left the flat, I said, if she asked us to leave it that is, and we rather hoped she wouldn't because we liked it here, then this would presumably be because she had decided to sell it, or had found someone else to live in it, and in either case the new occupant would want to take over the phone, wouldn't they?

'Not if they already have one in their own name elsewhere,' she came back. 'Or if they want to retain residency in another province.'

Who could have thought of this before starting the phone call? Then, when I had already given up and offered a cool *arrivederci*, she suggested by way of an olive branch: 'I don't mind writing to say that you live there, though, if you need to have *residenza* for other purposes.'

How explain the elusive yet all-important significance of 'residency' to a Brit who merely lives where he lives and acts accordingly? Can we hazard a definition? Residency means that the state now recognises that you live where you live, or say you live (for example, in the province of X at such-and-such an address) and henceforth will distinguish you from all the people who live in another province, or country, or who do, yes, live in X but whom the state does not recognise as living where they live (in X), either because those people want to be recognised as living elsewhere (where they don't live) and have managed by some wangle to achieve this, or because they can't get hold of some precious *documento* that would allow them to demonstrate that they do in fact live where they live (in X), and must thus continue to be recognised as living where they no longer live (in Y or Z, for example).

But does it actually matter? Well, yes. Once the state recognises that one lives where one lives, there are all kinds of benefits: the right to register your car in the area (otherwise you will have to travel to Y or Z to register it); the right to register with a local doctor; the right to apply for all kinds of local state jobs; the right to have access to certain services and benefits; the right to pay lower phone and utility bills; the right to vote; and, most importantly for us, a 2 per cent reduction on the amount of income tax withheld at source on free-lance services.

'*Va bene*,' I told Signora Marta, if she could write such a letter we would be very happy. '*La ringrazio*.'

But I was puzzled. She hadn't wanted a formal rent contract. I had half suspected that this was why she hadn't wanted the phone number in our name: she didn't want it to be in any way official that we lived here. And now, on the contrary, here she was offering to help us get residence. A calculated risk? Generosity?

'The flat,' Rita suggested, 'is officially owned by Maria Rosa, who is gaga in a nursing home. How is anybody to know that we are paying into Marta's account?'

Still . . . Life is complicated. In any event the drift seems to be that the government makes well-meaning but complicated laws and people very sensibly get smart and get round them. For example, there was this business Marta had mentioned that second homes carry much higher utility bills – a popular tax-the-rich measure. However, it is quite common in Italy for the middle and even lower-middle classes to rent their real home in the city where they work and possess a small holiday flat (second home) by the sea, by one of the lakes, or in the mountains. Result: many people register themselves or their wives or children as resident in the holiday home, so as to avoid higher bills. This in turn will create all kinds of other problems. On election day, the registered residents will have to travel a couple of hundred miles to go and vote in some place whose local politics they know nothing about. So they don't vote, you object. But, in Italy, if one doesn't vote three times in succession, one loses certain rights . . . etc. etc. Bureaucracy is a huge tangle of sticky string in which every attempt to loosen one knot tightens another.

And checks, or *accertamenti*, to make sure that each citizen is contributing his length of string to this tangle, are quite common. A few weeks after moving into Via Colombare, I went out on the balcony to see who had buzzed our bell and found a seriously fat man in uniform sitting on a moped with big dispatch boxes. Montecchio's local *vigile*. Taking some papers out of one of these boxes, he asked me something. I asked him if he could please speak Italian. He politely switched from dialect to something more comprehensible, upon which it emerged that he had been asking me whether I lived where quite obviously I was living (wearing pyjamas, a piece of toast in my hand). I said I did. He then asked if he could come and see. And in my kitchen he explained at length about the *tassa sui rifiuti*, the rubbish-collection tax. This apparently was paid, not by the owner or even renter of a property, but by the head of the household actually living there *whether or not resident* –that is, they wanted the money and red tape was not a problem (similarly, it is perfectly normal for a foreigner to file an income-tax return without having a work permit). The person in question was me, I said. I would pay. He scratched his head, cocked it to one side, eyed me carefully from his tubby face. '*Bon*,' he said.

The *vigile* then wrote something amazingly painstakingly on his sheet of paper. While he worked, I noticed how clean his uniform was, how well-ironed his shirt, how white the little pouch on his belt. It was another day of sultry heat. Despite the weight of flesh beneath all these clothes and accessories, he was not sweating.

He asked my name. Then asked me to spell it. Fair enough. We got through Parks quite rapidly, and were speeding through Timothy (Torino Imola Monza Otranto – I say it in my sleep sometimes) when we ran up against the age-old problem of Y which does not exist in the Italian alphabet. 'Hotel, Epsilon.' I finished. He hesitated, raised his head, blew out his cheeks and narrowed his eyes. What was epsilon? 'Epsilon,' I said, 'is a letter.' '*Ah sì?*' he said. It was clear that he was used to having his leg pulled, and so had developed these mannerisms – the suspicion, the slow questioning, the stare – to make himself seem less gullible.

Having studied me for a sufficient length of time, he decided I was not the type, said: '*Sì, Sì, sì, d'accordo*,' and scribbled something down, I didn't dare to ask him what. But then I had the idea of pulling out my English driving licence and offering it, *'per una verifica'*. Offended, he waved it away.

'Residenza?' he now enquired, for even if it had no bearing on my paying this tax or not it was important to write it down. Three or four times.

I was applying for it, I said.

'Stato di famiglia?' (a document describing relationships within the family – who is the mother, the father, the head of the household, who the breadwinner, who dependent).

I was waiting for my marriage certificate to arrive from England.

'Profession?' For everybody must be classified according to their profession.

I told him teacher. Rather flatteringly he wrote down *Professore*.

Then just as he was leaving I made the foolish mistake of remarking that we didn't have this residency business in England.

Again he was clearly concerned that he was being made fun of. There was the same cocking of the head, the puzzlement. He was one of those fat people who are terribly graceful, nimble almost, very aware of their bulk. He turned on his heel away from the door in almost a dance step, pushed back his cap and lowered himself on to a seat at my kitchen table. This was a serious matter.

How was it possible, he asked, for us not to have residency?

We didn't.

So what do you do? When you move.

You move, I said.

And the registration plates on the car?

You leave them as they are.

And your identity card?

There are no identity cards.

And the doctor?

You go and register at the nearest surgery.

He clearly didn't believe me. It couldn't be that easy. Not that I was lying. But I must be ingenuous. There was so much I hadn't understood. He was wondering how he could prove this to me. He had prickly, Latin black hair cut short under his cap and he scratched at it slowly, tugged at the tubby lobe of an ear. Then he had me.

How, he asked, would the post work?

In what sense?

How would they know where to bring it to, when you moved?

I tried to be equable, offhand. Somebody wrote your address on an envelope, affixed a stamp of the appropriate denomination and the postal service would hopefully take it to that address and ask no questions.

The man got up and left in polite disgust. Obviously it was not a country for *vigili*.

I was not surprised a few weeks later when the first refuse bill arrived addressed to Parks Thimothj. As for the phone, if you open Verona's very handsome telephone directory, you will still to this day find the name of Umberto Patuzzi covering up for whoever is enjoying the pleasure of SIP's services at Via Colombare 10, Flat 3. Doubtless the gas bills are still in his name too. And the electricity bills, despite the curious fact that these actually include the modest charge of 7,000 Lire a year for the votive light over his grave . . . (second home?).

7
L'animale domestico

July. Dog-days. The heat that is, and Vega.

We had settled down in the flat, bought a few 100-watt bulbs, only to realise what an attraction they were to the moths and mosquitoes. We had got used to the tock-tock of midnight ping-pong from across the street, discovered that something of a breeze could be created by opening all the windows of the flat simultaneously and waggling one of the communicating doors, eaten our way through mountains of water-melons (to every season its antidote), and dedicated a shelf of the fridge to bowls of sliced peaches swimming in Valpolicella.

We had even made our first tentative peace with Lucilla, offered our help around the house should she ever need it, assured her we would take no part in the court case pending in which Marta and Maria Rosa were to be accused of having dashed to *il Professore*'s bank security box only moments after his heart attack and burnt the will naming Lucilla as his sole heir.

'But who was *il professore*?'

'Why Umberto! Patuzzi! A wiser man never lived. A real *professore*.'

As I had been for the *vigile*.

'*Un uomo squisito*. His death was such a terrible blow.' Tears had a way of forming rapidly in Lucilla's veiny eyes. We shook our heads. And our assiduousness and sympathy (genuine, actually) had its reward in the reappearance, on about day ten, of the communal dustbin and the prospect of talks about one of those sacred spaces in the garage. Downstairs in the flat beneath our own (and hence opposite the Visentini) the more timid, perhaps dour Vittorina seemed ready to follow whatever lead her volcanic sister-in-law would suggest. All, or much, was coming right.

There was just the problem that night after night our sleep was ruined by the howls of Vega scrabbling at his master's shuttered door, while towards mid-afternoon, as I shifted from buttock to buttock in front of Patuzzi's huge desk, translating papers for an international conference on the decline of opera, it was impossible not to notice a slight odour of dog faeces rising from the small patch of ground where the creature was kept imprisoned. I mentioned this on the stairs one day to Giampaolo. His surprising reaction was to phone the local *carabinieri* immediately. They came out very promptly, confirmed that there was a potential health hazard and warned the one-armed, fiercely eye-browed Signor Negretti that he'd better clean up his dog's act.

Negretti came out on to the terrace with his two teenage boys and hosed down the grassy area below where the dog was sometimes chained, sometimes free to roam for four or five metres in any direction. He hosed it for perhaps ten or fifteen minutes, directed a last squirt at the shambling, excited dog itself, then went indoors. After which all was left as presumably it always had been.

Animals. Did I mention in the opening pages about somebody bundling a dog into the back of a car? Quite a normal sight on Via Colombare. The car will be a well-worn, dull green Fiat 128, the *contadino*'s car *par excellence;* the man will be wearing rubber boots and a straw hat with the name of the tractor company on its band. He will drive off with admirable caution, although without buckling his safety belt, if he has one. As the car passes you, muffled barking may be heard, or the thumping of the pointer's tail against the petrol tank.

But perhaps a better way into the relationship between Italians and animals might be to consider the normal translation of the English word 'pet'. The Italian expression is: *'animale domestico'*. *'Il cane è un animale domestico.'*

Well, in English one might feasibly say to one's girl-friend, boyfriend, wife, husband, son, daughter – 'What a pet you are!' meaning, what a delightful, friendly, cuddly bundle of fun, pleasure and loyal friendship around the cosy hearth. And of course we have the fine word 'petting', which I have so often tried to explain to puzzled students. But could one, in Italian, say to one's mate: *'Che animale domestico che sei!'* No, this would be inadvisable. For it would mean, first that they were *merely* an animal, as distinguished from the more elevated, thinking, speaking and shotgun-toting *Homo sapiens*, and second that they were submissive, knew their place, didn't bother anybody and barked only when supposed to. Even throwing in palliative adjectives – *'che bell'animale domestico . . . che animale domestico carino'* – would not help in the least, since these could only be perceived as irony, thus adding insult to injury.

In short, Italians think differently about their pets/ *animali domestici*. In 99 per cent of cases they keep them outside; they do not like them coming into their houses and would not dream of having them sleep say, at the foot of their beds. The idea of one's child being licked all over by a dog, as I was as a boy, would be unthinkably horrible to the modern Veronese mother (perhaps very reasonably so). But there is also something obsessive and exaggerated in this aversion, something which may have to do with the fact that it wasn't so very long ago that many families in the country around Montecchio had goats in the kitchen and the cow stall opening on to the sitting-room for warmth. Proximity to any but the most expensive 'luxury' animals has become a sign of social backwardness. And hunting dogs like Vega are a mere utility. You don't want them prancing into the house with their wet paws and dirty backsides. You use them when you go off shooting so they can bring back the *uccellini* which you eat in your *taverna* in nostalgic revelry at the joys of country life which you have wisely left behind. Otherwise you keep them chained in the yard.

Outside our window, Vega barked, howled, moaned deep into the night. With that extraordinary insistence dogs sometimes have. Bark, bark, bark, bark, for hours on end. What were we to do about it?

'Poison the thing,' a student suggested at once.

Poison. For weeks, months, it was to become an obsession. We noticed stories in the paper reporting dog poisonings. They seemed quite common. Almost the done thing. Somebody in a place called Bussolengo had killed more than twenty in a single evening. Well, we needn't go that far. And I read Sciascia's novel, *A ciascuno il suo*, where he mentions a whole Sicilian tradition of dog poisonings, a sort of low-order vendetta between rival huntsmen.

We considered rat poison. And bought some. We studied the dosages. Twenty or thirty pellets in a meatball should be enough. But what if a child were to pick it up? Occasionally the Negretti had guests with small children who were left to ramble about the defecated garden area. A student whose father was a vet cheerfully suggested the easier solution of a sponge soaked in meat juice. Apparently, the sponge expands enormously in the animal's gut, blocking intestines and eventually leading to death. He knew people who had found this method very effective. Well, we had a small sponge in the bathroom which overlooked Vega's little patch. Part of the Patuzzi heritage. Nothing would be easier.

We observed the animal's eating habits. She seemed perfectly used to having her food tossed at her from considerable distances. She was instinctively friendly, running to her master or his sons in the hope of a pat, which very occasionally, grudgingly, she got. Although sometimes it was kicks. On a sort of dry run, we tossed her a biscuit from the bathroom window. Immediately it was snapped up and appreciated.

'The only problem with the sponge', my knowledgeable student explained at another lesson, 'is that the creature will die in unspeakable agony, and you'll have to hear her howling like mad. Probably for a couple of days. Although of course it will be worth it in the end.'

We couldn't do it. At night, startled from sleep by bloodcurdling howls, we would feel that we could. I might go to the bathroom and squeeze the yellow sponge in my hand, feel how it contracted and expanded, sense how easy it would be, laden with the weight of the meat juice, to chuck it the three or four metres over the fence to the howling dog. But something prevented us. And we developed the alibi that it wasn't the animal's fault, it was the master's, and we would kill the master if only such things were feasible. As a poor substitute for serious action we took to phoning *casa Negretti* whenever the dog woke us. After a couple of nights they left the phone off the hook.

We talked to our neighbours about it. The Visentini weren't badly affected because they lived at the other side of the building and had installed elaborate double glazing. But the subject did allow for our first real contact with Vittorina. No sooner had we mentioned the dog than she was telling us how, when her husband had been dying the previous July, he had been unable to sleep because of the creature and she had begged Rocco Negretti to do something about it, to no avail. They were *gentaccia*, filth, no fate was bad enough for them. She burst into tears, remembering her husband's suffering and we were able to offer her coffee in our flat, where she amazed us by remarking that she had never been in here before. No, she and Lucilla had been good friends with *il professore*, but the hateful Maria Rosa was a city woman and believed herself above them. They had never been invited into the flat. *Il professore* had always taken his coffee at Lucilla's. While Maria Rosa did the shopping.

Vittorina was in her late sixties, big boned, only slightly overweight. With great dark rings about her eyes, she was obviously morose by nature, a lover of candlelit churches, superstition, mystery and gossip. But when she laughed it was with sudden heartiness and enthusiasm, a sort of profound natural health. She would go and tell Lucilla, she said, what nice people we were, because her sister-in-law was mad not wanting us to use *il professore*'s parking place after *il professore* had treated her so badly.

This was good progress, and terribly interesting of course (should we ask Vittorina about the photo taken near Prague), but it didn't solve the problem of Vega.

Until one Sunday we would wake at dawn to the celebratory crackle of gunfire. The hunting season had begun, the hunting season that litters the paths with spent cartridges and deposits as much lead on the national territory as all the Fiats, Alfa Romeos and Mercedes put together. And although we had never seen so much as a wild rabbit on our Montecchio walks, the surrounding hills echoed with sharp reports all morning. *Uccellini*, pigeons, purpose-bred pheasants were presumably tumbling from the sky. And Vega was quiet that night, having had some exercise at last.

8
Stile cimitero

August is a better month than July in the Veneto. The days are still scorchingly hot but, after a series of dramatic thunderstorms bringing hailstones as big as marbles and prompting radio and newspaper discussions as to whether farmers could ever have had all the crops they are claiming compensation for, the humidity finally fades like a bad dream; the days are drier and clearer and the welcome dusk comes that bit earlier.

It's a good time to take walks. The countryside assumes its dusty green long-suffering summer look: matt colours under sizzling light. The vines are thicker now, their shoots knotting swiftly across the system of wires between one row of posts and the next, completely shading the ground below. You can walk beneath them under a panoply of leaves through vineyard after vineyard up the valley toward the village of Mizzole, your hair brushing against berries that are just beginning to swell. In the scented green light a wealth of insect life goes about its business: you see extraordinary, bright yellow spiders spinning their threads fast from tendril to tendril. And through the still air and intense heat, you gradually become aware of a great silent seething all around, urgent and secretive, as if the whole world were concentrated on growth, growth, growth. One tends to fall silent oneself crossing vineyards on hot summer days. The plants don't want to be disturbed. There is so much still to be done before September.

On the plain to the south, the corn is already in and the *contadini* are burning the dusty stubble with a cavalier disregard for fire hazards. On the hill above us *il conte* (as most rich landowners seem to be known) loses an acre of woodland and there are whisperings of arson. Climbing a steep slope of stunted trees and scrub we find two men running around a large burnt area trying to stamp down flames every time they flare up: here, there, behind them, in front. The smoke has a pleasant smell and is thin and lazy in the shimmering air. The men's task seems hopeless, but, no, they say, they don't need help. We climb on and find the count's huge house, mansion rather: an ochre stucco, austere façade with travertine sills and plinths. Looking through the ironwork of the old gate we count six expensive cars. Rita reflects that Mussolini's round-up of iron for the war effort generally seems to have passed over the gates of the rich, while the *contadini* shelled out their saucepans. I feel we could do with another war effort to get rid of the thousands of kilometres of superfluous ironwork sprouting up in modern suburbia.

The radio begins to speak of drought and, in this our first year in Montecchio, the regional government ordered us to stop watering our gardens. Weeks passed. The ban was not lifted. But there was little sign of deterioration in the swelling tomatoes, aubergines and peppers which flourished in every vegetable patch. For the fat *vigile* entrusted with the business of enforcing the regulation, the same who had come to see if I was living where I was living, was not to be seen beyond six in the evening, while watering began more or less with the arrival of fresh air around midnight: old men and women pushing their hoses quietly between thick clods, the more arrogant new arrivals leaving it to their timers to turn on sprinkler systems under the stars. One thing the Italian politician perceives in a way his ingenuous English counterpart does not, is that it is the enforcement of a law which is unpopular, not the law itself, which is patently a good thing and the right response to whatever problem it is supposed to be solving. Just as it is right for the Pope to insist on chastity, as long as one is left to do as one pleases. In the model anarchic society, to which Italy frequently approximates, there will be rules without end whose value will never be questioned. And under this excellent cover everybody will live as he sees fit.

In the minty night air the water hissed. The aubergines plumped out with their dark mauve of secret flesh. Practised fingers tied up the pepper plants and fat salad tomatoes were left to ripen on stone windowsills. Growth was almost audible.

So that at number 10, poor Vittorina was perhaps the only person in all Montecchio who, out of some misguided sense of guilt or civic duty, actually bothered to carry out her dishwater in buckets and chuck it over our vegetable patch. With the result that one would find strands of spaghetti draped over the *radicchio rosso*, or a few bones of *baccalà* in amongst the parsley.

Giampaolo came out with a red colander, looked at the ground, frowned, went back in empty-handed.

Every condominium is galvanised by a sort of magnetic field of attractions and repulsions. Nowhere could these be more strongly and urgently felt at Via Colombare 10 than in attitudes to the large square communal garden to one side of the house. The truth is that the modern Italian has problems with his garden. He is not at ease with it yet as the Englishman is. Behind him he has centuries of a peasant culture which ended, if it has ended, not a hundred years ago, but yesterday. For him the ground means crops, the vines, the towering corn plants, tobacco, fruit trees, tomatoes. Quite simply, he has this in his blood. And there are many who buy or build huge villas on the slopes just outside Montecchio, with a swimming pool on the terrace, gymnasium in the basement and the most ornamental iron fence imaginable all around, and can then think of nothing to do with the garden but turn it into a vast cabbage and spinach patch, producing more than they could ever hope to eat or even give away. Out of a sort of nostalgia one assumes, or inertia, or lack of imagination.

On the other hand, there are those who feel ashamed of their peasant roots and see the garden as a means of expressing their arrival in the stylish world of office jobs, high tech and magazine-inspired domestic environments. In which case they attempt to reconstruct the traditional ornamental garden of the Italian aristocracy: dwarf cypresses, oleanders, religious statuettes and tiny stone paths, spiced up perhaps with a variety of exotic plants some garden centre is passing off as fashionable and which haven't a hope of surviving the cold Veneto winter. Once everything is planted and growing, such people don't play in their gardens as an English family might. They tend them, brush them and sweep them like some never-to-be-used front room, the way other people are forever cleaning cars they never take out of their garages. Until, with the sombre smell of the cypresses and a curious stony stasis of upright trees and crisscross flagging, the status-symbol garden begins to look like a little cemetery without the graves (but waiting for those of its owners perhaps). And house after house along Via Colombare, garden after garden, decorous little cemeteries alternate with vigorous pea and cabbage patches as each *capofamiglia* declares his particular response to the profound change that has taken place, the loss of that old obviousness that the land was for food which you needed to survive.

Vegetable garden, cemetery; chained dogs in the first, a Siamese cat perhaps in the second; nervous animals in uncertain patches of green marooned by the lava flow from the city as it solidifies day by day in streets and wrought-iron fences. The tall tall fences of Montecchio, *la fortuna del fabbro*, the blacksmith's jackpot. Nowhere, nowhere does one find that happy, relaxed, cosy, *ad hoc* floweriness of the suburban English garden. It must be one of the only areas of domestic civilisation where the British win hands down.

Lucilla and Vittorina were nostalgic for a peasant past. Understandably. They wanted those tomatoes and *peperoni*, lettuce and *radicchio rosso* too. But Lucilla was fat and lazy. And a little ashamed. She drew the line at vines, for example, and was famous for having torn down with her own hands an attractive *filare* that Vittorina's husband had set up. What's more, if there was a vegetable patch, it must be away from the road, secluded from the casual glance of passers-by. After all, the house itself was so stylish with its pretentious Californian eaves, *graffiato* finish, and big terrace balconies, gave such an impression of having arrived, it would be a crime to disabuse the passer-by with some humble salad crop.

So a thin strip of land away from the road and immediately beneath the wall of Negretti's house and terrace turned out to be the only place for productive cultivation. This annoyed Vittorina, who did the lion's share of work in the garden and got some real sense of recreation from it. It annoyed her because the ground below Negretti's three-storey windowless wall got no sunshine, little rain and was full of snails, indeed teeming with them. They bred in the unkept clutter and cracked cement of Negretti's terrace and then slithered down three metres of damp brickwork in the night to stake out number 10's lettuces and peas. So Vittorina would far rather have had a sunny patch over towards the road, to feel the sun warm on her back in the early morning as she tied up her tomatoes. She didn't care about the impression this would give to the neighbours, as she didn't care about being seen carrying out her dirty dishwater; she had none of Lucilla's obsession with social status.

But a difference of opinion between Vittorina and Lucilla was easily resolved. Lucilla stamped her small, fat high-heeled foot and, aside from a little dark muttering of a saint's name here and the Virgin's there, Vittorina inevitably succumbed. Along with her peasant's attachment to salad and vegetables, she also had the peasant's age-old submission, to master and bad weather. With her never perfectly plucked moustache and fierce temper, Lucilla resembled both.

No, the real problem with the garden in Via Colombare was that of integrating the old ladies' earthy mix of nostalgia and shame with the younger Visentini's more sophisticated, media-based, urban vision: an English lawn, shady trees, and, yes, a vegetable patch (because Giampaolo is a gourmet and fresh greens are tastier), but run along ecological, natural-food lines (because Giampaolo, like any modern man, is also something of a Green). Thus Vittorina not only had to work the communal vegetable patch under the tall bare wall of Negretti's grim house but, to add to her troubles, she wasn't allowed to poison the quite multitudinous snails. It all came out in the food, her younger neighbour scared her. We would all die of cancer.

And that was one battle Giampaolo won. Indeed, whenever Vittorina took up a position on something it was always clear she was going to lose. A bulky, heavy-breathing woman, she prayed a great deal, had Masses said for her husband, visited the cemetery almost daily and subscribed to such periodicals as *I miracoli di Sant'Antonio* and *La salvezza*. Her face had a morose wisdom which would occasionally light up in genuine friendliness. One suspected she was already resigned to losing the quarrels of this world, banking on the next. A pushover for the persuasive, courteous and always well-informed Giampaolo.

However, since Giampaolo only rented his flat, whereas the others owned, when it came to getting trees or bushes for the garden proper, Lucilla insisted on choosing and locating them herself (Giampaolo was quick to disclaim responsibility). The result was one of the very saddest collections of dwarf cypresses and ornamental mutants imaginable, unhealthy things picked up in sales and planted apparently at random across two hundred square metres of dry lawn. A funereal tone was everywhere apparent and, indeed, it occurred to us that Lucilla had probably never been into a garden that wasn't a cemetery. There were no gardens in her poverty-stricken youth and most of her life had been spent operating an industrial cleaning business from a small suburban flat. Whereas the early death of her husband and various relatives had made her all too familiar with cemeteries.

To her credit, Lucilla was aware that something was wrong with the garden at number 10, aware that this gloomy assortment of dull evergreens was not really what she was after. In the hope of achieving some improbable rightness, she would thus, Giampaolo explained, move the trees about year after year, dig one up, shift it a metre or two this way, dig up another, swop it with yet another, put this one in the shade, move that one out of it, and so on and so forth, so that the weary plants became sadder and sadder while the business of mowing the lawn in Via Colombare now involved a dizzy weaving back and forth through the lost labour of Lucilla's search for harmony.

And of course the lawn had to be mowed regularly. Giampaolo was strict about this. Regularly and very low. Because it had to be an *English* lawn, as the Italians imagine English lawns to be, an extension, that is, of the meticulous formal elegance of the Visentini's flat, licked clean from top to bottom day in day out with sacrificial anality. Yes, Giampaolo said at our first condominium meeting when my duties were outlined, the lawn had to be mowed twice or three times a week from spring through autumn and the cuttings had to be gathered with a rake and piled on a compost heap in the most hidden corner of the garden where shameful things like compost heaps are piled. It should be said here, in Giampaolo's defence, that most surrounding gardeners of the cemetery variety just had their grass taken away by the refuse men, and this was the easy solution that Lucilla, if not Vittorina, would undoubtedly have plumped for. But being a Green, Giampaolo rightly insisted that grass was a limited resource to be husbanded and utilised – along the snail-infested wall . . .

Never has good neighbourliness been more onerous, as, with the two ladies unable to handle the mower and no one willing to pay for a gardener, I was enlisted into the ritual twice-weekly mowing. And daily watering. For the lawn had to be watered assiduously throughout the hot summer, and most particularly it had to be watered at the front of the house where the terrace balconies of the two lower flats were only a metre or so above quite a few square metres of grass below, depriving the grass of water, but not light, since a low slanting sun shafted in of an evening to shrivel the poor plants up.

How we mowed and mowed that lawn. And how many hours I was to spend distractedly pointing a hose pipe at those doomed patches of grass beneath the balconies, which were so important of course, being amongst the most visible, through iron railings, from the dusty street. To make matters worse it was assumed that, being English, I would naturally know a great deal about lawns and my advice, as we settled in, would frequently be sought on dry patches, ringmoulds, moss, etc., as if such knowledge were carried in the genes. I thus got used to observing a genuine sense of disappointment when it was discovered that I knew nothing, but nothing about lawns. And what's more (to my shame now, actually) showed every sign of not greatly caring.

Giampaolo: 'What kind of fertiliser do you think we should put on the lawn toward the end of summer?'

Me, with a shake of the head: 'The cheapest.'

'Do you think we should leave the cut grass down this time, or rake it up?'

'Oh, let's leave it. Good idea.' But my enthusiasm was too evident, and very soon it was understood that my opinion could be ignored, and that I wouldn't even mind if it were not solicited. Which was a relief. And to salve any conscience I might have had, I reflected that at least I was doing my neighbours the favour of demonstrating the hollowness of national stereotypes.

9
La stagione è finita

Sometimes when I wasn't actually called upon to participate in the garden, I would watch the others from the big window in our *salotto*. For, ironically, ours was the only flat with a good upper-storey view of the garden. I thus observed that, while the old ladies followed the seasons, Giampaolo went by the book. Or rather, it wasn't quite the seasons Lucilla and Vittorina followed, but the rigid set of proverbs and rules a thousand years of peasant culture offered them. Some of which they themselves, having spent their adult lives in industrial cleaning, remembered only approximately. I recall in mid-September going out into the garden for a couple of tomatoes (just reward for all that mowing), to discover to my amazement that not only were there none left, but the plants themselves had gone, disappeared, been uprooted, the ground already forked over and raked.

'When Lucilla decides the season's over, she tears them up,' Orietta told me. Her voice was still completely neutral as it had been at all our early meetings. But now a half-smile played about the lips, suggesting the possibility of future confidences. 'She's pulled up the peppers too and the aubergines. It's the same every year.'

'But they were still growing.'

'Lucilla thought the season was over.'

Lucilla was an extreme, indeed manic case, but it has to be remembered that this is the country where, if you go swimming any time after September, even if the temperature is in the sweltering upper thirties, you will be looked on with surprise. *La stagione è finita*. The season is over.

Giampaolo, on the contrary, to plant a row of peas, brought out the encyclopaedia he was buying piecemeal and at considerable price. This would be at the weekend, since he had a regular office job. He laid the appropriate volume on a dry patch of ground and was careful not to touch it with earthy hands: if I happened to be around I would turn the pages for him and read. The spacing between one seed and another? Five centimetres. The depth of the hole? Three centimetres. Soil preparation . . . Brought up the last child of five in Venice, he knew nothing of the earth, but being a modern man he believed that information could be had from books. We planted the peas together. We did everything the book said. Most of them never came up. And the few that did were eaten overnight by the rampant snails.

The ladies sniggered. As indeed Giampaolo sniggered when they tore up tomato plants that still had a good couple of kilos in them. Lucilla would stop you on the stairs: 'Have Signor Giampaolo's carrots come up?' With that same half-smile around the corners of her lips, Orietta would say: 'Now they've pulled up the pepper plants.'

And yet . . . Giampaolo had considerable respect for the local peasant culture, because books teach this too. Parsley and spinach should be planted with a new moon, a lawn sown with a full moon, still wines bottled with a waning moon, etc. etc. And the old ladies in their turn had more than a sneaking admiration for anybody who could genuinely read a book and find something out. After all, it was Giampaolo who fixed their boilers when they burst, adjusted their cars and appliances, even if his peas never came up and the bulbs he planted didn't flower. In the garden, everybody watched each other in a delicious tension to see whose culture would prove the most effective. And in this respect the situation was typical of the small handkerchief of Italy I live in. There is such a collison of ancient ideas and new. Which will win? In a way it was not unlike Elija and the worshippers of Baal waiting to see whose sacrifice would burst into flames.

And in the meantime we were all watched by old Lovato, our neighbour on the Via Colombare side, whose tiny garden bordered on our own. Bald, towering, broad-shouldered, Lovato was one of the old guard, a never-say-die, pea-cabbage-tomato-and-pepper man, a retired farmer. His gaze, looking over the wall at our sad ornamental garden, was one of genuine puzzlement, turning to pity and just a hint of derision when his eye fell upon our miserable vegetable patch. In his own few poky metres he produced a quite prodigious abundance of vegetables in the way only the small farmer knows how: working the ground furiously and using obscene amounts of fertiliser, weedkiller, and pesticide. The snails must have felt sick if ever the faintest breeze blew from his direction.

Stolid, solid and quite unashamed of a businesslike shamble of pots, canes and cuttings all about him, Lovato watched. Through wire netting. For, above the waist-high dividing wall, he had unaccountably erected a fence reaching up a good three metres and lethally barbed on top, although sagging and rusting. I say unaccountably for intrusion from the direction of Via Colombare 10 was surely unlikely. But it was interesting that neither Giampaolo nor the old ladies found anything strange about his wanting to guard his property so determinedly. If an Englishman's house is his castle, an Italian's is his bunker. There is this obsession with self-defence: railings, remote-controlled gates, security cameras, bulletproof windows, armoured front doors . . . No, from the Via Colombare point of view, Lovato's attitude was understandable. But it absolutely must not be at the expense of the ornamental quality of number 10's garden. Railings, yes; rusty wire, no.

Lucilla and Vittorina had years ago asked Lovato to remove this *vergogna* (one is tempted to translate this as 'eyesore', but literally the word means 'shame', which is what they felt Lovato should feel). Lovato refused. Giampaolo more diplomatically referred to the fence as '*antiestetico*'. Lovato played deaf. He would not take the thing down. At which Giampaolo had suggested that the ladies buy a hedge which would grow up and cover it all. Yes, all three metres high of it, thus protecting the aesthetic qualities of number 10's cemetery. The hedge was duly planted. This had apparently infuriated Lovato, who claimed it would eventually rob all light from his small patch, although it's possible he was equally concerned about losing his pensioner's view of our miserable garden (which must have provided considerable entertainment). He would go to court, he said. There was a law about blocking other people's light. Giampaolo politely remarked that his ramshackle garage of breeze block and corrugated iron located to one end of the fence had surely not been erected with the appropriate building permission. Since this was where Lovato's son-in-law kept the Lancia Prisma of which the whole family was rightly proud, it seemed unlikely they would be willing to pull it down just in order to embark on uncertain litigation against number 10. When Rita and I arrived in Via Colombare the hedge was a metre high with everything still to play for.

To straighten out your topography then, we have the threatening hedge and nosy Lovato diametrically opposite the northern (and lateral) wall of the condominium which includes our living-room window where I sometimes stand beneath the elaborate, if dim, chandelier to look out on the world. To my left (and west) as I look out, is the long ironwork railing along Via Colombare, and to my right (never forgetting the mobile triffids in the garden between of course) Negretti's tall windowless wall. And here's a curiosity. Negretti's wall has a cinema screen on it, a huge rectangle of white, for before number 10 was built the present garden area had been a cinema. Yes, rural Montecchio had once had a cinema, albeit tiny. Now of course the screen was no more than cracking white paint surrounded by broken brickwork where the cinema had been demolished and Negretti's wall reinforced. Not a little of Negretti's intransigence with his dog, we discovered, his almost relishing the disturbance it caused, was the result of his having wished to buy the cinema himself, only to be outbid by these two old ladies, who then ignored building regulations to stick their own *palazzina* rather too close to his. In revenge he refused to do anything about the unsightly wall, the yellowing screen, the broken bricks. Lucilla and Vittorina offered to go halves to have it stuccoed, but Negretti, like Lovato, refused. And the more they showed that the wall bothered them, the more stubborn he would be. The ornamentality of number 10's garden was thus irretrievably compromised; for whereas Lovato's fence might one day be covered by that hedge, no ivy could really get a grip on the smooth white of that cinema screen. As for myself, wandering around in stifling heat, hosepipe in hand, doing my bit for the lawn, the snail-sad lettuce, the scorched earth beneath the terraces, I would look up at the screen and wish with all my heart that the cinema could have remained.

10
Il palo della cuccagna

Montecchio mornings late September. Seven o'clock. The tiles under bare feet are beginning to feel more than pleasantly cool. You go through to the kitchen, heave up the heavy plastic roll-down shutter, all the rage in the late seventies, but spurned now in the general return to natural materials. You have to be careful not to pull too hard or the thing will roll away through the slit and into its little box above the French window, to be retrieved only after hours of fiddling. On the outside, the plastic is peppered with holes where the wind hurled big hailstones in an August storm.

You step out on to the balcony, air fresh and glass clear. Number 10 is exactly half-way along the street. In a lacquered morning light you see the Madonnina in her niche with fake flowers a hundred metres away to the right, the derelict bottle factory the same distance to the left. Opposite, above the houses, rise two more, rather nobler nineteenth-century mills, likewise derelict, one with an attractive design of little pillars and arches just beneath the cornice some six floors up. Both buildings have been listed, their empty windows staring, innards gutted. And behind these again rises a low ridge of hills pushing south into the plain, with *Il castello di Montecchio* on top: a square tower, a wall, a taller tower, a wall, a third tower the same height as the first: Austrian defences. The Communist Party want to turn it into a sports and community centre. The Christian Democrats don't seem to be able to find the money, or the enthusiasm. At present, amid banks of blackberries going to waste, it's used only by the so-called *emarginati*: drug addicts, homosexuals, immigrants.

But what a splendid sight on a bright morning, with the larks still twittering high in the air, the most delicate fleecy clouds (*pecorelle* the Italians call them, little sheep) curdling in milky blue above, and the light green horizontal flow of the ridge beautifully pointed up by the sombre verticality of cypresses winding serpentine towards the sharp silhouette of the castle.

Down in the street, the old man who lives opposite slithers off his muddy bike. Giobatta Marini. Pushing eighty, hunched, flat-footed, fishing gear slung over his shoulder, he has his dawn catch in a plastic bag under his arm. The stout wife, who bore him all those table-tennis playing children, comes out in apron and slippers to meet her patriarch and whisk away the fish. An early lizard creeps between railings along the wall. And, leaning on the cool marble of the parapet, still in your pyjamas, you breathe deeply, as your father used to whenever he got a chance to be out in the country. 'How marvellous, what air!'

A boy in overalls, with bedraggled hair and pasty face, roars by on an ancient and deliberately unsilenced *motorino*. Leaving a cloud of oily blue behind. Well, OK. It's all part of the happy scene, not unpleasant really and he does boast the name of Raffaello. At the end of the street he revs quite violently – a bit of frustration, unsatisfied libido to burn up. Fair enough. He works in the mechanic's at the corner. But now he's turned the thing off, the cloud of exhaust has dispersed, and you can relax again, breathe in this beauty, and breathe deep: aah!

Until, quite suddenly, the whole marvellous morning is corrupted, tainted, transformed, by the most unpleasant smell.

It's sudden and overwhelming. One moment you didn't notice it, the next the whole picturesque scene – castle, fisherman, Madonnina – has become a deception, an enamel over something that reeks.

Words and smells don't go well together, but perhaps I could describe it as a corpse smell, a smell of something wrong, an abusive, acrid, clogging smell, and certainly a smell that one shouldn't be smelling at seven o'clock in the morning in a village in northern Italy. The chemical factory in the small industrial estate is letting off the fumes from its storage tanks. Go in, close the door and all the other windows too. Look at the fine morning through the glass you really ought to clean. And get the *espresso* pot on to drown that stench.

The following morning, if the pressure is suddenly low and fine mercurial clouds are thickening over the *castello*, it could well be a chicken-dung smell rolling down from the factory farms which have taken over the surrounding hills as the *contadini* beat their long retreat. An all-pervading smell which may last half the morning.

And the next day, if we imagine a rare breeze is flowing from the north after rainfall, it will be the smell of intensive pig farming further up the valley. Is this the worst? Or should pride of place go to the synthetic-fabric factory to the south whose methylated fumes, thank heaven, come only with the sirocco? But they're all bad. They all add to that constant threat of encroachment which typifies these villages. They all have to do with making money fast on territory which is cheap because it's being abandoned, territory which once provided a living, and little more. Unless perhaps a culture.

The evenings are more pleasurable. There are no particular smells. Your wineglasses are perched on the marble parapet of the balcony while from Patuzzi's abandoned armchair you watch huge moths whirr about the street-lights hanging from wires which run zigzag between the houses. The sound of Giampaolo's stubborn hose hisses from under the balconies, the old ladies call to each other up and down the stairs over the babble of their televisions: 'Cilla!' 'Rina!' Tock tock tock goes the Marini tribe's ping-pong. And a blackbird whistles quite beautifully at twilight. Over a period of a couple of months we get to know his call. We stand on the balcony and whistle. There is a pause, perhaps a minute. To tease you. Then he whistles back. And again. And again. 'Lest you should think he never could recapture . . .' but that was a thrush of course. The blackbird whistles, we answer him. It's upsetting to discover later that he sings so well because Giobatta has blinded him. For on the mornings he doesn't go fishing, old Marini will take the creature out into the country in its tiny cage, to attract other birds to the muzzle of his shotgun.

Perhaps it shouldn't be upsetting. This kind of thing has always gone on. This is the old way. Why am I so squeamish? Yet whenever I whistle to the bird now I can't help imagining the moment of its blinding, and I both want and don't want to know how it was done.

Giobatta, of course, is short for Giovanni Battista. When a friend of mine recently took his child to be baptised and said, 'Giovanni', the priest immediately came back, 'Evangelista or Battista?' There was no other choice. You would have thought with his namesake ending up the way he did, Giobatta might have been a shade more mindful about taking sharp instruments to creatures.

Night falls. But the gently swinging lights keep the street quite bright. In the glow, little girls are playing something like hopscotch. There is no bedtime here. They dodge about their chalk squares and shrill and argue. Comes the sound of clashing gears and a car scatters them, driving recklessly fast in the narrow space. Their parents playing ping-pong under the pergola do not seem concerned. A red light goes on above the Madonnina. Or perhaps it is always on but only noticeable in the dark. From the window below we can hear the ladies giggling together over their television. Comes the portentous sound of the pips. A woman's voice announces that it is 10.04 precisely, then the strain of the tune introducing the evening news programme. It is an endearing characteristic of Italian broadcasting that they are not overly concerned about starting programmes on the hour.

One Sunday, after a morning of particularly unpleasant smells, we walked to Montecchio's industrial estate to check the situation out. It lies just the other side of the cherry orchard behind the Madonnina. Sadly, the orchard is closed off by a ten-foot-high dry-stone wall some hundreds of years old. You skirt around this barrier and go by way of the bus terminus, where the driver is enjoying a few minutes in a bar before his return trip to Verona (termini always coincide with bars, which is as it should be). The road here is straight and narrow with tall ivy-bitten walls either side. A first iron gate on the right leads into an avenue of cypresses and the cemetery. Then, after a large tarred area, which trucks could presumably park in but never do, you turn into the industrial estate.

And are immediately surprised. For what you see is: attractive villa, followed by long low prefab; then, salubrious three-storey *palazzina*, followed by grubby factory; then, green-stuccoed terrace with cascading geraniums, followed by woodyard; and again, lavishly funereal garden, chemical plant; gnomed patio with barbecue, print-works; and on and on: expensive house, business, expensive house, business, expensive house, business for three hundred metres. All the local *padroni* live here with their factories and factory smells. How can we complain when they get the worst of it? Circulars from the Communist Party will later explain that the land was more or less given away allowing *imprenditori* to build cheap villas for themselves, their children, their grandchildren. 'Not a single job more was created,' they protest. Perhaps erroneously.

But as industrial areas go, and when the early morning smell of lucrative enterprise has subsided, this is not an unpleasant place. Well-dressed families are eating ice creams on balconies. There's a sound of chatter and children. A fat man in fashionable tracksuit is clearing up his toasting forks. The chained guard-dogs are asleep in the shade.

Then on our way home we stumbled upon *il palo della cuccagna*. In passing I might say that everything I have discovered in Montecchio I have stumbled on. It seems in keeping with the spirit of the place. And perhaps it was only because we saw them both on the same day that it occurred to me that this amusing celebration was not entirely unconnected with the mentality that produced the industrial zone.

We had planned to walk back a different way so that we could lounge on the Roman stones by Laghetto Squarà for a while, something that was becoming a favourite pastime: just sitting and watching, in the heat, by the water, with the sound of the spring gurgling across pebbles from under the broken church door. But the banks of the *laghetto* were packed this afternoon. A hundred and more people were shouting and cheering. As we approached, the cheering grew louder and louder, then a great splash. And more cheers, or jeers, before somebody called a name on a megaphone.

We climbed up on a stone. Into a drain hole in the bank, the trunk of a fir tree, perhaps twenty metres long, had been fixed so that it stretched out horizontally just above the water, supported half-way by a spike driven into the lake bottom. A small red flag fluttered right at the end where the pole was no more than four or five inches thick. On the bank, above the base of the trunk, stood a small gaggle of boys and men in swimming costume, shivering under towels. Beside them, on a high stool, sat the umpire.

The umpire calls out a name. The boy who serves me my *prosciutto crudo* in Brandoli's, the supermarket, lets himself down gingerly over the weedy stone on to the base of the pole, and begins to walk. All he has to do is reach the other end of the pole and grab the flag. This feat will transport him into the land of Cockaigne, that is, he will get a reward. In the event, despite the thickness of the pole at its base, he manages no more than three metres.

Because the whole pole has been thickly greased with soap.

There are about fifteen contestants and they go again and again in turns, slipping and slithering clownishly on the soap. If you refuse to go when it's your turn, you're out. And since the water rises right here from under the hills, it is not exactly warm. An older man, in his sixties perhaps, is shivering violently as he lifts his stomach on to the bank. A muscly exhibitionist clutches his crotch. There's a clammy weed in his hair. At each attempt, each contestant dissolves a little more of the soap, and then for four turns each is allowed to carry a handful of sand which he spreads in front of his feet. Thus some kind of progress is made, pushing further and further towards the flag, amidst the screams of girlfriends and mothers, and the chuckling of those men wise enough to appreciate that this is definitely a spectator sport.

It's interesting (and rather a shame) that no girls are competing.

At the end of the day (and we stay two hours and more), since it would be impossible to provide the winner with the real cockaigne of *palazzina* and family business beside, the prize, finally awarded to the lad who delivers bread from one of the village's bakeries, is 150,000 Lire's worth of petrol from our local petrol pump. As a vision of plenty, it says much perhaps. Though this archaic festival is obviously timed to coincide with the harvest.

11
Bepi

Orietta Visentini says that in twenty odd years she has never really been accepted in Montecchio. For she was born in Peschiera, on the southern shores of Lake Garda, forty kilometres away. People's friends here are their childhood friends, their family. Orietta sighs. They don't even know how to make friends, because they have never had to do so, and anyway, they can't imagine anybody being without their own circle.

What hope for me then?

Very little. I step off the bus outside the derelict bottle factory and walk down Via Colombare. I nod to people: to the grappa-scented car mechanic in his overalls whose work overflows on to the narrow street; to ancient be-capped Giobatta, the hunter and fisher, but working on his vines today along a sagging fence; I nod again to the slightly mongoloid-looking woman in black who puts her father out on a chair by the doorstep in the morning, squashes his straw hat on his head, and brings him in in the evening (surprisingly their dingy house, which opens directly on to the street, has an expensive aquarium in the window of a bare room with large table, wooden chairs, stone floor and nothing else). I salute the portly, heavy-jowled man in the light suit who finds climbing out of his Alfa 75 something of an effort, the more casual fellow who sells insurance in a Fiat 126, the stout, vigorous woman who every morning takes a twig brush to sweep the dust from the road outside her house and push it over toward her neighbour's. My greetings, which after all follow the traditional Italian style and which all these people exchange with each other every time they cross paths – *Buon giorno signora, buon giorno signore* – are met at first with embarrassment, perhaps even suspicion, since clearly I am part of that world which encroaches; later with returned nods, muttered courtesies. And perhaps that is quite enough. Only in the greengrocer's does a loud voice reply: ''ello, sir, 'ow are you!' And it is Bepi. My first friend in Montecchio.

I suppose Bepi fits into that class of Italians who are eager to know foreigners. One has to be careful not to be collected by these people. It's a group Giampaolo Visentini belongs to in a rather different, more sophisticated way. Not that these people have in any sense ceased to believe in the supremacy of Italian cooking, Italian wine, Italian style, and so forth, just that they are sensitive to a certain provincialism, eager to be associated with anything that lies outside their narrow circle. Perhaps they have been frustrated: Giampaolo by the stifling promotion procedures in the monolithic company he works for, Bepi by the obstacles put in the way of anybody without contacts who wishes to get a licence for a lucrative shop. Both feel they have ideas bigger than the narrow mentality of the people around them. But, interestingly, they don't feel this provincialism could be overcome by going to Rome, as a man stifled in Barnsley might head for Birmingham or London. On the contrary, Rome would be even worse, the locals would already have staked the place out for themselves. No, they look to the fairness and openmindedness of the efficient nations further north. Extraordinarily, they believe Britain to be such a nation. And can never understand what on earth I am doing here in Montecchio.

From behind his stone-topped counter, Bepi pumps my hand. He is 'very 'appy' to have an Englishman in his shop. He smiles broadly, he's my own age or thereabouts, but physically a much more impressive specimen: hugely solid, with thick shoulder-length curly hair, and such a look of eagerness about him, such a presence. Green green eyes. He sticks a couple of kiwis into my bag and doesn't want to be paid for them. *Per carità*!

As I turn to go, the priest walks in, Don Guido. I am thus able to witness the whole scene. In his black cassock, the priest stands there sniffing the air, a short, droll, old-woman of a man. He sniffs and sniffs, snub nose upturned as the other customers go about with their little plastic baskets picking up artichokes, peppers and what have you from the boxes around the wall. Then he lifts his shoulders sharply up and down in a gesture of impatience. The cassock has a shiny, worn look to it. 'Something smells rotten in here,' he announces out loud and with almost a threat in his voice.

Quite unperturbed giving or taking change, Bepi replies, 'Must be the carrion flesh of the last person to walk in.' '*Carogna*' is a common insult. At which the priest calmly proceeds with his shopping.

I never managed to get to the bottom of this dispute between our greengrocer and priest, a quarrel made attractive by its combination of intense animosity and total lack of consequence. And perhaps that is the essence of the Latin quarrel, at least on this level. It is almost enjoyed for its own sake. There is no feeling of any need to make up or resolve things, because no harm is being done. The priest came every day, ritual insults were exchanged, fruit and vegetables selected, money handed over, and that was that.

In a place like Montecchio, the indigenous population are, as Orietta had said, almost impenetrable. Because self-sufficient. Thus, being a newcomer and peripheral to village life, one inevitably gets to know other peripherals, people who like yourself have been washed up here, because at some particular moment this was where the current flowed, and the place turned out to be convenient. Bepi had tried for years to get a licence to open a supermarket – anywhere in the Province of Verona would do – until finally they allowed him to rent the downstairs of an unprepossessing old house on the outskirts of Montecchio – for a greengrocery.

Invited to dinner, he sits down, legs wide apart on his seat, his powerful body straining his clothes, and immediately, before I've even poured an *aperitivo*, announces: the man I call father in the shop is not my father.

In a country where reserve and formality are usually excessive on these occasions, it is certainly a dramatic opening. And embarrassing. He proceeds to tell us that he is the illegitimate child of a woman whose family threw her out. Not wanting her baby, his mother left him with a childless sister and her husband: the man he calls father and who helps in the shop.

He then goes on to tell us how, poverty-stricken, the family sold their house in Rivoli and came to live in a meagre flat in one of the downmarket residential areas of Verona. But he swore to buy back that house for the family to demonstrate that he was more than just an illegitimate child. And last year he finally did so.

If Bepi's abrupt, reductive autobiography is disconcerting, the obsession with family and home comes as no surprise. When an Italian leaves a place it's almost always with the intention of returning victorious and vindicated. Even if he believes that place to be hopelessly provincial.

How had he made his money? Bepi laughs. He taps a finger on his temples. All in here, he says, all in here. He tells the picaresque story of his entrepreneurial career. You know they're always saying Italian wine has no added sugar? Yes. And it's illegal to add sugar to wine in Italy? Yes. Well, I drove the truck that took the sugar to all the wine producers from Vicenza to Verona. At night of course. There are no police about at night. They only work office hours. He grins, he is very pleased with himself. For this was an act of *furbizia*, of cunning, and it paid very well. Spent all the money setting up a restaurant with a friend, near the main road to the lake, a big restaurant, for coach parties and the like. The mistake was doing it with somebody else. The friend couldn't see reason. Didn't have it up here. Bepi taps his forehead again. They went bust. There followed two or three other restaurants, then finally the licence for the shop. He had wanted a supermarket, but local shopkeepers always gang together and bother their political contacts to make sure no new licences are given. This is common practice, they have the politicians in their pockets, or they *are* the politicians. But Bepi will beat them at their own game in the end. Yes, he will. Sooner or later he'll have the knife by the handle . . .

As so often in conversations here, one notes this assumption of a fundamental lawlessness. The law is only one of the arms the individual uses in his essentially lawless struggle. Bepi talked at length about various court cases he was engaged in: with the phone company about stupidly high bills, with a neighbour about his (Bepi's) dog kennels, with INPS, the national-insurance people, about unpaid contributions for the girls in his shop, and there were others too which I forget now. Far from any desire to reform or change the situation, Bepi seemed pleased to have these various fights going on and not at all concerned he might lose them. As Negretti had seemed pleased when Visentini called the police about the stench of dog filth rising from his garden, as Lucilla was galvanised by her fight with Signora Marta. It is a bellicosity one finds hard to take at first, but which constant contact with other people, and above all the authorities, gradually tends to make more comprehensible, and even attractive. If there is an anarchical tradition here, there are certainly reasons for it.

Towards nine o'clock, his dinner barely over, Bepi simply falls asleep in the middle of a conversation on Patuzzi's cheap synthetic couch, one of the only modern items of furniture in the flat. The chandelier now has five small 60-watt bulbs casting sharper shadows from the fancy mouldings on the bookcase. But Bepi snores just the same. When we wake him he looks at his watch. *Diamine*, he has to drive thirty kilometres to Rivoli now to feed his dogs. Fifteen of them. Tomorrow he will be up at five to get to the vegetable market and pick up stuff for the shop, then in the evening he teaches a gym class at the abandoned church by Laghetto Squarà which he rents from Don Guido (the source of their quarrel perhaps?). Yes, he teaches gym on Mondays and Wednesdays, karate on Tuesdays and Thursdays. Do we want to come?

How can I say that after a day's teaching and translating I'm not sure if I'll have the energy?

12
L'uomo rinascimentale

We go out running with Bepi. He gathers about fifteen young people by the abandoned church beside the *laghetto*. Most of the group are girls, more than one with their eyes on Bepi. Off we trot out into the country, up the valley towards Mizzole. The evening air is cool. We run by the cherry orchards, leaves limp with a first suspicion of autumn. We run past the first long, low poultry farm. The stench is unbelievable. And on an empty box by the side of the road, I read: 'BEST CANADIAN CHURKEY EGGS – SEALED CONTAINER – FOR INCUBATION FOLLOW INSTRUCTIONS.'

Jogging (or 'footing' as the Italians unaccountably call it) along tractor paths, we pass through a large vineyard, the purple fruit almost ripe around our ears. Here, beneath the dense foliage, Bepi stops for some exercises, barking out orders with an unmistakeably authoritarian ring to his voice. *Flessioni*! And he's down on his stomach doing press ups. *Addominali*! He's on his back doing sit-ups, hands behind his head, legs bent at the knee. *Dorsali*! Over on our stomachs again. Such a desire for leadership! He flogs us. Showing off his macho dynamism. It's endearing. The girls titter, most of them making only token efforts. Footing again, we pass through a delightful old wine-stuccoed farm. There's an ancient well in the garden with stone top and swallows mustering for departure on the roof of the barn. Panting now, we run on through the picturesque village of Mizzole with the golden onion dome on its church. Posters tell us about pollution from pig farming, courses in secretarial skills, the imminent grape festival and the most recent deaths: Magnagatto Marta: ninety-two *anni*, much missed by her family. Graffiti on the stone walls, however, is mainly directed against a group of southerners from Reggio Calabria who have formed a cooperative and plan to build themselves some *villette a schiera* – terraced houses (a brand new fashion in Italy): '*Benvenuto a Reggio Mizzole*', has been scrawled over a road sign. Italians have a gift for grafitti. In the central square by the war memorial we read: 'Long live the government, long live taxes, long live the South . . . or no?' The work of the local separatists. Opposite, a sign over one of the village's two bars announces: Real American Cocktails, by Gianni.

We arrive back puffing and panting. Bepi wants to do some more exercises, but I've had enough. Perhaps anyway he is only waiting to see which groupie will hang on the longest. A process of natural selection. Walking home, past the millwheel, past a Roman arch, under which heavy trucks pass to two huge silage containers in a small yard, we reflect that if he votes at all, Bepi probably votes MSI, the not very reformed fascists.

Another evening we drop by the gym where he is teaching karate to a mixed group of all ages. Italians take their sport very seriously. Black belt tight round his waist, Bepi barks out commands in what we presume is Japanese, his body squatting low, making the impressive ritual movements with concentration etched on his features. 'All here,' he tells us afterwards, 'all here,' and he taps his forehead.

A few weeks later we are invited to the house Bepi has repurchased and is now renovating up in Rivoli. He drives us west through Verona and then strikes off north up the Valpolicella. It's *vendemmia* time, the grape harvest. The Alfettas and BMWs fret and fume behind tractors inching along with their cartloads of grapes; it's important that the fruit doesn't get too knocked about, so they're taking the road as slow as they can. The air is heavy with an extremely pleasant drunken smell, an almost tangible sweet stickiness. Midges swarm in quite unbelievable numbers. Storms and clouds of them. These *vendemmia* days, you find yourself breathing midges the way the whale simply swallows his plankton as he swims along.

We arrive in Rivoli, perched high on the hills above the Adige, site of one of Napoleon's famous victories. Bepi turns his grocery van into a narrow track, bumping steeply down. At the end, the old peasant house that has focused his enterprising mind for so long is unprepossessing: a humble two-storey rectangle divided into two small dwellings with chickens pecking about outside. Buying it back can have had only symbolic value. Especially seeing as Bepi doesn't want to live here himself, and can't even get on with the ancient grandmother he has installed there. On our arrival they exchange fierce insults, much as he did with the priest.

The grounds are large though, perhaps thirty or forty acres sloping steeply downward away from the house. Once laboriously terraced and cultivated, they are neglected now, like so much of this countryside. The vines are overgrown, the support walls crumbling, so that here and there a terrace has collapsed, showing how chalky white the soil is beneath. Bepi takes us down to his dog kennels, a low concrete building a good fifty metres long and full of big, black, barking dogs. Our host, apparently – he tells us himself – is the foremost breeder of Belgian Shepherds in the Veneto, if not in Italy. His neighbour, despite being out of sight and earshot of the dogs, has started a court case about the kennels because he is resentful that Bepi outbid him for possession of the house. The same old story. Bepi thus stands accused of having built them without planning permission. In typically belligerent fashion Bepi has turned the case on its head, sueing the local authorities for being so slow over granting permission that he was 'forced' to go ahead without in order to accommodate his business.

He releases a couple of dogs and lets them come with us. Disconcertingly, as we walk along, he barks at them in German. I ask him which language he prefers for his girlfriends. With touching honesty he tells us he hasn't as yet found the language that girls respond to best. I assure him it is not English.

Before going in for lunch, he takes us up to a ridge at the edge of the property where we have a breathtaking view northward up the Valpolicella to the Alps, their rocky peaks barely visible for the haze. Deep deep below in the valley a huge irrigation canal leaves the River Adige and disappears into a tunnel under the hill. Disused marble quarries now converted into mushroom farms are dotted all about. The vista is vast, open, inspiring. I remark rather banally that it seems out of this world, *fuori del mondo*. To which, quite naturally, Bepi replies that, yes, UFOs (Oofoes as the Italians call them) used to visit here quite often, but have now ceased to do so, ever since people became too violent. The Veneto, he says, along with parts of Russia, boasts the highest frequencies of UFO sightings in the world. He used to see the lights himself further up the valley. I feel it isn't the moment to say that the Veneto also shares with Russia one of the highest consumptions of alcohol in the world.

Returning to the house we find Bepi's delightful 'father', Vittorio, who has come out to the country for the day with his wife. Strong, squat, of great girth and irrepressibly merry, Vittorio is just the kind of jolly chap one tends to see interviewed in the local paper after a UFO sighting. Now he presides over the big wooden table in the kitchen, where he has lined up five or six bottles of wine and seems intent on opening all of them at once. Meanwhile, his wife, Gina, buxom, retiring and embarrassed about her poor Italian, has prepared the most wonderful lasagna from scratch. Oceans of it.

We sit down. Vittorio begins to describe the qualities of each of his bottles at considerable length. Since he speaks only dialect and, unlike his wife, isn't at all embarrassed about it, I can't understand. I pick up half of a jolly joke about a dog that only went for dead birds. 'Don't let him come near me then,' is the punchline. Bird in Italian also means John Thomas.

Midday. The abundant lasagna. The labelless wine bottles. The smoke from an unnecessary fire in the huge limestone grate. Big thick steaks, which of course Bepi gets through a friend of a friend who would never give him anything but *roba buona* – good stuff. Then *tiramisù*, again abundant, creamy, calorie-rich, cholesterol-rich, splendid. Alongside a treacly Recioto. And, finally, a score of different grappas to choose from after, or with, your *espresso*. Vittorio makes the grappa himself, with what's left after making the wine, flavouring it with such things as lemons, peaches, oranges, even coffee. The different brews are arrayed before us in the kind of tall, greasy, nameless bottles one expects to find in the garage with a couple of inches of brake fluid in the bottom. I try two or three and make a toast to the UFOs.

Going back in his greengrocer's van, Bepi tells me that what he'd like to do is study theology. The Church and the Masons still hold on to many of the deepest secrets of this world; only the initiated will ever be allowed to know anything worth knowing. He has applied to join a lodge and is studying the cabbala in the evening when he can stay awake. Vaguely it occurs to me that this is all part of the P2 mentality. And I wonder if Bepi isn't the closest I am ever likely to get to a Renaissance man.

13
Troppo gentile

To be earthquake-proof, modern Italian buildings are legally required to be constructed around a reinforced concrete frame. In the event of tremors, the whole structure should thus shift as one unit, rather than crumbling into its separate parts. And, indeed, as one walks about the outskirts of Montecchio and on into the surrounding hills, builders are eagerly pouring cement into columns of roughly nailed planks, in a hurry to get things done before the November rains.

Concrete the columns and the beams, where shortly before were olive trees; concrete the roofs, too, of these new *palazzine* and *case a schiera*; and likewise concrete the floors, all wires and plumbing laid forever inaccessible in the cement. Gaunt frames take over a vineyard. Up go the walls between one beam and the next. The roof is then topped with terracotta, the living-space inside tiled with ceramics: sombre colours and smaller tiles in the seventies, brighter gloss-finish colours and much larger tiles in the eighties.

It makes for some rather curious acoustics. With no wood, you are saved the creaking board, the moaning stair. If you want to sneak in to check on a sleeping baby, or, God forbid, sneak out on wife or husband, there is no danger of the floor betraying you. In stockinged feet you are soundless. On the other hand, a hard object dropped on that ceramic-on-concrete floor, even a coin, will be heard in every room in the building, volume and intensity depending on the vicinity to a loadbearing beam or column. Patent leather soles clicking across the tiles will thus click across all the floors and ceilings of the condominium. A lavatory flushing in the dead of night is an explosion, an act of terrorism. And if you should take a drill to the wall and, after penetrating the plaster, happen upon one of those steel-reinforced columns, then all over the building, from *taverna* to *solaio*, it will seem that the eventuality for which the structure was designed is in full swing. The air vibrates. Soundwaves oppress the ear. It is as if one were caught inside a guitar with some naughty Brobdingnagian child incessantly twanging the bass string.

We did experience a couple of small quakes in Via Colombare. The *palazzina* shuddered and sang. Patuzzi's wineglasses tinkled on their shelves. Apparently, columns of trucks were passing in the night, or ships' engines starting up in the basement.

Lying down to sleep of an October evening, thankful that we can now close the windows against the TVs, accordions and ping-pong of the velvety dark outside, we hear instead an unmistakeable fierce trickling, coming, well, presumably from below us. At eleven-thirty every night. Trickle trickle trickle, dribble dribble, drop, drop, stop. We hold our breath. But there is no explosion of flushing, for unspoken condominium etiquette requires that the toilets *tacciono* – fall silent – after eleven o'clock. It's a special kind of intimacy this concrete brings.

Trying to sleep again after being woken by Vega in the early hours, I begin to hear footsteps going back and forth in our *solaio* under the roof above. This is alarming. Slow heavy footsteps, back and forth, back and forth, above our heads. Rita confirms, they definitely come from our *solaio*, supposedly an empty attic. And in the dead of night one believes in *fantasmi*. Vega has been moaning rather than barking this evening, howling and wailing at the moon.

I get up, pull on a pair of trousers, then slippers against the cold tiles, and go out of the flat and up the stairs. Where I slip and fall on the highly polished marble. This particular flight to the roof is rarely used, but Lucilla waxes it regularly just the same. Everything must always be just so, a mausoleum odour. Cursing and rueful, I reach the iron door of the *solaio*, open it, and then remember I still haven't put a light bulb in. At which point the timed landing light goes out. I grope for the switch, but don't know where it is on this floor. So I go into the *solaio* blind.

I stare, waiting for my pupils to dilate, recognising a smell of geranium cuttings and thick dust. A dark, softly shifting light, filtering from the attic's one window, finally enables me to see the shadows of untidily piled boxes, an ancient bed, a crucifix, a pair of bellows unaccountably left on the windowsill, and rows and rows of *il professore's* old climbing boots. None of them moving, thank God. I cock my head. No sound.

But back downstairs, the footsteps go on and on above us.

Talking to Orietta, the quiet repository of all condominium gossip, we discover that Lucilla suffers from insomnia. The footsteps are hers, the ventriloquist building sends the sound where it will.

Orietta is loosening up. She is losing her suspicion of my Englishness. She recognises the advantage of having other non-Montecchiesi to make friends with. Giampaolo, she tells us, has frequently complained about those footsteps. Getting up in the night, it seems, Lucilla will put on her fur coat, partly against the cold, partly because she likes her fur coat; she finds its luxury comforting, its monied smell reassuring. But since she is small and bought the coat long, she puts her heels on so as not to have it trail on the floor. And paces up and down.

Another night it is the squeal of heavy furniture being scraped above our heads. Bumps and banging. Thud, scrape, squeal. Yes, Lucilla tells us brightly on the stairs, she decided to rearrange the sitting-room, do we want to come and see it?

Please would we come and see it?

Perhaps we would take a little drink with her? She has some *Lacryma Christi*.

Or perhaps we would like to have a piece of her *pastafrolla*?

Surely, if she isn't disturbing us, we would like to come and see her new curtains, eat her shortbread? Also, if we could explain something in the instruction book to her steam iron . . .

There is a scene in Fellini's film, *La voce della luna*, where a local politician, fallen upon hard times, is seen returning to his dreary flat in an old *palazzotto* in some tiny town of the Po valley. But every time he climbs the stairs and approaches his door, whether it be two in the afternoon or two in the morning, four ancient neighbours will appear at the door opposite and, like awful decaying sirens, try to lure him into their flat to share some old-fashioned dainty: a thimbleful of some sweet forgotten liqueur, a morsel of traditional crumbliness. Their faces are pictures of decrepit flattery and seduction. Close to obscenity. The furniture, dingily glimpsed behind them, is sombre and coffin-inspired with candlesticks in abundance, photographs of dead relatives on lace doilies. 'Would a small glass of sherry be to your liking, your honour? Would a small slice of *pan di spagna*, councillor, be acceptable as our humble offering?' Their veiny hands are outstretched in supplication. Which is immediately perceived as a trap, as if a whole culture were refusing to lie down in its grave, but were rising ghoulish to eat our contemporary flesh. Horrified and furious, the man manages to escape into his room, slams and bolts the door behind him. But already the four leathery faces are down by the keyhole. 'Would your honour be so kind as to take a glass of brandy with some humble folk . . .' They haunt his dreams. He sees their faces floating outside his window at night with the moon behind, luring him back into some archaic, provincial Italy of polished woodwork and thickly smoking candlewax, flattery, favours, back-stabbing.

Such, for me, were Lucilla's insistent invitations. So that I almost looked back with regret on her ravings from the balcony, her confiscation of the dustbin. Those days when I at least knew where I stood.

Barely has she got us inside her polished door – *troppo*

gentile, too kind, *Signor Tino* (she never registered the name Tim) – than she is leaning out into the stairwell calling down to Vittorina. She has a direct intercom connection with Vittorina's flat, but prefers to call down the stairwell, if only to remind all residents in the condominium of her existence. 'Rina! Rina! Come and have something to drink with *i signori inglesi*.' Is she calling up reinforcements? Or just increasing the size of her audience?

We walk in, and promptly slither on imitation animal-skin rugs strewn over the usual lethally waxed floor. Lucilla is clearly nostalgic for her cleaning days. The year before we arrived, she slipped on the rug in the entrance and broke her hip. But this has not deterred her. I all but come a cropper on the synthetic white hairy thing between low glass table and imitation leather sofa. Vittorina, who has now appeared in a nightgown, hair thinner than ever, frowns with the air of one who is wiser than the person she is used to being bossed about by. And indeed, she doesn't even try to remove her moustache as Lucilla does. A vanity beneath her.

We are shown round the flat. The walls are simple whitewash, as in almost every Italian house. The furniture is what a local Veronese would laughingly describe as *stile Bovolone*, Bovolone being an industrial settlement twenty kilometres away in the foggy *bassa* where scores of busy companies produce clunky replicas of antique furniture. A Louis XIV dresser, bright and new, features prominently in the entrance way. There is a Renaissance chest in polished pine, and Lucilla's is the first home, aside from paying visits to Waltham Abbey and Hatfield House, where I have seen a bed with a canopy curtain affair over the headboard, here upholstered in electric nylon pink. The room is about ten by twelve.

Il professore was a great man, she begins impulsively, having put little red glasses of *gingerino* in our hands. A great man. Of culture. She speaks in fierce dialect. I strain my ears to distinguish the words, my mind to understand. It is not unlike trying to make out a strange landscape through thick fog. Was that a house or a tree, a tail light or shop neon? And we are going so fast. My head starts to ache. Still, at the end of an hour or so of non-stop haranguing, I do manage to discern the following salient landmarks, if only because Lucilla goes round and round them so insistently, not unlike Pooh Bear following his own tracks in the snow: so, *il professore*, that is, Patuzzi, had written a will and put it in his deposit box in the bank (half of Montecchio seems to have a deposit box at the bank). He then died quite suddenly, of a heart attack, breathing his last on the ambulance stretcher right outside her door, *poveretto* (obligatory epithet for describing the dear departed). And what a fright for her! *Comunque*, the will had clearly stated that the wife would have use of the property only until her death, after which it would pass to her, Lucilla. Such an exquisite man, *il professore*. As had been agreed of course. Because it was her money, her money had paid for the *palazzina*. She had worked her fingers to the bone all her life. So cultured. We would have admired him immensely. But no sooner had he passed away than Signora Marta and Maria Rosa were off to the bank, had opened the deposit box and promptly burnt the will. For which they themselves would burn in hell. Whereas we would never meet anybody more *gentile*, more *generoso*, than *il professore*.

Lucilla's bosom began to heave, it wasn't clear whether out of love or anger or some dangerous blood-dark cocktail of the two. Then Maria Rosa had herself fallen ill and become infirm. Lucilla had looked after her, as was her duty towards another 'Christian', taking her meals which she handed over at the door whose threshold she was never to pass. Because that woman put on airs, while *il professore*, who might have had good reason to be haughty, was *dolcezza* itself. And when things got worse, Maria Rosa had come and more or less lived in her own, Lucilla's flat; slept there for months, being nursed and helped to the toilet and so on. Until, finally, Lucilla could cope no more and the woman had had to go into a home. But towards the end of that period, in a fit of remorse, Maria Rosa had told Lucilla the story of the will and how it had been burnt and had agreed to write a further will herself.

Lucilla fiddles under the flap of a rather oversized new Regency writing desk, bringing out a furry-grey piece of notepaper which she then waves under our noses. *'Ecco, legga, legga, Signor Tino.'* Her fingers are stubby and impressively bejewelled. I take the *documento* with due respect. Uncertain handwriting announces the last will and testament of Maria Rosa Griminelli. The whole of Via Colombare number 10 belongs and always has belonged to Lucilla Zambon who built it with her own money. There is a single indecipherable signature, no lawyer, only the beneficiary as a witness.

But Lucilla's hopes are pinned on that scrap of paper. She raises her voice. She is furious, defiant. Her bony teeth are in evidence. 'The flat is mine, mine, mine.' But we are nice people, and when she finally gets hold of the property, on Maria Rosa's death, she will allow us to stay, although she will have to ask us to buy it rather than rent. But we can discuss all this at a later date.

Would we like a *cioccolatino*, a San Pellegrino Bitter? Would we like to watch television with her of an evening? She would be grateful if we could adjust her set. There is a programme on Tele Montecarlo with a man just like her beloved husband, here he is in this photograph. *Così bello*! Why did the men always die first? But she can never get a good picture on Tele Montecarlo. Signor Giampaolo has put up that new motorised aerial on the roof and it is sucking all the goodness from hers. Do I know anything about aerials? And could Rita perhaps phone her lawyer for her to have him explain something she can't understand, and tell him to hurry up with the case.

Lucilla talks on and on. There is simply no chink in her verbal armour, no hesitation into which one might thrust the dagger of a request to leave. Vittorina watches, silent, dark, with those sudden smiles when she catches your eye, smiles which say she understands your suffering, but this is Lucilla, this is how she is, *porti pazienza*.

In desperation, we begin our long retreat. First simply getting to our feet, then edging out of the lounge and across the dining-room with its dark, dying plants, its sad canary, heading toward the entrance. Along a low wall is an array of those tiny twisted-glass Venetian ornaments, reminding me of my infancy in Blackpool, when we visited a Great-Aunt Esther who had row upon row of the things on a dresser.

Do we think she should ask for the *condono edilizio*, the building pardon? You see, she had this wall knocked down, that's why it is different from our flat, didn't we notice, between the entrance and the kitchen . . . So much more space. But without asking for planning permission . . . and now with this pardon . . .

Does she have the right lawyer? What do we think? Perhaps he isn't being tough enough. Surely the rent we are paying should go to her. How much are we paying? *Il professore* only left the flat to his wife for use while she wanted to live there, but any rent should go to her, Lucilla. And, of course, in that home Maria Rosa is in, Signora Marta is putting pressure on her to sign another will leaving everything to her. But it wouldn't be right, because Rosa isn't capable of exercising free will now. She is senile. Though the doctors are all *in complicità* clearly, with what's being paid for her to be there. All *il professore*'s fortune. The priest said . . .

Finally we make it to the hall. We are repeating *arrivedercis*, *buona nottes*, when I finally remember the purpose behind our visit, the subject I had originally come to broach. The nocturnal noises. We hope, I say, that we never, er, bother them, when we play our stereo, when we type late at night, when we have friends over. Noise carries so much in these buildings. One can hear everything. We wouldn't like . . . 'But no, Signor Tino, no, no, no, *troppo gentile, troppo gentile*! We like to hear noise. We like to hear footsteps, laughter, banging. The more the merrier. We're two old ladies. It keeps us company. We feel less lonely. *Ma troppo gentile, ma che signore*!'

And somehow Signor Tino just can't bring himself to say what he wants to say. The way he can never quite make up his mind to poison that dog.

14
Condono

The *condono edilizio* was first mooted in the early 1980s. The idea was to recognise that there are vast numbers of buildings in Italy which were put up without permission: villas and cottages in the north, whole blocks of flats down south. Since, officially, these buildings don't exist, they aren't paying the modest property tax (although they do of course receive electricity, water, post and so on, and residency certificates confidently assert that people do live in them and hence enjoy all the rights that go with officially living in a place). There are also, the new law would recognise, even greater numbers of buildings which have been altered in some way without permission: extended, restored, disfigured, rebuilt. Under the terms of the *condono*, the government would allow people to register these buildings or any changes made to them and thus get themselves *in regola* as they say, paying in return only a fraction of the fine they would otherwise have to pay if prosecuted. For the government this would mean a considerable *ad hoc* income and the prospect of larger regular revenues in the future.

No sooner had the splendid idea been put forward than building began in earnest all over the peninsula. Of course, the law would refer only to buildings completed some months before it was initially drawn up. But if a building isn't registered it is not always easy to say exactly when it was built. And perhaps the government didn't really care, since finances were such (are always such) that the larger the injection of cash, the better.

The law was passed by decree, quite normal practice, but a decree has to be ratified by parliament within sixty days. The *condono* was not ratified. Which was curious given the general enthusiasm. Some mischievous newspapers alleged that many of those MPs who voted against it were busy building their own illegal villas and eager to have them finished before the law was eventually passed, as they were sure it one day would be. But at the time, MPs had a secret vote in the Italian parliament, so it was impossible to tell who was involved.

Along Via Colombare somebody knocked down a handsome old barn and began feverish work on a luxury extension, which pretty well amounted to a second house. Passing of the law was again delayed. Almost opposite the luxury extension, the woman who swept the road regularly with her twig broom began to lay the foundations of a two-car garage with terrace roof leading through French windows to the first floor of her house. Wielding her broom, she bustled about the old workers in their dungarees with their bottles of wine and tupperware boxes full of cold pasta.

The law was now passed. But then the deadline for applications for the *condono* was waived on two or three occasions. To give a little respite. All over Italy the cement mixers rumbled; work went on apace. And I remember walking back along the more than usually dusty street one day, to find in number 10's postbox one of those magazines that somehow always find their way to ex-pats: *Investment International*, or some such title. They tell you how to send your children to English boarding schools, how to invest your money in offshore tax havens, how to prepare for the mental shock of return, how to let your Mayfair flat in your absence, etc. etc. On this particular occasion a review of European stockmarkets remarked, of la Borsa di Milano, that one could do no better than invest in Italcementi, the state-controlled cement company. Cement in Italy, the article said, had miraculously out-performed all other kinds of stock, thanks to the vigour, the creativity and the enterprising spirit of both manufacturers and building contractors. So much for the foreign perspective.

In Via Colombare we got a new fence to protect the really rather attractive beige-stuccoed, copper-drained three-bedroom extension which had replaced the old barn (beautiful, full of swallows nests, but no longer functional). The fence was made of tall, spiky, brown-painted iron railings sunk into a marble-topped cement wall, and it ended in a sheltered, terracotta-tiled entrance way complete with video-camera security. The tiny garden between the fence and the villa extension respected the cemetery style of dwarf cypresses and biblically inspired stucco statues. Opposite, the woman with the twig broom now swept her terrace of a morning, as well as the remaining half of the patio and a fair stretch of road outside.

But in the end this was a fairly innocuous form of anarchy. For around this time we took a week off to visit friends who live in the suburbs of Rome. Their house, a legal part of a new development, had simply been smothered by new building, much of it of the crudest variety, breeze blocks placed one on top of another with prefab roof, just enough to claim the *condono* and have the authorities accept the existence of a building which could then be developed in the future. Many houses were without utilities. Next door, the owner had converted the ground floor of his house into a bodywork repair outfit, blocking the narrow road outside with dented cars. Our friends had called the local *vigile* about the noise, the smell of spray paint, the inconvenience, reminding him that this was a residential area. The *vigile* went to talk with the culprit and apparently took a bribe.

Italian stories. One hears them more or less daily.

Back in number 10, there were various reasons for asking for the *condono*. The *palazzo* was a metre or so too near Negretti's house. Then the *solai*, for example, had tiled floors, whereas to remain in the tax bracket the house was in, they should have been left bare and 'non-inhabitable'. The same was true of the garage and the *taverna*. One has a building inspected, is the trick, its tax bracket declared, and then one changes it at will: peeling shutters in the city centre conceal luxury window fittings; pitted, flaking stucco is a front for polished parquet, granite and gold bathroom fittings. Everybody's at it. The humble façade, the lavish interior. Tall, glass-topped walls. Secretiveness.

Eventually, it was decided at condominium level (that is, by Lucilla) that number 10 would not ask for the *condono*. Because in the end it wasn't free, was it? However small, the fine would still have to be paid. And why bother? Lucilla was indignant. Nobody had really done anything wrong, had they? Nobody had hurt anybody. Anyway, the chances of the authorities ever catching you were infinitesimal; otherwise they would never have introduced the *condono* in the first place. And it was so dangerous to draw attention to yourself. Once they had your name in black and white, heaven knows what they might find out.

Lucilla was right. Some years later an income tax *condono* was passed by decree. People would 'reconstruct their tax careers', paying a modest fine. Thus the government would know how much tax to expect from such people in the future. But almost nobody applied for the pardon, since the very fact that the government had introduced it was an admission of their inability or unwillingness to catch anyone. Parliament then voted out the decree after the sixty days. This meant that while, over the previous two months, it had officially been the law, it was now considered never to have been the law at all. Upon which a few zealous magistrates attempted to prosecute those guilty few who had somewhat hastily confessed to their tax crimes in the hope of getting *in regola*. A lesson for the rest of us if ever there was one.

15
Discreto, valido, relativo

If Lucilla's most common expression was the flattering and subservient, *troppo gentile, troppo gentile,* a social tick she had presumably picked up in her deprived girlhood of floor-scrubbing and straightforward begging, Giampaolo Visentini's most characteristic utterances were always built around the three words: *discreto, valido, relativo.*

Imagine you are sitting in the Visentinis' tastefully and above all cautiously furnished sitting-room. You are drinking excellent *prosecco* which Giampaolo bottled himself, which he has put in the fridge three or four days before your planned evening get-together (in the back of the fridge, not the door, since that would involve its getting knocked around too much). Upon your arrival and acceptance of the offered treat, he has carried the bottle from kitchen through dining-room to sitting-room with the concentration of a bomb disposal expert shifting primed Semtex, has released the detonating cork ever so gently to prevent explosion, then tilted the bottle painstakingly slowly over an attractive pottery carafe bearing the name of some Sardinian seaside town – all this because it's so desperately important to avoid disturbing the sediment which is both the hallmark and curse of home-bottled wines. Giampaolo watches intently as he pours, brow knitted, long pale fingers strong and steady, his whole attitude conveying the slightly glazed worshipful concentration of the devotee. The contents froth out, the carafe fills, the sediment, which would have given the wine an unpleasant acidy taste, remains safely in the bottle and – *ecco fatto*, done it! Being bourgeois, it might be said, is never an easy way out in Italy.

Of course, if this is your first evening with the Visentini, if this is the first time you have drunk home-bottled *prosecco*, the whole elaborate rigmarole will seem nothing short of ridiculous. You can barely hold back a giggle. The caricatures are true, you're thinking. These Latins are obsessive about food and wine. What's going to change your mind is when you actually taste the *prosecco*.

And here at last it is. Lovingly as ever, but more relaxed now, Giampaolo pours from the carafe into tall slim glasses. '*Salute.*' You raise a crystal stem. The cold sharp taste stings the lips, demands attention. It's desperately dry, cutting like a knife through the sweetness of whatever goodies are being handed out. And as it fills your mouth, you become aware of wanting to hold it there. Bubbles froth on the palate. You are drinking something special.

So there you are, perched on geometrically arranged

chairs about a rug of soberly coloured squares and rectangles surrounded by polished tiles, chinking your tall glass with your host's. The Visentinis' daughter is there too: Lara, named after the heroine in *Dr Zhivago*. A strapping twelve-year-old, she giggles merrily when Rita cracks a joke. I'm offering compliments about the wine, asking if it is the same that we will be bottling together in the spring. There are the makings of a pleasant evening.

But Giampaolo is so solemn. And, perhaps not wishing to discuss wine with a layman, he launches into serious conversation. He's telling you about some new law. For he likes to talk about politics. Concerning drunk driving for example. Yes, the new law on drunk driving has been drawn up *discretamente* (quite well, with intelligence if not flair) and is in fact for the most part *valido* (sound, functional), but all of this is *relativo* (of only secondary importance) since the instruments for enforcing the law are not available, or if they are nobody has any intention of using them. He smiles, as if having performed a conjuring trick, takes a sparkling sip of *prosecco*, picks up another piece of *pastafrolla*.

And the formula, you discover as the evening progresses, can be applied to almost any area of life upon which Giampaolo cares to reflect. The Italian system of *autostrade*, he is telling you now, is definitely *discreto*, road surfaces and markings are always *valido*, but all this tends to be *relativo* since, with the exorbitant price of petrol and the very high tolls, one would need to be rich indeed before one could use it with any regularity.

Another long sip of this extraordinary wine.

Likewise efficiency in Italian companies, such as his own, is certainly *discreto*, the managerial class indubitably *valido*, but again these pluses are rendered *relativo* by a public sector which simply sucks blood from the rest of the economy.

And so, if you encourage him, he will go on all evening: the constitution, the electoral system, the TV networks; *discreto, valido, relativo*. It is a curious and, I believe, curiously Italian stalemate, in which ineradicable national pride (and why not?) exists side by side with a sense of cynicism (equally justifiable) and, at the end of the day, resignation. The judicial system has been 'conceived *discretamente bene*', and the constitution in this regard is undoubtedly *valido*, in that it establishes the total independence of the judiciary. But whatever the institutional make-up, it is inevitably only *relativo* given the endemic corruption that always allows the *mafiosi* to get off scot-free.

The mental pattern propagates itself like someone cutting pastry (or *pastafrolla*) with a die, or pouring wine into tall glasses. There is no question of simply showing anger or outrage for all the things that make the country a less attractive place to live than it might so easily be. The blunt analysis and sleeve-rolling gaucheness which forms the typical reaction of, for example, the English, inevitably carries the subtext that something could and should be done, and quickly: reform the poll tax, cut inflation, dump Thatcher, etc. etc. English people usually believe such things to be possible, or at least imaginable. But the Italian knows that nothing can or will be done in his country, and that if it is done it certainly will not be done quickly. This is his experience. After all, with all the shifting coalitions and merry-go-round of prime ministers, most people here haven't seen a real change of government in their lifetime. Thus an Italian's satisfaction, when he talks about politics, will lie in feeling that he has analysed the situation accurately, appreciated its ironies, seen the pros and the cons, absorbed the subtleties, and above all gone beyond the crude simplicity of foreigners who talk in ingenuous terms about changing things.

Discreto, valido, relativo – not one of them is a particularly complimentary or pejorative term. They are the cool words of the astute analyst, the man who looks at the whole show from a distance, then goes about his business as he would have done anyway, regardless, but happy to have had the chance to illustrate his powers of observation. In the final analysis: *'La legge non mi tange.'*

Fortunately there is Orietta's gossip to brighten up the evening. Lucilla has apparently called on the priest, Don Guido, to be a witness in the case she is bringing against Signora Marta. He has agreed. Which is interesting. And did we know that Lucilla has a fancy man? Simone, an ex-*carabiniere*. Yes, he comes three or four evenings a week. The daughter giggles and begins to explain about the vacuum cleaner. Lucilla has what must be a pre-war vacuum cleaner, but recently she has been borrowing Orietta's (Vittorina doesn't have one), claiming that her own is broken. Whereas, in fact, Lara, the daughter, saw Simone, the *carabiniere* fancy man, bumping down the stairs with the thing only a week ago.

To mend it? To use it? Can't he afford one?

Anyway, this is becoming a problem, Orietta says, since there's so much dust about these days with all the building going on in the street. She needs to use the thing herself two or three times a day.

Everybody nods gravely.

Orietta is small, doll-like, and clearly perfectly attuned to sedentary domestic life. She doesn't have a job, but every corner of the room shows evidence of her tireless cleaning. Only the other morning I watched her diligently polishing inch after inch of the long marble balustrade of the terrace balcony. There was concentration on her face, satisfaction, the devotion of the accolyte cleaning the altar. Not unlike her husband's expression while pouring his *prosecco*. Later we will discover that, when Giampaolo wanted to accept a more dynamic job in a much smaller company, Orietta forbade him. It wasn't safe.

She is also scared of earthquakes.

And of every possible disease. Thus, as so often with Italian acquaintances, we are not far into our first evening with the Visentini before Orietta is discussing her blood pressure. Which is a mite high. She shouldn't have more than two coffees a day. Also she occasionally gets attacks of tachycardia. She is appalled to discover that I don't even know my own blood pressure. As far as I know it has never been taken. Her face shows genuine concern. Apparently, we are touching on a real cultural difference here.

Orietta explains that after feeling somewhat faint a few days ago the doctor arranged for her to have an exhaustive series of blood and urine tests, together with an electrocardiogram and a heart scan. She has thus been getting up early every morning to get to the hospital, wait in all the queues, fill in all the forms and fix all the appointments. She remembers last time she had a blood test her bilirubin was way outside the norms indicated on the test sheet, whereas cholesterol A was thankfully low.

I remark that I have never, to my knowledge, had a blood test. I don't even know my group.

Lara had a rash a few weeks ago on face and chest.

Although this cleared up almost immediately, she too was sent off for complete blood and urine tests, including tests for such things as syphilis. It appeared that her *trigliceridi* were rather high.

I can't decide if this is surprisingly intimate or rather frightening, or both. And I remember our landlady, Signora Marta, fiddling with her keys at the gate that first day, talking about her gynaecological problems.

With the gravity of a Houyhnhnm, Giampaolo takes this opportunity to reflect that, on the whole, public hospitals in Verona function *discretamente bene*, when compared with hospitals in other areas of Italy, and of course the idea behind the health system as it was initially conceived is indubitably *valido*. However, it has to be admitted that the apparent success of the local system is *del tutto relativo* since, if all the people who presently go private were to turn to the public system, it would break down in a matter of days.

Lucilla for example, and Vittorina.

'Really? They go private? But they're not particularly well off, are they?'

Giampaolo explains that the old women go to a local health-service doctor whom they tip generously. When they have any tests to do, he always tells them to go to a private clinic, of which he, as it so happens, is a director. And they pay a lot of money. And say, *troppo gentile, Dottore, troppo gentile*.

We thus discover that it is not so much, or by no means only the upper middle class and the important executive who go private in Italy. Above all it is the ignorant, the workers and peasant class who have tucked something away in their deposit box or in a few government bonds.

They can't believe the public system can work and then, of course, it's a status symbol to say, I am going to my private gynaecologist, my private cardiologist, my private paediatrician. From whom, more often than not, they will get no receipt.

Rita tells a joke her mother made up when her father Adelmo kept going to the hospital for tests upon tests upon tests. It goes like this. What does a German do in the morning? He jumps out of bed, grabs a cup of coffee and rushes off to work. What does an American do in the morning? He climbs out of bed, sips a cup of coffee, reads the paper for ten minutes and strolls off to work. What does an Italian do?

Long pause. Puzzlement of the Visentini in their spic-and-span sitting-room.

Urinates in a bottle and sets off to the hospital!

Only Lara truly thinks this is funny. The others have a sort of pained smile. Health is so important. Not for nothing did we say '*Salute*' when we raised those glasses.

And Orietta touches her face. Do we think she should have her mole removed? This little one in the dimple on her cheek. She's afraid it may be growing. No it's not very visible because she powders it. Her doctor said to leave well alone, but she went for a second opinion and that doctor said to have a biopsy done. At a private clinic, Giampaolo adds.

Idly, Lara picks up the remote control and the television flicks on. With its usual brutality, the news is showing yet another Mafia killing. Corruption on a more impressive scale. The scene is always the same: the car caught at the traffic lights, riddled with bullets, the corpses in a heap on the front seats, perhaps an arm thrown out of the shattered window, blood trickling down on to the asphalt, spotlights all round for the TV cameras. They have shot General Dalla Chiesa, chief of police in Sicily.

Giampaolo plays with the controls to his motorised aerial on the roof to enable us to get a better view. Weeping relatives are being asked how they feel.

We finish our *prosecco* and go upstairs. Leaning out over the balcony to get some fresh air we are lucky enough to witness the departure of Simone, the ex-*carabiniere*. He's solid, sixtyish, thick head of bristling grey hair, and he has a package under his arm. Too small to be a vacuum cleaner though. He fiddles for the keys to his Fiat 128 parked a hair's breadth from our iron fence. Lucilla appears on her balcony, barely ten feet away across the façade of the building, although she hasn't noticed us. In the swinging light of the overhead streetlamp we can see she is heavily made up, dressed to the nines, wearing higher than usual heels, decidedly Felliniesque. She leans over the parapet and begins to whisper enticingly: 'Simone, Simone *caro*, when will you phone? Simone, when are you coming to dinner again?' One imagines him glimpsing her long teeth as he slides down into his car with the heavy sigh of one who has overeaten. *Ciao, bella*, he calls. She stands watching after him, pensive, huge breasts uplifted. It's sad to think of this woman being taken for a ride by her doctor. But then, as Rita remarks, she probably paid no tax in the good old days of the cleaning company, so it all works out in the end.

For the next few weeks I practise *discreto, valido* and *relativo* on any and every subject that comes up.

16
Una bustarella

They had shot General Dalla Chiesa, the man who had defeated terrorism, the man the government had appointed to defeat the Mafia. About the same time, a very close friend of mine paid his first bribe to a state official. These two facts are not perhaps entirely unrelated.

It's a complicated story, perhaps a little bit of a digression, but I'd like to tell it all the same because it shows how even the ingenuous foreigner who arrives here, as one arrives most places, more or less by chance, can so easily run up against the dark side of Italy.

This was an extremely close friend of mine. Like me he had arrived in Italy some time before, like me he lived in a little village not far from a sizeable town, like me he had grafted for a while with private lessons and commercial translations until good fortune had landed him one of the much sought-after jobs teaching English at the university, a position offering a decent, steady income for work that is pleasant and not overly taxing. He was delighted. Now he could relax a little. No more the breathless hurry to get from one lesson to the next, only to find the student has cancelled. No more the embarrassment of having to insist that patently rich people deign to pay one with a certain regularity. No more the smell of white-out in the early hours labouring over translations on the recycling of waste sludge in marble saw-mills, the unsurpassable tourist attractions of the nearby town. He was home and dry.

But the contract they made him sign at the university was a strange one. Although to all intents and purposes an employee, in the sense that he had a timetable and certain well-established duties, he was in fact officially free lance, the university retaining 18 per cent of his income as tax (had he not had *residenza* they would have retained 20 per cent), but paying no health contributions and requiring him to declare the money on a free-lance basis.

Now, since this friend of mine had a VAT number which he used for his translations, he went to the university accounts office to ask them what exactly his tax situation might be. Complicated, they said, and went into great detail. Which he didn't entirely understand. For Italian tax law might well be written in hieroglyphics for all the average citizen can understand of it. Never mind a foreigner. Rather than on actual income, everything seems to depend on the category of worker you are (artisan, lawyer, doctor, plumber, farmer, shopkeeper . . .) and the nature of the work you do (regular, casual, occasional, for one client, for various, etc. etc.), with different rules applying for each different category, different tax brackets, different deductions, different percentages for national insurance and so on and so forth. So that at the end of the explanation, which might also have been described with the much used Italian substantive, *mistificazione,* my sensible friend demanded to know the bottom line: could he retain his VAT number, do a few translations, and do the job at the university without paying VAT on it.

They said yes. And made him sign something. The usual *documento*. They also said that even if he did want to charge VAT on the job, they wouldn't pay it, but would deduct it from his salary.

Had any of the other thirty or so *lettori* opted for this alternative? he asked.

And was told none. Because it wasn't necessary.

But being a cautious lad, my friend also had an accountant. And went to see him. To clear the matter up. The accountant, however, could do nothing more than offer a second equally mystifying 'explanation' which simply defied comprehension, perhaps because, as the accountant readily admitted, the law in many areas was not only unclear, but frankly contradictory. It also changed with great regularity, and often government decrees, which were officially law, were not ratified by parliament and thus not only ceased to be law but were deemed never to have been law in the first place. Basically, my friend could do what he wanted. Since everybody else at the university was doing precisely that, my friend took this wise advice. He worked, he got paid and, at least in this regard, was happy.

Four years later he received a small white card in his mailbox. From the VAT office. He was required to present himself with great urgency, indeed within a date already past, for the printed card had taken more than a week to travel the six kilometres from the centre of town to his modest flat in the outlying village.

He got on his moped and rushed into town, found the VAT office, showed his card at reception, and was directed along a maze of corridors to a huge office whose walls were lined from floor to ceiling, door to door, with box files bulging with tax declarations. It quickly became apparent that the four moustached men behind four gun-metal desks were sorting through the VAT declarations of four years before.

My friend was breathing heavily because he had made it just in time. Like most offices in Italy, this one was open only in the morning since, unlike employees in the private sector, civil servants enjoy a 36-hour week, six mornings, six hours a day. It was now ten to one.

He handed his card to an older, weary, dusty, bespectacled man behind a huge, dusty heap of papers coloured the kind of garish pink and yellow that forms can be. In parenthesis, I find it is curious how colouring forms does nothing to make them more attractive. Rather the colours themselves, become, by association, somewhat frightening: those tissue blues, washed out mauves.

He apologised for the delay but the post had been slow. The man said the date was a formality and of no relevance. He then proceeded to look for the English teacher's VAT return out of the thousands, perhaps hundreds of thousands, which not only lined the wall, but were arrayed in great barriers of box files between the desks.

When the document was finally found, it emerged that while my friend had been wise perhaps to realise he needed an accountant, he had been unlucky in his choice. For the accountant had made a mistake. In the declaration of four years before, he had mentioned the university income and stated that it was exempt from VAT, but without indicating the code that would explain this exemption. The dusty old man now wanted my friend to tell him which code it was, so that he could write it in the space and the completed form be filed away and forgotten.

In passing, it's worth pointing out here that had the accountant filled in that space with any code, even a non-existent one, there would most likely have been no problem. For Italian tax inspection appears to be mainly involved in finding contradictory statements within any given declaration. Only very rarely do inspectors go out of their offices to see if the lifestyle of the taxpayer bears any resemblance to his declaration. Thus it is common and frequently repeated wisdom (in the bars in Montecchio for example) that it is far better to make no declaration at all than an incomplete or even minimally incorrect one. A line made all the more attractive by the fact that in this case one doesn't have to worry with an accountant. When Francesco Pazienza, a millionaire entrepreneur, was arrested in connection with the collapse of the Banco Ambrosiano and the death of director Roberto Calvi (hung under Blackfriars Bridge), it emerged that he had never made a tax declaration in his life, nor ever bothered with a tax code. He had thus never run up against the kind of problems experienced by my friend. And the same could probably be said of one or two people within striking distance of Via Colombare.

But the story that follows will offer a certain justification for that apparently antisocial kind of behaviour.

For my friend now made a terrible mistake. Lulled into a false sense of security by the bland innocuousness of this man with dust in his wrinkles and along the rims of his spectacles and peppering his anyway grey moustache, he said, truthfully, that he didn't know what code it might be. The man kindly suggested that he go away, consult his accountant, and return with this information inside a week or two. But here the young foreigner was quite criminally ingenuous, a born victim. He didn't want, he said, to have to return over such a small matter, nor to have to go and consult his accountant. It took him more than half an hour every time he came into town. Surely if he told the old man the nature of the work, he in turn could produce the code; they could then write it down and all would be over.

On the desk there was a little carousel of rubber stamps of all shapes and sizes, some adjustable, some not. The old man tapped the thing with his finger and it began to turn, squeaking slightly. Perhaps this was a warning.

Unheeded. My friend told him the nature of the work. Indeed of all his work. As a person who has nothing to fear from investigation and authority.

The older man became more interested, licked the dust off his lips, said he couldn't say offhand what code that would be; they would have to go and talk to a colleague.

The maze of passages again, grey carpets, fluorescent light. Indeed, apart from the occasional crucifix hanging under the heating pipes near the ceiling, this could perfectly well be an Inland Revenue office in Wapping or Huntingdon. But it isn't.

In another gloomy but more private office the colleague is of an entirely different variety. He is young, sanguine, peremptory and dust-free, despite the tomes and papers on his desk.

Such work, he pronounces, after hearing the story, should not have been exempt from VAT. There is no question of there being a code.

But my friend has a document provided for him by the university accountants whom he consulted precisely over this question.

Already he appreciates what a mistake he has made. But it is too late.

A document from the university? The younger man is scornful. No accountant worth his salt would be working at the university, getting only a million and a half a month. Would he? How could they advise him? In any event my friend, as a resident and contributor, is personally responsible for paying his taxes regardless of any advice received – even, the man adds triumphantly, if such incorrect advice were to come from this very office.

The dusty man has stayed to listen. Warming his hands over the radiator he looks out over the window at a building identical to the one the three of them are in, five, six stories, white concrete, regular square windows. In every room all the typewriters are supplied by Olivetti, as they should be.

'And you're still working at the university?' The sanguine inspector has assumed an interrogator's tone.

Yes.

So that this has been going on for four years?

Yes.

During which time your remuneration has been what?

My friend tells him. The other man's fingers are extraordinarily rapid on the keyboard of a calculator. 'You have evaded VAT for around nine million Lire,' he says.

But as the English teacher gasps, makes to protest, the inspector has suddenly become friendly. 'However, we should see this document you mentioned and your contract before we go into detail. Why don't you bring them in?'

He smiles, goes to pick up his coat. Is it because he's realised that it is time for him to go home for lunch? Or is there some other reason.

'When?'

'Oh, when you like. But don't forget.'

Leaving the building, my friend reflects that this kind of vagueness is more disconcerting than comforting. As was the unexpectedly pally smile on the young man's previously severe face. Extremely anxious as he is, he wants the matter settled at once, not left hanging over his head. And so he rushes things. When perhaps he might have been wiser to do what Orietta would no doubt have advised: had his blood pressure checked, waited till it had fallen.

In any event, he calls his accountant immediately, from a phone box outside the tax office, and tells him the story. At no point does the accountant apologise for his original mistake. If his client wishes, he says, he will go and talk to the tax office about it himself, but perhaps before he does so, it would be better if my friend got the document in question and the contract, took it to the inspectors, stressed his ingenuousness and insisted on his good faith. He has not, after all, pocketed any money in VAT and then avoided paying it to the state, as perhaps a shopkeeper might. He has merely omitted to charge the client VAT on top of the regular price, always assuming he was in fact supposed to do so. In this way he has not profited from the situation at all. Nor will the state have lost through the university's having detracted from their own VAT payments any monies supposedly paid to him.

My friend, however, is losing his nerve. He positively flaunts his anxiety by returning to the tax office with his documents the very next day. First there's the dusty man again, then the sanguine man, the one drily polite, apologetic, apparently innocuous, the other tougher, dismissive, immediately assuming the attitude of one who is fed up of hearing cock-and-bull stories.

Allora?

Here is the document.

The younger man looks at it; the older is window-gazing again. The document quotes three or four different laws, sections, paragraphs, amendments – convincing pomposity.

'*Incompetenti*' is the comment, and the VAT man opens a tome on his desk, finds a page, begins to read rapidly out loud from one of the laws cited. My friend, who is actually a dab hand at translating complex commercial insurance documents, can't quite follow it. Somehow it all depends on whether his non-university jobs are *continuativi* (regular) or *saltuari* (occasional). He earns, he says, about ten million a year from translations from a variety of clients, some new, some old, but he would be hard-pressed to say if this added up to *continuativo* or *saltuario*. The words surely require more precise definition.

The sanguine man undergoes one of his mistifying changes of behaviour. He smiles, he is relaxed. '*Sì, sì, sono d'accordo,*' he agrees. And adds: 'Five in ten people would probably feel you were in the right.'

'After all, given that I've made nothing out of it, no one can deny I'm in good faith.'

'D'accordo, d'accordo.'

The dusty man turns from the window to watch. My friend is smiling, seeing light at the end of the tunnel. The accountant seems to have advised him well.

Then the younger man lifts a hand to his face, touches his cheek, and says very politely: 'Though good faith is no defence under law, only a mitigating circumstance.'

'But . . .'

'And my interpretation remains, that you should have been paying VAT, that you have evaded VAT for a sum of approximately nine million Lire, and that you are thus subject to repayment of that sum, plus further payment of a fine.'

Flabbergasted, my friend can barely get out: 'How much?'

'Fines are usually equal to the amount evaded. A further nine million, with some reduction if you pay immediately, of course.'

A total of eighteen million Lire, or about eight thousand pounds. With his back to the window now the older man doesn't bat a dusty eyelid.

'But only a moment ago you said interpretation could go either way.'

'Naturally you could appeal against this and the judgement could indeed go either way. Which would clarify the law most usefully in situations of this kind. In the meantime you would be obliged to pay 33 per cent of monies due as a first instalment. You would also lose any possible reduction for immediate payment.'

My friend and the inspector are of about the same age and build. They stare at each other across the desk. One in disbelief, the other almost quizzical. And at last my friend plays his first smart move, even though his original idea is merely to gain time. He explains that some of his colleagues have recently fought and won a case to be recognised as employees of the university, not free-lance workers, this means that the job cannot be considered as subject to VAT. And recognition was retrospective. It would cover this period.

The sanguine man caresses his chin, narrows his eyes. He reminds my friend that in Italy the decision of a court does not establish precedence. It merely offers one interpretation of the existing law. The verdict in favour of his colleagues, if such a verdict exists, thus refers exclusively to those who fought the case, not to him. A second judge could perfectly well decide differently in his case. His status thus remains the same, and as far as he, the inspector, is concerned VAT has been evaded to the tune of 9 million. As an employee of the government he has a duty to collect evaded taxes and to punish those who evade them.

For the first time my friend lies, and this is another step forward. 'But I have begun my own case too,' he says. He is trembling.

'Ah?'

'So at present, in a way, everything is *sub iudice*.'

There is a long hard pause, much eye contact. The dusty man pouts, coughs drily. Finally the younger inspector politely invites my friend to come back once again, this time with a copy both of the sentence of the case won by his colleagues and of his lawyer's presentation of his own case to the *Tribunale del Lavoro*.

Which of course he hasn't got. Looking back at the building as he leaves, my friend remembers *The Castle*, the courtrooms of *The Trial*. Immediately, he phones his accountant. The avuncular man, in yet another cluttered office complete with crucifix, is kind and genuinely concerned. He hadn't initially wanted to go and speak to the tax people personally since, *'Finora io e te abbiamo sempre collaborato in modo amichevole'*: i.e., 'So far you have paid me under the table and I haven't given you a receipt for my services or in any way indicated in my books that you are a client of mine.' However, at this point he agrees it is time he went to talk to these people. Yes, he knows who it must be.

A nail-biting week. During which, to pass the time, and then, because, once there's an itch you have to scratch it, my friend goes to the university accounts office and again enquires, as if merely to reassure himself, about his tax position. Again he hears, as he did four years ago, that there is no need for him to pay VAT on his university income. He then tells the accountant, a forty-year-old man with the dress style of someone determined to stay young, an expensive mixture of Armani, Gianfranco Ferrè and Benetton, that the VAT office thinks otherwise and is at this very moment asking him to pay a heavy fine. To which the other man replies with great promptness that he can in no way be held responsible for the advice he gives. A brief slanging match follows, since this is one person, my friend feels, he can give a piece of his very worried mind to with impunity. As always, Christ looks on from his own particular cross. Plastic in this case.

Finally, the accountant phones. He has talked to the VAT people. Could my friend come into his office. They can't discuss it on the telephone.

And in the office he says: 'They want a Christmas present.'

'Prego?'

'Una bustarella.' A little envelope. A bribe.

'Did they say so?'

'God forbid.'

So how does he know?

He knows. And this burly accountant with thick bushy eyebrows now proceeds with nostalgic revelry to launch into the story of the very first time he offered a bribe. Oh, twenty years ago. He simply became so exasperated with the obtusity of the official he was dealing with that he said, 'OK, how much do you want?' and then fell silent, stunned by his own rashness. What if he had read the signals wrong? But he hadn't.

Later he learned the trick of dropping an envelope on the floor and asking the other if he had dropped it there. Another important indicator was if the official invited you out for a coffee.

It occurs to me, writing this down, that this sort of breathtaking breaking of cover – the dropping of the envelope, the invitation to coffee – is not unlike one's first declaration of attraction to a possible lover; there's sudden intimacy and self-exposure. It's exhilarating.

And, my friend tells me, his accountant was indeed exhilarated. In this case, the man began to explain, he had understood that they wanted a bribe, because otherwise they would have already proceeded to fill in the document requiring him to pay the fine. After which, there could be no turning back, the matter would be officially registered. And had my friend really evaded so much VAT, they would almost certainly have proceeded with the matter and nailed him. As it was, appreciating he was merely a victim of circumstance, they were inclined to let him off the hook in return for a small Christmas present . . .

'How much?'

Two days later the accountant phones to say the matter in question would cost 800,000 Lire. My friend should come to his office in a couple of days' time to say whether he intends to pay.

My friend is still very English. Though less than he was a month ago. In the past week he has joined a group of colleagues bringing a case against the university to be recognised as employees. So he now has a lawyer. An attractive young woman six months pregnant. And finding the idea of paying a bribe somehow offensive, the kind of awful initiation into a different way of life, a different state of mind, that theft or adultery might be, he phones this lawyer to discuss the problem. She is polite and patient, listening to the complex story. Until he gets to the bit about the little envelope, at which she suddenly becomes frantic. '*Per l'amore di Dio* we're talking on the phone.' Anyway, she will consult her accountant and ring back.

Which she duly does. Indeed, it's surprising how kind and helpful and civilised everybody is being. On the phone she's calm, matter of fact: 'The manner', she says – and my friend has written her circumlocutions down because he finds them so amusing – 'in which your accountant has chosen to resolve the particular difficulties in which, through no fault of your own, you find yourself, although perhaps not immediately attractive, and you do have my sympathy here, is nevertheless not so mistaken as you appear to think. If you follow his advice to the letter, I am sure you will be able to arrive at a *soluzione felice* without my help.'

But another anxious week has definitely italianised my friend that little bit more. For rather than simply shelling out the 800,000, as it now seems he will have to, he points out to his accountant that since the VAT office's complaint is based only on that one declaration of four years ago, they could perfectly well pull out the next declarations one by one, year by year, and have him over a barrel for the same amount again.

The accountant accepts this. It is agreed the 800,000 will be paid only if the VAT office can dig up the other declarations and allow the accountant to change them, otherwise the sum must be renegotiated. The VAT men, whom my friend never saw again, and whose names he does not know, are likewise reasonable. No they can't dig out the other declarations, yes they do appreciate the problem this represents, they will bring their request down to 400,000.

Pride satisfied, my friend pays.

'And 100,000 for me for negotiating the deal,' the accountant says, with still no apology for his initial mistake. And no receipt.

Before leaving the office, in the state of exhilaration that every initiation, every surrender of self, brings once one has decided to go through with it, my friend asks the accountant: 'But it's so little. Why would anyone corrupt themselves for so little?'

'No accountant worth his salt,' the burly man explains, 'would work in the VAT office. How much can they be getting, two million a month? They have to supplement it. A 100,000 from you, a half a million from me, it all adds up. And the rules are a lot simpler than the written ones.' Reflectively, as if this has occurred to him for the first time, he adds: 'There's only one person I know of in the VAT office who won't take something sometime. Lucky it wasn't him picked up your problem.'

My friend walks out into the bright street with the feeling of one waking up from a nightmare. In the end he's only lost two hundred and fifty odd quid. Not much to pay for a significant experience.

17
Una scampagnata

And when you do wake up from such occasional nightmares, when you turn off the TV with its bullet-ridden cars and improbable corpses (eight in a single village in Sicily the very morning I write this), when you close the newspapers with their intricate political scandals from top to toe of the peninsula, it will often seem that you are living in paradise.

There is no smell on the balcony this Montecchio morning. Perhaps because it is Sunday. The late October air has that look of water in a wineglass, so that one expects, on walking out of the front door, to step into a magic world. And magic it is. Old Marini's blackbird whistles brightly, perhaps remembering how fine the trees were on such sweet mornings, the sharp silhouettes of the hills, the nobly etched cypresses dark against the glowing gold of autumn cherry leaves.

We wait in the street for the old ladies to return from Mass, then set off with them, Orietta, Giampaolo and Lara on a *scampagnata*, a long walk up into the hills. We are going to see Lucilla's daughter, Marisa, who is not in fact her daughter, Lucilla now confides, but the child of a sister conceived and born adulterously while the husband was in prison and handed over to Lucilla at just a few weeks old to make the husband's release less turbulent. Lucilla's own and only child died at eighteen months, *poveretto*. From the long story she tells us about his illness it becomes clear that Lucilla quite probably provoked his death herself by applying scalding poultices to his entire body in an attempt to overcome some banal influenza. Shortly afterwards, a miscarriage led to her having *la totale* at only twenty. *La totale* is the grim Italian expression for a hysterectomy. Once again, I reflect that while people from the Veneto are generally reserved and formal, nevertheless when they get on to the subject of their health there is simply nothing, nothing they will not tell to the most casual acquaintance, from varicose veins to mastectomy, prostatitis to mere constipation. And, indeed, it's not long before Rita, Vittorina and Orietta are discussing various forms of tisane, or herb concoctions, which help to keep one regular. Vittorina has a plastic bag to put camomile plants in as she walks along. A new shop, it appears, is to open next to Bepi's and the girl is an excellent herbalist. She even has a mix for flatulence.

I remember how rigorously my own parents avoided discussion of such complaints. That was the English *omertà* perhaps, our own peculiar conspiracy of secrecy. Orietta is tackling an overabundant period now. Much confabulation.

To try Giampaolo on the subject, I remark that the other day the parent of a friend of ours informed us on very first meeting that her husband had only one testicle. Giampaolo neither laughs, nor winces, but with polite interest enquires: 'Tuberculosis, or war wound?'

We pass the Madonnina, at the end of the street, dead Christ on her lap, then a second tiny Madonna behind glass where the road leaving the village forks. *O Gesù salvaci!* – someone has attached a popular sticker to the wall just above. And how benign they are, these plaster guardians of dangerous junctions in their faded blue robes and dusty haloes, one hand inevitably raised in blessing. The glass has been polished. The Madonna is composed, wistful. A hundred metres further up the street, someone is still putting crysanthemums in a stone vase to mark the spot where a boy was killed on his *motorino* in the summer.

We climb steeply out of Montecchio to Olivè where so many parents send their children to the convent school because there are never any strikes and the Church is more efficient than the state. There is building work going on in what was recently an orchard, but the cement mixers are silent on Sunday. To the left, a fine old farmhouse has been restored with a warm beige stucco that has a honey look to it in the now yellow morning light. The white chairs and tables on the terrace outside, the patently movable dwarf trees and statues arranged in geometric design, offer, in what was once a farmyard, a last testimony to urban invasion. From here on *stile cimitero* gives way definitively to flourishing vegetable patches. Olivè is solidly indigenous.

A woman is attacking clothes with a soapstick at an outside sink. With every new fence a fierce dog barks. There's no pavement and, parked up against the walls, the cheaper Fiats predominate, with the occasional tractor. Weathered old men in trilbies and Sunday best descend to Montecchio for the second Mass, lighting cigarettes.

Then the asphalt gives way to dirt track. The road turns sharply left by a noble gate and goes into a steep cutting between high stone walls where a beautifully arched old bridge crosses above. With ivies hanging thick from the parapet, capers sprouting from the walls in vigorous tufts, the dust road almost white and the sky ever more deeply blue above, the scene seems made for one of those tiny paintings by Sisley or Pissarro that you find tucked away in the corners of rooms dedicated to grander canvases, paintings which convey such a sense of a single moment in a single place it is as if time has been made palpable. Even now, when I pass that turn in the road, I always remember it as it was that morning. It made such a picture.

Lucilla is volubly discussing *il professore* again. How often they used to come on walks like this! How cultured he was. How polite! Vittorina shakes her head, pouting silently, as if to tell us Lucilla is inventing. Clearly we are never going to get to the bottom of this. 'In my will,' the fat woman puffs, 'I've left everything to Marisa and Leone, but only on the understanding that they continue the case against Signora Marta.' She shakes her fist. Odd, I think, how despite her loathing she continues to refer to the woman so politely as Signora Marta. As if cowed by her urban credentials.

It's a long walk. We meet the main road climbing the side of the valley but, since it goes up in a series of tight bends, we merely cross it, following a little path that strikes up steeply from one hairpin to the next. The old ladies are surprisingly energetic, Lucilla amazingly managing perfectly well in high heels on the chalky white soil of the path. She has a posh coat on, although not her fur, plus a frilly blouse, a pearl necklace. Her bright make-up, I fear, will soon begin to melt.

Vittorina is plainer, but stalwart, peasant-solid with broad-brimmed straw hat, constantly bending down for her camomile. Orietta trails behind, already tired, limp. She hopes she won't have an attack of tachycardia. Giampaolo has that fine proud, upright, urban gait so admirable in Italian men. He wears a fashionable jacket, good walking shoes. Every Latin black hair is in place on his polished head. Lara is chattering about her homework. At twelve her Italian teacher has set her an essay entitled: '*La verità nella filosofia, nella matematica e nella fisica.*' It's mind-boggling. But not so tricky, perhaps, as *la verità* in the VAT office.

We are crossing another bend in the road when there is a sudden swishing sound, followed by grunts, heavy breathing. Turning round, it's to discover a pack of young and not-so-young men standing on the pedals of their sparkling racing bikes as they attack what seems an impossible slope. To a man they are fully kitted out with the cycling shoes, the elastic kneelength pants, the fluorescent sweat shirts, the caps . . . Not one without the perfect gear. A mobile love affair with sports equipment. One can do little but gasp with admiration at the energy with which they attack this slope.

'Not for someone with my blood pressure,' Orietta shakes her head.

'Or sloth,' says her daughter. Giampaolo maintains his reserve. Mentally I rehearse: as a sport, *valido*; the design of the bikes, *discreto*; but pleasure rendered *relativo* by the fact that by the time you get back you're fit for nothing but bath and bed.

Comes a sudden cry of '*Pista, pista!*' Make room! Out of the way! And from round the corner where the muscly backsides of the cyclists have just disappeared, flies a girl on wooden skis. The skis have small wheels at each end. The girl wobbles precariously, gives a heave on one of her ski-poles, and vanishes down the road – getting in vital practice for the season.

In sharp contrast to these healthy activities and all the talk of herbs and remedies, we now pass a cypress in a small clearing whose trunk is bristling with used syringes stabbed into the bark. Nobody has anything to say about this sad rejection of the usual social rituals. The old ladies shake their heads in incomprehension. Orietta worries that if the point of a discarded syringe should pierce the sole of her shoes, it could give her AIDS. But Giampaolo knows that the virus only lives for fifteen minutes outside the body. And we're back on safe ground discussing the reliability of the information they give us and whether the state should bow to Vatican pressure not to advise people to use condoms.

We trek on. The land, like that around Rivoli, is semi-abandoned. Elaborate stone terracing, now overgrown and ill-kept, reminds you that only fifteen, twenty years ago these hills were worked intensively. But not even the expensive blandishments of the Common Agricultural Policy have been able to keep the peasants at work up here. Now the only productive aspect of the landscape is the olive trees, their fantastically gnarled fairy-tale trunks and curious leaves, at once dull green and bright silver, adding a further touch of magic to the landscape, an autumnal play of stark, twisted, southern evergreen against paling breaks of deciduous copse. More prosaically, whenever the contours allow for it, there will be a long low prefab factory farm for chickens or churkeys. Approaching, you hear the sinister hum of electrics, then a busy clucking that explodes into excitement, or protest perhaps, as the birds sense your passing.

A couple of hours later, having reached the top of the ridge above the village, the whole fantastic landscape to the north opens up before us. Range after range of hills rise one after another to blue mountains. The panorama is vast, hugely open, intensely exhilarating. We stop and gaze. Two rapid reports from a shot-gun, then two more tell us hunters are about, although we have seen not a single wild animal along the walk, heard not a rustle. Bang bang, go the guns. Presumably aimed at some fluttering *uccellino*. *Poveretto*, says Vittorina, who enjoys cooking them so much. And, having absorbed the view, we press on toward the little village of Cancello.

When Lucilla retired she sold her cleaning company to a bigger one, but Marisa and husband Leone still work on in a management role. With the decent incomes these two no doubt deserve they have built themselves a house up on the hills. They would have liked to be nearer Montecchio but, unusually for Italians, they chose not to accept the offer of the flat immediately below Lucilla's. It is to this perversity that the Visentini owe their good fortune in occupying Flat 2.

At first sight, Marisa and Leone's *villetta* looks like an

English bungalow, for local zoning forbade them to build over a certain height. However the attic is *abitabile* – liveable – and opens on to a most attractive terrace cut in the roof. The ground floor is spacious and luxurious: tiles, parquet, rugs, two bathrooms, three bedrooms. But this wasn't enough for Marisa and Leone. Unable to build upwards, they decided to go down. The hills are limestone and easily cut. So there is a basement dug into the rock, comprising a garage for the Mercedes and then a huge *taverna* with absolutely all mod cons: TV, well-stocked bar, second dishwasher, fireplace of medieval castle proportions (including spit), etc. etc. And still it wasn't enough. For below that again, two floors beneath the rosemary, chives and minty grass of the hillside above, is the cellar. With bare rock walls, it is clammy, cool and abundantly stocked with wines labelled and labelless, alongside a variety of hams, salamis and sausages suspended from hooks in the ceiling.

Stiff Giampaolo is most impressed by it all. *Validissimo*, this idea of a second basement beneath the first. The temperature is just perfect. And the wine selection is certainly *discreto*. Whatever the inevitable 'relativity' of the situation may be, he chooses not to mention it in deference to our host.

We climb back up to the *taverna*. In bright and fashionable halogen lighting hidden in the false ceiling over the bar, I find myself surrounded by antlers, boars' heads, stuffed grouse and the like. And fleetingly I wonder what the same kind of people in England would aspire to. Perhaps the sort of showhouse I blundered into in South Wales on holiday last year: a simplified, wood-frame copy of some grand Victorian original, with twee furnishings, imitation Laura Ashley curtains, glass-covered bookshelves boasting leatherbound editions (surely fake) of Shakespeare and Dickens, and very sophisticated naughty underwear laid out on the pink silk lookalike counterpane in the masterbedroom.

But Leone and Marisa do nothing to hide their humble origins. They speak a broad dialect which I can't always follow. They have no cultural pretensions. If the floor is paved with a warm red *cotto*, it is because they like it. Likewise the designer tiles in the bathroom. They happen to like them. They have the money. And they are incorrigibly jolly as they serve us the usual abundant Sunday lunch of a pasta dish (*al pesto*), followed by various boiled meats and fatty red, quite delicious *cotechino* with *polenta* and salad. Then the inevitable *tiramisù*. And cheeses. A piece of Parmesan to sweeten the mouth? A piece of seasoned Piave? Or would you like some sheep's cheese? And now fruit of course: *uva moscata*, kiwis . . .

We are sitting around a table designed for thirty odd. There are photographs of big parties on the wall. But Leone's booming voice and merry stories make up for the lack of numbers. The wines come and go in the usual sequence, as they must: a Bardolino novello for the *aperitivo*, sharp and fresh from the vines, a smooth Barbera to bring out the flavour of the meat, a blood-red sickly Recioto for the sweet. And now a glass of grappa appears beside your coffee. There's giggling, backslapping. Even Vittorina is light-hearted, despite, at one point, some low-voiced conversation with Marisa about a Madonna who has been seen to cry recently in a church at Colognola Veneta. 'What about some chestnuts,' booms the incorrigible Leone. 'Chestnuts, chestnuts.' He's gathered them himself in some wood further north. Italians have always been off gathering or picking something for themselves. The chestnuts are placed over the grate on a sort of frying pan with holes, then wrapped in cloth in a basket and handed round. No salt. That would push the pressure up terribly. But another cork is pulled. It's all hugely pleasant and at the same time far far far too much.

'Troppo, troppo gentile,' Lucilla says at the door, appearing to forget that this is the girl she brought up as her daughter. *Troppo gentile*. Buxom Marisa in Sunday best winks at the others. Leone goes down to get the Mercedes.

But surprisingly, the seventy-year-old ladies are all for walking back. They don't want to be taken in the car. So we set out mid-afternoon in an atmosphere of dazed merriment and with a great deal of extra ballast to work off.

There is a lot more traffic about now as people return from their Sunday lunch in the surrounding trattorias. But not everybody is going straight back to Verona. Here and there, as we cross the road to follow the path, we find cars have pulled off the tarmac to park in the fields, and, while mother and children walk about looking for mushrooms, flowers and herbs, *papà* sits in the driving seat listening to the radio and nervously cracking his knuckles. Or alternatively, *papà* does go off walking with his wife and children, but all the while holding a tiny transistor to his ear, cracking his knuckles against his thighs. An elderly and very well-to-do couple stroll by: distinguished, snooty almost, arm in formal arm, mohair coats, traditional hats. But the man has his trannie at his ear. And he is biting the corner of his lips.

They are listening to the local football game. Across fields and slopes, it comes from behind, in front, above, below you – the sound of a nasal voice commentating play with the very same pomposity Lara is presumably supposed to bring to *La verità nella filosofia, nella matematica e nella fisica*. I overhear something like: 'The dynamic oscillation of mid-field deployment with interchangeable roles in zone configuration is indubitably sound when considered from an exclusively tactical perspective, but perhaps the precariously semi-advanced position of the two centre backs which this inevitably entails is not entirely suitable to the psychological tension in which players understandably though, it must be agreed, regrettably, approach a game that could prove the watershed of this intriguing championship.' It's bewildering and I for one certainly haven't the faintest idea what it means. But people are listening intently enough. After all, this is the place where the choice of referees for next week's games is announced together with political scandals and spiralling national debt on TV news headlines. The little radios hiss and crackle between the olives. Sunday afternoon. Verona are losing. Faces are long and severe.

We press on. Then, in the twilight of this beautiful day, hurrying down the hill paths, Lucilla begins to sing. She sings a sickly hymn tune: *Tu scendi dalle stelle, o re del cie-e-elo*! Then, more merrily, a grating old pop tune: *Ciao ciao bambina, un bacio ancora* . . . She is very loud, with a cracked, witch's voice, and completely tone deaf. The others join in, if only to drown out Lucilla. Then Rita and Giampaolo launch into some of the famous songs of the Alpini, the Italian mountain regiment. They are all First World War songs from when the regiment won a notable victory, turning back the Germans in the mountains with very great loss of life. There's a sort of spirited mournfulness to tune and words that reminds me of traditional Welsh singing. And the occasional refrain tells all: 'That long train that went to the frontier . . .'; 'On the bridge at Bassano, we'll hold hands'; 'Don't get yourself killed, soldier'; 'They are shelling Cortina'; 'Ta-pum, ta-pum, ta-pum'.

Italian friends tell me these old songs are corny, and yet I always find them desperately moving: the young men marching into the mountains, ill-equipped, to death and glory, for undoubtedly a certain sad glory there is to be had in such situations: 'But if I fall amongst flowers,' they sing, 'I don't care if I die.' 'Ta-pum, ta-pum,' go the guns. It always brings tears to my eyes. I must be hopelessly sentimental. And I can't listen any more. So I fall back a few paces to walk beside Orietta, who immediately asks me if I think it's wise of them to let Lara do so much volleyball. She's such a big girl already. Isn't there a danger she might get thick ankles, muscular legs . . .

We're still walking when night falls, although Montecchio isn't far below us now, the castle sharp against the glow of Verona behind. The radios have fallen silent. Ghostly among the hills, long thin lines of light flicker on. For the chickens its always fluorescent daytime. They produce more. I take Lucilla's arm as we negotiate our way along the last stretch of dirt track. She tucks my hand tight under her elbow. And so back home, after what must surely have been our most successful day as a condominium.

To hear, through the fence, from a hovering Lovato, the momentous news that *il professore's* wife, Maria Rosa died today. During our *scampagnata*. The battle for the inheritance of Via Colombare 10, Flat 4, opens in earnest.

18
Un panino due . . .

My first months at Via Colombare I bought my bread at Tosi's, a shop which is little more than a hole in the wall but still manages to sell every possible foodstuff in just ten square metres. There's a cash desk at the door, the wooden shelving is chock-a-block, the floor is made of old stone conglomerate, the cheapest, and, behind a cluttered deli at the back, old Tosi himself, bald head threatened by salamis above, cuts squares of pizza in the half dark and counts out bread rolls from bins. He always counts them out aloud. *'Otto mantovane, per favore'*, you say, and he begins: *'Un panino, due panini, tre panini, quattro panini . . .'* Before we learn his name, we always refer to him as *'Un panino due'*.

When he's tucked your rolls into a brown paper bag, this

lean old man scribbles something with a practised shopkeeper's smile and you turn to the wife at the desk to pay. They don't have a proper electronic till, which means they're declaring a very low turnover, since above something fairly pathetic VAT-approved cash registers have recently become obligatory. The *signora* doesn't have a head for sums and invariably gives you less change than she should. Meanwhile, Tosi is already counting out the next customer's rolls: '*Un panino, due panini* . . .' He has recently built a small estate of four *palazzine*, sixteen flats in all, opposite the petrol pump. They go for more than a million a square metre. A fortune. On the hill behind us he is building two much larger villas surrounded by elaborate iron fences for himself and his family. Rumour has it that in the hungrier years of the war he would give people bread in return for land. Certainly he now owns large areas of hillside, and is eagerly courted by the local building contractors. But for all his wealth, however gained, old Tosi continues to count out panini: *un panino, due panini* . . . And you say to his wife, '*Mi scusi*, Signora Tosi, you haven't given me enough change.' '*O davvero?*' she says. 'I am sorry.'

So when Bepi expands his greengrocery, adding a bread and deli counter, I'm happy to switch there. Which means I walk past Tosi's shop now, my plastic bag in my hand. Perhaps the old man has come out of his cave for a moment to stand on the steps beside the ancient enamelled blue sign that says, '*OLIO D'OLIVA. OLIO DI SEMI, ZUCCHERO* . . .' He has a soiled white shopkeeper's coat, arms folded. And to show that my betrayal is of no concern, he makes a point of smiling his scrubbed shopkeeper's smile from around a long hooked nose. For his old customers will never betray him. Old Marini and his wife will never betray him, never go to a shop run by a parvenu like Bepi. Lucilla and Vittorina will never betray him. They're in there. Despite the fact that everything is more expensive. *Troppo gentile, troppo gentile,* Lucilla says to Signora Tosi, not counting her change at the door.

Bepi is sorting through piles of paper as he takes your money at the till. Scores and scores of loose scraps of paper: green paper, yellow paper, blue paper, printed, typed, scribbled. 'What are they?' I ask him. '*Scartoffie,*' he says: rubbish. And he laughs his barrel-chested laugh. In fact, they are all delivery notes and invoices from suppliers: a farmer who brings goat's cheeses in jars of oil, an importer who sends him Swedish salmon, a processor who prepares olives and red peppers, again in oil. It's a serious deli.

Bepi has a blunt pencil behind his ear in thick hair. I ask him if he does his accounts himself. He says yes. I ask him how he can possibly manage this with his gym, his karate, his dogs, his court cases, his occult studies, the house he is renovating. Of course he can't, he says. But then if *he* can't, *they* certainly never will, will they? We both know who 'they' are. 'And if they bother you?' 'I'll prosecute them', he says, 'for harassment.' And he means it.

Rather than giving you too little change, Bepi usually rounds your bill down. 'Five thousand two hundred and fifty? Oh, just give me five thousand.' He has an electronic till, but doesn't always open it. After all, I'm a friend. The government, one might mention, agreed to pay shopkeepers a percentage of the cost of introducing approved electronic tills. Mainly produced by Olivetti.

Mopeds whizz round the bend in the road as I leave the shop. One towing a bicycle. Outside Tosi's shop there are now four or five youngsters sitting on the steps behind their bikes eating oily squares of pizza out of sheets of paper. I walk to the other end of the village to pick up my *Arena*, and outside the newsagents there are other youths perched on more mopeds; these ones drinking Coca-Cola and eating crisps. Moreno, the tiny halfwit in deerstalker cap, is trying to talk to them and they are gently making fun. Going past the church there are yet more youths, yet more mopeds, hanging around in the gardens there. They hang around till late in the evening, summer or winter. Generally they are well behaved, I don't get the impression they booze at all, but occasionally a phone box, *the* phone box, will get damaged – or a road sign. And they catch colds, of course. Because it's mid-October now.

Giampaolo protests at the first local council meeting I go to. Kids are hanging around all over the place vandalising things and freezing their feet because there are no facilities in Montecchio, no green spaces and nothing for people to do. Actually, Giampaolo is not really very worried about this, since for the moment his daughter always returns at a reasonable hour; but word has got about that the cherry orchard behind the Madonnina at the end of Via Colombare is not to become a public park and recreation area, as originally promised in the plan for the village, but a cooperative housing estate. Which will mean tripling the traffic along our narrow street.

Giampaolo is well spoken, polite, but forthright. A modern, liberal man. There are cries of '*Sì giustissimo!*' But the Christian Democrat leader in Montecchio, who is also the weasely fellow in charge of the post office, calmly dismisses him. There is volleyball some evenings in the school gym, and the church lays on meetings for young people one or two nights a week. The reason kids are out on the street vandalising things is because they are not being brought up with traditional Christian values in good strong families (murmurings of approval from the older contingent). And it is calumny, he says, to suggest that the Party is in the pockets of the building contractors.

The Christian Democrats' local office is in an old church on one of the main corners in the village. They poll around 70 per cent of the Montecchio vote. The Veneto in general has a higher Christian Democrat vote than anywhere in Italy, including Sicily. The old church has a small tree growing on its unkept roof. Below, on the grey wall above the flood overflow ditch which runs alongside, someone has spray-painted: 'FOREIGNERS OUT OF THE VENETO.'

Only two hundred metres away, the Communist Party headquarters is a dark, poky place on the main street opposite Pasticceria Maggia. On a hand-painted wooden board above the door, the hammer and sickle are fading fast. Through the window, old men can be glimpsed at a bare wooden table on which stands a labelless two-litre bottle of wine.

The very same men are also to be seen some mornings sitting under straw hats on a bedraggled couch under a fig tree against the sagging wire fence that surrounds their allotments. The two-litre bottle, however, from behind which they look out over lines of enormous cabbages, is doubtless a fresh one. Youths roar by on their mopeds, confabulate in knots at street corners. After dark, when their parents could not see even if they drove right by, they kiss.

A modest crop of unmarried mothers patrols the streets

with their baby carriages, and in general have the sympathy of the population.

The very attractive *barista* in Pasticceria Maggia is such a case. Her child is eight years old, and perhaps aptly called Luna. The *barista* serves the people coming out of church. Out of church and into the bar in their Sunday best, which means furs for the women now the cooler air gives them an excuse. There's a parade feeling about it all. From one institution to another: the host, the *brioche*.

The church has the largest car park in the village, aside from the supermarket's, which nobody uses. A capacity of around a hundred cars. It is full Saturday evening for the Mass for those who want to dash off skiing first thing Sunday morning, or those who'll be so long in the discothèque tonight they don't expect to make it tomorrow. And it is full again Sunday morning for the Mass for those who want to show off clothes and well-dressed children and get a *cappuccino* afterwards in the bar and buy attractively wrapped trays of pastries for visits to relatives. Some of these people drive from three or four hundred metres away.

The church car park is also full for funerals and weddings. A bride and groom come out. They have married in their late twenties after being boyfriend and girlfriend since puberty. A photographer is waiting on the steps. But the groom is already lighting a cigarette. Anyway, the real photos will be taken later in an ornamental park the other side of Verona where there is a lake and stone nymphs. The photographer will fade one face over the other against a pre-prepared full moon behind floating in the water. For the moment though, everyone is rushing out of church to try and get their cars out of the car-park before the crush. Since it's a wedding, they all honk.

Yes, it was certainly wise of the local government to provide such ample parking space, such a large area of asphalt in the middle of the village. But when there are first communions to be celebrated, even this space is unable to contain the flood of traffic and enthusiasm. The cars tuck in by the emergency overflow dike and down the embankment as far as the supermarket. The spiffily dressed relatives step out of black BMWs. Clean, *per bene*, as they say here: healthy, wealthy, right-thinking people. There is something almost Victorian about the overdressed children, the fussing mothers. Certainly they all know their catechism well enough, as one child after another is accepted into the community. And after the ceremony's over, it's off to a restaurant where a table has been reserved for twenty. The expensive festivities will go on all afternoon and the children will be given their golden chains and crucifixes and signet rings.

On his election poster, the local Christian Democrat uses a picture of himself and his wife standing with family and friends around a beautifully laid table with white embroidered tablecloth, tall glasses of bubbly, large slices of *panettone*. There is no message or slogan, just the candidate's name; but we can feel reasonably sure that this man supports all the best local aspirations, is the very avant-garde of the bourgeoisie perhaps.

The Christian Democrat's annual festival is called *La festa dell'amicizia*, The Festival of Friendship: good friends, good contacts, an aura of universal love and piety. With a subtle shift of emphasis, the Communists call theirs *La festa dell'unità*, The Festival of Unity. Conjuring up images of rump solidarity, a last stand. In the event, both festivals mean barbecue food and wine, dancing in front of a noisy band (the same one, quite probably) and lines of booths where trivial skills are rewarded with soft toys. If you go to the one you may as well go to the other too. As everybody does, in fact. Because both are a lot of fun.

My wife goes to see the priest who preaches to the faithful week in week out; Don Guido, the small, bespectacled, faintly squinting character who smelt something rotten in Bepi's shop. He sits behind his large desk in his modern *canonica* next to the new red-brick church which he himself had built.

What can he do to help?

Rita (for her sins perhaps?) is translating into Italian an American book about the papacy. The book quotes extensively in English from various encyclicals. Does Don Guido by any chance have copies of these encyclicals in Italian? She ought to use the originals, not translate them back herself. And she knows encyclicals are automatically sent out to all priests.

Don Guido has his black cassock on, loose about the shoulders, tight about the stomach. He makes a gesture, at once sly and resigned, of raising his hands, palms upwards. Yes, he gets all the encyclicals. And when they arrive he files them away – in the bin. He smiles. That's how it is. A modern priest doesn't have time for encyclicals, he has to deal with real life as it is.

While he is smiling, Rita notices something odd about the desk. Under that glass top he just raised his hands from to make his ironic gesture, are line upon line of tiny photographs. Photographs of faces. Passport size. And they are turned so as to look, not at the desk's usual occupant, but the other way, toward the supplicant, the interviewee. Rita recognises a face and draws a breath. They are Montecchio's recent dead staring up from the priest's glass-topped desk. '*Riflettete*,' says a little piece of card he has propped up: 'Think about it.'

Turning to leave she sees there is a photocopier in one corner. A notice says: 'Copies are free, but contributions are not refused.'

A popular private midwife in the village has the same line. Her prenatal examinations are free, but if people want to give her something . . . Women ask other women how much they should give. Not less than 50,000 a check-up.

Perhaps inevitably, the figure of the priest attracts all kind of stories, some probably apocryphal, some not. Famous for his careless driving, it is rumoured that late one night Don Guido had to call on a farmer to get a tractor to pull him out of a ditch. And in his car was an adolescent boy who had no cause to be there. Others maintain he has had more than one girl around the village. Recently, the *canonica* was robbed and poor Don Guido bound, beaten and gagged. All the same, he did not report the matter to the police. Why not? Because his son was involved, wasn't he . . .

Or so the rumour goes. But one quickly gets the impression that this is merely the kind of thing people like to say about village priests. The combination of celibate status and social prominence is too inviting for the fable-monger. And then it's important for the congregation that the priest be a wholesome sinner like themselves. Just as it is important for them that the men in the tax office take bribes . . . Certainly I have never met anyone who pretended to be shocked.

One evening in Via Colombare, Giampaolo adds a new

element to the Don Guido dossier by confirming that the priest has made something of a mission of going to preach to the prostitutes who hang around on the sheepskin seats of their white Mercedes near the station in Verona. Giampaolo admires him for this and feels he is *valido* as a priest and *discreto* as a preacher. The *relativo* aspect would appear to be that Giampaolo sees the Church as one of the conservative elements that keeps the local mentality so provincial. 'After all, prostitutes do have a social function,' he reminds us very seriously.

More prosaically, Don Guido keeps rabbits (also white and furry) behind the church, and hens and ducks too. When he meets children in the street he pulls boiled sweets from his pocket and tousles their hair. Then invites them to come and see his rabbits.

For Lucilla, Don Guido is a great religious intellectual, a kind, generous man, another person she can endlessly find *troppo gentile*. Especially now he has agreed to testify to how she nursed Maria Rosa those months after *il professore* died. A major point in her favour when it comes to authenticating the scribbled will.

Vittorina pays Don Guido to say Masses for her dead husband. She likes to light candles at twilight and mutter her rosary in the fat, waxy smoke. She buys any number of the religious publications displayed near the door. Miracles upon miracles of the saints.

Orietta is thankful to Don Guido because when, in confession, she told him she used contraceptives, he told her to act according to conscience. It was between her and God. There is concern and disbelief over another excellent bottle of Giampaolo's *prosecco*, when I point out that this is one of the main precepts of Protestantism.

But Don Guido is a little less Protestant when he goes to talk to Maria Grazia, the busty herbal specialist next to Bepi's who can advise such efficacious tisane. Her shop is officially a *sanitaria*, a sort of chemist's, but without the pharmaceutical side. It sells baby equipment, basic orthopaedic aids, elastic stockings, corsets, maternity bras, bandages, Elastoplast . . . and condoms. Don Guido complains that being the fine churchwoman she is, she shouldn't be selling contraceptives. Maria Grazia thus has the unenviable problem of trying to reconcile genuine religious devotion with social conscience and commercial flair. She goes on selling her condoms. And, what's more, at less than the manufacturer's list price. When the representative comes round, he tells her the local chemist has complained. He knows she is undercutting him on the price. He sent a spy to buy some. The representative says she will have to comply with the list price, or he won't bring them. But Maria Grazia continues to sell at the lower price to people she knows. Because it is ridiculous that a condom should cost twice or three times as much in Italy as it does in other parts of Europe.

Does the Pope's strong stand on contraceptives have anything to do with Don Guido's complaints? Or is he a good friend of the chemist's? In any event we discover that Maria Grazia rushed into marriage as a result of an unwanted pregnancy. She had meant to be a doctor.

The Scholl sandals representative also tells Maria Grazia that the chemist has complained about her undercutting him. It is *concorrenza sleale*, unfair competition. She must comply.

A *Corriere della Sera* article shows that Italian shopkeepers have the highest margins in Europe.

Maria Grazia tells us that when she opened her shop, the first *sanitaria* in Montecchio, she couldn't understand why so many old women would come in asking for large, sterilised sponge gloves, right handed. Later she realised it was because they did not want to touch themselves 'in that place', when they took their bidets.

When a tax inspector comes to see if Maria Grazia uses her electronic till and gives receipts that correspond to the price paid, you can always tell, she says, because they hang around a few minutes, looking a bit lost, then choose the cheapest item in the shop, the herbal chewing gum she has on the counter, for example. She gives the man his receipt and promptly phones up a couple of other shopkeepers to pass on the message. If they haven't already called her. But not the chemist. Who is opening his own herb section now.

The inspector then goes on to *Un panino due*'s and asks him if he has the *pane comune* whose price is fixed by the government and used to determine the rate of inflation. A baker is obliged by law to have this bread. So the old man pulls out the one bag he bakes a day just in case the inspector comes. The government has fixed the price too low and anyway nobody asks for the stuff. Maria Grazia says it has no bran in it and makes you constipated.

Speaking about health, I ask Giampaolo jokingly if he doesn't suffer from tachycardia like his wife. He drinks so much coffee. Perfectly poker-faced, he says no, he suffers from *extra sistole*. He is having a series of tests done at the hospital. I have to consult my dictionary later to discover that this simply means he sometimes misses a beat.

Orietta, meanwhile, has been missing more than one beat recently, because they have changed the refuse-collection system. In the past, a man came down Via

Colombare on a bicycle affair behind a huge bin. He emptied the street's rubbish into it, then pedalled off to unload the lot into a truck. There was something very Dickensian about it. But now they have introduced the *cassonetto*, a very large fibreglass container on wheels with lids opening on top and fluorescent reflectors on the side. There's one every twenty or so houses. You take out your rubbish and next day the truck comes by, lifts the container with automatic arms and tips it up into its press. A jet of hot water washes the fibreglass inside, then it is lowered back into place again.

All of which seems marvellously efficient to me. The best refuse service I have ever seen. The truck passes regularly three times a week.

But the woman at number 8, wails Orietta, keeps moving the wheeled *cassonetto* so that it's always opposite our flat. And when it gets full, the lid won't close any more. The smell could bring germs and disease and death!

Emptying her own rubbish, Orietta heaves the heavy container with rubber-gloved hands back toward number 8. Emptying hers, the mongol-looking woman at number 8 rolls it back toward number 10. Back and forth. Back and forth.

Don Guido drives by in his battered car to bless a house restored without building permission. He will also do exorcisms and disinfestations. On San Biagio's day he blesses the village's children so that they won't get sore throats. Just this week, though, he has installed the first two black people to arrive in Montecchio in one of the flats the church keeps for the poor. A gesture of true charity in racist Veneto.

'WE SAY NO TO A MULTIRACIAL SOCIETY' appears

on a wall by Laghetto Squarà near the flat. Other graffiti complain about pollution from chicken factory farms. A truck from Germany has parked behind, come to pick up the things that stink so much in the chemical plant, whose owner is prominent in Don Guido's congregation . . .

And so one could go on and on. Rambling back and forth through Montecchio, dodging the fast cars and wobbling bicycles. For everything links to everything else: the priest, the *sanitaria*, Bepi, the political parties, the *cassonetto*, the mopeds and the huddles of youths in the night . . .

There is no one characteristic which makes Montecchio Montecchio, Italy Italy, or the Italians Italian. And yet, as in any place, the slow accumulation of details does gradually form a sort of mesh or matrix. There is this constant entangling, as though in the weaving of a tapestry or net. And the more entangled and connected it all is, the more inevitable it comes to seem. It takes on the weight, the impenetrability of a dense contingent world. Yes, you tell yourself, it had to be so, because this is what this place is like. The barber believes himself a faith healer, but never gives you a receipt. You open an account at the bank and ask what the interest rate is but, instead of telling you, they say, what interest rate do you want, what do you do, who is your employer? Health is desperately, desperately important, but the air is laden with industrial smells every morning. Everybody likes the Pope, and racism thrives. But of course. What did you expect? This is Montecchio. And perhaps the best test of initiation is whether, on being presented with some new element, you immediately have a sense of its belonging here, of its being a new manifestation of the same matrix, rather than just another alien fact, another surprise.

On a mild autumn morning you see a young woman in a seal fur climb out of a sky-blue Panda and start to fight with her remote control driveway gate which won't open. And you understand why she has a fur and why she has a Panda and why she paid more for her coat than her car. You also understand why she has a huge iron remote-control gate outside a modest house. You even have a fairly good idea why it's not working. She salutes you with a friendly smile. She's nice. You help her. She curses in dialect. Finally, the thing starts rolling and she drives off the few hundred metres to church.

Then toward the end of October, as *I morti*, the Day of the Dead, approaches, flowers appear in one of the village's back streets decorating a little stone plaque in a wall, behind which a chained dog laps water from an old bidet. You hadn't noticed the plaque until the flowers appeared. It says: '*Qui, sotto piombo nemico, caddero due patrioti*.' 'Here died two patriots, slain by enemy lead.' And you think of the old men in the Communists' office behind their two-litre bottles, of Lucilla begging on the streets of Vicenza, and Tosi counting out his bread rolls for acres of land: '*Un panino, due . . .*'

19
I morti

To put your car in the garage under Via Colombare 10, you inch along a crazy-paved drive the opposite side of the *palazzina* to the garden, then down a steep ramp behind the building and sharp sharp left into the garage. Among the many early morning sounds, as I sit at my desk translating sales forecasts for marble granulates, comes the roaring of a small motor, tackling the ramp from the garage. Suddenly, the roar dies; instead there's a sharp whine, then a puttering, almost immediately beneath my window. Then the whole noisy business repeats itself.

I don't normally go out on to the back balcony above the ramp. I don't go out because, directly opposite, across Negretti's garden where Vega tugs her chain, is a thin, tall crooked house like something from a children's book; the witch's house: flaking stucco, battered shutters, grubby lace curtains awry. And at the window exactly on a level with mine, an old old woman with long face, skin shrunken on to her cheekbones, and black shawl pulled tight about her hair, is constantly looking out, so that if I step on to the balcony my eye inevitably meets hers. Upon which, a ghost, very definitely a ghost of a smile will cross her face. My salute is hollow. The experience is not unlike seeing Don Guido's photographs of the recently dead. And, in fact, today is All Saints' Day, or as the Italians more commonly call it, *I morti*, the dead.

But the unusual sound of this car – roar, whine, putter, putter, putter, roar, whine, putter, putter, putter – is too intriguing, and I head for the balcony, studiously avoiding that ancient gaze.

It is the first time in the four months since we came to Via Colombare that Lucilla has got her car out. From above I can just see that the back seat of the tiny Fiat is full of flowers. She has a fair few cemeteries to visit today.

If she can get the car up the ramp.

On the flat patch at the bottom outside the garage she revs it furiously. With the choke full out, the air turns Fiat blue. The engine is racing. And off comes the clutch with a jerk. The car shoots up the ramp. But at the top she must turn sharply right to fit in between the railings and the wall of the house. Racing up so fast, she loses her nerve and hits the brake. The car stalls and comes whining back down the ramp, careering about dangerously close to the outer wall that shores up the garden, coming to rest askew on the patch at the bottom. Immediately, she turns on the engine again, putter, putter, putter, and is presumably getting up courage for the next attack.

After watching the show through two or three times, I go down to help. The car isn't warm enough, she explains. I nod in agreement. Would she like me to try? *Troppo gentile, Signor Tino, troppo gentile*! Although the car is not old, the white paintwork is dull and cracked. Giampaolo has explained to me that this is because she uses some old industrial cleaning fluids she has to wash it. Lucilla's approach to cleaning is nothing if not radical. Only a few days ago we saw her wash out the canary cage by simply holding it under the garden tap. With the canary inside. Flapping about terrified.

The Fiat 126 is a minuscule car. Lucilla has the problem of reconciling the physical needs resulting from short legs and great girth. If she moves the seat too far back she can't touch the pedals, if she moves it too far forward she is squashed against the steering wheel. I telescope myself to about half my normal height and climb in. There is a fresh smell of crysanthemums: flowers for her dead husband, flowers for her dead child, flowers for her dead brother, Vittorina's husband, flowers for *il professore*, flowers for Maria Rosa. I waggle the gear stick. In the centre of the driving wheel she has stuck a crucifix, in the well of the speedometer, completely obscuring it, a Madonna.

When I've got the thing out on the street, like a teacher giving a good boy a reward, she says she'd been meaning to tell me that if I want to, I can start using the *professore*'s place in the garage now; yes, I can tuck in between the heap of firewood for *taverna* evenings and the pillars with their memorials of the dead. I am duly grateful. Vittorina arrives in a very sombre black coat with velvetty tassles and the two elderly women set off on their lugubrious rounds.

How the Italians love their dead! *I cari morticelli*, the dear deadikins! Shortly after lunch, out of curiosity, we wander along to the cemetery, which lies just to one side of the industrial estate. As with a first communion at the church, the small cemetery car park is full and scores of vehicles have overflowed into the villas and factories of the industrial estate, and even out on to the main road to Mizzole. It's a public holiday. Some cars have out-of-town plates from as far away as Tuscany, Piedmont. For it is important to visit your dead, however far afield they may be. And it is important to do so today, on this Day of the Dead. For one must have a sense of occasion, of formality, of rhythm. November is the dead time of the year; the leaves are falling, the soil is cold and bare; one visits one's dead. Giampaolo, for example, has taken his twin carburettor Giulietta to Venice to get a boat out to the island cemetery where his father is buried. Lucilla will even now be terrorising traffic on the road to Vicenza, Vittorina muttering her rosary beside her. One thus fulfils a duty, which is also a natural thing, not a burden, and then it is over. The fact that everybody else is doing the same duty at the same time certainly makes it more attractive.

The cemetery is rectangular and has tall walls, perhaps twenty feet high, like a little citadel. The crowd flows in from the car park, from the main road, from the pedestrian approach along an avenue of cypresses, and enters through the one big gate. Inside, there are white stone paths and more cypresses. The local authorities have cleaned everything up for the occasion. It's a job they've discovered the immigrants can do. The porticoes around the perimeter wall have been thoroughly swept. The marble is clean. Heading off directly to their loved ones' graves, people are dressed more or less as they would be for first communions, weddings and funerals: formally rather than sombrely. And they are all holding crysanthemums. Which have doubled in price this week.

The English, of course, bury or burn their dead and then largely forget them, at least after a few years. The main thing is to have them out of harm's way. But the Italians, like other Catholic nations I presume, behave differently. When I tell Orietta how my own father was cremated and his ashes scattered in the Thames from a plastic box whose colour and design seemed more suitable for the sale of ice cream, she is appalled, as if some awful sacrilege had been committed. But then he was a Protestant clergyman.

The fact is that Italians intend to remain on intimate terms with their dead for quite a while, and not merely by remembering loved ones as they were or placing framed photographs on mantelpiece or dresser. No, they want to sit by a grave and feel that there is a real whole body right there beneath them with whom they can somehow communicate. Setting up this privileged state of affairs in a busy modern world where space, and likewise health, are at a premium naturally requires some careful organisation, as immediately becomes apparent on entering a cemetery.

It is interesting, in this regard, how devotion and bureaucracy go hand in hand. On walking through the sombre iron gates past hooded statues and beneath the confidently engraved *RESURRECTURIS*, you find yourself in a fairly small space with graves in the ground before you and graves, or burial niches, in the walls around you. The niches are six high, the coffins being slotted into the honeycomb wall like drawers in a dresser. And the graves in the ground don't look quite like English graves either. There are none of those leaning tombstones, that tufty look, that precariousness of stone and affections sinking lop-sided into the clay, so gothic and so romantic. Here on the contrary, everything is neat, rigidly perpendicular, brushed clean, the atmosphere of some quiet, tidy courtyard in a government building after hours.

Almost at once, you notice that the graves in the ground are of two kinds: one where the covering tombstone is full length and more, one where it is smaller. Where the stone is full length, what you have is not a single grave with a single coffin six feet below in the earth and stones, but a cement vault in which as many as four coffins are stacked on shelves right up to the surface which is then sealed over by cement. These are usually owned by families. After thirty years, a coffin can, if more space is required, be lifted up, the bones removed and a new coffin with a fresh corpse introduced in its place. Obviously this makes for some interesting family politics.

Where the tombstone is smaller, we have something closer to the Anglo-Saxon tradition: a coffin in the cold ground. But even here the organisation is rather different. The graves are not dug individually. A long trench is opened up with an excavator. Starting from one end, a coffin is placed on the bottom of the trench and covered with earth. The earth is then shored up with planks to prevent it falling into the trench, which awaits the next occupant. This gives the whole process a rather industrial feel. But this is not a problem, since the Italians are more ritualistic about death than romantic. And ritual is by no means alien to mechanics.

The trench fills up. When all the coffins have been down there ten years or more, they are then all dug up together, the bones removed and the space once again available for the freshly dead. This obviously has immense advantages over the Anglo-Saxon system of leaving people in the ground more or less for ever. It also suggests that a grave is there for as long as it suits the living to go and visit it, not out of some eternal respect to the individual's remains. Cemeteries are a social phenomenon.

However, the practical considerations are more complicated than they may seem, and the authorities must be careful. If the same earth is used over and over, it becomes too rich and greasy; as a result of which rainwater ceases to drain away properly and the third or fourth round of corpses will not get enough air to decompose on schedule. One imagines that this makes their eventual exhumation rather unpleasant, not to say unhealthy. In order to avoid this state of affairs, sand and gravel are thus constantly added to the recycled soil to allow air and worms to pass through. If you are interested, the *Arena* will always keep you up to date on developments.

The cement vaults cost money. They are family-owned and the recycling of spaces is under family control. The graves in the earth are free, and considered much inferior, if only because they suggest that the family did not have enough money or respect to purchase a cement version. On one such grave we find a headstone clearly designed to head off complaints from indignant in-laws. 'He wanted to be buried in the earth,' the wife has had engraved on white marble, 'and I did as he asked.'

Naturally, since these graves are not paid for, the families of the dead have no control over their recycling. The authorities merely inform relatives some months before they plan to exhume the plot. Relatives then have the choice of having the bones boxed and placed in a very small burial niche at a small expense, or they can opt for the cemetery's communal ossary. If the relatives have moved, died, or otherwise disappeared, it's the ossary by default.

Thus for some people the Day of the Dead will hold a sad surprise. They come to find their loved ones and discover the grave is gone. The letter never arrived. Perhaps it was lost in the post. Bureaucracy is bureaucracy in the end. Things can go wrong. They scuttle this way and that about the cemetery, wondering if perhaps they haven't forgotten where Father was: then tears, protests, the search for whoever can be held responsible.

An equivalent problem for the very rich might be to have the remains of their dear departed stolen from the expensive family vault. Then a few days later comes the request for a ransom. It happens occasionally. The rich are inevitably churchgoers here. Indeed, it's an interesting party game to ask people if they know of any rich, famous businessman or celebrity who is not a practising Catholic. When the head of the Ferruzzi family refused to pay a few billion Lire for the corpse of his dead father-in-law, the kidnappers sent a message to the newspapers, denouncing the industrialist for his shameful lack of respect.

But a more mundane unpleasantness that might occur in Montecchio's cemetery on the Day of the Dead has to do with the *loculi*, the niches in the wall into which coffins are slid. Colloquially, these are known as *fornetti*, little ovens. Since there is no earth to cover the coffins, they have to have a metal lining inside and are sealed so as to be airtight. The corpse thus burns itself up under its own steam as it were.

But the unpleasantness has to do with the flowers. Each *loculo* has its little metal ring for a vase. You remove the vase, chuck the old flowers, put in the fresh ones and put the vase back. But for the upper rows of *loculi* you'll need a small step-ladder to get up to the vase. Step-ladders are provided, although you may have to wait. Worse still, you may find, especially on the Day of the Dead, that holders of the bottom *loculi* (notoriously wealthier) have invaded the floor space with an extravagance of flowers. This means it will be difficult for you to site your ladder. You move the flowers. The person who placed them there returns and complains. Arguments are not unusual. Voices echo round the stone walls. The *Arena* prints a story about a group of old men who came to blows in Verona's *cimitero monumentale*.

'Non fortuna, sed labor', claims pompous gold lettering in black marble referring to the exploits of some local entrepreneur. As with the graves in the ground there is a hierarchy with the *loculi*. You can have the cheaper variety where you are pushed feet first into a long deep niche, or the more expensive version where you are introduced sideways and have a whole two metres of façade space. Which lends itself well to declarations of undying love or long lists of achievements, grandiose claims: *Industria ed onestà*, boasts another marble slab. The more preposterous dead. But for the most part the stones are simple: the name, the dates, a photograph, a tiny red light or *lumino*. These lights were once candles, but are electric now. All the *loculi* and indeed the graves are wired up. It's part of the package. The electricity board sends the bill and gives warning before cutting you off.

We walk about. There's a buzz of low voices, the clipping of heels along the porticoes where flowers abound, the scraping of step-ladders. A subdued murmuring echoes back and forth between the high walls, the graves. The word '*poveretto*' can occasionally be heard. It is very civilised. Sober, but not gloomy. There are smiles, exclamations, perhaps some tears where a knot of well-dressed folk are visiting the more recently deceased. The day is bright, the flowers attractive, likewise the sun on clean stones. People come, pay their respects, go. Old attachments are at once acknowledged, distanced, given structure. There's a sort of serenity about it, which is charming in its way.

We find *il professore*'s *loculo*: Umberto Patuzzi. The photograph is recognisable, although one had almost expected to see him standing beside one of his road signs – to where? Purgatory? Paradise? With his little backpack. Instead, he is wearing a collar and tie like the people walking along the gravel paths around him. And he, or perhaps Maria Rosa, resisted the temptation to put in a photo of a much younger man. He looks his sixty something years. Whereas Lucilla has already chosen her grave snap; and shown it to us. A flirty, well-built young woman of thirty years before. 'They feel sorrier for you,' she explains.

Beside *il professore*'s small slab is a square of blank cement: the freshly inserted Maria Rosa, as yet without her stone. It's disgusting, Lucilla tells us that evening, that Signora Marta, being the niece and closest relative, hasn't even ordered a stone yet. It simply makes it clearer than ever that she never cared for the woman, she just wanted her money. Well, she'll never get it. Nor her flat. Never, never, never! After her day dutifully carrying flowers around, Lucilla is burning with rage again. 'Because the flat is mine, mine, mine,' she shrieks, giving me a key to the garage at last.

And indeed our position in Via Colombare appears to be getting more precarious. Following Maria Rosa's death, Signora Marta produced a will apparently written in the last days of the old woman's life. It leaves all the property to her and she is eager to sell the flat as soon as she has the title deed in her name. Fortunately, Lucilla has produced her will too and is contesting Marta's, saying the signature must have been assisted and is thus invalid. Indeed, she is now accusing Marta of corruption and fraud and her lawyer has asked for the opinion of a handwriting expert. But Lucilla wants to sell too if she wins. Either way we lose.

And we begin to get telephone calls. The woman with the twig broom and the garage extension doesn't want to be nosy, but is the flat for sale? And who owns it exactly? Her nephew will soon be finishing university and . . . For a couple of weeks we get one or even two such calls a day. So and so has mentioned to so and so that Flat 4 Via Colombare 10 may be for sale and since their daughter is shortly to be married . . .

From over his wall, where he is digging the ground to let the frost in, Lovato watches. He hangs around, and when I'm out there doing some condominium duty, he motions to me to show he wants to speak. Is the flat for sale? His daughter and son-in-law are cramped living with them. There's only one garage for two families, and if . . .

Thus, it occurs to us at last that when all those people came out on to the street that first day we arrived, it wasn't just because they wanted to enjoy the spectacle of Lucilla's raving. No, they all have designs on our flat. Pretty well every family in the street. If it becomes available they want to be able to buy it. For the dream of so many of these people is not only to remain at home, but to have their children and grandchildren remain at home too. They would do anything to stay in the same village and as near as possible to all their relatives from birth until death; and afterwards too, the attraction of the vault as opposed to the grave in the earth being precisely that proximity: Papà at the bottom, then Mamma, the brothers, the sisters, the children and all the long slow recycling afterwards.

Most of them seem to manage it – to stay at home that is. The local paper tells us that some 70 per cent of residents in Montecchio were born and bred here (the figure is disturbingly close to the Christian Democrat vote). For myself, I can never decide whether this indicates a sad lack of any sense of adventure, or the true flowering of wisdom. The way I can never decide if the formal atmosphere of annual cemetery visits is the height of civilisation, or merely a suffocating cultural inertia. In any event, the effect on house prices in a place where the population long outstripped new building will be obvious enough.

Lucilla's lawyer is bullish. So Lucilla asks us if we would mind prospective buyers coming in to look at the flat. She can thus have a contract drawn up even before the place is actually hers. This is nerve-racking. We suggest she might do better to show them her own flat which after all is the mirror image of ours, and, frankly, rather better furnished. She responds well to flattery. *Troppo gentile, Signor Tino.* And people gaggle round the top of the stairs being shown into her flat. Lucilla's is always the loudest voice. The words *valido* and *discreto* are heard, perhaps in unconscious imitation of Giampaolo. Viewers study the fittings, practised hands swing the front door to and fro to feel the weight. Clearly, it will need reinforcing, another security lock perhaps, but over all . . .

I point out to Lucilla that we might want to buy the flat ourselves and that she did once say she would be happy for us to do so. Then, from a legal point of view, as sitting tenants we surely have the right of first refusal. She is polite but uneasy. For selling also means doing a selected person or a selected family a favour. But yes, she says, if we are really interested of course we can buy. She hesitates, then names the kind of price that chased us out of London in the first place.

On the phone, Marta quite bluntly asks us if Lucilla is showing any signs of falling ill. Her blood pressure must be so high with her being overweight and always shouting. Then this business of turning the thing into a criminal fraud case is crazy and very ugly. Just an opportunity for the lawyers to get rich. Our rent isn't even covering her legal costs now. Do we realise that? *Mi scusi*? And, yes, if she, Marta, wins she might sell it to us, but actually she's rather changing her mind and probably won't sell at all now. Her sister's daughter has a boyfriend and they are planning to marry in three or four years time and . . .

In three or four years time . . . I'm bewildered how far ahead these Italians can plan their love lives. And it occurs to me there must be some intimate link between being able to choose your death photo before you're even ill, or decide which relative your corpse will replace in the family vault, and this ability to plan your marriage for some date that sounds to me like science fiction. Life is so carefully controlled here in the Veneto, so attractively wrapped up: *cappuccino* till ten, then *espresso; aperitivo* after twelve; your pasta, your meat, your *dolce* in bright packaging; light white wine, strong red wine, *prosecco*; baptism, first communion, marriage, funeral; *loculo, lumino*, exhumation.

Driving up into the hills of an evening, to a trattoria, one looks back down into the valley and sees the cemetery: a neat rectangle of glimmering red pinpoints in the night, the electricity board keeping the sacred lights burning in perpetuity. Or at least till your ten years are up.

20

Statali, dipendenti, autonomi . . .

Another way of wrapping up your life in Italy is to become a *statale*, a government employee, a civil servant. Of course, every nation has its own way of dividing itself up. The English have their classes, the Irish their religious denominations, the Americans their racial origins: Wasps, Japs and the like. In Italy, apart from the drastic north–south divide, one of the most deeply felt group distinctions is that of the *statali* and the *non-statali*: the government workers and the rest. Basically, as the rest of the population sees it, the *statali* enjoy a network of privileges so fantastic and far reaching as to establish them as a class apart, something almost approaching 'party status' as it was until recently in the Eastern Bloc. To truly understand your neighbours, then, you must appreciate their position *vis-à-vis* this conflict.

The privileges of the *statali* (as perceived, of course, by *non-statali*) may be listed as follows: they are not obliged to work; they are not even obliged to turn up at work with anything more than token regularity; mid-morning and mid-afternoon they can take a long coffee break in the nearest bar and combine it with a spot of shopping, or with filling in their pools coupon in their favourite *tabaccheria*; they enjoy shorter hours than the private sector, which means they have more time for moonlighting; they can get cheap holidays in hotels and camps reserved exclusively for themselves; they can get very low-interest mortgages directly from their employers while they are given higher interest rates on savings at the bank; they have quite unbelievable maternity and paternity rights; they have a better health-insurance scheme; they have the right (so important for an Italian) to be transferred to their home area after a number of years' work elsewhere; they enjoy the most extraordinary pension arrangements which often allow them to retire well before they're forty on a decent index-linked income; but above all, and it's worth all the rest put together – they are absolutely and utterly unfireable whatever they do, wherever they do it, whenever and how often, it doesn't matter, they simply cannot be fired. They have arrived.

In the protected world they live in, some *statale* exploits have become quite legendary. Given that managers in government offices are for the most part unable or unwilling to discipline their staff, when things get out of hand the police or *Carabinieri* will, once in the bluest of moons, arrive in force to check up on who is there and who isn't, perhaps prosecute a few dozen absentees. Thus the *Arena* tells us how in one administrative office the *Carabinieri* came across an expensive fur coat on the back of a chair, but no person in that chair. The employee in question had clocked in and then disappeared, as she did every morning, returning briefly in the afternoon to clock out. The following morning the *Carabinieri* followed her, to discover that she was working as a call girl in a flat directly opposite her office.

Stories like this strike a very deep chord. Naturally, the immediate reaction is one of disdain, of self-righteousness. '*Maria Santissima,*' Lucilla claps her hands, 'when you think how hard I worked all my life, Signor Tino.' But there is also profound admiration. How smart of her to have fooled the state like that for so many years. And they haven't even put her in prison or anything. How *furba* (sly, shrewd) she's been. Then look at the fur coat she put over her chair. 'Pure sable, Signor Tino!' What a smack in the face that was. Good taste too. Perhaps I should have been a *statale*.

And, at a deeper level still, people think: if that is how the state wastes its money, mismanages its affairs, then why should I be paying my taxes? The truth is that the *non-statale* has a psychological need for the *statale*. They are two sides to a coin that is common currency here. For just as the chaos and corruption of the south justify the peccadilloes of the north, so the lazy, absentee *statale* (who notoriously *is* a southerner, or so northerners will tell you), justifies the tax evasion of the *non-statale*.

Always assuming he is in a position to evade tax. For though the *non-statali*, the private sector, will present a united front in their disdain for *statali*, they themselves split into quite distinct factions when it comes to taxes. Leaving aside all the many nuances, there are basically two groups of *non-statali*: the *dipendenti*, i.e., employees, and the *autonomi*, the self-employed; and there is as much, if not more animosity between these two groups as between both of them and the *statali*. Indeed, the *dipendenti* and the *statali*, with their taxes deducted at source, may often form a united front against the *autonomi*, since they are convinced, and not without good reason, that the *autonomo* pays next to nothing in taxes and, what's more, earns a great deal more than either of them do. Everywhere jealousy is the key.

Three classic conversations result. The *autonomo* (perhaps our shopkeeper Bepi) meets the *dipendente* (let's say office-worker Giampaolo) and they complain about the *statale* (somebody in the post office for example), his benefits, his proverbial laziness and rudeness, his constant presence in the *pasticceria*, his twenty-day sick leave over a sore thumb, Italy's hopeless inefficiency in the public sector which is preventing it from becoming a truly important player on the European scene, etc. etc. etc.

Or the *statale* (Lovato's son-in-law, for example, with his Prisma in the illegal prefab garage) meets the *dipendente* (Giampaolo again) and they complain about the quite shameless acquisitiveness of the *autonomo*: never a receipt when you pay for your *cappuccino*, when you have the plumber in, when you see your heart specialist about your *extra sistole*. These people are unscrupulous. They steal from the community. We all have to pay more because they pay so little. It has to stop.

And when the *statale* meets the *autonomo*? Well, there's caution, obviously, but a certain mutual respect, too, an air of self-congratulation even, as of two people who have made the right decisions in life. And why are these miserable *dipendenti* always complaining? If they're not happy they should change their jobs. Or if the name of a mutual friend comes up, perhaps the word *poveretto* will be used, as of one who is lost, beyond hope. For it is generally agreed that the *dipendente* of a private company has the roughest deal. With his rigid hours, his limited opportunities for moonlighting, his difficulty justifying sick leave, his slavery to the market, his taxes always deducted and his comparatively low salary, the *dipendente* is undoubtedly the loser.

Hence, there is nothing the likes of *dipendente* Giampaolo can do but assume the rather stony moral high ground and talk about the citizen of the future and a society where everybody will one day have a sense of civic responsibility. This Giampaolo does with great dog-in-the-manger frequency. And England, for example, is much admired because there the social contract between government and people is truly *valido* and the level of fiscal honesty (yes, Italians talk that way) is *discreto*, even if all this is rendered *relativo* by gloomy weather, bad food and a general lack of taste. Never does Giampaolo like to distinguish himself more from the provincial, narrowminded aspects of Italy, than when talking about *dipendenti, autonomi* and *evasione*, as if his own fully paid-up taxes were some sort of avant-garde, internationalist creed, a measure of moral stature, rather than mere misfortune. Although in the *taverna*, one evening toward Christmas, barbecuing trout from Montecchio's fish farm and drinking rather more than he usually would (because *novello* is no good after December), we do get him to reminisce with obvious nostalgia about the good old days before PAYE was introduced (in the mid-seventies), the days when you declared next to nothing and nobody could do anything about it. So from his high ground, in the time machine of the *taverna*, the condominium *dipendente* will turn a wistful wine-soaked eye back on the cities of the plain. Which were, and for others still are, so much more fun.

I am tempted at this point to proceed to the rather grand reflection that thus, while the English have their lower classes, their middle classes and their upper classes, the Italians in turn have their *dipendenti*, their *statali*, their *autonomi*; so very deeply are these distinctions felt here, so bitter are the resentments, so sweet the triumphs. But the analogy could be nothing more than superficial. For this is not a hereditary system (a railway-union request that jobs be made hereditary was recently turned down), nor a family affair. On the contrary, father and son can all too easily be turned against each other. Old farmer Lovato, for example, with his years of hard autonomous (though mainly tax free) work on the soil, obviously feels not a little contempt for his wimpy son-in-law from the same background who has bagged a prize *statale* job as cook in a nursery school: just five mornings a week, plus all school holidays and the endless benefits: a day off to give blood, a day off for a union meeting, a day off for a urine test . . . The young *statale* pulls the Prisma out of the garage and cleans it meticulously beside his father-in-law's hard-worked cabbage patch. Or sits in the window opposite our lounge, building an elaborate nativity scene to grace the church porch a month hence. While old Lovato digs and eyes our flat . . .

Then there is more mobility between these groups than one would expect to find in a class structure. A *dipendente*, given the chance, or an *autonomo*, should his business take a dive, might well decide to become a *statale*. And a *statale*, on retiring at some ludicrously early age (*'i pensionati baby'*, they call them) might well become an *autonomo*, although he is unlikely, it must be pointed out, to want to become a *dipendente*.

Orietta, for example, a woman who has turned worrying into a fine art, who quakes when the ground trembles in Calabria, shivers when it snows in the Val d'Aosta, would very much like Giampaolo to become a *statale*, because then his job would be safe beyond any market logic for ever and ever and she could look forward to middle and old age with serenity in the full knowledge that the family will be able to pay for a well placed *loculo* at the end of the day. And Orietta is by no means the only wife pushing her husband in this direction. The search for security is an obsession here far far beyond anything I ever came into contact with in England or the States. I imagine this is linked to post-war insecurity, to the rapidity of economic change, the survival of a peasant culture forever seeking protection from bad weather. And, presumably, it's not unconnected to those frequent visits to the hospital for blood and urine tests, and then in a different way to the entrenched conservatism that surrounds all local customs and traditions here. Which is rather attractive. In any event, the more people despise the state, the more, nevertheless, they appear to wish to depend upon it, to become *statali*. As one dear southerner, Pasquale, self-declared anarchist and evening-school teacher explained to me: 'During the year the state cradles us, and in the summer holiday they just rock us to sleep.'

21
Concorsi

But how can Giampaolo become a *statale*? By doing a *concorso*. One appreciates that the reader may be getting weary of so many Italian words, but this is one that quite definitely defies straightforward translation. My dictionary, for example, offers a whole range of meanings: 'a throng of people', 'a coincidence', 'a competitive exam', 'complicity in a crime' . . . All of these, I fear, are appropriate.

The idea is as follows. A *statale*'s job is a very easy number, a meal-ticket for life. This the state tacitly acknowledges. Indeed, they have deliberately allowed this situation to develop in order to ingratiate themselves with the population. But, given the unfairness inherent in the fact that these jobs cannot be available for quite everyone, it becomes absolutely crucial that their allocation be seen to be fair. No favouritism must operate. Only merit will be considered. Merest merit.

Thus, the local railway station cannot, for example, simply put an advertisement in a local job centre saying they need three cleaning women and give out the jobs on a first come first served basis. Because then the station master might take on friends, or friends of friends – as a favour. Worse still, in the south, the Mafia would get control of things. So no, the railway has to hold a *concorso*, a public exam, and this must be announced at national level. Because again it would be unfair to exclude people from the south, even though they may, of course, after a couple of years, request transfer back home, thus contributing to overmanning there while reopening the vacancy in the north . . .

Our 'competitive exam' is thus announced in the papers and on posters inside and outside public buildings. Our 'throng of people' applies. Perhaps a thousand. Sometimes twenty thousand. Everybody wants to be a caretaker, a receptionist. 'Fifty Staff taken on to Process Applications for Dustbin Men', might be the typical headline of some small article in *Corriere della Sera*. It is never clear how these selecting staff were themselves selected. Whether there has been a *pre-concorso*, or what. It is as well, one suspects, not to enquire too precisely into the matter.

But what qualifies a person to be a dustbin man? Well, a certain level of intelligence, a certain mental attitude; so a written exam. Then a certain level of reliability, a certain personality; so an interview. But above all, health of course, and so a medical . . .

Which is where we come to the *concorso* as 'coincidence', or 'complicity in a crime'; or both.

The story I have in mind is Giampaolo's, a splendid Italian tale which I think sums up more or less everything that need be said about *dipendenti, statali* and *concorsi*. In one of the departments of Giampaolo's company works a highly skilled young technician who is very clever at his job. So clever that, under the table, the company is paying him more than his fellow workers to keep him. This lad's father is a Christian Democrat, has always held his membership card, and the son too is a member of the Party and lends a technical hand with Party activities, setting up the dais at the *Festa dell'amicizia* and such like.

After a few years at the company, the young technician marries. Both his own family and his wife's feel that the couple would be much more secure if he had a job as a *statale*. There are threats of recession. The State is the only organisation which will never fire you. Even if it means taking a cut in salary, security and peace of mind are the overriding concerns. And there will be the months of paid paternity leave when they have a child.

So the talented young man decides to take part in a *concorso* to become a bus-driver. And he goes along with his father to talk to his local Christian Democrat councillor. It is time the councillor did something for a family which has always voted for the Party and always been ready to help out. Otherwise what reason is there for being members? *D'accordo*, agrees the councillor, *va bene*. Which is as much as to say: Will do.

But our young technician is a conscientious, honest boy, with a sense of loyalty. He goes and warns his foreman that he will be leaving the company in six months or so, thus giving them time to train up someone else. Because he has applied to be a bus-driver, he explains. And, yes, he knows hundreds of people have applied, but he is sure he will be selected because he has spoken to Christian Democrat councillor X who knows Y who is on the committee.

The foreman promptly buttonholes the managing director. This boy is the cleverest and most efficient we've ever had, it will be a major setback if we lose him. The managing director, who is a Christian Democrat and friend of the same local councillor (here's our *concorso* as 'coincidence', although not such a great one perhaps), phones the said councillor. 'What is this, stealing our workers? It takes years to train someone to that level. How can a private company even begin to compete with the state with all the ridiculous benefits you're offering? I'm sorry, but this isn't on. You've got to stop him being selected.'

This places the councillor in a delicate position. The written exam and the interview have already been done, he explains. The boy is already through. He apologises profusely. 'I can't change those now, I'm afraid. If only I'd known.' Until at the last moment he has a brainwave: 'There's still the medical though.'

And we arrive at 'complicity in a crime'.

The doctor is looking at an X-ray. 'Don't you get any pain just above the pelvis sometimes?' The confident young technician says no, he never does. 'Really? Try and remember. In the small of the back. A dull ache?' 'No, never.' The doctor frowns, hangs the X-ray up on the viewing screen. 'Come and look at this. Here, you see, too much space between these lower vertebrae. Quite a common malformation, nothing to worry about in the normal way of things.' He is shaking his head. 'But I'm afraid it would soon result in disc hernia if you started driving a bus six hours a day.'

And incredibly everybody is happy: the doctor is happy because having done the councillor a favour he is now owed a favour in return, he has a card to play for the future; the councillor is happy because he has ingratiated himself with both young technician and managing director, they will see him as the right man to vote for, their own personal access to power; the managing director is happy because he has kept his worker and demonstrated his ability to wield influence; the skilled young man is happy because he never really wanted to be a bus-driver anyway.

Only the families of the young couple are left with a lingering feeling of regret, of wistfulness for that safe haven. A *dipendente*'s life is not an enviable one – he depends, as the very word suggests, on the whims of the market, the whims of his employer – and they had wanted the best for their children.

Whenever this story is told, by myself, by Giampaolo, people burst out laughing. The kind of laughter which greets those jokes that confirm a caricature. Yes, how they enjoy this harmless breach in the general *omertà*. And where could you get a story like that if everything was done in an honest, open way? According to merit. Or even if everything was done on a straightforward and acknowledged basis of nepotism and favouritism. No, it is the superimposition of the bureaucratic and apparently fair over the private and determinedly unfair, the public umbrella, we might say, over the personal intrigue, which breeds so many such stories, and which creates such a delicious tension in so many areas of Italian life. The rules are only a veneer, and indifferently glued on at that; like the Pope's diktats, or the catechism – no more than the thinnest coat of paint. While in the soft old wood beneath, the jolly worms honeycomb past each other in the dark. Busy and alive.

Curiously enough, I got confirmation of Giampaolo's story one December evening travelling back from town on the bus. It was rush-hour time, the bus was packed, so I went ahead to stand at the front behind the driver and watch the black countryside flinging by, the starkly twisted shapes of the bare vines against the twilight, the pinpoints of light rising up the hills to the north. In Borgo Venezia, another driver got on and came to stand beside his colleague. Barely a foot away from me, they talked about the most recent *concorso* for maintenance jobs in the garage. The new arrival had heard from someone in the know that these jobs were to be divided up equally on the basis of the local strength of the political parties; three people chosen by the Christian Democrats, one by the Socialists, one by the Communists . . . This made it unlikely that a friend of his would get in.

The speaker made no attempt to lower his voice to prevent me hearing. Nor did he show any sign of outrage or even unease that in this case a *concorso* was more a question of complicity than an exam. He might have been talking about a patch of dull weather, or the difficulty of finding fresh *tortellini* in the late afternoon, some irritating contingency. His colleague at the wheel drove on at great speed between the cement walls beside the flood ditches, stabbing at brake and accelerator as we hurtled through the narrow stretch where, if a bus or truck comes the other way, there is no room.

I moved back down the bus to the door. Two old women were knowledgeably comparing their blood sedimentation speeds as exhibited on the familiar health-service printouts. A group of fourteen-year-olds discussed whether horsemeat was nicer than beef, whether *polenta* was better with melted cheese or without. Then they argued about what kind of car Ruud Gullit drives. I climbed off. A bulldozer had been having a go at the old factory at one end of Via Colombare. A notice announced the construction of a complex of flats and shops. Reassuringly, the Madonnina was still in her place at the other end of the street, promising to protect us. Electric light gleamed on the more tangible security of iron railings. Simone's car was outside the gate at number 10, come for an abundant dinner: *baccalà, polenta*, Valpolicella. An electricity bill addressed to Patuzzi was in the postbox. The *cassonetto* had been pushed down toward number 8. Vega was barking, the TVs were on, and all was apparently well with the world.

22
Mussulmani

One of the sharpest images winter conjures up here is that of dry sticks. It will be hard, perhaps, to sing the beauties of dry sticks, but I shall try.

Maybe the fact that these sticks are seen against a blue sky is the first thing that need be said. For, after the autumn rains, much of winter in the Veneto is dry, bright and very blue: a crusty, colourless, cold ground under brilliant sunshine.

The leaves finally fall in late November. They fall from the vines, leaving strong, gnarled shapes behind. They fall from the fruit trees, the peach and cherry orchards. There is no wind and the thin dark branches are perfectly still against the heavens with an almost shiny blackness of polished bark. Often, tin cans and strips of plastic have been tied among the twigs – to scare the birds when there was fruit. Now they look like decorations for a ragman's ball. Along the edges of the fields, or winding along by ditches and streams, the fiercely cropped plane trees take on the despondent monumentality of surviving columns from some ruined portico.

In the smaller farms on the hill slopes above, the rows of vines are often supported by the cherry trees. A horizontal wooden slat is strapped to the tree; four or five wires are stretched from one slat to the next, one tree to the next, and the vines, twisting and splintery, cling on between. When winter comes and the luxuriant summer foliage of pergola and cherry leaf is gone, the rude peasant mechanics of these slats and wires is left stark in the bright light, like the tangled rigging of some beached clipper. There are the complex twists and turns of natural growth, branches and twigs curving back on each other, then the sharp manmade angles of sawn wood, and the graceful physics of sagging wire swooping from slat to slat, to end in small unused coils round the last cherry bough. All of which is seen against the terraced climb of the hill, the silver green of olives higher up and the sombre vertical dark of the cypresses.

Everywhere the *contadini* are cutting sticks. They prune the vines, moving slowly along the rows, arms constantly raised with knife and secateur. It must be tiring work. They bring out the year's now reddish brown tendrils, hardening into sticks, and burn them in low bonfires in the fields. At the bottom of the hill, along the ditches, they cut the young branches from the nobbly heads of the plane trees and tie them into bundles such as old women carry in fairytales, then leave them to soak in streams or big water tanks sunk in the ground. Kept pliable, they will do for tying up next year's vine shoots.

And they prune the fruit trees and the olives, sawing off whole branches, dragging away huge tangles of wood in their tractor trailors to be cut up for firewood on the powersaw in the farmyard. As we walk, the hills echo monotonously with the squeal of steel discs slicing through wood. There is something mournful about it, a lament for the lost summer, for last year's growth.

They cut longer sticks from poplar and birch trees, poles three metres long perhaps, and these they strip and leave standing in clumps in their farmyard, to serve as fence posts and railings, vine supports, shafts for pitchfork or shovel. Tall, leaning at an angle against a barn whose two main beams are themselves resting on the cleft branches of two ancient cherry trees, the birch wood is a smooth blue grey in winter sunlight. The walls of the barn are old packing cases, boards, strips of corrugated iron, an assortment of planks which once served other purposes, a sheet of pink plastic, an iron bar. On the other side of the building, a cable is taut between the tarpaulin roof and a concrete post driven into the hill. Unlike the thriving cemetery, there has been only token observance of such notions as perpendicularity here. Why doesn't the thing fall down, you wonder? Why doesn't it blow away? I stand and stare: the winter branches, the canes and cut sticks poking at the sky, the beams resting on the cherry tree, the tracery of crisscrossing wires; such a tangle of man and nature, the antique and the provisional, the old seasonal rhythms and the shamelessly makeshift. When the leaves are gone it's so clear.

We are in the farm, not far from Via Colombare, where

we pick up our eggs. A big German shepherd strains at the end of a chain which slides along a wire strung from barn to cowshed. Sixty plus, the farmer's wife is in her slippers and dark woollen stockings. She speaks good Italian and is bright and witty. Her husband is in the office, she laughs, and her thumb indicates the cowshed, which forms one side of the 'L' of the house. We go in to chat for a moment. In fact, there are two farmers here, brothers, pushing seventy. Their lease runs out in a few years and then the land will most probably cease to be a farm and the builders will move in. A builder bought the place some years ago and is pulling all the strings he can to get permission to put houses here. Sooner or later some contact he has, some favour he has done for priest or politician, will prove the winning card. For, although the regional plan designates the land as agricultural 'in perpetuity', no one has any illusions. After all, the surveyors are already marking out the orchard at the bottom of Via Colombare.

The cowshed is ancient, dark, with swallows' nests in the beams and soiled ropes knotted to iron rings in the stone wall, polythene over the windows. The smell of the eight cows standing in their straw and shit is overpowering. Here they stand and sit all year. They are never let out. The terraced land with its fruit trees, vines, and strips of wheat or maize is not suitable for grazing. The men go out to mow grass for feed in summer, and in winter there is the hay in the ramshackle barn. They have one milking machine and the two urns they fill stand in a little stream behind the shed to await collection. Perhaps this sort of arrangement explains why in summer the milk here sometimes goes off almost as soon as one has bought it.

Giuliano and Girolamo, they're called. They wear dirty

blue dungarees and brown felt hats. They speak in such fierce and garbled dialect that it is difficult to latch on to single words. One is merely left with a general impression of what has been said. Which may or may not be correct. Girolamo, the younger, but obviously the boss, is gritty and sarcastic. He likes to mock our city clothes and easy life. He scratches behind his ears, slaps a cow's thigh, smiles the smile of the old fox. Ailing and very bent, Giuliano is sweeter, although virtually toothless. He has just had his prostate removed – his *'prospera'* he amusingly calls it – and there are the usual detailed enquiries after health, all the more so because, before the operation, Rita recommended him to her brother who is a urologist at the hospital. Although this recommendation didn't improve Giuliano's lot in any significant way, a human contact is considered very important. It is a favour we have done them. Perhaps this is why they have agreed to sell us their eggs despite having an arrangement under which they're supposed to deliver them all to a local shop. Or maybe they say that to everyone.

Giuliano frequently carries a spade or hoe or just a pole around with him so he can lean on it. He is pleased I am English because it gives him an opportunity to reminisce about his prisoner-of-war years in Scotland and Wales, which seem to have been very happy ones. He lived with local farming people and they sent him out in the fields every day to do more or less what he does here: weed vegetables, cut grass. He settled in well. But when the war was over they gave him only twenty-four hours to decide whether to stay or return. And he would have stayed but for the thought of pasta. The thought of a plate of pasta put him on the boat back to Italy. I wonder if his toothless grin is meant to indicate that he appreciates what a caricature he is offering. Girolamo, on the other hand, returned from forced labour in a German factory, near dead with starvation. Even a plate of Scottish potatoes would have been good enough for him. He scorns his brother's sentimentality.

Because now Giuliano is complaining that the Ministry of Defence has stopped sending him his Christmas card. Every year after the war he used to get a Christmas card from the British government. Until that 'Tachair' came to power. She stopped it. Margaret's cuts, we discover, struck deep all over the Continent. But it would be unkind, one reflects, to speculate out loud on what would have happened to a farm like this had she ever got her way over the Common Agricultural Policy.

It's funny. These old farming people seem both suspicious of us and at the same time eager to take a break and have a chat. Occasionally, they invite us in for a glass of something. The big, nameless bottle with a strong dry wine stands in the middle of a long, scrubbed wooden table. The floor is bare stone, the walls powdery whitewash. There are straight-backed chairs and no armchair or sofa, but a huge colour television stands in one corner and two grandchildren are watching. It's curious how impervious everybody is to the Rome accent of all the announcers.

Since it's Sunday, the conversation – not at my prompting I can assure you – gets on to religion. Rita explains we don't go to church. The farmer's wife says brightly that their son-in-law doesn't go either, but that he is not a Jew. This is a little disconcerting, until we appreciate that all she means is that he is a believer, but that he doesn't go regularly, just at Christmas and Easter: i.e., the only imaginable non-believer in her universe is a Jew, and her son-in-law is not one of those. Nor, she clearly assumes, are we. Her warm smile suggests an indulgent subtext: you young people are understandably a bit lazy and selfish, but later you will go to Mass every week just as we do.

Rita, however, has an infuriating habit of being honest in conversations like this. 'That's not exactly the situation,' she says.

'You must be Protestants,' says the well-travelled Giuliano, perhaps remembering bare Presbyterian pews in war-torn Galloway, comrades carving images of the Madonna.

'Not exactly,' Rita says again.

'What then?' Girolamo is scratching vigorously behind his ear, smiling his mocking, foxy smile. Every Sunday morning, as we make for the *pasticceria*, we see him and Giuliano heading off to Mass, awkward in their old smokeblue suits and dark ties.

'Nothing,' I finally join in. 'We are nothing. We don't go and that's that.'

'But you must be something. Everybody has some religion.'

Girolamo turns out to have a conversational manner not unlike his German shepherd's way of straining threateningly back and forth on its chain. He begins to mock us. Everybody has some master, even if it's only money. What am I living for? I must be living for something, and that is my religion. So what is it? He sounds disconcertingly like sermons I used to listen to twenty-five years ago. But one feels it would be churlish and above all pointless to launch into an argument. For of course we both know what we know: his world of sticks and pruning, mine of town and translations.

'You must have some religion,' he insists, as if having cornered his prey. And he drains his wine belligerently.

I can't think what to say.

'We're *mussulmani*, Muslims,' Rita solves the momentary embarrassment and raises a laugh from everybody. Although Girolamo continues to eye us darkly. Going back out into the farmyard, trying to change the subject, I ask him if he ever lets the dog loose from its chain. To which the old man casually replies with the common expression: '*Non è mica un cristiano*. He's not a Christian, is he?' Similarly when you rebuke a naughty child you might say: 'So, are you a Christian, or a beast?' For these are the only two categories of living creatures the old idiom allows: Christians and beasts. Apart from the Jews that is. I almost forgot.

And when the world is going from bad to worse you can say: '*Non c'è più religione*.' There's no religion left any more. As if that were the problem. And you repeat it, shaking your head: '*Non c'è più religione*.' It's something Lucilla, with all her Madonnas and crucifixes and sacred hearts, has been saying a lot of late. Because Marta's lawyer has managed to have the hearing over the presumed forgery of her will postponed for another three months. For the moment, things appear to be going swimmingly for us parvenu *mussulmani*.

23
La tredicesima

Winter in Verona means chestnuts toasting over coal braziers in Piazza Erbe; it means the crowded market for Santa Lucia where suspicious-looking gypsy folk sell every kind of candy, nougat and dried fruit from brash mobile caravans. It means shops and supermarkets full of huge, colourfully packaged *panettoni* with special offers on Johnnie Walker and local brandies.

In Montecchio, winter means steam on the windows of the *pasticceria*, swollen watercourses, mist rising thick from Laghetto Squarà on frosty mornings, polythene bags over oleander bushes and lemon trees and Christmas decorations on the big cedar in the main square.

In Via Colombare, winter means the stout woman with the twig broom sweeping away the leaves almost before they have fallen. It means old Lovato digging his square handkerchief of vegetable garden down almost a metre to let the frost right in. It means the genuine mink of the woman whose husband drives the Alfa 75 and the fake mink of the mongol-looking woman opposite who cleans offices in town.

At number 10, winter means sweeping and mopping the stairs with the same monotonous regularity we watered the garden in summer. It means freezing to death because the roguish builder who put up this place installed tiny, inefficient radiators. It means a plastic Christmas tree appearing on the first landing and schlocky red and gold decorations pinned to the satin-finish wooden front doors. At night it means Vega wailing to the cold stars as he paces the frostbound soil outside, and the constant constant whine of Lucilla's central-heating pump.

Although each household has its own separate heating system, the boilers are not located in the flats but all together down in a tiny cellar; and Lucilla's is mounted against the outer wall in correspondence to one of those reinforced concrete pillars. Thus, every time her system starts up, the building hums. And she keeps it on all night.

Giampaolo goes upstairs to complain. As for everything else in Italy, there is a law about when you can and can't turn on your central heating. It was brought in after one of the oil crises. You can't turn on before 1 November and you must turn off after the end of March. During the day you can't turn on before six in the morning and you must turn off after eleven in the evening. And between six and eleven you can't have it on more than a total of twelve hours.

Naturally, like the emergency provision about watering gardens, this law is generally ignored, except perhaps by the stingy owners of large blocks of flats where the rent collected is supposed to cover the cost of heating. Giampaolo, however, hopes to use the rules to play on Lucilla's fears of authority and convince her to stop bothering us with the sound of her pump every night.

It is typical perhaps of a *dipendente*, an encyclopaedia reader and a modern man to appeal to the law. And Giampaolo does seem to know them all, how far they are *valido* and how far their value is *relativo*. I can hear him talking politely and persuasively to her at her door, right outside our own. But on this occasion Lucilla isn't impressed. Because her health is at stake. She has been coughing a lot. Then she is dieting, which makes her cold and constipated despite all the herb teas she is trying. When Giampaolo, polite as ever, backs down, she tells him he is *troppo gentile* and asks if he would like to come in and drink a glass of something with her. She is having trouble getting Telepace, the Vatican channel, on her TV . . .

Winter. I sit at Patuzzi's great desk where he must have leafed through many a sunny brochure on similarly bleak days, fantasising about the ever more exotic road signs he could pose beside. The temperature is well below zero, but the breath of the cadaverous woman opposite barely steams her window pane as she stares out with infinite patience. To one side, between her house and ours, a tangle of branches reaches up into the sky. It's the one tree in Negretti's garden. And on those branches are what I at first, in my ignorance, imagine to be oranges: beautiful big round abundant fruit hanging by invisible threads from a tracery of leafless black twigs above. In the staring twilight, they start to glow, reminding me of Marvell's lines: 'He hangs in shades the orange bright, Like golden lamps in a green night.'

But we're not in the Bermudas, despite Patuzzi's ghost. And the evening isn't green, but grey, a blue smoky grey. And of course these aren't oranges at all, but *cachi*, a very soft fruit with a peel like a plum's, only thicker, and inside a lush pulp with a tremendously sensual texture and sticky sweet taste. They are the only fruit I know of I've never seen in a London greengrocery. They are too delicate to travel. Even Bepi doesn't like stocking them because they ruin so easily. Negretti lets most of his fall to the ground in a blackening orange mush over dead leaves before telling his sons to go out and pick the last few. Then, one-handed as he is, he does a little pruning with a chainsaw. Twigs and branches fly. The old woman with her shawl watches impassive till evening deepens. Then she leans out and draws her decrepit shutters to, turning to give me a last wan smile before they close. It seems unlikely that her house has any central heating at all.

Vittorina comes out of her Christmas-decorated door to find me mopping the stairs. For it is our turn. She is obviously disturbed to find me doing this menial work rather than my wife. Is Rita ill? If I had told her, she would have taken our turn. 'No, she's fine, but she has a rush translation job on,' I explain. Clearly it is not sufficient explanation. Vittorina looks troubled; cleaning the stairs just isn't a man's job. Her husband Giosuè, for example, whose grave she is off to visit, never cleaned the stairs. I tell her how often I wish I'd been born into the world and values of fifty years before. She takes this perfectly seriously. And maybe it does have a little sniff of seriousness about it. For if there's one thing I hate it's cleaning these marble stairs, and reflecting how carefully Orietta and Giampaolo will look at them afterwards, how they notice if you don't get your mop into the corners or if you sweep dust under doormats. I have heard them criticising Vittorina's performance. There's something that spells death for me in obsessive cleaning. The cemetery is a clean place. Could it be the English let their cemeteries get untidy so that they won't remind us of death so much?

Giampaolo walks in with a carpenter holding a huge polished shelf about eight feet long and almost three inches thick. They apologise for muddying my stairs, but Giampaolo is paying for the carpenter's time. Then Lucilla comes out on to the stairs above. 'Rina! Rina!' she calls. I tell her Vittorina is out taking flowers to Giosuè. Lucilla asks if I would come up to her flat and help her with the Yellow Pages. She can't remember the name of her dressmaker and would I read out all the ones in the phone book. I lay down my mop.

For some reason, everybody is having something made for them. Perhaps it's because, with the world outside being so icy and damp, winter naturally becomes a time for home improvements. Giampaolo is changing the focus of his sitting-room, the position of the TV. Instead of having it on a raised platform in the far corner he has invited the same carpenter who previously did that job to relocate his impressive set alongside a row of equally impressive encyclopaedic volumes on one of two huge, specially made shelves which pin directly into the walls with no visible brackets. The whole plan is undertaken with the utmost seriousness. A plug socket will be moved to directly behind the TV so that no wires need be visible.

At the same time Vittorina, in the flat opposite, is getting another carpenter in the village to replace her kitchen furniture. There are long consultations as to the height and depth of cupboards, the position of the lights, the need to change the fridge so as to have one the right width for the new cupboards, etc. etc. People here seem to enjoy this so much more than just going to a store and buying the readymade thing. Over the years they establish a relationship with their carpenter and then during dinner-table or *taverna* conversation they will boast that he is the best in the *provincia* and they would give you his name and number if only he wasn't so busy he'd never have time to fit somebody new in. They talk about *il mio falegname di fiducia* (my trusted carpenter); and quite probably they have an electrician *di fiducia* too, and a bricklayer *di fiducia*, and a tailor or dressmaker *di fiducia*, and undoubtedly a butcher. Indeed, the Veronese rarely seem happier than when talking about their somebody *di fiducia*. A social status is implied, the status of the person who doesn't just buy what the market offers, nor stoops, as the Englishman might, to DIY, but discusses and creates together with his craftsman. It's the status, almost, of the patron.

But as in any relationship, there are drawbacks. The most common being that the somebody *di fiducia* is too busy. And the reason he is too busy is not just the enormous demand there is here to have everything done and made privately, but the fact that the somebody *di fiducia* is actually a *statale* working on the side in his spare time. Our postman, for example, is frequently to be seen about the village busily engaged in illegal masonry work or installing radio-controlled gates and garage doors. A man from the health clinic is trowelling on stucco. And this sort of situation can lead to a quite schizophrenic attitude on the part of the client, one moment praising the skill of his carpenter, or mason, or gardener *di fiducia*, and the next berating these *statali* and all their privileges and craftiness. Still, at least when the man gets his early retirement he will have more time for your domestic projects.

Inspired by the general enthusiasm, we have found a carpenter ourselves and are getting him to make a bed for us to replace the uncomfortable medieval thing which always makes me feel like I'm sleeping in the central panel of a triptych of tortures. Recommended by a student, our *falegname di fiducia* is young and enthusiastic, talks green politics more intelligently than most, rapidly produces an attractive design for a simple bed with bay oak surround, quotes us a price that is a good 30 per cent below anything in the shops and then disappears. He is so busy that we won't see the bed for another six months and more. It's the price you pay, Orietta says sagely, for using a good carpenter. But it's worth waiting.

I go up the stairs I have just mopped to help Lucilla rediscover her dressmaker. She had her kitchen furniture recarpented only a year or so ago. On a nut tabletop she has a pink *gingerino* waiting for me. 'Now, Signor Tino' – and with simpering and obviously relished embarrassment, shifting her tubby bulk from one slippered foot to another, she explains. She has to have her bras made for her specially. Yes. Otherwise they are not comfortable. You know? Normally she would ask her dressmaker '*di fiducia*' but the woman was too busy (this sad admission indicates that the client's importance is only *relativo*); so she went and asked somebody else, but has now forgotten the name. Seeing that the bras were due to be ready this week, perhaps I can find the name for her in the Yellow Pages, assuming it's there, since of course she didn't use the Yellow Pages herself to find this person, but got a friend to give her the name of her *sarta di fiducia*. And the friend is off on holiday.

I look up *'Sartorie per donna'*. It turns out there are about twenty in Verona. I ask Lucilla if she remembers the name of the street. Only that it was in the centre. But they all seem to be in the centre, more or less. We arrive at a name she thinks she recognises: Riccadonna. I dial the number for her and hand her the phone. She has her synthetic pink dressing-gown on, fluffy little-girl's slippers, a glimpse of varicose ankles. Her hair is in a sort of plastic cap, covering curlers, I assume. Perhaps Simone is coming tonight. When she gets through, she puts on the most extraordinarily servile, obsequious voice: *'Buon giorno, buon giorno,* I am Zambon, the signora of the seven bras, are you the dressmaker I ordered from?'

It is the number seven that somehow renders it so magically incongruous – seven seas, seven seals, seven bras.

The second place we try asks for specifications, which Lucilla duly gives, but I am not familiar with cup sizes. On the third, remarkably, we hit the jackpot. The seven bras are ready and waiting. I write down the name and address on the notepad in her kitchen. As I do so I notice out of the corner of my eye a covered birdcage next to the waste bin on the balcony. Lucilla has cleaned out her canary, *poveretto,* once too often.

'Troppo bravo,' she tells me at the door, as if I had been responsible for finding the right name. She is clearly pleased that Vittorina is out. She likes to have men do things for her. And she says, if only I could afford to buy the flat when she becomes our landlady she would be very happy indeed to have us stay.

Giampaolo, meanwhile, is not at all happy with his *falegname di fiducia*. Incredibly, this trusted man tried to install one of the big new shelves the wrong way round, couldn't understand why it didn't fit inside a piece of wall that juts out, and smashed off a very large piece of plaster. What's more he refuses to accept that the damage was his fault, claiming that he should have been told the alcove was not perpendicular to the main wall. They argue by the Visentini's door for ten minutes until the carpenter hurries off, lamely pleading another engagement. My mop in hand again (for I still have the last flight of stairs down to the garage to do), Giampaolo insists on taking me in to show me the damage. His long slender fingers probe the smashed plaster. What do I think? It doesn't look that bad, I tell him. But he shakes his head. Obviously, he will have to call in his mason *di fiducia*. Yes, there's a man who's done a variety of jobs for them in the past. Because one could never plaster a corner perfectly right oneself. People would always notice. Worse still, he's going to have to decide whether to fire his *falegname di fiducia* half-way through the job, or have him back. Again he shakes his head. The attachment to a person *di fiducia* is such a deep one, Giampaolo clearly sees the man's behaviour as a kind of betrayal. Not to mention the added cost of the mason. Which on a *dipendente*'s salary is a tough proposition. Orietta brings in the vacuum cleaner to take up all the dust and plaster. '*Grazie al cielo*,' she sighs, 'that we're getting near Christmas and there's the *tredicesima*.'

The *tredicesima*! Here's another little peephole into the heart of modern Italy. For what other country in the world has a *tredicesima*? None I'm sure, unless at the end of some very slippery pole the Land of Cockaigne truly does exist.

Or perhaps Italy is the Land of Cockaigne. It's something the Italians like to say sometimes. Or they say: 'Go to America? But Italy is America!'

The word *tredicesimo* means nothing more nor less than 'thirteenth'. But *la tredicesima,* the adjective turned feminine noun, means your thirteenth salary of the year. Thirteen, it's worth noting, is considered a lucky number in Italy.

What happens is that in the first weeks of December, the *statali* and *dipendenti* in general receive an extra month's salary. This is a legally required part of any employer–employee relationship. In the negotiations which originally brought the development about, I am told, back in the 1960s, the *tredicesima* was perceived as a productivity bonus to be paid only if the employee had behaved well, not been absent more than a certain amount, and so on. But given that almost nobody takes it upon themselves to judge the performance of anybody else, at least in the state system, payment soon became automatic. And some companies, notably banks, even introduced *la quattordicesima* and I believe in some cases a *quindicesima*.

Such extravagant arrangements give the hard-working *autonomo* perhaps his only real chance to gripe about the cushy lives of the *dipendenti* although since he is aware that most of the extra money will be spent on his goods and services in the general Christmas binge, he doesn't complain too much. Indeed, the imminent arrival of the *tredicesima* perhaps explains why Giampaolo and the ladies have all decided to get their carpenting done and bras made now. For, as pensioners, the ladies have their *tredicesima* too. They are briefly rich. Lucilla sets off into town for high heels and diamond-patterned black tights. Two men struggle up the stairs with Vittorina's new fridge. One can only wonder what they might do if they ever got the money they want for our flat. Give Giosuè a new headstone? Muffs and minks? A new sitting-room suite? Extra Masses said?

Going back down to replace the doormats after the stairs have dried, I hear the postman's Vespa arriving, as it usually does, toward lunchtime. I wait for him. Apart from some junk mail for Patuzzi, there is a magazine for Vittorina, *I fioretti di San Gaspare*. My dictionary translates *fioretto* as, 'an act of mortification'. The magazine is published by *L'ordine dei frati del preziosissimo sangue*, which the saint founded. Most of it involves stories of miracles following hard upon praying to the saint. One reader writes to say that, after years of painful prostatitis, his problem was resolved by a single supplication to San Gaspare. Perhaps old Giuliano should have been informed. And it occurs to me that Italians have a long and uninterrupted tradition of miracles. Of which maybe *la tredicesima* is just a recent and very civilised manifestation.

24
Viva, viva, Natale arriva!

It will seem odd perhaps that, having spent all my teens in London, I had to come to Italy to discover real fog. It is a peculiarity of the *bassa padana*, the Po valley. Protected by the Appennini from the prevailing west wind, the sun shines brightly on the vast triangular area of flat, damp soil between Milan, Venice and Bologna. The snow-covered mountains to the north keep a constant stream of icy air rolling down to meet the warmth steaming up from fields and ditches. And the result is the thickest fog imaginable stretching for mile after mile after mile. Sometimes lasting for weeks. The winter version of summer's *afa*.

Stepping out on to our balcony this December morning, the world is milky white and quite silent. The terraced hill has gone, the castle has gone, likewise the abandoned mill.

Along Via Colombare, the Madonnina has vanished and with her the woman with the twig broom, whose patient sweeping can nevertheless still be heard, pushing dirt she can barely see away into the fog. The dry sticks of Marini's vegetable patch opposite are sombre pointed shadows, spear tips of an army of wraiths. A few poplar poles lean against a spectral fig tree, eaves and balconies drip, and all the street's railings are hung with dew-soaked spiders' webs.

Leaning on the marble parapet we never polish, it's such a pleasure to breathe in this soft spongy air. It's as if the whole Veneto had been very gently, very efficiently anaesthetised. Even the smells have gone, smothered where they rise. Everything is whitely quiet, waiting.

Then into this beautiful, hushed world comes a sudden fierce jangling, turning the corner from the Madonnina end. A grating jingle blares through a megaphone, followed by a voice speaking in dialect: '*Mamme, bambini, ragazzi, ragazze*, come and see, come and see, three *panettoni* for the price of one, three *panettoni* for the price of one!' The voice stops with unnatural abruptness. The jingle plays again, harsh, idiotic, strident. When it stops there is the unmistakeable rumble of a diesel ticking over. The still, damp air begins to smell. And now I can just catch the ghostly shadow of a white Fiat Fiorino delivery van. Out blares the voice again, incredibly loud, the kind of volume one expects at the Last Judgement, booming through fog: '*Mamme, bambini, ragazzi, ragazze*!!!' Odd, I think, how he excludes fathers, unmarried adults and the like. The van stops three times along the two hundred metres of Via Colombare, sells a dozen or so *panettoni* and is gone.

As many as four or five of these *ambulanti* may pass down our semi-suburban, semi-rural street in a single day, summer or winter, rain or shine. There's the man who sells brooms, dustpans, brushes, kitchen mats, pan-scourers. He's a regular. He passes around ten o'clock, his wares piled on the top of his tiny Fiat 650 van. A broomstick lunges forward through the fog like a lance.

Another fellow sells mattresses. He has a dozen or so piled on the back of a small lorry. Like the *panettoni* man he has a recording crackling through an overloaded speaker system: *'Un' occasione d'oro per sogni d'oro.'* A golden opportunity for golden dreams. Every Tuesday without fail. He is burly, brisk, darkly moustached. But how many mattresses can he sell to thirty or so houses?

One suspects the knifesharpener of being wilfully picturesque. He has a grinding stone geared up to the drive of his moped and a little shelter affair arranged over the handlebars. He squints, hunched. In normal conditions you can see the sparks fly. Through the fog there's just the sinister shriek of metal on stone. You're reminded of the Green Knight, sharpening his axe; another sound heard in dead of winter.

Or there are the one-off *ambulanti* offering the most amazing deals. A huge lorry noses along the street, squeezing between parked cars, watching out for shutters left carelessly swinging. Four best-quality wooden kitchen chairs for 60,000 Lire. Just thirty pounds. Is that possible? Or on another lucky day you may get the chance to buy a whole terrace set of tables and fold-up chairs for 100,000 Lire. Sometimes I wonder if, rather than being behind the lorry when the stuff fell off, they didn't just take the whole lorry and start driving around the streets.

Of the regulars, the cheese duo are the most impressive. These two fat, jolly men have a super-long, purpose-built van which folds open at the side to reveal a cheese counter that wouldn't look out of place in Fortnum and Masons. Turning the corner by the Madonnina, they have to reverse and manoeuvre. The relaxed megaphoned announcement of '*Formaggi, formaggi, eccoci qua*' suggests far more confidence in their clientele. The vehicle ticks over in the fog. Orietta slips out in coat and scarf to buy some seasoned Asiago and Parmesan. It's cheaper, she says, than in the shops. I wonder why.

'Thieves,' is Bepi's only comment when I mention the *ambulanti* to him.

Coming back, Orietta makes her usual detour to the *cassonetto*, heaving it so far the other way it's almost lost in the grey damp.

The *marocchino* is even more discreet than the *formaggi* fellows. Officially, *marocchino* just means Moroccan. In reality, the word refers to a stock figure in Italian life, the Moroccan carpet pedlar. Male, anywhere between fifteen and fifty, he patrols the streets with a heap of carpets over his shoulder and colourful tablecloths on his arm. In summer one almost melts at the sight; if you bought anything it would surely be drenched in sweat. On winter days you suspect the carpets are worth their weight in gold. You're surprised he wants to sell them at all. In any event, the *marocchino* is admirably stoical. His face is a cipher. Apparently, he expects nothing, fears nothing.

The bell rings. Rather than buzzing somebody in immediately, or even quizzing them through the intercom, I have learnt to go out on the balcony for eye-to-eye contact. The Arabic man stands there in the damp cold, his rugs over his shoulders. Would I like to buy something? I say no, thank you. He doesn't insist. And this is another admirable side to the *marocchini*, they will never bother you, never shout anything or use a megaphone, never try hard to persuade. Perhaps this one might have done better if he had tried. For the truth is we could use a few rugs on our freezing tiles. It's just that I'm not used to buying this way.

He presses Lucilla's bell. We can hear. Inevitably, she lets him in. How many times have we been obliged to listen (for conversations on the stairs are audible everywhere), to Lucilla talking to Mormons, Jehovah's Witnesses, water-purifier salesmen, survey interviewers and the like. But this morning she actually lets the *marocchino* into her flat. He leaves about half an hour later, I fear without having sold anything. For a *marocchino* could never be *di fiducia*, the way the cheeseman is for Orietta. I hope at least Lucilla offered him a *gingerino* and told him he was *troppo gentile*.

From my balcony I watch the man walk stoically off into the fog. Even from this distance I can see that his carpets are not Moroccan at all. Most probably they are produced by some small sweatshop in Reggio Calabria operating from an illegally built prefab. He keeps a steady pace, stopping only at the house of the man with the Alfa 75 where the postman is mounting new railings on a low cement wall. Then the fog swallows him up. A short distance away there will be an old Fiat 128 serving as a base for himself and three others. They keep the carpets in the boot, move from village to village. Perhaps they sleep in the car too. The *marocchini* are rumoured to be homosexuals without exception. Certainly, they bring no women with them. And, curiously, they rarely aspire to a place in regular Italian life the way other immigrants do. I have never seen a *marocchino* here who did anything but sell carpets.

Since it's Christmas Eve, we drive into town for some last-minute shopping. On leaving the village, the fog is desperately thick along the narrow road, though no one is going particularly slowly. Each car hangs on to the tail lights of the one in front and hammers through, even though this means being far too close to avoid an accident if one had to brake. And since we are one of the only vehicles on the road without fog lights, the car behind has to hang on even closer to us than we to the car in front. What this means in terms of the dynamics of an eventual pile-up, I've no idea.

Suddenly a *carabiniere* looms right in front of our bonnet, waving a red stop sign. And we realise we haven't even seen the big traffic lights. Comes the sound of sharp braking all along the line. Four officers in fluorescent plastic jackets are risking their necks to keep the junction operating. I wonder, will we see a parking spot even if we pass one?

In town, the medieval and Renaissance buildings are splendidly mysterious. The illuminated clockface comes and goes in the fog at the top of the fourteenth-century Tower of the Lamberti. The Roman arena is sombre despite housing an exhibition of East European nativity scenes. Christmas carols, all English, are being efficiently cranked across the fog-draped trees of the main piazza, interrupted by the crackle of fireworks, illegal but abundant. Diving into the shopping streets the stuccoed façades have been bled of all colour by stabbing neon beneath. And anyway, nobody is looking up at them. They have things to buy.

But despite the *tredicesima*, Christmas is not quite the spree it is in England. This is partly because, at least in the Veneto, the children have already had their presents. Santa Lucia, 13 December, was the day. So the pavements are no longer choked with grandmothers determined to gratify excited infants. Decorations are everywhere evident, but fairly modest in the end: lights strung across the streets, red carpets on the cobbles outside shop windows, paper festoons in the three department stores. An unconvinced Father Christmas with the name of a shop on his armband is handing out sweets. And, of course, there is the everyday streetlife, which takes on a special poignancy at Christmas: a gypsy woman sits begging in a doorway, the baby in her arms swaddled against the fierce cold; young blacks proffer trays of cigarette lighters and pirated cassettes; despite numbed fingers, a tramp is playing a popular tune on some kind of bagpipes: *Viva, viva, Natale arriva . . .*

In Standa, the cheaper of the department stores, people are picking up a few last-minute details to add to their home-made nativity scenes: an extra sheep or two, fake hay they forgot to pick up for the plastic manger, a star with a little bulb in it. There's an array of polythene packages. The magi are available separately or as a group.

But most interest is concentrated on food. Serious food. The delicatessens are packed, despite prices that would raise eyebrows anywhere. There is no one traditional Christmas lunch in the Veneto, but it would be a mistake to imagine this indicates lack of interest in the occasion. On the contrary, it avoids any danger of getting into a rut. Parma hams and salamis are coming off their hooks at an extraordinary rate. All kinds of goodies – Russian salads, black olives, green olives, a sticky crystallising orange mixture which calls itself *mostarda vicentina* – are being spatula-ed into plastic tubs. A bristling old fellow picks up a whole form of Parmesan. For how much? A hundred pounds? Two butchers (*di fiducia* of course) are unloading duck, turkey, geese and chickens from the surrounding farms and factory farms, plus all the best beef cuts. The die-hard *contadini* are looking for *cotechini* and the wherewithal to make *polenta*. A curious shop window offers fresh pasta of every colour: green spinach pasta, swampy artichoke pasta, red pepper pasta, brown chocolate pasta . . .

We pick up the turkey we have promised our American friends and a few bottles of this and that from a display offering a remarkable range of cheap Scottish whiskies, many quite unheard of, I suspect, in Glasgow and Edinburgh. Glenlivet, however, is thankfully cheaper than it ever was back in London, although slightly watered down to meet local proof regulations. Driving back to Via Colombare just as twilight stiffens the fog, we find our astonishing postman still messing with stones, bricks and railings beside the Alfa 75, and we take the opportunity to give him his Christmas bottle of grappa.

He doesn't understand. He looks at us nonplussed in the foggy dark, his breath steaming warmly, white droplets on a black moustache. I explain that it's a tradition in England to give your postman something. The tracery of blood vessels on pink cheeks suggest that he is not unused to a glass or two. A token of our appreciation, I say, somewhat foolishly, for perhaps such words have never been addressed to a *statale* before. He takes the bottle, sets it down by the railings, thanks us, but remains somewhat wary, as if we must be expecting a favour in return. Perhaps in the end he will put it down to a fog mirage.

Giampaolo is unloading a Christmas tree from his car. In Italy they are not sold cut as in England, but with their roots in a pot. However, to get a cheap price, as every *dipendente* must, Giampaolo has driven some twenty kilometres to a hypermarket where they sell trees that, yes, have their roots, but tied in a plastic bag. Very *valido* as an idea and the price was *discreto*. He will plant it in a pot for Christmas, put it out on the balcony through January, then move it into the garden before the spring to join Lucilla's sad madrigal of ornamental evergreens. Orietta seems dubious as to its chances of making it that far. Probably it will have her hoovering pine needles every ten minutes right through the holiday. There must, after all, be something *relativo* about the deal.

Preparing tomorrow's food in the evening we turn on the radio. Rita has recently taken a liking to Radio Santa Teresa, our local religious channel. Or one of them. Two priests are discussing the Madonna's house believed to have been brought by angels to a convent in Loreto near the Adriatic coast. With sobre enlightenment, the priests explain that, in fact, this is a tenth-century Palestinian dwelling brought over from Bethlehem by the Crusaders. Having chatted for a while, they open the telephone lines for questions. Immediately, a woman's voice crackles through. She is very excited: 'Don Marcello, Don Marcello, do you remember me, Maria, from Nogarole Rocca?' Don Marcello doesn't remember her. 'You baptised my children.' From the cracked sound of her voice this must have been some considerable number of years before. 'Praise the blessed Virgin', Don Marcello says warmly.

Another woman phones, from Caprino this time, up in the mountains. She is so depressed, oh but so depressed. 'Actually,' Don Guglielmo reminds her gently, 'we were asking for questions about the blessed Madonna's house in Loreto and the value of devotional relics in general.' She bursts into tears. She is so depressed she doesn't think she can go on living. She would never have imagined life could be so awful. 'Unburden your sorrows on the Holy Virgin,' Don Marcello tells her. She has tried, she has tried, but she can't. It makes no difference. She honestly can't. She sobs loudly on our old valve radio. And it takes these two embarrassed men literally ten whole minutes to get her to agree to unburden her sorrows on the Virgin and get off the line. 'The Madonna be praised,' she finally sniffles. There's an audible sigh of relief from Don Guglielmo.

After which about a dozen more women call, at least half of whom seem to know one or other of the priests personally. Not one of them has anything to say about the tenth-century Palestinian remains in Loreto, or indeed about Christmas. Their menfolk, one suspects, are elsewhere.

Shortly after eleven we hear the clunk clunk clunk of the Visentini turning their security locks about two hundred times as they prepare to go out for midnight Mass. A few minutes later, Giampaolo comes up to our flat to inform us that our cat has got trapped in the garage and has walked all over his white Giulietta, which he had just cleaned. There are black paw marks all over it. The Italian distaste, on Orietta's face rather than Giampaolo's, for animals which are allowed to penetrate the four walls of the domestic bunker, is only too plain. I solemnly promise it won't happen again and mollify them both with Christmas gifts which they weren't expecting: a scarf for Giampaolo, simple brooch for Orietta, perfume for Lara. We have, as Italians say, made a *bella figura*, a good impression.

Best of friends, they offer to give us a lift to midnight Mass to save us getting our own car out. Although we hadn't been planning to go, we accept. Walking out into the street, we catch the familiar sound of a small engine revving wildly, shooting off as the clutch is released, then whining, dying and finally puttering into life again. Giampaolo goes down to help Lucilla get her car out.

The fog is impossibly dense, the traffic very brisk. The church car park, needless to say, is packed to overflowing. Inside, despite the fact that we're ten minutes early, the church is already a solid mass of fur coats. People obviously came some while ago to stake out their places and now there are no seats left. I am surprised at this lack of forward planning on the meticulous Giampaolo's part. Although perhaps the fault is our cat's.

We stand at the back near the nativity scene Lovato's son-in-law has been working on for so long. Stars wink in three phases, water runs in a little stream, ox and ass nod their heads. It's an elaborate affair. Although, as in all nativity scenes, there is no sign that the animals perform their natural functions. On the hill, the shepherds have a little carafe at their feet, which is a nice touch. They may not, after all, be so unused to UFOs.

More people crowd in. There's a buzz of chatter, greetings, handshaking, kisses. Everybody knows everybody. People you usually see smoking on street corners or double parking outside the bar are queuing up to light candles. Some of the youngsters are obviously dressed, under their coats, for the discothèques they will be heading off to as soon as the service is over.

Things get under way a few minutes late. Don Guido intones the liturgy in a style my father, an evangelical Anglican, would no doubt have scorned. But there are advantages. The quickly read, toneless words impose a sense of order and ritual without one having to pay attention to whatever they might mean. The congregation are prompt with their responses and know very well when to stand and sit. They move as one well-trained animal. And they enjoy this oneness. Since we are anyway obliged to stand, my ignorance passes unobserved.

Looking about, as the others mouth prayers they learnt in childhood, I can see Maria Grazia from the *sanitaria* who supplies contraceptives at below list price. To her left is Montecchio's most famous politician, presently Verona's councillor responsible for traffic. His wife has a nice full-length fur, although, surprisingly, the family are on the list for the co-operative housing to go up behind the Madonnina. Beyond them stands the builder who is putting up the luxury villas on the hill above Via Colombare. Giuliano and Girolamo are there too, and Un panino due, and the woman with the twig broom, again in a fur . . .

But these fur coats seem to be causing problems. For, although it's cold outside, it is desperately warm inside. Big modern radiators are pumping out heat. Before the altars, down the side of the nave, a thousand candles are burning. Orietta wriggles uncomfortably, frowns. But she hasn't put on anything sufficiently attractive underneath to be able to take her coat off.

Up in the chancel, a small choir of young people sing a very upbeat Christmas carol to the accompaniment of guitars and drums. Nobody seems to know the song.

There is very little tradition of Christmas carols here. And, anyway, nobody is invited to join in.

Don Guido preaches a sermon from the chancel steps with the aid of a microphone on a stand. He also has a microphone on the altar. This means he never has to raise his calm dull voice and assume a rousing evangelical tone. He is not a leader, but a medium, a go-between. Predictably, he preaches generosity. We must remember the poor at Christmas. Christ was born in a stable. There is absolutely no criticism, veiled or otherwise, toward his overwhelmingly bourgeois congregation. He is rehearsing the values on which their respectability rests. As so often with things traditional in Italy, I am unable to decide whether this is attractive or sinister, an expression of civilisation, or decadence. My Protestant truculence no doubt.

And after the sermon, we move into the Eucharist proper with the modern guitar band playing and a girl singing, very pleasantly and professionally. Indeed, it's a treat. People walk to the front, the host is popped into their mouths or placed in their hands. Moreno, the halfwit, goes up three times but is not turned away. To deal with such a huge congregation, Don Guido has four helpers, a younger priest, three nuns. Other young people, many of whom shoot by me every day on *motorini*, are walking up and down the aisles with baskets, collecting money.

Then Orietta faints. The heat was too much. She should have taken her coat off. Fortunately, there is such a crowd of people round her, she couldn't possibly fall. Giampaolo rushes her out to the car and off home. No doubt this will mean a fair number of tests at the hospital. We stay behind for the hot chocolate Don Guido advertised at the end of his sermon and discover that below the church there is a very large *taverna* complete with bar, and drinks. Now this is civilised! In the crush, we come across Vittorina and Lucilla, determined to show off their furs to the last, although Lucilla's thick make-up is running a little in the oppressive atmosphere. '*Auguri, auguri, Signor Tino!*' she calls, '*buon natale, buon natale*', then returns to her cemetery chat with other older widows. 'The stingy niece', I can hear her telling them, 'still hasn't ordered a stone for the *poveretta*. So I ordered one myself. To shame her. I told my lawyer to tell her lawyer I'd ordered it, and I didn't want to be paid, and do you know . . .'

Walking home in a freezing fog filled with car exhaust now as the worshippers disperse, I wonder where this morning's *marocchino* might be. Has he found a stable to sleep in perhaps? With ox and ass. Not unfeasible in these parts. And I remember an article I read in the *Arena* only a few days ago: in the recent cold weather many *marocchini* have been sleeping in the empty *loculi* in the walls of the city's main cemetery, wrapped in their carpets. Well, at least they won't have to hear Vega barking.

25
Buona fine, buon principio

The fog persists, thick and extraordinarily white – not the gritty, yellowish variety you occasionally encountered in London. Penetrating even the narrowest streets, it deadens the anyway dead days between Christmas and New Year, muffling the sound of fireworks children are letting off between slices of pizza outside Un panino due's. And when there is a deep frost the night of Santo Stefano, you wake the following morning to find every tree crystallised from roots to topmost twig: the clinging fog on their branches has turned to white ice. So that walking out in the country, breath tasting of blood in the throat, it's to find icing-sugar cypresses standing on a great cake of frostbitten landscape. The leafless vines have become disturbingly spectral, fields of crucifix-like contortions, bled white by frost and fog. The tall stone walls beside the road ring with the cold sound of voices. Figures approaching through the murk intone the end-of-year greeting: '*Buona fine, buon principio.*' Happy end, happy beginning. It's been a week and more perhaps since you saw the sky.

And yet, if you walk and walk, you can have that pleasure. For Montécchio is at the very northernmost extreme of the *bassa padana* and its fogs. The hills begin here, and you need only climb. Following more or less the same route we took with our neighbours in the mellow autumn, we head for Cancello, at the top of the ridge far above Via Colombare. And, after a mile or two, there's a sudden thinning of the atmosphere. The fog becomes merely mist and haze. A pale disc of sun comes and goes. The landscape takes on pastel shades, a faded tapestry of beiges and dull greens woven up and down the steep slopes where farmland is retreating before heath and thicket. Another few hundred metres and, almost before you realise it, here comes the explosion of colour and light: a sky more electrically blue than it ever is in summer, a low but whitely dazzling sun that immediately narrows the eyes, and, to the north, the vast, sharp panorama of the pre-Alps sparkling with snow.

There are cars parked by the side of the road. Well-dressed people are stretching their legs. '*Buona fine, buon principio.*' It's nice how these greetings are extended to every stranger one passes. Other cars race by with skis on their roofs. Immediately, the light encourages a mood of fun and sensual pleasure. And with the light comes heat. The air is full of the smells of damp earth and vegetation warming in the sun.

Turning back to look at the plain, you appreciate how the

fog stretches, like cloud cover seen from an aeroplane, as far as the eye can see: white, flat, monotonous, with just occasionally a church spire, or radio tower poking spookily through. And having made it up here and rediscovered such brilliant light and scented air, it makes you furious to think you'll soon have to walk back down to that underworld and live heaven knows how many more days in the half-light and cold. Indeed, if you were in the habit of dividing people into groups (and writers inevitably are), you could do worse than to distinguish between those Montecchiesi who are happy with their foggy lot, who sit it out stoically, like the Visentinis, seeking comfort in hearth, home improvement and fifteen TV channels; and those, on the other hand, who are obsessed by that bright paradise only a few kilometres away and who pass the entire winter with their ski-racks or bike-racks on the tops of their cars, counting the days to the next long weekend. In between the two extremes are the hunters, country folk, like old Marini, quite at home in the fog except that, if they're going to see anything to shoot at, they have to make the effort to get up here. Every few minutes the hills echo with gunfire. Little children gather the orange, yellow and blue cartridges along the path.

This silent winter fog, that suffocating summer *afa*, they must play their part in forming the local character. The seasons here don't offer the exhilarating heroism of battling through strong winds, horizontal sleet, deep floods and snow-drifts, the glorious centuries of stormy weather the British can boast. Instead, the inhabitant of the North Italian Plain faces these long long periods of relentless attrition, a loss of sunshine, of visual clarity, coupled with oppressive heat in summer and damp, penetrating cold in winter. Never the kaleidoscopic movement and brusque surprises of an English cloud formation. For day after day, heaven and earth remain inert, motionless, in an anaemic torpor. The taciturn Veneto, a research student at the hospital tells me, consumes twice as many pharmaceuticals per head as other more fortunate areas of the peninsula.

Orietta is popping pills for her tachycardia as we prepare for the New Year's Eve celebration in the *taverna*. Lucilla knocks on our door and asks Rita to come and read the instructions in tiny print inside the box of some medicine or other. For her blood pressure. Could it combine nastily with the other drugs she is taking for her constipation? Vittorina won't take the pills she has been prescribed for her low pressure, counting rather on San Gaspare. Giampaolo, meanwhile, is congratulating himself on having decided to go for the flu vaccination this year. Everybody at the office has been down but him. Taking sick leave most likely, Orietta thinks wrily, the *dipendente*'s only revenge. Sitting together in their flat, Giampaolo constantly fiddling with the remote control of the aerial on the roof, we watch the President's New Year message, in which, referring to the recent devastating bomb on a train in a tunnel between Florence and Bologna, he makes the famous remark: 'They tell me that the secret services are honest, they tell me they are working non-stop to find the culprits . . . ' Later there is to be something live from the Moulin Rouge which Giampaolo shows a lingering interest in. There's so much enticing soft porn on Italian TV. But now it's time to go down to the *taverna* for a big barbecue and plenty of wine and *prosecco*.

Towards midnight the fireworks begin to crackle in

earnest. It sounds like a gun battle. Nearer to home, the Negretti's adolescent boys have bought a full-scale discothèque outfit and installed it in their two-car garage where they are making other young Montecchiesi pay a couple of thousand Lire for the pleasure of sixteen-year-old Mario's disc-jockeying. Every time we stop talking in the *taverna* we are assailed by the line: 'Up, down, like a yo-yo, life is just a giddy up and go go.' Lara asks me what it means but I refuse to translate. It's too stupid. The reinforced cement columns throb. Heaven knows how Vittorina and Lucilla are managing to watch their variety shows upstairs. Giampaolo tells me that legally he could phone the *carabinieri* and get them over, since doubtless the noise is above legally established decibel thresholds and the Negretti certainly don't have a licence for holding public gatherings. However, he feels this would be unkind at New Year. I ask him how he decides whether to call the *carabinieri* rather than the *polizia*. Do they have different duties? He tells me that their duties are exactly the same, indeed they frequently compete, and refuse to share information in the hope of arriving at their criminal first. He calls the *carabinieri* merely from personal choice and because their station is a kilometre or two nearer. Isn't our Margaret Thatcher always talking about personal choice?

Towards one o'clock we go upstairs. The fog has lifted, as it sometimes will at night. The air is quite clear at four or five degrees below zero. From our balcony we can see rockets rising into the sky from surrounding villages. The restaurants offering their New Year's *cenone* at 200,000 Lire a head will still be packed. Tomorrow's news will tell us exactly how many people the fireworks and celebratory gunfire killed in Naples, how many people who paid for their *cenone* in advance turned up to find the restaurant closed, the proprietor gone forever, how many people driving back at dawn in thickening fog went into walls and ditches. Obliged to put up with Mario Negretti's disc-jockeying into the early hours, we while away the time with the 1,000 piece jigsaw the Visentini have given us, showing the snowy peaks north of this fog.

The following morning, the Visentini are off early to see their relatives in Venice, but Giampaolo has left precise instructions that I must go and see Lucilla before ten o'clock. I will be the only man in the house and it is bad luck for a woman to see another woman first on New Year's day. Thus, before Lucilla can go downstairs to chat with Vittorina, I will have to go and greet her. Interestingly, the more religious, mysterious Vittorina doesn't insist on observing this superstition, while for Lucilla it's a matter of life or death. When I mentioned this paradox to Vittorina a couple of weeks later, I actually got a squeaky giggle out of her. Cilla just wants to see a man, she said.

And, indeed, when I knocked and announced myself, Lucilla was in a state of suggestive *déshabillé* which twenty years ago might still have turned an *ambulante*'s head. *Buona fine, buon principio, troppo gentile, Signor Tino*. I bend down to kiss her on both made-up cheeks and she tells me she hasn't even been answering the phone in case it is a woman. Actually, she's not sure if the phone counts, but she thought she'd be safe. As always, she insists I come in. Do I know how best to look after the plants she has been given? Four *stelle di Natale* (poinsettias), a traditional Christmas gift, are lined up on the tiled floor, still in their transparent plastic wraps. They are so beautiful, but somehow she can never keep them for more than a month or so. *Sì, sì grazie,* she did get her seven bras, *troppo gentile* of me to ask, although she wasn't entirely satisfied. *Il professore,* on the other hand, knew everything about plants. He used to advise her as to how . . .

Two weeks after these New Year celebrations, we receive a letter from Lucilla's lawyer advising us in the most grandiloquent terms that from now on we are to pay our rent to her. We show our ignorance of such matters by not appreciating that we could perfectly well ignore this. I immediately telephone Signora Marta, who says she will get her lawyer to send us a further letter ordering us to continue to pay to her and quoting the various articles of the law which justify this approach. 'And how is the old lady?' she enquires as always. 'She must be seventy something after all, why doesn't she just enjoy her old age?' I tell her that while Vittorina has been quite ill of late, Lucilla is doing just fine. Marta says that she herself is so upset by having these criminal proceedings brought against her, she is now being forced to take an assortment of tranquillisers. When she wins the case she will sue Lucilla for damages.

After which, the legal war goes on with letter following letter. The first court hearing is finally held, then promptly adjourned – because Marta's lawyer doesn't turn up. A date some three months away is fixed. It is impossible for us not to reflect how all this is playing into our hands. Not only will nobody be able to sell the place until the case is settled, but it would take a very courageous Marta indeed to raise our rent in these circumstances. The affair seems to be without either *fine* or *principio* which can only be *buono* for us.

26
Strada delle zitelle

I date our final acceptance as first-class citizens of Via Colombare to the moment when it became generally known that Rita was to have a baby. It would have been Carnival time, February, the shops full of monster masks and d'Artagnan outfits for five-year-olds. It was also around then that we discovered the Centro Primo Maggio, a place which has always made me feel that little bit happier about living in Montecchio.

Rita wanted tests done at the hospital and asked Orietta how to go about it. No one could have been better informed. Nor more delighted about the news. A baby in number 10, *Meraviglioso*! Giampaolo, too, was genuinely delighted. His serious man's face broke up into excited boyishness. The vibrations in this spic-and-span, austerely stylish apartment were suddenly very cosy indeed. Lara almost jumped for joy. The little brother or sister she hadn't had, she cried!

Of course, the Visentini were discretion itself. They respected your privacy, spoke to no one. It was a point of honour. With them any remark, however banal was considered highly confidential. But about ten minutes after Rita had mentioned the development to Lucilla (since every secretive society must have its source of gossip), the whole of Via Colombare was informed. And our social status rose vertiginously. We were no longer two fly-by-nights who did strange jobs and brought queer visitors in scruffy cars with foreign plates. We were responsible people putting down roots. We were creating a family and thus probably Christian even if we didn't go to Mass. Walking along the street now, there was no question of people not responding to my *'buon giorno'* and *'buona sera'*. On the contrary, everybody smiled their complicity. Rita was buttonholed by women who had barely spoken to her before. When was it due? Was she suffering from morning sickness? Did we want a boy or a girl? Which hospital were we thinking of going to . . . Heads nodded sagely in the cold air. For there was no fog now, just a long dull wait for spring. After which, the baby.

Anyway, it would probably be a girl. Yes it would certainly be a girl. Why? Because every child born in Via Colombare in the last few years had been a girl. And oddly enough all their names started with 'M': Marta, Monica, Milena . . . Perhaps we could call ours Mariangela, or Miranda. Although not that many children had been born in the last ten years, of course, because not only was this the street of the little girls (at this very moment playing volleyball over railings in winter sunshine), but it was also *la strada delle zitelle*, the street of the old maids.

It hadn't occurred to us before, but now one came to think of it there was a marked preponderance of unmarried, middle-aged women in the street: the woman with the twig broom, for example, and her slimmer sister; then the dark-haired sprightly sister of the insurance pedlar; and the woman at the corner by the Madonnina who sat at her window behind a loom and had a dog on a chain outside which barked ferociously behind tall iron gates and appeared to answer to the name of Book.

'Perhaps it's because of the Virgin,' the woman with the twig broom laughed, all of a sudden on very easy terms. She had wiry permed blond hair and a fierce mole at the base of her nose. We didn't understand. 'The Madonnina,' she said, pointing to the statue with its patient sad face. And she added with a note of disappointment, 'I don't suppose you'll be leaving number 10 now, my nephew will have to buy in the co-operative.'

Walking back home, I objected to Rita that the Virgin had surely only been a virgin prior to the birth of Christ. After that she had had other children whom Jesus referred to as his brothers. It was thus unlikely that she would want to influence the women of Via Colombare to become old maids. Rita told me I was wrong. The Virgin had never had other children. But I have a whole youth of church attendance and Bible studies behind me. I was sure. 'And Joseph?' I asked. 'What became of him then?' We were walking by the low pink wall of old Marini's garden. He was pruning his fruit trees.

'Celibate.'

'But if . . . '

'Well, he could hardly go to bed with the mother of Christ, could he?'

I'd never thought about it quite in this crude way. I suggested we go and talk to Don Guido about it. Even if he chucked away his encyclicals he could surely clear up this one for us.

But in the end it was enough to enquire of an authority like Vittorina. Yes of course the Virgin had remained a virgin for the rest of her life. Anything else was unthinkable. Otherwise how could she be the model of virtue? She would come down to our level. The old woman, herself childless, seemed genuinely puzzled that anyone should have imagined otherwise.

I quote this banal misunderstanding merely to show how even a supposedly well-educated Protestant like myself can for so long be unaware of some key piece of dogma underpinning the Catholic culture he is living in. Joseph had thus been forgotten. Jesus hadn't had any brothers, as I had been taught. Mary was the model of celibacy, which was a blessed virtue. She had somehow managed to combine this self-denial with pious motherhood, thus making herself the perfect woman. Indeed, a statue of hers was still reputed to be crying in Cologna Veneta after more than three months, although the priests were refusing to allow the tears to be analysed. Radio Santa Teresa had discussed the matter, but without ever taking on the question as to why the virgin might be crying. Because she was still unhappy about her son's crucifixion despite his resurrection? Because the local congregation was sinful? Or to demonstrate that devotional images were more than mere blocks of wood or stone? Sometimes Radio Santa Teresa would broadcast a whole rosary repeating

Santa Maria, Madre di Dio, time after time. It was quite relaxing. And now the virgin was also being held responsible for the preponderance of female births in Via Colombare. And likewise for the fact that so many of the women in Via Colombare remained unmarried . . .

Naturally, I began to hope that our baby would be a boy (as the Virgin's had been, come to think of it).

But such a hope was precisely what was expected of me anyway. 'I imagine you'll be wanting a *maschio,* Signor Tino?' Lucilla said. 'It's only natural for a man to want a *maschio.*' And she laughed, as if to say, 'Too bad for you the creature was conceived in Via Colombare of all places.'

I thus decided to say to other inhabitants of the street that I would rather like to have a girl, while secretly hoping we would have a boy, and at the same time feeling irritated with myself for getting drawn into this superstitious mare's nest, which in the end nobody on Via Colombare particularly cared about, just as none of them particularly cared whether the Pope insisted that contraception was murder, or whether a visiting priest had once dared to tell them not to come forward for the host if they hadn't paid their taxes. There is this magical duplicity about Italians. I'll never get used to it. You think they're superstitious bigots, but then they're more open-minded than you are. None of them would ever have criticised Christ for plucking his ears of corn on the Sabbath. It's as if they were a nation of Protestants, or even free-thinkers, who just happened to be deeply attached, for reasons of style and aesthetics, to the Catholic way of worship. Because they appreciate its richness. It fills their lives.

But a more pressing question than the sex of the child was whether we should use public or private health care for this pregnancy. Giampaolo Visentini, being the new man, favoured use of a public health system which was, he claimed, extremely *valido*, although he appreciated that some people might doubt that. Indeed, he himself had paid privately when Lara had had to see a dermatologist over a rash she'd had, because the waiting list at the state hospital was so long. And he'd been furious, he added, when the consultant's secretary had not given him a receipt after he'd paid his 70,000 Lire.

The problem, Orietta explained, was that if you went to the hospital for your visits, you couldn't guarantee seeing the same gynaecologist every time, nor could you know whether he'd be there when the child was born. The doctors had plainly decided on this system in order to further their private practices outside the hospital.

We were thus persuaded to go private. A gynaecologist *di fiducia* was recommended by a friend and we went. Disconcertingly, despite having an appointment, we had to wait just as long as one usually waits in the doctor's surgery. Then at the end of his examination, the little man who went by the apt name of Dolcetta prescribed a list of tests so long we wondered if there would be time in the remaining six months to perform them all. And since a scan was urgent, he said, we should do that privately too, not waste time at the hospital; and he gave us the name of a clinic, where, we very quickly discovered, he himself worked, and presumably took a cut of the 100,000 or more they wanted for a scan. At which Rita decided to drop the man and go for the lowest of the low, a health service gynaecologist who came to the small public clinic in Montecchio once a week. Not being a hospital consultant or even a hospital doctor, his assistance was generally spurned and making an appointment was refreshingly easy. The man turned out to be a southerner with a light, jolly patter, and a determination, he surprisingly boasted, to make the public system work. We couldn't have been better served.

27
Centro Primo Maggio

It was accordion music which first drew us to Centro Primo Maggio. We were walking along a little footpath that leads off the main road behind the new church where Don Guido keeps his rabbits and hens. Running between two deep ditches, the path is ill-kept: to the left is a patchwork of vegetable allotments behind crumbling houses, plastic bags over warm-weather plants, plane trees pruned to knobbly trunks, dogs on chains, skulking cats, and a complex crisscrossing of lively streams. I am conscious, as I describe this, that it does not sound especially attractive, whereas in fact the rich haphazardness of it all and the general rejection of any recognisable geometry is constantly picturesque. Someone has built a little raft to push from one side of a ditch to the other: a chair strapped to a wooden door over petrol-can floats. There's an old man in his allotment asleep in a decaying armchair with a hat and a bottle of wine. A woman is dropping sprigs of rosemary into her apron. On precarious scaffolding, an older workman and young apprentice chip at the ruined stucco of a house. And there is bric-à-brac from the past: a complicated pattern of stone walls guides one of the streams into an old sheep dip; here and there steps lead from a house down to the water and a large, flat scouring stone. A sturdy middle-aged woman will appear, and descend the steps with a red plastic basket full of dirty laundry. Where the houses back right on to the water, you see pipes gushing out suspicious effluents into the stream. All these people have colour TVs and decent cars.

We had just begun to hear the strains of jolly accordion music when we came across the ascetic Lorenzo, standing thigh-deep in the larger of the two ditches, almost a river at this point, patiently hacking away under water with a sickle tied to a long metal pole.

He is cutting the choking underwater weeds, he explains, which are a result of excess oxygen in the water due to extravagant use of fertilisers up on the hills, plus the dumping of waste by pig breeders.

Off his own bat?

He laughs: he and some friends have formed a co-operative, a non-profitmaking company, which is paid by the council to keep the village's streams and ditches in good order. It's a victory won after a decade of protest about public lack of concern for the local ecology.

But isn't it cold in the ditch? A great clump of weeds detaches itself from the bottom and floats clear with the current. Lorenzo has a big bag tied to his belt into which he drops a muddy Coca-Cola bottle.

Not at all. The water is warmer than the air, and he has his waders on. He likes the job. But has decided to leave Montecchio.

Lorenzo has ginger hair, tightly curled, and a thin nose. Despite having left the Jesuits, his sharp features betray the stubbornness of the man with a cause.

Because the people here are so traditional, he says, so timid, so cynical, so set in their ways. They're never willing to get out there and fight the environmental battle. Lorenzo turns out to be another of those Italians who aspire to escape provincial claustrophobia.

'I'm thinking of going abroad,' he says, just as Bepi does, although the two people couldn't be more different.

First he tried the Church, he said, where they wouldn't allow you to have a single thought of your own. And now it's not much different in the end trying to improve the situation here in Montecchio. Every new idea is greeted with suspicion.

He begins to press us to come to the next meeting about the flyover the council are planning to build right by the hill with the castle. Feeling guilty, we agree to come – the cause is certainly a good one – but to change the subject we ask him what the accordion music is. Lorenzo gives us directions to the Centro Primo Maggio.

The path ends in a flight of steps climbing to a road where cars chase down a desperately narrow, crooked strip of tarmac with no space for a pavement below the tall walls of three- and four-storey houses. Opposite the path, however, the houses end and the road opens up into the village's second lake, which is much like the Laghetto Squarà, although without the Roman blocks. A battered crash barrier stops the hurrying cars from falling in. To the left of the lake are the gates to a large old factory covering acres of land. This was once a tannery. Now Mondadori, Italy's largest printers, are using it as a paper-storage warehouse. You thus step out from the path to find a huge German truck with two trailers rumbling back and forward to try and get out of the gate, around the crash barrier by the lake, and then on into the forbiddingly narrow canyon of the street beyond.

The other side of the lake there's a grassy pasture, and to the right, a group of *case popolari*, council flats. We walk down towards them and towards the sound of music. Other people are converging there too, in carnival outfit. Or, rather, the adults are for the most part in plain clothes while their little children are fairy queens and assault robots. Carnival is fairly tame in Montecchio. So tame we didn't even know the procession was today. In any event, no inhibitions are being dropped behind demonic masks. For a more extravagant celebration people will go to Verona, where bizarre floats wind through the streets for hours and youths cover shop windows in shaving foam.

The *case popolari* look really OK. True, the stucco is cracking here and there and the balconies are smaller than they might be, but by London standards they look fine. And the people living in them seem to be doing all right too. There are plenty of expensive cars about. Like the *statale* (and very often he is a *statale*), your *casa popolare* occupant is on to a good deal. He pays a rent way below the market rate and, after twenty-five years, the flat will automatically become his. Meanwhile, he polishes his Alfetta. The only drawback being that, ten years after the place was built, the council still hasn't found the money to put in pavements or asphalt the parking spaces. The ground is grit and stones. One thus has to wash one's Alfetta rather more often than even an Italian might want.

And the little princesses are getting their silver slippers dirty. The accordion speeds up. We follow a small d'Artagnan through the estate to find, on the other side, just where the country begins, a rusty green gate in a sagging fence and the legend, 'Centro Primo Maggio'. Inside, under a bare pergola, a small group of middle-aged men in Sunday best are playing accordion, guitar and drums. Despite changing tune every couple of minutes, the sound and rhythm is always the same: Der-der-der-der, di dum, diddy dum, diddy dum, der der der der, di dum, diddy dum, diddy dum . . . A table is stacked with paper cups; there are big plastic bottles of lemonade at one end and even bigger bottles of wine at the other. In the middle are plates of *galani*, fried dough cakes dunked in icing sugar. The children hurl handfuls of confetti, some of which gets in my wine. And a little boy bursts into tears because he has got his Zorro outfit dirty.

Then the Re Magnaron, the carnival leader, arrives. The *magnaron* is a tiny fish that swims about in the dikes and ditches here and once formed the traditional carnival dish. With his scaly head and sequinned cloak, the man playing the role looks like something from a Ben Jonson masque. Guffawing loudly, tossing clouds of confetti, he leads off the fifty or so cowboys, penguins, batmen and fairy queens on their infant procession through the village. But we have already fallen in love with the Centro Primo Maggio and decide to stay behind. There will be time for the parades when we have our own children.

It began as a Communist Party social club. Immediately to the left of the gate is a large low prefab with bar, cluttered tables, a pair of space-invader machines, a copy of *Unità*, the Communist paper, a poster of Berlinguer, a hammer and sickle, and an assortment of those ubiquitous old Montecchio men with their hats and wine bottles. Playing cards. Opposite the hut is the pergola, perhaps twenty yards long, vine tendrils stretching over a curving iron frame to offer a shady space on summer days and a small dance floor for festive evenings. There is a strip of cement for bowls, which is fenced in to prevent the heavy balls from flying out at passers by. A notice exhorts customers not to argue. Beyond, a very large scrubby lawn is scattered with rickety chairs and tables as far as the flood embankment and emergency ditch fifty yards away. To one side of this lawn a big barbecuing stand prepares hot sausage meat, *bruschetta* and aubergine slices on toast for lunch. Then there are a couple of tennis courts, a children's playground, a cement table for ping-pong and, at the very end of the complex, an ambitious dirt track for BMX bikes. For the Communists must appeal to the younger generation, too.

But it is not the facilities which make Centro Primo Maggio what it is. I haven't spent a hundred lazy Saturday afternoons here for that. It's the extremely attractive atmosphere of *laissez-faire*, the civilised and gentle nature of the people who use the place. There's nothing aggressive in the culture of Montecchio's working and peasant classes. At least, not that I have observed. And if they drink too much, they do it slowly, sitting on the veranda of the prefab, watching the crimson wink of Bardolino in the sunshine. They are at ease, relaxed, there is never the slightest threat of hurry or unpleasantness. Nor does one experience that sense of claustrophobia you get in downtown middle-class Verona, and even in Pasticceria Maggia sometimes, that obsession with fashion and elegance, fur and leather, the scrubbed faces of the men, the heavy make-up of the women, the crinkly dyed blond of respectable girls fanning out on to sheepskin shoulders, the hubbub of posh Veneto la-di-da.

None of this at Centro Primo Maggio. It's the sort of place, I have sometimes thought, that Orwell must have dreamed of. You salute your faith-healing barber who clearly appreciates you more now you have admitted to sensing a tingling feeling when his fingers touch your head. You salute the shoemender, who runs a little Elvis Presley fan club and has pictures of the King all over his tiny shop. You wave to the supermarket boys as they play tennis, the girls who serve in Bepi's shop. And Ercole, tall, lantern-jawed, who fills up your car at the local pump and ran as an *indipendente di Sinistra* at the last elections, nods to you as he helps the younger boys with their bikes. Prices are comparatively low, although it would be a mistake to buy a *cappuccino* here. Wine or *espresso* or both are the thing. Just inside the door of the prefab, a small space is made available for a couple of *marocchini* to show their wares without going about and bothering people. And there's a black man selling cheap leather goods and Russian watches. You pick up your wine, take it out into the garden and wonder how long you can resist the smell of sizzling pork and aubergines.

Not that there aren't encroachments from the modern yuppie Italy and its well-healed pieties: the anxious mothers, for example, who are watching their children do as tennis teacher tells them on the new, carefully groomed, clay courts; and then the bright young men who have just finished playing and are ordering, instead of beer or wine, the fashionable, healthy, super-vitaminised mineral drinks heavily advertised on television. They are so conscious of their virtue, these young men, as they discuss the technicalities of their game with TV-expert solemnity, I feel almost sorry for them. Outside, hordes of eight-year-olds in the uniform of the Montecchio biking club are strapping on their helmets before tackling the BMX course. Every single girl and boy has his or her special biking shoes, biking pants, biking gloves . . .

But it all coexists so happily at Centro Primo Maggio: as if the contemporary fads were nothing more than pink froth on the same old blood-red wine. And it's fun watching the bowls, or on summer evenings the people dancing to the squelchy tunes of the accordion beneath the now fragrant pergola: der der der der, di dum, diddy dum, diddy dum . . .

Whenever I go, I always feel this is Montecchio at its best.

28

Il frate indovino

Another thing that raised my status in Via Colombare, and at number 10 in particular, was the fact that I was the only man around one morning when disaster struck. We were sitting in the kitchen. The news was reminding us it was time to make our VAT declaration. It is touching the way the public service seeks to prod the citizens' memory in this way. Such and such a category, the newscaster tells you – artisans, shopkeepers, solicitors – has just three days to make such and such a declaration. Or: people with cars registered in January have just a week to pay their car tax, although there may be a reprieve since not enough forms are presently available.

The apologetic Roman voice was suddenly interrupted by a pounding on the front door. Lucilla, in her pink, brushed nylon dressing-gown, face harrowed by melodrama, was hopping from one foot to the other on the landing by the remains of her Christmas poinsettia. She had been unable to get Vittorina to come to her door.

This then was what all the shouting had been about earlier on.

Had she tried the phone? Vittorina has a phone by her bed. Lucilla rushed back into her flat and was so upset she couldn't dial the number. *'Che agitassión, che agitassión, Signor Tino!'* she cried. We helped her. A tubby hand grabbed the receiver. There was no answer.

Could Vittorina be out?

No. Lucilla claimed she had heard her moaning behind the door. At which Rita phoned for an ambulance while I rushed downstairs. Orietta came out, and whereas I would have imagined this was just the kind of thing that would have brought on her palpitations, she was in fact very cool and sensible. We must try and get into the flat. Lucilla's spare keys perhaps? But Vittorina had left her own in the door inside. So, a window, Orietta suggested.

I went outside and pulled myself up on to Vittorina's terrace balcony beneath which I had watered grass all the long summer before. Forcing apart the slats of her shutter just a crack, I was able to see that the french window behind was open to let some air in. I asked Orietta if she had such a thing as a breadknife and she hurried off to find one. It was late February. Rain was falling in the street behind me, and, unusually for these parts, there was wind with it. I remember the cheese van turned the corner with a coolly megaphoned *'Formaggi!'* Then Orietta brought out a selection of useful-looking knives and only a very few moments later I had sawed two small squares out of the plastic slats so as to be able to reach in and release the catches inside. I heaved the shutter up a little, crawled underneath, and found Vittorina stretched limply on her cold dining-room tiles in nineteenth-century underwear.

On being let in, Lucilla had a fit of hysteria. It was plain she could already see herself beating her fists on the coffin. She howled out loud and tugged at her short hennaed grey hair to feel the pain. Neighbours rushed in from the street. Together we got Vittorina into a sitting position on an armchair. The women rubbed her hands and feet. Others comforted Lucilla and helped her loosen off her girdle.

Somewhat embarrassed, I decided I had better retire to the kitchen until the ambulance came. It was thus that I found myself reading a rather odd calendar pinned to the door of one of Vittorina's freshly carpented cupboards. *Il calendario del frate indovino*, it said. And this immediately struck me as curious, for a *frate* is a priest, a friar (the calendar was published by a religious order), while an *indovino* is a decidedly secular fortune-teller. Another peculiar thing was the way the colours and graphics of the poster-size pages seemed to come straight out of the early sixties (old cornflakes-box illustrations spring to mind), whereas the dates referred unequivocally to today. In the middle of the page were the days of the month, each with its saint's name in bold type followed by runner-up saints in small print: i.e., 1 March, *SAN SILVIO*, Sant'Albino, Sant'Ercolano. Then, around the calendar proper, a series of different coloured boxes offered oodles of advice, predictions, maxims and mottoes, information for farmers, satirical jokes, cartoons and ominous sayings. Plenty for me to while away five minutes with:

'*Seeding*: given a waning moon, now is the time to plant peas, beets and spinach in a sheltered area.'

'*Women*: Die-hard reactionaries refuse to recognise that in a Christian society women have responsibilities as great as those of men, and sometimes greater. Like motherhood.'

I wondered quite who the reactionary here might be. And if the piece on seeding had been written by the *indovino* persona, was the comment on women the work of the *frate*? Vittorina of course had had no children, no motherhood to justify her femininity. Nor even virginity. Although she subscribed to this same potent mix of the religious and secular: the quote from the Bible and the day's horoscope beside. And then my eye caught this disquieting reflection:

'*Thought for the Day*. Every morning in Africa the gazelle wakes up and knows he will have to run faster than the lion if he is not to be killed. Every morning in Africa the lion wakes up and knows he will have to run faster than the gazelle if he is not to die of hunger. When the sun rises, it doesn't matter if you're a gazelle or a lion, you'd better start running.'

Clearly this boded ill indeed for poor Vittorina.

The Croce Verde ambulance arrived, an orderly offered a possible diagnosis of stroke, Vittorina was swathed in blankets and carried off. The stretcher-bearers refused to let the sobbing Lucilla into the vehicle so a neighbour, the insurance salesman's sister, one of Via Colombare's *zitelle*, travelled with her. At the last moment, Orietta hurried out with a plastic bag containing nightdress, cutlery, soap, towel and toilet paper, all of which Vittorina would need if she was to stay in hospital for any length of time. Lucilla retired to her bed with its pink canopies and called the doctor to come and measure her blood pressure, slipping the man 20,000 Lire for doing what the state already paid him to do. Imaginatively, he prescribed tranquillisers. *'Troppo gentile,'* Lucilla told him and called us in to ask if we would go and get her prescription.

The chemist is still a figure of some authority in provincial Italian society. A long queue of people with no time to go to the doctor were thus waiting for his advice. And, unfortunately, there is only one chemist in Montecchio since the local council has not given permission for another to open. This gives our chemist a powerful monopoly, especially since such simple products as aspirins, milk of magnesia and the like can only be sold by chemists. The prescription charge is around two pounds, then you pay a percentage of the cost of the product, this depending on the nature of the medicine required and your own particular status.

The process is complicated. The chemist has what looks like a plasticised log table on the counter and taps on a calculator, doing percentages, adding and subtracting. I wait, but then the woman in front of me doesn't have a prescription for the valium she wants. Which must only be sold under prescription of course. *Sotto voce,* a long argument begins. *Per favore, dottore,* she pleads. After furtive glances to check who is in the shop, he finally gives her what he shouldn't. At the full price. Then he asks me to sign two petitions, one to have the flood ditch outside paved over for more convenient parking, another to complain that the government is being very late in making its payments to chemists for medicines sold under prescription. Politely, I refuse. Down south, in Calabria, I think, there is an area where pretty well every chemist has been kidnapped at some time over the last few years. Ransom payments have not presented an insuperable problem. Walking home, I observe that I am already feeling that peculiarly Italian envy of the more fortunate employment categories.

We go and visit Vittorina in hospital. The building compares well with the National Health ones I knew, although there are a few beds in the corridors. The nurses are mainly small, slim, southern men and wear green pyjama affairs and slip-on clogs. At night Marisa has been sitting on a straight-backed chair by Vittorina's side. Almost everybody who is seriously ill has a relative spending the night with them.

But Vittorina is recovering fast. She's sitting up and smiling. It's just that she can't move her left arm or leg. In a slurred voice she is embarrassingly profuse in her thanks. She does hope Lucilla will let us keep the flat. And driving home, it occurs to us that, yes, we do have a strong card to play here. I will point out to Lucilla that since I mostly work at home I am generally on hand to deal with the kind of emergencies that might befall old and ailing women. Whereas a new tenant, even one as capable and *gentile* as Signor Giampaolo, would probably not be.

Always assuming Lucilla wins, or that the case is ever settled at all.

Arriving back in Montecchio, we noticed a small knot of people outside the church, elderly women and children, one or two of the latter furiously rubbing their foreheads. How odd. Until we recalled it was Ash Wednesday. 'From dust you came and to dust you shall return.' Don Guido had been signing the cross in ash on their foreheads. This was one religious festival that it was as well perhaps Vittorina had missed.

Although death, as they like to say, is not always unwelcome. And if the saga of Marta vs. Lucilla was to be interminable, it was not long after Vittorina's return home that the final curtain did at last fall on another long-running drama. The weather had turned rough: spring storms, March winds. And, at night, when the wind blew, you couldn't keep the shutters down because the plastic slats would rattle irksomely. This meant that if Vega chose to bark, five, six metres from our window, the noise was even louder. It seemed to ring in your skull.

One night we were kept awake for ages as the dog yelped, howled and bayed; railing at the stormy wind we imagined, participating in her doggy way in the change of the seasons, the approaching equinox. Right through the small hours it went on, urgent and tortured, as if the creature were barking inside your brain, tugging you back from the threshold of sleep with its teeth. How we moaned and swore and wondered at our own impotence. Until the following morning, wearily cleaning my own teeth before some lesson, I pushed open the frosted glass of the bathroom window, for no other reason really than to feel the air on my face and see the world I knew was there. Except that today it wasn't, quite. For under the budding *cachi* tree was stretched, as if in sacrificial offering, the horribly distorted corpse of our canine tormentor. Poisoned.

Rita! Rita! A moment's delighted celebration, an enthusiastic embrace. At last, at last! Someone had done for the mutt! How splendid life was going to be!

And then came the first doubts. Everybody must

imagine it was us. Oh no! The Negretti family were only too aware how much Vega disturbed us. We had talked quite openly about poisoning the creature. And there had been those phone calls we'd made. In the early hours. If nothing else they must make us the prime suspects. Not that we feared Rocco Negretti would go to the police. It wasn't his style. But what if some stupid vendetta were to begin? After all we had the cat now. Would it be safe for her to go out?

That evening we talked to Giampaolo and Orietta. Vega, they had heard through the grapevine, had definitely been poisoned, but nobody knew whom by. They looked at us intently. We denied any knowledge. There was a rumour, they said, that the animal had eaten some rat poison Negretti had used in his cellar. But this seemed extremely unlikely, given that the dog was never allowed into the house. Vittorina, grim faced, mouth twisted as she spoke, was mysterious: 'That animal got on one too many people's nerves,' she said darkly. Across from my study window, the old skull-face between lace curtains was sibylline as death itself.

Other inhabitants of Via Colombare seemed not so much reticent as genuinely uninterested. Who cared who had killed old Negretti's dog, as long as the next one he got didn't bark so much?

We mulled over this strange case of wish fulfilment for some time. And watched our cat carefully. Nothing happened. In the end our conclusion was that Negretti must have poisoned the animal himself to be rid of it. For only forty-eight hours after Vega's death he came home with a huge black Doberman and launched into a breeding experiment that is still going on to this day. The sight of the great black creature terrified us at first; how loud would this monster bark? Until we realised that a Montecchiese breeding a dog is quite a different proposition from a Montecchiese merely keeping a dog. For a breeding dog is worth money and hence deserves respect. With the result that first Ursa and later Sirio, Musca and Canope (this obsession with the night sky was one of the more attractive sides to Negretti's character) were well fed, regularly brushed, and barked very little at night.

29
Primavera

I don't know why, but I picked up a copy of the *frate indovino* calendar myself. I had noticed it hanging in three or four houses now. It seemed popular in a sort of Reader's Digest, ready-source-of-wisdom way. And who would be without a ready source of wisdom? Thus, come springtime, an entry entitled *Per Tutti* tells me: 'Remember that love exists regardless of age, and that the love that lasts longest is also the strongest. However, we should also remember that young people are a constant prey to sexual impulses, especially at certain times of the year. Fortunately, these can be quietened and actually disappear in individuals who manage to establish loyal relationships with their parents, their true friends, and their spiritual guides.'

A world where adolescents are not troubled by sexual impulses! One's first reaction is to burst out laughing, to assume that our *frate* is way out on a celibate limb here. Who could ever want such a thing? Yet when I begin to pay attention, it does seem that a very large proportion of my students at the university not only do seem to want, but actually appear to have achieved the God-fearing serenity he describes. And a fair number of youths in Montecchio too. There is a decorousness and calm about them at once admirable and disturbing. 'No, I don't want to leave home,' they tell you. 'I like living with *mamma e papà*. There's nothing I'd like to do that I can't do at home.' Or 'Francesca and I will get married and live together in about five years' time when I pass the state exam to become an accountant in my home village of Buttapietra.' They seem quite untroubled by matters sexual.

I ask how many of my students go to Mass (one can pretend this is a linguistic exercise when teaching English). More than half regularly and most of the rest occasionally. Yes, they go with their parents. Even their grandparents. (Of course, in a way, this is wonderful, even enviable.) I ask what they did last weekend, and hear from three or four students that they went on a spiritual retreat. To be together and pray for peace. The girls dress with Latin elegance and seem very self-composed. But Friday night they went to a discothèque. Oh yes, Federica, and what did you wear? (revision of chapter 4). Black skirt, black tights. And you Cristina? Black skirt, black tights. And you, Monica? Black skirt, black tights. Do the boys wear ties when they go to discothèques? Some do, some don't. And what did you have to drink? Fanta, Coca-Cola. No wine? No wine.

One constantly suspects that some cover-up job is going on. Something you can't understand is happening. Surely they can't all be like this, so very sure of themselves, untroubled by life's passing. And I ask questions at random. How did you get to the discothèque? In *papà*'s car. What kind of car does he have? A Mercedes estate. Oh, and how long did you stay? Till two in the morning. And does anything actually happen at these discothèques? What do you mean, happen?

Is this truly serenity, the wise calm of the youth who has a good relationship with loyal friends, sensible parents and spiritual guide? Or reticence and obtusity? And how does it square up with those unmarried mothers of Montecchio, disconsolately pushing their prams around the broken fountain of Piazza Buccari?

'By far the most widely practised method of contraception in Italy', explains Maria Grazia in her *sanitaria* (she loves these conversations), 'is *coitus interruptus*. You know? Not something young men are notoriously good at.' A rueful expression crosses her face. 'And then spring comes so suddenly here.'

It certainly does. Late March, early April's the time: San Francesco, San Sisto, Sant'Isidoro . . . The lingering mists, the cold colourless days, the heavy rains are suddenly gone. The sun powers through, so hot you find you're desperately overdressed. And the women would have loved to wear their furs just one last time. But it's too late. You wake one morning – San Celestino my calendar tells me – and the sky is awhirl with swifts and swallows. How they liven up the hills and farms and river bridges with their voracious, darting search for food, and sex presumably. Cherry and peach blossom simply explode. All the trees at once. Line after line of them up the hills between the still gaunt vines. Already the bees are crawling in and out of sugary petals. The polythene comes off the lemon trees. The earth releases all its pent-up smells. And in the evening dusk, white cherry flowers glow like beacons, to the croaking of a thousand frogs converging on Montecchio's ditches – to lay their spawn.

How loud those frogs will croak! It's obscene! And no wonder that one or two of the less-well-spiritually-guided tend to fall by the wayside: in the soft grass, the primroses and periwinkles. After all, the *frate indovino* did warn that there were vulnerable times of the year.

At number 10, a condominium garden committee agrees to have a man come in and prune all our flowering shrubs just before they can bloom. He cuts and clips, returning a year's growth to austere geometric shapes. And the buds had looked so promising. Rita is furious and sticks the cuttings in jars about the flat. If she had had more time, Lucilla says, she would have moved the hibiscus the other side of the little cypress. But what with Vittorina being ill . . .

On Palm Sunday everybody comes out of Mass with olive branches in their hands. Specially blessed by Don Guido. The children make a pretty picture. Their well-dressed parents look rather sheepish. *Il frate indovino* says:

La domenica dell'olivo, ogni ucello fa il suo nido,
e se gocciola la frasca, sarà bello il dì di Pasqua.
(On Palm Sunday, all the birds their nests do lay
And if the branch drips rain, Easter will be fine again.)

In the event, *la domenica dell'olivo* is fine this year, and likewise *Pasqua*. So much for our *indovino*.

On Easter Monday, *Pasquetta*, as it's called, the tradition is to set off into the hills for a mammoth picnic with barbecue equipment and bottles of wine. As always, the formula of religious festival plus heavy eating appears to be invincible. Everybody is on the move with hampers and ice-boxes. Marisa and Leone take the two old ladies up to Cancello. Bepi is throwing a party on his grounds at Rivoli. More modestly, we walk along the valley to Mizzole with Giampaolo, Orietta and a well-prepared picnic basket. As we cross the main road, a stream of cars drives by with sacks of charcoal strapped to luggage racks.

Outside the village, the valley is luridly green today and the spring light, you notice as you saunter along, is different from in England, somehow. At first you think it's clearer; perhaps because, after weeks of mist and rain, you can see the mountains again now, far far away. And it gives you a tremendous sense of space to see them there, still in their majestic winter white. But it's not really a question of clarity. Nothing could be clearer than the light in England when a gusting wind is blowing every scrap of haze and exhaust away so that you feel you could see the whole length of the Edgware Road, if only you wanted to. Anyway, by ten o'clock, as seen from Montecchio, the Alps have already disappeared in a gathering heat haze. Visibility soon loses that sharp edge it will keep all day in windier climes.

No, it's the suffusedness of the light which gives the spring its power here, its distinctly erotic feel. Quite simply, the light seems to have got in everywhere, to be on all sides of everything. Perhaps because it bounces off the pastel stuccoes so, and the white limestone of the window surrounds, simmers dazzling on terracotta roofs, shoots off dusty grey asphalt – a light that is glare, haze and heat all together. So that clothes simply fall off the women. In the space of a couple of weeks we've gone from furs to thin blouses and fashion T-shirts. People move bathed in fragrant brilliance, which somehow gives you a feeling that things are happening in slow motion. For the light has that effect too. Especially if you are in the habit of taking three bottles of wine on a picnic, stretching out under the first cherry blossom and simply watching as the more adventurous hikers push on.

And lying there, you hear your first cuckoo raise its cheeky call, and the larks twittering high in the sky, and the urgent hum of a thousand bees (for many orchards have their own hives), and the frogs and toads croaking shamelessly as they flop through the long grass to the water.

What chance for spiritual guides at moments like this? Surely even the best of biblical armour can offer no real immunity to such a strident call to be living and doing. What hope for Montecchio's Catholic youth? The *frate indovino* must be tearing his tonsure.

Then across the heavily scented grass comes an insistent modulated drone. Nearer and nearer, louder and louder. Until all at once a leatherclad figure bursts out of a nearby ditch, roars through the vineyard where we are picnicking, and attacks the first slope of the hill in a spray of dirt and stones. Followed by another, and another, and another . . .

For ironically, it's science that comes to the old Church's aid. There is the internal-combustion engine. With the same ritual inevitability that lifts the sun higher every day and draws the sap up in the trees, the local adolescents answer migrant birds and reawakened bees with a great shriek of unsilenced mopeds and motorbikes. Throttles are opened and closed, opened and closed, revving rhythmically in the spring air. Cannily, Don Guido, a man who knows the lesser of two evils when he sees it, permits the lads to go round and round the church car park in frenzied circles. Then they race to Un panino due's for a slice of pizza, then to Giulia's at the other side of the village for Coca-Cola fresh from the fridge. While, back in Via Colombare, the Negretti boys gun their mother's Cinquecento jerking back and forth, back and forth across the big terrace among the broken flowerpots and clothes pegs: three yards in reverse, a great screeching of brakes, three yards in first, three yards in reverse, three yards in first. The blue smell blots out all the stirring scents of the air. The noise drowns the seductive cries of the *ambulanti* with their seasonal offers of deckchairs and skimpy beachwear.

Walking the winding pavementless village streets to the bar of an evening becomes hazardous. Hoards of *motorini* scream by, rearing up on their back wheels, skidding and swerving. Could this be, one wonders, some pact between Fiat and the Holy See, a conspiracy to displace the libido of Latin adolescence and restrict casualties in the spring offensive to a minimum? Orietta confides that she and Giampaolo are now worried about Lara who has taken to hanging around with the moped brigade outside the church and is reported to have been seen holding the hand of a tall blond boy. I suggest she should consider herself reassured.

Mid-April. We cycle through a cherry-blossom countryside. Walking in the hills the hedgerows are so full of primroses, narcissi, violets, hyacinths, it's almost unbearable. The strips of winter corn are shooting up. Everybody's busy with their vegetable patches. The farmers are spraying their trees with the usual assortment of noxious chemicals.

And then it turns cold and rains again. Not only rains, but sleets, for an hour or two actually snows. The snow lies ice-white on the white cherry blossom. Old Marini shakes his head. Not a year for fruit, he says.

Giampaolo is shaking his head too. It is almost time for us to bottle the *prosecco* he has been keeping in three huge wicker-covered demijohns down in his cellar. The problem being that *prosecco* should always be bottled when the atmospheric pressure is high or rising. This sudden return to winter is a disaster.

But the weather is going to be good next week, I tell him. I have heard the long-range forecast. All we have to do is hang on and we'll have sun and blue skies again. The pressure will rise.

He frowns, twists his mouth.

What's the problem?

Prosecco should really be bottled with a waxing moon too, he says. And the full moon is Sunday. He knows the weather is supposed to be fine next week, but by then the moon will be waning.

I protest that I thought he was a man of science. Surely his encyclopaedia doesn't come any of this lunar stuff. This is the realm of the *frate indovino*.

Giampaolo is such a nice man because he knows when he is being ribbed and rather enjoys it, yet at the same time persists perfectly seriously with his line of argument. His encyclopaedia, he says, doesn't actually say anything about bottling *prosecco*. But the fact is that he has a certain amount of respect for popular wisdom. He believes that some day the scientists will find some reason behind the farmer's attention to the moon. More pertinently, we have spent quite a lot of money on our sixty litres of *prosecco* and he doesn't want to risk its coming out wrong.

But what could happen?

It might turn out flat, he tells me glumly. It's the waxing moon that makes it bubbly.

Well, I'm as anxious to avoid that as he is. For the next few days, every time I meet him, on the stairs, in the garage, or out on the lawn trying to remember where he put his bulbs so we won't mow over them (for we'll have to start mowing the lawn again now) – every time I meet him, our conversation is about rising and falling pressures, waxing and waning moons.

Couldn't we just wait for the next waxing moon?

We could. But that will take us to mid-May. It will be absolutely our last chance. Otherwise the fermentation process will have gone on for too long.

Giampaolo hangs a barometer on his balcony and wears a worried look. We discuss the expediency of bottling willy-nilly on the last day of this waxing moon, regardless of pressure. My own instinct is to bank on the atmospherics, rather than the moon. He looks at me, wondering if I know something. I hasten to assure him I don't. He must decide. Or perhaps he should ask old Marini. No, these Montecchiesi, Giampaolo tells me, only deal with local wines. They would have no idea what to do with a *prosecco*. Thus, while worrying about the moon, he nevertheless manages to express his Venetian, modern man's superiority to the provincial locals.

The days pass. The moon is now a perfect round silver

coin in the sky. How can it possibly affect our *prosecco*? I stand on the balcony, watching it rise full as full between rainclouds over the derelict factory. To wax no more. Mid-May it will have to be.

30
Il 25 Aprile

On 25 April flags hang from windows and balconies along the main street through Montecchio. It's Liberation Day. People whose homes face on to major thoroughfares are obliged to fly the flag. Most of them do. Somebody has forgetfully left a pink towel over the railings of their balcony. In a beam of sunshine it clashes gorgeously with the red, white and green.

Walking towards Centro Primo Maggio, for it's a public holiday, we hear the strains of a brass band. In dark uniform an endearing mix of adolescents and middle-aged stalwarts are playing a military march. They arrive at the monument to the fallen more or less as we do. Not the monument in the main square dedicated to the soldiers who died – they have already been there – but a more modest, modern affair located at the corner below the ex-tanning factory where another small estate of *case popolari* begins. Here a copper plate records the names of eleven civilian Montecchiesi killed in the bombing. A recycled wreath lies at its foot.

The band lower their instruments and a couple of youths in jeans are busy setting up an amplifier. A small crowd gathers, families in their Sunday best, shifting weight from one foot to the other, children tugging at coats. Every few minutes they have to part to let a car, or a team of racing cyclists through. On the opposite corner is one of the noisier bars for village youths, its window daubed with a cartoon view of the New York skyline, symbol of unimagined decadence.

An old, portly man in uniform, complete with medals, starts to speak into a microphone, although there are only thirty or so people. He begins with the normal introductory formalities employing the pompous Italian of public discourse, so that for a moment I imagine this will be one of those politician's speeches one grows accustomed to here where any possible message is obscured by an interminable clutter of qualifications and relative clauses. ('It depends' – I quote more or less at random from a newspaper by my side – 'if this development is to be seen in the light of a possible *rapprochement* between forces by their nature intrinsically unsympathetic to what I think one would have to call the future interests and indeed hopes of the nation, conceived as that group of people who, for reasons of history, race and culture, consider themselves to form an identity distinct from, though not opposed to, other national identities, or whether . . .')

But no. Having got over his carefully pre-prepared

introduction, his list of names to be thanked and organisations mentioned, the old man has given up on his notes and is talking in a very simple way about the war and the dead now. He remembers how Italy fought on the wrong side, how soldiers went to freezing Russia in light summer uniforms, how these civilians were killed by the bombs of their ex-allies. He pauses, clears a hoarse throat. 'If their death is to have any meaning at all,' he says, gesturing to the monument, 'it must lie in the kind of Italy that we have managed to build after the war, that we are able to build now. And at the moment, this Italy of Mafia, tax evasion and public corruption does not do honour to their names, we cannot feel we have built on their sacrifice.'

He continues in this remarkably strong vein, although speaking calmly and intelligently. His old man's sincerity is impressive, the more so because of his scrubbed red nose and the deep wrinkles, weather-, age- and drink-induced. He has none of the professional speaker's polish; he ers and ahs, feeling for what to say next. Turning round to the monument, having problems with his microphone, he begins to read out the names, one by one, as if they were people he knew. And maybe he did. 'Albertini Mario, Pizzini Giuseppe, Stefanelli Emanuele . . .' The little gathering listens gravely; and it's a moment of unusual candidness, this old man in the spring light, speaking hoarsely into a microphone, reading out the names of the dead, surname first, then Christian name, as if at some impossible roll-call. Then the band strikes up the national anthem and everybody disperses for their *cappuccinos*. On our way to the bar, we find a bunch of fresh daffodils has appeared by the plaque to the three who fell under enemy fire as the Germans retreated. It would be intriguing to know who put them there. The Dalmatian imprisoned behind jumps on and off the old bidet that serves as its waterbowl.

In the bar the price of our *cappuccino* has gone up another hundred Lire, but since this price is fixed by a government body, we can hardly complain at Pasticceria Maggia. The price of an *espresso* is fixed, the price of a *cappuccino* is fixed, the price of a newspaper is fixed, the price of petrol, diesel and heating oil is fixed, the price of bread is fixed. Is this in line, I ask Lorenzo, with the spirit of *Liberazione*? And paying at the till I ask the pretty Cinzia if the price of *brioches* is fixed too, since I notice they always cost the same everywhere. 'Not officially,' she smiles, and is careful to give me my receipt.

Returning to Via Colombare, it's to find Lucilla and Vittorina sitting on their backsides in the middle of the lawn, legs stretched wide apart in dark old wool skirts. Vittorina has her big straw hat against a sun that's getting perceptibly stronger every day. Each woman holds a knife and they have an old shopping basket between them. They thrust their knives into the lawn, wiggle them vigorously about and pull out the fresh young dandelion plants. The roots are cut off and tossed away and the leaves dropped into the shopping basket to be washed for salad or boiled like spinach. They chatter and sing as they work. I have never seen them so happy. Lucilla has put on a green kerchief, peasant fashion. When they've exhausted the garden, they say, they'll go off to the orchard and vineyard fields to try there. And indeed, walking about the countryside in spring, the meadows are full of crouched figures with plastic bags or shopping baskets, gathering dandelion and other leaves.

Giampaolo comes out to discuss lawnmowing rotas and they give him some of their harvest. *Vado Matto*, he grins, I'm crazy for them. We accept too, although I can't say I'm wildly enthusiastic. The locals have a taste for such rough, bitter salads: leaves with the texture of a cat's tongue and the taste of herb medicine. Terribly good for her constipation, Lucilla confides. To me it seems the kind of taste one could only have developed in darkest wartime.

Old Lovato watches us all from over the fence, wondering what we'll do with the garden this year, how much our hedge will grow and steal his light. Behind him, and stinking with fertiliser, his peas are already rising thick as Persian spears at Thermopylae. Meantime, with Vittorina not being able to do much after her stroke, Giampaolo's encyclopaedic, ecological approach has got us no further than a few weedy rows of snail-ridden spinach and salad. The sun may well follow its dazzling trajectory above Via Colombare, the railings and cement, vines and cypresses may drip and drip with light, but somehow that dank little patch below the old cinema wall and Negretti's terrace is always in the dark.

Incredibly, in May – but as a *dipendente* Giampaolo seems born to bad luck – the weather breaks again right on the new moon. Once more it seems the combination of rising pressure and waxing moon is to elude us. The brilliant Mediterranean sky is suddenly replaced by the kind of cloud you expect to find over Halifax or Slough. The rain is desperately heavy. Via Colombare is not cambered and surface water gurgles about looking for a gutter. Lovato stands at the window, staring at his peas, willing them to stand firm. Our lady of the twig broom cycles by under an umbrella, climbs off at her house and, despite the torrent, kicks a cigarette stub away from her gate. Old Signora Marini is another one pedalling under an umbrella. Lack of wind makes this possible as it would not be somewhere else I know. On the third day of uninterrupted rain, I even spy one-armed Negretti, his good hand on the right handlebar, his new dog Ursa tied to the left, and a red umbrella tucked under his stump.

Montecchio being on the water table for countless kilometres of limestone hills above, the ditches are soon full to overflowing. Even the emergency ditches begin to fill, something that happens only once or twice a year. The water is a muddy brown flecked with white as it bears away the heaps of litter people have thrown there. Before the week is out, water floods the section of road by the Cassa di Risparmio di Verona, Vicenza e Belluno, the village's one bank. The Communist Party is quick to get out posters complaining that, while the council has plenty of money to spend for all sorts of other projects, it has never solved this simple drainage problem. The head of the local Christian Democratic Party ducks (as it were) the question at a meeting held in the local library which is temporarily closed for book borrowing because the librarian is away for his military service. Finally, the rain becomes so violent that it fills the emergency ditch to the brim, bursting the stout wall that protects the main road and covering it with water and broken masonry.

How can we possibly bottle *prosecco* in this, Giampaolo complains. He taps his barometer. I've never seen it so low. We watch an evening's TV together over the last of the previous year's bottles. On one of the smaller channels there are frequent ads for talismans (by post) and the services of local astrologers, but nothing on how to get the right combination of atmospherics and lunar cycle for our sixty litres of bubbly. The news quotes the huge sum the government has already promised in compensation to keep the farmers sweet. Should we, perhaps, prepare a claim for our possibly ruined *prosecco*?

Then the miracle happens. The weather clears two days before the weathermen said it would. The pressure is suddenly rising. Giving us a twelve-hour window to do our stuff before the full moon.

31
L'imbottigliamento

Amidst ancient accountancy reviews and stacks of *Nuova Alta Tensione* in Patuzzi's cellar, stand about a hundred cobweb-ridden wine bottles. Giampaolo inspects them, turning them over in his hands, looking inside, putting his nose to the neck. There's a grave expression on his face. It's Friday night. Saturday is our last day for the waxing moon. His own bottles stand in sparkling ranks by his cellar door, each with a square of snap-wrap on top to keep out the dust. Clearly we should have thought of this problem before.

Our neighbour goes away and returns with a bottle full of metal shot and a big cast-iron tub. His instructions are precise. We boil the bottles ten at a time in the tub and for at least five minutes; we then half fill each bottle with the metal shot and, thumb over the top, shake vigorously, up and down and round and round. The shot must be rinsed between each bottle. After which the bottles can be washed in normal fashion, rinsed three or four times to remove the soap, and placed in a position where they can drain off thoroughly before tomorrow morning. Already I'm beginning to wonder if we mightn't perhaps have stuck with supermarket bubbly.

Rubber gloves are required. And infinite patience. But the radio has just the thing for us. As we work late into the evening there's a quiz show which involves people answering questions about intricacies of bureaucratic red tape: 'In what situation might you be asked for a document of *esistenza in vita*?' 'Should an application for a no parking sign for your garage or gate be made on plain paper, or stamped paper (and, if the latter, how much does the stamp cost?)' 'How many years less does a woman teacher have to work for her pension if she has three children?' 'When selling a second-hand car, is it sufficient for just one spouse to take an oath before the solicitor, or do both spouses have to go?' 'When given a prescription for an X-ray, for how long is it valid?' The respondents are quick on their buzzers. We try not to slosh too loudly because the answers are frequently surprising. Actually, it's a pretty useful programme.

Then Saturday morning early, a blond thumbprint of moon only a sliver away from being full, it's straight down to Giampaolo's cellar to do the deed. Like his mind, this tiny space of four or five square metres is admirably tidy and well ordered. There are two shelves of wine bottles, all carefully hand-labelled: the type of grape, the area they come from, the harvest year, the date of bottling: *Cabernet*

–Friuli – vendemmia 1981, imbottigliato il 2 Maggio, 1982; Traminer – Alto Adige – vendemmia 1982, imbottigliato il 15 Aprile 1983 . . . On the shelves below are boxes and cabinets full of tools, hardware supplies and the like. Again there are painstakingly prepared labels: 2 cm anchor nails, 1 cm self-tapping screws, 5 mm rawplugs . . . The air rarely moves down here. Along the top shelf are hundreds of editions of the topical magazine, *Panorama* (which may be worth something one day), plus twenty or so volumes of a now outdated but still formidable encyclopaedia. Almost at once I feel I'll have to be on my best behaviour.

Out comes the equipment, handled with the special care of the fetishistic object. A clear plastic siphon with a tap, lengthily boiled and rinsed the evening before. There's something disturbingly surgical about it. A corking tripod with handpumplike lever. As you bring this down the fat cork is squeezed pencil thin and forced into the top of the bottle. *Molto valido*, this piece of equipment, and a bargain at 50,000 Lire from a friend. The action is *discreto*. Although of course the quality of any corker is *relativo*, since what counts above all is the quality of your cork.

And we swing into a long lecture on the various corks the market offers. Giampaolo has purchased different kinds for the different wines he is planning to bottle, although there is also an element of experiment, he explains. He is eager to see how much effect different corks will have on the same wine bottled the same day from the same demijohn. He has corks made from a single piece of quality cork; these are the most expensive, since they retain their springiness and breathe well. Careful to wash your hands before touching them. Then there are some cheaper corks made from putting together pieces of cork in layers. These are OK as long as you're not planning to keep your bottle too long; they'll do for the *prosecco*, which will last a max of a year, but not for the Cabernet he's got which should improve with age. And, finally, he has a bag full of plastic stoppers, which have the advantage of being very cheap: you can insert them by hand and remove them by hand, but of course they don't breathe. It will be interesting to see if this makes any difference to the *prosecco*.

He's also going to do five corker of each wine he's got in clear rather than green glass, to check how far the light factor affects the quality. I point out that to do this he will have to open two bottles at once, otherwise he won't be able to make a direct comparison. But he's aware of that. When the in-laws come to lunch, it won't matter if one bottle is not quite up to scratch. Apparently, the tight space of the cellar is breeding a sense of complicity.

We lift the first demijohn on to a chair to get the height required for siphoning. This has to be done with immense delicacy so as not to disturb the sediment at the bottom. Bent over, muscles tense, it is as if we were shifting a tactical nuclear warhead. Then with the Murphy's-law cussedness which upsets even the best-laid plans, the chair turns out to be rickety, or the floor uneven, and the big jar tips perilously from side to side doubtless displacing clouds of sediment inside, like mud in a pond. There's a hunt for pieces of paper and cardboard to slip under the chairlegs, but the damage is done now and we will have to wait at least half an hour for the sediment to settle. In the meantime, we siphon off half a jugful, examine it for cloudiness, then pour a little in and out of our first ten bottles (dark green) to rinse and prime them. Immediately the dankish air down in the cellar takes on a very heady smell indeed.

We line up the bottles ready for action stations. There's a pleasantly conspiratorial feel to mucking about in a cellar that stinks of drink. We are beginning to enjoy ourselves, and at last the siphon is gently lowered into the demijohn. Giampaolo kneels on the cleanswept cement, head down low, to suck the precious liquor through.

At which precise moment, with a great banging of brooms, mops and buckets (the doors are iron down here and resound tremendously), fat Lucilla appears. And announces that she had planned to do the garage spring-clean today. There are a lot of tyremarks on the floor and one or two drops of oil. A rather shell-shocked, but determined Vittorina appears behind her, thinning hair tucked into a kerchief. They stand there in the doorway looking at us. Orietta has also been informed and press-ganged. Rita has pleaded the excuse of pregnancy. That is, having observed Lucilla's cleaning methods, she is concerned about exposure to noxious fumes.

So, at this extremely delicate and exciting moment, Giampaolo and I are obliged to go and move our cars out of the garage, where, hairy upper lip working nervously, Vittorina (despite all doctor's orders not to exert herself) is already sploshing detergent on orange bricks. Lucilla is strewing handfuls of sawdust. Orietta has a grim look. For the first time I notice a Sacred Heart above the four electricity meters. Cars removed, we excuse ourselves hurriedly.

Bottling turns out to be both boring and demanding. The siphon nozzle goes down into the first of a hundred and more bottles. The wine flows slowly, but you have to keep an eye on it so as to stop it at three or four centimetres from the top. Meantime, you're checking that the next bottle has been primed, or, once the process is underway, trying to cork the bottles you've already filled. With a dipstick, Giampaolo examines the wine in the other demijohns and tells bottling stories. How the year before last, for example, all but two of the *prosecco* bottles came out flat and were more or less undrinkable. Although he'd had excellent atmospheric and lunar co-operation. This is just one of those imponderables that make it so exciting.

I ask him why the *prosecco* I buy from the supermarket, admittedly at three times the price, is never flat, despite the fact that the bottling factory can hardly be observing the moon and the barometer. Additives, he says contemptuously. Sugar, fizzing agents. Give you a hangover. That's why shop-bought *prosecco* can never equal the perfect home-bottled variety, just as Bepi's vegetables are never at the same level as those grown in the garden without any pesticides.

Although this particular choice of comparison hardly seems to warrant the gleam of faith and enthusiasm now shining in Giampaolo's eyes, the delicious fumes are sufficient to quell any further objections and keep me more or less merrily at work for the rest of the morning. At least, I reflect, we have escaped the assault on the garage, which we might otherwise have been expected to get involved in. Leaving the cellar in a daze towards lunchtime, we find Lucilla shovelling up bleach-sodden sawdust in an atmosphere suggesting chemical warfare. The ferocious vapours cut right through our tipsiness, would quite probably clear the nose of a man long after he had ceased to be eligible for a certificate of *esistenza in vita*. 'Signor Giampaolo, Signor Tino!' the old woman calls to us. 'See, all the tyremarks and oil stains are gone!' Likewise gone is

Vittorina who apparently felt faint. Orietta has her kerchief round her mouth, her eyes streaming.

32
Fiaccolata

Is it a complete coincidence that the *fiaccolata* occurs toward the end of May, only a few days before tax declarations are due? 'The financial administration', says the form in front of me on the kitchen table, 'has tried to streamline and simplify the contributor's obligations . . .' There follow sixty-four pages of instructions on how I am to fill in my income-tax return, not many of them easily comprehensible, some referring me to paragraphs and articles of laws which I should apparently somehow procure and study. So that I am just reflecting that I will, after all, have to go to an accountant, when a faint murmur of *'Ave, Ave Maria,'* takes me out on to my balcony.

It's a balmy, almost summery evening. The cherry blossom has long gone. The foliage is thick on everything but vines and fig trees. Winter's dry sticks are no longer in evidence; new ivies twine the fences, smothering sharpness and starkness under soft leaves. And all the street's roses have flowered at once, small bright blossoms climbing up stuccoed walls. But not up the railings. Good iron railings must be kept clear. Our cat, who goes by the name of Toro, is scratching at Marini's cypress tree. The swallows whirl about the rooftops in a hurry to catch their supper before retiring. And Simone's car has just drawn up in the street below, when, from round the corner into the curdling twilight, turn the first of a candlelit procession, the *fiaccolata*.

They are coming from the village end of the street, the derelict factory end, led by Don Guido and chanting *Ave Maria*. They are enjoying holding their candles. Among them, as they approach our house, are most of the people I regularly see in the street: Mario, the insurance salesman and his *zitella* sister; old Marini, the Lovatos, man and wife, daughter and son-in-law; the salmon-faced mechanic; the wife and children of the man with the Alfa 75, although not the busy *imprenditore* himself; the elderly, bent, straw-hatted fellow who the mongol-looking woman plants on a chair outside her front door of a morning; Lara with various youths usually to be seen straddling their mopeds, bags of crisps in hand; the woman with the twig broom, of course.

With others from the village, there are perhaps a hundred people altogether, walking rather self-consciously along Via Colombare through the gathering dark towards the Madonnina at the far end. The patient little statue has been freshly painted and a small electric light adds to the halo effect. A bunch of spring flowers has been placed on the ledge below.

Vittorina goes down to join the chanters. Lucilla does not. She comes out on to her balcony for a moment to nod to everybody, then goes back inside where the business of entertaining ex-*carabiniere* Simone is doubtless a demanding one. The dirge grows louder and, as always at this hour, bats begin to flit back and forth, taking over the warm skies from the swallows in a peculiarly appropriate changing of the guard. They swoop below the eaves filling the darkness above the procession's slow candles with quick, demonic life.

Disappointingly, just as the picture is at its most evocative, the street lights go on, reducing the candles to pinpoints. And, immediately afterwards, any mystery that might have persisted is promptly dispelled when, having reached the Madonnina, an amplifier and microphone appear from somewhere for Don Guido to speak into. His uninspiring voice thus has a loud electronic ring to it, with now and then a whine of feedback. And he speaks for almost twenty minutes. What he actually says I don't know, for the words are as distorted as they are loud and uninflected and, after a few moments, I cease to pay attention. In any event, it seems unlikely he will have any useful advice on how I'm to fill in my tax forms. Nor do I imagine that my joining in the ceremony will afford me any particular protection against eventual errors I might make. And I go back inside to wade through the sixty-four pages of instructions.

The alignment of social forces *vis-à-vis* the payment of taxes is not quite perhaps what one would have imagined. Of course, the radio news has been reminding us with some insistency these last few days of our forthcoming civic duty as *contribuenti*. But not so the calendar of the *frate indovino*, who, despite his conservative attitudes on such questions as women and the family, despite his frequent appeals on behalf of all kinds of missions, does not hesitate to tell me at this crucial moment in the financial year that: 'Italy is not, as the Constitution claims, "a Republic founded on labour" (of which there is less every day), but a Republic founded on taxes (of which there are more every day).' Not satisfied with this inflammatory talk, he inserts, only shortly before the declaration deadline, the reflection: 'The criminal is not obliged to testify against himself. The taxpayer is.'

What is the Church's position here? Far from generating a sense of guilt in the would-be evader, the *frate indovino* seems to assume an attitude of solidarity with an oppressed population, as if we were still in the days when spendthrift Bourbon princes sent heavily escorted bailiffs about to wring the last *centesimo* out of a starving peasantry. The complicity will stop when we get back to sex of course, but on questions of rendering unto Caesar what is Caesar's, our Rovigo-based friar has a demagogue's infallible eye for the popular line. 'To make sure that VAT is collected,' he winds up the section entitled 'Predictions', 'the Italian government intends to subject the Italian people to a machine that most nearly approximates a meat mincer.' It's as if, tipping us a wink, he were saying, 'Don't worry folks, do as you feel with your declaration and the Church will be on hand to shrive your peccadilloes afterwards.'

Sometimes, when I pick up my bread of a morning at Bepi's, my friend invites me out for a quick *espresso*, and in these tense days towards the end of May we inevitably find ourselves discussing what is on everybody's mind. 'The government is a thief', he announces almost at once. It's a stock phrase, '*governo ladro*'. You frequently see it sprayed on walls and railway bridges. He shakes his shaggy head as though over an irretrievable and pitiful situation. I make the mistake of remarking a little piously that I do believe in a state where everybody pays what they have to, so that everybody can pay less, and I say I think the Church, with the hold it has over a lot of people, should tell them to cough up rather than conniving with them. Bepi's response is somewhere between the incredulous and the irate. Am I mad? His head-shaking speeds up. His scorn is all too apparent. But then it occurs to him that this is merely my Englishness talking – of course, I'm from a different world, I don't understand – and now he becomes concerned, his big forehead creases up, concerned that I may be about to make a big mistake and declare more than I need. He leans over the table, his voice urgent and conspiratorial: 'What you have to remember' – there's a bright light of conviction in his green eyes – 'what you have to remember is that they are attacking and you are defending. It's naked aggression. And self-defence is always legitimate.'

'The balance of indirect to direct taxation is fairly *valido*,' pronounces Giampaolo more reasonably that evening. He is weighing his words carefully in this sad period when last year's *prosecco* is already finished and the stuff we bottled last week isn't ready yet. 'Then the level of fiscal pressure has been established *discretamente bene*; but all this is rendered *relativo* by the fact that the government makes no serious attempt to collect. Except from *dipendenti*.'

And indeed the *dipendenti* have announced a protest to coincide with the tax-declaration deadline. They will be marching on the parliament in Rome, to demand draconian measures against the demonic *autonomi* who aren't paying their fair share. To hot things up, the newspapers amuse themselves by publishing figures indicating the average level of earnings as declared by various categories of *autonomi* the previous year. Your average jeweller claimed he earned just five thousand pounds, the average doctor even less, the average lawyer not much more, etc. etc. It's ludicrous. But everybody has their justification for behaving as they do, and the *dipendenti*'s protest is quickly followed by a series of articles showing how the government only wastes what it receives anyway, is generally corrupt and inefficient and always will be until Italy is more or less taken over by the European Community.

In the event, the administration of this year's income-tax collection does little to improve the government's image for fairness or efficiency. As May progresses and people go from one tobacconist's to another in search of the appropriate forms, it becomes clear that not enough have been printed. Or perhaps they have been printed, but they are certainly not being distributed. Then to make matters worse, somebody discovers that an important mistake has been made on one of the pages. We will have to return to the tobacconist's to buy a revised form. So that as well as reminding us of our civic duty, the radio is also talking about the possibility of a two-week postponement of the deadline for filing our returns. Indeed, this now seems more or less certain, the newscaster tells us, with a noticeably congratulatory tone to his voice. Just three days before we are supposed to pay, the Minister of Finance is interviewed and says that there will be no postponement, he has never mentioned such a thing, nor does he see why he should be obliged to deny any old rumour as soon as it starts circulating, even if it has been given credence by the public broadcasting network. People should never imagine anything has changed until he personally announces it has. And it hasn't. There will be absolutely no concessions to anybody, and people who don't file their returns inside the deadline will be fined in the regular fashion.

My accountant is thus in a state of desperation when I finally see him at nine in the evening the very day of the deadline. Out come all the invoices, the registers. His fingers incessantly tap the three-zeros button that distinguishes Italian calculators. As usual, I understand little of what he is saying about the various deductions available to me. I notice in my instruction book that if my wife was dependent on me I could reduce my taxable income by a splendid 120,000 Lire, or sixty pounds, and when I have a child I will be able to reduce it by a whole 48,000 Lire, twenty-four pounds.

Yet despite this evident meanness (there is no child benefit here), I am always surprised at how little I have to pay. 'First,' the accountant says briskly, 'we reduce your income by 14 per cent. Now, let's see.' Fourteen per cent! Why? 'Because in the category you fall into, or rather that we have chosen to put you into, taxable income is reduced by 14 per cent, which is considered to be your expenses. If the category were different, the reduction would be different. As would the percentage of national insurance you have to pay, and so on.'

When finally we get to the end of the whole business, it turns out the government actually owes me money. Which I can expect to be refunded in about four to five years' time, the accountant remarks. 'But you definitely will be refunded. With a modest interest. And it's always welcome when it comes, isn't it?' We finish towards eleven. The accountant has a whole stack of completed forms to be delivered to an office at the station which remains open until midnight the day of the deadline.

Then the following week the Minister of Finance calmly announces that, although he didn't postpone the deadline for filing returns, there will now be an amnesty for those who didn't get them in on time. They have until 14 June. Another two weeks. Perhaps the *fiaccolata* and the power of prayer are not entirely to be overlooked.

33
Mamma!!!

Given their enthusiasm for children, it will at first seem curious that Italians produce so few of them. Lara is an only child. Marta, the daughter of the mongol-looking cleaning woman is an only child. The woman with the twig broom has a little nephew who visits and at age six rushes up and down Via Colombare on a tiny motorbike with two-stroke engine making an awful racket. He is an only child. Many of my adult students have just one child. If they have any at all. The population is expected to fall by two or three million before the end of the millenium. Only in the house next to the cadaverous old lady does a very jolly *signora* have three children, all daughters. 'How many girls', claims an article in the newspaper, 'owe their existence to the elusive quest for a male child!'

It's interesting that those who prefer vegetable gardens to dwarf cypresses and do not clean too obsessionally, or have their blood pressure checked with fanatical regularity, tend to be those who produce more than one child. Again much seems to depend on the family's relationship to the rural past, the extent to which they are influenced by the general clamouring for security. For children are so expensive. They must be provided for from start to finish. First a gynaecologist *di fiducia* must be found, and then a paediatrician *di fiducia*. The little ones must spend their summers in *pensioni* or second homes by the sea to breathe the iodine, in winter they must go to the mountains to escape the fog. Very probably they will have to attend a Church rather than a state nursery, paying more. Then perhaps a private school, of which there are many. Everything they have must be new. Who would buy a second-hand pram or cot for their dear little child? Who would buy anything but the most expensive leather shoes for their toddler? And it will be a costly business sending heir or heiress to university, for this takes an absolute minimum of four years, usually much much longer, and there are no grants. Anyway the child will have a *fidanzata* or *fidanzato* by then, and very probably the family will have to buy them a flat, since they can't marry before they have been bought a flat, can they? And all the furniture. And all the appliances. Nor would it be wise for them to marry until family contacts, or personal prowess, have secured them a steady job. In the local area. It's a major undertaking.

'We didn't have another child', Orietta tells a rather bitter Lara, 'because it wouldn't have been fair to you. How could we have given you everything you need?'

A certain Antonio and Sabrina come to talk to Lucilla about the possibility of buying our flat. Their voices boom in the hallway. They now have jobs in the Banca Popolare di Verona in town. But they can't get married until they have bought a flat. And when they buy a flat it must be within walking distance of his parents. They have been looking for more than a year. Via Colombare would be ideal. Antonio's father is with them. A gruff dialect voice. Money isn't a problem, he says, and promises 'all in cash'.

The Veronese don't usually look for cheap 'first homes' as the English do. Indeed, the very notion of first and second is in naked contradiction to the word home, isn't it? Because a home is for always, for keeps. Looking for a 'first home' would thus be as absurd as looking for a 'first wife'. And while one might eventually fall out with one's wife and desire to change her, it's extremely unlikely that one would ever want to change one's home. Only a bomb could shift the people in Via Colombare from theirs. No, you protect your home with iron railings, remote-controlled gates, shock-resistant glass, armoured doors and locking shutters. It's your palace, your bunker, your life sentence. Even the modern Giampaolo will never leave Via Colombare, although his company has offered him positions in Rome and New York. For where would Orietta be without the marble and ceramics she has polished so often? The carefully chosen bathroom porcelain. '*Aggràppati al mattone,*' says a character in Natalia Ginzburg's, *La casa e la città*, when her brother announces he intends to sell his flat: 'Cling on to the bricks.'

The upshot is that most of the people buying in Montecchio are youngsters being eased (regretfully) out of the old nest (to a place not too far down the road).

Antonio's gruff father will pay a fortune to sort out his child. While he himself lives in a decrepit cave of a place off the main square. Because this is what parents must do for their children.

Understandably then, the people at the prenatal course we go to in town are all at their first child. And their last, is the general consensus. For the most part they are reserved and serious. Veronese. A poster shows a pregnant beauty in flimsy, fashionable nightdress looking out of a window into some spiritual distance of motherhood and self-realisation, the faintest smile on her face. On the wall opposite, a smaller photograph shows the blood and gore of birth itself. There is a crucifix of course, although I haven't spied a Madonna yet, which is odd.

An attractive woman social worker arrives and, sitting on a stool, discusses at length all the clothes we must prepare for the *esserino* when he arrives. She smiles constantly as she talks and a relentless use of diminutives generates a warm, cosy feeling in her audience. It's something I'm going to have to get used to over the next few years: *la gambina, la testina, il braccino, il piedino, le manine, i ditini, la boccucia, le spallucce, i ginocchietti, il nasino, il sederino*; and then the clothes: *la tutina, le scarpine, il vestitino, i guantini, il maglioncino, il giubbottino, i pantaloncini* . . . Together they create an overwhelming impression of lovable tininess to be cuddled and coddled and kissed and tweeked and generally thoroughly and triumphantly spoilt.

The previous evening we had seen a news programme showing Italian sailors setting off for their UN mission to Beirut. The camera zoomed in on a young southern boy weeping his heart out at the rail as his ship pulled away.

And it didn't take a lip reader to hear what he was screaming to that crowd on the dock. '*Mammaaaaa*! *Mammaaaaa*!' His face was broken up with fierce emotion. '*Mammina*!' In a way it's wonderful, this lack of shame.

And when we come out of the prenatal course at nine o'clock, full of warm feelings about our child to be, there are young conscript soldiers everywhere, monopolising the phones in the main square in an attempt to get a call through to *Mamma* before they have to return to their barracks. Verona is a big army town with two major barracks. One of these is out on the road to Montecchio, so that our bus going home is packed despite the hour. And the same boys who, five minutes ago, were desperately trying to get through to their mums are now rowdy and rough, jostling the one or two Montecchio girls on the bus, hoping perhaps to find the future mamma of their own only child. But the girls won't answer back. There seems to be a kind of rule that the locals will have nothing to do with the soldiers.

'Signor Tino, Signora Rita!' As our key clunks, Lucilla emerges from her door in a state of some excitement. She's in the pink brushed nylon dressing-gown, her television grinding out its variety show behind her. Do we know, she shouts, can we for one moment imagine, what Signora Marta has just done? Obviously we cannot. Do we know what she had the brazen cheek to do this very afternoon? No, it's beyond us. She telephoned, she telephoned to suggest that they both give up the court case, sell the flat and go halves on the money.

'*O Dio*!' Rita says coolly. I close my eyes. This is it. Eviction.

'It means she's guilty!' Lucilla is winding herself up into

her usual semi-hysteria. 'Guilty, guilty, guilty! It means she knows she can never win in court. Because the flat is mine. It's mine. It was built with my money and the *professore* left it to me, if only they hadn't destroyed his will. *È mio, mio, mio*!'

If she switched some of the time and resources presently allocated to cleaning to dental care, it would be much easier to talk to Lucilla at moments like this.

'So what did you do?' Rita asks.

I hold my breath.

'*Le ho detto mai* – never. *Mai mai mai mai*. Because she is evil. *Maligna*! *Una carogna*!'

And we are safe again. You can rely on Lucilla.

Upstairs my *frate indovino* tells me that I must be 'parsimonious with hatred', as hatred nourishes itself with my blood, my hopes , my life. I also notice that every single page of the calendar carries an ad for a book called '*Cara Mamma* . . .' written by none other than the *frate indovino* himself. On the page for May it says:

'Looking for a present for your sweetheart and mother-to-be . . . why not give her the fantastic, CARA MAMMA . . . It's worth more than any gold ring . . . and it costs much less.'

34
Giugno

The month of June is breathtaking, mainly because of the poppies. The corn stands thick in the broad fields of the *pianura*, or bristles in undulating strips between rows of cherry trees and vines up on the hills. It is light green at first, turning a duller, denser colour through May as it grows. Until, with the first truly hot days around the beginning of June, the green is suddenly transformed into a sizzling carpet of red, laid by some magical hand (while you were having your siesta it seems) to usher in the summer. It's quite overwhelming. We walk for hours up the valley to absorb field after field of it. Or we cycle southwards into the plain. The dazzling, dazzling red stretches majestically away, waving above the corn, miragelike, desperately intense, seductive, screaming life as colours will.

Giuliano and Girolamo are not impressed. It's a great pity these scientists haven't found a good spray to get the poppies without damaging the corn, they say. Or I think they say. I can never be 100 per cent sure I have understood these two old farmers. We find them up on the hill with their tractor, dousing the cherry trees one last time before harvest. The marginally younger Girolamo is at the wheel, steering between the terraces; bent forward at 45°, Giuliano stumbles along beside him. From a tank trailed behind the tractor, clouds of filthy-smelling chemicals steam up into thick foliage where here and there ripe cherries peep. I ask Girolamo how he measures the dosages he's giving. He shrugs his shoulders. He just sprays a lot, he says. They need a lot of spray to keep the maggots out. He comes down with us to mix the next tankload in the farmyard and it's clear he does so *ad occhio*, by guesswork. I remind myself I must tell the ecological Giampaolo just to see him shake his head. Giampaolo has now collected a huge number of snails from our sad lettuce patch and imprisoned them in a bucket with a pane of glass on top, but can't decide if it's worth the effort to wash and eat them.

Ciliegge avelenate – Poisoned Cherries – proclaim crudely daubed notices in all the orchards from Montecchio to Mizzole, trying to scare off scavengers by warning of noxious spraying. From the sound of giggling children in the leaves, the ruse would appear to be no more effective than the empty tin cans and strips of plastic strung up against the birds. *Ciliegge avelenate* – when Rita points it out, I am delighted to notice that the dialect-speaking locals have no better grasp of the use of double letters than I do. It should be, *ciliege avvelenate*.

Bepi doesn't stock cherries in his shop, because everybody, he says, either has a tree in their garden or steals from the orchards. As usual, his reflection comes complete with a tone and expression which suggest his disillusionment at the local situation (beneath contempt) and his confidence that he is smart enough to keep a step ahead all the same. Indeed, very few of the shops sell cherries. The farmers, it seems, mostly export their fruit to Austria and Germany. They have quotas to meet and the harvest was bad this year, thanks to that late flurry of snow. With the result that, despite all these hills upon hills of orchards, I personally end up eating very few cherries indeed. There are none at Via Colombare 10 of course, because fruit trees are very much a peasant thing, not part of a city person's garden . . .

'How long is it now?' the woman with the twig broom rushes out to ask, as we return from a shopping expedition. Everyone wants to talk to Rita. There is a ground swell of solidarity which rises with the curve of her belly. We are just a few yards from where the Madonnina is clutching her own son. Beside the statue, a notice has gone up to tell us the name of the builder who will be converting the orchard behind into terraced housing. Like all notices in Italy it gives the reference number, section and paragraph of whatever law it is sanctions whatever is being announced.

'Another two weeks,' Rita says. 'Election day more or less.'

This stout *zitella*'s brow knits as she thinks and calculates. 'The full moon won't be until a week after that. The third I think.'

I smile politely.

Lucilla and Vittorina are disappointed because they are going to be away. Their annual holiday. They have us over to say goodbye and show us photographs of a multi-storied modern hotel on the Adriatic coast north of Venice where they go every year. No more those magnificent adventures – Vienna, Prague – with *il professore*. Lucilla's wistful face is clownish this evening behind approximate make-up. The photo shows miles of beach and the usual evenly spaced rows of brilliant sunshades, ten deep, all the same green and purple pattern, like soldiers on parade. 'The sea air is so good for one's pressure,' Lucilla is confiding to Rita. 'That's why we go.' Vittorina, with her rather dazed post-ictus expression and ever thinning hair, manages a faint, squeaky laugh, twisting her mouth. 'Lucilla only goes for the men,' she croaks. 'Sitting in the bar chatting up men in the evening. And wearing her bikini on the beach naturally.' The image is so bizarre one would like to ask for confirmation. But how? Far from chiding her sister-in-law, Lucilla grins a grin of unqualified self-satisfaction. She has invested a lot in this image of herself as *femme fatale*. She and Vittorina are a good act.

But on popping downstairs to enquire of Giampaolo whether I can start opening my *prosecco* bottles yet, it is to find the Visentinis seriously concerned. And precisely about the question of Lucilla and Vittorina's holiday. Because, yes, sea air is good for high blood pressure, since the atmospherics tend to lower it, so the sea suits Lucilla and always has, but it is most definitely *controindicato*, i.e., a bad idea, for low blood pressure, which is Vittorina's more serious problem. Vittorina should really go to the mountains, since atmospherics there tend to raise pressure. Orietta can't understand why the doctor, who came today, hasn't explained this to them. There is general agreement that the man just takes his money and runs.

For a while voices are urgent and low. Giampaolo and Orietta see the situation as posing a real moral dilemma. Ought they to go and enlighten the two women, encourage them to change destination, at the risk of merely making Vittorina anxious without actually convincing Lucilla, who always has the last word and is very eager to go to the sea and talk volubly to bronzed widowers on deckchairs? Or should they leave be and let the women have their fun, despite concern that the climate could bring on the notoriously fatal second stroke? Really, it was up to the doctor to talk to them about this . . .

Forgetting my *prosecco*, I get drawn into a discussion about the Visentini's own holiday, still to be settled. And, like every Montecchio conversation on the subject, it soon develops into a rehearsal of the pros and cons of the invigorating mountains, the enervating sea. For any other destination is just too hot in holidaytime when factories and offices close. Only a foreigner, for example, would visit Florence or Rome in August, or embark on some walking tour of Tuscany.

Giampaolo declares himself for the mountains, the cool air, the great unspoilt panoramas, the brisk walks, the modern man's righteous ecological pride when he doesn't throw away a sandwich wrapper but tucks it back in his knapsack. Orietta is for the sea and lazy days under a sunshade which will never bring on her heart murmur, copies of her favourite women's magazines, evening barbecues with other members of the holiday village, in Puglia, Calabria, beneath palm trees. Lara just begs and begs to be sent somewhere else, anywhere, on some camp or something, it doesn't matter, so long as she can go on holiday without the family. But Orietta would worry too much.

In the end, as it turns out, Orietta will get her way on all fronts. Giampaolo will go to the travel agency at the last minute in a calculated piece of brinkmanship, hoping to pick up a cut-price place in an undersubscribed holiday village, a cancellation with any luck. Then, doing everything at the same time as they always do, he and twenty million other Italians will load the car in early August to face a seven-hundred kilometre drive in blazing sunshine with miles of tailbacks at every toll booth. But at least the expedition will justify the twin carburettor . . .

Bepi scorns them all, these provincials. For his first holiday since he set up shop, he goes off to the Seychelles. Where he meets more Italian greengrocers than he does at the market of a morning. Paradoxically, he seems quite pleased about this. He has made some useful contacts. New suppliers. Sheep's cheese from a distributor in Lessinia. And, on returning, he asks me to translate a letter for a friend he made there who wants to get in touch with a native girl he fell in love with. The letter is touchingly ingenuous, swearing the writer's determination to go back next year. Bepi seems very eager for me to finish it. His big burly presence and bright green eyes are extraordinary somehow against the funereal backdrop of Patuzzi's bookcase. I tap it out for him: the girl's beauty, their unending love. He watches the letters appear in sickly yellow on my processor screen. Is English the language he will have to learn to speak to girls? Somehow I already know he will not go back.

And, no, you can't open those bottles yet, Giampaolo

says, when I go down to ask him again. Not for another three weeks. There is an element of masochism about it, a casting about for virtue and self-esteem. His *dipendente*'s long-suffering life. If he just bought the stuff from the shop, he wouldn't have to survive this two-month period without. But having decided to bottle his own – because then it's the real thing, alive, not pasteurized and dead on a supermarket shelf – he will never go out and buy a case or so to tide him over. It's a point of honour. And he's rather disappointed when I do. Only to savour the difference when ours is ready, I tell him.

35
Elezioni

It is as summer gets into full swing that you are reminded you are living in a foreign country. A strange breed of wasps, more than an inch long, have made their nest in the eaves above our balcony and will occasionally whirr into the flat causing intense alarm. Opposite the church we see a snake, head held high, sliding rapidly along the wall of the flood-emergency dike. Typing away on *il professore*'s desk, I become aware that a baby lizard has come in through the french window and is soaking up the sunshine on the tiles by my feet. Outside, freed from their winter covers, lemon and orange trees flourish again in tubs by lowly back doors shrouded with bead curtains against the flies.

Meanwhile, Montecchio is being made ugly by preparations for the forthcoming general and local elections. It even seems possible that our child could be born right on polling day, although what kind of omen this might be I don't know. The local council erects long lines of ramshackle scaffolding outside the church and in the main square. These are then hung with laminated billboards rusting with age, thus giving the political parties free advertising space. At least fifty metres of scaffolding and sheet metal are required just to make sure that every party will get a look in. For, of course, there are many.

It was my first Italian general election and, despite the imminent domestic upheaval, I was eager to get a handle on the political life of my adopted country. I read all the editorials in national and local newspapers, I spoke about it to everybody I knew, I went to meetings in the local library. I thus passed from confusion, to disbelief, to further confusion, and, ultimately, a quiescent state of total disillusionment. Which I have maintained ever since.

Of course, every nation is disillusioned with its politicians. Everybody is half aware that a politician can never represent the people who voted for him, for the simple reason that anybody who stands for election is fundamentally different from the mass of people who don't. And if he isn't when he decides to stand, he most certainly will be once elected. The idea of a representative parliament is a pipedream. However, in the other countries I have lived in, one is at least left with the consolation of choosing between, if not different ideologies, then at least different emphases. This party will spend more, this less, this party believes in social security, this doesn't, etc. etc. So that elections can be expected to focus (reductively perhaps, but usefully) around some issue like, should we give more money to the health service, should we possess nuclear weapons, and so on. There is also the government's record. The governing party has done this, this and this. Do you like it, or don't you? Italian elections have none of this refreshing naïvety.

In the early days – heady May and the first half of June – most comment in the newspapers and on TV seemed to be concentrated on which member of the five-party coalition had been responsible for bringing the government down and provoking these early elections. Given that the public generally perceives elections as a great evil (if only because the squares are cluttered with scaffolding, and the TV monopolised by dull talk shows), this is a matter of some importance. Apportioning blame could prove a potentially effective weapon.

So, were the Socialists right to vote against such and such a clause of such and such a bill (usually something quite obscure)? Were the Christian Democrats right to insist on this clause and make it an issue of confidence when they knew the Socialists would vote against it and the Liberals abstain? Why did the Republican Party minister attack a government policy he had just subscribed to in a cabinet meeting? Why wouldn't the Social Democrats agree with the others as to who should be chairman of some bank or TV network? And so it goes on. Blame is never effectively apportioned. In the eyes of your average Montecchiese they are all responsible. They become responsible the moment they are elected. And anyway it wouldn't have mattered if such and such a clause of such a bill had been passed, since everybody would have ignored it just the same.

'The Socialists, a Modern Party for a Modern Italy' –

Bettino Craxi, their leader, is pictured with somebody behind him working on a computer. Despite the fact that their emblem is a carnation, the Socialists are using green posters this year to steal a march on the Greens. Who have unfortunately split into the Rainbow Greens and the Smiling Sun Greens and are arguing heatedly about who was responsible. 'A New Role for Women in a Fair Society', says the Communists' poster. But will it cut much ice in *la strada delle zitelle*?

All in all, there is a curious lack of imagination about this advertising. Especially given the Italians' usual verve and flare for such things. A weariness. As if none of it really mattered. 'Working toward a United Europe', boasts the Christian Democratic Party. But then so, if we're to take them at their word, are the Social Democrats. The Republicans trumpet their 'Honesty and Integrity', clearly hinting what everybody already knows, that the others have neither. But then do the Republicans? And is it what people want? The Movimento Sociale, inheritors of the fascist tradition, think it is. 'Firm Government and an End to Corruption', they proclaim. Well, it's a step forward from the '*Credere, Ubbidire, Combattere!*' – 'Believe, Obey, Fight!' – of their predecessors, a motto still provocatively visible under a thin coat of whitewash on the town hall of a nearby village. 'The Right Choice', say the Liberals about themselves, feeling that no further explanation is necessary. Or perhaps possible. 'Towards a Real Alternative', plead the Communists, their hammer and sickle reduced to a sixpence. 'Stability, Prosperity', thunder back the Christian Democrats, making much of their own emblem of the Crusader's red cross on a white shield. Well, who would ever argue with stability and prosperity?

In the end you have to turn to the extremist fringes to get any hint of policies. 'Rome = Mafia = Taxes', says the slogan of the separatist Liga Veneta. And another poster warns: 'Bringing Blacks to the Veneto = Slavery'. Obviously somebody has a penchant for perverse equations. At the other extreme, the Democratic Proletarian Party wants 'Nuclear Weapons Out Now'. The Pensioners' Party demands social justice for the elderly. Predictable stuff. The Radical Party, splendidly idealistic as ever, proclaims: 'No to World Famine.'

Responsible modern-man Giampaolo Visentini is thus profoundly depressed. 'They don't even bother trying to hoodwink us any more,' he observes. Bepi just snorts. He won't talk about it. It's too ridiculous. In the *sanitaria*, herbalist Maria Grazia's husband thunders for the Liga, the separatists. There are too many *meridionali* moving into the area. Have I heard that they're setting up yet another cooperative to build houses for themselves in Mizzole? Have I? With that and the new high-security prison going up next to the barracks, we'll have the Mafia here in no time. Amusingly, work on the prison is stopped the following week because it's discovered that the contractors involved paid bribes to politicians to get the job. A student of mine tells me she was a Democratic Proletarian activist once, but then she realised they were just the same as all the others.

Meanwhile, the debate on TV has switched to the technical question of whether parties should declare their allegiances *vis-à-vis* other parties before the election, so that people know what kind of coalition they are voting for. This is an age-old Christian Democrat ploy to have people suspect that the Socialists might desert the present government to form an alliance with the Communists after the election. Which would be the end of everything, of course. The Socialists insist that each party must simply present its policies and that is that. Whereas so far nobody has presented any. The Communists accuse the Church of using the pulpit to encourage people to vote Christian Democrat. The smaller parties try to have us all imagine that behind the scenes Christian Democrats and Communists are planning to get together and change the electoral system in such a way as to exclude all the others. There is an enormous amount of talking, much of it deployed about the furthest outposts of comprehensibility, and absolutely no debate. Nobody mentions interest rates, or inflation, or unemployment, or defence spending, or levels of housebuilding, or anything that might remotely have any bearing on day-to-day life. Nobody presents a programme or manifesto. As for the government's record, it is never considered, since each party in the coalition always claims that the other members were responsible for everything bad. Oddly, there are no opinion polls, no suggestion that things are running one way or another. If I could vote, I reflect, I would have absolutely no idea who to vote for.

Election day finally comes around. The baby is due now, but lying doggo. We wake to a perfect Sunday morning and hear the radio reminding the population that it's not just a right, but a duty to vote. They must get along to their polling station before dashing off to swim at the lake or picnic in the mountains. They mustn't let the election be won by apathy and indifference. 'And if you really can't vote today, remember that you have the right to take time off work to vote tomorrow morning. Up to two o'clock.'

The amount of concern suggests fears of an abysmal turnout. Which I would find only too understandable. We shall see.

Being a dutiful citizen, Rita sets off to vote. Who for, I have no idea. We follow the dusty road over the first and second bridges where people take the corners so courageously. The car park is full for early Mass. Six girls pass us on three bicycles. In each case the passenger stands on the saddle with her hands on the shoulders of the rider. One has an ice-lolly in her mouth, another a cigarette. The vines are stretching their tendrils across the pergola of the Bar Centrale in Piazza Buccari, where Moreno the halfwit, in deerstalker hat despite the heat, is cadging cigarettes and being gently mocked by men reading *La Gazzetta dello Sport*. And it's only half past eight. One learns to rise early here to get the best of the day.

We arrive at the other end of the village where the local school has been closed for the last three days to prepare it as a polling station. Although it's difficult to imagine why so much time was needed. In the main entrance, a computer printout has each person's name and, for some reason, their profession. There is an obsession about categorising people by profession. You then go to vote in one of a variety of classrooms, and in each classroom there are two *scrutatori* or observers. Not surprisingly, these are mainly the children of local bigwigs, glad to pick up the 80,000 Lire they get for their services. In the booth, you put a cross over the emblem of the party you want, and then, if you like, the name of one of the many many people who are standing for that party. Each constituency returns a number of deputies, and each party can offer a whole range of possible choices to fill those positions. Which means you can vote for someone in some particular faction of your chosen party, or for the man who has already done you a favour. Or is going to if he gets in. It makes counting terribly complicated.

Curiously absent from the whole process is any real suspense *vis-à-vis* the result. The evening news offers no 'swingometers', no eager experts discussing marginal states or constituencies, no surveys taken of people leaving polling stations. This is partly because the quite extreme system of proportional representation removes any see-saw effect. A swing of 5 per cent means nothing more than a swing of 5 per cent. Not the difference between one government and another. And anyway no such swings are likely to occur. Perhaps 2 or 3 per cent will leave this party, but only to disperse among five or six others. Perhaps at the end of the day one party will have crept forward the few points required to shout victory. But, in the main, the status quo will be left untouched. For the truth is that, disillusioned as they are, most Italians will always get out there and vote for the same party they always have. The football supporter mentality, Giampaolo calls it: 'You stay with them even when they're losing every game and charging you more to watch every time.'

Thus, despite the carefully deployed anxiety of the public broadcasting service before the event, and despite the fact that so many people hold residency and thus voting rights in cities far away from where they live, the turnout is a huge 90 per cent. This truly amazes me, and I bully everybody I know to try and extort some satisfactory explanation. To no avail. A love of secrecy, writing down the name of a friend of a friend in the polling booth perhaps? A residual concern that not voting might prejudice one's position in some *concorso* to become a teacher, or caretaker (Vittorina and Lucilla were both unaccountably worried about missing the election)? Genuine fear of a Communist government? Or perhaps – and it's the explanation I would plump for – perhaps, despite all disillusionment, a very profound, heartfelt satisfaction with the way things are and a determination that they should remain so. I plump for it because it has the hallmark of that profound schizophrenia, which is also the charm, of all matters Italian: the Pope adored and ignored, the law admired and flouted, politicians despised and re-elected. The gulf between officialdom's façade and private thought could not be greater than it is here. But in the secret of the ballot box that façade is always supported. Nothing changes. Italy, one sometimes thinks, is as if frozen in the high noon of its post-war prosperity.

I played a little game with my students on our last lesson of the year. I suggested they write down who they think their barber/hairdresser votes for and why. Normally responsive and fun to teach, my request left them nonplussed, diffident, reticent. It was as if one had asked some ancient Athenian to explain the Eleusinian mysteries. A completely taboo subject. Montecchio, in the event, returned the Christian Democrats with the usual 70 per cent of the vote, but I have yet to meet anyone here who will speak well of the party. 'The only good thing about elections' – Bepi deigned to mention the subject over an *espresso* with grappa at eight in the morning – 'is that the results are so complicated that for a month and more afterwards there's no government at all. And so for a while, *non possono rompere le palle*!' Which loosely translated means, They can't get on our fannies.

'If the country', comments *il frate indovino*, ear perfectly tuned to the popular mood, 'could buy politicians for what they're really worth and then sell them for what they claim they're worth, it could pay off its deficit in no time at all.'

Doubtless our witty priest votes Christian Democrat.

36
La luna

The baby was late. Rita was finding the heat and summer *afa* oppressive. We bought a fan and she sat at her typewriter in a stream of dusty air. When the Visentini got to know, Orietta felt it her duty to come upstairs and warn us that fans were *controindicati*. You sweated, then sat in the air from the fan, and inevitably caught a cold. She was also worried that we hadn't got rid of our cat. Cats could cause all kinds of diseases when one had a little baby in the house. I often wonder if perhaps Italian houses of the future won't be designed with some sort of disinfectant footbath in the entrance way. We liked our cat.

Meanwhile, whenever I bumped into anyone in Via Colombare an eyebrow would be raised. Any news yet? If there's anything I can do . . . Even the mechanic at the end of the street, smelling strongly of grappa after lunch as always, was in the know. Did I want my car looking over before the all-important trip? The last thing I needed was a breakdown on the way to the hospital . . . I thanked him and got filters, plugs and points changed at a very reasonable price. *'Buon giorno Signor Teem,'* said old Marini's wife 'and how is your *signora* this morning?'

What a far cry from the kind of reception I had been getting a year before! Clearly, I thought, a child is the ultimate passport to society here, a blank cheque to draw against vast reserves of Latin sentiment. Far from having my greetings rejected, I now had the opposite problem of having to discuss the relative merits of the various local hospitals with the vaguely mongol-looking woman, while the woman with the twig broom came to clap me on the back and tell ghastly stories about the gynaecologists at Borgo Roma where her sister-in-law had given birth. *'Macellai'*, she insisted. 'Butchers. They jump on your belly to push the child out.' And she asked who would be coming in to look after me while my wife was away at the hospital. I wondered for a moment if I had understood this correctly.

'Chi ti cucinerà?'

'Nobody, I can manage myself.'

She shook her head, whether in admiration, or despair at a changing world, I don't know. *'Troppo bravo, troppo bravo'*, she said. 'You English are so tough.' And she added by way of valediction: 'The full moon will be the night of the third.'

Inspired by the consultant gynaecologist who gave our prenatal course, we have decided to go to his hospital in the small town of Zevio. He appears to be the only consultant in the Italian state system practising the Leboyer method. Or so he says. Obviously, we've driven over there once or twice to check out the route: fifteen miles of twisting country roads, with the last stretch, unfortunately, being resurfaced and hence bumpy as hell. A useful stimulant perhaps, but also another complicating factor in that delicate equation: when to set off. We time the trip at thirty minutes. Getting out of the car to stretch our legs, we find a sleepy, overgrown village with a truly vast main square, in the middle of which is a villa-cum-castle surrounded by a moat. The rest of this inexplicably huge open area is just a desert of asphalt crisscrossed by fading white lines indicating where five or six roads might intersect. On Sundays, we discovered on our second trip, the space is packed to suffocation point with a bustling provincial market selling cheap clothes, fruit, vegetables, and adventurous underwear of mammoth proportions, presumably for ladies like Lucilla. The traffic was backed up for a kilometre and more. Another factor then, is that one must not go into labour on a Sunday morning.

The hot days drag on. We sit under the pergola at Centro Primo Maggio listening to the accordion. People with houses by the streams hang water-melons in the water to keep them cool. They're too big for the fridge. Despite the predictable election results, the politicians, as Bepi predicted, have so far been unable to come up with a government. Nobody's concerned. The shops begin to close as everybody goes off on holiday. There are the usual scandals about poor old people having to walk miles in suffocating heat to find a grocery open. By law, shops are obliged to run a rota system, but the fines are so small they tend to ignore the problem. You go to the post office and find it closes for the afternoon in July and August. There is alarmist talk about the unavailability of doctors in hospitals. We begin to get nervous.

And then the big day arrives at last. Or rather night. Towards two in the morning the terms of the equation are finally and ruthlessly satisfied: fierce contractions. We bundle into our despised orange car and head south across the *bassa* to Zevio. We're about half-way – San Martino, Campalto, Mambrotta – driving along roads that twist and turn unaccountably through perfectly flat countryside, when, over a distant dike, what should sail up into the sky but the moon, a perfectly round, splendid, shining white moon, full as full can be, and apparently drawing us to Zevio as the natal star to Bethlehem. How infuriating! I can just see the satisfied smirk on the face of our lady of the twig broom. Even Giampaolo will consider it as confirmation of his *prosecco*-bottling technique. Yet one feels strangely satisfied to see it too. *La luna*. So bright! So large! We speed on through field after field of silvery peach orchards under that presageful ghostliness lunar light tends to have, especially at important moments in your life. And it does cross my mind for a moment that perhaps the moon has more influence in Italy than it does back home. This would explain so much.

The Chiarenzi hospital in Zevio has long corridors paved with cheap black stone. The porter gives a direction with his thumb, barely looking away from a TV screen. In a spare room, a nurse with nun's headgear takes down the details. Then more corridors. At the entrance to the maternity ward a little waiting area is heaped with flowers and there is a small white statue of the Madonna. One gets to rely on her after a while: that simple passivity, absorbing all, at crossroads, hospital wards, cemeteries. Although somehow, through her very ubiquitousness, the quiescent figure becomes not so much a protecting presence as a reminder that, whatever happens, all will go on as before. Without her and her crucified son, usually much smaller and hidden away by some dusty central-heating pipe near the ceiling, you might imagine that what was happening to you here and now was unique, and desperately important.

Rather surprisingly, I find myself wondering if the Madonna doesn't have some quality in common with the moon.

In the ward, a bright young nurse speaks to us in dialect and listens to the baby's heartbeat through a wooden trumpet pressed against Rita's belly. Interestingly, she is called Stefania, which is the name we have chosen if the baby is a girl. Which no doubt it will be. I'm pretty well resigned to that now. Not that I in any way mind having a girl. On the contrary. What could be more delightful than a little girl? Just that I had hoped the Via Colombare influence would not be confirmed. I'd far rather have a random world than a determinist one, however benevolent.

We spend the night in a tiny room with Rita in labour and me fighting sleep. Enticingly, there's a *pasticceria* right across the street which will surely open at seven o'clock. Shortly after dawn, while a crow sits on a branch not a yard away, a priest leads four men carrying a rough wooden coffin out of the hospital into the street. I decide not to remark on this to Rita. And when a light goes on in the *pasticceria* around eight o'clock, I selfishly hurry out for a *cappuccino*, only to hear that the bar is closed for holidays. The man has merely come to do some decorating work.

And the *pasticceria* the other side of the village is always closed Monday mornings. A test of the extent of your Italianisation is whether you still grind your teeth when you hear that something is closed.

In the event, the low lights and soft music of the Leboyer method have to be forgotten because that room is already occupied. 'Full moon', explains the nurse. 'Haven't had a birth for a week and then six in a single night.' OK, OK, I give in. But the baby, when it finally shows up, is a big bouncy boy. We are both delighted.

The first duty of an Italian father is to buy a rosette, blue for a boy, pink for a girl, and stick it on some highly visible part of his house. Driving home that day, I found a *tabaccheria* in San Martino that sold me one for what seemed a rather expensive 10,000 Lire. The lady at the till was desperately eager to engage me in conversation about the joys of parenthood: *'Sì, sì, sì*, a great change in your life, you can't even imagine yet,' she says excitedly as I walk out in a daze without my receipt. Back in Via Colombare I taped the thing high on the front door of number 10 and hoped that all the *zitelle* in the street would see it immediately and eat their hearts out.

My second duty was to find two witnesses and take them along to register the birth. Since public offices are only open in the morning, this would have to wait till the following day. Giampaolo and Orietta were more than happy to help me out, and we set off early next morning so he wouldn't be too late for work.

Registration had to be in the village of birth, so it was back along the winding road to Zevio again. The *comune* was a baroque *palazzo* in the huge main square where traffic crisscrossed with impressive confidence across the open asphalt. At the top of flights of eighteenth-century stairs, a huge room with ornate ceiling and a long wooden counter was occupied by just two women toying with computers.

The man who registered births was out for a minute, they said. Could we wait?

I generally accept this kind of thing now. But Giampaolo looked at his watch. 'We'll give him five minutes,' he said ominously. As with his behaviour over Negretti and his dogs, phoning the police at the drop of a hat, I was surprised by his immediately tough, legalistic, although always reasonable approach. 'We have come to a public office', he told the women calmly. 'There is no queue, and hence no reason why we shouldn't be dealt with immediately.' Orietta tugged at his elbow. 'Giampaolo!' she muttered.

But after five minutes Giampaolo again politely demanded to be served. The younger of the women, lavishly if not seductively made up, fashionably if not attractively dressed, said the man couldn't possibly be much longer. Giampaolo asked where he was. The girl flustered. Nobody had registered a birth for a week or so, she said. And then they were so pushed still with the aftermath of the elections. Surely we could understand that? But if we were really in a hurry then she would try to handle the matter herself. Her voice echoed petulantly in the big room, designed, presumably, for nobler purposes. A great chandelier gathered dust above a VDU. The lighting was fluorescent.

We were in a hurry, Giampaolo said. We had come early because he had to get to work. People noticed, he remarked pointedly, when he was absent.

The girl, clearly resentful of the fact that her colleague

hadn't budged, came over to the counter, pulled a huge book out from a drawer beneath and asked us for our documents: Giampaolo's, Orietta's, my own. But when she saw the British passport she shook her head. Was I the father? She couldn't possibly take it upon herself to register a foreigner's birth. And she turned to the older woman: 'Do we have any special conventions with England?' The other didn't know. I suggested that the conventions would be the same as for all EC countries. 'Is England a member of the EC?' the girl asked her colleague. *'Credo di sì,'* came a monotone response. But the girl shook her head all the same. We would just have to wait for *il responsabile*.

'But where is he?' Giampaolo returned to the offensive. 'We have no intention of waiting here all morning.'

The girl looked to the woman behind for support. This dusty creature said sourly: 'Running an errand at the hospital.' And she wouldn't look up from her keyboard.

'Ring him up.'

My neighbour, I was discovering, had the disturbingly professional belligerence of somebody who not only knows when to pick a fight but is also perfectly confident of how he is going to go about winning it.

The two hesitated.

Giampaolo announced: 'This is a public service. The office is obliged to have somebody present who can register births. It is now officially open. You have admitted the man is not ill. At this point I am left with no alternative but to *sporgere una denuncia'* (i.e., report the matter to the police).

We had only been waiting ten minutes. It seemed perfectly normal to me.

'Giampaolo!' Orietta protested *sotto voce*.

Turning to us, the usually wooden Giampaolo grinned broadly and whispered: 'The man's in the bar. You'll see. He's having his breakfast.'

At the word '*denuncia*' the two women, rather than protesting or growing more hostile, had begun to confabulate quite urgently under the cover of their computer printer. After a moment they pulled out the phone book and began to leaf quickly through.

'They'd have the number to the hospital written down', Giampaolo whispered. I was all admiration.

The girl picked up the phone, dialled, asked if Lucio was there, hung on. And then the obvious occurred to me. 'It's because the *pasticceria* at this side of the village is closed. He's had to go to the one opposite the hospital and it's taking him longer than it usually does.'

And, indeed, just five minutes later Lucio could be heard hurrying up the stairs, icing sugar on the bristles of a fine moustache. '*Bene, Signori, vediamo.*' He smiled broadly, rubbed his hands together, and scribbled down my passport number as if he saw a dozen a day. To my relief the delay was not mentioned. Everybody was extremely polite and friendly and we all wished each other *buon giorno*. But Giampaolo, walking down to the car, was gloating. If there's one thing an impotent *dipendente* can do, it's demand his rights from a *statale*. Such was the world into which my child had now been officially introduced.

37
Manifesti funebri

So much gets said about the inefficiency of Italian public services that I feel it my duty toward the end of this book to remark on how extraordinarily fast, even in the holiday season, the Gas, Water and Cemeteries Board (AGSM) will authorise a death notice. On every wall or space where ads and announcements are pasted up in the villages of the Veneto – behind the bus-stop, or higgledy-piggledy on a wall at a crossroads – you always find a couple of these simple *manifesti funebri*, giving their sad news. And from time to time, while picking up your newspaper or going for a haircut, you will turn a corner and see a familiar name. You know in Montecchio when your neighbours die. The cemetery encroaches on the shopping streets. Rightly so perhaps. And, while birth may be a frilly silk-blue or pink, death has no sex and, of course, only one colour. So you quickly learn to recognise the black borders and Christ's upturned face with crown of thorns at the top in the centre. Across the middle of the poster there will be a name in large letters, and perhaps a nickname too, since nicknames are common in Italy (Dino Chiericatti, and beneath, *'detto, il capitano'*). The age is placed in brackets, likewise the married woman's maiden name. There is the time and date of the funeral, gratitude in advance for those who attend. And a brief comment such as: 'mourned by all her loved ones', or 'lost to the affection of family and friends' – some appropriate, conventional formula, nothing fanciful. 'Authorised by AGSM', they have stamped askew in the bottom left-hand corner. The very day after Vittorina died the posters were already up all over the village.

Rita returned from the hospital just two days after Michele's birth. In the meantime the old women had come back triumphantly sunburnt from their holiday and were fussing and clucking to see the child. We had barely laid the carrycot on the table before they were knocking on the door, bringing gifts in extravagant packages. They peeked under the covers, went into ecstasies: the first male child born on Via Colombare for heaven knows how long! A jinx had been broken! And again Lucilla made herself cry by recounting the story of her own little boy: the fever in the night, the hot poultices applied to *quel povero corpicino*. Again we said we were sure she had done everything that reasonably could be done. And I glanced up to check that I had written our paediatrician's number on the board by the phone.

Giampaolo came upstairs. He didn't want to disturb us. They would see the baby when we had all had time to settle down. He just wanted to let me know that I was released from my duties of watering and mowing the lawn for a little while. Then whenever we felt ready, we could pop the first of those bottles of *prosecco* together. He now had three in the back of the fridge.

The following afternoon, a day of stifling *afa*, Vittorina did not wake up from her siesta. Lucilla's yells brought me running. Leone and Marisa were visiting and the three of them had discovered the corpse together. When I got downstairs, Lucilla had already recovered sufficiently to start pulling open drawers and thumbing through papers. It was intriguing that, for all the closeness of their friendship, Vittorina had never told her where she kept the will.

Leone lowered the shutters. Marisa lit a candle each side of the bed. I withdrew. On the threshold of her spick-and-span flat, its millimetrically positioned lithographs, and carefully dusted knick-knacks, Orietta had tears in her eyes. That low pressure at the seaside had been a terrible, terrible mistake. Criminal, on the doctor's part. At which the culprit himself drew up in the road outside, a practised smile on his face as he stepped out of his Porsche. *Troppo, ma troppo gentile*, sobbed Lucilla. It occurred to me I had better remove the blue rosette from the door.

Today was Friday and the funeral couldn't be arranged until Monday. With Giampaolo still at work, Orietta came upstairs around fivish to say she was worried about the possible smell. No, the undertakers didn't take away the body here. The relatives had to pray over it until the funeral. They would put her in her coffin tomorrow, but the body would still be lying there until Monday and with this weather . . . Mightn't it cause some kind of disease?

After all, *la poveretta* was only just the other side of the wall from their own bed.

And the *cassonetto* with its rubbish was only the other side of the street.

Rita was trying to breastfeed the little baby. I couldn't imagine there was any serious health risk, I said. But it wasn't my field. Orietta, it appeared, had already consulted Giampaolo's encyclopaedia. And now she stayed in our flat to phone various offices of the health service. There was a corpse just the other side of her bedroom wall. Could it cause disease? Their reassuring answers didn't convince her. She would keep her windows tightly closed, however hot it got.

All Saturday and Sunday the people of Via Colombare trickled by to pay their respects to the deceased and offer *condoglianze*. Lucilla managed to be overdressed in mourning, bursting with energy and self-commiseration, playing the protagonist's part. *'Gradirebbe un gingerino, Signora Rosa, una tazza di tè?'* And yes, Vittorina had left the flat to her, although she didn't want to talk about that kind of thing now. Word spread like wildfire. Bankworkers Antonio and Sabrina stopped by with Antonio's father, all in black, although they had never known Vittorina.

It occurred to me that, with the flat downstairs to dispose of, the heat was probably off as far as we were concerned. And a baby is such an attraction.

Then on the Monday, perhaps a year and a month after we had arrived, I got to see another of Lucilla's balcony performances. About twenty or thirty of us had gathered in the street, trying to keep out of the mud a bulldozer had left, for they had just begun to plough down the cherry trees behind the Madonnina. More work for our lady of the twig broom. Perhaps because of the heat, people were not overly formal. Only Lovato, who had presided so long over Vittorina's gardening, had a suit and tie. Giampaolo had taken time off work and was smartly, although casually dressed. Faces were waxy with sweat. Don Guido arrived in his battered Renault, dents front, back and sides. There was subdued chatter, the bright whistle of a blind blackbird in the dusty morning air. Old Signora Marini whispered to me that we could come and get some figs when they were ripe. Black or green. She knew my wife liked figs. How was little Michele? Weight? Sleeping habits? *Che caro*!

The hearse turned the corner from the derelict factory end, its polished grey flanks bearing the sublimely comforting announcement: *Azienda Municipale Servizi Funebri* – another branch of AGSM. Men dressed in blue overalls went in beneath the Californian eaves of number 10 and lifted the coffin in the shuttered, candlelit room. They were careful with their feet on the polished marble. The ailing tropical plants were moved aside. Then out they came between the two dwarf cypresses that guarded the bourgeois spirit of the glass front door. In the street, one or two people stepped forward to place flowers on top but, as Vittorina had not been a Montecchiese by birth, it was not a big funeral. The hearse had long side windows cut specially low to make an elegant display of the polished wood. Don Guido had to slam his damaged car door twice.

And then, just as the hearse got into gear, just as the crowd was preparing to follow, Lucilla, with a perfect sense of timing, burst forth on her terrace balcony and began to shriek and tear her hair. She had been betrayed, betrayed, betrayed! By life, by death. Her only treasure had been taken from her. The only companion of her old age.

'Vittorina, Vittorina, *tesoro, cara,* how could you? How could you die on me? *Maria Santissima, oh Gesù, perchè, perchè?'* Curiously, there was at least as much anger as sorrow in the performance, as if her sister-in-law's death wasn't so very different from having been cheated out of *il professore*'s flat. Another loss, another encroachment. She bared her crooked teeth and howled, she pulled at her hair. Truly grief-stricken, and truly theatrical. She railed against God and spat. But this time one didn't feel inclined to find anything cartoonlike or caricaturish about it, as one had a year ago. One was part of the crowd now, and one watched and listened respectfully, offering the tubby woman the audience she needed. One reflected that there would always be occasions, many occasions, even in the modern, high-tech, all-problems-solved world Giampaolo yearned for, when appearance on one's balcony and a wild raw wail in stifling heat before a gathered crowd would be both understandable and appropriate.

Late that evening, we opened the first bottles of *prosecco* with the Visentini and wondered who our new neighbours would be. One bottle was flat. The second frothed splendidly. There was just no telling why. The moon, the pressure? '*Salute*! Health!' Orietta was quick to say, clinking glasses. '*Molto valido,*' I said taking my first sip. '*Discreto,*' Giampaolo nodded, not wanting to go overboard. 'But *relativo,*' Rita added, 'if only one bottle out of two is good.' Sharp young Lara giggled.

Afterword

Some four or five years after I arrived in Italy, in a moment of nostalgia for milk-floats and the busy racial mix of Acton High Street, I reread Browning's, *Oh to be in England*. It wasn't April and there are no melon flowers in Montecchio; nor, if there were, would I find them gaudy, for nothing pleases me more than bright colours. Then the things Browning remembered about England are not the things I remember. I go for the back seat up top of a Victoria-bound bus, or gusting wind on the upper Edgware Road. The orchard bough, the swallows, the thrush, are not part of my memories of home. And anyway, all these things can be found in abundance in both Tuscany and the Veneto. There is no need to feel nostalgic for what is all around you. So that perhaps, rather than making any real comparison between the two countries, all Browning was saying, in his very beautiful way, was that he was homesick. And also, by curious implication, that he was not coming home. For anyone whose homesickness can be so exquisitely relished, so effectively deployed, has long passed the point of no return. Browning remembers England the way a happily married man, surprised by a scent some warm spring evening, might remember an earlier girlfriend: with thanks, with pleasure, even a ghost of regret, but no real urgency. If this book is anything, I hope it suggests how I passed that point of no return. Which is a process of immersion in details, whether they be pleasant or unpleasant. For details are sticky as spider's silk; you are very soon caught. And rather than a travel book, perhaps if there were such a category in the libraries, I should call this an arrival book. For by the end, this small square handkerchief of Italy I live in has become home for me. Hopefully, for just a moment, the reader will have been able to feel at home here too.

AN ITALIAN EDUCATION

TIM PARKS

VINTAGE

Published by Vintage 1999

2 4 6 8 10 9 7 5 3 1

First published in Great Britain in 1996 by
Martin Secker & Warburg

Vintage
Random House, 20 Vauxhall Bridge Road,
London SW1V 2SA

Random House Australia (Pty) Limited
20 Alfred Street, Milsons Point, Sydney
New South Wales 2061, Australia

Random House New Zealand Limited
18 Poland Road, Glenfield, Auckland 10, New Zealand

Random House South Africa (Pty) Limited
Endulini, 5A Jubilee Road, Parktown 2193, South Africa

Random House, UK Limited Reg. No. 954009

A CIP catalogue record for this book
is available from the British Library

ISBN 0 7493 9626 1

Papers used by Random House UK Limited are natural, recyclable products made from wood grown in sustainable forests. The manufacturing processes conform to the environmental regulations of the country of origin

Printed and bound in Great Britain by
Mackays of Chatham plc, Chatham, Kent

Author's note

My editor is concerned that I may have used too many Italian words in this book. I am concerned myself. Rereading now, I see there are one or two, or sometimes three on every page. Even the chapter headings are in Italian. Clearly I should say something in my defence.

My first idea was that I might offer a little glossary. But this would be no solution. For if each of the words could be explained with a simple alternative in English, then I would never have felt inclined to leave them in Italian in the first place. I have been a translator for many years and one of the most galling aspects of that galling job is to realise, on translating a word, that you have offered only a tiny fraction of its meaning, only an empty semantic shell, since so often surface meaning is nothing more than the stony outcrop of a great mass of cultural bedrock beneath. Thus, if I write '*sacrifici*' in Italian, you will immediately guess that it means 'sacrifices', but unless you have lived in Italy you cannot imagine how often and in how many ways that word is used here, how it seals a crucial joint in the Latin mind frame, offers a vital stepping stone in the Catholic search for good conscience.

Our experience of another country is also an experience of its language, how similar it is to our own, how different. It once occurred to me that one way to talk about Italy would be simply to make a list of all those Italian words that are untranslatable, or whose translation tells you next to nothing, and then give dozens of anecdotes showing how they are used. I never got round to that. I'm not meticulous enough. But something of the project remains, in *Italian Neighbours* first, and now in this book dedicated to my children, my foreign children. For when my daughter exclaims *'O la Madonna!'*, or my son sticks out two fingers of each hand and whispers *'Facciamo le corna'*, it would seem superfluous to translate the first, while to write, 'Let's make horns' for the second isn't going to help anyone. This is language that has to be savoured, discovered, enjoyed. Dubbed movies are always disappointing.

Professionals in the publishing world have warned me that people don't want to read any word they've never seen before, or deal with any concepts they're not familiar with. I'm not convinced. I think when you've got the hang of expressions like *facciamo le corna* and *tengo famiglia* you're going to have a lot of fun with them. Mutter them to yourselves every day at the appropriate moments and you are guaranteed to feel, if only slightly, Italian. Anyhow, for those willing to make this small *sacrificio* I promise not to leave you out in the cold, if only because not being in the cold but becoming part of a privileged group, a family, is precisely what any Italian education is all about.

For Lucia

Cocco fresco

'Cocco! Cocco!'

It's a loud harsh voice from far away. At a quarter to nine the morning air is already vibrant with heat and light. Everywhere a steady brightness lies like a pressure on brilliant colour.

'Cocco! Cocco fresco!' The voice is getting louder, and it's recognisably a pedlar's voice, theatrical and coercive, the hard double 'c' extravagantly emphasised, the final 'o' almost stretching to two syllables. A young voice pretending to be old and bold.

'COC-CO-O!' You can hear the banging of a bucket now, as if against a leg at every step. *'Cocco fresco!'*

It's a geometric world we're in. First and furthest away lies the sea, behaving well today, a flat, undifferentiated dazzle, barely wrinkling where it meets an almost white sand. Coming closer, there are twenty measured metres between the water and the first row of sunshades. Old folks walk briskly here, parallel with the shoreline, their sagging or angular profiles sharp against brilliance beyond as they take their tonic morning stroll down the never-ending beach.

The voice is growing more insistent as it approaches.

'Cocco! Cocco fresco!'

The sea, the strip of sand, and then the sunshades: great green-and-orange umbrellas on this bathing station, tall and wide, each two and a half metres from the next, twenty-four in rows parallel to the sea, fourteen in rows perpendicular, with one space at the midpoint of each row in each direction to form a pathway from road to sea, a pathway across the beach (so that seen from above one imagines a bright sandy cross dividing a huge flag of colour). On the ground beneath the striped umbrellas, the sun, still low, though higher every minute, revolves slow pools of shadow around deck chairs and lounge beds, likewise green and orange. The sand is a rigidly patterned chiaroscuro where the early-morning bathers stretch their towels and unfold their newspapers, entirely ignoring the now imperative cry:

'COCCO!' Clank, clank clank. *'COCCO FRESCO!'*

A small child fussing in the sand with a spade says *'Cocco!'* in the sort of baby voice that repeats everything it hears. *'Cocco!'* He looks up from his spadework to where a lanky adolescent is now approaching through a blaze of light, a bucket clanking under each arm.

Bending to adjust the baby's sunhat, a woman's soft voice says, 'Yes, *cocco della mamma!'* Which is to say, 'Mummy's little darling, Mummy's cuddly little man.' But in perfect baby imitation of the young pedlar, now no more than a couple of metres away, the child shouts: 'No, *Cocco!*' Then, '*Cocco fwecco!*' As if he understood.

The mother laughs, twists on her deck chair and signals to the boy, who comes over with a grin. He is tall and straight with Latin-black hair and a smooth, bare, rather shrimpy chest already tanned to dark toast in early June.

'How much?' she asks.

He sets down his buckets on the sand and now we can see the slices of white coconut swimming in water.

'A thousand lire.'

This is extortionate, but once again the child, rocking back and forth on his nappy and bright red shorts manages, '*Cocco fwecco!*'

'Very clean,' the pedlar knows to insist. He has a gold crucifix round his neck, three bracelets, an earring, a diver's watch and a bright smile.

'*Va bene.*'

The deal is done. The boy pushes a crumpled note into the pocket of denim shorts and resumes his pedlar's cry among the sunshades. Meanwhile, the white coconut, whiter even than the light, dead white, is carefully washed from a bottle of still mineral water, then cut into tiny pieces so that a child can chew on it – my young child, Michele, gurgling in Adriatic light and heat, growing up Italian.

I remark to my wife, Rita, that where I was brought up, if you got down to the sea at 8.30 in the morning, you would freeze to death. But she is busy stopping Michele from picking up a crumb of coconut that has fallen in the sand. And now he's dug out a cigarette stub, too.

I remark that if you set up a sunshade on the beach at

Blackpool, where I lived as a child, the chances are it would be blown away. Even with a huge cement base. And assuming you wanted to set it up somewhere dry, that would mean you'd have to walk half a mile out before you got to the sea, with the danger that then the tide would come in so fast it would sweep the thing away. Though, of course, it would sweep away the cigarette stubs, too.

In Pescara, halfway down Italy's fancy boot on the right-hand side, the sea scarcely moves at all on summer days. Or it's as if a broad dishful of water were tipped ever so gently this way and that. Tiny wavelets creep up the beach a metre or two, only to creep respectfully back, leaving the strollers and sunshades and pedal-boats untouched. The sand Michele is crunching in baby hands a hundred yards from the shore has the soft fineness of sand in an hourglass, dry as desert bone, certainly too dry to make a sandcastle with, but good for tossing up in the air, or pouring over Daddy's legs. Fortunately, there's not a breath of wind today to blow it into your eyes.

A couple more families saunter along the pathway from the road and the bathing-station bar down to their sunshades. The pathway is paved with small, square flagstones, because it is wearisome walking far across soft, dry sand, and then it would be difficult to push a buggy through it. The sunshades have small red discs with numbers to avoid confusion.

I said families, but in fact there are no men in the groups, for it's not the weekend, and not really holiday time yet. Only late July and August are really holiday time. A harassed mother is carrying a huge inflated shark. Her two small boys drag a rubber boat full of toys.

They settle, as they always do, at the sunshade across the path from our own. For that is their sunshade. Rented for the whole summer. Number 34. But no, the boys can't go into the sea yet. No! *Per l'amore di Dio!* It's too early to go into the sea. Not before ten o'clock! Though the temperature must already have hit thirty . . . Certainly I stripped my shirt off long ago.

'If you waited,' I remark to my wife, 'till it got hotter than this to go into the sea at Blackpool, you'd never go in at all. Which might be just as well, because . . .'

But Rita's worried that Michele has sand in his nappy now, and she's debating whether to take it off. Is this early morning sun already too strong, perhaps, for his delicate skin? And if she puts cream on him, will the sand stick to it?

When you went swimming at Blackpool, you pulled off your clothes in a hurry and were shivering before you'd got your costume on. To fight the cold you ran fast across the beach through shallow water, or on a hard, ribbed sand that hurt your soles. Laughing and splashing, you plunged your goose pimples into a murky sea and fooled around in the waves for as long as you could without suffering serious exposure, then raced back out of the water to where Mother stood waiting with a big bath towel already opened. Father rubbed your hair furiously, distorting your vision of low cloud over the Edwardian seafront. The sand was damp and sticky and would never come out from all the body's secret corners, perhaps because the towels were never a hundred percent dry. The very air was wet and clung to you. Then there would be flasks of soup and tea and coffee, crouching in the shelter of a windbreak, sniffing and wiping your nose on a sandy wrist. Afterwards, fully dressed again, you dug channels and built dams for the water that lay just below the surface everywhere, all the time keeping a wary eye on a possible pincer movement of the tide, famous for carrying off the less experienced beachgoers. Your overall feeling on departure was one of battered heroism.

Rita laughs. She feels sorry for the English, but she also finds them rather ridiculous. Never once, in all our trips to England, has she braved an English sea, though she is an excellent swimmer.

In Pescara, the mothers bring their children early to the beach, to get the sun at its healthiest. Later they will let them go in the water when its coolness can only be a relief. And when the children come out, they don't change back into their clothes, shivering like wet dogs, teeth chattering, but into a second dry bathing costume. Or even a third . . .

Overhead and a few hundred yards out to sea, a light aeroplane flies low and parallel with the shoreline towing a long strip of orange plastic. It's advertising CRODINO, a soft fizzy drink. Nobody needs soup or hot tea here.

Michele spits out his piece of coconut. It appears he doesn't like it. '*Cocco*,' he says cheerily, apparently not having really made the connection. So I get to finish it up, perhaps my first piece of fresh coconut since the coconut shies of Lancashire funfairs twenty and more years ago. One thing about having children is that they remind you of so much. And having children in a foreign country gives you a new awareness of distance, a new dimension to your awayness.

After ten o'clock, as more and more people arrive, the sunshades become a warren of orange and green activity, most of it, at this hour, dedicated to the well-being of young children, who have to be undressed, smothered in sun cream, wriggled into their bathing costumes, and given a hat, which of course they take off, so it has to be put on again, then they take it off again, so then it has to be tied on, so that now they begin to cry – and perhaps the sun is already so hot that they could really use a T-shirt, or perhaps not, How hot is it already? and Don't throw sand, Matteo, Don't throw sand, Cristina, and no, you can't have *pizzetta*, it's too early for a *pizzetta*. Yes, I know I promised. Well, we'll go and get one at eleven o'clock. No, you can't go in the water yet. Not yet. For the moment just be quiet and play with your toys.

For they all have lots of toys. They have big plastic buckets and spades, and they have rakes and forks and then little plastic moulds to make bas-relief frogs and rabbits and dogs and cats of sand, except that the sand is too dry here, somebody will have to go and fetch a bucket of water, and they have plastic dolphins and rubber rings and water wings and goggles and snorkels and flippers, all in extremely bright colours, and tip-up trucks to move sand and excavators to dig it and rackets and balls and perhaps even a boomerang or a kite.

But they have no father to play with, to make their toys come alive, because father is in the office, or the factory, or even the fields, working. And for the most part they have no brothers or sisters to play with, because Italians of my generation rarely have more than one child.

The only children nose around their toys wondering what to do while their mothers chat.

For since the mothers always come to the same sunshade, which is *their* sunshade, they pretty soon get to know all the other mothers who have the adjacent shades, and they do this far quicker, it seems, than the children get to know the other children. After all, adults have had more practice.

The sunshades to our right are taken by two primary school teachers. Sitting on their lounge beds, creaming their stretchmarks, their small talk is inexhaustible: TV game shows, supermarket prices, medical tests, friends divorcing, celebrities divorcing, nappy rash, toddling, tortellini, teething. Nearby, the dear children they're more often than not talking about fret with their toys and, if they have a companion, begin to hit him, while the sun creeps up to the vertical, squeezing the shadows in beneath the sunshades.

'It's hard to see why they're at the beach at all,' I object as Michele clutches at my toes. Certainly I can't remember so much mere lounging when we were by the sea at Blackpool. We were always up and doing then. It was all games and eating, swimming and shivering and escape.

Rita is reading a publication called *Io e il mio bambino* – Me and My Baby. There was a free teething ring in it. Too late for Michele.

I repeat my complaint.

'Because of the sea air,' Rita explains. 'It's good for the children's lungs. The doctor tells them to come. There's quite a technical article about it here somewhere: the therapeutic action of iodine on the bronchi.'

'But you can't even smell the sea.'

'Not from here.'

This is remarkable. At least to me. Given the calmness of the water, the stillness of the warm air (and perhaps the ubiquity of suntan lotion), you can't actually smell that wonderful sea tang until you're almost in the water. Indeed, if you didn't look in that direction, you might well be in some sort of pleasure-ground Sahara.

The two teachers are comparing the peeling on their shoulders while their two children ignore each other. Not once in more than an hour have they said anything that might betray their professional interests. But Rita isn't impressed by my criticisms; she's reading an article about flat feet now. She's afraid Michele may have flat feet. She gets him to lie on his back and examines his soles, which only makes him giggle. To me they look like two nicely puffy bread rolls, and I decide it's time to take him down to the sea.

One can see why Italian mothers are not perhaps too unhappy about their husbands not being at the beach all day. By eleven o'clock the beach at Pescara has begun to take on a distinctly erotic feel of the variety that hardly encourages midlife monogamy. By eleven o'clock the adolescents have begun to arrive, and what can only be described as the serious sunbathers. Holding my toddler by the hand, I walk painfully slowly around a somewhat razzled mermaid, in a monokini that is no more than a thread of fluorescent green between tightly dark buttocks. Interestingly enough, she always comes with a fat elderly man, her grandfather perhaps, or perhaps not.

Upturned on his lounge bed, he is reading *La Gazzetta dello Sport* with not a trace of a smirk on his face. Summer is the transfer season, and one has to guess which players are going where.

Michele cries. The hot sand is burning his feet. I pick him up and carry him to the central path. On all sides now, amongst the shades, on the edge of deck chairs, sixteen- and seventeen-year-old girls are preening and preparing themselves for the solemn business of 'taking the sun'. They are local, Adriatic girls, smooth and darkly slim in what this year are brilliantly coloured costumes cut high on the thigh, though there is always the problem of changing costume from day to day, or even two or three times in the same day, so as to tan as low on the stomach and as high on the legs as possible.

I concentrate on keeping Michele's sunhat on, very aware that women and girls are all turning to look and smile, but not at me, no, at my golden little boy as he toddles blondly forward. For myself, I might as well be invisible. Children do this to you. Perhaps more so in Italy than elsewhere. Children are magnets for women's attention. I wouldn't be surprised if some unscrupulous fellows didn't use them the way others buy a fast car . . .

We break out of the sunshades into those twenty measured metres of empty sand before the sea. No doubt there is a regulation. And it's here that the action is, it's here that people come when they've had enough of their sunshades, when they can no longer just sizzle or chat or preen or read. The sand is beaten hard here, and there is even a metre or two that is darkly damp where the water laps. So you can walk with ease, and games can be played. Or really only one game, *tamburello*. For in Italy people are remarkable above all for their conformity, for all doing the same thing at the same time. The old folks stride by along the sea's edge, tummies toppling over tight costumes, the scars of their operations everywhere evident; the children rush into sheets of sparkling water; the mothers stand together on the shore to watch that they don't get far away, chatting to each other and occasionally shouting; while the adolescents, plus any able-bodied men who for some reason are not at work, or any women who for some reason do not have children, play *tamburello*.

If somebody is playing something else, then they are not Italian.

Tamburello is a game where, originally, you used a kind of wooden tambourine thing to hit a hard ball back and forth, but now you use a short, solid-plywood racket and a tennis ball. Of course, the ball isn't supposed to bounce, since it wouldn't come up from the sand. Which means you have to hit it hard . . . Ten or fifteen metres apart and parallel to the shoreline (to be on the flat), partners wham the thing at each other, scrambling about in the sand: pock, pock pock! The popularity of the game sometimes makes it tricky getting across this stretch of territory to the sea, especially with a young child. You wouldn't want him to be hit by a hurtling tennis ball or, even worse, by a young man diving with a swipe of wooden racket.

I make a significant detour round a pair of local boys slugging it out, then I sit Michele down at the sea's edge and proceed to dig out a little bathing pool for him. I must be about the only person doing this along five miles of busy beach, since this kind of heavy physical commitment does not form part of Italian beach-going traditions. Even Michele seems more inclined to watch than participate. Or he sits still staring at the glare of sky over sea, occasionally raising his arms, palms upward, as if in worship of that fantastically bright Mediterranean light. It's rather annoying when I am making the protestant effort to get involved and be a good father.

To my left as I dig, on a chair perched some two or three metres high at the top of a white stepladder contraption, the lifeguard in his red T-shirt is smoking a cigarette and likewise staring out to sea, though without Michele's rapture. Indeed, his attitude has discomfort and indecision written all over it; he can't seem to make up his mind which hand should cup his chin . . . Chatting on the sand below, and always ready to distract his attention, are two smooth young sirens; they have brightly coloured ties holding back raven hair, ankle bracelets, painted toenails. They giggle. They call to him mockingly, waiting for his descent, while he, a hefty healthy boy, gazes expressionless at the bathers. Summer affairs with the *bagnino*, the lifeguard and general dogsbody of the bathing station, are a staple of Italian beach mythology.

While Michele stamps about in a couple of inches of water, I take a break and watch the bathers. The previous summer, I remember, I had spent some weeks in the USA, where I visited a lake beach in New England. Here they had not one lifeguard but two, and for a much smaller area, since bathing was cordoned off to make sure people couldn't swim out into the distance and risk being torn to shreds by the richer folks with their motorboats. Doubtless this arrangement had much to do with American insurance laws and the genuine concern for safety such laws inspire. But all the same, as someone who loves to swim a distance rather than back and forth, I found the restriction depressing, especially since the rules were applied most rigidly, with whistles blown and arms waved and people screamed at and threatened with fines the moment they strayed from the fold.

At first glance, down on the beach at Pescara, the uninitiated might be led to believe that something of the same thing was going on. For only thirty feet out into the sandy wavelets a rusty pole emerges not quite vertical from the shallows and a notice on top announces: LIMITE DELLE ACQUE SICURE – end of safe water. To either side of the pole, a blue nylon rope sags between chunks of polystyrene to mark the line.

Suddenly a huge group of children are all rushing down to the water's edge. It's a *colonia,* a summer camp, and the children are being supervised by a not unattractive woman, in her early thirties, perhaps. The eight-to-ten-year-olds plunge into the shallow water, shoving and splashing each other and generally looking for fun and trouble. But '*Alt!*' screams the female voice. 'Not beyond *il limite delle acque sicure. Per l'amore di Dio!*' The poor children have to resign themselves to playing and fighting in water, which, at the line the blue rope traces, is barely more than two feet deep.

For the one thing I haven't told you about the geometry of the beach at Pescara is that some three hundred yards out to sea there is a series of huge breakwaters. Made up of great blocks of stone, they form humpy little islands of granite and weed and crabs. Each breakwater is diagonal to the land, though together they form a barrier parallel to the shore and arranged in such a way that the Adriatic's slow tide can bring sand in toward the beach, but can't take it out. The beach is thus getting bigger with every passing season, and the water shallower. When they put up that rusty warning, LIMITE DELLE ACQUE SICURE, God knows how long ago, it probably really meant something. Now you couldn't even drown a cat there. Hence, as so often in Italy, one finds oneself engaged with a system of rules or warnings that are now quite anachronistic. And the only positive thing one can say about this is that in general they're not enforced. Only the poor children of the *colonia* are forced to stay inside *il limite delle acque sicure*. Because here there are questions of supervision and insurance and responsibility. Everybody else simply ignores the leaning pole with its silly warning. Or children like to scrape up wet sand and throw it at the big red letters. And sometimes, rushing in or out of the water, or engaged in a splash fight, somebody will bang into it and hurt themselves. The pole is more dangerous than what it warns of.

The aeroplane with its advertisement flies back along the beach, and now the long strip of orange plastic reads OИIᗡOЯↃ. I have always wondered about the cost effectiveness of this kind of advertising.

The day passes. The sun is at the zenith. Sitting in the shallow water one casts no more than a sliver of a shadow. And it's too hot. Eventually I decide to do what Italian mothers do. I pick Michele up and wade out to sea. The mothers do this because a little further out across the water the iodine is even stronger, even more therapeutic. I just want to cool down.

Beyond the *colonia* and children fighting, when the bottom finally dips to four feet or so, there are very few people around, just a group of adolescents playing a watery game of volleyball, and then a man dredging for shells. He has a stout stick with a very large net at the end around a rigid semicircular frame. The flat part of the semicircle he pushes down into the sandy bottom to get at shells below the surface. He lifts the net. Michele is leaning out of my arms to see.

'Got anything?'

His old fat fingers sort rapidly through bits and pieces of weed and shell. His bald head is glowing with sunshine. By his side swings a battered old oilskin shoulderbag into which he occasionally slips something. He looks up. '*Che bellu citolo,*' he says, looking at Michele. '*Citolo*' means nothing at all to me, but he has that indulgent look older Italians inevitably reserve for the very young. It must be a local dialect. Reaching into another pocket he pulls out a tiny white whorl of a seashell and gives it to Michele. The baby's hand closes round it in that determined way babies have. '*'Azie,*' he says. For '*grazie*'.

The old man wades on. Some mornings I have seen him and others like him spend three or even four hours dredging the water, often right in amongst the children and the bathers. They take cockles and mussels home to make sauce for their pasta and their sons' and daughters' and grandsons' and granddaughters' pasta. Or the more enterprising will sell their harvest to the shops.

Then a voice is calling me. It's my father-in-law standing at the seashore. Rita has deserted the beach and gone shopping. '*Nonno!*' Michele cries. Grandfather!

Apparently he has been instructed to take over so that I can have a swim.

Carrying the boy back through the sunshades, I hear the cry of '*Cocco*' again. '*Cocco fresco!*' It makes you think how many people are weaving back and forth along this narrow stretch between land and sea: The coconut pedlar and a variety of immigrant trinket sellers, the old shellfishers, the aeroplane, the fatties looking for exercise, the asthmatics for air, back and forth, back and forth in beloved routine. For they will do exactly the same tomorrow. And the next day. And the next. '*Cocco!*' (The boy bangs his bucket, but my father-in-law isn't interested, already thinking of his *aperitivo* only half an hour away.) '*COCCO!*' And the aeroplane begins to drone again, joining a weft of sound and gesture over a warp of sharp colour.

Hurrying out to sea for my swim, it's suddenly very clear, the nature of this world my son is growing into: a world so regularly layered in its ranks of sunshades, its people, who are mothers with their children, or fathers out at work, or old men fishing, or lifeguards half-heartedly fighting off sirens, all without exception doing exactly what is expected of them. There's the neatly paved path, the stretch of hard sand (rushing head down between flying rackets this time), the fifty yards or so of milling children, the still water, and then beyond that the bastions of the whole thing, the outer wall of this geometric civilisation, those great stone breakwaters at their regular angles and intervals. I launch into a swim and clear them after ten minutes or so. A couple of men are sitting on top fishing, and a pedal-boat full of teenagers tips dangerously as the kids try to get onto the rocks without getting wet. On another rock, a boy is trying to do something with a girl . . .

But beyond the breakwaters, nothing. Never a swimmer out in the real sea with its long, slow swell. I swim a couple of hundred yards beyond the rocks. There are the marker buoys of a few crabbing pots, and on the horizon a ship of some kind. Further that way is, was, Yugoslavia with all that we know is happening there. Lying on my back, I can complacently reflect that Italy, for all its faults, must be one of the most civilised places in the world for a child to grow up. I shall write a book about it, I tell myself. Since that appears to be what people expect of me . . .

Prey-deek-torr

You think you will write a book, but then you think again. You delay. Years sometimes. The truth is I have always been suspicious of travel writing, of attempts to establish that elusive element which might or might not be national character, to say in sweeping and general terms, this place is like this, that place is like that. One always thinks: but I've met French people who weren't at all droll. Or: but I've been there and didn't find it at all romantic/squalid/interesting. Or worse still: how long has this author been there anyway? Two months, three? How can he possibly know anything deep about the place? How can he tell us anything more about it than the casual phenomena any traveller would notice, conversations in bars and things only half understood on the street. At which point it all becomes no more than an exercise in eloquent reportage, or like those novels by Dumas that speak so entertainingly of countries the author never visited.

When I arrived in Italy in 1981, more eager to escape friends and family and underachieve in peace than to go anywhere in particular, I swore I would never write about the place. There are so many books about Italy. Unpublished then, my only plan was to write one more novel before giving up and finding something sensible to do. I wasn't 'collecting material'.

And yet . . . places *are* different. Splendidly so. Perhaps that was something I hadn't fully appreciated then. And once one has discounted individual traits, class attitudes, generation gaps and, of course, the myriad manifestations of different personalities, still a substrate of national character does exist. The French *are* French somehow, the Germans are predictably German, the Italians, as I was slowly discovering, indisputably Italian. So that after I had been in this country – what, five years, six, seven? – rarely moving from the village where I lived, the small town of Verona where I worked, I gradually became aware of having all kinds of things to say and to tell that I couldn't put in any novel, or not the kind that I like to write. At that point, I only needed a publisher to come along and twist my arm, and there I was doing what I'd always said I wouldn't.

Still the question remained, how to get at this business of Italianness without falling into cliché, without merely appealing to what people already know? Perhaps this is not the kind of problem you can ever really put behind you, but the solution, so far as there was one, seemed to be to write only about those people and places I knew intimately, my neighbours, my street, my village, never to stray into the territory of the journalist, never to assume the eye of the traveller passing through. Which meant just the one travel book and then no more, I told myself as a sop to consistency, writing the last paragraphs of *Italian Neighbours*. After all, this was the only world I knew about in Italy. My condominium, my street. The only place I felt was really mine. What else would I ever write about here?

And then the following summer, floating in the Adriatic that morning with the way the southern sun heats up your brains even in deliciously cool water, it occurred to me that there was another world I knew here, or was getting to know: the world of children, my own boy, my neighbours' children, and, why not, the older children I have taught for years at the university. So one could write a book about that world and about everything peripheral to it: how it began, what it entails, where at some point it must end. And perhaps – the idea began to take on the urgency of a swift current tugging in the water, the obviousness of the sun's bright pressure on my closed eyes – yes, perhaps by the time we got to the last page of such a book, both the reader and, far more importantly myself, would have begun to understand how it happens that an Italian becomes Italian, how it turns out (as years later now it has turned out) that my own children are foreigners.

I swam back. The boy on the rocks had got his girlfriend to take her bra off, not imagining that anybody ever ventured beyond the breakwaters. Or perhaps not caring. In any event, I kept my head down, then had to look up again to avoid the gathering pedal-boats nearer the shore. I waded through the children from the *colonia*, bored with being in the water now but apparently not allowed to get out yet. They must spend a certain time in the water every day to get their iodine. Their mothers counted on it when they sent them there. As they likewise counted on the fact that they wouldn't drown. The attractive teacher was working hard inventing games that the children didn't want to play.

I hurried back to the sunshade, towelled down, returned all the beach clothes and toys and lotions and magazines to the bathing cabin, then joined my father-in-law for our *aperitivo.*

This is Mediterranean ritual at its lived and loved best. These are the times when I feel glad I came here. There is a big paved terrace shaded by a trellis of vines, a few video games mobbed by ten-year-olds, the majority straining to see over the shoulders of the few who have grabbed the action. There is a jukebox fed by a couple of adolescent girls in delightfully skimpy costumes and grinding out the inevitable summer songs: hoarse and husky voices in banally rhyming love. And there is lots of junk food to eat. Everybody has a *pizzetta* in their hands, a small round doughy pizza held in a couple of greasy napkins. My fat father-in-law, white sunhat tipped back on freckled baldness, puts one in Michele's eager hands, then sits back to enjoy his wine, his sausage meat stuffed with olives, and the spectacle of beautiful young people strutting and swaying back and forth from road to beach with next to no clothes on. Ah. These are our best moments together. We understand each other perfectly. The wine, then a cigarette perhaps. An extraordinary sense of well-being, the little boy relatively quiet for a change with his face full of pizza.

I tell my father-in-law about the book I plan to write. He's enthusiastic, says I should put in some stuff about how different childhood was in his time. When his father went to bed he used to put a pencil mark on the salami to show where it had been eaten up to, so that none of the ten children could chew on it during the night. Nobody had been feeding *him* pizzas at one and a half!

Like many Italians, my father-in-law has a genius for appearing hard-done-by. I point out to him that he has more than made up for this deprivation since. He laughs. The man is never in a better humour than when eating and drinking away from his womenfolk. He calls over a waitress, who, of course, knows him and all his likes and dislikes, and another plate of munchies is ordered, another couple of glasses of wine. Why not? When Michele finishes his *pizzetta* and begins to nag, Grandfather sticks a couple of tokens in his hand and tells him to go over to the motorised rocking horse. That nice girl there will put the money in for him. This gives the old man a chance to tip his hat at a tubby twelve-year-old and make all sorts of signs and gestures to get her to play babysitter. Michele toddles confidently away.

We are just settling into this summer bliss when my wife arrives. This, I must say, is most unusual. *Aperitivo* time in Pescara is supposed to be her break, when the men 'look after the child', buying, as Michele was quick to discover, his cooperation in every possible way. Perhaps she has come because today is the last day; tomorrow morning we will be driving back north to the oppressive heat of a Veronese summer.

Rita sits down smiling and, amazingly, does not scold us for having farmed the kid off to a little girl. I had been expecting the worst. Nor for smoking in his presence. Amazingly again, she orders not a glass of wine, but a *gingerino*: bittersweet, red, treacly, over-priced. She shouldn't drink alcohol, she says.

This is not like her. Generously, I ask if the shops were crowded.

She didn't go shopping, she said. Mamma, hers, is preparing *pasta e fagioli* for lunch. Pasta and beans. Not my favourite. And now she bursts out laughing. She left the beach to check her *predictor*, she says. And it was positive.

Her what? I haven't understood because she's pronounced the word Italian fashion – *preydeektorr* – as she must when speaking Italian to her father.

Her *predictor*. She switches accent. And slowly it dawns. My father-in-law, when he understands, is aghast. This is a big mistake. What about Rita's career? Big families are decidedly a thing of the past. Nobody can afford more than one child now. Do we want to be putting marks on the salami again, the wine bottles? Etc., etc. My book is set back six years or so . . .

Contro corrente

'Pregnancy,' Dr Maroni says with a solemn smile, 'is not a pathology.'

Dr Maroni, later forced into retirement and investigated for criminal neglect, is clearly *contro corrente*, very much against the swim of things.

'Pregnancy is not an illness,' he insists. 'Childbirth is the most natural thing in the world.'

In order to prepare the mothers, and incidentally the fathers, for this extremely natural event, he proposes to teach them a method of self-hypnosis that will allow them to blank out their minds and let the body's normal and natural animal functions have their way. Underlining the substantial scientific underpinning to what he teaches, he mentions French and Russian experts, American research centres. Such references score highly in an insecure country that doesn't quite believe it could itself be responsible for any major scientific discovery. Or not these days.

The young men and women, arm in nervous arm on awkward chairs, are impressed.

Yes, considerable research on the extent to which contractions can or cannot be consciously controlled has been carried out in California, Dr Maroni explains. He speaks in great technical detail, and always with an extravagant and tubby smile, of all the various chemical and physiological changes that take place during child-birth, the extraordinary fact that the child's head is actually wider than the space it has to pass through, the importance therefore of the screw effect caused by the child's turning in the birth canal, the consequent danger that the umbilical cord will become twisted around his or her neck.

This is the wonderful mechanism, he smiles, that God and nature have devised for bringing us into this world. And above all it is *perfectly natural*.

To me, sitting in a row of pregnant mothers, the whole thing begins to seem more and more frightening. The word 'natural' after all can very appropriately be applied to such phenomena as earthquakes, volcanoes, and, most commonly, death.

Dr Maroni is a big man, bulky, heavy breathing, but with a hypnotic voice. Relax, he tells his middle-class audience when he has got them properly scared: what we are experiencing is the tension caused by the conscious mind's awareness of danger, our unnatural intellectual awareness of a natural process; this blocks what would otherwise be the body's natural reactions and so provokes the very danger it has imagined and seeks to avoid. What we have to do then is to re-learn a primitive innocence.

He begins his autogenous training. The tone is oddly biblical: 'Let each one of us say unto ourselves: I am relaxed, I am serene, I am calm, I am at peace . . .'

We are in a small, institutionally spare room of square-backed chairs and posters inviting women to have their breasts examined for cancer, or to get themselves tested for AIDS, or to discuss their marital difficulties. For this is Verona's Consultorio Familiare. '*Vieni, donna,*' says a huge poster, '*vieni al consultorio.*' Come woman, come to the clinic. The abrupt rhetoric reminds me of those dull programmes one occasionally tunes into on the BBC World Service, where well-spoken announcers talk worthily about educating peasant folk in the Third World. Notably, there is no publicity for contraceptives. Nor abortion. The Pope will have his sops.

'Let each one of us say unto ourselves, I am at peace, there is nothing I need to think about, there is nothing irritating me, nothing I need to do . . .'

Everybody closes their eyes and sets about this impossible business of relaxing. Above their bowed heads, the Madonna presides, a small, rather gaudy ceramic on the wall to the doctor's left. Like most modern Italian mothers, she has had (in the Catholic version of the story) only one child, and, as we are being advised, she opted for the most natural of births: simple surroundings, the freedom to adopt any position felt to be desirable. The light, in particular, one imagines, despite the extravagant star, must have been kept fairly low. (Dr Maroni has let us know of his enormous contempt for the bright neon used in most hospital delivery rooms, which he believes makes a baby's arrival into the world unnecessarily traumatic, like being woken by a searchlight.) Joseph, of course, does not appear in the ceramic. If he was present and supportive at the birth, as a good modern husband should be, he certainly did the disappearing trick later. As likewise the real father. But this again is more or less the norm in Italy. I know of very few men here who have actually changed many soiled swaddling clothes. And I envy them.

The doctor, who always makes a point of letting us know that he is not paid for his evangelical encouragement of a return to nature, has an immensely hypnotic, self-assured, complacent voice: 'Let each of us say unto ourselves, I am the skin on my fingertips, the softer flesh beneath, the wrinkles over my knuckles, the veins on the back of my hands . . .'

The game is to concentrate on various parts of the body, minutely, one by one, and relax them. I concentrate, and, as is my way when I concentrate, grow more conscious and, if possible with all the coffee I drink, more tense.

'Let each of us imagine,' says the doctor's slow, sage voice, 'that we are entering our own bodies through our vaginas. First the outer lips open, then the redder inner lips. There, we are now inside the vagina. We have reached the neck of the uterus. We are entering our own wombs where our baby swims in his amniotic fluid . . .'

It's at moments like this that I can't help wondering at the good doctor's insistence that the husbands must attend these sessions. Unable to relax my uterus, I decide to concentrate on the bizarre grammar deployed to achieve some of the effects he is after, imagining literal translations of the variety: Let each of us reflect to ourselves on how much to us changes the cutaneous surface passing from the smooth dark of the groin to the swelling rough and hair of the pubic zone . . .

There's the click of somebody's cassette recorder reaching the end of its tape. The doctor's voice is raised a little in obvious irritation. He hates interruptions, especially when the spell is approaching its climax: '*Ecco*, we are entering the womb to embrace our own tiny *bambino*, who is part of us and not part of us. We are at one with our *bambino* who is at one with us . . .'

A little later and we are more chastely located inside our lungs. Indeed, we *are* our lungs and our whole being is no more and no less than the rhythm of our breathing. He lets this continue for some time, the voice becoming more and more soporific, while at the same time he occasionally snaps his fingers to see if we respond with that small instinctive intake of breath that betrays the breathing of sleep, or hypnosis. Noticeably, my wife responds perfectly. Then he wakes us up with a clap of his hands.

How had we fared, he asks.

Into the inevitable embarrassed silence that attends such occasions, Rita says that she has no problem achieving this super-relaxed state when she comes to these sessions and indeed when she practises on the sofa at home as he suggests, but that when she actually gave birth the first time she was unable to do so. This is why she is repeating the course, because she feels it would be useful, if only she could do it at the crucial moment when it was required.

There is a sharp intake of breath around us that has nothing to do with sleep now: partly because the idea of having a second child is so momentous in contemporary Italy as to be seen, depending on your orientation, either as a form of conspicuous consumption or as a Catholic rebuke to those who are clearly not doing what the Pope says they should, and partly because her experience appears to challenge the authoritative, almost authoritarian doctor's claims that his training will prove invaluable at the dramatic moment.

Dr Maroni has a way of twiddling his thumbs while smiling in an avuncular, slightly priestly fashion. He asks her what exactly she felt went wrong. She describes the appalling back pains she experienced, the terrible contractions, then the feeling of desolation in the small and rather shabby *sala travaglio*, the labour room.

'Was your husband there?'

'Yes, but in the end a pain is a pain,' she says, rather too ambiguously it seems to me.

The doctor will not stop smiling, his face all reassurance. 'It's a question of practice,' he says. 'Practice, practice, practice . . .' I fervently hope my wife won't feel she needs to repeat events of this kind ad infinitum until she has mastered the technique.

Then a voice from the back asks the question that is uppermost on everybody's mind: is it true that there is no *sala rianimazione* at the doctor's small provincial hospital, no intensive care unit, and no facility for immediate heart surgery on the newborn child in the event of this being necessary?

The doctor frowns. After stressing the naturalness of childbirth this is not the kind of question he wanted to hear, but to duck it would be to lose almost his entire following. There wouldn't be another birth in his hospital for the next hundred years. In the event of an emergency, he says, and it is costing him some effort now to maintain his smile, there is a helicopter at the hospital of Borgo Trento in Verona that can be at his hospital in approximately five minutes and back at Borgo Trento in a further five. Since it takes at least forty minutes to set up an operating theatre and find the necessary surgeons for a delicate operation, the baby is thus just as safe being born out of town as in the centre. If not safer, since there they tend to induce birth with a drip and use every technological barbarity to impose their will on this natural event, rather than simply letting it happen. Not to mention those fierce lights when the baby emerges . . .

While many further questions are asked about the nature of muscle contractions and its relation to breathing, about diet, about the value of red lighting and low music and nice soft double beds in the delivery room, it's clear that what most people in the group are meditating upon as the evening draws to a close are those crucial seconds when somebody decides to call the emergency service at Borgo Trento, when somebody else has to start a helicopter engine, when doctors have to rush out onto the dark tarmac in the cold night air with a tiny newborn child in their arms . . .

Because for Italians pregnancy is, inescapably, a pathology, and childbirth its crisis and resolution. The lengths Dr Maroni has to go to convince us to the contrary can only serve as confirmation. His is a voice crying in the wilderness, defining the wilderness for those who hadn't noticed it. The couples we met at his little sessions used him the way some people use homeopathic medicines: as a sort of fashionable and politically correct addition to the real thing, but not a basket one would seriously consider putting very many eggs in. And if the man is under investigation now for neglect, which I am sure he is not guilty of, it can only be because somebody who had a sad experience is convinced, and was probably always convinced, that childbirth should only take place in the centre of a huge concentration of technological resources and expertise. If it went okay for the Madonna in her stable that was merely because she was delivering the son of God. After all, she never tried again, did she? To those conceived by more orthodox methods the state owes every possible logistical support (as afterwards it owes every child an education, medical care, a steady job, a pension, TV entertainment and a funeral). Nowhere could a nation's determination to forget the precariousness of its peasant past and embrace the protective mystique of modern science be more evident than in Italian attitudes to childbirth . . . after which infancy may be seen as a long and carefully guarded period of convalescence.

Facciamo le corna

Contrary to popular belief, then, the Italian child is not born into a splendid world of spontaneity, fun and sensual delight, but into a tight space of immense caution, inhibition, and a suffocating awareness of everything, but everything, that can go wrong.

Not to mention how much it will all cost.

It was thus that I was persuaded, by solemn neighbours and employers, and of course my concerned father-in-law, that if I insisted on having a second child (folly became madness when we arrived at a third), the time had come for me to take the whole question of insurance more seriously. My accountant agreed, remarking that in terms of tax relief I would save only the equivalent of about twenty-five pounds a year by having another bundle of joy (there is no Child Benefit in Italy). He pointed out the advantages of being able to reduce my taxable income by the few million lire I would pay into an insurance scheme, and he recommended, as Italians in their eagerness to do favours always will, someone I could go to: an agent, Ragioniere Nascimbeni. Since Nascimbeni means 'well-born' I decided to take this as a good omen.

I telephoned Ragioniere Nascimbeni. Generally, it is not easy to make appointments in Italy, since it is important for the person offering a service to appear to be extremely busy, and hence successful. Any shortcomings in the service, in terms of slowness, will thus seem to be a guarantee of its qualities. I have even had a courier service in Verona tell me that they cannot come to pick up a package for forty-eight hours because they are so busy, and of course they are so busy because they are so fast. It seems pointless arguing with such logic. Nascimbeni, however, and to his immense credit, must be one of the most amenable men in the world. He was extremely, yes, extremely busy, there was simply no point in my going to his office where he was 'under an avalanche of work', but he would come to our house immediately he had finished for the day. Yes, that very evening. Would nine-thirty be too late? I was suitably impressed.

Ragioniere Nascimbeni (*ragioniere* means accountant, or more precisely, someone who has completed the kind of high school that concentrates most of all on accountancy. It does not mean that the person in question is a full-blooded accountant, since that would entail a university degree which would confer the more enviable *Dottore*. *Ragioniere* is thus the least impressive of those titles – *Ingegnere, Avvocato, Architetto, Professore,* etc. – that Italians like to place before their names to confer a little importance and pomposity, in this case so little importance and so hollow a pomposity that one feels it might be wiser not to draw attention to the fact at all) . . .

Ragioniere Nascimbeni arrives right on time. I buzz him in and stand outside the door at the top of the marble stairs to guide him to the right apartment. He comes up with an unusual clatter, a curious, rolling gait. I watch with interest as he attacks the first flight, disappears, then sways into view on the second. By the time I'm face to face with him at the top of the fourth, I'm beginning to appreciate why this man is genuinely so busy and successful in his field: he is himself a walking advertisement for just how much can go wrong in life, the perfect contradiction of the happy providence suggested by his name. One look at Nascimbeni and you *know* you need insurance. And perhaps he comes to your house, rather than seeing you from behind his desk in town, just to remind you how difficult it can be for a man to climb stairs, to cross a room, to find a comfortable chair.

I said 'walking advertisement', but I should have said 'lurching'. Nascimbeni has the built-up shoe of the polio victim. He throws his limp leg forward, leaning on it only when it is rigidly straight, bringing round his good leg as rapidly as possible. The impression is of someone negotiating a ship's deck in a storm. His eyes behind thick glasses squint severely. Every few seconds he blows his nose, breathing hard.

'Bella zona,' he says automatically of the dusty street outside, *'bella palazzina, bell'apartamento. Molto bello.'* His voice is nasal, obstructed, adenoidal. We offer him the sofa, but he would prefer to sit at a table. His leg isn't comfortable on sofas. Not the right position. Then he must take notes, of course. Yes, the kitchen table is fine. 'Many a

family I go where the kitchen table is the only surface to write on,' he laughs. No, he can't accept a coffee, his blood pressure is too high. Got to be careful. Had to have a bypass last year. Looking at him carefully, he doesn't look a day over forty. The baldness is premature.

'Bene, allora?' He has pulled out a notebook, a series of brochures, an impressive pocket computer. He puts his hands together in a pantomime gesture of attentiveness. Every few seconds a tic obliges him to twist his neck to the right, together with a slight down-and-up rotation.

I explain that we are about to have our second child, and we thought . . .

'Però!' He exclaims, which is as much as to say, Who would have thought – what courage! *'Complimenti, Signora,'* he adds to Rita, smiling generously and blowing his nose.

Then he begins to expound his various life insurance schemes. The point is, hmm, with my still being so young, hmm that if, he hesitates, if . . . He hesitates again, he looks at me across the kitchen table, squinting, smiling, 'Yes, if anything should, er, *happen* to you . . .' Immediately he says this he lifts both hands from the table and makes two fists but with the forefingers and little fingers protruding and pointing upwards. 'If anything should happen to you – *facciamo le corna* – it's likely to be an, er, accident – *facciamo le corna* – rather than, er, an illness. Isn't it?'

Facciamo le corna, literally tranlated ('let's make the horns') refers to his gesture of the closed fists with pointing fingers at each side. For some reason this is supposed to ward off evil luck. One might make it, for example, when seeing a hearse pass, or when contemplating the possibility of one's favourite football team losing a big match, or just at the mention, during dinner table conversation, of some normally unmentionable disease (pregnancy?). Ragioniere Nascimbeni must combine expression and gesture, often simultaneous with the tic that twists his neck to one side, about a hundred times a day . . .

'Yes, I mean the most common cause of, er, yes, decease, among men of your age, is a road accident, *facciamo le corna.*'

And he does. The fingers point quite automatically but always eloquently from his two fists, accompanied by an apologetic smile. He is trying to explain to me, it seems, that it would be wise for me to take out a special kind of policy that would pay out very large amounts if *something happens to me*, above all in my car, and rather less, or at least in the early years, if I die a natural (that word again) death. But I am so mesmerised by his constant *corna* punching the air across the table that I'm finding it hard to concentrate. Without thinking, I ask, 'And do they pay out if it's the result of drinking?'

'What?'

'If I'm drinking and driving. Or, I don't know, if I didn't have my safety belt on and should have. Would they pay just the same?'

He looks at me with the concern of someone whose job is to be understanding but who finds this difficult when he hasn't understood. It's something to do with my being a foreigner perhaps. Then he gets it. He laughs. '*Per carità*, nobody ever *checks* whether anybody's been drinking and driving when there's an accident! *O dio, no.*' Then he frowns. 'Actually the insurance companies are presently taking the government to court precisely *because* they don't enforce the drink-driving law. But not so that they can avoid paying out. Oh no no no, *per l'amore di Dio*. But because if the government did enforce the law, there would be fewer accidents, there would be fewer sad occasions on which they were obliged to pay out . . .'

'Ah.'

'Now, where were we, yes, accidents. Hmm. Yes, so if, on the other hand,' he picks up his thread, 'if you should, er, be, er, be disabled in some way – *facciamo le corna naturalmente* – then the . . .'

Smiling, Rita intervenes. He doesn't need to beat around the bush so much and keep making his *corna*. We know that insurance is about illness and death. We just want the appropriate coverage for the children. We're doing this for the children.

Ragioniere Nascimbeni squints at her through his thick glasses, then relaxes. He has a round, pleasant face, rounder still for that receding hairline. He seems relieved. There are many houses he goes to, he explains, where people actually get angry if he even uses the word death, because they think it can bring them bad luck. He blows his nose. It is almost the hardest part of his job, he says earnestly. Blowing his nose yet again, he apologises that he suffers from allergies, against which, it seems, one cannot insure.

Much cheered by our non-superstitious attitude, he now proceeds more brutally. Yes, my most likely death would be in a car accident, though he can't imagine that I drink and drive, ha ha, hmm, anyway, no, in the event of such an accident, I, or rather, he laughs apologetically, no, my wife or children, would receive exactly, under this particular policy, four times the amount I would get by death from illness. Good. Well, if one accepts this kind of policy there is no need for a medical. If one wants a larger amount for death by illness, then one has to accept a medical. He looks up sadly: 'Not because we imagine you are trying to trick the company, already having an illness and not saying anything, but just in case, *facciamo le corna*, you have a condition without being aware of it.'

Holding back my laughter, I ask him if he has children, and if so what provision he has made. I do this because an article in *Il Sole 24 Ore*, the financial paper, once suggested that the best way to deal with any investment or insurance agent is to ask them how they behave. They know all the best deals. Nascimbeni, however, shakes his head. He and his wife long ago decided that children were too risky a business. Too many things can happen. But having said this very solemnly, he suddenly becomes aware that it could be understood as foreseeing bad luck for ourselves. Rita comes to his rescue. '*Facciamo le corna*,' she says. Out spring her forefinger and little finger. I'm stifling laughter. And at exactly the same moment Michele begins to cry in the other room – furiously, a great bloodcurdling yell. Nascimbeni comes out with a nervous cough, as if to suggest that our irreverence might somehow be responsible. He blows his nose again and, as my wife goes off to get the boy, begins to talk about a saving scheme for children. One of the major problems with children, and again he deprecates the fact that he always has to be imagining problems, is that when they get to eighteen or so one has to pay for their university education, which could last what, five, six, even seven years, and then help them to set up home when they get married, buy an apartment and so on. Well, by paying a fairly modest amount monthly into an entirely tax-free investment fund, one can be sure that come their eighteenth birthday . . .

'Nobody bought me an apartment,' I remark. 'We don't own this one.'

'No, of course not, me neither.' Nascimbeni twists his neck to one side and smiles. He looks about him, apparently appreciatively, at the window fittings, the quality of the tiles, the workmanship. 'Perhaps you should buy it now. Or another apartment.' He hesitates. 'I mean home ownership is the only way really to insure yourself against, er, against the event of eviction, which with young children, of course, would be, er, disastrous. Anyway, if you did want to buy a house, I would certainly be willing to help you with the mortgage . . .'

Rita walks through the room with Michele in her arms and takes him out through the French window onto the balcony. The cool evening air will calm him down. Outside on the street children are kicking a ball at each other, standing to one side every time a car races past. Not a situation, I imagine, that Nascimbeni would wish to contemplate. Except in business terms.

'And house insurance,' the agent continues. 'In fact, there's one very interesting policy that might be of use to you now, in the sense that it covers not only against damage to household belongings, but any damage your children might do to somebody else, or their property. Imagine, for example, that your little boy, when he's a bit older, was to push that basil plant off the balcony so it fell on somebody's head. They could then sue you for damages, something this policy would cover, and the wonderful thing about it is that the premium remains the same however many children you have, so . . .'

When he has gone, we roll about on the bed laughing and *facendo le corna* at all the possible things that could go wrong, a satellite falling on our apartment, the leaning Tower of Pisa collapsing precisely the day we go up, etc. Until it occurs to me that *fare le corna* can also mean to betray one's spouse (in the same way that, in Elizabethan English, horns were supposed to be visible, to the eye of faith, on a cuckold's forehead). *Facciamo le corna* could thus mean, let's betray your (or my) partner, and people here actually say: 'Yes, so and so is away again, no doubt putting horns on her poor husband . . .' Though one could hardly accuse poor Nascimbeni of having meant this double entendre. On the other hand, it is an eventuality against which no meaningful insurance cover can be offered. As with almost all the serious things in life.

I remember some years later the shock of recognition when, upon warning young Michele that by the time we got to the *pasticceria* there might not be any chocolate croissants left, he raised his two chubby fists, shot out forefinger and pinkie, and earnestly declared, '*Facciamo le corna, Papà!*'

Casa

Nascimbeni's comments on house buying had not fallen on stony ground. As part of the obsession with security that manifests itself in tall iron fences defending bristling vegetable patches, prescriptions for every medical test under the sun and an instinctive fear of any food that does not form part of the traditional national diet, it has become a generally acknowledged truth in Italy that a couple should not embark upon a family until they own the bricks and mortar they live in. Perhaps this has to do with the fact that the language makes no distinction between the idea of house, the physical place, and home, the emotional base. Both are contained in the word *casa*, as if the family didn't really exist apart from the physical place where its various components meet. *In gioia e in lutto la casa è tutto*, says the proverb – In joy and in grief, the home is chief.

As feckless foreigners (not being from the Veneto, Rita, though Italian, was considered a foreigner), we had been able to ignore this craving for ownership on the production of our first child. Indeed, we had caused some surprise by having a child not only while renting, but while renting in precarious circumstances, in furnished property, and without the proper contract and strict rent control enjoyed by most tenants. But in the end we were not immune. The desire to have our children safely tucked up in a house that was home – *casa*, in short – finally got to us. The second pregnancy marked the house-buying adventure. Thus was our second child born into a world of maximum stress in order that she be safe. What could be more appropriate by way of initiation?

Through the summer months after that Pescara holiday, Rita and I walked the length and breadth of the village and various other villages, pushing little Michele in his MacClaren buggy, which sells in Italy with the added extra of a sunshade on a flexible pole, something fussy mothers adjust this way and that at every corner they turn. We walked back and forth along the slalom of Montecchio's main road, the crumbling façades and demotic brickwork of the older village, the more ordered and boring streets of recent developments, in search of property to buy.

When one thinks of London's suburbs, with a FOR SALE sign on every third or fourth house and at least one estate agent in every row of shops, it seems that a search of this variety should not be too difficult. But in all the years I've been in Italy, while the housing market in the UK has gone through the roof and then under the floor, I think I can safely say that property here has always been a seller's market, so greedily is it desired, so rarely sold once gained, so much money have the middle classes accumulated by avoiding tax and hoarding the high-yield bonds the government is forced to issue in its inability, or unwillingness, to collect.

In short, there was nothing for us to buy. Not that there weren't empty apartments. Every now and then we would be advised to enquire after this or that uninhabited flat. But in the event it had always been promised to a son, a daughter, niece or nephew, marrying in a year's time, in two, in three. And the refrain was always the same: *bisogna fare sacrifici per i figli* – one has to make sacrifices for one's children. One has to buy them a flat and keep it empty for whenever they may be ready to use it. Sometimes it seems the whole Italian property market is frozen in indulgent expectation of the next generation, who will move into the home prepared for them at precisely the moment when they're expected to produce the next generation again.

No, the only way to buy a house, our friends advised, was to buy a place that didn't exist yet. To buy new, maybe to buy cooperative.

We push Michele's buggy through the broken terrain and rubble of what was once the cherry orchard at the bottom of our street to arrive at Stefano and Marta's new house on a cooperative housing project. They're old friends, former language students; I just bought his nearly new Opel as he moved up-market to a very serious Passat Estate. The wealth implied by this switch and by the fact that he runs a successful accounts consultancy, and again by the impeccably dapper way this little man dresses, makes it difficult for me to understand why he went for the cooperative option. Is it just a question of its cheapness, of the low tax rate, of the Italian belief that interest, when you're paying it rather than getting it, is theft? I'm intrigued.

To buy cooperative you join a group of people who have been allotted a particular piece of land designated for cheap housing. A builder is engaged and a price for the project fixed. Building starts when everybody has paid a certain amount and continues in fits and starts depending on everybody's ability to pay until completion, if you're lucky, not more than a year or two late.

But there are all kinds of rules that make the proposition less than attractive. One has to have been resident in the area concerned for a certain period; one must agree not to sell the house for ten years; one cannot easily drop out once the project is under way. Then the house itself cannot be more than a certain size, there is a limit to the area and the number of bathrooms, etc., and a large number of houses must be fitted into the land allotted.

Stefano and Marta's house stands in a terrace and has three (low) floors with a garage beneath. Since the terrace is back to back with another terrace, all the light must come from one north-facing façade. But the stucco outside is a deep salmon pink and the guttering is all in bright copper – expensive – while inside Stefano didn't accept any of the materials stipulated by the builder when he fixed the price, because in that case the fittings would have been the same down-market trash as in everybody else's house. No, the entire ground floor of Stefano and Marta's house, we discover, is paved in Tuscan *cotto*, a beautiful rust-red matte-finish tile, set off just here and there by the odd Persian rug.

The apparent modesty involved in buying cooperative turns out to be only apparent. In the event, not one of the purchasers on this project accepted the standard materials in the contract. Though none, Stefano has a satisfied smile, have installed his wonderful *cotto* . . .

When we get inside we appreciate why. There's consternation in the air. *Cotto*, unlike regular ceramics, stains; and the workers, Marta explains, holding their own little boy in her arms, the workers who installed the antique stone fireplace that is, must have brought some pasta with them and eaten it sitting on the floor. 'Look here.' She shows us where a few strands of pasta have left a definite dark scribble on a tile right by the fireplace. For an expert it might even be possible to tell whether they were eating lasagnette or tagliatelle. Stefano and Marta's *cotto* is thus ruined even before they can begin to enjoy it.

'Isn't Beppe bound to drop things?' I ask of their little boy, wriggling to be out of mother's arms. 'Food and all? Then there'll be more stains. God knows, Michele throws his food around enough.'

'Not on the *cotto*,' the child's mother says confidently. Instinctively, Rita picks up Michele who was struggling to get out of his buggy.

For although people here must have a house in order to give their children security, it is certainly not with an eye to offering the little fellows freedom. Just as later they will give them the money to go to university, and give it to them for as many years as it takes, five perhaps, perhaps even ten, but not let them choose what they are going to study. They must study economics and business. They must study engineering. If the remarkable social stability of provincial Italy can be an enviably decorous thing, it is not bought cheap.

Stefano is a chubby-faced man who invariably displays a corpulent gravitas, just occasionally belied by a dimpling cheerfulness about salt-and-pepper moustaches. But this pasta stain has got the better of him. Grimly tugging his moustache, he warns us that we are bound to face something of the same problem, whatever kind of house we buy. 'Because Italian workers are simply imbeciles.' And he shows us what happened to his designer switches. They are lovely big matte-black switches in a matte-black frame, very handsome, silk-finished, and with a splendid soft click when you turn them on and off. More than a hundred thousand lire each, it seems, but of course one only buys these things once in one's life . . . Anyway, they come with a protective adhesive sheet over them which is supposed to be left on until *after* the whitewashing is completed. Instead, Stefano complains, the fool took the protective plastic off as soon as he'd installed the switches, and the idiot *imbianchino*, the whitewasher, for all houses are whitewashed, didn't notice and just sprayed the whole lot with his machine. As a result, although Stefano has now managed after patient hours to get the paint off the flat surface, when you turn on a switch, the part that comes slightly outward can be seen to have a white edge to it – *ecco*, there! – which is most unsightly.

Isn't it?

I have to stoop to notice the offence, a hairline frosting on the deep silky black. Instinctively I know that I will never be able to reach such standards. I will never be modern enough or Italian enough to care about a small stain on a tile or a smudge of paint on a switch. Thus I will never really face the dilemma that confronts most contemporary Italian parents: how can I be an obsessive anal hedonist in a restricted space and at the same time spoil my children rotten. One partial answer, of course, is to have only one child.

Young Beppe wriggles even harder to be away. Marta, petite to the point of seeming packaged, complains that he has already put fingermarks on the fresh whitewash. When we look round, clutching Michele so tight he screams, and say, no, the place looks dazzlingly white, we are told that they have all been carefully wiped off. She has found that if you use a dry cloth and . . .

When I ask Stefano for a few more details about these sizing restrictions for *case cooperative*, he puts on his gravest face and takes me upstairs to show me a tiny bathroom. ''*Orribile*, no? Far too small. But,' he knocks on the wall and just fleetingly his cheeks dimple in a smile, 'behind here there is an empty space. As soon as the inspectors are gone we can pull down this wall and put in a proper bath.' His face has rediscovered its serious mask: '*Sai com'è?*' he says almost apologetically – You know how it is? – and what he means is, this is the kind of subterfuge the state reduces us to. Except you can see he loves it, really. And I imagine him saying the same thing to all his clients when they present their tax problems. *Sai com'è?* Meaning, of course we all know how bad things are, but I can sort out your problems for you. Suddenly I understand why he bought cooperative. It was not quite in order to save, though he has saved something, nor quite in order to surround himself in luxury, though he has bought some beautiful fittings: no, it was to bask in what luxury he has *in defiance of all the rules*, in the teeth of government provisions. It makes the pleasure so much sweeter.

We retreat down the stairs, a cramped spiral of polished stones that Stefano chose himself, he explains, for the way their olive-green colour contrasts with the dark wood of the banister. To me it seems the whole thing is designed for children to fall and break their necks down.

Back on the *cotto* by the fireplace, Beppino has finally been released . . . into a baby pen.

We drink a glass of wine together on a polished granite table top, admiring the fitted kitchen, the halogen lighting sunk in the ceiling. There is some talk about the relative performances of the Opel and the new Passat, which Stefano believes is extremely stylish, while Marta complains it looks like a hearse. But of course there is nothing mutually exclusive in Latin culture about funerals and style. Everybody turns to look at the huge black thing through the kitchen window. First there's a tiny garden surrounded by stout iron railings, then this great gleaming piece of German technology, then a wasteland of mud and discarded building materials. I ask when they're likely to put in the road and the pavements. It's been a while now, hasn't it? Stefano sighs. The gravitas again. One of the things you have to put up with when you buy cooperative, he explains, is that the local council, rather than the builders, are responsible for the road and pavements. So, who knows? He makes a gesture of resignation. *'Sai com'è?'* And this time his favourite expression means There's no way round this one.

Five years after that conversation there is still no pavement outside the cherry orchard cooperative. But I had already decided to find some less exhausting way of buying.

Mella

It is not common to see Italian men pushing kids' buggies around the streets. If they are doing so, it will be in the company of their wives, usually with a slightly bent and beaten posture, waiting to be free. For a writer, on the other hand, the fact that a kid is making too much noise and your wife is busy with some translation or other, gives you an excuse for a walk. And you can always say you're heading off to look at some new house-building project.

You strap the little fellow into the buggy, get out into the street and start fooling with the sunshade. It's August, the heat is overpowering and above all sultry. In his buggy Michele strains this way and that, little hands clasping for a butterfly – brown and purple – then a hornet. I try to discourage him. A big, somehow shiny boy, blond and pink, he has a round pork-pie face and almost Michelin arms of white lard, which he clasps tight to his chest for fear of the sunbaked metal of the buggy's struts. Rita would have remembered to tie a towel round them.

Walking towards the village alongside the flood-overflow ditch, I see a snake raise its head and move rapidly through the ivies on top of the wall. I try to point it out to the boy, swinging the buggy round, insisting on the direction. But he can't see. The snake rustles quickly through the ivy and disappears. Then a great green lizard darts off a stuccoed wall, quick as a thought lost before it surfaced, certainly too quick for a two-year-old. It's one aspect of Italy that can hardly be affecting him – yet.

What he can see though are the madly racing cars, and to every changing note of acceleration and deceleration round the tight curves of the village streets he responds with a furious 'brum-brum' between fat lips. The words he most enjoys at the moment are 'Alfa Trenta-Tre'. He repeats them lovingly despite considerable difficulty with the 'r's, and what he's referring to, of course, is the smartly designed Alfa 33, a bright red version of which always sits right here outside the greengrocer's.

'Alfa Tenta Re!' Michele shouts. He strains against the buggy's safety belt.

Loading up cases of fruit against the wall, Salvatore, who owns the place, laughs and pulls the boy's cap over his eyes, and gives him a peach to eat. Rather than saying thank you, Michele twists in his seat to gaze back at this car he has unaccountably fallen in love with, 'Alfa Renta Te!' When I try to adjust the sunshade, the pole is sticky with peach juice.

Then, in the supermarket, they haven't got the thirty lire change, so they give Michele a sweet. '*Che caro!*' the two girls at the tills say. What a darling! Serena at the far desk slips off her chair to come round and get a proper look and ruffle his blonde hair. They have a little supply of sweets by the supermarket tills to cover the change when it gets down under fifty lire, since nobody bothers with the smaller coins, or is even sure whether they're current any more. But even when the change is right, the girls still give the sweets away to little children. They like to be nice, to think perhaps of the moment when they will finally be leaving the supermarket to have a child themselves. So now, as well as having a *caramella* in his mouth, Michele gets another to clutch in his hand. I try to protest. His teeth, his sugar levels . . . Serena says that her sister feeds her little baby spoonfuls of sugar. It's good for children. Since her own teeth are unashamedly grey, I can't even make the remark about it being good for dentists, too.

In the centre of the village I walk fairly fast and don't always let people catch my eye. That way I'm only stopped, what, three times . . . *'Che bel butin! Che boceto! Che biondin!'* The elderly ladies use little dialect words to express their affection. Babies are public property. They tweak his nose and pinch his cheeks. And if the boy doesn't get a sweet in the newsagent's, it's only because I manage to spirit the thing away with my copy of the local paper and the obligatory *Io e il mio bambino*. Meanwhile, a girl is kissing him and putting his cap straight and feeling how chubby his knees are. Clearly it is quite wonderful being an infant in Italy, so much so that one fears nothing will ever be quite so good again . . .

I hurry the buggy along the street in search of some shade and play space. Piazza Buccari, the main square, has two small patches of dry grass with a patch of cracked asphalt between and an oval pool with marble surrounds in the middle. Released, Michele scurries straight across to stuff his fingers in the nozzles that send hoops of water from one side of the pool to the other. Safe in the knowledge that his mother cannot see him, I settle down to the papers.

There's an article about an electronic pocket rosary invented by a certain Pasquale Silla, Rector of the Sanctuary of Divine Love in Rome, a fascinating device with a *misteri* button to select the desired mysteries and then an *Ave Maria* button to call up the appropriate prayers on a tiny liquid crystal screen: the invention is highly recommended for children.

Io e il mio bambino, on the other hand, has a long correspondence about prejudice against baby girls. One letter remarks that whenever a boy is born people say, *È nato un maschio* – it's a male – but when a girl is born they say, *È nata una bella bambina* – it's a nice little girl – adding the 'nice' to make people feel better.

Frankly, with one *maschio* already sending the water in the fountain squirting all over the piazza and brum-brumming with every car that passes, I'm crossing my fingers for a *bella bambina*.

Then I have just embarked on an extremely serious horoscope purporting to analyse my future baby's character depending on what time of what day the dear little creature is born, when Iacopo comes along, heading for the *pasticceria*.

Iacopo is an artist, a bull of a man, tall and broad with big shoulders and a big square face, a beard he has found some way of keeping forever at a length of exactly two virile millimetres. He paints. He thus feels a kindred soul to someone who is a writer, someone with whom he can complain about how desperately provincial the Veneto is, how an artist can never be accepted here, how his minutely detailed still-lifes of modern bric-a-brac – a *telefonino* by an aubergine, a madonna reflected in a microwave (which are indeed very witty) – will never be recognised. Whereas if we were in Rome . . .

Speaking to Iacopo, I always get the disconcerting feeling that we are rehearsing for an Italianized version of *The Three Sisters*. And yes, he insists that I have a cappuccino with him. My little boy – what's he called again? – can have an ice cream.

So, after the peach and the two sweets, Michele is dragged away from the fountain, screaming, to be kept quiet, or almost, with, in the end and on his own insistence, a *bomba*, a doughnut, while Iacopo complains to me that to make money he's presently having to paint the dullest mother-and-baby portraits. All people seem to want is pictures of themselves getting married or themselves holding their babies. Meanwhile, the girl at the bar becomes the nth person this morning to ruffle my little lad's hair and kiss his forehead. Should I ask Iacopo to paint his picture? The girl bends prettily, cleavage in evidence, to cut the boy's doughnut for him and whisper in his ear and tuck in his shirt and say what a little darling he is and slip a *caramella* in his pocket. I often wonder if Michele has already learnt to distinguish the generosity of men, chiefly aimed at buying space for themselves, and that of women, which presumably has to do with their yearnings for maternity. And if so, which he prefers. With any sense, I suppose, he will learn to exploit both.

Iacopo tells me he finds it very difficult to work because his own small baby keeps him awake at night and his wife is less amenable than she used to be. He has even taken to sleeping on a pallet in his studio on occasion. In return, I offer him the story of when, shortly after Michele's birth, I heard my wife's voice calling '*Amore?*' from the kitchen. To which I replied '*Si cara?*' Only to have to hear: 'I wasn't talking to you, *stupido*.'

Iacopo laughs. '*I sacrifici*,' he says. 'Oh, the sacrifices we have to make for our children!'

This reminds me that I am supposed to be house hunting. I explain our dilemma. We are expecting a second child and . . . Iacopo pouts and frowns, as he did when complaining about the local lack of taste. A second child! Really . . . But then in that way Italians have of always feeling they personally are being called upon to help, to show their ability to do you a favour, he gives me the fatal piece of information. 'Walk out of the village on Via Segheria,' he says. 'There are some *villette* going up on the hill there.'

Standing at the bar to pay, I am just forcing Michele back into his buggy again (child rearing is such a muddle of caress and coercion) when the boy comes out with the word '*mella*'.

'What was that?' I ask. For this is a new word.

'*Mella*.'

'What?'

'*Mella!*' he yells from a pained red face, reaching up, panting, showing dangerous signs of bursting into tears. In explanation, the girl behind the till reaches over to him with a piece of silver-blue cellophane in her hand. '*Caramella*,' she says. ' '*Azie*,' Michele says. And that makes four. With a little more dedication, I suppose, I would be using the occasion to teach him to count.

Naturalmente

Sega means saw, *segheria*, sawmill. Sawmill Road. In the mid-nineteenth century Montecchio was a flourishing industrial area, mainly because of the scores of streams that rise here, providing power for mills and water for the tanning business. Heading south out of the village, Via Segheria begins with a long line of abandoned and partially abandoned factory buildings of the more picturesque variety, one with a fine red-brick chimney some eighty feet high. Opposite this, on the lower slopes of the hill, a builder is putting up twenty or so *palazzine* of various designs, each forming a pair of semidetached houses, or four of five apartments. Without exception, the roofs are tiled red, the buildings stuccoed white, and each sits in a pool of dove-grey cement surrounded by a garden and properly enclosed by a cement wall topped with sturdy iron railings painted brown. The garage doors are likewise iron and brown. But the volume of the houses is more generous than is usually the case and the spacing decent and above all not of an obvious geometry. I decide to look for the builder, who, according to a sign painted at the bottom of the new road they have opened, is called Righetti, Guglielmo.

Michele is attracted to the sound of a bulldozer digging its way into the hillside. He tugs at my trousers and brum brums. A cement mixer churns merrily, ready to still the whole landscape in a crust of grey. We climb the new road and in one of a line of garages built into the side of a three-storey block, I come across four workmen. They are taking advantage of the shade for an early lunch. There's the inevitable two-litre wine bottle on an upturned box. They are all in their mid and late fifties, grizzled, weather-beaten, inarticulate. It comes to me that it's always the older peasant generation doing the actual building here, the hard labour, and doing it mainly for the younger, upwardly mobile generation, who may often be their children. So perhaps, despite having made all the *sacrifici* in the world to make sure their own children can afford the luxuries of modern housing, these men occasionally drop a little spaghetti on the *cotto* on purpose, out of a vague resentment, or even, in the teeth of Iacopo's claims, a sense of humour. The garage, I notice, is quite unnecessarily paved with bright gloss-grey tiles designed to resemble Sardinian granite. It's the kind of material an English family would feel proud to have in their kitchen.

The extravagant paving of garages . . . The discrete flaunting of the sensibly superfluous . . . In such impossible collocations lies the contemporary Italian aesthetic, wealth freezing a world of luxury so still that little children who are all movement can grow up there safe and frustrated.

When I ask the workers a question, they answer in a dialect so strong it's hard to follow. They come from another time than the one they're building.

'Signor Righetti?'

But now there's the roar of a poorly tuned car and a tiny 126 screeches up in a puff of exhaust. Out climbs a lean young man in yellow shorts and no shirt, battered running shoes on his feet, sardonic smile on smarmy face. *Buon giorno, buon giorno*. 'Guglielmo Righetti,' he says, 'a pleasure,' and, immediately, he bends down to go through the who's-this-fine-young-fella routine with Michele, whom the older men have more soberly ignored. His torso is flat and smooth, wiry rather than muscular. And yes, *naturalmente* he'll show me one of the houses. What am I after? Yes, *naturalmente* the prices are very reasonable. For the kind of quality he's offering, that is; none of your cooperative rubbish. He launches into a well-rehearsed spiel about all the problems involved in buying cooperatives. It was extremely intelligent of me, it seems, not to get tempted into a cooperative. He tells a few horror stories about people losing all their money. 'And the materials they use!' Walking along beside him, though, I notice that the drainpipes on his houses are not of copper, as on Stefano's. When he asks me about my accent and discovers I'm English, he wants to know whether it's true that the English and Americans still build with wood: wooden frames, wooden floors. Is such a thing possible? Really? The only thing he uses wood for is to make a casing to pour the cement into. Ha, ha! How far behind we must be. And what about the rain? Do they really build in the rain? He shakes his head. The future is in concrete and steel. Erected, *naturalmente*, under a scorching sun . . .

Righetti's style is to mix a too obvious bonhomie with demonstrations of professional superiority. As so often, before I have time to go away and think about it, I'm impressed.

He takes me to a rather attractive-looking building at the top of the street, designed in an L shape. There are three floors, with three apartments on the ground floor and then three more on the next, but these upper apartments have access via spiral staircases to an additional duplex floor under the roof. He shows me one of the larger apartments. We have to go up the space where the staircase will be with a ladder, which sends Michele wild with delight. And it's curious inside to see how all the pipes and wires are simply set directly into cement then to be covered by tiles or bricks. What will happen if a pipe bursts? 'My pipes don't burst,' Righetti tells me confidently. 'And my workers are the best in the Veneto. I don't let just anybody work for me.' Remembering the men drinking directly from the bottle in the garage, I wonder what the worst workers must be like, and grab Michele just before he plunges down through the hole back to the first floor.

Or am I being unfair? Certainly the windows are solid and handsomely double-glazed. The shutters are the sensible, traditional wooden variety. Looking out from a bedroom, Michele firmly in my arms now (and I fish out a *mella* from his pocket to keep him quiet), I see that this flat would have an excellent view across a hillside of vines and cherry trees, were it not for the fact that Righetti Guglielmo has started building another large and exactly similar block about fifty yards away, the last in the complex by the looks of it, for there is a perimeter fence just beyond. In particular, it seems to me that the large terrace balcony off the kitchen would be a lovely place to sit if, instead of looking towards it, it was on the other side of that other building.

'Price?'

'The place is about 170 square metres,' he tells me.

Italians tend to judge whether a place is expensive or not on the relationship of price to square metre. Had I been a little more experienced I would have known to bring this size assessment down by about ten percent since, in retrospect, telling me the metres first was a ploy to make the price seem cheap.

'Yes, but the price?'

'Less than a million a square metre.' It's one of those psychological barriers. Or was, before it became two million a square metre.

'Can't you give me the exact figure?'

'I'd have to do some sums,' he says cautiously. He talks with a very strong nasal accent and has to make an effort not to slip into the dialect he speaks with his workers. He'll phone me, he says, this evening, if I'll give him my number.

'Look, okay,' I agree, 'I'd be interested in this flat, but only if it were in the other building, the one looking out over the country. There must be an identical flat there.'

'*Naturalmente*,' he laughs, shaking his head in a knowing way. 'And how many people have said the same thing! But unfortunately it's already taken. Inevitable, really.' Righetti has a way of shifting his weight from one foot to another and generally looking more boyish and innocent than he can possibly be. My age? A year or two more or less. His hands are folded on his chest, which is the colour almost of Stefano's *cotto*. I should think it over anyway, he says. I won't find any better apartment than this in Montecchio. And these, he repeats, these are professional people's apartments, not cooperatives. 'People who live here,' he confides, 'might perfectly well buy a Mercedes . . .'

Outside he tousles Michele's hair once again, tells me he is soon to be a father himself and how important it is, how absolutely vital, in fact, to feel that one owns one's own house when one has children. '*In gioia e in lutto la casa è tutto!* Or no?' He laughs. It's the kind of proverb you'd expect a builder to know. Then he races off in his rusty white 126, an attractive touch in someone who is obviously making money 'in shovelfuls', as they say here. Later I would come to associate that car with the man's outrageous meanness.

'I can't imagine,' I tell Rita later, 'why Michele's off his food, he certainly didn't have anything when he was out with me . . .'

The boy sits in his highchair on the balcony looking out across the street where other children are playing a kind of hopskotch now between the passing cars. He picks up a bit of egg and throws it over the parapet. Could egg stain the marble of the parapet below? Perhaps I should have got Nascimbeni's insurance after all. And I insist: 'I just can't understand it.'

Rita frowns. She agrees entirely with me that we are not going to pay God knows how many million just to stare into the garages of another apartment block. However expensively paved. If we want to do that we may as well go and live in the city. So that evening when Righetti phones to say 158 million, we tell him we would only be interested if it was in the other apartment, and he rings off.

Then rings back a month later. We still haven't told him what we'd decided about that flat.

Which flat? Ah, yes. No, we said we'd only be interested if it was in the *palazzina* looking over the country.

But haven't we decided whether to buy it yet or not?

Sorry, but hadn't he said it wasn't free?

Not at all. *Naturalmente* it's free. It hasn't even been built yet, has it?

One of the problems of living in a foreign country is that there is always half a chance you didn't understand something properly. In this sense it is perhaps not entirely unlike being partially deaf. Had Righetti been having me on, or hadn't he?

'All payments to be made in cash,' the voice was now saying, '*naturalmente.*'

Un riassetto . . .

Can there be anything particularly Italian about a birth? We are driving fast across the flat country to the south of the village on a winter night. The contractions arrived very suddenly and were immediately fast and rhythmical. Earlier on in the day there had been no warning whatsoever. So much so that we spent the afternoon in a dull office in the centre of town while a solicitor read out the conditions of a contract of purchase at a price of one hundred and ten million lire, all of which had been fully paid. This for the authorities. To avoid some taxes. Then he read out a second contract that said that despite what had been said in the first contract, we still owed Righetti & Co. fifty million lire. This for us and while Michele examined the entire length of the skirting, and Christ surveyed the scene with weary indifference from above a handsomely framed scroll declaring the solicitor's credentials (credential: 'giving a title to belief or credit' – Chambers). This second contract, which is probably still in the glove compartment of the car as we drive cross-country to the hospital, includes a self-destruct clause that says we agree to tear it up in the presence of the other signatories as soon as the money is paid. Hence, there will be no record of what we really paid. With that safely settled and behind us, the poker faces of builder and credit-worthy solicitor broke into broad complicitous smiles and wished Rita *auguroni* – big wishes – for the birth of the child.

Which is now quite suddenly upon us.

It's a cold frost-hard night: patches of fog on a dark flat landscape, narrow empty provincial roads. Rita urges me to drive faster. She feels things are moving more rapidly than they should. But with the winter's heavy frost the asphalt is broken and potholed. The car shudders. At 100 kph it bounces fiercely. One can appreciate why Stefano switched to his funereal Passat. Rita cries out. And another bump . . . It's an interesting question whether we're more likely to reach the hospital 'in time' driving faster or slower. What kind of parameters would one need to know to work this out, I ask her. But Rita is rehearsing names again.

'Okay, so if it's another boy we call him Filippo, right?'

'Right.'

'And if it's a girl, Stefania.'

Both names translate easily into English. No trouble for the relatives. Steer clear of Girolamo, Giuseppe, Amalia and the like.

I'm already half wishing we had steered clear of Guglielmo . . .

'And if it's a Marocchino?' Rita asks, mooting the notion of a possible infidelity with one of the Moroccans who walk the streets here selling rugs and tablecloths. Or if it has a peg leg and makes *le corna?* She tries to laugh gritting her teeth at the same time, while I am reminded that we have still to see Nascimbeni about the new house insurance. Already children have made the man a staple in my life.

'Esposito,' I suggest. It was the name given to children abandoned at the church door, and it means, literally, 'exposed'. As opposed, of course, to protected, like all the other babies in the safely owned bricks and mortar of Nascimbeni's cautious world. There have been a spate of babies abandoned recently, usually and so sadly in the *cassonetti,* the big communal bins on the street where one has to take one's rubbish. And just yesterday a newborn fell through the lavatory tube of the Milan–Venice Rapido as it left the station of Vicenza . . .

But these are not helpful thoughts on such an occasion. So I turn on the radio, just in time to hear a sentence so remarkable that despite our own dramatic situation, Rita and I make a point of remembering it. The late news on Rai 1, the main public station, announces the arrest of a killer who it described as: '*un sicario di spicco molto attivo durante il riassetto degli organigrammi gerarchici della camorra nei primi anni ottanta*' – a notable hitman particularly active during the re-equilibration of the organizational hierarchy of the Neapolitan mafia in the early 1980s.

Will our children ever learn how to speak like that? Do we want them to? And what kind of nation is it that speaks about its criminals as if they were just another large bureaucratic corporation?

The car hits another pothole. At the same time we have to hear of yet another case of TB in Naples because people haven't been bothering to vaccinate their children. And gypsies have been stealing little girls again and selling them as prostitutes . . .

'Basta!' Rita says. She switches it off.

'Childbirth is entirely natural,' I insist as we hit another bump. Car transport less so.

We cross the river Adige and arrive in Castellano. The hospital has all the welcoming features of a mental institution built in the twenties: gloomy stone-paved corridors and special public-sector lighting effects, though at least it is easy to park when you arrive after midnight. In the porter's office a man is busy watching dancing girls on TV and waves us vaguely along the corridor towards *Maternità*.

We are welcomed in a tiny office by a little nun with glasses, who sets about filling in a long form, steeped in precisely the kind of vocabulary we have just been laughing at on the radio. Rita tells her that she thinks the matter is getting somewhat urgent, the contractions are fierce, but the nun very correctly points out that the form will have to be filled in first: age, place of birth, parents' occupations, place of residence, phone number, first or second or whatever number offspring. The office is a cupboard with two chairs, a desk and the inevitable framed certificates testifying competence.

Rita groans and complains that things are getting very serious indeed. She still has her big brown overcoat on. And, *'O dio,'* she gasps at a particularly brutal contraction.

Particulars of first born. Nature of presentation. Weight at birth. Miscarriages in the intervening period. Date of last menstruation. Results of tests undergone since then. Data of own birth. Profession. The list seems endless.

O dio!

Dr Maroni, as I recall, did not tell his class how to get into self-hypnosis while filling out a form.

Address, postal code, phone number (work, home) . . .

Finally, we are directed down a corridor past a full-size white stucco statue of Our Lady to the delivery rooms. Since Rita has gone to Maroni's class, we get the new super-modern, politically correct room, the advantage here being that this place has none of the heavy equipment, the complicated gear and the leg straps that make a normal delivery room look like an emergency ward in Bosnia. No, here there is nothing more than a big double bed with plenty of pillows to be arranged at will. The light is low and pink, suitable one imagines, for brothels, though the music would hardly be popular: Vivaldi's Concerto in Re Maggiore for Two Mandolins.

Since we actually have a very similar bed at home, not to mention a quantity of pillows and cushions and the facility for generating low red light and the Deutsche Gramophone's version of this particular concerto (how else would I have recognized it?), it occurs to me that we might very well have stayed at home and saved ourself the nun's interrogation. Though in the event of trouble, the helicopter might find it difficult to locate our part of Via Segheria, since there are no streetlamps yet.

At home, I reflect, a husband might know what to do. Or, more pertinently, where to go when there was nothing for him to do. This is not the case in hospital. In hospital one is obliged to play the role of the modern husband supporting his wife at birth, and this is particularly important in Italy, which has only recently discovered such healthy concepts (the range goes from gay rights to bottle recycling) and thus practises them with the eagerness of the neophyte.

But what exactly is a man supposed to do at his wife's childbirth, apart from be there wondering what to do and holding her hand if it helps? Which I am abruptly told it does not.

'Let each one of us say unto ourselves . . .' I begin in a low voice, as Rita settles on the bed. 'I am calm, I am serene . . .' But this only makes her giggle, in the middle of a long groan. Annoyed, she sets about breathing deeply.

The nurse arrives, a dark local girl who speaks a fierce dialect and carries a clipboard and another form to fill in, a form that in many ways, too many ways, resembles the first, it being a principle of bureaucracy, I suppose, that no person can be believed until he has answered the same question in the same way at least three times.

'*O dio!*' Rita shouts. 'I think it's coming.'

'They all think that,' the nurse says complacently. The least, one feels, a husband might be able to do is to fill in the form while they get on with the business of childbirth . . .

But now it's the nurse's turn to scream *O Dio* because the baby is indeed arriving. She rushes to the cupboard for rubber gloves, scissors, cotton wool and the like (one presumes). Boxes and cellophane packets spill from a high shelf onto the floor. '*O la Madonna*!' she screams (not inappropriately now), dropping everything, then remembering she has to press an emergency button to call the doctor. By the time she has fumbled her gloves on, the baby has already arrived, is kicking and whining and dirtying the sheets.

I only pray that my newborn child will always be able to deal so peremptorily and effectively with bureaucracy in the future. Here is a re-equilibration of the organizational hierarchy, if ever there was one.

But Dr Maroni, when he arrives, is furious. However natural childbirth may be – and this performance was close to perfection – a doctor is supposed to be present. That's the law of the land. Was it my wife's fault or the nurse's?

Rita isn't listening. She's simply delighted that it's a . . . *bella bambina*: Stefania. Within five minutes of its birth the child has already been smothered in diminutives, many invented: *sinfolina, ciccolina, ciccina* . . . It must be one of the areas where Italian most excels: the cooing excited caress over the tiny creature, *uccellina, tartarughina* . . . Little birdie, little turtle. Rita is ecstatic.

'What was your other child?' the nurse asks me, trying to divert the conversation away from the late arrival of the doctor. 'A boy,' I tell her. 'And what's the age difference?' 'Two and a half years.' 'Excellent,' she smiles, 'he'll bring older boys home for her, and she younger girls for him. The boy should always be older . . .'

Who would bother arguing with such conservative ideas at such a moment? Invited to cut the umbilical cord myself, I decline. I'm overawed, and nervous and a little squeamish. Just at the moment I wouldn't trust myself with a pair of scissors.

Rosa e blu

Pink and blue. Blue rosette for *un maschio*, pink rosette for *una bella bambina*. You pin them on the door, the main door of the *palazzina* that gives onto the street so that passers-by will see, so that friends will be informed without having to ask. Thus, the family lets the people round about know that there is one more amongst them, just as the sombre death notices pasted up with other posters about the village inform them that someone has been taken away.

But the rosette business is difficult in our new flat since it stands at the very end of Righetti's as yet unfinished development. The road bends to the right climbing the steep hill and stops abruptly in a rusty wire fence. Even sticking the rosette on the gate rather than the door will only inform my own immediate neighbours.

My new neighbours. Five families have moved in so far, including ourselves. All youngish couples, all of them with one *maschio*. The arrival of a *femmina*, and so soon after everybody has moved in, is thus an occasion for celebration.

'Ah,' says Silvio (downstairs flat, north-facing), seeing me fixing the rosette on the railings: 'It's a *bella bambina.*' He smiles: 'Well, you've already got your *maschio.*'

With willing new-neighbourliness he stops to talk. Then his wife arrives with their little boy, Giovanni, a mutinous two-year-old. The jollity is such that I ask whether they're intending to have another themselves (that irritating way parents have of always wanting others to have the same number they do). Silvio begins a pantomime of embarrassed gestures, as if to say, Ah, wouldn't it be wonderful. But so expensive. Because then Sabrina would have to stop working. '*I sacrifici,*' he says vaguely.

Would he feel the same, I wonder, if they'd had a nice little girl first? So many only children here are boys . . .

Then he goes on to talk, far more enthusiastically, about the garden, which for the moment is just a thousand square metres of torn up hillside. He wants to get a small bulldozer in to take out the line of vines and the four cherry trees. Those kind of things don't belong in a garden. I'm so busy thinking about my new baby I don't even protest.

After which, some terracing will have to be done, to take the steepness off the slope, and then there will be a lot of plants to buy – oleanders, hibiscus, azaleas – plus the trees, of course; he has something Japanese in mind for that corner by the main door, though they don't come cheap, unfortunately. Then before we do that we'll have to get in a sprinkler system, for which we will need a small excavator. The ground is too tough to dig trenches because Righetti parked his machines here for a year and more. 'We still have to get a quotation for that.' Plus Mario (bigger upstairs apartment) has suggested that while we're about it we may as well lay down the cable for some garden lighting . . .

I have finished fixing the rosette. '*Complimenti,*' he says again. And shakes his head. He is a very handsome young man, Silvio, foreman in a factory that produces picture-frame mouldings. He speaks with disarming straightforwardness. It would be so expensive to have another child . . .

Rosa e blu . . . There is an extraordinary conflict of cultures going on today in this little corner of the world that is provincial Veneto. Or at least so it seems at first glance. There are the old structures of a peasant, Catholic, superstitious Italy, physically present in the roadside shrines and Madonnas, in the vineyards and olive groves of the terraced hillsides, in the row of vines my neighbours are determined to tear down, in the cracked infrastructure of the old village, its tall stone walls and millwheels, its complex system of streams and irrigation canals dividing the many springs that rise here. Battered tractors muddy the streets. Heaps of manure steam on vegetable patches. Dogs are chained outside.

And it's present, too, in those people, whether young or old, who seem to have preserved an ancient mentality intact: the men pushing their dogs into the boot of the car, the little children who serve you in far-flung trattorias, working hard at only nine or ten, the hunters with their battered hats and shotguns tramping the undergrowth, the grizzled cardplayers in the Bar Centrale with their red wine and untipped cigarettes, the women riding rusty bicycles to the cemetery, or doing their shopping in their slippers, the young mothers who cry when they hear they've had a girl rather than a boy, the teenagers who visit palmists, cartomancers and fortune tellers various to discover the astrological sign of the man they should marry. All these good people can be seen together in their Sunday best for Mass, of course.

But then there is the new Italy of fast roads and bright cars, the chase of polished steel, the new ersatz *palazzine* springing up around this village and filled for the most part with office workers from the town, so well behaved, so carefully dressed, oh not formally, in the way English people alternate stiff office suits for work with shabby casual wear at home, but with studied elegance, with a deep magazine-and-television-bred appreciation of what is fashionable, and therefore necessary.

This is the world of the *telefonino* – the portable phone – and the *donna manager* in her crisp *tailleur*, the fitted kitchen and the halogen lamp, the Japanese umbrella tree and the satellite dish. At the newsagent's kiosk *Casa bella* and *Elettronica* rival *Famiglia Cristiana* and *The Mortifications of San Gaspare*; the computer game takes over from the rosary (and hence the desire to invent a rosary that *is* a computer game).

But aside from the obvious outward phenomena, vices and virtues are shifting, too. Missing Mass is no longer a terrible crime, but spanking your children, or firing a worker, or even using unleaded petrol in a car without a catalytic converter, are atrocious, unthinkable acts. Most of all, of course, there is NO DIFFERENCE AT ALL between races white and black, between people who have handicaps and people who don't, people who have AIDS and people who don't. No, we are all and always and forever equal, especially men and women . . .

Yet little boys still get a blue rosette at birth, and nice little girls a pink. So gender conditioning begins, delightfully, at birth, in the teeth of the new orthodoxy, and in the modern home as much as in the traditional. Little Stefania, or Francesca, or Cristina will get her pink rosette, her pink hat, her pink shoes, her pink sleep suit. Little Enrico, or Gigi, or Maurizio will be clad in blue and given more aggressive rattles. Isabella will clutch a Little Pony with a golden mane. Giovanni's first toy car will coincide with Antonella's first doll. Marco will be furiously attacking the pedals of his plastic tricycle when Marzia is tottering about pushing her first baby buggy.

The fragile structures of modern piety soon crumble before something so deeply felt as child rearing, though the most strenuous attempts will be made to inculcate the dear little things with the very values the parents are ignoring, whether Christian or secular. The children will all be baptized and sent to catechism by parents who would never dream of darkening the proverbial door. The nursery will deny to the last that they divide the children up for boys' games and girls' games, that they teach them anything but the strictest parity of the sexes, whereas I have seen teachers protesting vigorously with one young fellow that little boys must never tie ribbons in their hair.

No, the remarkable thing about the Veneto is not its still engrained Catholicism, nor its rapturous embrace of all things modern, but the fact that these two should so happily and profitably coexist. Until it begins to dawn on you that there is no conflict of cultures at all here – that was an Anglo-Saxon presumption – no conflict, but a superimposition. As if values were held more for their aesthetic properties than anything else, and thus could no more be in conflict than Armani and Krizia, Michelangelo and Picasso. You can believe fervently that men and women should be equal – it's an attractive thing to believe – but if a pink frilly rosette is likewise attractive, then by all means stick it up. Where's the problem? Once determined to avoid gender conditioning at all costs, I personally succumbed long ago. Having fixed my rosette securely on the railings, I fluff up the net circles and smooth out the two sheeny ribbons that hang down almost to the wall. Honestly, it looks splendid . . .

La visione del bambino

I'm just going back into the house after my encounter with Silvio when Righetti arrives in his tiny car and climbs out with a pickaxe in his hand. He has seen the rosette and extends his warmest congratulations. 'Of course,' he says, 'you already have *un maschio*.' It's a line I shall have to get used to.

'And the mortgage? Has it come through yet?' He is worried because I still owe him fifty million lire. I explain that the matter has been delayed because the bank insists on not only seeing but also keeping an original marriage certificate, which in England has to be made up by hand.

He shakes his head over our backwardness. Wooden houses, handwritten marriage certificates. It seems pointless trying to explain that in other countries some things are taken on trust. Or at worst photocopied.

'And the rent for the garage?' Since I am unable to buy the garage right now, he is renting it to me, so long as I undertake to buy it within a certain number of years. He has promised to hold the price steady.

'I haven't been in a week yet,' I remind him.

'Rent is always paid in advance.'

With his pickaxe Righetti climbs the broken terrain of our future garden to where a piece of plastic piping no more than two feet long is trapped in a discarded chunk of cement. Then, while I rustle myself up a quick family-free lunch (Michele is staying with Marta, Stefano and Beppe), he hacks away at that cement until finally he has freed the piece of pipe. Whistling contentedly, he picks it up and walks back to his battered 126, having saved himself, I imagine, something like five or ten pounds.

I then spend about double that on flowers and set off back to the hospital – only to discover that I'm not allowed to leave flowers in the wards. Flowers are unhygienic. I shall have to take them home with me. And I'll have to do it now, because I'm not allowed to see my wife or my baby. Visiting hours are strictly three to four in the afternoon and eight to nine in the evening. Naturalness obviously ended, somewhat acrimoniously, with Dr Maroni in the delivery room.

As a husband, though, I do have the very special privilege of coming in at seven-thirty to see mother nursing baby. Then, before eight, the little ones will be removed and other visitors will be let in to discuss the gruesome birth details with *mamma*. But they don't get to see the baby.

In the evening Stefano and Marta come early with me in the hope they'll be let in at the privileged husband's time, too. Apparently, a close friend of Stefano's works on one of the wards, and Stefano is convinced that with a little manipulation they can wangle their way round the restrictions. *Sai com'è?* Stefano's tubby moustache bristles. Marta, elegantly petite as ever, is almost beside herself with excitement. She loves babies, though she feels she should warn me that the chaos we'll have to deal with at home with two of them will be horrific . . .

Outside the hospital Stefano calls his doctor friend in General Surgery on his mobile phone. The man promises he will talk to the duty nurse immediately. Stefano sketches a smirk and is solidly confident as we take the lift to the third floor. Marta wants to see the baby; he wants to get round the regulations.

But it's not to be. As the lift doors open, we find ourselves pushing through a considerable crowd milling on the landing and up and down the stairs. All of them are watching the glass-and-aluminium door to which we're headed. It's locked. There is a bell beside the door, but underneath it says to ring only in emergencies. Stefano immediately says to ring. I hesitate. 'Ring,' Stefano says, 'they just write that kind of thing to scare people.' 'But . . .' Somebody behind explains that, though it says nothing about this on the door, it is generally understood that husbands are allowed to ring now that it's past seven-thirty. So I do. Nothing. 'Ring again,' Stefano insists. After about two minutes a nurse appears. Who are we? In a perfectly relaxed fashion Stefano begins to explain that he just had a chat with Silvano Benigni who works in General Surgery, and he . . . The nurse doesn't even let him finish. It is already an extraordinary concession, she says, that the husbands are allowed to see the babies feeding, an extraordinary and, frankly, she thinks, foolish concession. If they started letting others in, where would it end . . . ?

Oxen, asses, foreign kings?

As I slip through the door, I leave Stefano and Marta in a huge crowd of eager grandparents, aunts, uncles, sisters, brothers, friends, all of whom, I now realise, hoped to be considered an exception to the rule, hoped that some contact they had would get them through that institutional door to the magic world of mother and child. There's a grumble of discontent as the nurse turns the lock behind me.

In England, I've noticed, one can more or less wander into a maternity ward when and how one likes. The babies stay with their mothers all day. Their friends come and chat to them. There is no climate of crisis. But here I have to put on a green coat over my clothes and two elasticated plastic bags over my shoes. For this is why the others are excluded, of course. It's the modern obsession with hygiene, with technique, with management, with control – the babies must not by any means be exposed to the outside world. Everything must be clinical and safe, while on the other side of that door behind me, as I fumble with the ties of my green coat, seethes the old world of Latin sentiment and immeasurable affection, the blind determination to get a sighting of the new child, to adore it, to bring it gifts: gold, gold and more gold these days, spices and oils being now cheaply supplied by the chemicals industry. As I walk off down the corridor to Rita's room, the emergency bell is punished with monotonous and impatient regularity.

How can such an unfortunate clash be resolved? How can a grandmother see her newborn grandchild without feeling that she has prejudiced the dear babe's health? The answer is simple, and they've written it right there on the panel by the door that explains the visiting hours. For beneath the numbers that limit access to the mother are the words:

VISIONE DEL BAMBINO
8.30 – 9.00 p.m.

Visione! What a pregnant word that is. *Visione della Madonna. Visione del bambino* . . .

In the corridor a woman with a decidedly southern accent is arguing heatedly with the nurse. Her baby boy has been brought to her in a pink tunic. Pink! The nurse tries to explain that since the hospital insists on dressing the babies in their own, the hospital's, sterilised baby clothes, they can't always guarantee that they will have sufficient tunics of the right colour. A lot of boys have been born in the last couple of days and . . .

'Consider yourself lucky,' the woman says ominously, 'that my husband is in Germany . . .'

I find Rita chatting to the wife of a local bus driver in a room with only two beds. The babies have already had a first shot at sucking and are now dozing. The women chat, faintly euphoric, though nothing like the restive crowd outside. Then the bus driver himself arrives, nervous, young, long-haired, bringing packages. He sits down and squeezes his hands together in endearing embarrassment. The women go on chatting. I and the other husband are more or less ignored. Our duty is merely to watch, to wonder at the dear little creature rocked in Mamma's arms, occasionally to pick something up, open a bottle of mineral water, explain that all is quiet back home on the domestic front.

The other woman, Fausta, talks about her other children. Yes, three others! With a shy smile the (now amazingly) young husband pushes his hand through greasy hair. (Should the nurse have provided us with hats perhaps?) When I congratulate them, Fausta laughs: '*Figliole e fritelle, più se ne fanno, più vengono belle.*' 'Little girls and pancakes, the more you cook the better they look.'

How do Italians remember all the proverbs they use?

Suddenly, from the corridor, the same southern voice I heard arguing with the nurse a few minutes before, shrieks, 'Salvatore! O Salvatò!' It's a dramatic Latin yell, as though over a grave. At the same time there are sounds of bustle and protest at the main door along the corridor. The noise is so loud as to actually remove the seraphic look from the nursing mothers' faces. What's happening? The bus driver and I head for the door to discover that there is indeed a way of getting somebody else to join you when you come to see wife and baby: you handcuff yourself to the person and have him dress up as a *carabiniere*. It appears the southern woman's husband was not in Germany at all . . .

Despite the handcuffs the couple embrace. Smaller than his wife and perhaps younger, the convict is at once surly and embarrassed. A second *carabiniere* is in attendance. Nobody is asked to wear a green coat. They disappear into her room. The protests a moment later must be when Salvatore discovers his *maschio* is wearing a *femmina*'s pink tunic . . .

But husbands and *carabinieri* aside, most mortals who want to see the baby have to wait, as I said, for *la visione del bambino* . . .

It works like this. At five to eight the nurses come and whisk the babies away. As soon as they are safely off in the service lift, the ward doors can be opened and the crowd admitted to visit the mother. That serves as a kind of appetizer, a teaser, a holding operation. Yes, he's big, yes with lots of hair, and Nonno's nose, yes, to a T . . . Then, as half past eight approaches, the visitors suddenly desert the ward and charge down the stairs to the nursery on the floor below, where the babies will now have been arranged in their see-through cots behind a great wall of glass . . . Here comes the *visione.*

Infected by the general excitement, Stefano, Marta and I hurry down, too. We push through the doors to the nursery. But for the moment the wall of glass is obscured from within by a venetian blind in dull institutional green. A crowd has formed, perhaps forty or fifty strong, all frantically waiting for the stroke of eight-thirty when the blind will be lifted and the miracle revealed. People mill impatiently in the limited space. A Donald Duck sticker warns us: DON'T KNOCK ON THE GLASS!

Then comes the raising of the blind. The crowd surges, as at a football match. They press against the glass. To see what? Four rows of pink- or blue-clad babies just about visible in their cots, if turned the right way round, and even then identifiable only by the large black numbers glued on the perspex. Ours is 16.

But people aren't disappointed. The air is filled with oohs and aahs and coos and laughter and isn't he just his uncle, isn't he, isn't he? – this of a tiny creature almost three yards away with his arm across his face. True, there's a little frustration amongst those who can't get to the front, or who have got to the front, but the number of the cot they're after is way at the back; but that can be resolved by going off to find a nurse: Nurse, please can you move cot 12 to the front for a few minutes, please Nurse, please . . .

For my own part, I'm amazed at Marta and Stefano's eagerness as they stare at cot 16 where little Stefania is facing the other way, so that all you can see is a surprisingly full head of dark hair. Then someone begins to complain that his videocamera has been jostled. He was trying to video his nephew (age twelve hours) through the glass when . . .

Such fanaticism! Such enthusiasm! Such a desire to worship, to devour the object of worship . . . It reminds me of when the wooden Madonna in the village church of Cologna Veneta starting crying. Rita and I went along to see the miracle but gave up because of the press of people outside, so many of them with expensive photographic equipment. And I realise now that access to the maternity ward is denied not just out of a sense of hygiene, but in order to enhance the notion of the child's sacredness.

Stefano and Marta seem satisfied now. The nurse has turned the cot round and they can see that Stefania Angela has dark eyes and an old man's face. We drive back. I let myself in just in time to catch a ringing phone. From three hundred miles away Rita's mother demands: 'Is it a boy?'

Sogni d'oro

Perhaps it is appropriate that the day after Stefania's birth is also the day of the first condominium meeting. My own family increases and I myself am admitted to the larger family of the *palazzina*.

Turning off the main road that afternoon as I drive back from the three-to-four visiting spot, I notice that a road sign has been set up in the mud at the bottom of the development announcing that the slick question mark of asphalt that climbs the hillside to embrace Righetti's various building sites is no longer to be known as Via Segheria. It has now been renamed Via delle Primule, Primrose Way. On the face of it this ought to be a good omen, redolent of youth and pleasure. But something niggles. What is it? Shakespearian warnings as to the unhappy consequences of hedonism – the primrose path of dalliance? Or a certain blind tweeness that as always unnerved me in such names as Buttercup Lane and

Cowslip Cottage? Needless to say, this is not a street where anybody has ever seen a primrose.

The condo get-together is to be held at 9.30 p.m. in the flat below mine, the Cremoneses'. Here the mild Francesco and morose Francesca live with their only child, Gigi, aged, at that point, four and a half. The first thing that needs to be said about Gigi is that he is enormous. He's a *bufalo*, as they say here, charging riotously around an apartment that is trying desperately hard to look old, if not antique, even before the whitewash is dry. The effect is achieved mostly by the tiles, which are a dark rust-red, immediately making the space look far smaller than it is, and above all dull, though Francesco is complaining that at least half of these tiles will have to be replaced since they are defective.

He draws us over to one side so that we can see. Basically, you have to crouch down in the doorway to the kitchen and look slantwise, your eyes at toddler height, between a chunky dark brown leather armchair and fat soft sofa. In this position, and only in this position, the light from an old-fashioned candelabra affair above, all chains and brass arms and gloomy glass beads, catches the rust-red-floor in such a way as to reveal that the glazing on many of the tiles is indeed broken and pitted . . .

Everybody shakes their head and agrees they'll have to go. *Fondi di magazzino*, Silvio says knowingly, meaning, warehouse leftovers. But this interpretation presents Francesco with the alarming prospect that there may not be a sufficient number of good tiles left to replace those that are defective. Perhaps this colour isn't being produced any more. Did Righetti pass off the very last tile of this type on him?

Mario, who has just arrived – stout, solid, businesslike – announces that he has decided to change all the doors in his apartment because the wood is such poor quality. A litany begins: electrical fittings, mixer taps, shutter catches . . . Since a builder must always be anathema no sooner than one has bought from him, I propose a toast: that Righetti's child, when it arrives, be a little daughter. '*Cattivo!*' they all shout, which is to say, 'Unkind!' or to a child, 'Naughty!' But everybody is smiling. After all, they all have *maschietti*. Let Righetti eat his heart out over a girl.

Running round the sofa, Gigi knocks a lamp off a low table. Francesca shouts at him. '*Smettila!*' Stop it! Despite the accident, the blond and chubbily handsome Gigi continues to rush around. Half-heartedly Francesco suggests that the boy, his son, might like to go to bed, an idea that nobody else picks up in the general fussing to see if the lamp is broken. Nor is the notion proposed again as we finally arrange ourselves around the table to talk. At ten-fifteen Gigi continues to whoop in and out of the kitchen, helping himself from the fridge.

Where is my Michele, Silvio's wife, Sabrina, asks. How on earth am I managing alone? When I reply that Michele is in bed, others at the table show a mixture of awe and concern.

'You have left him alone in bed at only two and a half?'

I point out that it's late for a little boy, and I am just about to go on to say that his bedtime is seven o'clock, when I remember that there is no word or expression to translate 'bedtime' into Italian. There is something coercive about the notion of a 'bedtime'. It suggests that there comes a moment when parents actually force their little children to go to bed and will not take no for an answer, something unthinkable in these more indulgent climes. In explanation, I have to say that Michele 'habitually goes to bed at seven o'clock', which gives quite a different impression, and Francesca in particular marvels at what a wonderful little boy my Michele must be hurrying off to his bed so early, not realising that I had to pin the chap down for half an hour or more while I sang to him and told stories and said that Mummy would be back very soon, until finally he got more bored than I was and tired of all the crying he'd done and fell asleep. On more than one occasion I have heard such behaviour described by Italians as cruelty.

'But what if he wakes up?' Sabrina asks. *'Poverino!'* (Their own two-year-old, Giovanni, they have left with his grandparents.)

I remark that it is only two short flights of stairs away from my flat and the door is open. I will hear if he cries.

'The door is open? To the apartment?'

'Yes.'

There is now considerable concern that someone might get in and do something awful.

'But the front door to the *palazzina* is closed,' I point out. 'We would hear if anybody came in or went out.'

'The doors to the apartments are good,' Silvio says, sitting down at the place offered to him, and obviously making a contrast with the other fittings we have been criticising; he shakes his head, 'but not the main door to the block.'

The word 'good' here, as used by Silvio, means safe against thieves. The front door to a Righetti apartment weighs two hundred kilos and has an armoured steel core and security locks top and bottom that bolt into the steel frame on both sides. It is one of the first things the builder shows prospective customers, inviting them to swing it from side to side and feel its weight, to examine the dark holes in the armoured frame where the security bolts go deep deep deep as you turn each lock not once, not twice, but three times. In stark contrast, the front door to the whole *palazzina* is a stylish affair, with little glass panes. Child's play to put a brick through and turn the handle inside. Without actually saying it, Silvio is telling me that I am relying on the wrong defence to keep out trouble.

'And the shutters on the ground floor need bars on them,' he goes on to tell Francesco, 'otherwise a thief could just unscrew them from their hinges and lift them off.'

Francesco immediately gets up to go and look. All the men follow, crowding out on the terrace balcony above our wasteland garden with fields and vineyards beyond. And yes, Silvio is right, a thief armed with a screwdriver need only remove some forty woodscrews to lift off the shutters and get going on the shatter-proof double-glazing. From the distant barracks comes the whine of a bugle sounding the change of the guard. The village behind us is quiet under a frosty moon. The men discuss the positioning of steel bars. It seems pointless to remark that nobody even has any shutters in England. In any event, it is with these sober reflections on all that remains to be done to protect ourselves in Primrose Way that the meeting at last begins.

We sit down round an old-fashioned table to tall glasses of something *frizzante*, which young Gigi insists on trying, as indeed he tries all the various kinds of *dolce* that people have brought to celebrate. Not because his parents are indulgent. On the contrary, they protest with seeming vigour. It is late, they say. Gigi should be in his bed. He is too young to drink wine. He has already had some chestnut cake after his dinner. Etc., etc. All the same, Gigi gets a little wine poured and grabs a pastry.

Everybody laughs, and it occurs to me how seriously instructive this must be for a young child, how precisely it enables him to grasp the absence of any relation between what 'should' and what 'can' be, between rules and reality. How often does one wake up in Italy to hear that some new law is being introduced, some back-seat safety-belt requirement, tax on government certificates, tax on visiting your doctor, so that one sits up and takes note and makes the appropriate arrangements, only to hear a week later that as a result of public protest the government has revoked the law or the tax or whatever it was, or reduced it, or postponed it, which amounts to the same thing, with the result that you are one of only five or six percent in the whole country who actually bothered to do anything about it. This kind of scenario has happened to me any number of times and will probably happen again, but not, I think, watching him guzzle a bowl of *tiramisu*, to Gigi. He will never pay until it is quite clear that everybody else will. He knows it is a mistake to obey a command immediately.

'He'll go to bed when we go,' Francesco says wrily. Nor is the man ashamed to tell me the whole sad truth. 'Or rather, he'll insist on coming into our bed, so in the end I'll go and sleep in his. Otherwise, I'd never be fit for work in the morning.'

Francesco is a delightful man, slightly stooped, phlegmatic, flexible, amiable, alert. His face, beneath closely cropped unmanageable hair, is dark with a beard that seems gloomy rather than virile. But this only makes it all the more attractive when his features light up in a bright smile. Francesco is a damage inspector for the car insurance division of a big financial company. He takes pictures of ruined BMWs, Fiats, Alfa Romeos. He knows the value of materials that crumple without breaking. He knows that often customers are claiming for damage and repairs that have nothing to do with the accident in question and for which his company is not theoretically liable. But he also knows that except in truly outrageous cases his company will pay. After all, that is why car insurance is so expensive. So that everyone can exploit it. Clearly, Francesco is infinitely better equipped than I am to give an Italian child an education. Worrying about a name like Via delle Primule, indeed! Everybody else seems delighted with it. Anyway, Sabrina says, all the new streets in the village have flower names: Via dei Ciclamini, Via delle Rose, Via dei Garofani. And they don't have any cyclamens, roses or carnations. Why should our street be any different?

There are seven of us round the table this evening: myself, the hosts Francesco and Francesca, then Silvio and Sabrina from the adjacent apartment, Giorgio from the apartment next to mine, a tubby, happy-go-lucky, slow-spoken fellow, and finally (since one of the apartments, though paid for, is still empty) Mario, the man who is changing the doors (and light switches as it turns out, and door frames, and the spiral staircase . . .). Mario is altogether a more forceful personality. He has come along armed with four or five gardening catalogues full of photographs of plants we can buy. With our glasses of bubbly, and doing our best to ignore the shrieking Gigi, we set about creating a little paradise . . . for our children.

'Which brings us,' Silvio announces, 'to the question of the gates.' Inevitably, it turns out that the first thing to be established about paradise is, once again, how it is to be protected.

'The gates?' I enquire. What could there possibly be to say about the gates, except that I have just hung a pink rosette on them?

'Some people have been forgetting to lock the gate,' Silvio says, rather solemnly for such a handsome young man.

This is true. The big double gate that has to be opened to take a car out has a lock of dubious utility, which my fellow condominium owners insist should always be left locked. This means that one must first get out of one's car to unlock and open it, return to the car, drive through, then get out again to close and lock it. Some people, including myself, it must be confessed, have been 'forgetting' the last part of this operation. Though not as often as I would like.

And this is dangerous, Silvio insists, because it means a thief could easily get in. He exchanges glances with Mario and with Francesco. It's clear that there is already some kind of understanding with them about this.

I feel I'm being put on the spot and so point out that a thief could easily get in anyway. The railing is not high, and the pedestrian gate can be buzzed open by reaching a hand over the low wall and pressing the little plastic button, which is not even carefully hidden on the other side. Child's play.

But if the main gate is open, Silvio says, somebody could

bring in a van or even a truck and take away an enormous number of things.

Perhaps I should say at this point that, since all the owners are locals, condominium meetings at Via delle Primule 6 are conducted in dialect, not 'proper' Italian. As a result, it occurs to me now, as once before with Righetti, that I may have misunderstood, so bizarre do Silvio's fears appear to be. But no, he now launches into an explanation of how, in summer, when doubtless many of us will be away on holiday at the same time, a truck could come in through the gates, park by the garages below his apartment on the ground floor above and load everything he has into the back. Thus while Righetti's workers are almost expected to be careless and while the government can to a very great extent be ignored, thieves are assumed to be diabolically efficient and effective.

I apologise if I have occasionally left the gate unlocked. Doubtless this has been because I have been very taken up with the birth of Stefania . . . One of the wonderful things in Italy is that children are accepted as an excuse for more or less anything. I have even heard one man excuse an infidelity on the grounds that he was so happy his wife had just given birth to a . . . son.

Francesco now remarks how wearisome it is getting in and out of the car to fiddle with the gate when it is raining. Given that it hasn't rained at all in the few days since people moved in, I imagine this must be a gesture of reconciliation towards me. But it turns out to be only a set-up for what he and Mario and Silvio have presumably agreed between them. Later I would appreciate that I am really the only one who comes cold to condominium meetings.

'That's why,' Mario says, 'I was thinking that we should invest in *un cancello telecomandato*' – a remote-controlled gate.

I have often wondered about the etymology of *cancello*, the Italian word for gate, since *cancellare*, the verb, means to cancel, annul, or erase, rub out, efface. Is there, to some extent, the residual idea that upon closing one's gate one erases the outside world with all its contingent dangers? What better, then, than to have an automatic gate to cancel the world . . . automatically.

'With a *cancello telecomandato*,' Mario earnestly confirms, 'we won't have to bother remembering to lock the gate, since it closes and locks itself on its own.'

Thus, in order to avoid the inconvenience of getting in and out of the car, we are now about to spend three million lire, of which I and Giorgio, since we own the largest apartments, will be called upon to pay the lion's share, expenses being based on floor area occupied. Giorgio, guarded, polite, but capable of a certain taciturn belligerence, objects. He sells tickets at the local railway station and though hardly overworked is not overpaid, either.

But the other camp are compact and well organized. And in a majority. The fact is they want to have their *cancello telecomandato*. They really, really want it. And not just for the sake of security. Having bought their brand new white-stuccoed flats, they want to show they have arrived. In this sense the remote control gate is at once as superfluous and essential, or essentially superfluous, as the sprinkler system and the lawn lighting and the determination to cut down the cherry trees and remove the vines and have expensive tiles in the garage.

'They already have a *telecomandato* at number 4,' someone says, as though to clinch the matter.

But I'm dead against. In the wealthy American suburbs, I point out, they don't, as I recall it, put fences round houses at all. The gardens just run down to the pavement. If we really want to save ourselves trouble, we could just remove the railings and the gate altogether. They would never present any real obstacle to a determined thief anyway.

Everybody laughs heartily, as when I suggested I hoped Righetti would have a baby daughter. What a great *senso dell'umorismo* the English have . . .

The rest of the evening is then spent choosing plants from Mario's garden catalogues, with Gigi, showing no signs of sleepiness, pointing his chubby fingers at the glossy pages – 'But I want this one, I want that one' – then showing us the money in his wallet, then a scar on the back of his leg. At which the perfect defence suddenly comes to me.

'They're dangerous for children!' I announce.

'What?'

'Automatic gates! There was a case in the *Arena* [the local paper] just the other week of a kid being killed when a gate closed around his neck.'

This is actually true. Remembering Nascimbeni, I make the *corna* gesture to ward off bad luck and am pleased to notice that nobody laughs at this.

'I bought an apartment at the end of a quiet cul de sac so that the kids would be able to run out and play on their own,' I go on with dreadful self-righteousness, 'not so that I'd have to hang around worrying about a remote-controlled gate.' In short, I don't want the kids *cancellati* by the *cancello* . . .

Silence. In a rare moment of intuition, I have set two Italian ideals at loggerheads, or perhaps three: on one side, protection of the property, in this case reinforced by the fashionability of remote-controlled gates with flashing yellow lights on top and little beep boxes you can keep on the dashboard of your car; on the other, the safety of your only, high-investment child. It's not unlike the collision of priorities that brought about the *visione del bambino* at the hospital. A tough one . . . Giorgio sends grateful glances across the table. Silvio admits he will have to investigate the safety aspect. The meeting is adjourned, and finally Gigi can retire to his, or rather his mother's, bed.

Upstairs, there's a message on the answering machine. Rita is already fed up with the hospital. The incessant sound of the emergency bell is driving her crazy. She has persuaded the doctors to let her come home tomorrow morning instead of making her stay the required three days. Can I perform accordingly?

In his room Michele is sound asleep. Looking at him, I reflect that at birth, as Stefania is just born, the child's experience must be more or less universal. At what point then do they actually become Italian? I have seen Michele fiddling with the little button inside the perimeter wall that buzzes open the pedestrian gate out onto the street. It is put there for people departing, so they won't have to use a key, but Michele has learnt that even on coming back to the house, people reach their hands over the wall and use it, including people who have never been to our house before but who know that such things are common. So, there is a lock on the gate and even a spring-shut device to keep out intruders. But for convenience sake, and because electrical things are attractive, there is a button on the wall that everybody can use to open the gate, intruders included; just as children should go to bed at eight, but don't because they don't want to, and as there are excellent rules about all kinds of things that for convenience sake everybody disobeys.

Has my son taken this in yet? At two and a half? Does he appreciate how absurd and attractive it is? Or does he not rather just enjoy seeing the gate slam itself shut and then buzzing the button with his pudgy little fingers to make it snap open again? And will he finally, as a result of experiences of this variety, approach that triumph of expediency that involves holding two separate and mutually contradictory propositions simultaneously, so as not to have to go through the anguish of rejecting either of them? Gate with lock for protection. Lock easy for everybody to open for convenience. Who knows?

He still wears a nappy at night. I check it, change it. The front of his little sleep suit says, in English, 'Dreams of Gold', an excellent literal translation of the Italian expression for 'sweet dreams', *sogni d'oro*. I wonder are Silvio and Mario perhaps at this very moment dreaming of golden gates, *telecomandati*, of course, and does that genitive in 'dreams of gold' mean that the dreams are golden or that they are about gold? Would this in modern Italy amount to the same thing? The size-tag at the back of the sleep suit has also been written in English to enhance the possibility of foreign sales. 'For the kids great', it says. That is: large size. My Michele, like Gigi, shows every sign of being a whopper. Or perhaps I should say, wopper.

Ninne nanne

Very early in the morning, I get a knock on my door. It's Francesco with the bad news that there's a damp patch rapidly forming on his bathroom ceiling. One of the pipes in my floor must be leaking. On the phone Righetti pretends incredulity. Hard to say '*naturalmente*' to this one. And when I arrive back from the hospital with Rita and tiny Stefania, it's to find that despite having taken up four floor tiles, the builder and his worker still haven't found the problem. Apparently, no record was kept of exactly where the pipes were laid. In any event, they certainly weren't golden. The men bang on the tiles with mallet and punch. The baby cries. Rita curses. On his way out in the late afternoon, Righetti takes the opportunity to remind me once again that I still haven't paid the first month's rent on the garage.

In the evening Stefano and Marta call with baby Beppe, to see both new house and new baby. And while I try to explain – and I feel almost apologetic – that we've decided it's okay if the children put fingermarks on the paint in the kids' room, which, of course, Michele already abundantly has, Stefano shakes a professional head over the rush job in the bathroom and wonders whether the floor can ever really be perfectly flat again. Once something has gone wrong . . . to put it right . . . *sai com'è?*

But the baby, Marta says, is a *spettacolo* – a spectacle, a show. Oh, she really is. *Un vero spettacolo!* It's worth noting what positive connotations that word attracts in Italian. After all, what would Marta wish you to say of her own carefully kept house, her *cotto* floor and *pietra serena* fireplace, her lounge that she keeps locked shut to prevent Beppe getting at it, if not that it is *uno spettacolo?* Whereas my mother always used to say: 'Tim, for heaven's sake, don't make a spectacle of yourself!' Meaning, don't draw attention to yourself. And meaning, little children should be seen and not heard, or better still neither seen nor heard.

Over the coming weeks and months, I'm afraid, it was my mother's pejorative use of the word that turned out to be the most appropriate for our new baby. Stefi made a most awful spectacle of herself not just during the day but at one and two and three and four of almost every night and morning, moaning and wriggling and vomiting and never never never going to sleep. Every manual and magazine was consulted, every possibly dangerous element was removed from the mother's diet, including artichokes and *peperoni*. One doctor even prescribed, as doctors notoriously will in the Veneto, that we give the child Valium. Whether this would have worked or not, I don't know, for we baulked at that. Certainly, nothing else did. The nights were spent, as the Italians say, *in bianco* – in white – awake. Though wakefulness would be a flattering description of the semicomatose state in which I moved, night and day, over the coming months. For not only was I continually shattered from sleep by Stefi's nagging scream, but likewise constantly narcotised by my wife's *ninne nanne*, her lullabies. I remember listening endlessly to the one with the chorus that goes:

Ninna nanna, ninna nanna,
La bambina è della mamma,
Della mamma e di Gesù,
La bambina non piange più . . .

Lullaby, lullaby,
The baby is mother's,
Mother's and Jesus's,
The baby cries no more . . .

This turned out not to be true. Whether Mother's or Jesus's or both, the baby was still crying fiercely. In that near delirious state in which one drifts in such circumstances, I remember managing to feel irritated that the baby for which I was making such huge *sacrifici* appeared to be everybody's but mine . . .

My wife sang:

Sorridi alla tua mamma amore
Che sempre veglierà per te . . .

Smile at your mummy, my love
She will always stay awake for you . . .

But this wasn't true either. For as every parent knows, the person most susceptible to the soporific effect of a lullaby is the person obliged to sing it. Many a night Rita's head would collapse red-haired on the pillow leaving that fellow never mentioned in any lullaby – Dad – to hold the baby and sing those more bizarre English songs that rather sadistically imagine babies swinging from precarious treetops.

To avoid singing for hours, one of the solutions we resorted to was a tape of lullabies. A languid southern croon offered some seriously sedative, even dirge-like pieces (most satisfactory) but inexplicably intercut with brighter, jollier things from unformed little girl voices backed up by an irritating accordion line of the kind one invariably picks up on the radio in Austria. This was entirely counterproductive, as if whoever had planned the tape wanted to put you to sleep only to wake you up again. Needless to say, there were no male voices.

How many times I listened to that cassette! One of the jollier songs told how the Madonna went off to market leaving Bambino Gesù with . . . guess who? Easier to guess who she didn't leave him with, isn't it? Lucky Giuseppe. No, she calls on a group of angels with incongruously Italian names who happily agree to babysit. But in her absence Jesus wakes and begins to squall. The angels try more or less everything we ourselves had been trying to get our own little baby back to sleep. Angelo Lilla tries *camomilla*. The *angelo d'oro* suggests a *bel coro* – a choir. Various other rhyming spirits propose easing off the swaddling clothes, massaging the little fellow's tum, playing the violin, pulling faces at him, etc. But still the baby cries *disperato*, still the Madonna remains *al mercato* (grabbing a cappuccino if she was my wife). Finally, back comes Maria to announce that Gesù is just a smidgin hungry. She sends the angels off to market for something she has unaccountably forgotten, but by the time they get back with the goods the Son of God is, of course, asleep in the Madonna's arms.

One says 'the Son of God', but minor details of this variety have no place in the endless Italian lullabies that feature the Virgin and her little boy. Very soon you begin to appreciate that, contrary to the Anglican tales I was told as a child at Sunday School, Jesus's claim to prominence depends only very marginally on his being the Son of God and far more importantly on his having the Madonna for his mother. In any event, the only vitally defining factor about these two is that he is her *bambino* and she is his *mamma*. She has no other men after him and he no other women. This is what has remained sacred. Everything else is accidental.

But the lullabies I like most are the ones that allow the sad truth of their generative context to sneak into the lines themselves. The brutally simple *'Fa la nanna e la nanna faremo . . .'* (Go to sleep, then we can all go to sleep) is something I might well have made up myself around the end of the third week with Stefi. While rhyming bargaining gambits of the variety: *Non fare più capricci / se no sarann' pasticci* (Come on, don't fool about / or there'll be trouble no doubt), followed up by the rather more threatening *Alla tua mamma dài già tante pene / potrebbe creder che non le vuoi bene* (You already make things so hard for your mother / she might end up thinking you don't really love her), are the sort of thing I might have tried another week or so on. But the *ninna nanna* I finally began to identify with, say, by the end of a month or two, is the one that goes as follows:

Nanna O, nanno O
Il mio bambino a chi lo do?
Lo darò al suo angiolino
Che lo tenga fino al mattino

I make no apologies for my inability to rhyme the translation . . .

Lullaby, lullaby
Who shall I give my baby to?
I'll give him to his little angel
Who'll keep him till the morning

In short, here's a mother who's reached that point where all she wants to do is find somebody else who'll look after her child . . .

Nanna O, nanna O
Il mio bambino a chi lo do?
Lo darò al suo cherubino
Che lo tenga a se vicino

Lullaby, lullaby
Who shall I give my baby to?
I'll give him to his little cherub
Who'll keep him close by his side.

The poor mother then goes through a list of possible surrogates for herself including, notably the *befana*, an ugly but kindly witch, and at the last, inevitably, Gesù and Maria, this final solution rhyming with *e così sia* – so be it, as if to say: at this point I wash my hands of the whole miserable affair.

The tone of the song, in minor key, is insuperably plaintive, at once desperate and desperately resigned, perhaps faintly vindictive in places, especially when the *befana* is invited to keep the child a *settimana*, a whole week, and again, though more subtly, when the singer lights on the idea of unloading her sleepless brat on the Madonna and child, as if the whole awful situation were somehow entirely their fault in the first place. Not the father's at all. And apparently father is a more unlikely babysitter than all these supernatural candidates. In any event, he's never mentioned, not a whisper of *papà*, not even a plea that the fellow do his duty. So that pacing up and down with Stefi in the small hours and listening to those southern voices rolling their sad 'r's and dragging out doleful vowel sounds through heartbreaking, accordion-wheezed cadences, I felt I had good reason to wish I'd been born in the times when those lullabies were written. For in that case I would probably have never had to hear them at all.

One day I remarked to Marta, while Michele and Beppe were fooling around with their model cars together in the still huge pile of rubble outside their house, on this total absence of fathers in lullabies. Not true, she objected. I couldn't have heard 'Ninna nanna al mio papà' – Lullaby for my dad. Sing it to me, I said. Instead, she went and got a tape from a shelf arranged in the kind of meticulous order my things will be in only after my final departure. Here, listen, she said. Very sure of herself. And, with bated breath, I did. It turned out to be one of those splendid cases of the exception that not only proves the rule but insists on it. Sung by the most winsome infant voices, here is how it goes:

Ninna nanna al mio papà
Al più buono e al più caro dei papà
Dormi, dormi, mio papà,
Il tuo bimbo a te vicino resterà

Lullaby lullaby for my dad
For the best and the dearest of dads
Sleepy byes, sleepy byes, Daddy,
Your little boy is by your side.

In short, rather than Daddy helping to get baby to sleep, this is baby, or little boy, singing Daddy to sleep. Rather than being the sufferer struggling to have someone else accept the embrace of Morpheus, Dad is himself the baby, the object of soothing vocal caresses. A mad fantasy, you might think, a hallucination spawned from the exasperated nerves of the modern and politically correct father in the middle of another night *in bianco*. But I'm afraid not. No, I suspect the generative context of this little song is quite different and once again far less flattering to the paternal figure. For we're in Italy, remember, and this must be siesta time. Dad is back from work, he wants a nap after lunch before starting his long afternoon, and quite probably he's threatened the kids, now somewhat older, with God knows what if they don't shut up and let him sleep. (Why else the appeasing 'for the best and dearest of dads'?) Nobody is interested here whether the children sleep or not, so long as they don't bother Papà. Thus, after the verse above, all that remains of the song is a soft spoken, almost fearful whisper:

Dormi, dormi, Papà
Io sono qui vicino a te
Zitto zitto, senza fare rumore

Sleep, Dad, sleep,
I'm here beside you
Quiet, quiet, without making a sound . . .

The whole song lasts exactly one minute and eighteen seconds, about twice as long as it would have taken me to get to sleep had Stefi been capable of doing the honours. Laughing with Marta, I asked her if Stefano had ever spent the night awake looking after the baby. But she said his work was far too important for that. When Beppe was little, he moved into the spare bedroom.

I could almost hear him saying, '*Sai com'è,*' which this time can only mean 'I bet you wish you did know how it is for me.'

Maybe three or four months into this *via crucis,* I remember discussing the problem on the phone with my ever resourceful mother-in-law three hundred miles away in Pescara. And she said, '*Ma Tim, le hai dato il sonno?*' Literally, 'But Tim, have you given her the sleep?' For a moment I wondered if she might be referring to some drug I wasn't aware of. Or perhaps it was merely that I hadn't understood again.

'I beg your pardon?'

Then she recalled that although I know Italian, I am not Italian.

'Given her sleep. That means you put money somewhere in their clothes.'

'Oh? Money?'

'It gives them a feeling of security,' she explained.

Why didn't Nascimbeni tell me this? Or perhaps it was so obvious . . .

So one night in a volatile mental state between hilarity and despair, we decided to try this proverbial remedy. You never know. A five-hundred-lire coin in each sock and a fifty-thousand-lire note tucked into the top of her nappy, as if she were some kind of precocious belly dancer. It didn't work. But then as Rita pointed out, I had forgotten to ask exactly how much money was required these days. *Un milione? Un miliardo?*

If I'd had it, I would have given it.

Ricatti

In the paediatrician's waiting room, a little girl, perhaps four or five, tips over the low table holding the magazines, then begins to pick up the publications and toss them in the air. The mother shakes her head, says, '*Smettila, Jesseeca*' (after Jessica Lange presumably), then rights the table. Other mothers smile indulgently. How can one control the dear little things? Since it doesn't seem to bother anybody, I let Michele wander around singing to himself, pushing and poking the other toddlers, and in the meantime I pick up a copy of *Donna & Mamma* from the floor. The letter on the first page reads as follows:

> We are two parents, aged 29 and 31, and we have a three-year-old girl who is getting us very worried indeed. Francesca was a first child, first grandchild, and, in fact, the first baby in a whole circle of friends. So she is surrounded by an army of people (grandparents, aunts and uncles, relatives, friends,

and most of all ourselves, her parents) all ready to go into ecstasies over her. We both work only half days, so we can spend a lot of time with her and all four grandparents are very helpful. Result: Francesca is extremely fractious, bossy, moody . . .

Meanwhile, at the paediatrician's, Jessica has managed to stand on a chair and is pulling a notice off the notice board announcing a lecture – 'Intra and Extra Family Communications in a Pluralist Society' – to be given in the town hall by some professor or other. The mother hurries to replace the torn notice and suggests that Jessica might like to play with some of the many toys that have been brought along: the frog that croaks, the doll that cries unless you keep a bottle stuck down its throat, etc. Jessica is not convinced. She wants to tear that notice down. Perhaps she's not happy about living in a pluralist society.

In *Donna & Mamma* the letter goes on to say how, in response to every parental veto ('and we can assure you we restrict these to the absolute minimum'), young Francesca goes crazy, shouts, bangs doors, even attacks her parents physically.

Somebody looks in from the street, sees there are too many people (four at the paediatrician's means at least an hour's wait), and goes out again.

'The only thing that seems to work,' continue the two desperate parents, 'and please don't be too shocked, is *ricatti*, blackmail. "Be a good girl, otherwise we won't take you to the playground." "Don't shout, otherwise we won't let you see a video." "Do us a favour and we'll do you one . . ." '

But this is a method these conscientious parents really don't want to use. It is *poco educativo* – not very educational

– in the sense of not bringing up the children as one should. How can one, they wonder, sink to blackmailing a three-year-old child? And they complain that the girl's fractiousness is beginning to affect them. They are getting more and more irritable themselves, less and less willing to try 'to understand her'. 'Even though we adore Francesca,' their missive finishes.

Jessica has just begun to attack the carpet with a pencil when the door to the surgery opens and the mother can grab her by the hand and take her in.

'*Bella bambina*,' says one of the other women appreciatively.

'Very lively,' I agree.

Then before I can stop her, the other woman, who I recognise as the cashier in the butcher's, is giving Michele a *caramella*. His teeth will thus be filthy when the paediatrician looks in his throat.

I decide to study the expert's answer to the case of little Francesca and notice that in more than a page and a half (for this is the 'in-depth, case-of-the-week letter') the word 'spanking' is mentioned only once, and noticeably it's the more unpleasant word *picchiare* – to beat – that is used (i.e. something totally unconscionable), rather than the blander, less frightening *botte* (smackies).

'Sometimes,' the learned man says, 'some parents even get so frustrated with children like Francesca that they *even hit them* [his italics], and then of course they feel like "worms" for treating the child so badly and perhaps causing her a serious trauma . . .'

Nascimbeni no doubt would make his *corna*. For my own part, I can't help thinking that while the trend away from formal discipline is clearly general across the Western world, no people is perhaps as perplexed as the Italians with the whole problem of how to make a child do what it does not want to do. Perhaps because Italian parents so rarely find any good reasons for not doing what *they* want to do.

'You must,' our expert in *Donna & Mamma* concludes, 'firmly disapprove of any behaviour you think is unacceptable, even if this does not immediately give noticeable results. You must, however heart-rending it is, be willing to hear her cry . . .'

O la Madonna!

But *ricatti*, the paediatrician insists, are out. And particularly *ricatti* to do with food. The little girl must never be told that if she doesn't eat something she won't get something else. She must never be bribed . . .

How curious and unnatural all this is! And how comic in a society that seems to hang together above all on *ricatti* and a strict tit-for-tat system of favours done and returned. I accept an invitation to dinner only to be scolded by my wife because 'Now we will have to invite *them*.' My professor at the university offers me a weekday off, but then friends suggest I should not accept because 'Then you will be obliged to do him a favour when he asks. And you don't know what that favour is.' My bank gives me a mortgage, but then is furious when I close my account to move it elsewhere. 'You were ready to come to me when you needed a favour,' the bank manager almost shouts, 'and now you ditch me just like that. When I thought the British were so civilised!' Michele is dispatched with a Christmas present for one of our neighbours, only to return with a ten-thousand-lire note in his hand. Disturbingly, they felt the need to discharge their debt once more.

But perhaps it is because society is so comprehensively established on *ricatti* that parents try to spare their little ones the experience, that Jessica, for example, isn't threatened with the loss of some treat or other when she starts tearing posters down from the wall. My own feeling, though, is that parenthood would be impossible without blackmail. 'You better behave,' I tell Michele before we go into the paediatrician's office, 'otherwise you can forget any ice cream afterwards. Okay?' But I tell him in English so that the mothers won't have to hear anything so *poco educativo*.

The door has opened, and Jessica's mother is being eased out. Jessica herself runs straight across the floor and grabs another mother's shopping trolley. *'Che bambina vivace!'* everybody says. What a lively little girl.

One of the excellent things about the Italian health system is its strict separation between your GP and your paediatrician. It represents the positive side of taking children seriously. Our paediatrician, a petite, peppy woman exactly my own age, is a pleasure to deal with. She has called Michele in for the check-up automatically carried out on three-year-olds.

'What a buffalo!' she says as he comes through the door. She has a boy the same age who is about half his size. She gets Michele to strip and weighs and measures him and looks at her chart on the wall. She shows me the relationship between the various parameters: age, height, weight. Michele is way ovcr even the maximum; his figures are those of a five-year-old. I'm rather concerned. I don't want the boy to be one of those poor giants who lumber around at school feeling embarrassed about how big they are. But the paediatrician reassures me. The charts we're looking at were based on children in Rome in the early 1960s. The first such charts came out in the fifties and all the Italians were worried how small their offspring were, because the charts had been based on studies of Swedish children and then distributed internationally. So the Italians made up their own charts for their own much smaller children, only to catch up and perhaps even overtake the Swedes in just a couple of vitamin-crazed decades.

'A supernourished age,' the paediatrician says, shaking her head. But when we go over Michele's diet, she can see nothing wrong: a big mug of warm milk and a piece of toast for breakfast; fruit mid morning; meat and vegetables at lunch, or mozzarella and boiled eggs and tomatoes; two or three whole peaches or a big bowl of cherries in the afternoon; pasta in ragout for dinner; an ice cream or two here and there along the way. It's not excessive, she feels. They're just big children. I stress Rita's care in making sure the children get the right things, though I don't add how appalled she is when we visit English friends who let their shrimpy offspring get away with a couple of bread soldiers with honey. The truth is that Italians go on spoon-feeding their children years after the English have stopped, just to make sure they have enough of everything. It's almost the only issue over which they seem willing to stoop to physical coercion. Marta will tie Beppe in his chair so she can force him to get what is good for him, then let him run as wild as he likes. Outside, of course.

'Occhio alle merendine,' the paediatrician says. Watch out for the snacks.

'*Magari,*' the little boy says. I wish. 'Daddy never lets me have them even when he promised, because I'm always naughty . . .'

The paediatrian frowns. I can see I shall have to add the further *ricatto* that if he tells other people about our *ricatti* it's as if he'd broken his side of the bargain before he started. We can discuss the matter over his ice cream.

Barbecue

Speaking of food, there's a fine smell when we get back to Via delle Primule. It's a warm spring evening and Silvio is inaugurating his barbecue (a neologism here, pronounced ba-bey-coo). This is not any old barbecue, such as one might pull out from a car boot for a picnic, tossing a little lighter fluid over those specially prepared barbecue nuggets. This is a deluxe item.

We walk round the back of the *palazzina* to admire it. Silvio has the good fortune to have a door in the back of his apartment which gives directly onto his garden, and he is already way ahead of anybody else in turning this into a patch of paradise. He got the grass down in late March and now, in early May, it's already tough enough to walk on. The secret to this, he tells me, is the use of three times the amount of fertiliser suggested on the bag. The grass, I notice, does have a curious, chemical blue colour, and likewise the little laurel hedge he has planted all around it.

The barbecue stands at the far end of the lawn against the perimeter wall. Built in some white stone conglomerate, about two metres high, it looks like something in the so-called Monumental Cemetery in Verona, some kind of pompous headstone, or tomb. It even has a little terracotta roof around it with the big chimney passing through. The expression 'charnel house' immediately flickers to mind. Silvio already has some dead flesh on the grill, comfortably arranged about waist height over a space for storing split logs in the picturesque manner typical of Swiss farms. The meat sizzles in the warm spring air. '*Che profumino,*' I say politely.

Waving a long thin stick, Silvio's little boy, Giovanni, is running wildly round and round the garden inside the laurel hedge, which has begun to divide the patch from the other gardens. His wife, Sabrina, a very tall and attractive woman, is bringing a tray of garlic bread out of the kitchen to be barbecued with aubergines and olive oil. Hearing Michele and Giovanni shouting and playing together, big Gigi arrives carrying a plastic bag full of model cars. The kids start to play in the dirt where other people have yet to begin any serious gardening. Then Mario comes, and Francesco, and then Marcello, the boy whose family have bought the last remaining apartment for him and his girlfriend to live in as soon as they are married, in a year's time.

Much technical discussion ensues as to the merits of this Rolls Royce of barbecues, its main advantage apparently being the draught its very large chimney creates, which allows the food to cook more quickly and cleanly. Inevitably, we are asked to hang around for at least an *antipasto.* We do. Rita comes down with Stefi on her shoulder, wailing. Seats are brought out, brand new folding garden chairs, which sink into the damp ground. Silvio looks with some concern at his bluish grass, which he plans to cut for the first time next week. Could it be that too much fertiliser will burn the roots? 'Of the trees,' Mario says knowingly, 'but not the grass.' Silvio has planted three ornamental fruit trees in a perfectly straight line in the exact middle of his lawn, the distance between the central tree and the two extremes of the line being exactly the same as between the latter and the neat rows of laurels that define the territory. Everywhere, in the perfect right angles of the hedge, the fierce pruning to shape the trees, the stiff verticality of the barbecue and the rectangular precision of the flower bed, one senses that modern love of an all-anaesthetizing symmetry that spreads outwards from the pages of design magazines, the sharply framed world of the television. It's not unlike, it occurs to me, the fiercely geometric arrangements of the beach at Pescara, a charade of order in which everybody does more or less what they want – and most of all the children.

For now, right in the middle of a useful discussion as to which plants must go where and when, Giovanni suddenly starts throwing the small metal cars at the other boys and then at us. Silvio shouts, '*Smettila!*' Giovanni ignores him. Silvio, a big muscular man who has been considering renting one of the semi-basement cellars in the condominium to set up a little gym for himself and his dumbbells, threatens, in fierce dialect, to hit the boy. Giovanni ignores him. Then, giggling satanically, the boy pulls his pants down and makes to pee on the lawn no more than a couple of yards away.

Somebody laughs.

Silvio shouts, *'Ti farò a pezzi!'* I'll chop you in bits. But despite this fighting talk, so far from the tone of *Donna & Mamma,* he still hasn't moved from his elegantly striped chair. Giovanni pees, with that glorious golden trajectory infants have, pointing his *pistolino,* as they say here, up to the sky.

More laughter.

'Good fertiliser,' Mario says, lips dripping with olive oil. 'No danger of burning out the tree roots.'

'Well, I never,' Silvio protests. 'What can you do with a kid like that?' Clearly, he's somewhat embarrassed by his impotence, yet at the same time perversely proud of his child's boldness. Looking round at the rest of us, his face seems to protest that he did everything possible. Meanwhile, Sabrina goes over to the boy and scolds him quietly. Giovanni scampers off giggling.

Then, just as the shadows are lengthening and the barbecue flames are brightening and the glass of wine I've drunk is beginning to take a few corners off the world, as Stefania finally nods off for a few moments and Silvio insists that Rita try a piece of sizzled sausage, Mario reopens the whole question of the automatic gate. He has checked with a company that produces a totally child-safe gate with light-sensitive trigger devices on *both* sides, so that it can never close if something is there. Never. The mechanism costs only two million lire, over and above the three million for the basic system, plus sixty thousand each for the remote controls.

His timing is perfect. What with the hospitality we have just accepted putting us in a weak position (*ricatto*), the pleasantness of the early evening, a general desire to please these generous people, and perhaps a new feeling that maybe if a child or two does have a close call with the gate that might not be a bad thing after all, Rita and I suddenly don't feel like fighting a serious battle over this one. Especially when it comes out that the others have already enlisted Marcello on their side and are thus four against two. Rita, however, astutely feels that capitulation on our part should not come without concession. She suggests that since we have only one car and one garage, while they all have two, we should not pay more than a sixth of the price for the gate, despite having one of the two bigger apartments. With their Italian flair for compromise, and perhaps even imagining that this was our only reason for objecting to the project in the first place, Silvio and Mario accept at once, so that all things considered, it's not quite clear who has blackmailed whom. In any event, everybody clinks glasses while the children are mildly told off for getting their clothes dirty.

A couple of weeks later, Michele tugs me by the hand and leads me to his little bedroom, whose window looks over the back of the house and the individual gardens (as opposed to the big communal garden round the side of the house). What he wants to show me is that a barbecue has appeared on Mario's patch at the top of the territory, a barbecue identical to Silvio's barbecue and arranged, as regards positioning and orientation, in exactly the same way. A month later it will be Marcello, who, though he still hasn't moved into his apartment, has a third barbecue appear exactly midway between the other two.

So the charnel-house pattern spreads outward. So the children learn the importance of having what other people have. Michele thinks it is wonderful. He loves barbecues. But when is Papà going to get one?

And when is Papà going to get a TV?

When is Papà going to get a mountain bike?

Plenty of chance for *ricatti* here.

Wiser than *Donna & Mamma* my *Frate Indovino*, a sort of calendar cum almanac, says:

'Your son. From nought to five he is your master, from five to ten your servant, from ten to fifteen your secret counsellor, and after that, your friend – or your enemy.'

Well, I can't wait until Michele's five.

Alto Adige

One year, and still Stefania not only wasn't sleeping but was still keeping us awake all night. Our paediatrician now suggested a trip to the mountains. The fresh air at a thousand metres and more was supposed to work wonders for a child's sleep. All our neighbours confirmed this, were suprised we hadn't gone up there before. So photographs show us blearily pushing a pram on the high plateau of the Alpe di Siusi in Alto Adige, a hundred miles to the north, with Michele sitting on my shoulders or clutching his mother's coat.

Alto Adige is officially part of Italy, but nowhere could be less Italian. The men wear lederhosen over bony knees and have feathers in felt hats. The women have round, rosy, weather-beaten faces. Orange or pink geraniums, but never both, adorn every wooden balcony, banks and banks of them, in rigidly straight lines. The cobbles are carefully swept. The gates are wooden, and the fences are wooden, and the tables in the bars are wooden, and the road signs likewise. Indeed, if anything can be made of wood, it will be. And if they make a pizza here, they make it with speck, or sausage, not aubergines or artichokes. Ethnically, they're German. They speak German. They call the place the Südtirol. One evening something happened here that had to do with Stefi's not sleeping, something that reminded me how different the Italians are from the Germans, and how tolerant, both to babies who won't sleep, and to parents suffering from babies who won't sleep.

It was March. Easter. In the afternoon we had taken a ride on a horse-drawn sleigh up on the glacier. They give you blankets for your laps, and we held Stefi between us while Michele sat up front beside the old peasant driver and the horse heaved us through a wonderfully slanting sunshine that sparkled off snow cliffs and turned meadows thousands of feet below to carpets of green gold. Stefi howled the whole way. And howled likewise in the crowded restaurant afterwards, where Michele fell off his chair twice, taking a plate of dumplings with him on the second attempt. Winding up my strudel, I became aware that I was rapidly reaching that point where accumulated tiredness turns into bad temper. Another few minutes and I would do something crazy. In desperation I decided a little indulgence might still save the day, and went and bought a pack of cigarettes. I must say I do this only rarely and only, for reasons I have never understood, when I am away from home. The children still whining, I lit up, deliciously, over coffee and a grappa. Likewise Rita.

We had been enjoying the smoke, nicotine and sundry poisons for about ten seconds, when to my shock and surprise a huge fat woman on her way out suddenly addressed us in demotic Italian: we should be ashamed of ourselves, she said fiercely, ashamed of ourselves, smoking in the presence of our children! The lady's accent was of the Teutonic variety unlikely to endear itself to anyone born south of Trento. What's more, there was a definite suggestion of racial superiority in her tone, as if those of German descent would never smoke anywhere near a young child. Her face, after she'd finished speaking, had a frightening severity to it. She didn't move on but just stared at us, apparently demanding a response. Nor did she try to make her attack more palatable by smiling at Michele or cooing over Stefi, as some elderly Italian bigot might, just told us straight, and she repeated her complaint, that we were behaving badly.

I lost my temper. In an extravagant and quite unforgiveable fit of rage, I shrieked at the woman that I was smoking *because* of the children, I was smoking *because they were making my life impossible*, because they refused to sleep, because I myself hadn't slept for months. For months. For months! Did she understand? Could she even conceive what that meant? And I said that if anybody else came and bothered me about it, I would only smoke all the more. Indeed, I would smoke a million cigarettes tonight if she didn't mind her own damn business.

The woman was not at all put off by this lamentable loss of self-control, as if she expected no better from someone she imagined to be Italian. If my children didn't sleep, she told me, still speaking in the same clipped, hectoring tones, it was because I spoilt them. I should *leave them to cry*, she explained. For however long it took. It would be a far kinder thing than blowing cigarette smoke all over them.

This time I didn't reply but grimly lit another cigarette, blowing the smoke quite definitely in her direction. She turned and left, speaking loud words to her husband, and one of those words was *italienische*, which set off a murmur of voices from the tables around us. Appropriately, Stefi howled. For perhaps the first time I was grateful for it.

Children, Rita remarked when the woman was gone, were perhaps healthier in German-speaking countries, but certainly sadder. For my own part, I was somewhat consoled by the fact that I had actually been mistaken for an Italian, if only by a non-native speaker. Or perhaps it was just that after a good argument I felt more relaxed. Ready for another night *in bianco*, with 'Lullaby, lullaby, Who shall I give my baby to . . .'

For neither the fresh air of the mountains nor a whiff of tobacco smoke had had any effect at all on Stefi.

Breaking off her crooning in the dead of night, Rita laughed, 'I know who we should give her to!'

Who? Was she hallucinating angels?

'The German *befana* in the restaurant.' The old witch. 'We should let her try and babysit Stefi for a night.'

But for all her difficulties we cared for our dear daughter far too much to abandon her to such a formidable figure. Though I remember we did once try to leave the little girl to cry, giving up after perhaps half an hour of constant yelling. Exactly one year and nine months after our daughter was born, Rita noted in her diary: 'Stefi sleeps four hours without break. First time . . .'

Capitomboli

When English children begin to crawl they find carpets on the floor, carelessly turned up at the corners. They find walls soft with wallpaper, thick curtains they can haul themselves up on, deep sofas smothered in cushions, big quilts on top of the bed, fluff and dustballs beneath. The English domestic world is a soft, soft place. Perhaps there is a hearthrug. Perhaps there is a cat or a dog on the rug. The child moves from one softness to another.

When Italian children begin to crawl they find tiles, or at best polished wood. Carpets are too hot for hot summers and unhygienic. Every day a wet cloth spreads disinfectant on shiny ceramics. There is no soft paper on the walls but rough whitewash, or solid waxed stucco, which is the fashion now. The stairs to the outer world are polished stone. The windows are shuttered. It's a harder, cleaner, smoother, more controlled environment, bright by day, jet dark at night. With the shutters tight, no shadows flit softly about the curtain hem. Bang your head on the window ledge and you find marble. Take a tumble, or *capitombolo*, as they say here, on ceramics and the bruises go deep.

At six months Stefi manages to roll off her changing table ... and cries for hours. At ten months she is discovering how many sharp edges Righetti built into his stylish spiral staircase. The small balcony tiles, our builder assured us, were baked specially hard to resist the fiercest heat, to stay cool. But when a tiny girl pulls herself up on the railing, she soon finds that the metal is scorching. In honour of Nascimbeni she tosses all her toys down between the bars, but never manages to hit anyone. Only gloomy Francesca in the apartment below complains about finding Pinocchio and Topo Gigio and an incongruous Big Bird amongst the underwear she hangs out from the balcony on a projecting clothes horse.

Hard surfaces make for hard noises. Windows opened in sultry heat suddenly bang when the sirocco rises. A loose shutter rattles. Reaching up to swing on a door, one-year-old Stefi finds it's stuck. The handle behind is tied with a handbag strap to the coat hanger to stop it slamming, to let the blessed breeze pass through the house. The bathroom door is tied to a dressing gown on a peg. The air stirs in the house, bringing with it the shrill cries of Gigi and Giovanni and Michele, shouting at each other from respective balconies, then Stefi's shriek when a door suddenly gives and her head crashes back on the tiles. '*O che capitombolo!*' echoes Mother's voice. What a tumble that was!

Through the afternoon dropped toys and wooden bricks ring on the ceramics. When a child rolls a wooden ball at skittles in some other apartment the noise is of distant thunder, then comes the explosion if the ball's on target. Outside, the harsh drone of the cicalas is as compact as waxed stucco. And after twilight the jarring trill of the crickets . . . Oh, for the soft tinkle of the ice cream van in a mild London suburb!

I take the children to the bar for ice creams. At eighteen months, Stefi is remarkably precocious in the handling of *pistacchio* and *stracciatella*. Michele still gets his *zabaione* all over his pudding face. On the tables round about young men and old are drinking beer and wine and grappa. Michele tries mine sometimes, a sip now and then, a little gulp. There will be no momentous initiation into the world of alcohol for these children, as when my friends and I first ventured into pubs to get the oldest-looking amongst us to buy a beer. There is no mystique to drinking here. Which is perhaps why so many of the young people are still tamely swallowing Coke and Fanta. They tried Papà's beer and didn't like it.

Leaving the bar, Stefi trips on the base of a sunshade and goes down on her face. At least a dozen people rush to lift her up, men and women alike. And *O che capitombolo! Che povera povera piccina!* Poor little thing! They're so sure she's hurt herself, the girl wails in fright.

In town the big churches offer occasional protection from the heat. They have the same gloom the house has when you half close shutters against direct sunlight. They have the same hard surfaces, the stone floor, stone steps, the same sudden sharp sounds when a sacristan starts to move some chairs, when an elegant woman's heels scrape as she genuflects. After all, there is a lot in common between *casa* and *chiesa*. Both are sacred. I have seen Marta polish the parapet of her balcony with the same sacrificial intensity of the old women who bring out the shine on the altar rail here in San Zeno. Certainly, Stefano decants his home-bottled wine with more reverence than the acolytes who carry the Host. Here the drone of the cicalas is replaced by the monotone of a priest reading some special Mass in a side chapel. Apparently for one long dead. I try to get Michele to behave, to show respect, to just sit and enjoy the cool, but suddenly he hoists himself up on the baptismal font to get a look inside, and, slipping on the smooth stone, catches his chin, bites his tongue, falls. A nun rushes from her prayers. *O povero povero bambino!* The boy wails even louder. The sympathy grows correspondingly. *O povero piccolino!* Now Michele's howl fills the huge church. Then Stefi cries, imagining something awful has happened to her Lele, as she calls him. They make an incredible noise. But nobody complains. Neither the huddle in the little side chapel, nor the old women kneeling. Nobody tries to hush them, as I suspect the good folk would if we were in the Südtirol. No, it's I who attract frowns of disapproval when I insist the boy get back on his feet again and pull himself together, when I tell him how silly it was to go climbing up the font. Only after I had been in Italy a very long time did I begin to appreciate that weeping is something to be savoured rather than curtailed. There is so much quality in a child's tears.

At almost two Stefi chases a lizard across the floor upstairs. It must have fallen in through a skylight. Its little feet slither on the shiny surface of Righetti's titles. Its tail curls this way and that. Wildly excited, Stefi runs straight into Rita's desk. '*O che capitombolo!*' I tell her, going to gather

her up. She howls and shrieks. '*O povera, povera Stefi!*' It seems I've converted.

In the main piazza of the village, Michele dances round the oval parapet of the fountain. It's bright winter weather now, the light icily, harshly brilliant as it never can be in England. We've just come out of the *pasticceria*. Rita has gone off to the greengrocer who sells the best grapes. I'm sitting on a bench with Stefi in my arms under bare trees, and 'Don't fall in, Michele!' I shout, 'Don't fall in!' But I pride myself on not being one of those parents who frustrate their children's desire for adventure.

Michele runs around the cheap marble waving his arms and shrieking and bending down to splash the water hooping from low jets. His blue overalls, made in Italy, announce 'CALIFORNIA DAYS'.

'Don't fall in!'

Then Iacopo arrives. You can set your watch by Iacopo's arrival at the *pasticceria*. He's on a huge black motorbike today. Perhaps because he has just left his wife and child. And he says he would like me to have a coffee with him to discuss matters. How can an artist, he demands, be expected to pay much in the way of alimony? His wife comes from a rich family, they . . .

I'm just trying to explain that I've already indulged (in coffee), when there's a splash, a big splash. Michele's in, with the algae and the lollipop sticks, and floating litter and freezing cold. He stands there knee-deep in dazed disbelief that things really can go wrong in life. Then begins to wail. '*Che capitombolo!*' Iacopo breathes, unusually aware of something outside of himself. For my own part, what I'm most aware of is that there is no man in greater trouble than an Italian husband who has been careless enough to let a child catch a cold. It's far, far worse than mere desertion or problems with alimony.

Six months later, with Michele almost five and Stefi two and a half, he sits on a seat attached behind the handlebars of my bike and she on a seat on Rita's. There is no better way to travel. Little hands flail to touch each other as we ride side by side. Little songs are sung. 'Lele,' Stefi shouts, 'Stefi,' he answers, and they love to feel the breeze on their faces. The road is flat, narrow, dusty with summer sun. Swallow shadows flit quick across the asphalt. There's a sensible, flat green stillness about the broad landscape as it sits out another long summer day, quietly, patiently. The corn doesn't wave, it waits. The trees are silent. Only lizards scuttle in the leaves, and sparrows perhaps. Until, round a bend, we find men by a stream, too many men, one after another: a fishing competition. Suddenly the road is lined with their cars. We slow down.

And now something's coming up behind too. Honking. We fall quickly into single file in the narrow space. It's the car leading a bike race. It honks furiously, as if outraged to find parked cars and other cyclists on the route. The fishermen turn annoyed from their tackle. Then they forget their own competition and begin to cheer. *Forza Dino!* Come on! *Forza Montecchio!* We have to stop. The men, young and old, sweat by with their plastic crash-helmets and fancy fluorescent pants. How they love sports equipment! How they love having the name of their team on their shirts! Pedalling harder for the spectators, they flash past in a pack and are gone. The children applaud the *spettacolo*. Then we're just speeding up again ourselves into the stillness of that flat countryside, when all at once something shocking happens. All at once I'm doing a somersault in the air, quite high in the air, actually. I go up and up and over and crash down on my bicycle, Michele underneath. After three years' perfectly happy cycling on that seat, the boy has finally decided to poke his foot between the moving spokes. We might as well have been shot from behind.

The casualty ward, when a car gets us there, has a children's section. They're very kind. They make no criticism or comment. A dozen of these accidents a day. All Italians carry their children on bikes and mopeds and scooters. What better way to see the world! They put a couple of stitches in Michele's leg. He screams, despite local anaesthetics. Nobody tells him to be a man. But the nurse shakes her head. '*Che capitombolo*,' she tells him indulgently.

When they're not off on a trip, after ice creams, or on biking expeditions, the children are naked in summer. They spend far more time naked than an English child ever could, and naked without shivering. Does this kind of thing really influence the character as much as one suspects it might?

Michele and Stefi roll about naked on a sheet on the tiles in the sitting room. They are naked on the lawn in a paddling pool while Rita pours buckets of water on them from twenty feet above. Giovanni joins in. And Gigi and little Martino, Giorgio's son, and Gianluca, Mario's little boy. Gianluca's Serbian babysitter, who arrived to escape the war, stands and watches in a garden transformed from rubble to the lush pages of a magazine, the inverse process of what is happening in her country.

The children are naked, too, on our annual holiday in

Pescara, where the toddling Stefi kneels in the great stone sink outside the house and showers herself with cold water under a fierce sun. They are naked at night in bed under a thin sheet. Too naked now. For one of the characteristic sounds of their childhood must be the dreadful whine of the mosquito over their fragrantly plump bodies. *Zanzara,* the Italian word for the beast, is more onomatopoeic, as befits a language historically closer to the menace. The children's smooth brown nakedness is broken by the great red blotches of mosquito bites. How angry it makes them when they're irritated with the heat! They scream for you to shut the windows, shut the doors. Despite the suffocating closeness. Then, 'Papà, Papà, there's a *zanzara* in the room! Come and kill it!' I come in and perform with a copy of *Io e il mio bambino.* Righetti's whitewashed wall has tiny blotches of blood. I wonder how my old friends Stefano and Marta get round this one, how do they keep those walls so free of fingerprints and blood?

In the middle of the night there's a terrific bang and scream. Michele has tried to imitate Papà. Climbing naked over the furniture, brandishing a toy catalogue, he has crashlanded in his Duplo. Its sharp corners and little studs are printed all over his naked body. Like the grappa drinkers in the bar and the nun in San Zeno and the nurse at the casualty ward, Stefi rushes to help, and she wails: *'Lele, Lele, che ca-i-omolo!'*

Nonni

My mail-order calendar-almanac, *Il Frate Indovino* (literally, *The Fortune-telling Friar*), which I waste hours and hours consulting, has a section for every month entitled '*DONNE*', WOMEN. The heading is scrawled large in awfully cheap calligraphy, yellow on green or pink on blue, and in the circle of the big 'D' of '*DONNE*', or in a small space after the 'E', there will be the tiny illustration of a baby, or a plate with knives and forks on it, or an iron, or a washing machine. The Cappuccino priest who writes the thing clearly has no interest in glamorizing the sex he manfully renounced.

'*DONNE*' usually kicks off with endearing remarks of the variety 'If we really considered the work that you women do every day in the home (11 million of you in Italy and 120 million in Europe) we would understand how much we need you, since without you the whole political, social and economic system would collapse. The housewife should be recognised as a productive worker and rewarded accordingly.' It's the kind of vague blandishment that for so many years won so many votes for the Christian Democratic party, always a great supporter of salaries for housewives, and indeed for everybody, if only there were enough money . . .

Inside this little section (which rubs shoulders with other sections entitled 'Farming Tips' or 'The Stars Speak Out' or 'Did You Know?') is a small subsection (yes, every month!) entitled 'Children, or not?', and this little paragraph is packed with considerations clearly designed to stop the demographic slide and maintain the Friar's reading public in the future. This month's offering observes:

'To have children or not? Here is a problem that obsesses and frightens every couple. Why? Usually it's just selfishness: we don't want to make any *sacrifici*.'

Sacrifici again. The word comes back obsessively.

But apart from buying their house and taking out life insurance (which I very much expect they would do anyway), how many *sacrifici* does the Italian couple really make when they embark on child-rearing? What follows was published as a prize-winning letter in one of the mother and baby magazines . . .

LETTER FROM A GRANDMOTHER TO HER NEWBORN GRANDCHILD

Dearest Anna,

I shan't explain to you who I am because it's too complicated, but when you're big you'll understand. Oh, I don't mean really big, but a little bit big, when I'll be playing with you and passing the time with you telling you fables and fairy stories, just the way I did with your mother . . .

Speaking of which, your mother and father were so happy when they knew you were going to be born because they also knew that they would be giving you to me to look after, and your mother remembers how much time and energy I spent to bring her up good and kind. Of course I was able to spend all that time on her because I only did the housework, while your mother will soon have to leave you to me; she has to work outside the home to help make ends meet (that means buying everything necessary for eating, dressing and having fun on a level with everyone else. That's what life's like today, Anna. Your mother says that if there hadn't been me, she probably wouldn't have been able to bring you into the world, knowing how difficult it would have been for her and your father) . . .

Well, I'd say Rita and I had been in our Via delle Primule *palazzina* no more than a week before we became fascinated by the constant coming and going of certain solid respectable folk in late middle age. They would arrive with admirable regularity in their small Fiats or on puttering old Vespas either to pick up a young child and take him off for the day, or to stay with him for the evening, while the parents went out. Only a few months later and we had learnt to recognise and more or less place all these good people – exactly four per family – until greeting them had become a staple of condominium routine. For all the parents in the building work, mothers and fathers alike. Otherwise, how could they eat and dress and have fun (and drive cars) 'on a level with everyone else', i.e. a level considerably above that of their own parents, these grandmothers and grandfathers, who more than anybody else appear to be the ones making all the *sacrifici* . . .

A road sign near the school in the village warns cars to slow down. There is a silhouette of an adult holding a child's hand as they cross the road. The child is the internationally stylized little girl with pigtails and skipping legs. The adult is bent with age and wears the kind of hat only old men wear: unmistakably Grandfather . . .

The whys and wherefores of this abundant availability of grandparents are easy enough to understand. The first thing is that Italians tend not to move unless they really have to, and since Verona is in an extremely affluent area with a low unemployment rate, very few are so obliged. In thirteen years of living in this village, I can think of nobody who has left to go and live elsewhere on a permanent basis, though some who did go away in the fifties and sixties have come back.

Then, it is popular wisdom in Italy that marriages to the girl next door are more successful than marriages to partners from afar. *Corriere della Sera* once ran an interesting feature on this subject, with detailed statistics to show that divorce rates were higher amongst international marriages than national ones, and again amongst interregional marriages than local ones. A crucial reason for this latter statistic, according to the newspaper, was to be found in the problem of cuisine. Once the 'romance period' was over, the man would feel unhappy to find that the meal on his plate was cooked, not as mother cooked it in Rome, but as Laura cooks it in Rovigo, the salad tossed not as Mamma tossed it in Palermo, but as Monica sees fit in Parma. For women are not thought of as good cooks or bad, but merely, or more importantly, as cooking in the way one does in a particular area: good cooking being by definition the cooking of the place you were born and bred. In any event, the paper implied, the only possible consequence of such radical dissatisfaction was divorce.

Assuming then that the boy remembers the determining importance of food and various other local mores and hence is wise enough to marry the girl next door, it clearly becomes much easier for all the parents to get together and buy an apartment. But if they are to make this generous gesture, it is also very clearly their right to insist (leaving aside the next-door image) that the new apartment be midway between their respective houses. Parents, after all, are entitled to enjoy their children and get some return on the effort spent bringing them up. The natural result of this is that even in these modern times a large majority of Italian couples have all four grandparents at their beck and call.

The availability of *nonne* – grandmothers – is then further increased by the fact that women in Italy retire at fifty-five (in the civil service the age is fifty), and in fact have all sorts of incentives for getting out even earlier, thus leaving millions of healthy and frighteningly energetic middle-aged grannies with nothing but time on their hands. Imagining, then, that their offspring (my generation) stick, as they usually do, to an average of just one child, and assuming that they don't have too many brothers and sisters playing the same game, it is clear that these lucky young parents will have a never-ending source of babysitting at their disposal. Indeed, the problem for the modern Italian couple is not finding somebody to babysit, but avoiding giving offence to whichever of the grandparents is asked to babysit least, and then, of course, having to deal with the children after they have been spoilt and over-protected and stuffed full of *caramelle* and sat in front of the television all day and given the kind of expensive, battery-operated, showy and above all fragile toys that grandparents, in their determination to leave an impression on the last generation they are likely to know much about, do tend to buy.

No sooner, then, have I got to know the handsome Silvio and his equally handsome little boy, Giovanni, than I begin to see the little lad all around the village with his grandmother, most notably in the play area at Primo Maggio, the ex-Communist social club, where, even at four, the boy will still be forbidden to use either the slide or the bigger of the climbing frames, but will always able to get Nonna to buy him a lolly. 'Still pees in his bed at night,' she confides to me. 'Just like his *papà*, oh you wouldn't believe for how long. Eighteen or nineteen years old he was before he stopped.' Having established her maternal authority over the little boys of two generations, she smiles fondly. Then shouts: '*Smettila,* Giovà, you'll get your trousers dirty!'

But Granny's condescension aside, how I envy little Giovanni's parents! Having dropped off their boy with Nonna, they are setting off for a pleasant game of tennis at the local sports club, while I have to watch Michele losing his temper because there's something he can't do on the climbing frame and Stefi crying because she's banged her head on the slide.

Likewise, no sooner have I got to know Giorgio and Donatella, who have the apartment next to ours, a chubbily pleasant and supremely relaxed couple if ever there was one, than I begin to recognise the happy grandparents on her side who arrive daily to carry off little Martino for the day while our neighbours go off to work, and the happy grandparents on his side who arrive in the evening (rarely without a new toy) to look after darling Martino while they go out for a drink, or even while they stay in and watch TV. Again, how I envy these two, who, like the French aristocracy of the eighteenth century, appear to have discovered, rediscovered, the ideal method for bringing up children: having someone else bring them up for you. It was the dream expressed in the lullaby after all. Indeed, the modern Italian seems to have gone one better than the old French artistocracy in having chosen for the delicate task the most reliable servants in the world: those responsible for their own upbringing (with the not inconsiderable advantage that they don't have to pay them anything for it). One only fears that if ever they (my generation) have to look after their own grandchildren, they won't be equipped for it, having had so little experience. No, when it comes to parenthood, the younger generation will be out there on their own, reinventing the wheel all over again.

But most of all I envy Silvio and Sabrina, Giorgio and Donatella, because all our relatives, Rita's and mine, are either in England or in Pescara, or dead. In any event, unavailable. Consequently, I very often, and especially in the first sleepless months of Stefi's life, would find myself typing with a cot on the desk beside me or, later, with a child crawling on the cold tiles round my feet; and one disastrous day when I myself had simply fallen asleep over the keyboard, I woke to find that a bottle of ink had been poured over a freshly printed typescript. 'Where,' I cried, 'where are those *nonni*?'

I wasn't quite the only one in Italy suffering this plight. Turning on the radio one fraught morning, I hear the presenter announcing a phone-in entitled 'Intergenerational Solidarity and the Unnatural Grandparent'. Who would not listen to such a programme? What it turned out to be, however, was no more than an invitation to call up a group of 'experts' and complain of grandparents who were not doing what was expected of them, not, that is, writing cloying letters to their newborn grandchildren or arriving with proper regularity in their little Fiats so that their own children could drive off in their BMWs.

Almost immediately an outraged voice was on the line from somewhere like Ravenna or Cesena: 'But since we've had the child, you understand, after all that was said beforehand, since we've actually had the child, I mean, they, my parents, have only offered to babysit, what, twice in two years, and they absolutely *refuse* to keep him while I'm out at work . . .' The presenter and his panel are duly shocked. The legal specialist in particular informs us that a recent groundbreaking court ruling has established that grandparents have the legal right to see their grandchildren even if the parents don't wish them to. This demonstrates the importance of the grandparent-grandchild bond and the unnaturalness of those who neglect it. For where there is a right, says the expert, there is inevitably a duty, too.

Someone phones to say that her mother will look after the grandchild but then perversely refuses to change him. As a result, she feels cruel leaving the little boy with his grandmother for more than, say, a couple of hours.

'We could phone in ourselves,' I suggest to Rita. 'Surely there must be some law that denies grandparents the right to live more than twenty miles away from their grandchildren.'

From her position on the sofa Rita opens one comatose eye. 'You hate it when they come,' she says.

She's right . . .

Fare festa

Imagine a dull afternoon late February. The doorbell makes you jump. You pick up the intercom, ready to tell the Jehovah's Witnesses that you don't want to discuss the end of the world, you believe it happened long ago. Or it could be Righetti, who has a way of turning up at the most inappropriate moments asking for that rent on his garage, which was supposed to be a mere formality but now turns out to be deadly serious, especially since we're now supposed to buy the thing but can't afford to. Far from keeping the price steady, as pledged, he has increased it in line with the general property boom, *naturalmente*. We forgot to get him to write something down. He claims never to have made any such promise.

The intercom crackles, but no one is there. '*Chi è? Chi è?*' Nobody. Children mucking around, you think, more relieved than angry. You're just putting the thing down when from far away a voice calls 'It's us!' Because what my in-laws do is get out of the car and ring the bell, to get gate and door buzzed open, then go back to the car to unpack. But this is also a call for help. They will have lots and lots of things to carry . . .

I run down with Michele, now five years old, perhaps, clumsily quick and wildly excited at the prospect of an unannounced visit from those great, if only occasional, benefactors, his grandparents. Outside a freezing twilight is stiffening to fog. The garden is a huge trench because, after repeated flooding, a solemn condominium meeting decided to link all the drainpipes from the gutters to the central sewage system. This is illegal for some reason I don't understand, but common practice, not to worry.

Nonno Adelmo, my father-in-law, drives an ancient Ford Fiesta, bought second-hand when he and Nonna Maria returned to Italy to retire some years ago. Despite boasting that this remarkable car has done more than three hundred thousand kilometres, Nonno would clearly like something more comfortable. Nonna, however, still lives in a post-war mentality where things that work have to be made to go on working, and on and on and on, just as food on the plate has to be finished, not thrown away, and just as the rather unattractive fruit from the old trees they have on their acre of land in Pescara has to be gathered, to the very last sour plum and pippy grape, and given to friends and relatives and even the merest acquaintances. So as well as having to drive an ancient car, Nonno now has to fiddle in the back of it to tug out two big crates of homemade jams – fig, apricot, and medlar – plus bottle upon bottle of laboriously prepared tomato preserve for pasta.

The curiosity about Nonna Maria is that she mixes this

obsessive peasant parsimony with a flamboyant love of style. Her father was a cinema projectionist in Rimini; she grew up with the fashion-saturated films of the twenties and thirties. Early photographs always show her assuming extravagant poses, perhaps draped over the parapet at the seafront or simpering beside some monument in Rome, her fine-boned face set in a smirk of insuperable complacency. Even now, stepping out of this ramshackle car at almost seventy, she is wearing a wide-brimmed green felt hat with big pin and an attractive shawl tied with a silver broach. The fact that both are battered and somewhat the worse for wear and tear gives her a decidedly raffish look in the thickening fog as she lifts Michele into her arms. She smells of sweet scents and applies make-up generously, frequently disappearing with Rita's perfumes and lipsticks when a visit is over.

It would truly be hard to exaggerate the cooing and crying and sighing and kissing and nose-tweaking and exclamations and tears and tickles and cuddles that now have to take place. The children must imagine they are the only people in the whole universe. Nonna lifts up Michele and dances round and round with him and '*O che bel bambino! O che ometto splendido! O che spettacolo!*' She holds him up to her hawkish face, rubs noses (losing some powder from hers), then swirls him round again, then crouches down to put her own old cheeks next to his. And now Stefi catches up, toddling and waddling down the path, and the whole extravagant process has to be repeated: the whirling in the air, the nose rubbing, the kissing.

It's what the Italians enthusiastically call *fare festa a qualcuno*, which, literally translated, means 'to make a party for someone', and combines the ideas of welcoming them and smothering them with physical affection. Comparison of this expression with the slightly disapproving 'to make a fuss of' speaks worlds about the difference between Italian and English approaches to such occasions.

'Michelino, look what we've got for you!' Nonno shouts, pulling more packets from the car. 'Stefi, look what's here!'

Michele immediately frees himself from Nonna to run to Nonno.

'Are you mad Adelmo?' Nonna demands. 'The children will freeze if they start fiddling with their presents out here. *Poveretti*, they're both so thin!'

This is patently not true. Michele is nothing if not a hefty fellow. Already I'm asking him to ease up when he jumps off the sofa onto my neck as I read. Stefi shows every sign of being equally robust. In any event, the children have now grabbed two big presents from Grandfather and are fighting with the wrapping paper shopgirls always apply so attractively and efficiently here, thus denying you the problem and pleasure of wrapping them yourself. Still protesting the children will catch their deaths, Nonna somehow grabs both of them, presents and all, and with considerable effort starts to heave and coerce them toward the house. As she sways up the front path in the fog, dragging them by their wrists, we can hear her launching into some story or other with her favourite expression: '*Bambini*, you know what *my* grandmother used to say? Do you? She used to say that little children should always . . .'

Nonno shakes his head, clearly annoyed that he is to be excluded from the present-opening scene which can only occur the very moment the children are through the door and Nonna frees their hands. Easier to keep a dog off red meat than a child from wrapping paper. He had obviously been looking forward to that.

Good journey? I ask, taking hold of a whole box of medlar jam, which I truly loathe. Nonno cheers up telling me that they found a service station with an excellent restaurant, just this side of Bologna. In that way Europeans have of getting back at us for our linguistic hegemony by inventing awful English words that aren't really English, the service station is called the Auto-grill, pronounced Owtoe greel. Apparently in no hurry to get indoors out of the cold, he finds his trilby and overcoat on the back seat, puts them on, then leans on the top of the Fiesta to enjoy a cigarette. 'Women,' he signs with extravagant eloquence, and already he is looking for that male complicity which can at once bind in-laws together while keeping the family as a whole in galvanized tension.

'By the way,' he says, nodding at the crate I've got stuck holding, 'you don't need to actually eat that stuff. Just wait till we've gone before throwing it away.' I laugh, but to be on the safe side thank him just the same. He shakes his old trilbied head. Obviously it hasn't been an easy journey. Foolishly, I ask why they didn't announce their arrival. 'Women,' he repeats. 'What do you want?'

It's his favourite and impregnable cover.

As we're walking to the house, in response to some imperceptible dwindling of the twilight or thickening of the fog, five globes of halogen ignite simultaneously in the garden. Mario and Silvio insisted that the garden must be lit, partly for the ornamental effect but, more importantly, to prevent intruders from creeping near the house unobserved. Nonno laughs at this ludicrous expense, as older Italians do laugh at their young before giving them everything they want. Under Perspex fishbowls on metre-high poles, the halogen gives off the kind of blaze that blinds without illuminating. Even the trench collecting the gutters is thankfully invisible. The fog is suddenly thick as milk.

Upstairs, Stefi has run off to her room with a Sicilian doll and Michele is playing with a huge battery-operated jeep, clearly bought in the same auto-grill where Nonno and Nonna had such (and they're still talking about it) an excellent lunch.

'Do you like your present?' Nonno flops on the sofa. He has taken his overcoat off, but not his trilby. His body is remarkably spherical, yet taut. He doesn't give an impression of flabbiness, more of a properly inflated balloon. Or serious salami.

'Do you like it?' he repeats.

Michele now finds time from having the thing crawl over a sofa cushion, in reverse, to say yes.

'Your grandad bought it for you,' Nonno says. He scratches the baldness where the trilby rubs.

Michele plays on, fascinated by the lever that toggles forward and reverse gears.

'Do you like what your granddad bought you?' Nonno enquires.

After another pause filled with Michele's splutter and spittle – the noise the thing makes itself clearly isn't enough – Nonno again insists: 'You wouldn't have had it if Nonno hadn't bought it.'

The boy doesn't appear to have noticed.

'Your *nonno*,' my father-in-law begins again . . .

'Michele!' I scream. I can't bear it. 'Michele, for God's sake, say thank you and give your *nonno* a hug.'

The little boy turns in surprise, his infant mind trying to make the necessary connections. Then he leaves his toy, rushes to his grandfather, kisses him, thanks him, and heads straight back to the jeep.

The scene reminds me, particularly as the February evening proceeds, of the surprise I experienced the first times I was present at Baldassarre family reunions; before, that is, I knew Italy or Italian or the Italians. For these people, mother and father, sons and daughters, all criticise each other endlessly, all and always have something to complain about, often bitterly, even resentfully; yet when they meet, when the Baldassarres are actually face to face, the gestures of affection, the extravagant *fare festa*, the gratitude expressed when gifts are exchanged, could not be more voluble or enthusiastic.

My wife embraces her mother rapturously. And her father. Michele watches them. Everybody does seem perfectly happy and delighted to see each other. The *nonni* are here! *Evviva!* Yet Michele is surely aware, even at five, that we complain a great deal about these unannounced trips, about not knowing how long Nonno and Nonna are going to stay, about the problems that arise if we have other guests. And surely when alone with his grandparents he will have heard them levelling all kinds of criticisms against ourselves, for they are nothing if not indiscreet. Then as we sit down together at table, everybody will talk critically about Rita's brothers, Uncle Berto here in Verona, Uncle Renato down in Rome, will complain of the former's love of expensive clothes he can't afford, the latter's tendency to send his mechanic's bills to his father. Why do these boys have to borrow so much? Why do they never pay back? Why do they apparently believe that everything is owed to them? Yet later in the evening, when Roberto arrives – orange Benetton sweater loosely tied round the collar of a Gianfranco Ferrè shirt, beautifully creased wool trousers, shoes he might even now be trying on in some expensive store in central Verona – when Roberto arrives with his fierce mane of hair and proud Roman nose, everybody will rush to give him those same rapturous embraces they recently gave each other, everybody will laugh themselves silly, hand-clapping, back-clapping, hugging and kissing. Wine will be poured and then more wine, and Nonna, almost expiring with pride at having such a tall handsome son, and a doctor to boot, will notice that there's only a 'finger' left in the brandy bottle in the glass cabinet. And she will complain what poor taste it is to leave just a finger in a bottle of brandy: her grandmother always said never to leave a drop in the bottom of a bottle, it brings bad luck, though of course nothing good can be thrown out . . . So then she will drink the brandy herself, she feels obliged to, or she will share it round, and the grappa too, seeing as there's some grappa, and everybody will be the best of friends, passing young Stefania from arm to arm and turning her upside down and picking Michele up to tickle him and toss him on the couch and so on, despite its being far too soon after their dinners for that kind of thing.

Yes, no doubt the children take all this in, this wonderful *spettacolo* of affection, this carefully choreographed *festa*. And perhaps somewhere deep down they are learning to associate it with the fact that they must remember to say a huge and quite extravagant thank you to Nonno when he remembers to bring them a present, albeit picked up on an exceedingly full stomach as he staggered out of his favourite auto-grill. Yes, they must put on a good show of gratitude, they must give Nonno his reward and his due, then everything will be given and forgiven them, as everything is given and forgiven to Zio Berto.

I have often wondered, in this regard, whether Italians can really appreciate a story like *King Lear*. Why didn't Cordelia put on a bit more of a show for her foolish old father? Surely that was wrong of her. For there are times when a little falsehood is expected of you, and can be engaged in quite sincerely, because appearance has a value in itself, indicates, precisely, your willingness to keep up an appearance. All the world is appearance. Cordelia was wrong. Equally, those heart-breaking modern American short stories where family members finally and painfully confess to each other the sad truth about their infidelities and resentments, can mean little in Italy, where people are instinctively familiar, from the kind of childhood Michele and Stefania are now enjoying, with all that unpleasantly and inevitably underlies our getting on together. They know this, but are wise enough to put on a good show and enjoy it.

'Don't send the children to bed!' Nonna protests. 'It's so early! How can you do that? You know, Michele, my own grandmother always used to say how important it was for children to experience the fun of being up at night. She said that if . . .'

The children love this. Michele, like Gigi in that condominium meeting of time ago, like children all over Italy, is helping himself to everybody's wine, grabbing pieces of a *panettone* left over from Christmas. The huge brightly red box, complete with silvering and ribbon, in which this insubstantial and rather dull cake was presented, speaks tinsel worlds. Another *spettacolo*. When I insist it's their bedtime and I've had enough of them, Nonna starts muttering about that notorious English coldness, that awful British reserve. Why can't the children have some more cake? Why can't they stay up? Listen to the poor things wailing! They don't want to go to bed. It's only nine o'clock.

But I long since learned how to get round this one. I lean over my mother-in-law's excessively perfumed shoulders and hug her. I tell her how wonderful it is to see her again, which actually it is. Then I tell her, laughingly, lovingly, to mind her own damn business. She responds well to this. She laughs. She admires a man who can be frank and speak his mind, she says. Then she entirely forgets the children despite their tortured yells as they're dragged away to the horror of a warm bed, and concentrates instead on telling Roberto how a doctor should behave. Because a doctor is a doctor, she suddenly announces very severely, and should cut a certain figure, even when he's a urologist.

Roberto looks at her with blank complacency, dipping *panettone* in his wine. He has no idea what she is talking about. So she has to spell it out: she was appalled, yes, totally appalled, in Pescara last summer when they brought a neighbour's relative for him to see, yes, for their son and doctor to see, about the poor man's prostate, and he, Berto, appeared *in his bathing shorts*. He saw the man in his bathing shorts! What a terrible loss of face. Her grandmother, Nonna Matilda, used to say that . . .

There is an advert on Italian television that shows a young man in a supermarket queue buying onions, potatoes, vegetables various. The cashier, an unfashionably fleshy beauty, plumply pale under the blackest jet curls, asks the fellow if he is making a minestrone. 'Yes,' he admits shyly. And what a sympathetic smile the dear girl has as she leans her big breasts forward over her electronic till to tell him not to forget the leeks. No, don't forget the leeks . . . Her grandmother always used to say that leeks were the secret to a good minestrone . . . Meanwhile, a caption floats up across vegetables, whose generous roundness is somehow underlined by proximity to those breasts, to the effect that you always get the human touch in Conad (yes, Conad) supermarkets.

So now Roberto, having to hear for the thousandth time what his mother's grandmother may or may not have said about how doctors should behave (for it may be that 'my grandmother said' is only a way of lending ancestral authority to a private and self-interested opinion), Roberto shouts, *'Sì Mamma, sì Mamma*, anything you say, *Mamma,'* but laughing; and just as both children return to beg a last glass of water and to go round kissing everybody again, he begins to recount a spoof of this television advert, which he has seen on some late night satirical programme.

So, in the spoof everybody in the supermarket queue begins to say what their grandmother put in her minestrone, a huge list of vegetables, some of them most unlikely, with one customer insisting, against all reason, that the real secret to a good minestrone was . . . watermelon. Yes, watermelon, in the minestrone. An argument flares up, while other customers who are eager to be served and to get along home begin to shout in frustration, until one woman cries out loud, 'You know what my grandmother did? You want to know what my grandmother put in her minestrone? My grandmother pissed in her minestrone, that's what she did.' To which the woman's antagonist replies, 'And my grandmother pissed in your grandmother's minestrone . . .'

Berto bangs his fist down on the table three times. Everybody laughs. Nonna included. Rushing off to bed both Michele and Stefi are repeating – 'My grandmother pissed in your grandmother's minestrone, my grandmother pissed in your grandmother's minestrone' – and giggling their little heads off.

Then Nonna draws a deep breath and, quite unembarrassed, insists that what her Nonna Matilda used to say was that a doctor, like a priest . . .

Berto covers his face with freckled hands showing a gold signet ring and gold bracelet. But for all this mock despair, just two minutes later he is bothering somebody else in exactly the same way his mother has been bothering him, though his appeal is to a different type of authority. No sooner has Nonno Adelmo cut himself a slice of *panettone* than Roberto begins to criticise and advise him about his diet, to tell him what, according to the latest research, he should eat and what he shouldn't eat, the dangers of obesity, his chances of heart attack. Nonno shakes his head as though in melancholy irritation with somebody who, like his wife, has understood so little about life he isn't even worth arguing with. But then only a few moments later it will be his turn to advise us, Rita and myself that is, as to how we should proceed with some changes he feels need making to our apartment, tools we need to buy, a product that would be very good for protecting the shutters against weathering. Not to be left out, Rita responds by advising her parents against taking holiday-makers in their spare apartment in Pescara over the summer. It tires them out so much. They would be much better advised to . . .

What Berto didn't mention when he recounted the story of the supermarket spoof was the caption that floated up at the end of it. For I saw the programme, too. It said, if I rightly recall, 'Conad, the supermarket where nobody minds their own business.' Well, nobody minds their own business in the Italian family, nor is expected to. Everybody's behaviour is fair game for everybody else. Even the long dead grandparents of the grandparents are still there, having their say by proxy, turning in their graves, insisting on tradition. If the original Conad advertisement is effective, it's because it plays on a situation everybody recognises. If the spoof makes people laugh, it's because things are just beginning to change.

Our family evening thus proceeds in a sort of merry-go-round of well-meant advice, every last word of which is just so much form, so much water off another duck's back. But these ducks swim in such water. They like to feel it running down their feathers. Towards eleven o'clock, after very generous embracing, Nonna and Nonno retire to the spare room upstairs and we to the main bedroom downstairs, while Berto retreats into the fog to buzz open the doors of his extravagant Lancia Thema, everybody thinking exactly what they like about everybody else, and having quite forgotten every single word of advice given or received.

These visits from the grandparents last two or three days on average, though on arrival they often speak of staying two or three weeks. Perhaps this is just part of the show. Nonno gets up before seven to go out and buy fresh croissants for our breakfast, plus two or three newspapers to read, a gesture that scores very highly with me. It also gives him the chance to smoke a private morning cigarette. Not that he can't smoke inside the house, quite the contrary, but he doesn't like his wife to see him indulging, though of course she knows that this is why he goes out. After breakfast he takes the children to school or nursery and together with Nonna retrieves them in the evening. Then he buys them sweets and ice cream and cakes and toys while she fusses over them, her voice squeezing itself into little trills and warbles of affection which puff off into the emotional air as though shot through the hot fissure of one of those volcanoes that for all their furious activity never quite erupt.

One of these visits, I remember, coincided, most appropriately, with carnival time. Michele and Stefi were dressed up as Batman and Isabella Queen of Spain in costumes peer pressure forces you to buy ready-made and unwashable from Standa, the department store. Nonno and Nonna took them into town to see the carnival procession with all the floats and clowns and pretty fairies tossing *caramelle* through freezing February air into a sea of little angels and devils and Japanese robots and D'Artagnans and Tarzans, all wondering how exactly their costumes should inspire them to act. When hero and royalty came back, full of sweets and soda, it occurred to me there could be nobody better suited to take a child to carnival than Nonno and Nonna, nobody more profoundly in tune with the spirit of the thing.

Then, on the third or fourth morning, their own show is suddenly over. It's been a short run. They're leaving, as unexpectedly as they arrived: usual departure time, six-thirty a.m. You'll be fast asleep and they'll wake you all to tell you they're off. The children stand flat-footed on icy tiles, rubbing their eyes. 'Oh, but why do you have to go, Nonno? You promised you'd take us to the mountains. But you promised. Please don't go.' If the kids occasionally forget to say thank you, they have no trouble in playing this part. They love their grandparents so.

'I'm afraid,' Nonna bends down to whisper dramatically, 'that we've got to go and see a person we've just heard is very sick.'

This is a monstrous lie, invented entirely on the spot and only because it is unthinkable for Nonna to disappoint the little ones with the simple truth, that these old folks have had enough of children and grandchildren for a while; they want to be home. 'We're so upset to leave you, children,' she says, 'but Zia Bice has been taken very ill. She fell down the stairs and broke her hip. We'll be back soon!'

Whether this final remark is true or not remains to be seen. But then, it doesn't matter, since it's the impression being created now, at this very moment, that matters, not how the kids feel later when their grandparents don't in fact return. My in-laws are consummate politicians, issuing promises like pretend currency (and in this perhaps not entirely unlike Righetti and his fixed price for the garage). It's an interesting debate afterwards between myself and Rita as to whether we should tell the children that there are no sick friends, no help to be given to a neighbour redecorating his house, no urgent consulting work that Nonno is doing for a building company, only two old people who want to be well thought of at a low price. Curiously, it's the cold old protestant Englishman who doesn't want to tell the kids, can't see the point. At least about one's grandparents one ought to be able to cultivate illusions. After all, they won't be around long enough to oblige you to think otherwise. When it comes to builders, on the other hand, it's very much a question of caveat emptor . . .

Nido

Let's return to that pressing and so pertinent question my favourite lullaby posed: who can I give my baby to? There are, as I have said, the grandparents, generally more available, useful and conservative in other families than in our own; but then there is also the state nursery, the so-called *nido*. One would have imagined, given the near ubiquity of grandparents and their eagerness to muck in, and given too, the disastrous state of public finances in this country, that the Italian government would have been only too happy to have saved itself the expense of child minding and left the old folks to get on with it. But no. On the contrary, it is remarkable how far the state has gone in order to lighten even further the already light burden on this new generation of Italian parents. For Italy has the most generous maternity leave regulations and the most enlightened system of pre-school care of any country I know. Everything, it seems, is done to make child rearing easy and attractive. And still the birthrate falls.

The word *nido* means nest, but in recent years it has come to mean the first of two levels of state nursery schools, the one going from age six months to three years. I remember being amazed when I heard about the *nido*. It seemed so marvellous that there was a place where one's child would be fed, changed and looked after from eight in the morning till four in the evening. True there were fees to be paid, but they were modest. I could not believe how bountiful the state was proving to be. The only problem, I then discovered, was that the number of places was limited.

We applied – this is going back to when Michele was about a year old – hoping to have at least the morning free to work. As so often in Italy, there was no pre-printed form, but Rita wrote a letter on expensively stamped legal paper and backed it up with the necessary certificates (of residency, of family relationships, of birth, of marriage, etc.) plus copies of our recent tax declaration. Soon afterwards a man came round to our house and asked searching questions about how many hours I worked at the university, questions to which I answered truthfully. He was polite but clearly looking for trouble, eyeing all around him, which in that particular apartment, before we moved to Righetti's empire, amounted to no more than great icebergs of ugly fifties furniture frozen in a time unlikely to be remembered for its sense of grace, or even practicality. How big was the apartment, he asked, how many rooms were there, what kind of car did I have? His face was discouraging, sceptical. Clearly every answer was the wrong answer. Did I have a VAT number? he asked. I said I did. But this apparently was an indicator of wealth, rather than a token of bondage, and likewise the fact that we were renting furnished accommodation, since rents are high.

In any event, we were refused a place. Apparently, we earnt too much money and we spent a lot of our time working at home. But our real crime, as Stefano with his experience of accountancy explained, was that we were self-employed. What we should have done was start a company and then be employees of ourselves. He tapped his nose. '*Sai com'è?*' he said. 'It is easier for a camel to pass through the eye of a needle than for a self-employed worker to get his child into a state nursery.' He laughed. Young Beppe was spending his pre-school days with his grandmother.

Is it worth going into this admission process in just a little more detail? I think so, if only to appreciate the tendency the Italian authorities have of offering everybody a prize (to endear themselves to the electorate) and then, since they can't actually afford to give it to everybody, setting up a maze, or obstacle race, to make sure that only those who really haggle for it (not those who need it) actually get it. It's a mentality every Italian child will one day have to learn to react to, a touchstone situation around which many a personality will form, especially at that critical moment when young people leave school and have to fend for themselves. The question is, are you willing to fight for your gravy train, or aren't you?

Back to the *nido*. Inevitably, there is a points system, in order to establish a *graduatoria*, i.e. a hierarchy of entitlement, a waiting list, or perhaps more simply a pecking order. Equally inevitably, the exact way in which points are allotted is obscure. The truth is that volumes could be written on the various *graduatorie* in Italian society – to get into a college hostel, to get a low-interest mortgage, a place in a housing project, a job. This very day I read an article on a *graduatoria* establishing the order in which, in a little village down south, those who have suffered the ignominy of being buried in the ground (considered plebeian) can expect to be shifted into *loculi* – grave niches in the wall – as soon as places become available in the municipal cemetery. A row has been sparked off because many of the relatives of the dear but ill-treated departed fear that the points system is being abused in order to favour people – corpses or their relatives? – with political contacts in the local authorities.

As for the *nido*'s points system, I never met anyone who understood exactly how it worked. Questions are asked about whether one's parents were refugees from Fiume (the area of Italy returned to Yugoslavia in 1947), or war orphans, and clearly these are extremely advantageous positions to be in. Bizarre anachronisms aside, however, it is no secret that there are points for being a *dipendente*, an employee, and above all for being a *statale*, a state employee. Logically, the state looks after the child in order to be able to count on the presence at work of the parents. Not for nothing is the state often referred to here as *mamma stato* . . .

Desperately behind with deadlines, when Michele was perhaps eighteen months, Rita wrote a long letter to the selection committee for the local nurseries. She pointed out that it is impossible to translate with a child crawling over your typewriter. She remarked that work was work whether it happened at home or not. She drew their attention to the fact that we had no relatives in the immediate vicinity and that the income tax declaration we had showed them did not demonstrate excessive wealth; evasion could not just be assumed.

Eventually we got a reply, which came as rather a surprise, saying that our case had been reconsidered and we were now on the *graduatoria* for the four *nidos* in the area, albeit around number twenty-something of those excluded. There is always room in Italy for the special case. It is always worth screaming and making a noise, as most children know so well. All the same, we suspected that number twenty-something was as good as total exclusion.

We were wrong. Less than a month later we were already being offered a place, not in the local *nido* but in the bigger nearby suburb of San Michele, an ugly ribbon development along the road and railway running east from Verona to Vicenza. The speed with which twenty people had come off that waiting list should perhaps have warned us. For it meant that twenty children had been withdrawn. As it was, we accepted gratefully, even thought of ourselves as having scored a little victory.

The drive from Montecchio to San Michele is about seven kilometres. You leave the vaguely scenic village set off by steep hills, even mountains when the weather is clear; there's the picturesque *castello* on the hillside to your right and one or two attractive villas with iron gates and ivy and wisteria. But as you turn left and south away from the hills, the scenery changes. On the right now is the long, high wall of a barracks, to the left the grey geometry of a top-security prison. Finally, the last glimpses of country give way to the most amorphous of suburban landscapes: interminable apartment blocks that all share the same fittings, the same mass-produced memories of nobler marbles and woods, while on the street outside, as outside Stefano's house, the pavements are still unlaid, the weeds growing tall.

The nursery is a low prefab opposite a building site. Dropping-off time in the morning is from seven-thirty on, but most parents arrive, bleary-eyed, around eight. You are greeted by a girl, who 'welcomes the baby'. She is not one of the senior staff, who will arrive only towards nine; she is a new and raw recruit. The girl takes a baby and smiles as she wrestles with it, inviting, begging, the mother to leave. Babies stop crying when their mothers are actually gone, she insists. But the mother, carefully made up, in fur coat and high heels (did the means inspector notice these things?), can't bring herself to walk out on a crying child. Then another baby is brought in. The girl is supposed to welcome this child as well. And there is a two-year-old being led in by a man in a leather jacket, both of them sneezing fiercely. The girl is supposed to interview this man and ascertain whether it really is wise for him to leave his sneezing and doubtless infectious infant at a nursery full of tiny tots. But she is overwhelmed, she doesn't know where to turn.

With this harrowing scenario repeated every morning, the only reasonable policy was to go in to the nursery itself, get Michele toddling about on a play mattress with plenty of toys and perhaps a couple of friends, wait till he was calm, then disappear. At first we were scolded for doing this, since hygiene demands that parents do not enter the play area with their shoes on. That's why there is a girl on the threshold to welcome them. But it turned out this was one of those sensible rules that have to be broken from time to time (daily) in the name of convenience. The scolding wasn't serious. Rosanna, as I discovered she was called, was grateful that one baby wasn't yelling.

So much for the welcoming of the *bambino*. What the older and more experienced teachers then did with the children all day would remain a mystery to me and something I felt it might be wiser not to enquire into too closely. What does one do with tiny children all day? I continued to take Michele in in the morning and pick him up in the evening, and he didn't seem any the worse for wear and tear. On the contrary. And I was assured, without asking for assurance, that there was no gender conditioning; I was assured that the children were spoken to in Italian and not dialect, though I'm sceptical on that point. I remember arriving one afternoon to hear the *maestra* singing a little song called 'The Bells of Bovolon', in celebration of a tiny village way off in the fog-bound plain. The song was in dialect and almost entirely incomprehensible to someone who only knew Italian, yet Michele understood it perfectly, waved his arms and cheered. I must say I was delighted. One takes great pleasure in seeing children acquire skills one does not have, seeing them become, thankfully, different from oneself.

But by far the most important thing a parent had to do when recovering his or her child was to look at the notice boards that gave the menu and the *scariche*.

The menu as one might expect, indicated what went into the children, the food being cooked on site from, we are assured and I do believe, the freshest ingredients. Minestrones, pastas and risottos, perhaps prepared according to Nonna's secret recipe, were the regular fare for those old enough to eat them (the *graduatoria* for being a cook in one of these places is, I am told, quite endless). *Scariche*, on the other hand, means 'discharges' and referred to what came out of the children at the other end, as it were. A normal day's notice board (scribbled in felt tip on plastic) might read:

MENU
purè, minestrone
yogurt, frutta

and, appropriately, underneath:

SCARICHE

Marco	:	*uno bene*
Stefania	:	*due bene*
Simonetta	:	*due (liquido)*
Thomas	:	–
Gigi	:	*uno (abbondante)*
Marzia	:	*uno (duro)*
Paola	:	*diarrea*
Francesca	:	*uno (scarso)*

For this alone, this observation and disposal of the faeces, I could have forgiven these nursery school teachers anything. They could have talked to my child in dialect all day and engaged in any gender distinction they chose, and it would not have bothered me at all. In the entrance, mothers would gaze long at the day's results, as at other times of life into a lover's eyes, then hurry into the class to discuss the finer points of *due bene* or *uno abbondante* with the poor *maestra*. I always used to hope that I would find the miraculous *due bene* and know that it was unlikely Michele would perform again that day.

One afternoon, however, another notice board appeared

in the little porch to the school, a board that was to be the source of much contention. The authorities had decided to raise the amount of money we paid for the nursery service, basing payment on income (declared income, what else?). Perhaps it was merely in order to inform us what the new fees were that they decided to announce them in a complex table on a notice board. Or perhaps there was some provocative intent. You never know. In any event, all of a sudden everyone could see what everyone else was paying.

I thus discovered, Michele in my arms, that our own contribution was to be more than doubled to four hundred thousand lire per month, the maximum, worth at that time about two hundred pounds. One other person was paying this amount. One person was paying three hundred thousand; two or three, two hundred thousand; while the vast majority were paying about a hundred thousand, and some as little as fifty.

Annoyed, running through rapid calculations in my mind, I went outside and stood Michele on a low wall where he could brum brum to the diggers in the building site opposite, and I could watch the comings and goings of the parents. Some of them, it's true, did arrive in little Fiat 126s. Some of them were not parents at all but grandparents wobbling on bicycles or slow old mopeds: an old woman sitting a child directly on the handlebars, an old man with a *borsalino* propping up a two-year-old on the transmission shaft of his Vespa. This was fair enough. But what was one to make of the arrival of perhaps twenty Volvos, BMWs, Mercedes in little over ten minutes?

One of the most characteristic Italian emotions, it seems to me, is that mixture of envy, perplexity and wonder that comes when one realises that others are working the system far more effectively than oneself – *sai com'è?* – this together with the knowledge that they are doing so and will continue to do so with absolute impunity. Until it dawns on you that the system was invented in order to be worked in this way . . . A black Saab rolled up. A man with gold wristwatch and mobile phone climbed out. Clearly, I had filled in some form or other wrongly.

A few months into this, after our next tax declaration and after the four hundred thousand a month had begun to bite, I managed to uncover a tiny office in a health administration centre in town, where a small woman looked through my file, sighed, then, at last, explained. As an *autonomo* – a self-employed person – I paid a straight ten percent of my salary in nursery fees, up to a maximum of four hundred thousand. If I had been a *dipendente*, I could have paid ten percent of seventy percent, and had I been a *statale*, I could have paid ten percent of fifty percent.

When I burst out laughing, she asked me why, and we had the tedious discussion as to whether such uneven treatment in fact legitimises tax evasion on the part of *autonomi*. In a recent conversation with a member of the railway police, I told her, I had heard that even they were paid their overtime under the table, tax free, yes, even the police, and of course *statali* were notorious for having other jobs in their plentiful spare time. This office, I remarked, was open only two hours a day on alternate days.

As I produced all this provocative talk, I was aware of having suddenly become a little bit more Italian, aware of the society and its language speaking through me, aware that I, like my son, was growing Italian, if not exactly growing up. There was a certain theatricality about it. It was exactly the show expected of an *autonomo* wounded in his wallet.

Far from being offended by my attack on *statali*, the polite, middle-aged but chiefly bored secretary was sympathetic. She remarked, whether in corroboration or opposition wasn't clear, that she had noticed an interesting thing about this year's declarations: they were lower than last year's, lower, that is, than those presented before the new system of income-related fees was introduced.

I was taken aback. Why lower? Then I caught on. But it was surely unlikely, I said, that people would alter their whole income tax declaration merely in order to lower their nursery payments.

The declarations, she said, submitted for the purpose of calculating nursery fees were only photocopies, not originals. She smiled brightly. In front of her on the desk she had the usual impressive assortment of rubber stamps, perhaps fifteen or twenty on two revolving carousels. She gave them both a wry twirl.

'But they could be compared with the orginals.'

She shrugged her shoulders. 'Why should they be?'

What she was suggesting, then, was that people were writing out a different, lower tax declaration for the purposes of the *nido* fees, and from her tone of voice I shall never understand whether she wasn't perhaps encouraging me to do this myself in future, or whether she just felt like mentioning something that she probably felt she couldn't mention in the official way of things. To show that she had her eyes open.

I went to a parents' meeting and brought up the

question. It was one of those dingy affairs where everybody sits on tiny infant seats in their overcoats because the time-switch for the heating has gone off. I said the new way of calculating fees penalized *autonomi*, as if we were all without exception tax evaders. 'You are!' somebody immediately shouted. When I mentioned what the woman in the fees office had said about lower declarations, I was immediately interrupted by the chair, an ostentatiously unshaven fellow, not to mention furious objections from the floor. It was not an experience I shall ever wish to repeat, if only because I felt so ingenuous and foolish afterwards. Given that I was the only parent there who was an *autonomo*, what solidarity could I expect from the others? Clearly the important thing now was to evade the amount of tax that would set this matter to rights . . .

But nursery fees were not to be an issue in my life for very much longer. Around that time something happened that decided us to withdraw Michele from the *nido*, and made sure that we never sent Stefi at all.

It was winter. Michele had been ill off and on for some weeks. Finally, when he was better, I took him in again. The weather was cold, and on driving towards San Michele the air slowly thickened to the inevitable fog. There was a horse in a little scrub of field by the barracks, and Michele would always twist in his seat to see this horse and shout *'Cavallo!'* It made him feel good, especially when the creature had a kind of jacket affair on, an old red rug strapped round its back. Then he would shout, *'Cavallo con pullover!'* – 'pullover' being one of the less likely words the Italians have borrowed from us, though with a mysterious shift of stress from the 'u' to the 'o'. *'Cavallo con pullòver!'* Michele yelled. That put him in an excellent mood. But this morning the horse was lost in a grey fuzz. Michele was glum.

In the little parking space, I drew up beside the black Saab, from which man and child were emerging into the fog in paroxysms of coughing. I arrived in the porch immediately after them. The little boy was feverish, his eyes streaming. The girl 'welcoming' was, as always, new, and I hadn't yet learnt her name. Very timidly she asked if the child wasn't ill.

Fiercely, the man said no.

'But . . .'

The boy had a bit of a temperature, but nothing serious, he insisted. Anyway, he personally was going to work even if he didn't feel well. He and his wife couldn't just take time off, they had a company to run . . .

The girl wanted to protest, but didn't, and the little boy was left holding her hand. 'Come on, Thomas,' I heard her saying as the toddler stood there in a daze of fever.

I had already taken Michele's coat and hat off, but now, instead of going in with him, I walked over to the notice board that listed people's fees, imagining that, for all English names are fashionable here, it is unlikely there would be more than one Thomas. I was right, and thus discovered that Thomas's busy *papà* was paying only a hundred and ten thousand lire to use the *nido* not only as a nursery but as a nursing home.

Driving a Saab, he was declaring an income decidedly less than half my own, which at that time was hardly handsome.

In a little pique of self-righteousness I decided to take Michele home.

Santa patata!

I'm at that stage in a book where you stop and wonder what kind of impression you're giving. Will it seem from these pages that I have nothing but condescension for how Italians bring up their children, how they run their nurseries, that I believe the little Latin rascals are at once spoilt and frustrated, likely, if following their parents' and grandparents' example, to become woefully superficial, at once emotional and Machiavellian? Nothing could be further from the truth. A chapter on Zia and all she stands for should set this to rights.

It might be said in passing, however, that the newspapers in Italy would tend to agree with the negative line (so long as it's not elaborated by a foreigner). Their pages are full of horror stories about modern youth, its lack of spirituality, respect, and (surprise, surprise) basic values. Oddly, it is often those who represent the best in society, or at least the most solid and stable, those who are a proof that much is still as Pope and *Frate Indovino* would have it, who seem most ready to lament the ill wind that is abroad. Thus, almost every time I take baby Stefi or strapping Michele to Zia's she has some horror story for me.

Zia means no more and no less than aunt, or auntie, and as such is used in Italy, as elsewhere, to refer to those people we all feel should be relatives, but sadly are not. Zia Natalina is the person who substituted for the *nido* for us. Of the two, she certainly came closest to offering what one expects from an institution.

Determined not to send Stefi to the first-level nursery, not to have to decipher the difference between *due bene* and *uno abbondante* and gaze with envy at how little others were paying, Rita looked for a babysitter in the way one does these things here. One asks the people in the shops, who know everybody and everything, until sure enough one morning a tall solid sensible girl arrived and wheeled Stefi off in her blue *carrozzino* for a fine spring walk out of doors. Indeed, as I recall, this would have been right around the time that the back garden was taking on its crematorium appearance and perhaps the very day that a small van arrived with all kinds of complicated electronics and hydraulics to attach to the gate.

Milena, the girl's name was, and she was training to look after handicapped children. She helped with the church's summer school. In the afternoons she looked after a very beautiful, sadly retarded girl. On Saturday night she went to the disco, as it sometimes seems the whole of Italian youth does, but on Sunday she was always up in time for Mass. When the Pope came to Verona, she was one of the thousands filling the Arena, the old Roman amphitheatre, and listening, where lions once mauled Christians, to his peculiar homilies about not having sex, but how if you do have it, it's better without contraceptives. How does he know? In any event, she had no boyfriend. What better sort of babysitter could one ask for?

A couple of hours after Milena left with Stefi, we received a telephone call. Our little girl had had one of her totally hysterical screaming fits, the kind of thing we were so used to at one and two and three o'clock at night. However, the person explaining this to us was not Milena, but her mother, Natalina. Yes, Stefi had gone quite wild for an hour. Was it all right if she looked after the child herself, and at her own house, rather than having Milena keep her outside? Somehow, just hearing the brisk warmth of that sensible voice down the phone one knew at once that this was the person to give the baby to, streets ahead of guardian angels and *befane*.

Very soon Zia Natalina was a fixture in our lives, a figure of monumental maternity to both children, somewhere between mother and grandmother, overwhelmingly wholesome without being bigoted. Of all the Italians I know, she is perhaps the only one, who, while pursuing the time-honoured Italian tradition of spoiling children rotten, manages nevertheless to get them to do as she wishes. It is a skill there is no question of acquiring, but has to do with such imponderables as presence and good will and complete freedom from neurosis or pretension, a total at-homeness with oneself. It has to do with being Zia.

You climb out of the car, perhaps with both children, always excited to be on their way to see Zia. The house is in the part of the village built in the 1950s, a big detached thing clumsily approximating some period image of luxury. There's an extravagant Californian roof of big concrete beams sloping over a huge terraced balcony that never gets the sun.

You stand outside the black railing and buzz the bell to the upstairs flat, since, like so many Italian houses, this one is divided into a downstairs for Grandfather and an upstairs for the family. In the middle of the little front garden stands a tall cedar that has outgrown its original ornamental purposes and now threatens to obscure every window.

As always, Zia appears on the balcony. She beams. Michele waves and shouts: 'Zia! Zia! Zia!' Stefi says, 'Tia!' In a loose dress Zia puts her fists on ample hips. 'Well, *santa patata!* look who it is!'

Zia is I think the only person I have ever heard who actually uses the expression *santa patata*. Holy potato. So determined is she to be harmless. At the same time I can't imagine she is one of those people who put up DON'T BLASPHEME stickers on so many lampposts and buses.

You walk up weathered crazy paving to an unprepossessing door at the side of the house. On the wall by the door there is a huge fly, perhaps two feet long, done in wrought iron, and in the porch an even bigger spider, a good metre of him, crawling metallic up the whitewash. The children marvel at these things at once impressive and ugly. Zia's husband made them.

You climb the stairs past the spider. The staircase is extravagantly wide and airy, but dark and cold too, being made of polished limestone laid over cement. The rooms, when you get into the apartment, are surprisingly small and ungracious. The kitchen, in particular, where everything happens, is so poky you wonder where all that space you imagined from outside could have gone, as if in one of those science fiction scenarios where things are different sizes without and within. Basically, there is a long wooden table, straight-backed chairs, cupboards of crockery, a television, and then a folding plastic screen to hide – as if it were a source of shame – a tiny space with cramped oven and sink. As late as the 1950s they still hadn't seen the advantages of selling comfortable environments to women. And Zia hasn't bothered to change things. She is not of the Via delle Primule generation.

While treating the children to whatever baking she has done, and in particular her Carnival *galani* – airy slivers of batter drenched in icing sugar – Natalina launches into one of her horror stories about the way society is going. So and so, the man across the street, you know, with the hardware shop, has left his wife, *poveretta*, and two young children, *poverini*, to run off after another woman, silly girl. And, 'I don't know, Signor Teem,' Zia says, shaking her head, 'I don't know how anyone can do that. *I bambini!* Signor Teem! *I bambini!* How can a man leave his children?'

The conclusion, as always, is that people are becoming monstrously selfish. *'Non c'è più religione,'* she sighs, offering the children another *galano*. No, there is no more religion.

In other company I might remark that, hardly devout myself, I still haven't run off with one of my students. But the last thing I want is to get into a serious discussion, or dry up a valuable source of information. It was from Zia, after all, that I first heard the excellent news that Righetti had just had a baby girl, and then very soon afterwards that the wife was pregnant again, in search no doubt of a baby boy.

So I just nod my head in agreement. Then to feed her

dismay, I tell her about an article I have read in the paper about police speed traps. The Italian police use the photograph method. When the *autovelox*, as it's called, snaps someone speeding, a copy of the photo indicating date and place is sent to the motorist's home along with, of course, a notice of the fine. But this led to a lot of wives discovering that their husbands were not quite where they were supposed to be, nor alone, either. A number of divorces resulted. Now, today's paper tells me, the police have decided to send, not the photo and request for payment, but merely a letter that calls you along to the police station to discuss an unspecified traffic offence.

'*Santa patata*, Signor Teem,' Zia says, shaking her head. 'I just don't know. I don't know what the world is coming to . . .'

For my own part, I can't help marvelling at this Latin gesture of male solidarity. It's only another way of defending the family, after all, I tell her, and I can see my father-in-law laughing and clapping me on the back, or Nascimbeni now making more ambiguous *corna*.

Then she tells me to tell Rita that a certain Marco something or other, the husband of one of Rita's friends, has died. It's so ironic. He left his wife three years ago, set up with someone else, then died suddenly of a stroke. So it was all for nothing! In fact, the stress probably led to his death. And the poor wife had suffered so much, been in and out of mental hospital at a certain point . . .

Again, with other people one might get into some kind of argument over these subjects, one might start saying what a tough proposition marriage is, or how people can change and become incompatible, or how remarkable I find it that sixty or seventy percent of marriages do survive. But Zia is so convincing in her straightforward moral topography that I can't help feeling that she is basically right. Invariably, there is a copy of *Famiglia cristiana* on the table, though she doesn't go overboard for the more bizarre religious publications.

Her own husband, Zio Mauro, when he comes in, is a friendly hulk of a fellow, with huge thick red hands of the kind one can say are *rubate all'agricoltura*, stolen from the fields. He's a mechanic with a partnership in a small garage where no doubt he makes his ironwork creations in his spare time (upstairs is a deer's head with great antlers). Sometimes I see him playing bowls in his Sunday best at Centro Primo Maggio. He's shy with me, and when he does speak it's in a dialect so strong that I'm lost. Certainly, one can hardly imagine him walking out on his wife now, so that is not the problem. In any event, you can see he loves the children, always ruffles Michele's hair, chats to him, even after a tough morning's work.

Or is it that Zia is afraid Milena will be the silly girl who robs some other wife of her husband? The daughter does have a big solidly beautiful body when she wanders about the house in her pyjamas. But all she talks about are the difficulties of getting a job in the state sector. She has done a state exam, but everybody knows these are fixed, so much so that she is only thirty-somethingth on the *graduatoria* despite having heard from an inside informer that she scored far higher than various people further up . . .

Zia shakes her head and pouts, but fixing state jobs clearly isn't as bad as men walking out on their families.

Michele drags himself away from the *galani* to find the remote control for the TV and switch it on.

'*Santa patata*,' Zia exclaims at this precocity. 'I'll spank you, I will!' But you can tell she doesn't really see it as a misdemeanour at all.

The television is showing Japanese cartoons dubbed with Roman accents. Our modern ecumenicism. The Italians seem to make no programmes of their own for younger children, though they don't miss the opportunity of using the advertising space to sell the whole range of consumer goods. Apparently studies have shown that it is more and more the children who are responsible for the choice of purchases in Italian households, even when it comes to such things as video recorders and cars. Back in Via delle Primule there is certainly much rivalry between the boys about which car Papà has.

'*Vacca!*' young Michele shouts when a Japanese giant ray guns the knee-joints off a robot. '*Bravissimo!*' the teeny voice of a rescued girl with Caucasian features cries.

'*Vacca!*' Michele repeats. But this is embarrassing. *Vacca* means no more than 'cow', but it is a short form for *porca vacca*, pig cow, or filthy cow, with all sorts of unpleasant connotations along the lines of women of easy virtue.

'Michele!'

Zia says, '*Santa patata*, Michele, you better not use that language with me.'

She turns to me and winks.

'You better not,' she insists, at once smiling and serious. Somehow it seems to work. '*Scusami*, Zia,' he says.

Then it's handicapped children we're discussing, Milena's chosen field, the deaf in particular, which inevitably brings Zia to our mutual doctor's husband, who has left his wife alone with their handicapped boy after running off with some silly girl he met doing amateur dramatics.

Finishing the fierce espresso I'm always offered, I remark, in line with the general tone of the conversation, that it is indeed a hard environment for a child to be born into. I've even heard, I say, of people using this as an explanation for not having kids at all.

But here Zia will not follow. This is merely a façade for selfishness. '*Ogni bambino ha il suo cestino*,' she announces, with *Frate Indovino* facility. Literally translated this proverb means 'Every baby has his own little basket.' I ask for an explanation.

'Every baby,' she explains, picking up a very solid Stefi, 'is born with what it needs to survive.'

On this supremely optimistic vision of providence, I escape, meeting on the stairs Nonno Ernesto, who is coming up to eat his lunch. He eats his meals upstairs, is fed and served, then returns to his downstairs flat. He's looked after, but doesn't bother. I wonder why these happy solutions are so rare in my own country.

As I climb into the car, the children come out on the big terrace balcony to wave goodbye to me and say not to come and pick them up too soon. Later they will go out into the garden at the back, where Checca the raven lives in a cage the size of a gazebo and knows how to say '*ciao*' to you hopping from perch to dirty perch, so they will say '*ciao*' to each other there for a good ten minutes, with Checca teasing by making these monotonous humans wait for the response. Then they will be allowed to water all Nonno Ernesto's huge vegetables that grow in military parade rows between neat walkways of paving. Under a blistering sun they will fight over a watering can of the variety Peter Rabbit fell into, while noble tomatoes, portly aubergines and fat young peppers stand to shiny attention before them. When no one is looking, Michele will toss some water over the big tortoises to see them pull in their scaly heads from the lettuce they've been thrown.

Other pleasures of Zia's household, particularly when the sun is too hot and the radio warns you to keep children indoors, are the huge model railway up in the loft and the go-kart which one can pedal round the garage and the basement. Both these toys are twenty years old, but benefit from a strict maintenance routine; Zio Mauro, as his ancient 128 testifies, is another of those, like my mother-in-law, who find their vocation in preventing inanimate things from dying. While Stefi makes heart shapes out of pastry in the kitchen, Michele goes down to watch the man working in his dark basement workshop, filing railway lines, or replacing ball joints, or perhaps working on a large wrought-iron frog or some such thing. Towards Christmas there is a big nativity scene that has to be re-wired, the holy family put in the shell of an old TV with papier-mâché landscape and three-phase lighting. My son and the mechanic speak dialect to each other, surrounded by cases of unlabelled wine bottles, the little boy all wonder at the man's skills, not perceiving how firmly they place him amongst an older breed of Italians, which Zia's own son, Nino, who occasionally passes by in a gleaming white Lancia Dedra, has already left behind.

I walk over to get them at five o'clock to find they are playing Scopa with Zia over a glass of Fanta. It's a game of cards you usually see old men playing under dusty pergolas around bottles of the variety Zio Mauro has down in the cellar. Judiciously, Zia is losing.

Sauntering back home, Michele tells me that if I leave Mamma, he'll kill me.

I beg your pardon.

'If you leave Mamma, I'll kill you! And he adds: 'Francesca Tuppini's *papà* has left her *mamma.*'

'Well, *santa patata,* Michele,' I have to exclaim, 'what has that Zia been telling you!'

Nor was the possibility of parental separation the only hard fact my boy must have learnt from Natalina. About a year after the children had started going to Zia's, I remember crossing the road with him one day and hearing him remark that we would have to do this carefully if we didn't want to end up like that little boy at the cemetery. Careful questioning revealed that Zia regularly put him on the handlebars of her bike when she went to place flowers on her mother's grave at the cemetery (at least once a week). Once there, she always made a point of explaining to him that all the people whose photographs he could see on the tombstones and the grave niches were dead people, people who had been alive and living here in Montecchio for the most part (and often she could tell him the streets and houses where they lived), but who were now dead and confined in their coffins, until, after twenty years or so, they would be pulled out and someone new put in. The little red lights, she explained, beside the photographs, the *lumini,* were to indicate the presence of God. In particular, she showed him the grave and photograph of a little boy his own age who had been killed in a street accident in Piazza Buccari a couple of years before. This photograph made a big impression on Michele, who was clearly less impressed by the spiritual comfort of the little lights than by the thought of how drear and cold the graves were and how frightening to think of the once-alive-now-dead people inside them.

'You have to look when you cross,' he tells me solemnly, 'if you don't want your photo in the cemetery.'

Another place Zia regularly took Michele and, even more so, Stefi as she grew up, since Stefi was to go to Zia every weekday for two years and more, was the church, a large amorphous red-brick construction from the outside, but bright and airy within. She took them when she went just to pray and light a candle and she took them when she went to funerals. And Zia went to a lot of funerals. Indeed, I can think of nobody who goes to more funerals than Zia. Unless it was just that these were unfortunate years. Michele and Stefi got fairly used to the ceremony and learnt to insist on lighting candles. Stefi, as she grew into a little girl, became terribly impressed by how well everybody dressed at church, which she very soon realised was one of the main and best reasons for going there. If we passed a church on our walks, she would protest loudly until we went in and lit a candle. When she was around three and we took a holiday in England, she was most upset that there were no candles to light. And on the same holiday, when my mother was trying so delicately to explain why she didn't have her beloved dog any more, using expressions like 'Laddie isn't with us now' and 'Laddie's gone away to a better place,' Michele said to Stefi with great frankness, 'She means the dog's dead. He must have tried to cross the road.'

Biancaneve

In the beginning, then, there was the *nido*, then Zia, though Zia will never be entirely eclipsed, and finally the *scuola materna*, a sort of second-level nursery for three-to-six-year-olds, still optional, but as you only pay for the food, much more widely used than the *nido*. It's here they start to teach the children things, including, though you may opt out, religion (Catholic, vocational); but if you do opt out, your child will be alone, unless perhaps there is an *extra-comunitario*, meaning a little black boy who is a moslem. Or another way of putting it would be to say that if you opt out – have your children opt out – you are yourself a moslem, a term that can be used to describe anyone beyond the pale. Not that the majority in the village are 'staunch' Catholics, or bigoted, or even, in most cases, remotely interested in matters religious, merely that they would no more dream of opting out of the catechism than of not greeting their parents with the appropriate, time-honoured embraces. Catholicism is still the default setting for those without preference in a supremely hedonistic Italy.

I asked the woman who was Michele's and later Stefi's teacher at the *scuola materna* what they actually did during the so-called *ora di religione*, the hour of religion (which, when you investigate, turns out to be two hours). Immediately, she began to apologise; she began to say that they hadn't yet been granted a specific teacher for religion, so they found it difficult to cover the whole programme, established apparently in liaison with the church and including every major issue of faith. They found it difficult, she said, to teach the little children everything they were supposed to. I smiled to think that this slim, gaunt woman, who likes to wear a stooped, professional, worried look, had imagined that I, protestant by birth and sentiment, atheist by conviction, was one of those who worried that the children weren't getting enough religion. At the parents' meeting there are always one or two mothers who fuss that the tiny tots don't know their catechism yet. Somebody's dear boy hadn't even realised that Jesus was the son of God! Though the thing that mothers most complain about is the wonderful food. At one meeting I went to a woman needed to know why the children couldn't have salmon from time to time. The others present did not laugh. Nor did anyone mention that we were only paying fifty thousand lire a month for twenty meals and snacks.

Outside the nursery school every morning, first Michele and then Stefi would insist on stopping with the mothers to have me read, and later read themselves with furrowed brow, the little board where someone writes out the day's menu in black felt-tip. Pasta with tomato sauce, boiled beef and polenta. Fruit. Not risotto, *grazie a Dio!* At four years old, Stefi seems to know the cook very well and waves to her and calls her by her name. She always asks for second helpings and always complains that they give her too much. Michele, on the other hand, can never remember what he's eaten and sometimes will ask if dinner's ready only ten minutes after he's finished it. Or he will wake up and ask 'Have I had my breakfast yet?'

Beside the menu there are other notices. Something typed and official looking today. The headed paper shows it's from the Commissione per la pubblica istruzione della VII Circoscrizione, the committee of the local authority responsible for education. I ask Stefi if she can read it. She's at that wonderful stage where children pronounce each letter then syllable before putting the word together. Fortunately, Italian spelling and phonetics is such that this is possible. There are no grimly chaotic words, like 'thoroughly' to deal with, or 'mightn't'. The note says:

> Protocol code: a/2473
> Re. Gratitude
> Having convened in open session on 5 April 1991 and having been apprised of the donation of no. 1 swing to the Monte d'Oro Council Nursery School, the Local Authority Education Committee extends its most heartfelt gratitude to the Parents Committee of the aforementioned school for their interest and generosity.

Beneath is the kind of signature one might expect from a committee: a bumpy line tugging in various directions. Still, I can't deny feeling pleased on reading this notice, since I was one of those at the parents' meeting that first suggested the donation. Then when am I ever going to see

'Re. Gratitude' at the top of a memo again? Stefi, who spelt the thing out, understood nothing. Nor seems unduly concerned. An important step.

The parents' meetings are less formal at the *scuola materna* than at the *nido* and are held class by class so that you get to know the other parents, which is nice. Or I should say you get to know the other mothers, since I am the only father who ever, occasionally, goes, not out of virtue, but pure curiosity.

First the teacher explains the theme of the year to which everything they are teaching is linked. This year it is difference: difference between colours, tastes, smells, measurements, difference between languages, and difference between opposites, big-small, sick-healthy, black-white (the little moslem boy?), girl-boy, child-adult. Listening to the gaunt teacher expound this, I can't work out whether the intention is to be politically correct (aware of all the different kinds of person), dangerously honest (people are not 'equal') or merely informative.

In any event, the story they have chosen to anchor their theme around is *Biancaneve e i sette nani – Snow White and the Seven Dwarfs* – an excellent choice offering the whole gamut of human emotions and inequalities in just those seven names, Grumpy, Dopey, Happy . . ., which, whatever the language (Brontolo, Pisolo, Gongolo) one can never remember quite all of. As if to remind us that difference is endless, beyond our grasp.

Warming to her idea, explaining how the Mirror-mirror-on-the-wall bit will allow them to introduce the idea of comparatives and gradations of difference (who is the fairest of them all?), Irma, the gaunt teacher with long thin arms and knotty elbows, guides our attention to the walls (we're sitting on embarrassingly small seats again, creating all kinds of problems for those in dresses and skirts), where there are scores of children's drawings depicting moments in the *Biancaneve* story, including the part where the woodsman takes back a deer's heart instead of Snow White's. On each drawing the teacher has written such appropriate things as, Tall-Small, Beautiful-Ugly, Cruel-Kind, Rich-Poor, Fat-Slim, Animal-Human . . . It's fascinating reflecting how these simple contrasts must fill the children's minds, establish all sorts of conditioning, moral and aesthetic, that they can then swim with or fight against (certainly Stefi always has a second helping because she likes eating, but then says they gave her too much because she is aware that it is wrong to be fat).

The parents, however, or rather, the mothers, apart from their preoccupation with keeping their legs tightly closed, seem very little interested in all this, as if any teaching to four- and five-year-olds were a hopeless gimmick, especially if it drags in old Disney movies like *Biancaneve*. As people begin to chat or gaze out of the window at our no. 1 new swing, I feel a yearning to cheer up poor Irma with some expression of appreciation. Difference and its distinction, I might say from my tiny chair, is at the basis of all human learning and is always to be distinguished from discrimination. It's what travel books are about. I keep my mouth shut.

But now *Biancaneve* and the year's curriculum are behind us. It's complaints time. One mother is concerned that the climbing frame (floor smothered with mattresses beneath) is not being properly supervised. Then Righetti's wife, Monica, says she feels that the transition in the morning from the calm of the family to the shrieking mass of children tearing around the play area before they split into classes is proving traumatic for her little Lauretta. Other mothers nod in sage agreement. One morning, Monica says, when she just heard the noise, when she just realised how *loud* everybody was screaming there in the play area, she turned back and took the girl to her grandparents. Carefully, Irma remarks that she will do what she can, though she has never actually noticed Lauretta looking upset. Now, however, she says, we must hurry on with the agenda. For the main and truly serious business at this first parents' meeting of the new year is the election, by secret ballot, of our class representative, that vital person who will liaise with the teacher on behalf of the parents whenever anything crops up.

Here is an experience: the election of the Monte d'Oro Nursery School's Second-Year Class Representative. A secret ballot, of course, implies the need for a properly democratic contest, implies that without secrecy there would be attempts to sway the voters' decisions, difficulty in expressing one's true desires, corruption. A secret ballot is an essential precaution where much is at stake. It guarantees that something is being taken seriously. Thus the rules for electing the class representatives in schools, and even nurseries, form part of that complex machinery that Italians have righteously put in place (the endless *graduatorie*) precisely because experience tells them that things are normally decided by personal influence and favouritism (*ricatti*), though it is common knowledge that such machinery very often becomes little more than a cover for what it was designed to eliminate. *Pilotato* is a favourite word in the Italian press. It refers to the way some decision-taking process may be secretly manipulated – piloted – by those with personal interests, a sort of sophisticated technical euphemism for the more brutal English 'fix'.

Was this true in the case of the Monte d'Oro Nursery School election for our class representative? Was this election fixed for ulterior motives? Not exactly, and yet . . .

The first thing that must be said is that one of the many implications of a secret ballot is that there be at least two candidates, that there be competition. Without competition, who needs secrecy? And it was here that the election of the class representative differed (something to be taught to the children?), and differed radically (gradations of difference?), from your average political election.

Unsurprisingly, indeed reassuringly, none of those who had turned up for the meeting were eager to take on a thankless role that mainly involves collecting money to buy materials for the children's end-of-term *spettacolo*, and then, even worse, getting everybody to agree on the choice of, and again collect money for, an end-of-year present for the teacher, something that may well cost in the region of a hundred pounds, so important a figure and so capable of influencing the life of one's child is the teacher perceived to be.

Irma, whose long legs, sensibly trousered, seem to stretch metres from her tiny chair, announces, with great formality, that she will now absent herself from the room while we select our candidates, since it is important, she reminds us, that the teacher not be thought of as influencing the choice of the person she will have to liaise with (is she afraid we might otherwise suspect her of attempting to increase the value of her end-of-year present?). So Irma leaves, closing the door on total silence. We all sit on our infant chairs surrounded by those pictures of the ugly old witch offering the poisoned apple. And nobody wants to bite. Nobody wants to be the class representative. Everybody has quite enough work to do at home with dwarfs various. Though nobody, you can feel sure, has seven.

'Well, somebody will have to volunteer,' a small woman says, but in a tone that makes it perfectly clear that that somebody will not be her. Indeed, exactly in announcing that harsh reality, she has excluded herself. The pressure grows. It's not unlike those games where you stare at each other waiting to see who will be the first to break down and laugh, or worse still those open prayer meetings I went to as a child where everyone would wait for everyone else to make a contribution. Finally, a bright blonde brittle woman breaks down and confesses that she is willing to do the job, but only, and she is suddenly quite adamant about this (as if having earnt the right to be), only if she has another person as an assistant, someone who can help her or even take over from her if things get too much. Upon which, another mother, perhaps already regretting that she had not been the first to volunteer (the blonde woman is certainly getting some very warm smiles), announces that she is willing to be the assistant.

Ecco! Settled. There is a huge and understandable sigh of relief. At the same time I notice that one method Irma is using to teach the concept of difference is that of getting the children to draw a circle, probably round the base of a tin, and then a small figure either inside it or out. Then on these drawings she has written, 'ME INSIDE THE CIRCLE' and 'ME OUTSIDE THE CIRCLE'. Very ominous. Though I'm pleased to reflect that class representative is one little circle I have always managed to keep out of.

With everybody feeling happy and relaxed and talkative (we have a candidate we can now, secretly, of course, all vote for!), Irma is invited back in. The blonde woman, who has assumed the authority of a spokeswoman, announces our decision. But Irma frowns. It's her I-take-things-desperately-seriously frown, as when I quizzed her about what was taught in the *ora di religione*. She then informs us that the class representative is an official, legally recognized position and that the school's statute makes no provision for the role of an assistant. This will not do.

There is something wonderful about watching people coming to grips with rules that are totally inappropriate to the situation in hand, as when one observes a gaggle of Germans waiting in pouring rain for the green pedestrian light that will allow them to cross a road where there is absolutely no traffic nor any sign of traffic. As the rain dribbles from their umbrellas to their shoulders, or bounces off the pavement onto their sensible shoes, you can see them hesitating, growing tense and wondering whether for just once in their lives they mightn't cross a road (but it's such a big road!) with the light on red. Which is illegal! Until at last the light changes anyway and they are relieved of this terrible dilemma, yet at the same time perhaps annoyed that they didn't make up their own minds first, that they didn't make that gesture of awful daring . . .

There was very little hesitation, however, when it came to Italian Montecchio and the Monte d'Oro's second-year class representative. People are not so respectful of authority here. Nevertheless, it is remarkable to see quite how far some will go to get round a rule without actually breaking it. For cunning lies not in ignoring rules, breaking boundaries, but moving as it were in a different dimension, where they become irrelevant. I wish Stefano had come along.

What if, somebody said, the vote for the representative was a perfect tie? What would happen then? Surely the two candidates would have to share the job, either alternating, or one operating as the other's assistant?

Irma was unsure. Perhaps in that case . . .

A tie was impossible, I pointed out, given that there were eleven of us and . . .

One vote gets wasted on a third candidate, I was quickly enlightened. My own most probably. How could I ever have imagined this was a problem?

We thus, in the absence of any known provisions for an exact tie, proceed as follows: half of us, and that is Miriam, Cristina, Anna, Silvia and Orietta, will vote for the first candidate, the blonde (fake blonde, I now realise) Cristina; while the other half, Monica, Mariuccia, Paola, Mariella and Daniela, will vote for the second candidate, the minute and nervous Paola; while I, and only I, will vote for a candidate of convenience. Who? Why not Daniela, a very dark young mother, who I find rather attractive? But to vote we must know the respective surnames, while the candidates themselves have to fill in the inevitable form giving particulars. Memories of childbirth. Still a lot to do . . .

We are in a hurry now, because apparently the teachers leading the various class meetings want to leave. Dinner time beckons. There is much busy laughter and joking, but also a lot of serious casting about for pens and jotting down of names and surnames on scraps of paper, and 'Who am I voting for? Cristina?' 'No, Paola.' 'But I thought . . .' 'It's Paola's surname is Preti, not Cristina's. Cristina is Chieppe.' Organized at last, everybody quite sure now who they and everybody else are voting for, our teacher herds us out into the big open area between the classrooms where our children have been playing during the meeting, rolling about on big cylindrical cushions and falling off the climbing frame on purpose to plunge onto the mattresses below. We then cross to the kitchens, where three very serious ballot boxes are lined up on a big wooden-topped table full of chopping marks. The plump cook hands us our ballot papers and in great secrecy each scribbles down his, or rather her, decision, everybody now assuming exactly that formal hesitant concern people have as they make their way into polling booths. The papers are folded against possible intrusion and posted in the black box.

What would happen, I wonder, as I'm about to scribble down Daniela's surname, Nerozzi, what would happen if I exercised *my legal right* to put down a different name than that agreed on, to jot down Cristina Chieppe, for example, and saddle the poor woman with the entire and onerous responsibility of being our *rappresentante di classe?* The problem is that if I break trust the others would know who had done the deed (there would be no vote for Daniela), whereas if any of the others decided to upset our arrangements there would be the secrecy of being one of a group. How could anybody know who had voted for Chieppe instead of Preti? Or vice versa. On the other hand, I am the only one in a position to 'favour' either candidate. On reflection, this is the most interesting election I have ever taken part in. And the most harmless.

Meanwhile, the children have gathered round, very impressed by this ritual of making a sign (*different* signs, children) on a piece of paper, hiding it, putting it in a box. At what age, one wonders, will they realise what a farce it is? For the moment, the teachers will have their work cut out explaining the difference between Bashful and Dopey, between the variously poisoned apples, between the resurrection of Snow White and that of Our Lord – if they have time to get on to that part of their program this year.

Com'è il tempo?

'Com'è il tempo?' says the voice in the phone. What's the weather like?

How should I reply to this? Outside a blue sky is just lightly curdled here and there in creamy flecks of cloud. Good, you would say, the weather is good. But no. Even my children already know that this is not so. The weather is decidedly not good. For the air is very moist. It is humid. The temperature is not much over sixteen or seventeen degrees. What's more, there is a forecast of a light cloud cover for later on in the afternoon. Worst of all, it rained during the night, which means the ground is damp. Michele and Stefi are desperately disappointed. For today should be Michele's school outing. He is now at the *scuola elementare*, the primary school.

'Com'è il tempo?' the voice repeats. It's Stefano. I tell him cautiously, 'Well, very much as it is where you are, I

suppose.' Stefano and Marta and Beppe, now Michele's closest friend, live no more than half a mile away.

'We haven't opened the shutters yet,' Stefano says.

'Ah. Well, do.'

All in good time. The only thing is, he says, are we planning to let our Michele go on the walk, or not? Because they're worried about letting Beppe go. He had a cold a couple of weeks ago.

Just as the Italian household must be perfectly clean before one can relax in it, so the sky must be scrubbed an immaculate blue, every smudge of cloud polished away, before one can feel safe, before one can feel that the universe is behaving as it should, that things are fair, that the celestial *graduatoria* hasn't been fixed.

'The bad weather continues,' apologises the man in air force uniform who reads the forecast on TV. And you think: 'What bad weather?' then remember a brief shower shortly before lunch. We once took a holiday with Stefano and Marta to the tiny Mediterranean island of Capraia, sharing the rent of a cottage. They insisted we all pull out after only a week because they felt the weather had let us down. It had rained twice and there had been some brisk wind. As we left, the temperature was up in the mid thirties and the water dazzling with light. But there was a forecast of gathering cloud, Marta pointed out, for the late afternoon . . .

Now Stefano remarks that Marta is particularly worried about Beppe getting his feet wet.

'What are you going to do?' he asks again. It's part of the local genius for living in groups that everybody wants to know how everybody else is going to behave before they decide themselves. Ten or fifteen families may phone each other before deciding not to go for a picnic.

The children are squirming on the sofa. *'Per favore, Papà!'* they whine. *'Per favore,* we want to go.'

Michele is a big boy now, nearly seven years old, a strapping lad, blond, ungainly, tiggerish. At four-and-a-bit, Stefi is just losing her baby plumpness. *'Per favore Papà,'* they beg, and both children cross themselves, which is a gesture they have seen Gianluca Vialli make on TV before he takes a penalty.

'Well, we'll certainly be taking our kids,' I tell Stefano. 'They can put their rain jackets and boots on.'

There's a brief silence at the other end of the line. The idea that a walk will require protective clothing already relegates it to worse than second best. But at this end the children are cheering and jumping about – sometimes it's worth having an English dad, even if he does send you to bed early. Amid the whooping, Stefi remembers to cross herself again, as Vialli does, if he scores. Sometimes I fear she may want to become a nun one day, just for the theatricality of it all.

'But what if none of the others turn up,' Stefano insists, and adds, 'I suppose I could call Morazzoni and Castelli.'

'The teachers will have to turn up,' I point out, 'since they arranged it. Then there's ourselves. Worst comes to the worst there'll be six or seven of us.'

Stefano says: 'Look, I think Marta should talk to Rita.' Clearly, it's a question for mothers to decide.

In the event, it only takes Rita about fifteen minutes to persuade Marta that it will be safe to go on this walk, that there are plenty of places to take refuge if it rains, that the chosen picnic spot has benches so we won't need to sit on the wet ground. My wife has considerable powers of persuasion.

Outside the school, about twenty minutes after the official rendezvous time, almost half the children have turned up as have a fair number of parents. By common telephonic consent, everybody has brought umbrellas and jackets with hoods, for there are still two or three clouds in the sky. As always in Italy, every pair of shoulders sports a small fluorescent backpack full of all kinds of emergency equipment.

It's Saturday morning and Michele's class, which goes to school from eight till four, five days a week, jeers at the other class, indistinctly to be seen through high windows beyond a fence, who go to school from eight till one, six days a week. Many parents are convinced that their children will suffer if they don't eat at home and that they are anyway incapable of being away from their mothers for more than five hours at a time, so they choose the solution of the six-day week. Schools thus offer two completely different timetables, no doubt causing all kinds of complex logistical problems, though conveniently leading to the employment of more teachers than might otherwise be necessary.

Michele and Beppe wave sticks that are really swords at the window where their companions are working. Michele has become D'Artagnan, while Beppe is all three of the musketeers at once. In character, Beppe has a long, punk ponytail where his hair has been allowed to grow out of the fringe at the back. Stefano hates this, but since Beppe, at seven, says he wouldn't feel himself without it, his mother won't hear of his wishes being violated. We should not try to appropriate our children's bodies . . .

The boys wave their sticks. They shout mild abuse. But when Michele pulls out the big catapult Nonno made him – one of the only kept promises I can recall – I have to intervene. No, not even a small stone.

On all country walks Michele carries his catapult, his penknife, a pack of cards showing high-performance cars and a long, pointed stick. He is obsessed by the fear of *vipere*, adders; the hills are full of *vipere* whose poisonous fangs will kill him stone dead if ever they get within range. Everybody knows that, he says, and almost the only thing he seems to catch on the radio news is rare cases of tourists rushed to hospital with snake bites. After thirteen years in Italy, I myself have still to see a *vipera*. On the other hand, I have seen plenty of high-performance cars.

Stefi carries her Topo Gigio shoulder purse and her Polly Pocket. 'Polly Pocket – *la tua amica piccina*', the ad says. All over the world, English is everywhere in a child's life. The unnatural thing is understanding it.

We walk out of the village towards the *castello*. The scene is extravagantly picturesque, as if in some kind of postcard conspiracy: ahead of us are turreted villas up a steep slope, mellow stuccos, ivy walls, iron gates overwhelmed by wisteria. A zigzag of tall cypresses shows the way. To the right and north lies the long valley of the Val Squaranto, narrowing to steep woodland. Above and behind range the bright white peaks of the Alps, sharp and clean as good ceramics in a top cupboard. 'There'll be a chill wind before long,' Marta worries, noticing how last night's rain fell as snow on Monte Tomba.

This castle on its hilltop, this long dark valley, these mountains . . . what we are walking into here is the romantic landscape of Stefi's drawings, endlessly repeated in broad felt-tip with only a swift turnover of foreground protagonists for differentiation: Snow White and the Seven Dwarfs in the second year of the *scuola materna*; the angel and the Virgin when despite poor staffing the *ora di religione* got that far; Nonno and Nonna after one of their rare visits (recognisable from Nonno's paunch and trilby); Zia Natalina feeding Checca; and on one occasion, I remember, after reading some heavily abridged classics together, Iphigenia sacrificed to Zeus (sitting on top of the *castello*). But default settings for the figures in Stefi's drawings are Mamma and Papà, or a prince and princess, two couples who are frequently and flatteringly confused.

Michele, on the other hand, doesn't see the castle, the valley, the mountains. His fantasy world is fed by the fast road we have just crossed that marks the end of the village. Give him colours and a piece of paper and he will stretch out its chase of polished steel into supersonic racing monsters perfectly capable of sprouting wings. And every sports car that goes by is a red Ferrari . . .

We follow a path which immediately steepens for the climb to the castle, upon which the children start to complain that they're tired. Marta wonders if Stefano shouldn't carry Beppe. Stefano refuses.

Marta is a curious creature. Petite without quite being frail, she falls into the category of those who despite having an obsession with cleanliness and safety nevertheless do want to have a second child. An unusual scenario. But for some reason she, or he, can't. So they are trying to adopt. Only, adoption takes so long in Italy. There are so many rules. The child has to be safeguarded in so many ways that he ends up not being adopted at all. Twice they've been promised a child and then denied it at the last minute, the last time when the government suddenly introduced the rule that neither parent could be more than forty years older than the child. Since Stefano is now forty-two (his moustache is peppered white), this is making things impossible.

However sad, it is amusing to hear Marta complaining about this, since her own protectiveness, which so often prevents Beppe from going out (he cannot sleep over at our house because 'he has never spent a night away from his mother'), is very much part of the same mentality that framed that rule.

Along with another couple of parents and Maestra Elena, Michele's teacher, we fall to discussing the bizarre case of a couple in Trento who are being denied the right to adopt. The local social services object that the man, a successful interior designer, wears an earring and openly states that he does not believe in God, while his wife has recently shown signs of capricious imbalance by giving up a steady job in one of the town hall offices.

How dangerous it is to put yourself outside the group mentality in Italy! To declare that God doesn't exist, to jump off the gravy train of a state job! (Is it just me, or is there something similar about these crimes?) For all comment, Marta merely insists that her husband does not wear an earring, that they do go to church, and that she would never give up her job and the security it brings her. Then, although Stefano is clearly a little nervous about this, she tells everybody that they are thinking of going to Africa or South America to find a child to adopt. It's a major and very courageous step. There's a moment's silence as people grope for the right response. At the same time we turn a corner of stones and brambles to arrive at the outer wall of the castle where somebody has painted the ambiguous graffiti PORTARE I NEGRI NEL VENETO È SCHIAVITÙ – Bringing blacks to the Veneto is slavery. Above and below this are the more forthright and commonplace 'Foreigners out of the Veneto' and '*Eviva la Repubblica Veneta*', with a primitive lion, symbol of the old Venetian Republic, sketched above one crumbling portal. Somebody has even invented:

Ruggisce il leone
Trema il terrone

The northern lion roars
The southern peasant trembles

I wish Stefano and Marta all the luck they will need . . .

Gathering the children to talk on the clearing inside the castle walls, Maestra Elena makes no comment on the disturbing graffiti, but tells us that the castle used to have nine towers, not just three as at present, and that the beautiful cypress trees around it had not even been introduced into Italy when the first settlement was started on this hill.

An Italy without cypresses. I had never imagined.

We stop for a picnic further along the ridge of the hill where, in the general drift yuppiewards, an old farm is being turned into a riding school. They have agreed to let us sit on their benches, which is kind of them, though the grass is quite dry now. The weather, generally commented on as miserable, is a soft breeze shunting puffy little clouds back and forth above, while a thick haze has obscured the mountains to the north.

Out comes the tupperware, the knives and forks. Some of

the picnics are quite elaborate. Aubergines in oil, zucchinis, salads. Many of the mothers have wisely told father to arrive at the top of the hill with the car so that big bottles of wine, dishes and cakes can be easily provided. Someone has brought a guitar. After lunch the children sing:

Io son contadinella
alla campagna bella
se fossi una regina
sarei incoronata

I'm a little farm girl
In lovely fields around
But if I was queen
By now I would be crowned

Stefi loves this song. She gets so excited, as her own drawings suggest, by the idea of transformation, country girl to queen, Mummy and Daddy to prince and princess. Perhaps growing up is waiting for metamorphosis. The same song then continues, unaccountably, with this little riddle:

E cinquecento cavalieri
Con la testa insanguinata
Con la spada rovinata
Indovina che cos'è!

Five hundred cavalr-ee
Their heads all bloody
Their swords all broken
Riddle me riddle me ree

And then the riddle's answer:

Sono solo le ciliegie
Sono solo le ciliegie
Sono solo le ciliegie
Che maturano al sol.

They're only cherries
They're only cherries
They're only cherries
Ripening in the sun.

Are they the cherries the farm girl was picking perhaps? Was she planning to crown herself by weaving their stems together, the way little girls do sometimes in this country of cherry trees? It's a lovely song. The children yell it out to a slightly mistuned guitar (Marta is singing very loudly and happily, too), while some of the men have gathered together to discuss football over the wine and one or two boys are sneaking off into the bushes with their sticks and catapults. Then between a song here and there from the adults, the children start telling jokes, most of insuperable silliness, most about *carabinieri*, often in voices breathless with embarrassment. Finally, it's Stefi's turn. She stands on a stone in the middle of the circle. She is younger than the others, not a member of the class, only here because she is a little sister. She has short dress, plump knees, big red boots. Like most Italian girls of her age she wears earrings already under tight pigtails.

'There are a Frenchman, an Englishman and an Italian,' she begins excitedly, 'in a train compartment. And a *terrone* . . .'

My first reaction is dismay. *Terrone* – a southern peasant – is just too derogatory, the territory, as we have seen, of graffiti and insult. It's going to be a racist joke. Nobody seems upset.

'They're in a train compartment and the *Americano* pulls out . . .'

'The who?' Everybody laughs.

'The *Americano* . . .'

'But there was no . . .'

'The *Americano*,' Stefi insists, 'pulls out a cigar and he smokes a couple of puffs' – she imitates, delightfully, making a big pouting round of her lips – 'and then he pulls down the window and tosses it out, and the Italian says, "Why did you do that, you hardly smoked it at all," and the *Americano* says, "Oh, we've got so many cigars in America!" '

For the moment here she seems to forget what comes next. She scratches her head, tugs a pigtail. 'Then the Scotsman . . .'

'The who?'

'The Scotsman pulls out . . .'

Again there are light-hearted protests, though everybody knows perfectly well that the only two who matter in this joke are the Italian, in whom popular wisdom recognises a northerner, and the *terrone*. The others are only there to symbolise that First World, which tradition always has it is richer and more plentiful than home.

'The Scotsman pulls out a bottle of whisky and he drinks a couple of sips,' again the imitation, 'and then he pulls down the window and tosses the bottle out. And the Italian says, "Why did you do that, you hardly drank any of it at all," and he says, "Oh, we've got so much whisky in France." '

'Scotland,' everybody shouts.

Stefi gets annoyed. She puts her hands on her hips, it's a gesture she's learnt from Zia, and bellows, '*Santa patata*, let me finish! And then,' – but she stops now and smiles sweetly, perhaps remembering to be more the princess than the farm girl. For my own part, I have already seen the end coming. I feel amused and appalled.

'Then the Italian: the Italian suddenly picks up the *terrone* and tosses him out of the window. And the German says, "Why did you do that, he didn't do anything," and the Italian says' – here Stefi holds both hands out, palms upward, in the age-old Latin gesture of explanation, conciliation, regret – 'he says, "Oh, we've got so many, many *terroni* in Italy." '

People laugh, though there is just a little nervousness, suggesting that such things are closer to the bone here than, say, jokes about the Irish in London. And what am I to do? Do I give her a lecture on the return trip about how southerners are just as much human beings as anybody else? Or should I say that you can tell jokes like that for fun, but not in public, in case people take them the wrong way. After all, little Pasquale's parents are southerners . . .

'Listen, Stefi,' I begin when I've got her on her own for a minute on the return trip – there aren't as many of us now because, after letting the kids play for an hour, many mothers felt they would be too tired for the walk back, and so have departed with fathers and tupperware and wine bottles in the cars – 'Listen, you do know what *terrone* means, don't you?'

'Of course,' she says, 'someone who comes from the south.'

'And . . .'

But she interrupts: 'Papà, is Nonno a *terrone*? Francesca Piva says my *nonno* is a *terrone* if he comes from Pescara. I'll be furious with him if he's a *terrone*.'

Foolishly, instead of pointing out how ridiculous it is for her to change her opinion of her *caro nonno* according to where he comes from, I get involved in a technical discussion of where exactly people begin to be called *terroni*. Much further south than Pescara, I point out. Pescara isn't considered the south at all. Then realising that one only validates this kind of prejudice by caring about its exact geography, I say, 'Anyway, if Nonno is a *terrone* that just shows that they are as nice as anyone else, doesn't it, and that there's no reason to dislike them or start tossing them out of train windows.'

'He never keeps his promises,' she says grimly. 'He was supposed to come at Easter and he didn't. You can't deny that.'

Just as one can never deny that people did laugh at her joke.

We return by a different path, snaking steeply down the hill to Mizzole. There are kilometres of young vines planted here, with black plastic stretching in lines across their roots to keep in the moisture. Knowledgeably, Stefano tells me that there have never been vines before on this hill. The wine will be awful. It's just tax write-offs and EC subsidies. *Sai com'è?* Same with the sunflowers they've started growing at the bottom. Who ever saw sunflowers in the Val Squaranto before?

Further down the valley the fortunately eternal cherry trees are on the point of blossoming. All the little cavalry-men, Maestra Elena tells the children, are waiting to get out and wave their swords. From across the valley come the regular explosions of clay-pigeon shooting, an incomprehensible sport, but always better than hunting for sparrows and blackbirds. One of the little girls has collected a small bagful of cartridges in six different colours. Apparently, she likes to make decorations with them at home. Marta is afraid of lead poisoning.

D'Artagnan and All-three-musketeers find an early lizard with one leg missing and there is the usual discussion about whether to put the thing out of its misery or not. Whereas, if D'Artagnan ever comes across a *vipera*, of course, it will be mercilessly hacked to bits with sharp stick and penknife. Occasionaly the hero pokes in the leaves by the side of the path, but finds no more than primroses and periwinkles and long discarded Coke cans.

In Mizzole we stop in the square, for an ice cream. This square is just thirty metres by thirty of cheap paving, but there's a bar the other side of the road which has its tables under big white sunshades on the piazza. The proprietor looks carefully up and down the dusty road before crossing with a tray of drinks.

The children eat their ice creams. For entertainment there's an old field gun anchored in cement by a miserable war memorial of grey concrete, black railings and artificial carnations. One of the fathers shows the kids how to winch up the barrel of the gun, how to aim it. Stefano remarks to me that he managed to avoid military service thanks to the only-son-of-widowed-mother rule. Marta says she hopes conscription will be abolished by the time Beppe gets there. Michele, Rita says, will no doubt enjoy his military service, and most likely Stefi would, too, if she got the chance. She's now arguing furiously for a chance to sit on the barrel. Maestra Elena tries to get the children away from the gun to talk for a moment about the war memorial, but there are only seven children left now, at once tired and rowdy, and the monument is short on information:

MIZZOLE, AI SUOI CADUTI, it says: to her fallen soldiers. The list of names beneath gives no indication of which war they died in. D'Artagnan hits the top of the monument with his catapult and I have to confiscate it.

When the adults sit to have coffee, Maestra Elena pulls out a pack of cigarettes. She's an efficient-looking woman in her early forties with a couple of children of her own and just the right mixture of kindness and discipline, earnestness and fun. She puffs. Immediately, two of the children start singing one of those indoctrinating songs the school is full of these days:

Papà non fumare
Papà non fumare
Perchè il fumo ti fa tanto male

Daddy don't smoke
Daddy don't smoke
Because smoke is so bad for you

The song goes on and on jollily rhyming pipes and cigars with the miseries of cancer and heart disease. But Maestra Elena, who may well have been responsible at some point for teaching them this stuff, only smiles. 'It doesn't do them any harm,' she says, 'to know that teacher has a vice or two.' How different from the South Tyrol!

The last stop is Mizzole's famous shrine with the tree growing out of it. There's a tall, dry-stone wall at the end of the village with a tiny chapel built into it, no more than two metres by two. It has a miniature dome on top and is open at the front with just a low wall and black gate to defend it. Through the middle of that wall, obscuring an altar and statue behind, explodes a gnarled and stunted ash tree, and through its branches you can just read: SANT'EUROSIA – VERGINE E. M.

Michele asks me what 'E. M.' means. I don't know. Nervous about seeming ignorant, I ask Rita in a low voice. She explains, '*e martire*' – and martyr. So why didn't they write it, Michele asks. Because they ran out of space. And Rita says *vergine* gets written in full because it's more important than being a martyr. In the end it goes without saying that a saint is a martyr, though none of those present knows exactly what Sant'Eurosia did to get herself martyred . . .

The gate beside the tree has a latch but no lock, so all the children immediately crowd through into the tiny space where a life-size white statue stands on the altar, head in the dome. One of the girls reads from a typed information sheet under cracked perspex on the altar. She has that monotonous reading voice children have, the others interrupting, Maestra Elena correcting. But still we learn nothing of Sant'Eurosia, only that her image was first brought here by Spanish soldiers in the sixteenth century, that the villagers erected this statue to her and planted the ash tree in 1630 in the belief it would protect them from the plague, and then that 'This miracle came true, for no one in Mizzole died of the plague.' Later, reads the little girl, in 'an undetermined period', the ash tree died. The villagers decided to remove it. But when they came to cut it next morning, it had miraculously sprouted.

The present shrine, however, is as recent as 1947. 'When the townsfolk were evacuated here from Verona to avoid bombing, they made a vow that if the saint saved all of them they would build a handsome chapel around the old *capitello*. Once again the miracle came true.'

I must say I have always felt a certain admiration for those who introduce 'if' clauses into their dealings with the divine, as though bargaining from a position of strength. Little Beppe says: 'But the names in the village square died. The ones on the monument.' A rather attractive young mother explains patiently and sincerely that that was precisely because they weren't here in Mizzole under the protection of Sant'Eurosia.

Where were they then?

In Russia, most probably. Unarmed, without winter clothes . . .

Still crowded in the chapel, Stefi says she'd like to light a candle. Actually, there are already two candles alight on the altar, but they're of the big cylinder variety covered in red plastic so that the wax can't escape and is guaranteed to burn for something like a hundred hours, come hell or high water. They're designed for cemeteries, these monster candles. A label on the side of the plastic announces that the brand name is Santa Chiara – the religious goods trade is not without its wit. Whoever put the candles there didn't trouble themselves to remove the supermarket bar code.

There are no candles for visitors to light, however. Nothing for Stefi, that is, who protests. D'Artagnan says, 'Why don't we blow these candles out, then light them again with Maestra Elena's cigarette lighter?' But here the parents object, and anyway All-three-musketeers tells his companion bluntly: 'It's no good you lighting a candle, because you're going to hell anyway, because you don't believe in God.'

Michele's friends have been telling him he'll go to hell ever since he became one of only two in his class to opt out of the *ora di religione*. 'At least I don't have to go to catechism,' he replies staunchily. Obviously, he feels it's a fair trade. None of the parents make any comment.

Then from Mizzole it's all along the flood overflow ditch and the busy road back to Montecchio: nothing to look at and parents screaming at their kids to keep in single file away from the traffic. 'What terrible weather,' Marta says, 'so sticky, so hot. Poor Beppe is sweating like a pig.' Under his sweater and rainproof jacket . . .

Somebody who wasn't sweating, however, as we were very soon to discover, was our new and, it has to be said, unwanted tenant at Via delle Primule, no. 6. On our return from the walk I sent Michele down to the cellar with his and my boots. Every apartment has a little cellar at semi-basement level where you can store such things as gardening tools, skis, bottling equipment, barbecue forks and the like. In just a moment the little boy came running back breathless to say there was a man down there in the cellars, a man he had never met before. Living down there, he said . . .

I hurried down myself. As well as six cellars for the six apartments, there were also the two small *taverne*, semi-basement rooms with chimney attachments for winter barbecue parties. Silvio had rented one of these for his weight-lifting machines, but the other, larger *taverna* was, as far as I knew, still free. Now, when I got down to the narrow corridor beneath the *palazzina*, it was to find the door to this *taverna* open and a young man inside. He had a camp bed on the floor, a sleeping bag and a battered suitcase, and he wore blue jeans and a tattered shirt. Silvio was already down there trying to talk to him. But the man spoke almost no Italian. *'Mio nome, Hristo,'* he said. He smiled. Then he tried English: 'Name. Hristo.' His physiognomy shouted Slav. He seemed harmless, charming and totally indigent. Clearly, he was cold.

We phoned Righetti. Righetti claimed he knew nothing about Hristo. He had rented the *taverna* to a local *imbianchino*, a whitewasher, to store some of his stuff in. This was perfectly legitimate, he said. If none of us wanted to rent or buy the room, he could give it to whoever he liked. We phoned the whitewasher, who spoke in fierce dialect and said Hristo was working for him, and that this was a very temporary arrangement, until the boy found somewhere to live.

'But where does he do his wee, Papa? Where does he poo?' Michele asked. Indeed! The children were fascinated. The Yugoslavia they had vaguely seen on the TV had come to our basement; and as with the blacks who try to clean your windscreens for money at the crossroads, it was difficult to explain that your annoyance was directed not at them, who were legitimate objects of charity, but at the people who thrust them on your doorstep, indeed under your doorstep. At a condominium meeting we all agreed we must be charitable to Hristo, while declaring a full scale war of our own against Righetti and the *imbianchino*.

O la Madonna!

Walks. I've described just one, but since in the children's minds, as in my own memories of childhood, all walks will probably muddle into the one long walk of growing up, perhaps now is the time to mention some others. Let's start with the one we most commonly take, the path with the stream on one side and the irrigation ditch on the other that goes from Montecchio to the Ferrazze. It's a walk of long wet grass full of croaking frogs, of sluices raised or lowered either side of you, of channels fanning out across the fields, and if you sit on one of the occasional cement slabs that bridge the irrigation ditch, you can dangle your feet just above the water and at evening time watch swallows dive into the line of the water and skim the lily leaves straight at you. Here they come, look, fast and low, flapping madly. Then at the last moment they sheer off above your heads. I think of *The Dam Busters*. Michele thinks of *Star Wars*. He makes the appropriate noises of lasering them down. Further on, attached to a branch with a piece of wire above an abandoned scooter, Stefi spies a small colour print of San Bernardino of Sienna. He is bending down to hold a lantern by a locked door. The children ask what the saint did, why is the picture hung on the tree. I don't know, any more than I knew who Sant'Eurosia was. But I can explain the bunch of fresh flowers by the kerb where the path comes out onto the street again at the Ferrazze. That's to mark where a young man died when he fell off his moped some years ago. Above the flowers in wobbly hand on fading board someone belatedly wrote the words, *Maria proteggici!* Mary, protect us!

Or there's the silent walk striking up through a pathless wooded gulch above San Martino Buon Albergo. Here in winter it seems the frost never thaws, the deep undergrowth cracks beneath your feet, so that you stop and listen to the stillness, because this is trespassing. You tell the children not to breathe a word – they love that – 'Move quietly, Stefi, *piano!*' – and at the top, in the high, old, dry stone wall that marks off a once aristocratic domain, hunters have set snares at regular intervals, fitting loops of wire round those holes that wooden scaffolding once went into. The wire is attached to a brick or heavy pipe which is then balanced on a piece of wood set between the stones. They're hare traps. Inside the old stone wall is a nature reserve set up by the Glaxo drug company. Michele likes to dismantle all these traps, with a very severe look on his face, ripping out the wire, throwing the bricks into the wood, as if he were Christ turning over the tables in the temple, or some classical hero of the stories we've been reading, hacking at a monster's scales.

'How many hares do you think we have saved?' he asks, breathlessly, already looking for the next. Like all little boys he is obsessed by measurements. How many kilometres have we walked? How far away is the sun? How many metres have we climbed? How much does the mountain weigh? How long have we been walking? How many *vipere* are there in a square kilometre? How many sandwiches have we brought? As if by answering these questions something might be explained.

Stefi, on the other hand, gathers flowers, though she leaves the wild cyclamens because Mamma has told her they're rare. She never asks how many flowers there are in the wood.

On the other side of the reserve, if we have the courage to climb the wall and cross it (you shin a tree right beside, get on top, then drop down a good three metres into grass and move quietly quietly through the bushes) – on the other side, where three paths cross, there is a little shrine or *capitello* with the Madonna and her child, the latter braving the winter weather in just his swaddling clothes. PREGA PER NOI, the stonemason has chipped, and then ANNO MARIANO 1979. So they're still at it, you realise. It's not just another lost tradition.

Further on, if you take the path up the ridge northwards, there's a shrine to Sant'Antonio, a local saint – as one has local papers and local TV stations – and further on still . . . The Italian countryside is never just landscape or nature trails, never just a stroll, but full of roadside gods, reminders, little idols, so that you can hardly take your children out of the house here without discussing religion, life, death, and, above all, miracles.

'How many miracles did San Rocco do?' Michele wants to know. Why Sant'Antonio, Papà? Why San Giuseppe? In this niche in the rock? Why San Bernardino? Why San Francesco? Time to ask him how long a piece of string is.

On the precipitous path on that other walk that leads down from the tall hill above Pigozzo to Santa Maria in Stelle, a full-size Jesus stands with his back to crumbling rock, arm raised in stony blessing above a pond not more than a couple of metres across, where *contadini* soak the prunings they have cut so that they can use them later as ties for vines. Inevitably – because this is a spring walk – the frogs croak, crickets whirr, swallows flit across the chalk-white path. 'How ugly he is!' Stefi says of the haggard Christ.

When the summer weather gets unbearable the thing to do is to drive the forty minutes up to the fresh air of the first mountains above Velo. Here Jesus and Mary huddle under birdhouse roofs of wood or flaky stone to tell you where someone was lost in a blizzard or, in one place high up above the treeline, struck by lightning. GESÙ PROTEGGICI! the stonemason carved. I love it when they put the exclamation mark.

'A hundred days of indulgence,' announces a small shrine above Tecchie, 'for a prayer to Maria.' You'd think such strict after-life accountancy went back to the Middle Ages, but no, the date is 1894. In thick woods at fifteen hundred exhausting metres an overgrown stone cross suggests: 'Take one step back with your right foot in honour of Jesus, who here resides.'

Wherever we walk we find these things. And the children always stop and look. They always want to read about the disaster or the miracle (the one invites the other). Or the hopes of indulgence. They'll wander across meadows and dangerously leave paths to decipher the engraving and puzzle over misspelt words with no spaces between them: PERSUADIVOZIONE, one cross says, 'Out of his devotion'.

Why not count the images? It's not a bad game. Twenty-seven one day in a walk on the mountain above Giazza, from the big chapel to San Francesco at the bottom to the tiny Madonna behind a rusty grating high up on the cliff face (a rosary – not electronic – is wound round one iron bar). Then, if you lose your way and get back late, you can count the great neon crosses harshly white on the high ridges above you.

The children ask me about obscure saints. They compute thousands of years of indulgences. And of course it doesn't matter whether they are Christian or not, whether they attend the *ora di religione* or not. Either way, they can see the countryside is full of spirits. It's obvious. And somehow or other they will fit in with this Italian vision. They will be more polytheistic than I was. Less likely to make a god of just one thing. They'll know there's a saint for every condition, every corner, a moment to turn this way, a moment to turn that. No absolute. So when Plutarch wrote his *Quaestiones Graecae* he discovered that the Greeks most faithfully kept those religious traditions whose origins they couldn't remember. What group psychology could be more stable, or more functional?

North of Velo, where stone gives way to wood, there are more crucifixes, fewer Madonnas, first inklings of the Teutonic in the tortured contortions of the body. And there are more picnickers, too, almost always in big groups of extended families, or established friends, or whole condominiums. The backs of their cars are open to unpack all the barbecue equipment; their chairs are set up in the stony beds of dry streams. Like us they've come north for the day to escape from the heat.

How many degrees cooler is it up here, Papà? And why does it get cooler if you're nearer the sun? Shouldn't it get hotter? Wasn't that why Icarus fell? And why do you get more indulgence praying in front of one image rather than another? These walks are such a mix of science and mysticism. It almost seems done on purpose to illustrate the two paths to knowledge. Just the other side of a big busy farm, we pass two boys and their girlfriends on the grass kissing – not ten yards from a stinking manure heap. It's extraordinary. And one boy has the radio on with the football commentary because it's Sunday. While all around, the country is empty except for its shrines, its irritating cattle with their tinkling bells.

'Yuck!' Michele says.

'Yes, that's quite a smell.'

'No, I mean the kissing!'

But a goal breaks that off. The boys are up on their feet cheering. The girls smile. This may be a sentimental people, but rarely romantic.

'Mummy said we had to be back by seven so you could do your homework,' I tell Michele on one memorable walk.

'But I haven't got any,' he insists.

'Why not? They always give you something.'

This is true. It's incredible how early schools start giving hours of homework in Italy, how seriously and traditionally they teach grammar and maths. It warms a parent's heart.

'There's no homework,' Michele says, 'because the others have got to practise for their first communion this evening. They've got to say their first confession.'

So, I think, the teacher hasn't given homework because the priest has told her that the children will be busy. Fair enough. I ask: 'What would you confess, Michele, if you had to?'

'Can we stay out then?' he asks.

'Please!' Stefi begs.

They want to go to a place where we found a sheep's skull some time ago. They want to see if it's still buried under the leaves where we left it.

'Yes, but tell me, what would you confess?'

Michele ponders. He's so earnest. 'Oh, being naughty. Hitting Stefi. Lying. Taking Gigi's toys. Swearing. Being mean to Mamma when she's tired.'

It's an impressive list.

'And how does confession help?'

'You say Ave Maria and Paternoster, you feel sorry and God forgets about it.'

'And you never do it again.'

'You try not to,' Michele ponders, 'but in the end you're bound to.'

'So then you confess it again?'

'Every time you take communion.'

Which might be every day. Like our dear ex-Prime Minister Andreotti, now accused of mafia crimes. Clearly, my son has very little need of catechism. The news is in the air. We set off to dig up our *memento mori*.

And it would have been about this time, I suppose, though on quite a different walk, that Don Guido, the local priest, stopped in his car one afternoon to talk to us. We were standing – myself, Michele and Stefi – by one of the village's endless streams trying to fish out a small Ferrari of Michele's that Stefi had accidently dropped in the water (provoking Michele to commit one of those inevitable sins). The Ferrari lay bright and red on the stones beneath lazily clear water, but our arms weren't long enough. Either we waded in, or we went home and got a net.

I stood up and at once a car drew up beside me, blocking the road. The priest wound down his window. He has a small round flabby face with rimless glasses. Although we had never spoken to each other before, he announced very abruptly: 'Isn't it about time your son took his first communion?' I think he knew Michele from when Zia took him to all her funerals. Certainly Michele knew him because Don Guido sometimes comes to talk to their class.

'Communion?' I was taken aback. 'My son isn't even baptised.'

Rather than being shocked the priest said very practically: 'Well, we can baptise him then.' The drowned car forgotten, the children were all ears now. They are perfectly aware that something is up as far as their parents and religion is concerned, something that separates them from the other children. For myself, I was annoyed at the man's presumption. I said, 'As I recall, if my son is baptised before he comes of age, I have to make promises about bringing him up in a Christian fashion, promises I can't possibly keep and don't mean to.'

This time the priest did seem surprised. Indeed, so much so that after staring at me half a moment in almost wonder, he wound up his window and was gone without so much as a *buona sera*. Didn't I understand, he must have been asking himself, that it was the form that mattered, rather than the content? That it is the image of Sant'Eurosia and our devotion to her that are important, not whatever it was she did. The emotion attaches itself to the form, the gesture, as when my in-laws embrace everybody so warmly before disappearing into months of silence and broken promises. It was frankly churlish of me to start talking in this dogmatic fashion about the details of the baptism service, thus excluding my children from the community merely for the sake of some ridiculous pride that attached itself to dubious notions of sincerity and coherence. But it would take me another while yet in Italy to appreciate that. Or perhaps it's writing about it that gets you there. As a rule of thumb, the more you write, the less sure you feel about your point of view. One hopes that's as it should be.

But not to digress too much, let's finish with a walk that takes you high up into the hills above Novaglie. Here, on a blistering day in August we found a place where the jet from a farmer's huge water cannon strays out onto the road. You can stand there by the fence and at intervals of two to three minutes you get the gentlest of gentle showers. We stood there laughing. In low sunshine the pumping water was white and very bright against the dusty blue grass and scrub of the hillside beyond. Until, in between sprays, there came a whistle, sudden and very sharp. I whistled back. The whistle came again with a slightly different modulation. On the other side of the road, just visible through a chink in a cypress hedge, the children found a mynah bird in a cage the size of Sant'Eurosia's shrine.

'Like Checca!' Stefi cried. But this bird was far more skilled.

'Try some words on it,' I said.

'*Ciao!*' the children shouted.

The mynah bird said '*Ciao.*' It didn't seem very interested and launched into a most complicated whistle.

'*Pronto,*' Michele said.

'*Pronto ciao,*' the bird said. '*Pronto ciao.*' As some will say when they answer the phone.

'Try some other words,' I said. So they ran through the following:

Hello	–	no reply
Santa patata!	–	no reply
Buon giorno	–	'*Buon giorno,*' said the bird.
O la miseria!	–	no reply
Porca vacca!	–	no reply
Pizza	–	no reply
Merda	–	no reply

Clearly this is a conservative, sensibly fed, well-educated bird, I thought. Then in perfect imitation of Zia Natalina, Stefi sang out: '*O la Madonna!*'

'*O la Madonna!*' the bird came back. As if to say, 'How long it took you!'

Mamma

'Have you ever thought that the first word Jesus, the Man-God ever pronounced was "Mamma"?'

One of the many publications the *Frate Indovino* tries to sell you through his calendar/almanac is *Cara Mamma*, 'a marvellously illustrated volume that speaks to the heart about *la mamma*, that person whom the whole world esteems, whom children seek and love, the Bible celebrates, the saints venerate, churchmen honour, monks do not forget, nuns emulate, the suffering invoke, the poets sing of, writers exalt . . .'

What are all those images the children find along their walks if not a mother and her son, Hristo? And the first word, *Cara Mamma* tells us, the very first word that the one ever pronounced was the name of the other, Mamma!

In Italian, I shouldn't be surprised.

Cara Mamma also tells us things like: 'When God realised his task was great, he created *la mamma* . . .' And again,

'Few children are worth what their *mamma* suffers for them.' There are colour illustrations of yearning, generous faces – modern photographs or Renaissance Madonnas (often surprisingly similar) – and these are placed alongside embarrassing poems by the venerable likes of Pascoli, Ungaretti and D'Annunzio: 'Cry no more,' writes the latter. 'Your favourite son is coming home . . . !'

It is one of the curiosities of Italy that even in the heyday of feminism, even in times when the only child is left with his grandparents while mother is off to work, the *mamma* mystique has lost none of its attraction and power.

At the *scuola materna* the children are always at work on what they call *lavoretti*, little practical projects, like making a basket of flowers with paste and paper, or a rag doll, or a pastry plaque in the shape of an angel with tinsel eyes. On Mother's Day, May 12th in Italy, Stefi's *lavoretto* is a piece of paper with her handprints all over it in different coloured paints. But the paint is not so thick as to obscure the poem that the ever serious Irma has had computer printed on every child's paper:

Cara Mamma,
quante volte ti arrabbi
vedendo dappertutto
le impronte
delle mie manine!
Scusa,
se anche oggi per la tua festa
te li regalo.
Conservale,
e un giorno ben lontano,
rivedendole,
ti ricorderai

quanto erano piccole le mie manine
quando cercavano le tue.

Dear Mummy,
How often you get angry
seeing the prints of my little hands
everywhere.
Forgive me,
if I bring them to you
even today, Mother's Day.
Keep them
and one day far in the future,
looking at them again,
you'll remember
how very small my little hands were,
when they reached out for yours.

It is noticeable that, as with family greetings, when it comes to the subject of *mamma*, reticence is not at a premium. 'Earned emotion' is not an idea I have ever heard mentioned in Italy. Any extravagance of sentiment is legitimate. This seems to be as true of the great poets as of the minor. The following stanza of a poem by D'Annunzio is addressed to his mother, not to one of his many mistresses:

Ti scrivo qui, seduto al balconcino
della mia cameretta, in faccia al mare,
e bacio ogni momento il mazzolino
che ieri mi mandasti a regalare.

I write to you from the balcony
Of my room, looking out to sea,
And kiss and kiss the little bouquet
You sent me as a present yesterday.

Somewhat less eloquently, after a family argument which has to do with Rita and her brothers having forgotten to give Nonna a present on Mother's Day, Rita's father sends one of his circular letters to all his children, beginning with the all too stock expression: 'Children, one only has one mother in this world, so I don't see why you can't . . .'

You never hear what would seem to be the obvious correlative: 'One only has one father in this world,' perhaps because, as for the baby in his shrines by the roadside, this isn't quite true. You don't have a father at all. Joseph is merely a stand-in. God is the father, and that fellow's most distinguishing trait has always been his absence.

On Sunday Silvio rises at four o'clock in the morning to set off fishing. He likes to drive with friends twenty or thirty miles away and fish in remote streams. At six years old, his little Giovanni is clamouring to go with him but isn't allowed. Or invited.

My friend Stefano also loves fishing, though he spends most of his Sundays cycling. He and his brother put the bikes on the car, drive as far as Boscochiesanuova, then set off on gruelling rides in the mountains panting right up to fifteen hundred metres in their fluorescent cycling strips. So Stefano claims. Marta, keeping Beppino from putting his fingerprints on the wall or his snots on the new crystal tabletop, remarks that it doesn't seem to be doing much for Stefano's paunch.

Now that his second child is getting old enough to cause trouble, Giorgio, my immediate neighbour, tells me he has been dreaming of leaving his safe job at the railways to collect and sell the rare fossils and minerals you can find in the mountains here. He would hunt for this or that crystal in the old quarries of Lessinia, for silver in the Carso . . . There is even a little gold, he tells me, above Turin. One would have to be away for days at a time, he explains, with a tent and a stove, and when you weren't discovering minerals, there would be mushrooms to pick, truffles to unearth, and chestnuts in November and December. All far, far from home. Giorgio's eyes are wistful. He knows he will never really leave his safe job with all its benefits, though he would probably love to be fired. For the moment he escapes from his children through intensive gardening. More exotic trees have been bought to replace those that died in last year's frost. An elaborate plan has been hatched to pass the sprinkler system under the main driveway so as to take in the tiny strip of grass beyond the garages.

Mario also gardens: not the main condominium garden, like Giorgio, but his own patch at the back, which he has turned into an impressive display of shrubs, flowerbeds and lawn complete with pergola and barbecue and an electric socket for the TV on warm summer nights. But his apartment is round the front of the condominium, while his private patch of lawn is the furthest away of all at the back. When he goes out to do some gardening he is entirely out of sight and earshot of wife and child. He might just as well be off fishing in the watery Bassa or cycling in the rugged mountains, or prospecting in Piedmonte. I have never heard him complain about this arrangement.

Of course, in England the women often do the gardening. But not here. Here it's the man's escape. Monks are famous for their gardening. On Sunday afternoon the gardens of Via delle Primule are a-buzz with radios commentating the football match; likewise the strips of grit for playing bowls at Centro Primo Maggio, where Zia Natalina's husband spends his free hours. It's hard to spot a man with his child . . .

In the early and even late evening, when he might be at home with his wife and daughters (for the second baby was a *bella bambina*, too, and now a third is on the way), Righetti can be seen roaming round the various estates he's built, showing flats to eager young couples or collecting rents, for garages, *taverne*, cellars. But since the whole business about Hristo began, he hasn't bothered us. Hristo, it turns out, has left a wife and two children in Bosnia, the better to be able to provide for them. Everybody is very understanding about that. In reply to our threat of legal action, we have been told that if we insist, this will mean chucking the poor man out on the street, which is hardly Christian of us with him having all those mouths to feed.

In the *pasticceria* I commiserate with Iacopo on the mess his private life has become. He now rides a very big motorbike and is seriously into leather. He seems infinitely depressed. But no, he admits, no, there is no problem over access to his little boy. He taps his Raybans on the tablecloth, indicating that his time with young Sandro is no consolation. *La visione del bambino* is not his obsession. This is not America, and Iacopo is no Mrs Doubtfire. No, the problem is that there is alimony to pay. Unable to make ends meet with his creative paintings, he has started doing some things to order, which he despises. Portraits mainly, of wedding couples, of mother and baby . . . His new girlfriend, frighteningly slim and haggard and likewise into leather, looks old enough to be his . . .

'Mamma!' comes a shout from the apartment below us. Voices are raised. It's nearly midnight of a hot night in July. Time for Francesco to capitulate and surrender the double bed to young Gigi . . .

I take the children to see Robin Williams' *Hook* in a *cinema parrocchiale* in Borgo Venezia. It's fascinating to observe how the story takes its spring from a father's guilt at not having spent enough time with his children. This is mildly ludicrous, you can't help feeling, in Italy, where there's simply no need to feel guilty about such things. Your children always have their . . .

'Mamma!' Stefi calls in the night. 'Mamma!' As I'm awake, I get up myself and walk across the passage to see what the matter is. The little girl is on the lower of two bunk beds. '*Cara*,' I begin. 'Mamma!' she screams. 'I said I wanted Mamma.' The situation is almost symmetrical to the time Rita called out '*Amore*' from the kitchen and I was a fool to reply '*Sì*,' since it's obvious that when a mother calls out Amore without further specification, she is calling for her son. On this particular night it turns out that Stefi's merely afraid because there's a moth in the room. When Rita has finally woken up and got this information out of her, Papà has to go and kill the thing. Mamma refuses to do that.

'*Chi chiama mamma*,' announces the sibylline *Frate Indovino*, '*non s'inganna*.' In rough translation this might read: You can never go wrong when you call for Mamma.

Michele takes this proverb very literally. Doing his homework, he shouts from his room: 'Mamma, what's three times seven?' If I happen to be in the vicinity, I reply:

'Twenty-one.' 'No, I want Mamma to tell me,' he insists. 'But I can do sums just as well as your mother!' 'I want Mamma to tell me. MAMMA! What's three times seven?' From some distant balcony Rita calls, 'Twenty-one!' And he is satisfied.

But what is it exactly that the Italian mother does to generate this extraordinary bond, this wonderful and wonderfully sick phenomenon that the Italians call *mammismo*? And when they talk about it they're at once complacent and concerned, as when they talk about the public debt, or about rampant corruption. It's one of those staples of Italian life you have to get used to. There's hardly much point in asking whether it's good or bad. In this sense it has the same status as British weather, or cooking . . .

Well, I suppose most of all what Mamma does is be there. Sabrina is there when Silvio is fishing, Marta is there when Stefano is cycling, Donatella is there when Giorgio is gardening. Mothers may be away at work during the week, but they are there during the weekends when Daddy isn't. Of course, you think, why don't these women get furious with their husbands for not taking the children with them? The answer to that is that they don't want them to. They don't want the children to be out in the hot sun, in the cold air, they don't want the children to be over-tired, to fall off a mountain, fall in the river, or, even worse, miss a proper meal. When a father does take the children out, on his return he will have to hear: 'Oh, but he's exhausted, he'll be ill; oh, but look at the scratch on his elbow; oh, but look at the bruise on his knee; oh, but he hasn't eaten any fruit. Did he take a bidet when he . . . ?' A father taking his child out on a walk, on a trip, is a man on probation. His wife's thoughts stalk him everywhere.

For a mother isn't just always there, but always protecting. The roadside images show the woman with tiny child or dying man. In both cases her gesture is the same: the encircling arms.

'Don't run!' screams Francesca as Gigi dashes out of the house. 'You can't run in this heat. You'll sweat!' Everybody knows that sweating is dangerous. Especially if there are draughts about. In blistering July anxious mothers close the last crack of the train compartment window to prevent their child getting a *colpo d'aria*, a draught. Everybody else understands and sits there patiently, near dying of asphyxiation as the sun beats on the pane. Or in winter mothers lean out of windows waving woollen sweaters or scarves and hats. 'You'll get cold, you'll catch your death . . .' In a country where the wind-chill factor is unheard of, big boys set off in fur, mittens and muffs, to walk the twenty yards round the back of the condominium to Papà's car, for the four-hundred-yard trip to school. Not surprisingly, hypochondria is rife. When Gigi doesn't want to go somewhere, he likes to complain of a pain in his knee. His parents rush him to hospital for tests . . .

Can hypochondria be extended to cover the morbid anxiety that one is in need, not only of medical attention, but also of cash? Believing one is ill and believing one is indigent are akin somehow, and both closely related to one's relationship with . . .

'Mamma!' Zio Berto cries, embracing Nonna on one of those family reunions. They hug. Then she steps back. 'Oh, but you've lost weight,' she protests. 'Oh, but you're not eating well.' Her boy is thirty-four years old now and has his wife beside him. As he is leaving after dinner she slips an envelope in his pocket with a million lire in it, though Nonno has sworn blind he will not give the children any more money. Why does the boy still need money when he's a doctor? But the old woman explains indulgently: 'As my grandmother always used to say, "*All'amore dei figli, non c'è amore che somigli.*" ' To the love of children, no other love can compare.

Certainly not the love between husband and wife. In the Anglo-Saxon world, you might say, complicity traditionally, or at least ideally, resides in the relationship between the parents. In Italy it is crucially shifted towards the relationship between mother and child. 'Don't tell your father I did your homework for you,' Marta tells Beppino, pulling his little ponytail. 'He'd be angry with me . . .'

But beyond diet and swaddling and coddling and funding, Mamma has something else to offer: a suffused eroticism. All those beautiful Madonnas, all the embracing, all the games near naked in the summer heat, the family siestas on the big bed with the shutters closed against a scorching sun, the nights together with Papà relegated to the kid's room. When Nonna hugs Zio Berto, she squeezes hard and perhaps tickles him. There are no evasive euphemisms here for those dangerous parts of the body one always suspected as an English child could never really be mentioned to one's parents, since one's parents never spoke openly of them to you. Here everything is properly caressed, properly talked about, thoroughly tickled. 'My soul full of desire for love,' writes D'Annunzio, 'I think of your kiss, your trembling sighs, your gaze, your quiet laugh.' One can't imagine even the most sentimental Englishman writing such lines to his mother. On the other hand, it's not for nothing that Italy has some of the leading theorists in group psychotherapy for families, not surprising that some young men have an extraordinarily inflated, mother-fed opinion of themselves and what is owed to them. It can be tough on Papà. On the day I write this, the radio has reported the case of a boy who, when his father refused him the keys to the faster of the two family cars, hit the man repeatedly over the head with a hammer. Mother tended to give him what he wanted . . .

Yet in the normal way of things, all goes smoothly enough, despite some extraordinary situations. I first met Stefano and Marta before they were married, when I gave them English lessons as a couple. They both felt they needed it for work, he to read *The Economist*, she to deal with foreign customers in her shop. One day I was going through the routine household objects. What do you have in your bedroom, Stefano? Desk, chair, bedside table . . . What do you have on the bedside table? Hesitation. Alarm clock. Ah, so, you use that for waking up? Pause. A little confusion. Stefano was already in his early thirties at the time. He already had his own business. Marriage to the girl he had known for fifteen years was just a question of when. 'To wake up? No,' he smiled. 'No, you see, I don't actually sleep in my bedroom. I sleep with my mother.' Not apologising, but explaining, he added: 'Always. Ever since I was a little boy, when Father died.' Marta did not seem at all embarrassed that this had come out. When, eight and more years on, we go over to visit them one Sunday afternoon and he's not there, I ask: 'Cycling over the Alpine passes?' and she says, 'No, he's gone to visit his mamma.'

'Oh, is she ill?' I couldn't understand why he'd gone without the family, or not invited his mother over to their place.

'No, he just wanted to spend the afternoon with his . . .'

'Mamma,' Stefi shouts. 'Yes?' I go through into the bathroom. 'No, Dado' – my daughter calls me Dado – 'I only want Mamma to clean me.'

There are some advantages.

Non essere fiscale

Can a child or person really have two nationalities, express the traits, that is, of two national characters? Or doesn't one inevitably exclude the other? Or worse still, they simply destroy each other, so that rather than being English and Italian, my children with their mix of languages and habits, are neither one nor the other. These are imponderables. But there are moments when even imponderables are wonderfully incarnated. This tiny chapter remembers two of them . . .

It's eight in the evening. I've just come into the room to send the kids to bed. Stefi is sitting on the floor playing with her dolls and singing a song: 'Mary Had a Little Lamb'. She sings it in the well-to-do, upper-middle-class accent of the little children who made the English tape she has. Instead of her normal raucous tones, her voice is wavering and twee, as befits songs about little girls and their woolly little animal friends. Stefi loves to sing as she plays:

> She took the lamb to school one day,
> School one day, school one day.
> She took the lamb to school one day.
> It was against the rules!

But when Stefi gets to this line – 'It was against the rules' – she suddenly makes a violent gesture. Her chubby right hand becomes a fist that shoots up from the elbow as the left hand slaps down on the right forearm to stop it and give the gesture its fierce tension. Like the sign of the cross, it's another piece of behavioural bric-a-brac she's perhaps learnt watching football on TV with Dad. If you don't want to be so rude as to actually make that gesture, an Italian can say, 'You know where my Grandfather kept his umbrella, don't you . . .' (Those grandparents again!)

But the funny thing is how Stefi knows to make that rebellious, disrespectful gesture at just the point where dear little Mary breaks the rules and brings her lambkins to school come hell or high water. 'There,' her crooked elbow and clenched fist says, 'see how much I care about your stupid rules.' It's not a sentiment I get from listening to the tape.

Then Michele comes in and says to me, in English, 'Oh, don't be so fiscal, Daddy. Don't be so fiscal.'

He's complaining about my sending them to bed on time, and what he means is *fiscale. Non essere fiscale, Papà.* Look at a dictionary and it will tell you that the word derives from the Latin *fiscus*, a basket, then came in Italian to be *fisco*, the coffers of the state, and then, by unpleasant association, the people responsible for filling those coffers.

In short, the tax collectors. So that *fiscale* means, as fiscal does in English: having to do with taxes. But given Italian feeling about rules in general and taxes most particularly, the etymology could hardly stop there. So what was originally a basket in the days of Caesar's empire had come to mean, by the days of Benito's, 'severe', 'exacting', and then, by inevitable slippage, 'too severe', and even 'perversely exacting'.

'Don't be fiscal,' Michele says, knowing I like him to speak English. 'We'll be good if you let us stay up.' What he means is, these rules (which he doesn't know are typically English) don't need to be applied to the letter (a flexibility typically Italian). Then, still dealing in English institutions – this time the fact that I read to them most evenings before going to bed, something which, since they don't actually send their children to bed but merely succumb to sleep along with them, Italian parents hardly have the opportunity to do – Michele throws in a juicy *ricatto*: 'If you let us stay up another half an hour, we'll go to bed without being read to.' Finally, with an exact perception of my obsessive protestant work ethic, which he will never share, he adds, 'That way you can translate a bit more . . .' He has thus managed to arrive at a trade by which I actually get to work more by not sending them to bed . . .

Meanwhile, Stefi has reached the last verse. And beyond. She has modified the English nursery rhyme.

> So Mary found another lamb,
> 'Nother lamb, 'nother lamb.
> Mary found another lamb,
> Better than the first.

She's very proud of this addition. What a miserable sad ending the English version has. Hers is so much sunnier.

I let them stay up. The story of my fatherhood has been that of a long strategic retreat from the systems I hoped to impose. (*Tristram Shandy* is another book that must remain largely incomprehensible to the Italian spirit.) But then neither have my attitudes to the *fisco* remained as solid as they were. If my children are inevitably acquiring an Italian education, they force me to acquire one, too. At least up to a point. And when I protest that there's no point in having rules unless they're enforced, inventing a bedtime without imposing it, Rita says complacently, 'Why don't we sit out on the balcony a bit and have a drink?' So you sit there in the late twilight with a thin cloud cover veiling the moon, a light breeze stirring the cherry blossom and a swelling chorus of frogs croaking their way to the pools at the bottom of the valley. And your wife says: 'Miserable weather, *non è vero*?'

Centenario

'Then the headmistress will take one step back,' Michele is eagerly explaining, 'after which the president steps forward and takes the floor.'

'Does what?'

'Takes the floor.'

'Starts speaking.'

'Teacher said, takes the floor.'

But to me, 'takes the floor' sounds ridiculous in the mouth of an eight-year-old. 'Starts speaking,' I insist. 'That's what it means after all.'

Michele shakes his head. 'You're not Italian,' he observes sadly.

We are in the courtyard behind his school where he is showing me a strip of fresh turf a couple of metres wide and thirty metres long, linking three small newly planted trees in a narrow carpet of pea green, surrounded on every side by swept concrete.

'The grass was laid only yesterday,' he tells me excitedly. Indeed, the gridwork of squares is all too obvious, the last-minute search for a cosmetic effect endearingly evident. For today is the hundredth anniversary of Montecchio's elementary school. It's eight-thirty in the morning, and we have just brought along a big carton full of sodas and munchies for the celebrations later in the day.

'Anyway, then the president takes the floor and . . .'

'Which president?'

Michele thinks. 'The president of the republic.'

'What?!'

'The president of the republic.'

For a moment I almost believe him. In one of those hateful pre-election PR jobs where public figures like to be seen mucking in with the people and above all kissing little children: the president of the republic, Oscar Luigi Scalfaro (newscasters must be under instructions never to spare us the Oscar Luigi) turns up in the small village of Montecchio with three thousand bodyguards and journalists to celebrate the *centenario* of the elementary school and shake everybody's hand while pretending to be unaware of a battery of television cameras. Then the absurdity of it comes home to me.

'No, Michele. If the president of the republic was coming, the place would have been under siege for weeks.'

'Oh.' He looks puzzled, probably doesn't understand 'under siege'. Then he remembers. 'The president of the *circoscrizione*,' which is to say, of one of the eight local districts that form the municipal area of Verona. This seems more likely.

'And Poggiolini,' he adds thoughtfully.

'Poggiolini?'

'Yes, he is going to make a speech.'

But the only Poggiolini I know of is a prominent national figure recently arrested for his part in a complex scandal having to do with taking kickbacks for inserting second-rate pharmaceuticals on the list of those medicines that can be obtained by subsidised prescription. Presumably, Michele has been getting the news mixed up with whatever his teacher has been telling him.

We are back in the entrance of the building now, where my son is showing me the commemorative plaque to be unveiled in the presence of various notables.

But not Poggiolini. I explain that Poggiolini is in gaol.

'But he is an important man.' Michele is sure he was coming.

'He's in gaol. There are lots of important men in gaol.'

'But why?'

'For stealing.'

'But why do they steal?'

'Perhaps because they have so much opportunity.'

'But why?'

'Because important people have to spend all the money that people pay in taxes, and sometimes they spend it on themselves.'

This is a conversation we have had to go through any number of times since corruption scandals both local and national started filling up ninety percent of news programmes. It's been going on for more than a year now and I am still not sure if Michele has grasped the mechanics of it. Nor I, perhaps. Nor the lawyers.

After a moment's reflection, Michele assures me that when he becomes an important public figure he will not steal. I say, '*Benissimo*.'

Maestra Elena arrives, dressed to the nines in dark blue *tailleur* and puffy flesh-coloured blouse, her hair freshly coiffeured, sprayed, fixed, helmety, the same sort of obvious obeisance to the big occasion as is suggested in the neat geometry of fresh turf. Parents, mainly mothers, are busily coming and going with contributions of wine, crisps and nuts, bowls for putting the food in. Nervously jolly, Elena thanks me for the box of edibles we have brought, but I can see a glint of concern in her eyes at my somewhat bleary, unshaven state and scruffy clothes. There's a jittery, before-the-event mentality in the air, a mixture of elation and worry. Elena wants everything and everybody to be just so. I almost catch myself reassuring her that we still have an hour to get home and brush up before the solemnities begin.

In the event, when we arrive back at the school *en famille* and in somewhat better shape right at ten o'clock, only a few people have so far gathered outside the gate. We wait. The school is a solid two-storey building in fading fleshy yellow stucco with wearily noble surrounds to door and windows. When first built, it seems the central part of the construction was used as a town hall and only a few rooms in the wings were given over to lessons. Now, brushed-steel window fittings seem to leap out from the stone like bright metal in greying teeth. The shutters, which are always closed in the evening against possible vandals, are dark green.

Most parents arrive a respectful ten minutes late. But still the ceremony doesn't begin. It turns out there are logistical problems as to where everybody is to stand. The school is set back from the road and sensibly protected by a low wall topped with tall green railings reinforced with ancient wire netting. Just inside the gate a double flight of stairs leads up, from right and left, to the main entrance where the still-veiled plaque is. Since there is precious little space between railings and school, people are warned that they will have to stay outside the gate for the first part of the ceremony. The children, meanwhile, those who are pupils at the school, have gone inside to put the last touches on the songs and poems they are to perform. A few well-chosen specimens, all girls, are leaning over the balcony above the porch whence the Italian tricolour will be raised at the appropriate moment. The parents mill below, as they do when they wait each evening for their kids to come out. I can see Francesco and Francesca, our downstairs neighbours, and Silvio and Sabrina. They tell me they have discovered that Hristo is using a Camping Gaz in the basement. What's more, he's now surrounded by drums of paint, since it seems the *imbianchino* didn't have enough space for all his materials in his own garage. 'Is the paint flammable?' Francesco asks. Could the whole condominium explode when Hristo cooks his beans? Silvio makes the *corna* gesture, but his smile is grim. We will have to have another condominium meeting . . .

Iacopo the painter calls to me. He's in leather again, but his new woman isn't with him, perhaps wisely, for I saw the wife about somewhere. I notice he now has a ridiculously tiny beard, which extends no more than half an inch below his lower lip in an inverted equilateral triangle. The rest of his face is unusually cleanly shaven. Brushing an extravagant curl from his forehead, he complains that they've asked him to paint a picture of the event. 'Can you believe it?' he grumbles. That's why he's had to lug along this enormous camera. But he could have spared himself that explanation. Every self-respecting father has at least half a million's worth of Japanese technology strung about his neck.

The band arrives. They arrange themselves in a rather cramped fashion by the front steps between the school and the fence. We are now running some thirty minutes late. A man with tweed jacket and red pullover, head of the 'parents' representatives' (is there a secret ballot for this position?), stands on top of the steps by the entrance and, fiddling with a microphone, tells us that the band will play some music until all the various luminaries and authorities have arrived. While he is speaking, the parents chat amongst themselves, largely indifferent to the exact turn events may take. Our Saturday morning is already lost, may as well catch up on gossip. To a mood of cheerful resignation the band strikes up some unexpectedly slurpy fifties music.

They're a curious lot, the band. Stefi, who's too young for school yet, still at the *scuola materna*, insists that we get as close as possible. She wants to stand on the wall clutching the fence above as some other little children are doing. I take her over there and lift her up, but in the only space left by a line of other children there's a saucer of milk and a cracked bowl of dirty cat food. The tradition of feeding stray cats is old and strong all over Italy, but it does seem curious to find offerings here on the school wall on such a red-letter day. I manage to persuade another young fellow to move over a foot or two.

There are about a dozen players in the band, and much to my amusement they're known as Il Piccolo Manchester. I grew up in Manchester and Blackpool, and remember

Whitsun marches behind much bigger bands, much bigger banners. *Piccolo* seems just about right.

They all have dark blue uniforms, which only accentuate, as uniforms will, what a motley group they are. Playing the flute at the front are two rather attractive girls, a blonde and a brunette, having trouble with the music stands clipped on their left arms. The blonde keeps losing hers, has to break off her playing to put it back. But the flutes are drowned out by the brass anyway. Then there are two or three young men: a trombonist with his hair tied behind in a ponytail that forces up his cap at the back so that the peak tips down over his eyes; a thuggish unhealthy-looking fellow who bangs a snare drum with determined boredom; and a very earnest lad with a clarinet. All the others are oldies, men who learnt to play in the army, most probably, patriarchs with noble white moustaches and cheeks blown out round trumpets and horns, solid paunches beneath. Holding two great cymbals in white-gloved hands, a thin and very dry old man wears antiquated tortoise-shell glasses and sports one of those truly huge moustaches that sprout from right inside the nose to fan out downwards across the whole mouth, giving the curious cartoon impression that he has no lips at all. Comically, whenever he gets the chance to clash his cymbals, he does so with great panache, hurling his arms up in the air in grand operatic gestures. Beside him sways a blue banner announcing in silver lettering that the band was formed in 1876. When the thing suddenly sags to one side and you catch a glimpse of the fellow holding it up, he's so old and infirm you feel he might have been there the very day Il Piccolo Manchester sounded its first brassy notes in a newly united Italy.

Only when it's far too late do I realise that the fence is filthy. And rusty. Stefi is getting dirty. The cosmetic effort for the centenary got no further than the one or two strips of fresh turf. 'And we know what will happen to that this summer!' Stefano has arrived and come to stand beside me, portly and in good spirits, relieved that Beppe is out of their hands and thus doesn't have to be worried about. 'Nobody will ever come and water it once the big occasion's over.'

This time I manage to get in with a *Sai com'è* before he does, and lift Stefi down.

'Still, it's the big occasion that matters,' he then goes on to reflect. 'Who really cares what happens to the turf in summer?'

The band finish their preliminary medley. The luminaries, however, have still not arrived. The musicians strike up again. Stefano tells me that the fellow with the dramatic manner with the cymbals and the big moustache is known as Il Pesce, The Fish, apparently because of the harelip his moustache is hiding. But everybody has a nickname here. Michele recently told me that he is known as Fax. Partly because the Italians pronounce Parks as Pax, and partly because Michele once tried to explain to his friends that his father had bought a machine that sent paper through the telephone.

Stefi turns round to tell me that her favourite member of the band is a very plump chap with cheeks like two big salad tomatoes. I try to draw her attention to the handsome, earnest young clarinettist with his polished black hair and shining eyes, but Stefi is adamant.

Finally, the bigwigs are all assembled at the top of the

steps: the head of the parents' representatives, the president of the district, the headmistress, the priest, two teachers, and a local politician who is councillor for traffic in Verona.

The parents' representative kicks off. It is desperately important, he says, gripping a red microphone and after almost no preliminaries, that we citizens come along to give support to 'one of those very few public institutions that are still sound.' The reference to the political scandals that recently led to the collapse of Verona's local government is clear enough and would be deeply embarrassing, one imagines, for the councillor, who is implicated, if only people were paying attention. But they're not. I can see Silvio's and Francesco's heads together, no doubt over the interminable Balkan crisis. And Iacopo has now taken something from his pocket to show it to an attractive young mother. On official occasions Italians come out of a sense of politeness, and to be part of *lo spettacolo*, but not to listen. The headmistress's speech suggests why.

Like Maestra Elena, the headmistress wears a dark *tailleur* with a brightly fluffy cravat and has a hairstyle reminiscent of early Thatcher days: medium wavy and lacquered to death. But any possible likeness to the Iron Lady dissolves when it comes to performance. She takes the microphone, smiles nervously, almost trips over the wire, then gets hopelessly tangled. The parents' representative has to crouch down to sort her out, unwrapping the wire from around her white tights. Then after a few words of nervous welcome, she moves the thing too far from her mouth, so that one has that curious effect of illusion interrupted, as when an opened door allows light into a cinema. Her voice is suddenly natural and distant and touchingly incomprehensible. Again the representative, who appears to be the factotum of the event, springs to her aid.

'I'm so *emozionata*,' she apologises, which is to say, at once excited and nervous and moved. A very Italian word. 'After all, it's not every day that one celebrates the centenary of one's school, is it?'

Nobody laughs at this delightful truism, for once again nobody is paying attention.

The headmistress opens her handbag and pulls out her speech. There are various sheets of typewritten paper. And she proceeds to read, as all public speakers do in Italy, for there is no merit attached here to the ability to think and speak on one's feet. On the contrary, it's as if the effort of writing the piece down word for word was a guarantee of gravitas rather than ineptitude. I always find it curious that though Italians are wonderful performers in their private lives, in public they actually strive to plod.

The headmistress reads. With the slight spring breeze she finds it difficult to keep the papers in order in one hand while holding the microphone in the other. She drops the papers. The microphone wanders nearer and further from her mouth. The parents' representative does what he can.

She is reading a history of education in Italy and at this school in particular. The school leaving age in 1894 was ten ... School became obligatory for girls at the turn of the century ... Nationwide state-controlled schooling came in only in 1959 ...

She reads quickly, giving the kind of details that might be interesting at an academic conference but making no attempt to have them come alive for her present audience. Then after a tricky, breeze-blown turn of the page, she starts talking more generally about the goals of education today. We have to reaffirm our *indirizzi culturali* – our cultural orientation – within the framework of *una civilità umanistica* – a humanist civilisation. They are the sort of buzz words of contemporary orthodoxy that are on everybody's lips all over the West. I remember when I went to the parents' meeting held prior to the children starting at the school, I asked what my son would be doing if I signed for him to be exempted from religious instruction. 'Something similar,' the headmistress replied mysteriously. Then she explained that all the children who opted out, of whatever age, were put together in one class, some seven or eight out of two hundred. 'But what will they do exactly?' I asked. 'Peace Studies, for example,' she replied, as if this subject had long been a well-established academic discipline. To my shame, I was unable to hold back a smile, almost a laugh. The headmistress was most upset. What, she asked me, as if I were a naughty child, was so funny about Peace Studies? But it seemed pointless trying to explain my sense of the emptiness of those words in front of twenty parents for the most part concerned, as always, with the quality of the food. I made a gesture of apology and begged her to continue.

Now she is explaining how children's education is structured in a modern elementary school. For one cannot have, she says, or rather reads, a *percorso educativo* – a curriculum, one presumes – without *progettualità*. *Progettualità*! Never heard that word before! I ask Stefano what it means. Planning ability, he explains. And indeed the headmistress says that whereas when the school first opened they taught only religion, Italian and mathematics, now they have a full range of subjects to timetable, including, as from this year – and for the first time she reads with a little more animation – Computer Studies!

Ah!

The children by the flag on the balcony are making faces at their mothers and fathers below. Two members of the band have sidled round the corner of the building out of sight of the luminaries to light a cigarette. Brass players, too . . . The headmistress is just pronouncing the words 'recent advances in didactic methodology' when a bus passes, entirely drowning out the inefficient PA. At which it occurs to me that, for better or worse, the most important thing that children bring home from these events is a profound indifference to the content of public discourse. It is important for the headmistress to speak, of course. But who cares what she says.

'Hope this is the last page,' Stefano mutters, as the woman once again flusters with her script in the wind, though her hair is majestically still. She waves the microphone about as the papers refuse to behave. But barely has Stefano made his remark than she has finished, without any forewarning, any sense of conclusion. And quite suddenly it is just as Michele predicted. The headmistress takes one step back and the president of the district steps forward to take the floor . . .

The president of the district is a postman from a nearby village. His long speech is dedicated to a meticulous reconstruction of the district's decision to support the celebration and sponsor the wonderful exhibition of 'A Hundred Years of Elementary Education', which we will find in the assembly hall. But I lose most of this in crouching down to tell Stefi that she will, honestly, get crisps and Fanta at the end if only she holds on. I promise.

Then just when I'm least expecting it – BOM BOM B-BOM!!! BUM BUM B-BUM!!! – the band explodes into a rendering of the national anthem made all the more feisty for the twenty minutes of tedium we have just put up with – BOOM BOOM B-BOOM, BOM B-BOOM BUM B-BAMMM!

The parents' representative tells us the great moment has come, the plaque is now being unveiled by the youngest child in the school. Unfortunately, we can't see this, because it's inside the entrance, but he will give us a running commentary. 'So, yes, the little boy has grabbed hold of the cord. Yes. He is pulling it. Now! Now! Yes, well, the drape seems to be more firmly fixed than expected. Oh. But the little fellow is still pulling. Is it, is it, yes! There it comes! A handsome white stone commemorating a hundred years of the Cesare Bettelone Elementary School! And now for the flag raising!'

The girls on the balcony are busily doing their stuff. The tricolour runs up a flagpole that points forward from the parapet, as if from the bow of a grounded ship. It flutters handsomely in the breeze. The anthem strikes up again. The band go for it with renewed vigour. Il Pesce clashes his cymbals in great style. Then, unexpectedly, a second flag appears, not on the pole but draped over the parapet as is the style on Liberation Day: the yellow stars and deep blue background of the European Community! What a wonderful ideal Europe is! Only yesterday I heard that four new countries were to be added, four new stars in a great constellation of political correctness. And indeed instead of Peace Studies what they finally decided to call the lesson for those who opt out of religion was *'Osservazione all' Europa'* – 'Looking to Europe.'

The anthem ends abruptly. The priest, Don Guido, steps forward in a fine black cassock and purple patterned stole. He reads a long prayer, then puts the headmistress to shame by displaying an enviable ability to juggle missal and microphone as he whips a phial of holy water from his pocket, unstoppers it, and, holding it in the same hand as the microphone, turns to the doorway to make sprinkling gestures over the portals. Since this involves stretching his arm out suddenly in the direction of the amplifier, located immediately inside the porch, each sprinkle of holy water is accompanied by a sudden sharp squeal of feedback. Unless it was the demons in flight. Though frankly you would have thought they'd have left long ago, out of boredom.

Du bi du dan

Announcing the opening of the town-hall-cum-school in 1894, the local newspaper could not have praised the architect more highly: 'a grandiose, elegant modern building, well-provided, especially in the schools, with all the necessary comforts and hygiene requirements.'

He used the plural, 'schools', because while the main body of the building, 'in simple style with ashlar facing,' was to house the town hall, the two lower buildings forming a 'U' around the courtyard behind were to house one the girls and the other the boys. For those were the days when the sexes weren't allowed to mix even before puberty. It reminds me of the oddity of my own upbringing where we were allowed to mix before puberty at elementary school, when we didn't really want to, but not afterwards at secondary school, when we did; and of course what one fears sometimes is that one's whole life has been conditioned by such bizarrerie . . .

The first part of the ceremony now over, we file round the back of this 'grandiose modern building' to the spacious courtyard and the children . . .

The children. How easily they get forgotten in events of this kind! So far, apart from the prettily dressed girls pouting on the balcony, we haven't seen any of them. Nobody has complained. Now, as we round the corner, there they all are in a great phalange in the middle of the courtyard, ready to do their stuff. And with surprising efficiency, the band are already sitting on their chairs beside them, spirited through the main building presumably while we walked round. The amplifier has likewise been brought through, so that already the speeches are beginning again. The headmistress. Again. The president of the district. Again. The councillor under investigation (he is refreshingly brief). Old teachers at the school.

Copying their parents, the children chatter and ignore the whole thing. Without even lowering his voice Stefano explains to me that when he was a kid, in the early fifties, they celebrated the school's birthday every year. And all kinds of other birthdays too: the president's, the republic's. They had oodles of these events. They were always standing in courtyards waiting to recite poetry. Stefano seems more amused at this than upset. But no, he doesn't remember a single poem . . .

We're jerked out of our conversation by a bell. The caretaker, the oldest member of staff at the school, is waving a handbell around to show how he used to announce lesson changes some twenty years ago. Then some old pupils of times gone by are invited to the front and given a 'diploma' while the band plays 'Oh, When the Saints' with creditable vigour.

How Italians love diplomas, commemorative documents of every kind! Diplomas for having gone to a skating course, for having taken part in a volleyball competition, for being present at the inauguration of some institution or other. It's rare to do anything in a group in Italy and not end up with a diploma. Perhaps they like them so much because these fancy pieces of paper parody those documents that are so vital in Italian life and which, in the event, are so hard won: school finishing exams, your degree . . .

After the ex-pupils, the caretaker is called back and he is awarded a diploma, too. A caretaker's diploma! It's a small red-orange scroll with a white ribbon tied around. Very attractive. He smiles, laughs, nods, but thankfully refuses to 'take the floor'. Instead, he waves his diploma in the air and returns clownishly to his place, receiving great cheers from the children.

Now at last we are to hear the poem that Michele has been reciting so irritatingly for the past week (without my ever really listening). The centenary poem. But not all the kids, it turns out, will get a chance to say it. Six have been chosen and each will recite a few lines. Holding the now infamous microphone.

The poem is written in the local dialect. For although dialect is frowned upon in public discourse, considered uneducated, too domestic and direct (so that the headmistress, for example, would never address us in dialect and the postman president did his best not to), nevertheless it is apparently appropriate for poetry, for quaint and harmless expressions of pride in cultural identity. It's interesting that, for all his love of the Romans and their lingua franca, Mussolini encouraged the use of dialects, perhaps understanding how they warmed people's hearts, gave them a link with a more immediate past, a sense of community. And indeed the wonderful thing about dialect is that it has not been touched by new-speak of the likes of *progettualità* and *percorsi didattici* and *attività psicomotoria* (gym). No, the local dialect is as earthy as the broadest Yorkshire and brutally adenoidal, with the result that it always seems funny in the mouths of children, like watching a toddler trying to use a crowbar. In any event, it's the dialect poem that gives us the day's first attempt at humour, the first retreat from the façade of civic piety.

'Our school is an 'undred year old,' a very small chap begins, 'but bearin' up well despite all 'er colds.'

A girl with chubbily trembling knees goes on to suggest that a little beauty treatment of the poor lady's cracked and yellowing old skin would not come amiss. But since they can hardly take her to a health clinic, whispers a bespectacled little boy, the pupils will do their best to keep her young at heart. Then a very self-assured young maiden explains that if the school ever feels lonely, the children will always be there shouting and playing to cheer her up. But will always, interrupts another, give her a nice long rest in summer. (Clearly the poetess has equated the school with *i nonni*.) Towards the end of fifty and more similarly cosy lines, the biggest boy in the oldest class is allowed the exclamation: 'What a bore it is, 'aving to study!' a line which he shouts with great enthusiasm, raising a yell of support from the other pupils and thunderous applause from the parents, who for the first time this morning have actually listened to something.

Twelve o'clock is almost upon us, well-synchronised tummies are beginning to rumble. But just before we go we are to get an example of what I can only call the other extreme of Italian speech . . . After the jolly, homespun, dialect poem, the main group of the children finally get their chance to do something. They are going to sing a song written by a teacher who goes by the noble name of Gino d'Arezzo. It is called 'Imparare in Liberta' – 'Learning in Liberty'.

I said sing, but I should have said chant. Gino comes out front to conduct them. There's a second's silence, then rather tinnily (after the band) some taped music rattles out. But this is only to give the children rhythm. The minute they start to shout their lines, the tape is lost. Gino d'Arezzo waves his arms urgently. The first verse goes:

Nella scuola il mio domani c'è
leggo, scrivo, studio: serve a me
dal sapere nascerà una nuova società
società-à-à-à-à-à-à-à-à!

Which rather depressingly translates as:

The school is my tomorrow, my future
Reading, writing, studying, it's so useful
From this knowledge born will be
A new society-ee-ee-ee!

Gino is obviously the kind of fellow who in English would be rhyming words like 'ebony' and 'ivory'. The second verse goes:

Nella mente tante cose già
ideali ricchi di bontà
la cultura non sarà fonte di rivalità
civiltà-à-à-à-à questa è civiltà

This, in a now very poor translation, might go something like:

> So much already in my mind
> Fine ideals good and kind
> Culture won't breed competition
> Civiliza-a-a-shun. That's civiliza-a-a-shun!

I must confess I wasn't ready for this. I feel thrown. Rather than being filled with fine ideals, my mind becomes the setting for a three-cornered tussle between hilarity, embarrassment and depression. The poem is awful, infinitely worse than the church choruses I remember singing as a child – 'Red and yellow, black and white, all are precious in His sight,' etc. Perhaps the problem is that Gino's piety is not even underwritten by a formal religion, with all that religions imply in terms of mystery and our not really understanding the world: Sant'Eurosia's miracles, appearances of the Madonna, and the like. No, Gino, his poem suggests, has it all worked out: one simply needs to be good and to tell the children to be good (and look to Europe). But the little boys and girls do belt the words out with such enthusiasm that one can see how Gino might imagine his *percorso didattico* is working.

Civiltà-à-à-à, questa è civiltà-à-à-à! The children holler and clap. It reminds me of those well-marshalled groups of Chinese children one used to see repeating (presumably) idiocies about the advantages of communism. And the text itself is not far off the kind of thing I occasionally used to tune into on Radio Tirana in the good old days when nearby Albania was still a museum to Stalinism. In fact, the next verse of the poem is going to mention the formation of the New Man, which was always one of Radio Tirana's obsessions when they weren't reading reports from *The Black Book of Western Imperialism*.

But before we get to that, the song is interrupted by a kind of chorus. For this is an extremely modern song/poem/chant with a rap beat, and now in the middle the kids all break off (so that one hears the tinny whine of the tape again). With perfect timing, or almost, they shout: 'O! O! O! DAN, DAN, DAN, DUBI, DAN DAN!'

This is repeated several times, the 'dubi', written here as spelt in the Italian copy of the song, which I later got hold of, being presumably some kind of corruption of Sinatra's 'do be do be do . . .'

'O! O! O!' they scream. 'DAN, DAN, DAN, DUBI DAN DAN!'

The hollered doggerel is actually something of a relief after all those serious thoughts, if only because the children are getting off on it so much. One small girl, a lovely, solid little creature with two pretty blonde pigtails and a rumpled skirt, is going almost crazy in the front row, jumping up and down in manic Muppet fashion and bellowing the refrain. 'DAN DAN DUBI DAN DAN!!!'

The third verse is a little harder to catch, since half the children are still chanting 'dubi dan dan' while the others recite the words. But, I later found that copies of the poem were sensibly provided in a handout:

Ogni bimbo studierà
O! – in completa libertà
O! – solo questo basterà
ed un uomo nuovo si farà-à-à-à-à

The nearest I can get to this is as follows:

Every child will stud-ee
Oh! – in total libert-ee
Oh! – this is what it will take
The new man to cre-e-ate.

In defence of the rather lame half-rhyme – take/create – I can only invite the reader to observe how easy it is to rhyme in Italian (in this case merely by using the same inflected verb ending) and how miserably difficult in English. However, the thinking, if such it can be considered, is clear enough. Encouragingly, when the children repeat the verse after another round of 'dubi dan dan's (I should have said that all the verses were repeated), more than one little boy, and I suspect my Michele is amongst them, has begun to replace the words *uomo nuovo* (new man) with the rather less nebulous concept *uovo sodo* (hard-boiled egg).

Oh – this is what it will take
The hard-boiled egg to cre-e-ate.

My father-in-law once told me that when as teenagers he and his schoolmates had to sing the many fascist songs at the Saturday morning gym sessions Mussolini instituted, they always changed the words to make them ridiculous, even those who were eager supporters of fascism. It's as if such songs naturally invited their own parody.

But this is speculation. More to the point is that the headmistress has announced that our revels are now ended. The band wind up the event with a lively tango, a tune one can only assume they usually use at rather different occasions. 'Thank God for the band,' Stefano observes as we file into the school for our well-deserved snack. 'Without them . . .'

Anno fascista

The nice thing about these occasions in Italian schools is that there is wine available. It's every parent to his or her own child's classroom, then tuck in: cakes and munchies, Coke and Fanta. And Soave and Custoza and Lugano. Stefano and I very quickly fill up big plastic cups. The walls of the classroom are covered with giant demonstrations of mathematical rules and explanations of where to put the apostrophe when writing Italian, something I should really study a little more carefully myself. A large chart shows how the children are getting on at their various subjects. There are the names of the pupils along the vertical axis, the subjects on the horizontal and then different colours filling the squares defined by the meeting of name and subject: red for excellent, blue for good, green for average, yellow for not good enough. It's a remarkably open system, brutal for those who are doing badly. I can see that Iacopo's child has problems with composition, while Stefano's Beppe is the best at maths. Michele, I choose to think, with the kind of parental jealousy one always hoped one wouldn't have, is hanging in there like a good long distance runner, in the pack behind the leaders. All his squares are blue. So much for Gino d'Arezzo's 'Culture won't breed competition.'

Having made sure Stefi has one hand round a glass of Fanta and another in a bowl of crisps (my part of the *ricatto*), I now escape from the children to go and look at the centenary exhibition, set up very seriously and professionally in one corridor and classroom.

Any historical exhibition held in the village of Montecchio begins with the same five or six old photographs of the village as it was in the early 1900s. Today's is no exception. Conveniently enough, one of these photos shows the school, then town hall. Certainly, it was more impressive in those days without the railings and carpark in front. Its scale and volume were more right somehow. The effect might be that of seeing a long-lost temple cleared of surrounding jungle. Then there are the photos I must have seen a hundred times of the day the first tram arrived in Montecchio in 1928. The square was just a large open space without any of its present pavements and war memorials, its scrubby patches of railed-off grass and litter-bound fountain. There wasn't even any asphalt, just a dusty expanse between school and stuccoed houses where the tram rolled in beneath strings of bunting. How much more gracious spaces were before the motorcar took over and forced everything into its urgent geometry of channels and lanes! The tram was the vanguard. It was 1928. The village was about to change. The people waved their hats and cheered. No doubt they were right.

Another memorable photograph shows six 1930s children playing on and around a Vespa. It reminds me of the facetious headline people used to joke about: 'Cinquecento collides with scooter, fifteen dead.' Nowadays most mothers pick up their only child in the family's second car.

Two old women are standing in front of the first exhibit proper, giggling. It shows a series of school reports, the first dating back to 1895 and offering an impressive combination of scrolls, pillars, angels, rubber stamps, and noble calligraphy to announce the occasion of Adelina Chiavegato's leaving school. Interestingly, it doesn't use words such as 'maturity' and 'graduation' as would become the fashion later; it speaks of Adelina's being granted IL PROSCIOGLIMENTO DELL'OBBLIGO, her 'release from obligation', meaning quite simply that she has done enough not to have to come to school anymore. She has passed her final exams. Age ten. Now she can go and work in the fields, or in a factory, or wait at home till someone marries her.

I ask the two ladies what they're laughing about. They're wearing heavy coats, despite the spring weather. Their hair is white, teeth, as so often in this part of the world, grey: grandmothers presumably, in need, like the school, of an overhaul. They point to a report from the year 1931/2, except that here there's a second entry for the date that says: *Anno IX Era Fascista* – Ninth Year of the Fascist Era . . . How galvanising it must have seemed to have written Year IX! And how astute of Mussolini not to try to eliminate the Christian calendar, but to have the two live side by side on every printed document, 1931 and Anno IX, not unlike the catechism and '*Osservazione all'Europa*'.

In spidery handwriting at the top of the report is the

name Elvira Avanzi. 'That's me,' one of the women says, fiddling with reading glasses.

It's a report to be proud of, and made all the more so by the fact that the fascists substituted the system of grading from one to ten with the more morally loaded system of *giudizi* – judgments. Thus we have the possibilities of *lodevole* (praiseworthy), *buono* (good), then *sufficiente* (passed by a whisker) then *insufficiente* (fail).

The entries read:

Lavori manuali, lavori donneschi (manual work, women's work)	– *lodevole*
Igiene e pulizia della persona (hygiene and personal cleanliness)	– *lodevole*
Nozioni di matematica	– *buono*
Nozioni di geografia	– *buono*
Religione	– *lodevole*
Calligrafia	– *lodevole*
Comportamento morale e civile (moral and civil behaviour)	– *lodevole*

But they are laughing, Elvira explains, 'Because everybody got *lodevole* for hygiene. You didn't have to do anything to get *lodevole* for hygiene. It was automatic. Even when you came from cleaning the chickens. Everybody got it.' Just like the caretaker's diploma . . .

But the certificate display has its darker side, too. To the right of Elvira's school report, a futuristic design of three boxes springing out from a sheet of grey paper frames the initials ONB, Opera Nazionale Balilla, the fascist movement that organized children at elementary school. Balilla was the nickname for Giovanni Battista Perasso, a boy who in 1746 threw a stone at a group of Austrian soldiers in Genoa, thus sparking off (so they say) an uprising that expelled the Austrians from Liguria. Clearly this was a fine example for the schoolboys of two hundred years later to follow, though quite who they were to throw their stones at must have been unclear at first. Leave Michele alone with his catapult and God knows what uprising might occur.

Attendance of the assemblies of the Opera Nazionale Balilla was obligatory, so that as well as having to deal with two dating systems, children also had to collect two school reports. Underneath Elvira's *lodevole*s there are four or five ONB certificates. The graphics are extravagantly *1984*ish, with the words Ministero Educazione Nazionale and Partito Nazionale Fascista featuring portentously in storm-torn skies. Below them, an angel holds sword aloft as she strides across a landscape of planes, tanks and smoking power stations. In the centre of this piece of paper that only fifty years ago was handed out to little children with, on the back, some comment on their 'performance' is the single word (in very large capitals), VINCERE, which I suppose one would have to translate as TO VICTORY! I can imagine my Michele being very proud indeed of receiving such a piece of paper. He has been going through a phase recently of drawing the most elaborate weapons of war, frequently mounted on the back of high-performance sports cars.

On a display opposite these old reports is a huge piece of paper with the large, even handwriting of a teacher, offering information that claims to come as the result of research made by the fifth year. It reads as follows:

> *'Mens sana in corpore sano,'* said Mussolini and every Saturday morning the children at the Cesare Betteloni

> school had to come to the playground to do exercises and drills. Often they would prepare shows and take part in competitions.

A black-and-white photograph beside shows the courtyard of the school and the children exercising in their white smocks. A rather attractive young teacher is bending to touch her toes, long dark hair falling forward. The research report continues:

> Before being a teacher here, Maestro Ferdinando Ruffo was also a pupil at this school, though he never got a higher grade than *sufficiente*. The floors were made of wood then and there were smoking stoves in every classroom. The desks were heavy and wooden with fold-down seats and holes for inkwells. Sometimes there were four children to a desk and forty-five to a class, not twenty like today. In 1943 the school was occupied by the Germans in flight. The lessons were stopped. The more fortunate children went to study with the nuns in the nearby village of Olivè. Maestro Ruffo, however, was able to complete his studies thanks to a kind friend of the family who tutored him gratis, and in 1945, when the school reopened, he passed his final elementary school exam.

I'm surprised to hear that the school was occupied by the Germans; I didn't know that at all. I ask Stefano if he knew, but he didn't. His family is not from this village. I wonder if it is churlish of me to ask myself whether perhaps the headmistress shouldn't have mentioned at least in passing how the courtyard we were standing in this morning was once the scene of Mussolini's Saturday morning exercises, how the school was closed for two of its hundred years as the Germans fought their long and bloody rearguard action up the peninsula. (How discreet that 'in flight' is!) Or was this simply so self-evident it didn't need to be said? Or perhaps there *was* some passing reference and I missed it in the general chat. But I don't think so. That was not the tone of the morning at all. The mildly worrying thing about it, if one wishes to worry about these things, is how close in spirit the chanting of Gino d'Arezzo's poem is to much that went on on those mornings. Doubtless many of the children loved it.

There is a mill of parents and kids round the exhibits, spilling wine and Coke, marvelling at how their village used to be, reminding each other of buildings that have changed, wondering at the old cars that sneak into the corners of the frames, sighing over the pretty children's smock uniforms that made them all look like choirboys, looking for friends' school reports amongst the more recent post-war exhibits, where the assessment system, I notice, has now retreated from *lodevole, buono*, etc., back to plain numbers: *Uno, due, tre, quattro, cinque, sex . . .*

'What's this *sex*?' I ask Stefano.

'Six,' he tells me. 'The grading was one to ten.'

'Yes, but I mean why is it written *sex* instead of *sei*?'

Stefano strokes his chin. He has a nice tubby chin and a tubby man's moustache. But this is one thing he doesn't know. His brow furrows earnestly. No, he doesn't know, only remembers that they always wrote it that way.

We ask one or two others. They don't know. Iacopo doesn't know. Marta doesn't know. So I don't find out about this until I ask Rita later. Rita has a disturbing way of knowing everything. It was *sex* instead of *sei*, she explains, because the children could very easily have turned an 'i' into a 't' and so transformed *sei* into *sette*, before showing the thing to their parents, but with the 'x' there it was impossible. Italians do have a way of assuming that one's planning to cheat . . .

Elvira, Adelina, Ida, Elvira again, Maggia, Libera . . . It's mainly the women who have kept their school reports and brought them along. And what fine old names. Arselide, Egidia, Amalia. Turning my head to where another exhibit lists the names of children in the various classes today, I spy two Thomases, a Michael, a Jessica, and, for Italians, an unpronounceable Hilary. All with local surnames. Alongside the names, a brief history of school-leaving ages and leavers' accomplishments shows that only two of the forty-four parents of the present fifth year (ten-year olds) went to university while twelve of the twenty-one children wish to go. The present school-leaving age is fourteen.

Michele arrives with a cake in one hand and a fistful of cheese biscuits in the other. Speaking with his mouth full, he's eager to show me a puppet-making project he's been involved in and leads me into a classroom where the exhibition continues. Arranged down the middle are five ancient desks, painted a dirty blue-green and more or less fitting the description of the desks in Ferdinando Ruffo's hard times. An assortment of old text and copybooks is laid out on top. Michele drags me to the wall where his puppets are displayed under the rather depressing heading CREATIVITY AND MANUALITY TODAY.

But at this point, with one o'clock approaching and that Italian propriety that demands that an *aperitivo* be followed promptly by a meal, everybody begins to make their escape. I have just begun to look at a row of black-and-blue witches, their lumpy papier-mâché faces squeezed into extravagant grimaces and smiles when

Maestra Elena comes in to tell us they want to close. Michele is furious, to the point of tears. So I promise him, and myself, that I will come back during the week to look at the show again. And indeed, what follows in the next chapter are fragments of this, as it turned out, excellent exhibition, a sort of dialogue between the printed page put in front of the children and what they themselves wrote down in their copybooks. Perhaps I should add that it was while poring over these exhibits with notebook and dictaphone that I got for the first time an acute sense of that national and moral history that my children, like all other Italians, will inevitably absorb, the attitudes and mental gestures society makes available to them. As so often when looking at anything that has to do with the past, I was surprised at once by how very much and how very little has changed. What year is it now? 1994? Or *Anno Fascista LXXII* . . .

Prima composizione

First Composition Lesson, 1915:

> *Daddy works* is a simple sentence to which other words or *complements* may be added in order to complete the sense. For example:
>
> *Daddy works happily*
> where *happily* is a complement, or
> *Daddy works happily from morning till night*
> where *from morning till night* is another complement, or
> *Daddy, out of love for his family, works happily in his workshop from morning till night*
> *out of love for his family* and *in his workshop* are two more complements.

Daddy, out of love for his family, works happily in his workshop from morning till night . . . The whole mythology of Italian bourgeois life is presented in a nutshell in the very first *lezione di composizione*: the small-time artisan slaving (but creatively, in his own workshop) for the sake of his wife and children. Not unlike dear San Giuseppe, patron saint of carpenters. The word *sacrifici* need not even be mentioned. The child will be aware that he should be grateful and should emulate. But the key fact here is that Daddy is out of the house, absent (we presume, and for convenience's sake everybody agrees, at the workshop).

I remember that one of the first compositions Michele had to write was about people's occupations. He wrote: 'The baker bakes bread, sells it and makes money. The carpenter makes cupboards, sells them and makes money. The farmer makes food, sells it and makes money.' Clearly there are moments when lucidity pierces even the densest of orthodoxies.

The second composition in 1915 put down another corner-stone of the Italian's mental architecture:

> Blessed is that family where there are old people, says an ancient proverb, and happy the children who heed the counsel of the old, for it's as if they had already enjoyed a long life. Love your grandparents, children, for they love you as the sons and daughters of their sons and daughters, and hence with a double tenderness. If you see they love your company, don't leave them alone, and when it's their birthday, never forget to wish them many happy returns, 'A hundred more happy returns, Granny and Granddad!'
>
> Don't forget, Michele and Stefi!

Today, in the 1990s, the school's end-of-term plays, whether it be Christmas or summer, always include a figure with pipe and straw hat who complains that nobody cares about the old anymore. And Stefi objects: 'Oh, but I do care, if only they would visit . . .'

In 1906 a child noted down in his copybook the following PATRIOTIC AND RELIGIOUS ANNIVERSARIES AND FESTIVALS for the month of March:

1. 1st March 1896, The Battle of Adua, Africa
2. 4th March 1848, Carlo Alberto grants the constitution
3. 7th March 1785, birth of Manzoni
4. 10th March 1872, death of Mazzini
5. 11th March 1544, birth of Tasso
6. 17th March 1861, proclamation in Turin of the new Kingdom of Italy
7. 18th March 1848, Milan rises against the Austrians, beginning of the glorious period known as the Five Days
8. 19th March, San Giuseppe's Day
9. 22th March 1848, Austrians chased out of Milan and Venice
10. 23rd March 1849, beginning of the glorious Ten Days of Brescia in the rising against the Austrians
11. 25th March, *Annunciazione di N.S.G.C. [Nostro Signore Gesù Cristo]*
12. 28th March 1483, birth in Urbino of the painter Raphaele Sanzio, known as 'The Divine'. *The Transfiguration* was his last painting, and his most sublime.

One notes: 3 battles against Austrian imperialism, 1 for Italian imperialism (lost, against the Ethiopians, at Adua); 3 anniversaries for poets, 2 for the church, 1 for a painter, 1 for the constitution; 2 uses of the word 'glorious' (for Italian resistance to Austria, but not Ethiopian resistance to

Italy), 1 use of 'sublime', notably in the confident superlative, 'the most sublime' (does 'the least sublime' exist?); and, finally, 0 mentions of women, unless by allusion in the Annunciation . . .

With this total absence of female role models, a book entitled *Operaia e massaia – Woman Worker and Housewife* (1915) – was still having to explain exactly why women should bother getting an education at all:

> There was a time, not long ago, impossible as it may seem, when people believed that education wasn't necessary for women. There were even people who said it was dangerous. And this prejudice has still not been entirely overcome. I say that it may seem impossible, because, if education is necessary for men, then it's even more necessary for women, since they are destined to become the first teachers of their men children. An uneducated woman cannot be free from prejudices and she will communicate these to her children. An illiterate woman cannot experience the sweet comfort of watching over and helping her little boy in the first steps of his education. And what is more beautiful and poetic than the mother who holds her little son's hand as he does his first writing exercises or as she listens to him repeating his first little school lessons. Does not a young woman lose much of her beauty and grace if she can't read either those books that lift the soul to God, or those magazines that teach so many things both for domestic life and for the execution of housewifely tasks? And if she isn't married and her loved one is far away, in order to write to him she will have to turn to a third person and admit him to her most intimate secrets. What humiliation! What mortification!

So women have become educated in order: 1. to teach their male children; 2. to devote their minds to God; 3. to learn how to be in fashion; 4. to keep house and to . . . write to their boyfriends. When over lunch my own daughter Stefi announces that she wishes to be an airline pilot, big brother Michele tells her she can't. Because she's a woman. I remark that on the contrary Stefi can do anything she wants. But Michele gets angry, because at school, he claims, he has been told that women can't be pilots. Or racing drivers. And at school they must be right. No, women can do anything, I insist, Stefi can do anything she wants. My son sits there glaring at me. Women can't be priests, he says. He is right.

But they can be teachers. And the irony surrounding *Operaia e massaia* is that very soon it would be the girls who had the most obvious and immediate role model in the classroom, *la maestra* herself. Schools, particularly at the lower levels, are now an almost exclusively female domain. Having missed Gino d'Arezzo at the *scuola elementare*, my son will probably reach adolescence without ever being in class with a male teacher.

But having become teachers, what kind of model do these women offer? A little girl's exercise book from 1970 is open at the following composition:

MY SIGNORINA HAS GONE!

Today, 25 March 1970, was the last day that our *maestra*, Signora Argentina Zanoll will take our lessons. Some children, even when the lessons had only just begun, threw rice over her to celebrate her promotion. For us it was a rather sad morning because we knew that after three years of lessons with this *maestra* we would have to leave her. The saddest moment was when the

> bell rang to go home. The Signorina gave each one of us a kiss, almost all the girls were crying and the Signorina with tears in her eyes tried to console them. She said she would always remember all of us and that she will often come to say hello and that the new *maestra* would love us just as much as she did. Having left the classroom, we set off home with happy memories of our good *maestra*, who, for all this time, has been just like a *mamma* to us.

Just like a *mamma* ... Why is it that Italians, men and women alike, find it so difficult to think about a woman without that word popping up. For all its championing the female right to education, *Operaia e massaia* is no exception in seeing woman as a nurturer of protagonists, rather than a protagonist herself.

> You future Italian mothers, future educators of a new generation, encourage with calm and mild words the tendency towards peace among nations, inspire in all the hearts that surround you the horror of war that makes men crueller than beasts. But should your brothers and fathers and husbands one day have to run to defend the sacred borders of our land, then kiss them with smiles of love and hope. It is your fine and holy mission, oh Women, to preach peace, peace in the family, peace in the state, peace among nations. But it is also your duty, and a no less holy duty, to rouse spirits when men must fight in the name of independence and liberty, and to give your praise to valour, but valour demonstrated in a legitimate struggle.

Is this an exercise in having your cake and eating it? The Italians have a lovely expression for getting things both ways, they talk about having 'your wife drunk and the barrel full'; i.e. she's off your back *and* you can drink to your heart's content. Or, you've made your wife happy without even spending anything . . . The funny thing is hearing women use this irretrievably sexist expression.

A six-year-old's exercise book, lying on one of the old school desks, gives the child's (guided) reaction to this heady mixture of patriotism and feminine sweetness. We're in 1926 now:

> Page one: a cut-out photo of the king.
> Page two: (in huge handwriting) 'Mamma I love you lots and lots, I promise I will be good.'
> Page three: a cut-out photo of Il Duce.
> Page four: 'December 8th, I love and worship Maria.'
> Page five: 'December 13th, Santa Lucia has brought me a pram with a pretty doll.' (Santa Lucia is the Veronese children's Father Christmas, of which more anon.)
> Page six: 'Dear Baby Jesus please help me to be good.'
> Page seven: 'January 6th, the three kings brought Jesus gold, frankincense and myrrh.'
> Page eight: 'Long live the Queen and Empress, Elena of Savoy.'

Beside it, another notebook of an older child lists the main events of the same year:

> 26 January: Agreements between Italy and Great Britain on the repayment of the national debt.
> 18 August: Second attempt in Rome on the life of President Benito Mussolini, carried out by the British subject Violet Albina Gibson. The president is lightly wounded in the nose.
> 11 September: Pesaro agreement, vital for the stabilisation of the Lira.
> [date missing]: Third attempt in Rome on President

Benito Mussolini's life, carried out by political exile and anarchist Gino Luccetti; his bomb hits the presidential car but only explodes after rebounding on the ground.

31 October: Fourth attempt in Bologna on the life of President Benito Mussolini, carried out by Anteo Zamboni, immediately lynched by the outraged crowd. The leader of the Black Shirts is grazed by the bullet but unhurt.

Was this a particularly bad year for Benito? And what did the children make of the bizarre behaviour of British women, their attraction to the Italian male nose? But if this led to any confusion as to the nature of male and female roles, it would soon be cleared up. The peace mission of the 'future mothers of Italy' does not play a prominent role in this reading for the fourth-year elementary class of 1938, though it's amusing that while men are at the centre of all the action, Italy itself always gets feminine pronouns:

> From 3 October 1935 to 5 May 1936 fascist Italy conquered the Abyssinian Empire. In seven months the Italian legionnaires conquered the vast Abyssinian army and occupied a country four times the size of Italy. Fifty-two nations opposed this campaign and fascist Italy alone took on and conquered all her enemies.
>
> How did she conquer them? First and foremost by faith, faith in the justice of her cause, faith in the king, faith in Il Duce. Then with the strength and valour of her race; the strength and valour of her legionnaires, who with constant heroism overcame the most arduous tasks; the strength and valour of all Italian men and all Italian women who accepted any and every sacrifice, even donating their wedding rings to the cause of the Italian motherland. They won with their valour and

their genius, the achievements of the legionnaires being supported by powerful weapons of war used on a grand scale for the first time in the Ethiopian campaign: aeroplanes, tanks, radio. These mighty and modern instruments of war, precious in peace and terrible in conflict, were the product of Italian genius. The aeroplane was conceived by the Italian Leonardo da Vinci; this great inventor likewise studied the possibility of the propeller, but the application of the propeller to a flying machine was made possible only after the invention of the internal combustion engine, first constructed by the Italian Eugenio Barsanti. The tank was also conceived and designed by Leonardo da Vinci. The tank is neither more nor less than a small automobile armoured with steel, the automobile moving by virtue of Barsanti's internal combustion engine. Then came the radio, through which news can fly at the speed of lightning. The radio, too, is an exclusively Italian invention, conceived by Guglielmo Marconi. Thus, Italy truly did everything alone; she conquered her Empire not only with her heroism, but also with her genius. Entrusted to the marvellous talents of the Italian race, this is the Empire of justice, of genius, of work, the empire of civilisation . . .

The text must have made heavy reading indeed on the smoky winter benches of the Cesare Betteloni school in Montecchio. But then the compositions couldn't have been much fun either. 'You are looking at a portrait of Il Duce,' suggests another textbook of the time. 'Record your feelings (of pride and admiration).'

The parenthetical prompt is less out of date than one would imagine. Perhaps it is part of the language's rhetorical vocation, I don't know, but so much schooling in

Italy seems to depend on encouraging children to have orthodox ideas and then express them in extravagant tones. It's remarkable, after all, how much of the basic emotional gesturing is the same in the woman's textbook of 1915, the eulogy to fascist enterprise in 1938 and Gino d'Arezzo's 1994 poem on the construction of the New Man. There's a confidence, an exhortatory pride, a radical piety which admits of no contradiction, or even indifference. A textbook entitled *Pagine gaie* (Gay Pages), published not in 1930 but in 1960, has a reading that begins as follows.

> Italy My Homeland
>
> Italy, people of artists, martyrs, saints, of warriors, heroes and sailors, people of arduous achievement bent over their daily tasks, intent on constructing without pause, with muscles and spirit, a new civilisation in the world.

But it's not just textbook and teacher telling the kids how they should think about things. When Maestra Elena stops in the exhibition room a moment to chat to me, she complains that almost all of the children's essays show signs of parental, meaning maternal, interference. Immediately, I think of Michele screaming: 'Mamma, but what can I say about my summer holiday? Mamma, what can I say about carnival? Mamma, what can I say about Bosnia?' 'Michele,' I tell him, 'just write what you think.' 'I said Mamma, not Papà! MAMMA . . .'

I ask Maestra Elena how she can tell there's been interference. Is it that they always get their grammar right, that they don't make any spelling mistakes? No, she says, far from it. No, it's because they always say *the right things*.

The interesting thing is how my son's teacher no more doubts that these are the right things than she would question the declensions of a verb. It's just that she wants the kids to get there on their own. Talking to my father-in-law about this, he laughs and tells me that he and his friends always finished whatever essay they wrote with a quote from Il Duce. That way they could feel sure of a *lodevole* . . . Things are a little more subtle today but not much, if the following composition is anything to go by. Conscientiously dated February 27th 1970, it's entitled, 'If I had a nice big sum of money . . .'

> If I had a nice big sum of money, I'd spend it like this: half I would give to the missionaries to build hospitals, homes, schools, churches for poor people. I would also send it so they could have running water and gas. I would send it willingly, just seeing in the newspaper and on television those poor black children with their swollen stomachs and their heads big from hunger. They are so hungry they eat lizards and ants.
>
> The other half of the money I would save for my future.

Perhaps the child who wrote this had *nonni* in the house whose advice he had taken. Certainly, as the 1915 textbook says, 'it's as if he'd already enjoyed a long life.' He knows how to please. Though the truth about my own children and those of all my friends is that they clamour endlessly (and understandably) for new toys. I can't imagine a nice big sum of money would last very long in their hands.

A large, serious and forbidding book published in the early 1920s was already very much aware of the dangers of this split between rhetoric and reality. Perhaps it is part of any nation's stable schizophrenia to be aware of a characteristic and perverse trait and then to persist in it anyway. This passage could have been taken, only very slightly altered and updated, from any contemporary newspaper.

> The Italian flair for craft and cunning has exalted the use of rhetoric with which the unscrupulous seek to mislead the masses. It is deplorable what little authority over people the men of reason and figures enjoy in comparison with the speech-mongers. From small societies right up to parliament the prevalence of men gifted only in speaking is distressing. There are too many lawyers, too many orators holding positions of power . . .

But what a relief to get away from all this seriousness to the poems the children learn. For while the Italian language has a very long and strong suit in crafty rhetoric, perhaps its real trump card lies with the simplest and most innocent lyricism. A book from the 1920s is open at this little gem:

Cavallino trotta trotta
Che ti salto sulla groppa
Trotta trotta in Gran Bretagna
A pigliare il pan di Spagna

Trotta trotta in Delfinato
A pigliare il pan peppato
Trotta trotta e torna qui
Che c'è il pan di tutti i dì.

Again with all due apologies for my limitations as a translator of poetry, here is an approximation:

Trotalong, trotalong, pony bold
On your back I'll jump and hold
Trot away to Britain Great
To get yourself some nice bread cake

Trot away to Picardy
To get some bread that's nice and spicy
Then trot right back to Italy
For the bread of everyday.

The thoughtful teacher who laid out the exhibition has placed the poem alongside a reading that expresses the same moral rather more brutally. A little boy refuses to eat his regular bread roll in the morning because he wants a piece of cake. Upon which Breadroll answers back and gives the boy a very thorough lecture on the virtues of humble routine and simple pleasures (from morning to night – happily – in his workshop . . .)

Growing up anywhere in the world, I suppose, is partly a question of absorbing the lesson that you can't always get what you want. But Italian children do get a great deal, as witness this most charming of all the poems, written, perhaps not so surprisingly, at the frenetic height of fascist grandiloquence. I say not surprisingly because sometimes I feel that the two extremes of Italian expression are there to counterbalance each other. These little verses were typed rather than appearing in a book; they were composed for the Cesare Betteloni end-of-term school play in 1930. Quite probably this is their first publication.

Ciliegie rosse e belle
lucenti e tenerelle
volete voi gustar
volete voi comprar

ciliegie eccole qua
tra la là la lalà lalà tralalà

Di queste perle rare
mi voglio incoronare
regina mi farò
gran ballo vi darò
guardate tutti qua
lalà lalà lalà lalà

Orecchini pendenti
bei visetti ridenti
mazzi giocondi e vivi
per abiti festivi
come stan bene qua
come stan bene là
lalà lalà lalà lalà

How perfect these silvery little rhythms are for expressing childlike joy, these even syllables and endless vowels. The resources of English lie elsewhere, I'm afraid . . .

Cherries red and fine
With their juicy shine
Do you want to try
Do you want to buy
Cherries! Here they are!
Tra la la, tra la la

With these pearls so rare
I'm going to crown my hair
I'll make myself a queen
Throw a dance you've never seen
Look everybody, over here
Tra la la, tra la la

Ear-rings a-dangling
Pretty faces smiling
Bunches bright and gay
On clothes for holiday
How nice they look here!
There, how nice they are!
Tra la la, tra la la

One of the best snapshots we have of our own children is that of their two faces cheek to cheek in the orchard just beyond the house with freshly picked cherries draped dangling over their ears . . .

At this point my long mooching about the exhibition was interrupted by the teacher who had arranged it, none other than Gino d'Arezzo. Nervous, red-faced, he has brought a photographer along to take detailed photographs that will preserve his work forever. For never again, he feels, never again will it be possible to assemble such a collection of old books. The two are carrying a stepladder to help them get aerial shots from above the display tables. 'Go ahead, go ahead,' he tells me rather extravagantly, seeming at once put about and flattered that somebody is taking his exhibits seriously. I compliment him sincerely, on an excellent show, upon which, between moving the stepladder back and forth for the photographer and turning the light on and off to see how it will affect various exhibits, he explains that he feels the exhibition is important because people don't realise how much school has changed. They are in danger of losing touch with their children. They don't appreciate how modern and technical school has become. Light years away from their own days. I wonder if perhaps the teachers of the 1930s wouldn't have said the same thing.

'From next year the fourth and fifth years will be learning the computer,' he reminds me.

I remember when I was sixteen the grand fanfare for the introduction of computer programming in my grammar school. Everything we learnt is now hopelessly out of date.

The photographer is trying to work out some way of screwing a small tripod to the stepladder. These technicalities . . .

'And everything's so much more analytical these days,' Gino goes on earnestly, as if I had to be converted somehow, to become a New Man, perhaps. He draws my attention to a project the children have just completed on the village of Montecchio. 'Methodology of Research,' it begins. 'To stimulate the capacity for orientation in vital space . . .' Beneath are the children's accounts of how they get to and from school through the village streets. Mainly by car . . .

The photographer decides that there is too much glare from the window and that he will have to use artificial light. Why, one wonders, don't they just take photocopies of all the books, since almost all the exhibitis are books? In any event, having congratulated Gino d'Arezzo once again, I feel it is time to demonstrate my own capacity for orientation in vital space by finding my way back home. In the porch I stop to note the new commemorative stone unveiled the previous day. It reads:

ON THE FIRST CENTENARY
OF THE INSTITUTION OF THE CESARE BETTELONI SCHOOL
THE SCHOLASTIC COMMUNITY, THE CITIZENRY,
AND THE CIVIL AUTHORITIES
CELEBRATE AND REMEMBER
14 MARCH 1994

Opposite, is the stone unveiled a hundred years ago:

ON THE 50TH BIRTHDAY OF H.M. UMBERTO I
KING OF ITALY
THE COUNCIL REPRESENTATIVE OF MONTECCHIO VERONESE,
THE MAYOR, COUNT DR GIUSEPPE RIZZARDI,
IN THE PRESENCE OF SENATOR COUNT LUIGI SORMANI-MORETTI
PREFECT OF VERONA,
INAUGURATED THIS BUILDING,
WHICH ON THE DESIGN OF ENGINEER GIOVANNI MOSCONI
AND WITH THE ASSISTANCE OF THE GOVERNMENT
WAS RAISED AS A GRACIOUS HOME
FOR THE TOWN HALL AND SCHOOLS
14 MARCH 1894

While kings and counts, multiple titles and double-barrelled names have clearly gone out of fashion, one can't help feeling a strong sense of continuity. Outside, a soft March rain is falling and somebody rides by on a bike under an open umbrella. Walking home I glimpse into a mechanic's dark workshop to find that he is indeed working away from morning till night for the sake of his family. Whether happily or not it's hard to tell when a man is under a car. But he does have two young teenagers as apprentices. Boys, of course. Though not Slavs in this case. Back home Mario tells me that he, Silvio and Francesco are determined to proceed with formal legal action against Righetti. We can't go on forever with someone living in our basement. 'Only it could take years,' he worries, the legal system being what it is. Not a hundred, I hope.

Come si deve

When I went to primary school, I carried no bag, because the books were all there, inside my desk. Or if I did, it was a pump bag for gym, or for games. Later, when there was homework, one carried a little briefcase, which went with the collar and tie – we were little businessmen, little accountants and executives, travelling to school on bus and tube – and inside that bag it smelt of sandwiches because the school meals were so awful you opted out.

In Italian schools only essential texts are provided and only up to a certain age. Others are bought by the parents. They're expensive. This means that if they were left in the school, people would be afraid of their being stolen, afraid of having to pay for them again, afraid of losing all the places they have underlined them and written notes in the margin. There are no lockers.

So the children carry all their books to school every day – from six years old to eighteen. Not in briefcases, which probably wouldn't be big enough and certainly wouldn't go with the casual clothing the children wear. Instead, they have backpacks of fluorescent pink and yellow with 'Invicta' written on them and shiny plastic buckles, the same as they will carry years later about the streets of Rome and Paris and London when their mothers finally feel able to let them go away for a few days on a school journey. I weighed Michele's school backpack one morning. Five kilos of books . . .

But however heavy they may be, their backpacks will never smell of sandwiches, because the food is so good no one would ever dream of opting out of school meals. Or rather, the mothers would never dream of letting the authorities let the food get so bad that anyone would want to opt out.

And they'll never smell of football boots either. For school offers no games, no extracurricular activities. There are no music lessons, no singing lessons, no school choir, no carpentry for the boys and cookery for the girls, no hockey, no cricket, no netball, no basketball, no football, no swimming, no athletics, no sports day, no school teams. The school doesn't, as it does in England, pretend to offer a community that might in any way supplant the family, or rival Mamma. That's important. It doesn't, and later on the university won't either, try to create in the child the impression of belonging to a large social unit with its own identity. There is no assembly in the morning, no hymn singing, no prayers, no speech day. Apart from the centenary, which, as the headmistress pointed out, can hardly happen every day, school, for Stefi at six, for Michele at eight, is no more and no less than reading and writing and mathematics, geography and science, oh, and

English (just introduced) and, of course, *l'ora di religione*, or, in my children's case, 'Osservazione all'Europa', where they have now learnt that one of the things that unites European nations is, not our school, not our state, but our . . . religion.

The Reformation can wait.

No, if children want extracurricular activity of any kind, they have to go outside school; the parents have to look for it, and take them there . . . and pay. Late afternoons become full of *sacrifici* of time and money.

Gigi La Magna, who cuts Michele's hair, plays for the local football team, A. C. Montecchio. He talks to friends who hang about the shop while he cuts hair. He complains about decisions the coach has made. He tells Michele he once played with Roberto Baggio. It was a friendly match in the village of Illasi. He scored that day and Baggio didn't.

Is this a true story?

Gigi's father, Giobatta, claims he has healing powers that are transmitted through his fingertips, sometimes merely when he is cutting hair. Yes, once he healed a person who was terminally ill without even knowing, merely by cutting his hair.

Is this a true story?

In any event, it's a relief that Michele's trips to the barber only encourage him to start playing football, not to become a faith-healer. The trophies on the shelves, after all, that so impress him, come from football . . .

When I was a child, to play football we headed for the nearest public park or waste ground after school and kicked the ball at each other. Or we played with a tennis ball in the playground. Sometimes there would be two or three games of different age groups all crossing each other, up and down, right to left on the bumpy tarmac. On games afternoons the Maths teacher or the R.I. teacher would split us into eleven against eleven, or however many we happened to be, and let us loose on the playing fields. Playing, we learnt to play, and I seem to remember having a good time, too. But apparently this was wrong. Or so the young fellow who takes the inscriptions at A. C. Montecchio tells me. Apparently, this was terribly ingenuous of us and explains why English football is now so backward. No, no, no, they take their sport much more seriously, he assures me, in Italy. Or perhaps it's just the times that have changed.

In any event, there are no playing fields at the primary school, or the *scuola media*, the next one up, and there are no public spaces here where kids can just play. To play football on grass your kid has to enroll in A. C. Montecchio . . .

You take your boy along to the village's only field, surrounded by a cypress hedge and tall fences and a gate to lock it up when it's not being used officially. That's an important concept. You pay up. Not much. Your son is given a kit bag in the team's colour with the name of the team on the side, a team shirt and team shorts. A. C. Montecchio has a new coach this year, a man, incredibly, who used to play for the Hungarian national side, or so the big posters they've put out around the village claim. But this celebrity only teaches the older teams. Then his wisdom is passed down through team members to the infant groups. And what it mainly involves is drilling. Because it's not worth starting to play football until you have done hours of drilling, hours upon hours, just as there's no point in playing the piano until you've done all your scales, major and minor, backwards and forwards.

You go to pick the boy up at five-thirty perhaps on an October evening. It's deep twilight, and they're still running about touching their toes and jumping in the air, then practising penalties, then practising headers. At the end there's only time for a ten-minute game, under the dim glare of one of four floodlights now. By December, whoever's in goal freezes to death, though he does have the official team gloves. The trainer screams and shrieks for the kids to pass. 'Pass, *per l'amore di Dio!* The way I told you in the drill!' He blows his whistle a lot, though rarely for fouls. He sends one boy off for holding onto the ball too long. Then he sends another off for saying *porca vacca!* Good job it wasn't Michele.

Training's supposed to end at six, but drags on and on. They want us to know that they take it very, very seriously and are developing our children's talents. These pieties are in the air, which otherwise is icy now. Frankly, I'm shivering. In fact, I'm savouring the word *sacrifici*, rolling it over and over on my tongue, while from the touchline other waiting parents are yelling complicated advice into the gloom. *'Devi gestire lo spazio in modo dinamico!'* You have to have a dynamic sense of territorial control! Little Mirko doesn't even look up, idling in an offside position. The parents wave their arms. Generally, both mothers and fathers are disappointed with their sons' performances. They shout things even worse than *porca vacca*. Why can't the kids do it like on TV? God knows they watch enough! Michele gets the ball full and hard in his face and keels over on the frosty grass.

The gate to the pitch is at the end of Zia Natalina's street and going back we pick up Stefi, who is inside in the warm learning to cut pieces of folded paper so that they will come out as angels with joined hands. '*Santa patata*, Michele,' Zia says, 'you look like the abominable snowman.' Actually, his face is bright red. Very soon he will decide he doesn't like football. He will tell me so over a restorative hot chocolate in the *pasticceria*. He doesn't know why, but he just doesn't like it. He shakes his head solemnly. Even if Gigi La Magna did once play with Roberto Baggio. 'You do exactly as you please,' I tell him generously, warming icy hands round my cup. 'There's no pressure on you at all.' Open on another table the pink *Gazzetta dello Sport* has a huge headline to announce that someone has paid fifty billion lire for someone. But I feel I can let that pass.

My friend Iacopo is not so lucky. His little Renzo is turning into an infant ace. To the envy of all Renzo's friends, Iacopo takes the boy home from the field on the back of his Moto Guzzi, before shooting off to a new woman, a *mamma* figure again, but pleasantly florid this time. In the bar he confides, somewhat embarrassed, that he is doing the boy a small painting of himself scoring a goal, for his birthday present. The frame is the goal, from behind, and the child diving across the picture to head home. Privately, I think this ridiculous, but when one day I take Michele to play with Renzo and see the thing, it turns out to be very good: the provincial twilight, the boys too small for the goal, that sense of comedy and poignancy you often get when watching children play an adult sport. Iacopo is talented, though for some reason the school has never hung his picture of the centenary.

Having given up the national sport (so young!), Michele

toys for a while with baseball, which Stefano's boy Beppe does, with American football, which Francesco's Gigi does, and then with tennis, which Silvio's Giovanni does. There's nothing like the private sector for providing the full range of choice. Your only child must be accomplished, he must have confidence in himself, he must achieve. For a season, both Stefi and Michele go to courses at the swimming pool, where mothers jostle fiercely the whole morning on inscriptions day – there are so few places – but then don't let their kids go to half the lessons because they have a blocked nose or a cough. A good fifteen minutes of the forty is spent on preparatory gymnastics. And 'No playing in the pool!'

Finally, both children fall in love with roller skating, or with the tall sweet girl, Ilaria, who teaches it on the basketball rectangle that belongs to the church. It's another occasion for buying expensive equipment: boot-skates, kneepads, elbowpads. There's just the small problem for Michele that he is the only boy in the course. So strong is the gender conditioning in this country, where no tall black males skate gracefully through the parks or along city sidewalks, that everybody imagines skating is just for girls. So now not only is Michele going to hell because he doesn't do the *ora di religione*, but he is considered effeminate because he likes skating. It's funny, because there is absolutely nothing feminine about the way Michele skates, lumbering around pulling girls' pigtails and pushing them in the back. The teacher spends half the lesson screaming at him. At least, he tells Beppe, he doesn't have a ponytail. And he doesn't go to dance class. He may skate, but he would never dance. *Che schifo!* What yuck! he laughs at Stefi, who loves to dance. She loves her little pink shoes and her little pink leotard that make her look so cherubically chubby when she whirls about her class, where there are no boys at all. For myself, I rather like the dance teacher; she is in her forties, separated, has rather a razzled look about her and always arrives stubbing out a cigarette. She doesn't have that complacent righteousness that seems to infect most of those running children's activities here, no doubt borrowed from the church. She doesn't make a show of trying too hard.

Ilaria, on the other hand, like the football instructor, protracts her lesson deep into the winter evening, making the children practise pirouettes and balancing acts various. But at least watching fifteen little girls skate is infinitely preferable to watching a score of boys thump a wet ball at each other. It's a pleasure to see how their faces glow in the dusk as the street lamps flicker on and the hills about the village suddenly loom. Sometimes Don Guido comes out of the *canonica* and watches them, too. After all, they're on his property. Behind him, at exactly six, the fake bells in the red brick church start up. I suppose they must be on a timer. They contrive to be at once deafening and twee as they grind out the hymn:

> *E' l'ora che pia la squilla fedel,*
> *le note ci invia dell'ave del ciel . . .*
>
> The hour the faithful bell rings out
> Heaven's Ave Maria to us devout . . .

Does anybody actually say the angelus when the plodding tune chimes? Does Don Guido? He stands thoughtfully amongst the parked cars watching the skaters. When he greets me now, he seems resigned to my family's nonconformity, reinforced perhaps by Michele's towering presence amongst the skating girls. In any event, he nods pleasantly and makes no mention of catechism, and afterwards he is perfectly happy if some of the children want to go and see his rabbits and guinea pigs in hutches by the tall brick wall of the church. Stefi likes to do that. She loves soft furry things. And she likes it if he gives her a *caramella*. But she does not like being pinched. Why does this priest feel he has to pinch little children . . . ?

Sometimes I wonder if all their lives the angelus, heard everywhere in Italy at six o'clock, will remind my children of nothing more, nothing less, *per carità*, than roller skating at winter dusk.

Michele's piano teacher is also called Ilaria. We bought a piano because we hoped the children would learn. Indeed, we would learn ourselves. And this was very un-Italian of us, for almost nobody in Italy has a piano. Trying to explain the exorbitant prices, the man who sold it to us insisted the English bought ten times the number of pianos, of musical instruments in general, the Italians did. I suspect this has to do with the obsession here, which is also a modern obsession, that it's simply not worth doing anything unless you can do it at the highest level. You play football seriously from the earliest age. Or not at all. You emulate Roberto Baggio, or whoever is the hero of the day – Gianluca Vialli, Beppe Signori – your parents shrieking from the touchline, waving bottles of expensive mineral drinks that will improve your performance and protect your health. Or you go swimming to join the swimming team. You do the appropriate exercises. In case you wanted just to play, the pools are strictly divided into lanes. And if you go to the BMX course as Michele did one year to use the ambitious dirt track they have at Centro

Primo Maggio, then you must take part in the races, with your crash helmet and fashionable stretch pants and kneeguards, until in your teens you graduate to one of the sports bikes that race through the village and up into the gruelling mountains almost every Sunday in summer. You must be hailed by megaphones as you pass the makeshift grandstand in the *piazza*, preceded and followed by fat ex-champions on motorbikes keeping people out of your way. You must win cups and medals and feature on expensively framed team photographs (the barber's shop is full of them and likewise a thousand bars). You must do your sport, whatever it is, like they do it on TV. Otherwise, it's not worth it. It's just not worth the *sacrifici*. Don't even start. Hence the frustration of so many parents on the touchline – not like that, like this! – and hence, ultimately, the child's withdrawal to the computer games in the Bar Centrale, where it's not quite so difficult to excel. There is always a band of burnt-out teenagers in front of the screens, and the game they have now, Michele tells me excitedly, for he loves computer games, is that if you do everything right, a video woman takes all her clothes off. Big Gigi, the boy downstairs, is scornful of Michele: if you want to see naked women, all you have to is turn on the TV late at night. On Channel Seven . . .

At their age the only notions I had of naked women came from the pages of the *National Geographic* showing tribal dances and Amazon pygmies.

Since the piano is notoriously hard to get good at, since the powers that be hardly ever show it on TV and never on computer games (the girl does not undress on a piano or to piano music), since no-one listens to that kind of stuff any more anyway, it's not surprising that nobody in Italy buys them, and that it's miserably difficult to find a teacher. Who would bother to learn the piano just to teach someone else, particularly if they show no signs of being a star? Particularly if there are no state jobs available teaching piano in schools.

Our first discovery, Marzia, was a brilliant pianist but contemptuous. Everything you learnt, it was as if you had taken a step back. You had only discovered how much more there was to know. '*Non è come si deve,*' she would shake her head when you played some new piece you'd learnt. It's not as it should be. The way when Baggio and company are sending us to sleep with some particularly dull performance, the commentator will say, '*Questo non è calcio come si deve.*' Not football as it should be.

The second teacher, Gaetano, was merely indifferent. He nodded vaguely. He might say *bravo* in a flat voice you imagined was ironic until you realised how utterly distant he was. Then he had the irritating habit of saying, 'Now what?' and he would open the book some fifty pages on and play some hugely complicated piece right through and absolutely *come si deve*. Nothing could be more humiliating.

At which point enter the minute Ilaria, with her hoarse boyish voice and dialect accent. The reason Ilaria is teaching, and doing it quite well, is that she herself got the worst of both worlds, the old and the new, as far as attitudes to achievement are concerned. One of five children from a quarrying family in the mountains, she showed an unaccountable interest in the piano as a little girl, taking lessons from the local priest. He saw she was good and encouraged her. It was one of the more positive roles the church once had. Throughout her teens she gave maths lessons to younger children to save up for piano lessons from a proper teacher. Four maths lessons to one piano lesson. Her parents would not pay for the lessons, not because they didn't have the money, but because then they would have to give the other children something equivalent. That age-old obsession with tit-for-tat accountancy. Anyway, this was before concern with one's children's advancement became so fashionable, before one only had one child.

Eventually she got to the academy, but didn't have the financial support to finish quickly. She did other jobs to stay alive, graduated late, missed any chance of becoming a professional. So now with the modern mentality that anything you do must be done perfectly, she has a low opinion of herself. She insists, playing brilliantly, that she doesn't play very well. She imagines you want to play the most difficult pieces in the shortest possible time. It took quite a while before we could make clear to her that we were perfectly happy even with the slowest bumbling progress, as long as the children felt happy about it, as long as they learnt to savour the music a little. After a year Stefi plays a fairly decent 'Mary Had a Little Lamb', while Michele finds that yet another 'effeminate' activity can be fun. And he feels no nostalgia at all for the now flood-lit field where Iacopo has to shiver on the sidelines waiting for little Renzo to score his goals.

It's curious, because I remember as a child giving up my own piano lessons to play football. And I would now, too, if only there was anybody to play with without becoming a fanatic . . .

Four-fifteen. The parents wait around the school gates. Everywhere there are cars double-parked. It's problematic because the road is narrow just here, and cars are getting bigger. Then the bell goes and the children burst out with their lumpy backpacks. Another five minutes and the traffic is chaotic, fighting its way to a score of destinations: the swimming pool, the tennis courts, the gym in the other school where Stefi dances, the basketball rectangle for skating. One child is playing baseball while another is on his BMX. One learns archery while another is at pre-ski classes.

The cars weave back and forth across the piazza. It's hectic. Mainly mothers at the wheel. Or grandmothers. They are wondering if the tennis racket they have bought is expensive enough, if Giovanni will make the team, if Chiara has the right physique for it, pampering and tormenting this new generation of Italians with their own vision of what the good life might be.

The fake church bells chime. The twee sound spreads across the village like runny treacle. *È l'ora che pia* . . . It drowns out Ilaria showing the kids how to lift one skate and pirouette, distracts the football trainer explaining the Hungarian's method of springing the offside trap, irritates the BMX instructor teaching the kids how to start from a grid. The mothers wait in their cars. How much time will the children have to eat their dinners and be dressed *come si deve* for catechism?

Walking back up the path from the gate on a Wednesday night in winter I am carrying Stefi's dance bag, two pairs of skates, and the plastic case with the music books in it. Everything seems to happen on Wednesday. I spend two hours shuttling everybody around. I climb the path. And there, wrapped in his coat, sitting beside one of our ridiculous garden lights, is Hristo, our refugee. He has come out to smoke a cigarette, because someone has objected to the smell of cigarettes from the cellar invading the stairwell. The children stop to talk to him. His Italian is much better now. Shivering, he grins. And sometimes he kicks a ball around with the children on the cement behind the garage. Michele likes playing football with Hristo and the other boys in the condominium on the cement behind the garage. Silvio joins in. And me. Hristo plays with a cigarette in his mouth, which is definitely not *come si deve*, though he certainly knows how to play.

'How many times can you kick the ball up in the air without it touching the ground?' Michele asks. Hristo shows, hopping about on Righetti's rough cement after a day's whitewashing, ash falling from his cigarette. Twenty-five! Silvio is even better. I only manage seventeen. Sometimes it seems one doesn't need teachers to get a little exercise. . .

Though how, Silvio wants to know, climbing the stairs, is Hristo heating himself down there in the cellar, with all that flammable paint around him? And how, even if we pursue the legal line (the lawyers have exchanged letters), can we chuck him out on the street? Generously, he invites the Slav up to watch television with him in the evenings, to hear the news, which inevitably spends an inordinate amount of time presenting the achievements of the nation's football team, or basketball team, or volleyball team (world champions), or water polo team (world champions), or their athletes, or their tennis players, or even, recently, their rugby team. '*Miracolo!*' the announcer claims, borrowing a word from another strong suit in Italian traditions. *Miracolo di Pescosolido* – the tennis player has beaten Edberg. *Miracolo della Ferrari* – they have won their first race in years. *Miracolo di Benvenuti* – he has won the eight hundred metres at the European games. *Che spettacolo!* And you know it's not a miracle at all. It's the result of all the *sacrifici* that parents made ferrying their kids back and forth from one activity to another, doing things *come si deve.*

Tengo famiglia

Along with his penknife, catapult and sharp stick, scourge of all vipers, another thing Michele now carries around with him on his walks is his wallet. Because the children get pocket money now. Five thousand lire a week. But Stefi doesn't carry around her pocket money because she spends it all at once. Or allows Michele to 'save it for her'. A very dubious procedure. However, even if he always and unfailingly carries it round with him all the time, money is quite safe with Michele. He will never forget it because it is never far from his mind. He likes to gloat over it. He likes to count it, blue-eyed and eager. His endless questions have found a new focus.

'How many lire in a *miliardo*, Papà?'

'*Un miliardo*, of course.'

'But how much is that?'

'A thousand million.'

More innocent still, Stefi asks, 'And how much is a million?'

'A thousand thousand.'

'So I need a thousand of these,' Michele holds up an extremely battered note, 'to make a million.'

'Right.'

'*Cavolo!*' Stefi says. Cabbage! Which is to say, Wow!

'But how many zeros in a *miliardo*?' Michele persists, now counting the noughts on his ten-thousand-lire note.

'Nine.' It's important to have children get used to these big numbers. It's important to get used to them yourself.

'And a *miliardo di miliardi*?' he asks.

I laugh: 'That would be the national debt, or thereabouts.' That number beyond which there are no others.

'The what?' He's puzzled, of course. Shall I tell him that every Italian man, woman and child owes something like thirty million lire, more than his pocket money can ever amount to? There seems no point in going into the matter too deeply just at the moment. After all, the government never has, and if they did . . .

Michele has a pound coin in his wallet, too, that he keeps from last holiday in Somerset.

'How many lire is it worth, Papà?'

'Today, you mean?' I explain the concept of exchange rates. Would that I hadn't.

'Two thousand and fifty lire.'

'And today?'

'Two thousand one hundred lire.'

'And today?'

'Two thousand three hundred lire.'

'And today?'

'Two thousand four hundred and fifty lire.'

'And . . .'

Thank God the kid doesn't have a deutschmark. Otherwise, we might have a thoroughgoing neurotic on our hands. I'm jealously guarding the secret that his savings are losing value every day, the way I've tried for so long to hide the fact that it is us and not Santa Lucia who bring them their presents just before Christmas.

Sitting together in their jackets on the blue-green grass of a hilltop for a November picnic, the children lay out all their money on a stone and stare at it, something that, like the picnic, would be impossible in a windier country. For it's a currency made up almost entirely of notes, light as air. The biggest coin amounts to no more than twenty pence.

And it's a colourful currency, too, as packaging here is very colourful, and religious images. The thousand-lire notes are grey or pink, the two thousand-lire notes are orange and brown, the ten thousand-lire notes are a lovely blue, the fifty thousands are pink again, but softer and bigger than the one thousand, and the hundred-thousand lire note is an impressive *spettacolo* of pastel browns and greens with hints of blue. Unlike the dull, utilitarian dollar, such a currency does lend a certain enchantment to the business of spending.

Stefi loves the pictures on the notes, the horses, the bowls of fruit, ships, children studying. And the faces that go with them. Whose faces? I have to explain who Giuseppe Verdi was, and Bellini. That's why the picture is an opera house. You see, La Scala. I promise Stefi we'll go to see *L'Aida* in the Arena when she's bigger, though not, I don't think, *I puritani*. I explain that Maria Montessori, on the one-thousand note, invented a new method for teaching children, yes, which they use in their *scuola elementare* to a certain extent, when they give them all those projects to do where you're supposed to learn on your own rather than be told things. And then they tell you what you're supposed to have learnt. Michele already knows everything about Guglielmo Marconi on the two-thousand note, about his radio call to America, though not that the scientist became a fascist in later life and was happy, it seems, to see his name in school-books as the inventor of something that helped conquer the vast Abyssinian army. But we can spare the boy that. On the ten-thousand note there's Count Alessandro Giuseppe Antonio Anastasio Volta. 'Think if you had to use his whole name!' Stefi says, when I explain (approximately) what he discovered.

Then on the fifty-thousand lire there's the delightful Bernini with his extravagant moustache and goatee. More talk. More history. Turning to my wallet, rather than Michele's, a very intense Caravaggio glares out from the hundred-thousand note, the biggest. Caravaggio, who killed a man, I warn my son, after an argument over a tennis game. Michele also has a filthy temper and after a few knock-abouts with Zio Berto is clamouring for tennis lessons to add to skating and piano . . .

On every banknote it says, 'THE LAW PUNISHES THE MANUFACTURERS AND DISTRIBUTORS OF COUNTERFEIT NOTES'. It's one of those warnings that, rather than instilling terror, just reminds you how common the crime is, suggests it almost, and it's funny thinking of all the forgers having to copy the different typefaces this is written in on the different denominations.

But now Michele is concerned about other things

written on his notes. There are biro scribblings on two of the one-thousand lires. *'Terroni e statali, siete tutti parassiti!'* Southerners and state workers, you're all parasites! And on another. *'Bestemmiare è vilta.'* Blasphemy is vile. On one of my notes someone has jotted down: *'Pane, vino, Arena,'* *L'Arena* being the name of the local newspaper.

Does the writing reduce their value? Michele asks. And if so by how much?

I reassure him. It doesn't matter what people write on notes, they're always worth just what the number of zeros says they're worth. Sometimes I'll scribble down a phone number on a thousand lire myself if I don't have any other paper. Though it's interesting to note that people rarely write on the bigger denominations. Some things are still sacred.

We're on the hill by the old *castello*. The children turn the notes over and over on a stone. The colours, the heroes, the graffiti. 'Italy, people of artists, martyrs, saints and warriors . . .' Everywhere the culture reproduces itself, reflects itself, as in a hall of mirrors – the landscape, the language, the currency, all bouncing off each other, recreating each other – and in the midst of those mirrors, both reflected and projecting, stands the child, discovering himself in these castle walls, these terraced hills, the liquid words he speaks, and now in this coloured paper, too.

Michele gathers up the notes and organizes them carefully in order of value. Divided Italy. State-bound Italy. Priest-ridden Italy. Bread-and-wine Italy. Inflationary Italy. Operatic Italy. Artistic Italy. Genial Italy. It's all there in the little boy's wallet. He possesses it all and is possessed by it. At eight he is Italian, to all intents and purposes.

Though actually I should have said that it is very un-Italian of me to be giving the children regular pocket money. Five thousand lire every week, paid on a Sunday, if they have been good, and with always the possibility of that terrible sanction – No pocket money! – if they are not good.

Italian parents tend not to do this. The Italian word for pocket money is *mancia*, which is also the word for tip. And tips, at least here, are something given absolutely at the giver's discretion. They might be big, they might be small, or they might not be given at all. There's no question, as in America, of percentages. Or you might give a tip once, but then not the next time. Or vice versa. Tips are given out of warmth, not routine. Crucially, they are capricious. They depend on mood. And like all things capricious they emphasise the power of he who exercises the caprice, he who feels affectionate one day, perhaps less so the next.

Years ago, when Zio Berto was at university, and later too when he had to work unpaid for some time as so many Italian doctors do, Nonno and Nonna were abroad. With no income, Berto spent money like water. He was always in debt. Nonno supported him. But Berto never knew when the money was going to arrive. Nor how much. In the meantime, he might borrow from us. Or others. Every attempt on our part (not Berto's, it must be said) to persuade Nonno that an allowance paid regularly into a bank account with the understanding *this much and no more* would force Berto, allow Berto, to be more responsible was dismissed with the sharp retort: 'I am not a bank. I give when I want to give . . .' So the day came when Berto split up with a girlfriend of long standing and Nonno had to pay her off the very considerable debt that had accumulated. Nonna, it appears, who in this case was Mamma, of course, and hence a crucial element in the equation, had no access to a bank account, but when they were back in Italy, there was always an envelope with all the money she could find in it. She slipped it into Berto's pocket when Nonno wasn't watching. If giving is a personal thing, then there are two parents, two sources of income . . .

So Michele and Stefi's friends don't receive regular pocket money, which is a very Anglo-Saxon, puritan thing, with its obsession with system and clarity, benefits and punishments, its perverse desire to have little children learn to manage given amounts of money over given periods of time. No, they get a *mancia* from Papà, perhaps when they ask for it, perhaps when they don't, and then a *mancia* from Mamma, perhaps when they least expect it, perhaps with the express injunction not to mention it to Papà. What better way to learn about life, and about all the intrigues that lie ahead. Then Beppino and Giovanni and Gigi get lots of *mance* from grandfathers and grandmothers, on both sides of the family. Some clandestinely, perhaps. Some not. And here my children are unfortunate, for visiting rarely as they do, the grandparents are not around to give *mance*, and they would never dream of sending anything through the post (like their English grannie, my mother, does). No, not even at Christmas or their birthdays. What would be the point of giving a *mancia*, or anything else, if one were not there in person to reap the reward of gratitude, to enjoy the child's pleasure? Nonno and Nonna may come twice one month, then not again for six months. Even then they don't always give something. But sometimes their gifts are indeed spectacular, since spectacle is precisely what they are aiming at. The fifty thousand lire note which still holds pride of place in

Michele's wallet, but which disappeared from Stefi's the day after it was given, came as Nonno and Nonna were making a sudden escape one visit, announcing, entirely out of the blue, or rather the grey, of a winter dawn, that they had to go down to Rome to see an apartment Berto's brother Renato was thinking of buying. Nonno had already hurried downstairs with his trilby on to warm the car and smoke a cigarette, and at the door, repeating their excuse to the children, Nonna suddenly reached into a once-elegant handbag she still won't throw away, rummaged amongst all the odds and ends of make-up she had 'borrowed' from Rita and found the two fifty thousand lire notes. By now the children had learnt to show immediate and immense gratitude, and to ask no further questions as to the whys and wherefores of yet another sudden departure.

Then, halfway down the stairs, Nonna turned back and produced a further thirty thousand lire and gave it all to Michele. Yes, all to Michele. She would give the same to Stefi when she came next time, she said. In just a week or so. Inevitably, no sooner was the door shut behind her than this gift was the cause of very serious discord. Should the thirty thousand be equally split now, or not? Would Nonna really come again in just a week or two? Would she ever remember what she promised even if she did come? Stefi wept, Michele was sullen when we insisted he share. Such is the power of he, of she, who gives without system.

But even this kind of capricious giving is not quite the norm here. For rather than a *mancia* the Italian parent much prefers to give gifts, things. By putting money in a child's hand, however small the sum, you are giving him power. You are inviting him to compare the price of things in toy shops with the coloured notes in his wallet, an excitement Stefi took to far more quickly than Michele, rapidly adjusting her choice of purchase to the exact and total amount of money in her purse, or, alternately, dividing it into two purchases on the rare occasions when there was something she badly wanted that cost less than what she had. It is understood that when Stefi goes into a shop, she will have no money left when she comes out. And she comes out beaming, delighted. For, whatever Stefi's money can buy, she is always pleased with it. *Chi si accontenta, gode,* as the Italians never tire of saying – he who makes do, enjoys – though linguistically the Italian is much closer to the tautological, as perhaps good maxims should be: he who is happy with what's available, is happy. And Stefi is always that.

For Michele, on the other hand, the difference between the number of noughts on a price tag and that of the notes in his wallet has always been a source of anguish, and he frets and saves and tries to get Stefi to save with him, which she will only do when whatever money she has is exactly enough to tip the scales and buy that expensive thing they both want immediately.

So, with my English pocket-money system Stefi buys a lot of junk, while Michele suffers and works himself into a lather calculating weeks against fives and tens of thousands. 'Mamma, how many five thousands in eighty-six thousand?' 'Seventeen and one over,' I tell him. 'No, I want Mamma to say, MAMMA!' 'Seventeen and one over,' she says. And then he suffers, he suffers terribly, wondering if he could ever be good enough to get his pocket money seventeen weeks on the trot (at which point Stefi will grant the one over), or whether he shouldn't build into his calculation the inevitability that we will catch him kicking Stefi or using his catapult where he shouldn't at least once a month and cut his pocket money, and it's really too bad he can't just be cleared of little misdemeanours like that with a couple of Paternosters the way the other boys can.

How much wiser those parents like Stefano and Marta, who just give their children gifts, a huge Lego set, a pair of skis, a proper bow and arrow, whenever and for whatever reason it occurs to them to do so. How much more fortunate those children whose grandparents are a constant shower of remote-controlled jeeps and dolls that cry and pee. Silvio's Giovanni appears one day on a miniature mountain bike with more gears than he can probably count. Is it his birthday? No, it isn't. But he asked for it. Or rather, he asked for something else, but they gave him this. Ask and something else shall be given. Another time I find him going back and forth behind the garages on a small electric car. No wonder Silvio felt he couldn't afford another child. Later, as these children grow up it will be the splendid sports bike, the moped, the shiny Vespa, then the thrill of car keys, the small Fiat, the bigger Fiat, and finally, when the awful die is cast, the gold rings, the apartment, the furniture . . .

But no cash.

So the young Italian couple will eventually find themselves safely installed amid all that their parents have bought for them. At last, at last, they will be able to begin an independent life and start saving up their own money . . . to give things to their children. The first time they buy a property themselves will be when the first or, more probably, the only child marries.

Great generosity, total control. It's a heady (even divine)

mixture, and one that gives rise to another triumphantly Italian expression. For it allows the father, returning from that workshop where he slaves for love of his family from morn till night, to say proudly to anyone who questions him, '*Tengo famiglia*,' which translates, 'I support a family.' But no, no, it's more than that. Translation is helpless here in the face of the vast mental iceberg sailing beneath this apparently harmless semantic tip. For *tengo famiglia* lies at the crossroads of so many cultural highways. *Tengo* comes from *tenere*, to hold. The expression means, I hold a family, in the sense of both I support it and I control it. It contains the notions both of *sacrifici* and of power. Then given the sacred nature of the family in a Catholic society, where every family is a holy family, it also means, I am a pillar of the establishment, I am doing my social duty. So that if anyone ever asks what you have achieved in life, you need say no more than *tengo famiglia* to be beyond any possible reproach, and when the judge is about to pass sentence on you for theft or political corruption, your lawyer will always plead, 'But your honour, my client *tiene famiglia*!' He supports a family. And this both excuses him for what he stole (he stole it for his family!) and makes it more difficult to put him in gaol (what would become of his children?).

The more gifts you give, and the less cash, the more you can claim *tengo famiglia*.

Righetti has once again increased the price of the garage I am still not quite able to buy. Rather ingenuously, I accuse him of being an unprincipled property speculator. At which he protests, probably rightly, 'I am only doing what any other builder would do, selling at market prices.' Then with that way he has of pretending he is not rich, is just a modest employee of his father's, he adds, *'Tengo famiglia anch'io sai.'* I support a family, too, you know.

'Naturalmente,' I reply. Bitterly.

My only consolation is that the man's wife has just produced yet another *bella bambina*. A third. Silvio, Francesco, Giorgio and I had a very good long laugh about it. That'll teach him for putting a refugee in our basement! Righetti is just not modern enough to imagine a girl running his company. Even if it would be him holding all the purse strings . . .

Santa Lucia

If you undo the strings of Stefi's purse, you may not find any money, but you will often find a little letter. Now that she has learnt to write, she is obsessed by letters: 'MAMATIVOLIOBENEANCEQANDOFACIOLACATIVA' reads a very early one. Stefi prefers the technique the stonemasons use on hillside crosses of saving space by missing out the gaps. She also has the Veneto tendency to drop the double letters. A translation might read: 'MUMYILUVYUEVENWENIMNORTY.' It's interesting how early Michele and Stefi have become accustomed to these contradictory notions, enshrined for the other children in the confessional. Later, they will be able to feel they love Daddy even when they take a few thousand lire from his wallet, and later still that they are all good citizens even when they don't pay taxes. Let he who has no sin throw the first stone.

Another letter might be addressed to Santa Lucia. The day the good saint hands out her presents is December

13th, but Stefi's letters begin around Easter, and she stores them all in her purse before deciding which one to send:

> DearSantaLucia, for SantaLucia I want a Carabambola [a brand of doll] with her highchair and pushchair. [Fair enough.] And if they don't have that, or if your mule can't carry such big things, then I would like a Lego set, but not any of the ones Michele has already got. I mean not the pirates and not the extraterrestrials. Buy any of the others. *Millegrazie.* STEFI.

It's impressive how much children are willing to write when it comes to letters to Santa Lucia. At eight, however, Michele's missives show a sad and growing suspicion that all is not as he has been told.

'Santa Lucia,' he starts one of the last letters in the run up to the big day, 'if you really exist, if it's not just my dad and mum who sneak in at night . . .' Thus people continue to send messages to God, just in case he might be there, or letters to old lovers, just in case they still care, or they make complex applications for state jobs, just in case the selection process might not be fixed.

> Cara Santa Lucia, if you're there and a hundredandtwentythousandlire is not too much [numbers are always written attached together in this cautious country to prevent anybody adding anything in between], then I would like a fishing rod and, if possible after that, all the things that go with a fishing rod like a reel and the line and hooks and weights and floats because I want to go out and catch lots of fish like my friend Beppino or like Huckleberry Finn [children's literature, as indeed adult literature here, is almost all foreign]. I will try to be a good boy as much as I can. I

was good all last week. *Grazie*. MICHELE. PS It must be a freshwater fishing rod, not a sea fishing rod because Beppe says they're different.

They show these letters to Mamma to check that Santa Lucia will be able to understand. Though Michele may now have other motives . . .

Rita says, 'But Michele, what's the point of asking for a fishing rod in winter when it's too cold to go fishing?'

'We had a picnic with Papà last week,' he says.

This is true. The temperature in November can be very mild, even warm at midday when the sun is high in a paper-blue sky, then suddenly freezing in the evening when you have to stand around watching your kids play football, or skate, or ride their bicycles round the BMX track.

Michele ponders. Mamma is right. People don't go fishing so much in winter. So perhaps he could try horse riding. 'Beppe's started horse riding,' he says. 'And he's got everything. The jodhpurs, the boots, the helmet, even the whip. Perhaps I could ask Santa Lucia for those.'

Has or has not Michele grasped the idea of the richer categories of professions yet? I thought he had. When complaining that Beppe had gone off to the mountains one week to learn how to ski, I did hear him say to Gigi downstairs: 'But then his father's an accountant. Accountants can do anything.' Yes, I think he has grasped that. So is it that he doesn't realise how much jodhpurs, boots, helmet, whip and, of course, riding lessons cost, or is it that he imagines there's no limit to Santa Lucia's purse? But then he did write, 'if onehundredandtwentythousand lire is not too much . . .' Perhaps everything hangs on whether he does or does not believe deep down that Santa Lucia exists.

'Look, if a fishing rod's what you really want,' Rita

decides to stay on the safe side, 'ask Santa Lucia for that. After all, it will always keep till spring . . .'

The truth is that Michele is going through something of a crisis with regards to the existence or otherwise of the blessed saint. Some of the boys at school have insisted that it really is just their parents bringing the presents. Indeed, their parents, perhaps eager to exact gratitude, since it's galling past a certain point to have the children thanking the wrong person, have told them so. These kids know the score, and they laugh when Michele gets angry about it and says on the contrary he *knows* Santa Lucia exists. How does he know? Partly because his *mamma* says she does, and partly because when he got up in the middle of the night to do a wee last year he caught a glimpse of her shadow behind the window. She was just like in the pictures, tall and dressed in a long white robe with a crown on her head. The other boys laugh at him. He, being bigger, hits them. The funny thing is that they laugh at Michele for not believing in God and hell, not believing in visions of the Madonna and the secrets of Fatima, and here they are laughing at him again for believing in something much more pleasant and attractive, and in the end hardly more far-fetched: that a phantom saint travels about on her mule on a December night carrying presents to all the little boys and girls.

At the school gate one evening Michele sheepishly tells Rita that Maestra Elena wants to see her, immediately. Inside the classroom, the teacher makes the boy wait outside. Apparently she had to intervene to stop Michele punching and kicking two other boys. Protesting at being sent out of class, he demanded confirmation from her as to the existence of Santa Lucia. The boys had been taunting him for believing . . .

What did she tell him? Rita asked. This is getting to be a major issue. We don't know how to behave.

Maestra Elena smiles. She has a lot of experience in this kind of thing. She told him if he believed in it all, then it would come true, and if he didn't believe in it, then his parents would give him toys instead of Santa Lucia.

One can't help admiring the dexterity of a can't-lose formulation like this, the kind of thing that sanctions more or less any combination of belief and disbelief, that will later allow a person to believe that contraception is murder, but only for those who believe it is murder; the Pope is infallible, even when he's wrong for me, etc. In this particular case the solution allows Michele to go on writing some heartfelt last-minute letters to Santa Lucia . . .

The great day approaches. The children adjust their requirements and become painstakingly specific: the push-chair before the highchair for Carabambola, if it's got to be one or the other; a ten-kilo line and trout tackle, if possible.

They place their letters, carefully folded, on the sill outside the window, where the tooth fairy leaves ten-thousand-lire notes (Alessandro Volta) whenever appropriate. The paper doesn't blow away because the shutters are closed. During the night Santa Lucia comes along, somehow opens the shutters from the outside (the scenario my neighbours always fear), removes the letters and, on the last few nights before the big day, replaces them with chocolates. Immediately on waking the children rush through a mess of toys to the window . . .

One day the good saint forgets. 'Papà, Papà, the letter's still there!' Oh no! I force myself out of sleep, Michele's going to have another crisis of faith. But I'm thinking quickly today. I sit up in bed. 'You must have been naughty, Michele.' 'No, I wasn't.' 'Oh, but *I* was,' wails Stefi. We remember she threw a knife across the table yesterday and broke a glass. Santa Lucia's credibility rating soars. Immediately, I feel guilty for having reinforced the notion of divine (semidivine) retribution. Stefi is now begging Michele's forgiveness. She's even offering to put her next pocket money in with his.

Anyway, the following night we're back on duty again, substituting (how often one's obliged to do this one way or another) for the absent supernatural. Or rather, Rita is. Inevitably it's *le mamme* who do all these things, who open the window, remove the letters, then store them in some hiding place for memorabilia, along with Stefi's old handprints and an assortment of milk teeth and drawings of princes and princesses and fast cars with bazookas and MAMATIVOLIOBENEANCEQANDOFACIOLACATIVA.

So it's appropriate really that Santa Lucia, distributor of presents, should be a woman, and I really can't understand why the good lady doesn't hold sway in the whole of Italy, but limits her largesse to the Veneto. Babbo Natale – Father Christmas – fat and jolly with his white beard and tasteless red outfit, is such a conspicuously northern import, less Italian somehow than the *marocchini* or the slogan on Stefi's new winter jacket (made in Vicenza) that says, in English, 'BIG OUTSIDE'. Why should we have reindeer in what is patently mule country?

Then because Santa Lucia is only a local saint, when the great day comes, the children have to go to school just the same. It's as if an English child had to go to school on Christmas Day because the national religion were Hindu or something. They wake desperately early and rush to open their presents, which Santa Lucia leaves in the sitting room despite the absence of chimney or any possible entrance through the heavy shutters, not to mention the automatic gate. This year the saint has been attentive to their demands. There's a box with all you need to see off a shoal of trout, and Carabambola comes with both high-chair and pushchair. *Come si deve*. Then it's breakfast and straight off to school.

It's interesting that this business of Santa Lucia's being local doesn't seem to be instrumental in shaking Michele's faith. He doesn't ask himself why she has such a highly developed sense of regionalism, the way churchfolk never wonder why the Madonna just will not appear to Tibetans. Perhaps all those roadside shrines have prepared him for the locally divine. Santa Lucia has power . . . here!

Still, that old spoilsport, reason, does get the boy to the truth in the end. Reason and, as it turns out, Zia, who is anything but a spoilsport. For on the evening of December 13th Zia Natalina is there at the school gate to give the children Santa Lucia presents of her own: a compendium of boardgames for both, an aeroplane kit for Michele, a cosmetics set – lipsticks, eyeshadows, powders – for the six-year-old Stefi. She's enthralled. I'm appalled. Especially when the gift comes from this woman who's always complaining about younger women running off with older men. But Michele returns home thoughtful.

He says: 'Zia gave me a present, Papà, for Santa Lucia.'

'Great.'

'It must have cost at least fifty thousand lire.'

'That's very generous of her. I must phone and thank her.'

'Last year, when Nonno came, he gave me a car.'

'Yes, that's right, he did. That was very kind of him.'

He pauses: 'But you and Mamma didn't give me anything . . .'

'Ah.'

Rita comes in.

'Other people give me things, but you never do.'

Rita and I exchange glances. What can we say? We admit we're ungenerous, or we admit that Santa Lucia . . .

Michele smiles. He sidles up to us. He's big, healthy, ungainly, ready to face the trauma now. He hugs his mother. 'You gave me the fishing rod, didn't you?'

What can one do at this point but capitulate? 'But don't tell Stefi,' we insist. 'You mustn't tell Stefi. Don't spoil it for her, yet.'

Thus does one spread the Western idea that the real initiate is he who knows there is nothing to know: Father Christmas today, true love tomorrow. The very next morning, while sharing breakfast with her Carabambola, who's rather romantically been christened Stellina, Stefi says, 'Thank you so much for giving me the pushchair as well, Papà. Michele told me.' And you can see that for her it hasn't been a trauma at all. *Chi si accontenta . . .*

Nor will it stop Stefi writing letters to the saint. Only she writes with a little more shrewdness now, a little more awareness of how much can be spent. Indeed, she's already suggesting they should write letters to Babbo Natale. Michele, with a sidelong glance at me, agrees. They start: 'Caro Babbo Natale . . .' The charade, it appears, is attractive, even when you know it is a charade, and though in past years we've told them that Santa Lucia and Father Christmas have agreed on a strict territorial divide, and hence they can't expect any more from the old fellow than they can from Nonno, who never comes at Christmas, this year we decide to let them write the letters with the strict injunction that they must appreciate that Father Christmas has very little left to spend . . .

It takes Michele about ten seconds to start putting together a scaffolding of reasoning for this innovation. 'After all,' he tells me, 'we're English as well as Italian, so we have to get something from Father Christmas too.'

'Write the letter in English, then,' I tell him, 'and he might be more generous.'

Back to *ricatti* . . . Michele thus writes his first words in English. Endearingly, he employs Italian phonetics: 'Dir Fava Crissmas, mi an Stefi hav torccd an we ar agri that wan a sled so Dady can teik us to the maountins. Giust won present for to is not veri costos an yu laik sno so much am scior you will giv us a sled . . .'

He does. We take it up beyond the snow line above Velo Veronese on Christmas afternoon and park next to the cross that guarantees whoever prays there a hundred-day indulgence. We slide down the slopes with a thousand other people on sleds and toboggans and lorry inner tubes and plastic bags. The air is full of shrill *Madonna!*s and *Dio Santo!*s, and *Santa Patata!*s and *O Gesù!*s as our sled turns over in an explosion of powdery snow.

But our real Christmas present comes as a result of an entirely different kind of appeal. On picking up the children from skating the last day of school, Rita falls into conversation with Don Guido, and it occurs to her to mention poor Hristo to him, cooking for himself in our basement with all that paint around that could blow up any minute and nowhere to go to the toilet. It's incredible how long it's been going on. Every week, Righetti promises that the *imbianchino* has promised that the man is about to leave, but he never does, and it's not hygienic and with all those children in the condominium, all those families, however nice a boy he is . . .

Don Guido asks: 'Why didn't you tell me this before?' As though to say, Oh ye of little faith. Or perhaps, There are advantages to being initiates in this community you know. Or even, If only the Catholic Church had already existed, no way Christ would have been born in a stable . . . And in very short order the priest finds a home for the delighted Hristo. He's persuaded someone to let a room at a reasonable price, perhaps to accumulate a little indulgence . . .

Meanwhile, back in Via delle Primule – where every middle-class sitting room has a little nativity scene and Stefi, despite her determination to opt out of the *ora di religione*, has been spending all her money on oxen and asses and a golden angel who hangs by an almost invisible thread from a bookshelf above the infant Christ – back in Via delle Primule, everybody in the condominium gets together and we decide we will rent the cellar ourselves as a group, thus pushing out the *imbianchino* (since Righetti gives condominium owners priority) before he can move in any more Christ figures. 'That's probably all Righetti intended in the first place,' Francesco says knowingly. 'To force us to rent the place. To maximize his investment.' *Naturalmente.*

But the children are sad to see Hristo go. He played football and ruffled their hair and Michele said he reminded him of Jim in *Huckleberry Finn*. As does Michele's written English for me . . .

La passione

There are those who catch fish and there are those who do not. I am one of those who do not. I have never in my life caught a fish, unless perhaps it was minnows and tiddlers in a net as a child. Even then they had a miserable habit of slipping through the holes. But Michele?

Michele has fallen in love with the idea of fishing because so many of our neighbours and friends depart early on Sunday mornings, returning towards lunch with bags full of trout. Silvio has had a big sink installed in his garage so he can wash them there beside the second car he has bought now that he is certain a second child is financially beyond him. Giovanni and Gigi and my Michele and Martino and Stefi and Gianluca jostle about him as the sleek things come slapping and slithering out onto the shiny porcelain. They peer and wonder as Silvio plunges his strong thumbs deep inside a pale belly. Then he has every imaginable gadget and tool for finishing the job, things I shall never know the name of in any language.

The children love it. They know that the surrounding landscape is crisscrossed with streams and ditches; they know that when you cycle by on a Sunday every stream has a score of fishermen along it with their waders and bristling tackle boxes, their catch nets trailing in the current. Fishermen, I must insist. Not fisherpersons. Women here don't fish. Santa Lucia has brought Michele a present that will initiate a new relationship with Papà, an introduction into an exclusively male world. If only Papà knew anything about fishing . . .

The first thing we need, Silvio explains, is a licence. He details the complications, the expense, patiently but with half a smile on his handsome face. There are different licences for different kinds of fishing, different numbers of rods, different territory. And for children and adults. Of course, he explains, the child's licence is much cheaper, the problem being that if I then accompany Michele, how can I convincingly demonstrate to a possible inspector that it is really the boy fishing with his rod and not myself taking advantage of his licence to fish on the cheap. Especially if the inspector should come along right at the moment when I'm holding the rod while Michele pees or something . . . In the end I may as well get another rod for myself and my own licence and do things seriously.

'*Sì*, Papà, *sì*!' Michele is leaping and hopping at my elbow.

But this is one sacrifice I have no intention of making. Absolutely not. For secretly I loathe fishing, I loathe even the idea of fishing, of pulling up live and scaly creatures by a hook in their mouths. Frankly, I'd even prefer mountain cycling to fishing; and my unconfessed, unconfessable, long-term strategy is to get Michele started by exploiting the help of my friends, in particular Stefano, then, as soon as he is old enough, to send him off fishing on his own or with his schoolmates.

Alternatively, Silvio says, we could go to one of the gravel pits where they actually put the fish in the water themselves and you pay each time you go. The expression almost of pain on Silvio's face as he mentions the gravel pits shows what he thinks of such places. 'But it *is* easier,' he says.

'Oh,' says Michele. He's puzzled, because his reading of *Huckleberry Finn*, in Italian, has given him the impression that you only have to leave a hook in any river overnight and a huge Mississippi catfish will come and grab it. I know otherwise. Indeed, here Silvio has touched on another half hope that remains unconfessed: that Michele will find the realities of fishing so disheartening that he will give up the whole idea, or at least until he is old enough to try again on his own. Though I feel a bit of a worm feeling this.

Which brings us to the question of bait.

It depends what we're going for. Silvio waves his arms vaguely. How can he be expected to sum up a lifetime's experience in a few words. It could be maggots, it could be worms from the garden. It could be a certain type of worm – he uses a dialect word – that we can only get in the shops. Or it could be as simple as a couple of pieces of sweet corn. There are any number of factors, of combinations of factors. But the first problem to solve is what sort of fish you're going for and where and when, and that brings you back to deciding whether to get your licence or not, and again he explains the complicated procedure and the various documents required – the *certificato di residenza, certificato di stato di famiglia,* and, since Michele's not old enough for a regular identity card, a *certificato di nascita,* a birth certificate. Without forgetting the problem that I should really get a licence myself if I'm going to be with him . . .

If only Santa Lucia could have sorted all this out, too! Michele hops from foot to foot impatiently. I note in Silvio's innocent face that complacency Italians have when they have completed a bureaucratic procedure and you have not, the secret desire they have that you should go through the same hell they did. Not unlike the way parents of more than one child always want everybody else to have more than one child, too.

'But do these inspectors really come along?'

As with every discussion about laws and rules, there comes the moment when one must examine the question of enforcement . . .

For example: Do I really need a regulation child seat for the back of my car?

No.

Do I have to wear my safety belt?

Only if I don't want to be thrown against the windscreen . . .

Do I have to have a TV licence?

Not if they don't bother me about it.

Do I have to get an official sign on my gate saying that it is illegal to park in front of it?

Yes. Yes, amazingly, yes. Because this particular rule involves a local tax, and the local government is desperate for cash, and because it's the easiest thing in the world to see whether you've paid or not: a *vigile* rides around checking if there are official no-parking signs on your driveway gate. I must pay this tax.

Now Silvio is insisting that it's the same with fishing. The inspectors are terrible. Just when you least expect it, there they are. They even work odd hours! After dark. Sunday mornings . . .

Michele, who has already fretted through the cold winter months barely kept at bay with the sop of weekend sledding, who has cast his rod from the top of his bunk bed to fish toys from the floor and examined all the worms in the garden, is nearly out of his mind with impatience. 'But Papà, Papà, I want to go *now*.'

Upon which, with extraordinary charm, Silvio belies all he has just said and announces: '*Va bene*, let's go now!' A little 'raid', he says, as Italians will, pronouncing the word 'ride' and meaning, a sortie, a brief adventure. Apparently, some element in Michele's hot-headed boyish character has called to Silvio. He too wants to go fishing *now*.

It's a March evening. Spring is already in the air. And it must be a Friday, since every other day Michele is skating or playing the piano or riding round the BMX course. Silvio doesn't take us far. We load the rods and tackle in his second car, the new Panda, and drive no more than a kilometre round to the other side of Centro Primo Maggio. Here, following an untarred track, we arrive at a big ditch, perhaps twenty feet across, with some miserable and unpromisingly weedy water in the bottom, all hedged about by huge bulrushes. It must be part of the village's flood overflow system, picking up a mix of rainwater, effluent and surplus from the local streams. An old wheelbarrow tyre is half submerged in scum. We scramble through tall grasses down a steep bank and tuck in amongst trees and bushes on the mud at the bottom. There's myself, Michele, Silvio, Silvio's ever-mischievous Giovanni, and Stefi, who threw a fit when we almost didn't take her, though I can see Silvio is decidedly against the presence of little girls on fishing expeditions.

It's past five and almost twilight. In a delirium of excitement Michele has forgotten – and this is rare – to ask whether there are vipers here. He doesn't even have his viper stick, for heaven's sake. He extends his rod. Then Silvio shows him how to arm it, while Giovanni gives a running commentary in the urgent stutter he has and shouts and chases up and down the bank, and Stefi asks how many fish we are going to catch and crosses herself as she always does now when she is excited. Our feet sink into the mud. I realise that when I get back there will be something like hell to pay, since an Italian father can make no greater mistake than not making sure his children have the appropriate footwear for any trip that takes them away from their mothers. The kids' school shoes are already filthy. Worse, their little feet will be damp.

'What if the inspectors come?' Michele asks breathless.

'They won't,' Silvio says. He slips two bright yellow pieces of sweet corn on the hook.

But how can he be so sure? I want to know. After all he just said . . .

Silvio turns to me and, over Michele's busy blond head, winks and pulls a face, as though to say, I don't want to explain why in front of the children, but believe me it's okay, no inspectors will come. Then he shouts at his own son to shut up and stay still, he's frightening the fish away by yelling and running about. Everybody starts to say SHSHSHSHSH! so urgently I imagine even the fish will feel chastened. 'Shush!' screams Michele. The murky water is obediently silent.

The light is failing. A chill creeps into the air. And the problem with casting here, Silvio explains, is first the overhead trees, then getting the hook to go down in an area without weeds, and lastly the fact that the depth varies a great deal, so you often have to reel in immediately and raise or lower your float, because the bait has to sit just above the bottom for these fish . . .

Michele isn't listening to any of this. He's suddenly become afraid that it will be too dark if we don't get going now.

'*Presto, presto, presto!*' he urges in a super-hushed, super-fierce voice. Already I'm suffering for his imminent disappointment, savouring it sadly ahead of time. 'Michele,' I say, repeating what every father must sooner or later say to every son. 'Michele, remember fishing is a question of patience. You may have to wait hours and hours. This isn't the Mississippi in 1860.'

'The fish are *f-furbi*!' Giovanni shouts. They're smart! '*F-furbi, furbi, furbi!* You'll never catch them!'

'Shush!!'

'Sometimes you don't catch anything at all,' Silvio warns him. Then he adds seriously: 'What matters is *la passione*.' It's a word he uses when I compliment him on his extraordinary gardening achievements and confess my own incompetence. You have to have *la passione*, he says. If you have *la passione* you will be willing to make any *sacrificio*, and even if things don't come right first time you will go on till they do. But *la passione* is a mystical thing. 'Either you have it or you don't,' Silvio warns.

'I know, I know,' Michele whispers. *'Presto!'*

Silvio casts with a delicacy and grace you would never expect from his thick, muscly forearms. He then hands the rod to Michele and begins to sort out his own. 'Watch the float all the time,' he says sternly. 'If it starts to bob, tell me and I'll show you what to do.'

The light is dying. It's bleeding out of the sky where dark branches are suddenly darker, evergreen leaves bereft of their gloss. Already the float has a slightly fluorescent look to it. And with the dusk comes a smell, or awareness, of damp and stagnancy. There's something dreadfully inauspicious about this situation: five people huddled around a filthy, weedy ditch. Deep in my heart, I know nothing can come of it. Then, in a low whisper Michele cries: 'It's bobbing!'

Silvio doesn't even look up. He's straining his eyes over loops and twists of line in the half light. After all, barely a minute has passed since he cast.

'It's bobbing!'

'No, it isn't.' I hardly bother looking myself. I'm thinking how the place at least looks a bit more picturesque now the shadows have wiped out the wheelbarrow tyre and the beer cans on the other side.

'Porca vacca!' Michele screams. 'It's bobbing!'

'O la Madonna!' Stefi crosses herself.

Giovanni yells: *'Pesce, ha preso un pesce!'*

And sure enough, Michele had caught a fish. Silvio grabbed the rod, struck, and reeled it in with his fingers round the boy's. It was a muddy-looking fish, somewhat tubby and far from graceful, perhaps eight inches long, but undeniably a fish. In the distance Don Guido's recorded bells began to chime, *È l'ora che pia . . .*

Over the next hour seven fish were caught, four on Michele's rod. Oh, the fish in that ditch were far from *furbi*. Either that, or they'd been a long time without seeing canned sweet corn. And I thought how deeply an experience of this kind could affect one's character. It would be like getting one's first novel published by the first publisher you sent it to and becoming famous overnight. Or having the very first girl you ever approached fall immediately into bed with you. Michele is surely in danger of becoming a wildly optimistic, ingenuous fellow. And I know nothing could keep him away from fishing now, not even a nest of vipers.

Not even mother's fury when we get home plastered in mud and with seven fish to clean, since Silvio claims they already have a fridge full of fish. Not being a fisherman, *come si deve*, I have no idea how to clean the things. But both children are adamant that we have to eat them.

'What are they called?' Rita asks.

'He said some dialect name. I can't remember.'

'They certainly stink enough.'

Grilled, these fish turn out to be greasy and infinitely bony, and they taste exactly the way the water they lived in suggested they would. Putrid. Had the kids been fed such food in the normal way of things they would surely have thrust away their plates in disgust. Had the *scuola materna* served up such fare, the *rappresentanti di classe* would have been overwhelmed with telephone calls and a protest meeting immediately arranged. But on that particular evening Michele and Stefi gobbled the whole lot down. Without even a drop of ketchup. Later I learnt from Silvio that no inspector would ever go to that ditch, precisely because there are no fish there that anyone would want to eat.

'I do think though,' he added grinning, 'that your boy has *la passione*.'

Diobon

So that was the year I got to know the anglers' shop in San Michele Extra. The place has the air of one of those farm goods stores they used to show in old Westerns, where an elderly father and three willing sons serve a rough-and-ready clientele in a cluttered ambience of bristling tools, sagging open-mouthed sacks, and large dogs that sniff at everybody and each other, or lie asleep between two barrels and a dustpan. The shop is narrow and long, its walls lined with rods and tripods and nets and wading boots, then stacked to a high ceiling with nondescript boxes and arcane equipment of every variety. At the far end, people in overalls who all seem to know each other jostle at the counter for the attention of the men serving, or the advice of the old patriarch who stands to one side discussing finer technicalities, the rarer experiences, occasionally deigning to satisfy someone's curiosity on such routine matters as float shapes, line weights, spinner sizes. All things I know nothing about.

The men are all talking in dialect, with absolutely no exception, and amongst men dialect always seems to go with a booming timbre, an extravagant, effortless, candid loudness. The older men are the same one might see playing bocce at the Centro Primo Maggio or transporting demijohns of rough wine in Fiat 128s with straw hats tipped back on white hair and a hunting dog in the boot. The younger men are their sons, but here the variety is greater, ranging from those who spend all day at polished desks choosing which phone to answer, to those who create complications at the counters of state offices and those who labour from morning till night in their workshops or at the wheel of their trucks.

Inevitably, given the social nature of the occasion, someone is performing. One voice booms louder than all the rest. I recognise its owner as the man with the bodyshop where I got my car fixed when it was run into from behind, a mishap he turned into something of a bonanza at the expense of the insurance company.

He has come to pick up a rod he's had repaired. The thing is so monstrously long that when he opens it out to examine what they've done, he has to do so lengthwise down the shop, so that two people are holding the base at the back of the queue while the tip has disappeared into the storeroom behind the counter.

Carlon, I remember they call him, which is to say, Big Carlo . . .

And he is big. Perhaps not even thirty, Carlon has the swaggering bravado and huge barrel chest of the kind of testosterone-stuffed fellow you imagine taking part in arm-wrestling competitions to win an evening's free beer. But there's something self-consciously flamboyant and almost camp about him, too. His overalls are blue, as no doubt his father's were before him, but his shirt is a neon pink unbuttoned on a froth of blond chest hair, and from under a battered bush-hat more long blond curls fall freshly shampooed onto his shoulders. His big moustaches are likewise blond, *idem* his goatee, while the tattoos on thick forearms show, not anchors or naked girls, but two very large and colourful butterflies. The final touch comes with the sunglasses: Carlon has blue mirror shades with silver frames which he has hooked over the thick gold chain around his neck. The crucified Christ at the end of that chain is thus reduced to a silhouette behind winking reflections of heavy-duty waterproofs in a V of blond-fringed pink.

Carlon is talking – perhaps with the excuse of his newly repaired rod extending through the crowd – to the whole shop, and the whole shop is listening; and every other word Carlon says is 'Diobon', the dialectal version of 'Good God' and the most common and irritating blasphemy in the Veneto.

'Rascal was so big, *Diobon*, so big, and me that's not used to sea fishing, *Diobon, Diobon,* I was determined to work him, because the line was too light, *Diobon,* see what I mean, I mean, *Diobon,* if I'd waited and played him like I might another time, *Diobon,* that fellow would'a chewed through the whole tackle, *Diobon.*'

His dialect is so thick I'm having to invent half of what I'm hearing. The others in the shop are laughing and throwing in suggestions, and they know he's hamming it up, he's lying, and that anybody who breaks a great big expensive rod like that must have made some kind of stupid mistake, but they're enjoying it anyway, and the man behind the counter is assuring him the rod is fixed so well he could catch a whale with it now. A whale he could catch, *Diobon!* The shopkeeper is winking at everybody else and Carlon has seen him winking and shouts, '*Diobon*, if nobody believes me I'll break all your heads, *Diobon!*' And it's clear of course that they're all old friends and probably spend every Friday evening telling tall stories like this. Because Friday evening is when everybody comes to stock up on bait for the weekend.

Halfway down the queue, Michele is all ears, doubtless understanding Carlon far better than I do, or at least the content, if not perhaps the context. 'That big!' he whispers to me, innocent eyes wide. 'A fish that big!' (That is, as big as himself.) In wonder he adds, '*Diobon*', which starts me wondering how in all conscience I can stop him using this language when my own is hardly impeccable in English, if somewhat less repetitive.

We've come to buy bait and a variety of other things for our first fishing trip *alone*. We've been to a gravel pit now three times with Stefano and Beppino. It's one of the places where you pay to catch trout bred in a fish farm. Stefano is an expert fisherman, operating, as no doubt he does his accounts, with a sort of routine, well-informed cunning. He knows when you have to arrive, which are the best places, what time they throw the fish in, and when the creatures will want to start eating. He even knows when you can afford to take time out for a cappuccino in the bar since none of the fish are biting any more. '*Sai com'è?*' he says, very pleased that you don't. So when you go fishing with Stefano you always catch at least six fat trout, something that can only have served to reinforce Michele's *passione*, especially since nobody has yet asked him to contribute any pocket money to the entrance fee.

But there are problems. Despite his evident familiarity with the gravel pits, Stefano claims to despise them. He only goes, he says, because he and Marta feel it would be too dangerous to take Beppino to a river, because he might fall in and drown. (It's interesting that Stefano never mentions the hang up of the licence.) Of course, the boy might perfectly well fall in the gravel pit, too, but it's the nature of gravel pit fishing that there are lots of people around and hence someone would be able to pull him out. Stefano couldn't do it himself because like many Italians of his age he can't swim; he never learnt. Ironically, Beppino can swim very well, having been to swimming courses (as he can likewise ride a horse and pitch a baseball), but this doesn't stop Stefano from having a nervous breakdown every time the boy goes near the water, and going near the water is something that does tend to happen when fishing.

Perhaps as a result of this nervousness on his parents' part, Beppino shows no sign of developing the *passione* now raging in Michele's boyish breast. He skips around by the water's edge, his long ponytail dangling; he leans over to see what other anglers have in their nets; he deliberately crouches with his nose almost in the water and thus keeps Stefano in a state of constant tension. 'Don't fall in! What will Mamma say!' As always what Stefano really means is, 'What will Mamma say to me.' And as always he knows perfectly well what she will say. She will say, 'I told you the boy should have stayed home!'

Discouraged, denied any initiative or responsibility, Beppino ends up lying down on the grass with a copy of

Topolino, alias Mickey Mouse, a comic that borrows all the Disney figures but is entirely written and produced in Italy. He brings three or four with him. Then, rather than leaving well alone, Stefano will protest: 'You wanted to come fishing, and now you're not even watching your float. It wasn't worth bringing you!' (Read: risking your mother's wrath.) In reply Beppino shouts rudely, Zap! or Wroom! or Snap! or Gulp! (pronounced goolp). For although *Topolino* is written and drawn in Italy, kids are so used to the English exclamations buried in the pictures of translated comics that these have been kept, though somewhat domesticated here – Tlack! Sgrunt!

When Stefano gets quite furious on one occasion, Beppino giggles and starts saying something that sounds like 'Moombeley, Moombeley!' Laughing, Michele joins in. 'Moombeley, Moombeley, Moombeley!' Stefano is beside himself. It's only later that I realise that this is how the children pronounce those little balloons in comics that say 'Mumble, mumble.' They have mistakenly imagined the words are some kind of awful mockery. 'Moombeley, moombeley!'

To cap all these difficulties with the ultimate insult, Marta will not allow Stefano to clean the fish (caught in such trying circumstances) in her gleaming kitchen sink (they haven't as yet installed a sink in their garage), as a result of which he insists at the end of each expedition that we keep all the fish he has caught, something that can only serve to increase Michele's enthusiasm and dampen Beppino's. So I have decided that if Michele insists on fishing, then we should go alone from now on. And here we are at the angler's shop in San Michele to buy bait.

We get the maggots, the worms, the white polystyrene

foam balls to attract the trout's attention and a landing net. Only as we're leaving does it occur to me that we've forgotten the gadget you use to pull the hook out of their mouths. It's something Stefano has always done so far. Then I reflect that without Stefano we probably won't catch anything anyway, so it hardly matters. Outside on the main road Carlon is trying and failing to start a bright red, open-topped Golf.

The gravel pit is flatteringly called I Laghetti, the little lakes. Like that ditch where Michele landed his first fish, it is drearily unattractive. But this only makes one aware of how little children care about the aesthetic quality of such experiences. They don't even notice. They don't see. All Michele is thinking of is fish, *Diobon* . . .

You get up at six-thirty and drive away from the hills towards the *bassa*, past Michele's old nursery school where they used to write *due bene* and make him sing 'The Bells of Bovolon'. The horse in the red coat has apparently died since we used to make this trip years ago.

In San Michele you cross the main Verona–Venice trunk road and head off down the bypass toward the *autostrada*. Then just when a landscape of heathland and provincial decay has made the idea of fishing almost unimaginable, seems fit only for fast roads streaking to better places, you take a sharp right turn along a narrow track and tumble over an embankment to where a series of erstwhile gravel pits have been allowed to fill with water. Between two of these pits, as the car slithers down a landslide of slime and sharp stones, you see a long, low, wooden shed with a tarpaulin roof and smoking iron chimney. There is a veranda at the entrance, and the windows have the unusual (and hence ominous) accessory of mosquito screens. Above the door a sign says: I LAGHETTI, RISTORANTE, TRATTORIA, PIZZERIA. It's a description that would appear to cover every preference, yet I suspect this may be the only restaurant in the whole of Italy where no foreign tourist has ever penetrated. I remember going to I Laghetti one winter night to find every one of its hundred-odd tables occupied and ever diner wearing an overcoat, and in some cases even a hat. Wooden, damp and above all primitive, the place has only a couple of old paraffin heaters. Clearly, the owners felt the mosquito screens were a more urgent investment.

But it's only seven in the morning now and we're not here to eat, but to catch our food for lunch and dinner. Another notice on the side of the shed announces: AZIENDA AGRICOLA ITTICA – Ichthyic Agricultural Venture – which is the pompous way they have now discovered for saying fish farm. Beneath, it says: 'Sale of Live Trout and Sports Fishing'. Whenever I see that notice, I always think that the only good sports in all this are the trout . . .

You park on a rise above the pools and dash for a place. Italians are nothing if not early risers, and the bank is already more than half full. The pit to the left is reserved for a competition, and here the men are thick as maggots in a bait box, standing elbow to elbow, their lines admirably parallel, unshaven faces tense with concentration. In the right-hand pit, where we're going, things are a bit more relaxed, though even here there are already a dozen and more men and boys scattered around the twenty by twenty metres of still black water. Immediately, Michele is frantically anxious, flustering with nets and tackle box and rod. 'Hurry, Papà, hurry!'

There's a mud path through wet grass and trodden camomile, with the water on one side and a barbed-wire fence on the other, or where there isn't the fence there's a steep bank rising to wet fields above. You pick your way round people mainly fishing in threes and fours, since even this solitary sport is never quite solitary here. The men set out their rods – most have at least two – and then they go and sit together with their friends and speak softly – so as not to disturb the fish from their task of finding the hooks – and they smoke, since smoke doesn't disturb fish, and they eat crisps, or sandwiches, or pre-packaged croissants, and drink water or wine, or even a slug or two of grappa, and keep the corners of their eyes on their floats, occasionally pulling out a big farm-bred fish, twisting and sparkling in the bright morning air. We pick our way past them and the mud is littered with cigarette stubs and abandoned tangles of fishing line, and every two metres or less there is a little concrete block you can sit on, with a deep hole in the side of it where you can rest your rod once you've cast.

We seize one of the last blocks on the far side. '*Grazie a Dio,*' says atheist Michele and, borrowing the gesture from Stefi, crosses himself. Having successfully found a place, he immediately relaxes. Indeed, I'm amazed at his confidence as he sets up the rod as Stefano has taught him. At least four fish, he promises himself. As on the first occasion, I'm now afraid for his imminent disappointment. In my pockets I make the sign of the *corna,* though I'm not sure it works if made in pockets. I reflect that whereas that first time in the lonely ditch any failure would have been limited to the business of catching, or rather not catching, any fish, here there is the further danger that we will *fare una brutta figura*, figure badly, look ridiculous in front of a score of other fishermen. Myself especially. For very soon it will be evident to everybody here that I have no idea at all about fishing. Doubtless one of the things that draws people to come to places like this, rather than setting off to find some isolated stream or deep-running river, is that here they can watch everybody else, learn from them, perhaps, or, better still, laugh at them.

A man appears to our left, taking up a position between our concrete block and the next. Which is rather too close for comfort. By the time Michele's boyish fingers have fumbled through all the tackle, the fellow has already cast twice with a determination not presently being shown by the other anglers, two or three of whom are actually reading the paper. Funnily enough, I find the complacence of the paper readers and the businesslike manner of the newcomer equally unnerving. Each seems so sure of what he knows, while I only know that I know nothing.

Then Michele refuses to hook on the maggots because he's squeamish. He may have *la passione*, but he won't touch a maggot. So I have to do that. As their white bodies squish and pop under the barb and their yellowy blood or sap or pus or whatever it is oozes out of them, I am seized by the conviction that they are dying in vain. There is no way I and my son will ever catch a fish. Meanwhile, on his fourth cast, for he seems to be trawling without a float, the man to our left catches a large trout. It's the first since we've arrived. So expert is he at playing the thing in and gathering it in his net, so dexterous and skilled is he at wrapping it in a floor cloth to whip out the hook before dropping it in a second net, which he secures to a peg banged into the bank, that he has cast yet again, a fifth time, before we are ready for even our first attempt. The newspaper readers raise their eyes from the pink print of *La Gazzetta dello Sport*, consider this solitary diligence, and return to their chat. Their floats are motionless on a glassy surface, their lines beautifully curved in parallel as the sluggish current draws them ever so slowly from left to right.

Michele goes for a really big cast in an attempt to get his hook right in the middle of the pit, but he misses his timing and the float falls ignominiously a couple of metres from the muddy shore. Still, I tell him, you're as likely to catch a fish there as elsewhere, and I suggest he hang on to the rod while I nip into I Laghetti to pay for our right to fish.

'Papààààà!' I've got about halfway down the cigarette stubs and bursting tackle boxes when a huge voice calls me back.

'A bite! A BITE!'

Conditioned now into believing myself forever wrong and my son forever lucky, I race back to deal with this unexpected and frankly alarming eventuality. The float is indeed bobbing. Foolishly, I insist on striking myself, which I have never done in my life before. The line flies out of the water and way back over my head to tangle on the barbed-wire fence behind. There is no fish on the end of it and no maggots either. Some minnows have merely nibbled the things off. Copies of *La Gazzetta* rustle. Faces stare. The efficient man to our left turns and frowns to show displeasure at all the noise we are making. For Michele is shrieking: *'Diobon, Papà, Diobon non così!'* Not like that!

Michele is convinced there was a fish and I lost it. *'Porco*

Giuda, Papà!' he screams. Pig Judah! It's seriously bad language and he's loud enough to frighten off every trout in the Veneto. Humiliated, I lose my temper and tell him with my now sharp eye for a possible *ricatto* that if he shouts at me again he can forget any more fishing adventures. Ever! But all at once I'm aware of the fact that my speaking in English can only rouse the others' curiosity and most probably their desire to find me incompetent. An Englishman who doesn't know how to fish! With all the water they have! Then I'm furious with myself for caring what these people think, which it suddenly seems to me is a peculiarly Italian anxiety. I never used to worry so much in London, I never used to tie myself in knots over situations like this.

Knots . . . It would be a polite way to describe the condition our line is in now. First we have to unravel it from the barbed-wire fence, then it takes us about twenty minutes of cursing and told-you-so's before we manage to get it untangled and back in the water. Once again I head off to pay for the pleasure we're having using I Laghetti's gravel pit . . .

This time I make it round the cluttered path and into the giant shack of the *ristorante, trattoria, pizzeria* without being called back. There is a wooden veranda that has an almost backwoods New England feel to it, then immediately inside swing doors that seem to wait a moment before swinging back, there are a couple of ancient pinball machines. I haven't seen a pinball machine in years. Time must have stood still at I Laghetti ever since somebody was persuaded to give them the licence to build this horror. Still, the dings and clunks of pinball are a good deal less abrasive than the outer-space laser fire of the screen-based games Michele loves. I just find it curious that a bunch of adolescents should be playing these machines deep in the swampy countryside at something before eight in the morning. Why aren't they crouched over their rods?

On the wooden walls around me are sad stuffed animals and a couple of framed fish, then one or two certificates, the inevitable shelf of cycling, angling and football trophies, and a corner dedicated to muddled photographs of parties apparently held in the *ristorante*. The bar amounts to six scattered tables with red-and-white check plastic cloths and a game of table football.

I go to the counter to pay, but there's nobody there. I wait and notice a board over the till that gives the fishing prices. For one rod, twelve thousand; for two, fifteen, for three, eighteen. No wonder the others come in groups!

A girl appears. She's small, surely too young to be working. And indeed she can't give me my ticket, she says. But then it turns out that she can make me a cappuccino. I decide to go for it. With no alternative, I take one of the prepackaged croissants from a display that seems to be made out of fifties dish racks.

The *Arena* is lying open on a table, so I may as well sit down and read till someone comes to take my money. I spoon sugar in my coffee, then have a fight with the packaging of the croissant. Just when I'm finally set to enjoy myself for a couple of minutes, I discover that the coffee has been made with long-life milk. I hate long-life milk. Despite which – is this possible? – it seems to be off. This is awful. But then it occurs to me that the bar probably hasn't had to serve a cappuccino for years. The adolescents by the pinball machine are drinking Coca Cola and the one or two older men wine, or coffee with wine in it. The croissant has the consistency of overboiled potatoes.

But the paper has a story to cheer me up. A man in some small town in Piedmont phoned his wife with a strangled voice to say he had been kidnapped. She must await further instructions and on no account phone the police. She phoned the police. The police made enquiries and discovered that the husband had warned his boss and work colleagues that he would be away from the office for the week. Within twelve hours they had found the man with his young and, one trusts, delightful mistress in a seaside resort on the coast above Genova. In a statement the man admits to having made a *brutta figura* . . .

Then amazingly, because this is generally an asphyxiatingly Catholic paper, the journalist proceeds to enthuse about how such stories demonstrate that the sun has still to set on traditional Latin passion and imagination. In what other country in the world, he asks, could such a thing happen? Indeed. For my own part I am already rehearsing my presentation of the story across Zia Natalina's kitchen table. '*Santa patata*, Signor Teem,' she will say, '*davvero non c'è piu religione!*' And I will say: 'When he could have just pretended he was off on a fishing trip . . .' Far from imagination, it sounds like folly to me.

An unsavoury young fellow appears at the till. He has long hair in a thick ponytail and wears clogs that he deliberately drags on the floorboards, even when standing still. His tattoo is an eagle, and he has three earrings in one ear and a St Christopher round his neck. He gives me a small square piece of yellow paper, puts a cross in the square where it says 1 rod and then writes the date. Already guilty that I've been too long, I stuff the thing in my pocket, buy Michele a bar of chocolate for his breakfast and head off.

About a hundred people have arrived since I went into the bar. Poor Michele is now seriously hedged in with a new fellow on his right tending three rods and having thus paid eighteen thousand to our twelve. Everybody has denim jackets over overalls, and most have little peaked caps with the name of a football team or tractor company. There are chuckles of laughter and upturned canteens. Nobody seems to be taking the fishing very seriously except for the fellow on our left, the only one constantly casting and winding in. Michele, poignantly holding the rod, limp line drifting near the bank, whispers, outraged, to tell me the man has already caught four big trout, while minnows have eaten all his bait as many times! And he has mosquito bites all over his feet. I should never have told him to wear sandals.

There are tears in the boy's eyes. Then the fellow with the three rods to our right, unanswerably large and burly, complains that Michele's line is drifting into his. Michele winds in and casts again in bitter silence. To cheer him up I point out that at least he is casting well now. He shrugs his shoulders and refuses to speak to me, munching his chocolate with the rod tucked under one arm.

Fifteen fruitless minutes later I finally get the explanation to the morning's various enigmas: Why were some men round the pit reading the *La Gazetta dello Sport* as if they hadn't come to fish at all? Why were the adolescents playing pinball instead of sitting by their rods? Why did one hundred people arrive between eight and eight-fifteen?

Answer: because eight-thirty is the time when, on

Saturday (we have only been on Easter holiday weekdays with Stefano), they throw in the fish. Only now will the feast begin. The kill . . .

An old tin dinghy appears from the top end of the pool. The same long-haired fellow who took my money revs the outboard unnecessarily sending the boat swerving into the centre of the pool so that everybody has to hurry to their lines. In his haste Michele jerks his out of the water and gets it tangled round the fence again. Now he really is crying with rage. Because now is the moment we could have caught something, and if only . . .

I don't wait to hear but set about slicing through an impossible tangle and setting up from scratch.

The long-haired fellow kills his outboard and stands with great panache in his wobbly boat. He dips a bucket into two big plastic tubs, fore and aft, full of trout. He chucks the wriggling fish now over the front of the boat, now over the back, now to one side, now to the other, in a very approximate gesture of fair distribution, while the men who have dropped their chat and their papers and jumped to their feet, all shout, '*Diobon*, chuck a few over here, over here, *Diobon* . . .' With a snigger the lad running the Ichthyic Agricultural Venture tugs his outboard into a roar that sends a cloud of oil smoke drifting across the pit and races back five metres to the shore. Presumably, he doesn't have a paddle in the boat.

Working feverishly, I have the rod re-armed before anybody has caught more than three fish, though the terribly earnest fellow to our left is just pulling in a fourth. Michele is beside himself, but casts beautifully. He gets his little float right in the middle of the pool, just as the wild flurry calms down. Apparently, the remaining fish have realised that it might be unwise to snatch at all those maggots. We wait. Nothing. But by now I've lost all concern about Michele's disappointment. The worst has already happened. There's nothing to be done. No, now I'm positively savouring how awful it all is, secretly hoping that we will never have to come to this barbaric place again.

'Another half an hour and we're off,' I tell him. He nods, miserably, gripping the rod tight. He helps himself to another piece of chocolate, staring tearfully at the now motionless water. I watch an oil stain ever so gently uncurl. Half an hour, then I can leave. All around the successful fishermen are beginning to relax and chat. One or two head off. Others are examining their sandwich boxes and wondering if three fish is enough to explain themselves to their wives.

Such, and so desolate, is the situation when Michele gets a bite.

There can be no mistaking it. The float goes down like a stone. I'm all nerves again.

'You!' Michele shouts. 'Papà, you do it! *Diobon!*'

His mixture of Italian and English has everybody looking at us again. But I'm not going to be held responsible for another debacle.

'You do it, son,' I tell him, as if this were some kind of major concession, an extraordinary gesture of trust.

So Michele does it. He strikes beautifully, with a dexterity I would never have imagined. Immediately, the rod bends fiercely. The thing must be big. And without any instructions from me, Michele starts to play it, by instinct, letting out a little line, winding in a little more. The men on both sides of us are watching intently. I grab the big net I bought and slither down the bank. There's a splash of tail, but Michele is careful not to lift it out of the water. He steers it towards me, slowly, surely. His eyes are so intent! In just one more minute we have caught a truly huge trout, perhaps the biggest anybody has caught this morning. As I lift the net, the thing is leaping and twisting and wriggling on the line. Michele's face is ecstasy and triumph. To our left the efficient fellow who already has a dozen takes precious time out to say '*Bravo!*' I could kiss him . . . for being so kind as to leave one for us.

But now I remember I didn't buy the gadget for pulling out the hook. And I don't have a cloth to hold the creature in, either. Nor do we have the net for keeping him alive under water while we go on fishing. We'll have to kill him right away. Michele is down on his knees by the net *diobon*ing and admiring and saying he wonders if Huck Finn ever caught a fish so big. But when he takes the trout out, he can't hold it. It leaps out of his hands into the muddy grass. For a moment it seems it might even make it back to the water. Overreacting, I trap the bastard with a full press that sinks him deep and slimy into the mud, then I force his mouth open and try to get the hook out. It's brutal. I'm not used to this kind of thing. The trout bites me. The hook won't come. Finally the line comes, but without the hook. And then I have to bang the monster's head about a hundred times on a stone before he's still enough to be forced into a plastic bag. '*Bravo, Diobon,*' Michele says. Other people are sniggering. Frankly, I feel about as exhausted as a first-time murderer.

The fellow on our left catches another. He has it in his net in less than thirty seconds. Michele wants to go on fishing, but I suggest, with a little exaggeration, that the fish we've caught is big enough for the whole family. Let's leave when things are going well and come back on a weekday when there aren't so many people. He agrees. He picks up the plastic bag and walks very proudly through the clutter of the path, showing the fish to anyone who is interested.

It's as I'm sitting in the car again, waiting for Michele to take a pee in the bushes, that the day's last mystery is cleared up. Pulling out the car keys from my pocket, I find the keys have become tangled up with the little yellow ticket they gave me with its picture of a trout leaping out of the water after a fly. To pass a couple of seconds I set about reading the small print on the back:

REGULATIONS

No licence is required. Buy this permit before fishing and keep it with you. Those found without a permit will be charged double. The permit is personal and is valid for a whole morning or afternoon. Fishing is permitted only with one rod and one hook. Behave in a correct fashion. Weight and number of catch is unlimited.

The curiosity here is that on the other side of the same ticket there are actually squares to be checked to indicate one rod, two or even three . . . But it is the section '*Divieti*', i.e. what you are not allowed to do, that really wakes me up.

It is forbidden to feed the fish in any way whatsoever.

It is forbidden to use a teaspoon and anchor to hook the fish [not something I was planning on].

All natural baits are allowed, but it is forbidden to use any metallic lure of any kind.

Transgressors of the above rule will be invited to

leave the pool and their catch will be shared out amongst the other people fishing.

'Michele! Michele!' He comes running. I read him the rules. I explain to him that man to our left was definitely using a spinner, a metallic lure. We saw it every time he pulled in a fish. Theoretically, we could just go along and tell the long-haired fellow with the earrings and the man's catch would be confiscated. They'd have to share it out, and since we reported him, we would surely be entitled to at least one more trout.

Michele is all for acting at once. He begins to shout. *Ladro!* Thief! But now I've got him excited, I have to go on to explain that, on second thoughts, there would probably be no point in reporting the matter to the long-haired fellow. It's just a rule, Michele, I explain. Everybody there must have seen he was using a spinner, and nobody said anything. Nobody gives a damn . . .

Michele is disappointed in me. He thinks I'm just scared. But then I tell him that, actually, thinking about it, Stefano always had a spinner on one of his rods, didn't he?

'*Sai com'è*, Michele,' I say. He pouts and nods wisely. Perhaps he is beginning to understand . . .

In tiny print below the *divieti* it says: 'The management cannot be held responsible for any theft that takes place on the premises. Damages to things and persons are covered by RAS insurance.' Oddly enough, that is Nascimbeni's company. I imagine the man hobbling down the bank to warn the management that a gravel pit is the kind of place where people could come to blows and hurt each other and then make claims against the management for not having imposed the rules properly.

At home Silvio applauds Michele on having caught a

spectacular fish. *La passione* helped him do it. Silvio's smile turns to a frown. 'Just too bad the thing got smashed up so badly when you killed it.'

'That was Papà,' Michele confides. 'Papà doesn't know anything about fishing.'

The following day, Sunday, Michele chose our fishing trip as the subject for his weekend homework composition. For me it was a chance to observe how he saw events. Or at least how he felt those events should be presented. He wrote:

FISHING

When you go fishing you have to be very careful not to get tangled up with the line.

If you use a rod with a float it's more boring because all you have to do is watch the float to see if it moves.

But if you use a small false metal fin then you have to keep turning the reel, and you get more fish.

You have to know how deep the water is where you're fishing and you have to know how to cast.

WHEN THE FISH BITES

When the fish bites you see the float jump up and down in the water.

First you have to make a little tug with the rod and then you have to wind in the line until you can see the fish darting about in the water. Then you get the fish in the net. Then you get the fish with a cloth and you give it a bang on the head to kill it.

After that you put the fish in another net that goes in the water to keep the fish fresh.

Before that though, when you kill the fish you have to take the hook out of its mouth.

Then you start fishing again.

NECESSARY EQUIPMENT

Rod, weights, hooks, worms (bait), float, two nets, line.

How knowledgeable it all sounds. As if it were a lesson he'd learnt. How experienced, too, and technical. And how reticent . . . Clearly, Michele has understood a great deal more than I imagined.

Il cambio della guardia

A curiosity of car travel is how it confuses the seasons. We are travelling south across the Pianura Padana, that great triangle of flat, chemically-fed farmland south of the Alps and east of the Apennines. The landscape is an oppressive geometry of rectangular fields laid out in rigid lines of maize or wheat or vines, unrelieved by hill or hedgerow. Even the fruit trees have been trained to spread their branches at right angles through only two dimensions, so that they look more like Jewish candlesticks than anything organic. Above them, the crisscross bristle of giant pylons is so in tune with the rest it might be just another machine-managed crop at a higher level of evolution.

We drive on. As the morning passes, the sense of oppression is intensified by a blinding glare of summer light, a light that strips the land bare and leaves it vulnerable, simmering, as if heated to boiling point in some monstrous industrial process. The *autostrada* shoots across it straight and white as a white-hot poker, flashing with the dazzle of sunlight on racing windscreens. In the car, the fan blows warm, sticky air through the ventilator ducts. Excited and fractious, the children fight over sunscreens to stick on the windows. Rita distributes fruit juices from the freeze box.

Yet in the midst of this blinding heat, the road signs are warning you of fog. White blobs at the side of the road measure out stretches of a hundred metres each. If visibility is down to three blobs, reduce speed to eighty kilometres an hour. If to two, sixty. If to one, forty. When you cross a bridge, another sign says to watch out for ice. There is the little image of the skidding car. Further south, past Bologna and then Rimini, when you've joined the great Adriatico highway that pushes right down to Bari, it's the wind they tell you to be careful of, coming out of the long tunnels or crossing the huge viaducts that span dry river valleys above a shimmering blur of sea. Danger, gusts of wind! There is a little picture of a hump-backed car careening on two wheels. But the only wind today comes from the polished chase of bright metal packed with holiday-makers heading south. Then even that peters out as the traffic slows and sticks in a viscous summer jam. The children fight and scratch over a water bottle. An incongruous triangle tells me that if it's snowing I must have chains on my wheels.

Hot weather, cold signs . . . It's as if they were trying to remind you of the great epic of the turning seasons, how the country lies still under fog and frost in winter, then boils in summer's vertical sunshine. Or perhaps the signs are there to console us that July heat is only fleeting, as unimaginable in mid-winter as snowflakes are today. Or perhaps, again, somebody wants to have you reflect that the road is always there even when you aren't, embraces a range of experience you know nothing of. But this is hardly a conversation one can hope to divert the children with. Just as it would be pointless to tell them how this reminder of life's different seasons prompts memories of English family holidays years ago when my parents, brother, sister and I set out on a Ribble bus from Blackpool (incredibly, the service was known as the Gay Hostess), peering through rain on the windows at a Lancashire landscape whose lush wetness was always perceived as a challenge. How would we manage to survive in tent, or cottage or caravan for three windswept seaside weeks? What adventures would we have in our determination to stick it out? Cows glowered in fields, huddled against a wind that blew winter and summer alike in that country. And perhaps on some mental highway, as one clutched the handrail of the seat in front, there might have been incongruous signs referring to other periods of life, waiting for other seasons to be relevant, signs saying: in the event of marriage, reduce speed and drive with due caution; in the event of children, steer right and proceed with immense patience.

For Michele and Stefi are now pulling each other's hair over which of the soft toys Zia has given them is whose. Rita tries to sort them out, kindly at first, then furiously. The heat and light are getting on everybody's nerves. As a father, however, squinting against this impossible glare, I can rejoice in another difference between these holidays and those of my own youth: in those days, in England, Father was present all holiday, he saw and suffered it all, while I, like so many Italian men, am just driving my family down to the sea, the better to escape back home to a month's steady work and solitary amusement. When in Rome do as the Romans, especially when they have a tradition that turns out to be so convenient.

School ends the second week in June. The children hang up their fluorescent backpacks, perform end-of-school plays that mix self-congratulatory and politically correct messages. Stefi's is about a treasure hunt with all kinds of colourful people fighting over what is announced by a wizard to be the ultimate treasure. When finally discovered, the booty is in the form of a huge egg. The greedy treasure hunters break it open only to discover, inside, a papier mâché dove with the word '*PACE*' written on it . . . peace. An army of father photographers record their infants' bewilderment.

Meanwhile, the sun blazes mercilessly down on Via della Primule where Mario and Silvio are fixing up a television on Mario's terrace so they can watch the World Cup outside, of an evening. The children take refuge from the heat by splashing in a big paddling pool, into which, from our balcony two storeys up, Rita tips buckets of cold water. The children shout and wrestle. But as soon as they are out of the water, the sun is too hot to stay in the garden. It's thirty-seven degrees and wickedly humid. They have to return to the gloom of their rooms, where half-closed shutters keep out the sun.

The heat is all conditioning. It's not the clean heat of sharp light and shade but the sultry, dog-day variety. The sun is a blotchy white impurity in a molten metal sky. The air presses around you, so that it is more difficult to leave the house now than in the bitterest winter weather. Everybody buys big roll-down awnings to protect their balconies, and there's the problem that these must all be the same colour to preserve the aesthetic harmony of Righetti's white-stuccoed *palazzi*. In the end the decision is for grey and yellow stripes. And still it's too hot to stay out on the balcony, except perhaps late in the evening.

As July sets in, a long and elegant species of wasp arrives. The locals call them *matonsin* – little bricks. At five-minute intervals they drift in through the kitchen window and buzz loudly across the sitting room to the bottom of the stairs. In her smartest summer dress, Stefi goes to open the small, pretty, pink wool handbag she likes to carry when she goes to the *pasticceria* or more occasionally with her *nonna* to Mass, or with Natalina to the cemetery. Only to drop it in fright. There are two of those fearful beasts in there! And a horrible big lump of dirt. They have been building a nest. They are called *matonsin* because they carry little bricks of mud between their long legs. Stefi cries. She pokes her bag with a plastic arrow. It's hard when a vanity accessory turns out to be a den of stings.

On the other hand, Michele does have the pleasure of seeing a *vipera* at last. It slithers across the tarmac just beyond the automatic gate and disappears into a crack before he can find a stick. So he claims. And it was that long, *Diobon!* He talks about it for days and refuses to go out without his knife.

The cicalas drone, so loudly. All night the crickets whirr. With the windows open to get some air you have to listen to other people's televisions now dragged out onto balconies and terraces. Later, dogs bark nervously. After midnight the still air seems to hold and prolong the sound . . . of samba tonight, from the Centro Primo Maggio. It's incredibly loud! Unable to sleep for the heat, I decide to walk down to see what's going on, perhaps enjoy myself. Five adolescents are dancing without enthusiasm in front of huge loudspeakers. Village life . . .

It's hard to get the children to bed. One treat they have learnt to insist on is what Rita calls *il cambio della guardia,* the changing of the guard. It's something you can see from the big terrace balcony. Around nine-thirty, the swallows are still swooping and diving and twittering across the cornfield just beyond the garden. They have a wonderful way of making the twilight seethe, making dusk seem busy and optimistic. Michele and Stefi watch, rapt, gloating over their escape from bed, sucking iced tea through straws. Then, at some imperceptible deepening of the shadows, or cooling of the air, the swallows are no longer there. Or are they? The space beyond the balcony is still full of diving and swooping. But it's different now. In the twinkling of an eye the swallows have metamorphosed into bats. *Il cambio della guardia!* It's remarkable how similar yet how different the two movements are, the swallows communicating joy, light-heartedness, the bats, with their mothy flittering, nervousness and unease. Stefi, at six, tells me the day is like the swallows, the night is like the bats . . .

At midnight, everybody in bed at last, the lawn sprinkler system comes to life with an enormous explosive splutter and hiss, then settles into the soft shushing and ticking of modern plumbing. Stefi uses it as an excuse to get into our bed. Waking at two in the morning, I look at the thermometer in the sitting room and find it is thirty-two degrees – in the house! There's a little giggle. Turning round, I find both Michele and Stefi naked on the tiles. They can't sleep. It's too hot, it's suffocating. But I've had enough of this misery. 'Time for Mamma to take you to the sea,' I announce.

So southwards in the car. To Pescara, to *i nonni*, to the beach. First across the flat blazing haze of the Bassa Padana, then the busy stretch of road between Bologna and Rimini with its ribbon development of paint and ceramics factories in stylish modern prefabs. Until finally you're running along the Adriatic coast, and here there are tunnels and steep slopes with dramatic hilltop villages, and *campanili* and castles. Down the central reservation of the *autostrada*, a ribbon of oleanders trembles white, pink and cream in the breeze of racing cars, an astonishing gift of colour, while the fields above the road are small hillside puzzle pieces of dusty corn or towering sunflowers. How intense their yellow is, how it focuses the day's diffuse light! Rita explains to the children that sunflowers all turn like so many soldiers on parade to follow the sunshine riding high. 'Unless it's the sunshine following them,' Stefi says. The little girl is developing a flair for the poetic, or absurd. Technical Michele immediately points out that when the sunflowers aren't there the sun goes round just the same, so it can't be the sun following them. There follows a long discussion on astronomy: the sun fixed, the earth moving, the sunflowers torn between the two. Stefi gapes and says she's dying of thirst.

We're approaching Senigallia when the radio sees fit to warn us that it would be wiser not to set out on a journey in this heat. I have turned to the motorway information station, which mainly plays Muzak, reminds you to stop regularly for coffee, and unfailingly alerts you to traffic jams when you're already in them. Yes, a knowing voice says, this heat is definitely *controindicato*. It is so easy to get fractious, or even fall asleep. Don't set out unless you absolutely have to. 'But we did absolutely have to,' Michele protests. So did everybody else. The road is packed.

'Are we travelling down the boot, Mamma?' Stefi asks. 'Have we got to the heel yet?' Michele is contemptuous. 'We're not going any further than mid-calf and we're not half way there yet.'

Further south, on a hillside above the dark mouth of a tunnel, wheat has been planted in a large heart shape to decorate the steep slope of alfalfa. The children get so excited by this: a huge tawny yellow heart on the glistening green hill! And there's another! And another! The farmers must be paid by the tourist board, Rita remarks. No! Stefi immediately waxes sentimental. A heart means love, she insists. The farmers put the hearts there to say they love nature. It sounds exactly like a line from one of her school plays. Passing into a long, deep tunnel below one of those hearts, we are suddenly met by flashing hazard lights. There's a desperate screeching of brakes, the traffic grinds to a halt. Here we stay put for more than an hour.

There's been an accident up ahead. People walk up and down the tunnel. Mainly they're families going on holiday or men going to spend the weekend with families already on holiday. They fraternise. They complain. The mothers can't decide whether it's better to be stopped inside the tunnel, where at least we have the cool, or outside, where fumes can't get trapped like this. Exploring the narrow service passage between our own tunnel and the north-bound one, the children are fascinated and frightened.

Popping our heads out the other end, we see the traffic thundering by as though through the night . . .

Back in the car, Michele remarks angrily. 'This would never happen up north.' 'Never,' Stefi complains. Apparently their conditioning is now so complete there's nothing Rita or I can do to stop it. But it's interesting that when we do finally arrive in Pescara neither of the children appears to notice the things that do distinguish the streets here from those up north: the larger, more garish, more American billboards and neon; pavements absent or broken; white stop lines only a memory . . .

But the children can be forgiven their substitution of prejudice for observation. For what they are seeing, as any child should, is that we are now running along the seafront with its scores of bathing stations, its thousands upon thousands of sunshades, its white sand, its mill of happy people. We have arrived; we are on holiday. And though the sunshine is just as hot in Pescara as it was up north, the air here is fresh and vibrant. Everywhere you have the impression of zest and clarity, so that, looking left, all the brilliant colours of beach life seem to have been scissored out of sharp light and neatly pasted on the kitsch blue sea behind. You can breathe here in Pescara, you can enjoy yourself. The children don't think of any of this, but they immediately perk up and even begin to show some affection for each other. Michele will help Stefi to learn how to swim, he says. She will feed in the tokens, she promises, when he is playing his seaside computer games. For my own part, I imagine how the locals here would suffer any amount of disorganization and insult rather than move to our suffocating world of straight lines and sultry heat up north.

Stesso mare

It might be the following morning, walking down to the sea, that Stefi sings the famous little sixties song:

Per quest'anno non cambiare,
Stessa spiaggia, stesso mare.

I'd love to give the translation of this the same trite rhyme and rhythm the Italian has, since triteness, or a sort of sentimental affection for all the cosy simplicity that triteness entails, is exactly what these lines are about. But it can't be done. I'll just offer the bare bones of the thing, leaving you to look at the Italian again – *stessa spiaggia, stesso mare* – and imagine it being sung to a plonky tune by a rosy six-year-old already in her bathing costume and swinging bucket and spade in her hand, the bucket full of all kinds of little plastic moulds for making rabbits and dogs and ducks and cats of sand.

This year, don't change,
Same beach, same sea.

She repeats it over and over, having forgotten, as almost everybody has, the rest of the song.

This year, don't change,
Same beach, same sea.

Her little girl's eyes are bright jewels of pleasure as she hums Pooh-bear-like and holds hands along a street where grass grows through a seasick pavement, where a mechanic has brought his work obtrusively out of his garage – so that we have to walk round overalled legs beside a dusty Alfetta – where a railway line dismantled fifteen years ago still crosses the tarmac, still hasn't been turned, in either overgrown direction, to any more use than the feckless know to find for it late at night. Ring pulls, butt ends, syringes and used condoms abound in the grubby shale. I hurry the children past, though bougainvillea is brilliant on the broken masonry of something abandoned and there are geraniums growing wild between sleepers. Incongruously, an Arctic husky dog barks as we pass. Already suffering from the heat at eight-thirty in the morning, the fashionable animal is chained in the shade of a hanging ball of colour, a flesh-pink oleander trained up into a tree. The stench of cats at a corner is nauseating . . .

This is the Pescara scene then, its pleasures and irritations, between the exotic and the squalid. Yet the important thing, as Italians, really the only important thing, is that we have come back to the same place: *stessa spiaggia, stesso mare*, same beach, same sea. We have come here every year now since the children were born. And we will continue to come. Already Stefi is celebrating this decidedly Latin pleasure.

In Pescara when you see cars with German plates, you can feel fairly sure they're not driven by Germans. They are the cars of those who chose to give up home to find work. Like migratory birds they're always back for their summer holidays. And further down the Italian boot, where life is wilder, in Calabria or Puglia, the newspapers will report on mafia bosses being arrested because they have come home to spend their holidays by the beach they like best, near their mothers . . . The Mediterranean epic, from Ulysses on, was ever one of return.

So, what normally happens, as I said, is that Papà takes wife and family down to the beach, to an apartment, a pensione, a relative, in Jesolo, in Rimini, in Cesenatico – broad safe Adriatic beaches, shallow seas, low prices – then escapes to spend his summer at home, at least until his office or factory closes down in August and he can go and join his loved ones. Naturally, there are countless stories of infidelity; naturally, there is lots of men's talk in gyms and bars. Inevitably the media carries out useful surveys of the variety: does a prostitute's business increase during June and July when men are freer, or fall off because, being freer, they are more able to see or seek a mistress? This year, though, there's a more interesting scandal, the kind that never becomes a standing joke, because it involves . . . female infidelity. It turns out that a number of young mothers on their own with their children in Rimini have been lured into affairs with an engaging young man encountered on the beach. The man, impressively, has an apartment right on the front, where he invites them to make love to him. What they don't know is that there is a concealed video camera in the bedroom. Soon they will be receiving blackmail threats. Finally, somebody goes to the police and the story comes out, but still all the mothers remark on how affectionate the man was, how gentle, what a good lover. Unfortunately, none of the papers seems interested in finding out what the women did with their children during these assignments, something surely uppermost in many an envious reader's mind.

You flick through the summer pages. Magazines bristle with advice on holiday affairs. Nobody takes the moral line. Miraculously, the Pope knows to keep quiet for once. Apropos of some photographs of a nude newscaster with the wrong woman, a celebrity is quoted as saying he thinks that in summer everybody should have the opportunity to 'put horns on their partner in peace and quiet'.

This, then, the routine holiday, this the tang the air has for the adults, at once domestic and salty, while the children, free at last from school, catechism, oppressive heat and mud wasps, measure their distance from Mother's apron strings along the endless beach . . .

But what I'm going to tell you about now is a different summer; the summer seven years after the one that started this book. For this year, my wife, well advanced in a third pregnancy and thus beyond every contemporary Italian pale of measure and caution, was unable to come to the beach. So Papà became Mamma and took the children to the sea alone. It was the year of role reversal, the year, for me, of an initiation into an Italian world that takes up such a large space in a child's memories. It was also the year I fell in love . . . no, not with the Lolitas on the beach (with whom one is always in love), but with Pescara, an apparently unprepossessing seaside town with all the qualities of triteness and banality suggested by that little song Stefi sings as we walk out in the morning, but a town all the same that I believe has more to tell us about Italy today than all the monuments of Florence, Rome and Venice put together.

L'avventura

Same beach, same sea . . . At the bottom of the sleepy, dirty road my in-laws have inhabited since longer than anyone wishes to remember, lies the beach. We walk down there every morning, buckets and spades in hand. But before the beach one has to cross the *lungomare*, the seafront road. Aerial photographs would no doubt be able to show that there are still traces of zebra crossings every hundred metres or so along this busy road, but local drivers are cheerfully unaware of this, and the authorities do not seem eager to remind them. We stand there, Michele, Stefi and I, on the kerb as the cars race by. Nobody stops. After a few minutes' pointless patience, I make the *corna* gesture with both fists, grab the children one in each hand and walk right into the flow. Like the waters of the Red Sea, the cars respond to this gesture of mad faith. But only to this. Nothing less than complete recklessness will ever work that miracle of getting you across the seafront road at

Pescara. The children are quick to take note. South of Bologna, it sometimes seems there is no rule but gesture and response. Fortunately, on the other side you do indeed arrive in the promised land . . .

First, there's a thin line of slightly raised grass plots held in broken marble surrounds. Arrive in June and the grass is still uncut, perhaps two feet high, as if this were some ghost resort, untended for years. They get to it just before or just after the season officially begins in July. Spaced every ten yards or so in the coarse prickly grass stand the seafront palms. Some are old and majestic, some new and fresh, and some so young they seem no more than the fat tops of giant pineapples pushing out of the earth. But however old or young, these palm trees always seem to have the same size fronds, and it's this that gives the seafront its solid geometry, its sense of repeating the same pattern on and on and on, every ten yards, tree after tree after tree as far as the eye can see. Their scaly barks make you think of snakes and reptiles, of drowsy survival in torrid heat. I always feel more 'away from home' when I see a line of palm trees.

Not so the children, who ignore them.

Between the palms and grass plots there are posts bearing rusty frames for holding posters. Again, one every ten yards. Without exception the posters advertise breasts and bottoms bursting from designer bathing costumes, or young lips kissing ice creams under a lover's gaze. The images, like so much advertising in Italy, particularly summer advertising, have a slightly fifties, distinctly nostalgic feel to them – the dramatic make-up, the extravagant breasts – as if there were always some heyday to be remembered, some mythical past to be recalled and repeated ad infinitum.

Beyond the grass and the palms there's a sort of avenue, a seafront promenade, where bicycles pass, and – illegally – mopeds and scooters. At the weekends cars invade the space and park there, again illegally, and sometimes the police or the *carabinieri* come and move them all away and fine everybody and are desperately rigid and unpleasant, and sometimes they don't. The drivers risk it.

I get the kids down to the front by eight or eight-thirty. Already this is a bit lazy of me, since both my wife and *Io e il mio bambino* have insisted that the sun is best at seven-thirty. Best, of course, means healthiest, the vitamins without the ultra-violet, since the key to every official discussion about an Italian holiday is pretending that it is undertaken entirely for health purposes, whereas all the images you actually see, on those posters, on TV, and later on the beach itself, are screaming Fun, Pleasure, Sex . . .

The children want to walk along the parapet a couple of metres above the beach. In this way we proceed past the Delfino verde (the Green Dolphin), then the Orsa maggiore (the Great Bear) until we come to the Medusa. These are the bathing concessions, and the children know all their names on and on along the front towards the centre – Calipso, Sette pini, La Sirena, Belvedere, Miramare, Aurora – all their names and all their various advantages and disadvantages: the bar at the Delfino verde doesn't have fresh brioches, but the hot showers are truly hot and even have a windscreen of bamboo, an unusual feature in a country where most people will desert the beach if the breeze does anything more than stir the tassels on the sunshades. The Orsa maggiore has hot showers too, and you don't even have to pay here. But there is no windscreen, and the attendant hangs around to see that you don't push the time switch down more than twice. You get two spurts of no more than forty seconds each. The Medusa has freezing cold showers lined up in a row on a block of cement. They deliver unbelievably icy water in great swishing jets that still the heart as you step under them from burning sand. But the Medusa also has the best terrace bar, with the best *pizzette*, and the best computer games.

'And the colour of the sunshades, kids? Do you remember the colour of the sunshades on the different concessions?'

It's the first day. We're passing the Orsa maggiore and I'm holding Stefi's hand as she walks the parapet. Michele likes to lead the way, as little boys will. 'Close your eyes, now, don't cheat. See if you can remember them from last year. Oh, but you'll have to stop walking a moment if you close your eyes!'

Although the children are reasonably bilingual, there are some categories of things they will always return to Italian for: the days of the week, the months, numbers, colours, all things that have some kind of order, funnily enough, some rigid formality.

So Michele now begins: 'Delfino verde, *verde e arancione*.' Green and orange.

And Stefi: 'Orsa maggiore, *rosso e giallo*.' Red and yellow. But they argue about this because Michele thinks it is *rosso e bianco*. They stand there above me, eyes screwed shut arguing about the colours of the sunshades. On the parapet below them I notice an obscene graffiti. It says: *I peli della figa istupidiscono la gente*. Literally: 'Cunt hair drives people crazy.' Fair comment. But for the moment I say: 'Okay, we'll check the Orsa maggiore in a minute. What about the Medusa?' Immediately, the children sing: '*Bianco e blu*', and they're right, of course, because it is to the Medusa we go every year. The Medusa is the best. It is our bathing concession. Same beach, same sea. Never, never change.

I'm thinking now that perhaps the best way I can tell you about Pescara, about Italian holidays in general, is just to take you through a day, one day. Because a day in Pescara is many days, and everybody's day. And not just in Pescara either, but in Rimini, Cesenatico and Jesolo, too, and in Senigallia and Riccione and San Benedetto and every last seaside resort along the Adriatic. A day in Pescara is triumphantly representative; it reproduces itself, like the palm trees and sunshades, endlessly in time and space. For this is not a holiday such as those I remember from my own childhood where the first thing Mother and Father did was to buy an ordnance survey map and track down the places mentioned in the brochures you'd find left on a shelf by the door in boarding house or rented caravan. Then each day we would have to decide what we were doing, which walks to take, which villages to explore, museums to see, rocks to scale, all the time scrutinising the sky and saying, 'It's nice now, but how will it be in half an hour?' or more often, 'It's miserable now, but with this wind there's no reason why it shouldn't be beautiful later on,' so that in the end you set out anyway, rain or shine, often visiting a museum when the sun was powering down, or the beach when gales blew your towels away – wonderful holidays of discovery in windswept Welsh bays or nosing about those noble homes the aristocracy was just opening to the likes of us so that they could continue to enjoy their heritage at our expense; holidays of adventure and risk, of foaming surf, hard shale, precipitous paths; holidays where you might get caught in a thunderstorm far from home with father cleaning his glasses vigorously on his shirt tails and saying, 'But on the map this definitely goes on through that thicket and back to the cottage' – he prided himself on his map reading – whereas in reality the track petered out in dense bramble where an Austin A40 had been abandoned, and you would have to backtrack a mile and more under heavy rain in waterproofs that never were, and when you finally got back, exhausted from exposure, Mother heated soup from tins, fussing with the Calor Gas, and invariably she would say, 'Well, that was a good trek,' or, 'Well that was a walk and a half, wasn't it? Now, what shall we do tomorrow?' Those were holidays that made a hero of you, that made you proud of our glorious centuries of miserable weather, holidays that made you . . . English.

Pescara is not that kind of holiday.

In Pescara you don't consult maps. You don't wonder what you will do. You don't scrutinise the sky, which you know will be blue and blistering. You don't discover anything. Or not the things my parents would have considered discoveries. For although steep hills rise directly behind the town to peak in a red-and-white communications beacon that my father, like so many Englishmen, would immediately have wanted to climb to, nobody does that here. The temperature is in the high thirties, the hillside has been defaced by ugly and probably illegal second homes made from great slabs of cement and defended by barbed wire and railings and thick cypress hedges. Nobody takes walks around the town. And very few people venture up the tortuous roads to the ancient villages of the hinterland, where parking is difficult and shade at a premium. Charming these places may very well be when you get there, but who has the energy to look for them in this heat? No, when in Pescara, you stay in Pescara. Or more precisely you stay the other side of that hectic road that marks off the town from the seafront. In short, you stay on the beach, where the discoveries you may make, as that all too eloquent graffiti daubed on the seafront parapet suggests, are ultimately those that my parents would have done anything to prevent us even imagining . . .

'Adventure' – in English – a hazardous enterprise, a risk, an exciting experience, with positive and above all respectable connotations of courage and bravado on the part of he or she who risks.

'*Avventura*' – in vernacular Italian – a brief affair.

But leaving aside, if we can, the steamier aspects, the fact is that in Pescara, on this Italian holiday, you are saved the awful business of trying to get a number of people to decide on what the day's 'projects' will be. In Pescara you head off to the sea. Everybody heads off to the sea. The only decisions are: shall we take the masks and flippers as well as the buckets and spades and the air bed, and, who is going to carry what?

First day then, eight-thirty: we've remembered the names of the bathing stations, we've remembered the colours of their sunshades and now we pass through a vine-twisted arch into the Medusa, the name written deco-style in cleverly twisted metal. Here, unusually, I decide I need a cappuccino. The kids, I tell them, can walk through to where there are tall swings on the first part of the beach. They aren't happy about this. They want me immediately. They want to be in the water now! But I need a break, I'm not into the rhythm of this yet. I deploy the classic *ricatto*. If Michele wants his tokens for the computer game after our swim, if Stefi wants me to build her a sand castle, I deserve, don't I, having dressed and breakfasted them, a few moments *pausa* to get my head together at the beginning of a long, hot holiday.

The staff behind the bar welcome me. Yes, of course they recognise me from the year before. How is my wife, my father-in-law, my mother-in-law, my children? Same beach, same sea ... Same pleasant people taking your money.

I sit down at a table and stir a sprinkle of sugar into my foam. The terrace is deserted, people tend not to breakfast here. There's the softest breeze among tamarisk trees which provide a chequer of shade around the plastic tables – just as well, since I've forgotten my sunglasses. I'm just beginning to wonder how long I can leave the kids on the swings when a young mother appears with, perhaps, a four-year-old boy. Instead of walking through the terrace and down to the beach as everybody else does, she passes by my table to get to the jukebox beneath the bamboo awning against the wall that ends the terrace.

She sets the child down. She is in her late twenties and wears a lime green shift that just fringes buttocks left naked by her tanga costume. Not quite the buttocks of a girl, but almost. The child is eager to get to the beach, already whining and tugging her hand. But Mamma is stooped over the jukebox, her finger moving carefully over the titles, like someone looking for an elusive name in a big phone directory. Then she's found it. Her money must be in one of those fashionable little fluorescent pouches that tie round the waist, for she fiddles a moment under her shift. And she must be a regular frequenter of the Medusa because I know this machine takes tokens you buy at the bar, not coins. She has some. She slips one in. 'Listen to this, *ciccio*,' she says to the little boy. He deigns to stop a moment. She stands, one heel in beach sandals off the ground, one forearm raised, the position of a girl about to dance. Nothing happens. She gives the machine a little push. It doesn't go. Under her breath she says what she shouldn't – *porca puttana*! She pushes the machine a little harder. Nothing happens. The child has started to wander off now, knowing Mamma will follow. But apparently it is very important for Mamma to hear this song. Seeing the fat man who runs the concession coming in from the road, she goes over to him. Like everybody else in Pescara they exchange the greetings of people who have known each other since at least the beginning of this life. The tubby man, in red shorts and a tank top, waddles over to the machine and fiddles with something behind. The speakers crackle to life.

So what kind of song is it that our young mother wants to listen to, wants her little boy to listen to? Some nostalgic thing, like '*Stessa spiaggia*'? Or the sexier:

> *Sapore di sale, sapore di mare,*
> *hai sulla pelle il sapore del sole.*
>
> Salt taste, sea taste
> Your skin has a sun taste.

This in a languorous male voice with just the right catch in it?

Or is she going to put on some more contemporary song, perhaps thinking of the husband left behind in Milan or Turin? *'Non c'è, non c'è il profumo di te . . .'* – Not here, not here, your smell this year . . . – this one sung in a passionate woman's voice of the more uninhibited, sadly-obliged-to-pleasure-herself-alone variety.

Or even a song for someone she has just met on the beach, someone she has begun a holiday *avventura* with? *'Sei un mito'* perhaps. *'Sei un mito, sei un mito . . .'* – 'You're a myth, you're a myth . . .' – with all that word's ambiguous aura of the *non plus ultra* and the untrue.

No. She puts on none of these Italian songs, whether traditional or contemporary. She presses the buttons again and hurries off to grab her little son as the music clashes to life. There's an ominous grinding of synthesized guitars, far too loud, then an equally ersatz, parodically urgent drum beat, over which, unnecessarily raw and abrasive, an English, indeed a cockney voice starts to shout something like: 'What y'gonna be, what y' gonna do? Don't you know I gotta have you? Gotta have you! Gotta have you!' The child – dark curly hair, big brown eyes – gapes in amazement and incomprehension, seems on the brink of tears. But Mamma has started to dance. At eight-thirty-five a.m. on the empty terrace of the Medusa, she twists and turns with enviable grace by the jukebox beside the palm tree that rises from a mass of geraniums. Her shift lifts. She waves her arms. Her eyes are closed in concentrated pleasure. She doesn't even see that her little son has run off. A few minutes later, when she catches up with him halfway across the beach, I can hear her shrill voice shouting, *'Non era bellisimo?'* – Wasn't that wonderful? As I leave, the fat proprietor exchanges a fat and knowing smile.

We track down our sunshade. It's three rows from the front, four in from the walkway. Remember that, Michele, three from the front, four from the walkway. And then I notice that the jukebox mother is only two rows behind us. She's rubbing cream into herself on the lounge bed and ignoring her little boy's fussing in the sand. Sorting out the deck chairs, it occurs to me that here is a mother who will never pore over ordnance survey maps and the contents of provincial museums, who will never use expressions like, 'So what's our project for today?' or 'Well, that was a trek and a half, wasn't it!' Like the mothers in Moravia's *Agostino*, or Morante's *Aracoeli*, it is she herself who is there for the child to discover . . . an area, I suspect, where I shall be a rather poor stand-in for my wife.

La Medusa

I ask the children if they know how to say *medusa* in English. Stefi at once says jellyfish. And she is right. Medusa means jellyfish. But Michele knows that Medusa was also a sea monster with snakes for hair and eyes that could turn you to stone.

'So why are the Medusa's colours blue and white?'

They are puzzled by this. Every morning I use this kind of chat to put off the moment when I'll have to run into the sea.

'I mean why aren't they pink, which is the colour of jellyfish, or some horrible snaky grey and blood red, for Medusa?'

Michele, who is perhaps pounding on my chest or trying to bury my legs in the sand, makes the mistake of actually trying to think this one through, so seductive is the notion of relations between words and things. 'If Medusa was a sea goddess,' he begins, 'wouldn't blue and white . . .'

With more female intuition, examining painted toenails, Stefi tells me, 'Because they are nice colours.'

And they are. The Medusa is blue and white. All the big sunshades are blue and white. In segments. The deck chairs and lounge beds are blue and white. The low wall round the terrace, the bathing huts, the pedal-boats and skiffs for hire, everything is obsessively blue and white. In exactly even doses, at exactly equal distances.

In the morning when you arrive, the sunshades are still closed, limp, like still-closed sunflowers along the *autostrada* at dawn. But already the *bagnino*, the lifeguard and general dogsbody, is coming round to open them, popping them out one by one, not all together as the sun would. Each sunshade is exactly two and a half metres from the next, and at this early hour with the sunshine slanting from the sea, the shade from your shade is almost beneath the shade behind. Should we sit there, I ask Michele, in their deck chair but in our shade – the shade from our shade – or here on our deck chair but in the next person's shade, the shade from his shade? 'Oh come in the sea, Papà,' he shouts. 'Come in the sea. I'm going to tear you to pieces and feed you to the fish.'

During the day the shade rotates elliptically, as it must, starting boldly out in the open, hiding right under the great blue-and-white umbrella when the sun is hottest, then stealing off seaward as the afternoon progresses and the sun falls towards the hills. Thousands of holidaymakers drag deck chairs and sunbeds after it, or away from it, depending on the state of their tans. The beach is in constant movement.

The *bagnino* comes round to open our shade. He is followed by a girl, perhaps no more than fifteen. Tall, slim, very well endowed, she doesn't help him, doesn't even talk to him, but drapes herself on objects round about. He is eighteen, perhaps, blond and bright. They are both very aware of each other's presence, and aware of other people's awareness of that.

He opens our shade and our lounge bed and, because it is our first day, introduces himself. Then he moves on to open the other shades. His girlfriend follows, finds somewhere to drape herself, watches.

Suddenly I stand up and dash through the sunshades screaming, 'The sea! The sea!' The children come hurtling after. Behind me, La Signora Jukebox is paring her nails, or examining a mole, or searching for split ends. The sea, as we splash into it, is perfectly flat and still.

When I try to describe Pescara to English friends, when I try to persuade them to join me here, they are always unimpressed, even the ones who love Italy and who will visit Florence and Rome and Venice a thousand times. It is this gridwork of sunshades that depresses them, this routine of rented deck chairs and lounge beds, the machinery of it, the beach bureaucracy. They remember their experiences on crowded English beaches those few days when real heat miraculously coincided with a weekend or bank holiday. They remember their fear of encroachment when people laid their towels between themselves and another family who had already seemed much too near, so that they could smell the steam from their coffee flasks, the oil on their skin. It's a scene I remember all too well myself. A dog sniffs at your foot. A ball bounces over your wife's legs. And where can you let your own children play cricket? On your back, eyes closed, you sense the sunshine being constantly darkened by people threading their way through the little encampments, all but treading on your towel, as you too will all but tread on the towels of others when you return from the sea, worried that you're going to drip cold water on lobster backs or shaved arms and legs. And now there's a teabag in the sand, and here a sandwich wrapper that someone is clumsily chasing after as the breeze blows it over alarmed sunbathers . . .

On the Adriatic beach, precisely the regular distance between ample shades prevents all this. Nobody can come any closer than that, those two and a half metres. It's near, I know. But it's not too near. Anyway, most shades are rented for the summer by locals, who only come at the weekend or after work. And nobody else can take them over when they're not in use. For this is another of the *bagnino*'s jobs: to keep out freeloaders. As for sandwich wrappers, who would ever dream of bringing sandwiches when there is the bar, the lovely terrace, just a hundred metres away? People don't even possess thermos flasks, probably wouldn't even know what they were. For the litter there are litter bins every four shades or so, regularly emptied, not to mention an army of boys employed by the bathing station to keep the place clean. Every evening they go by with a small industrial machine that lifts up the top inch or so of sand and passes it through a sieve before dropping it back on the beach. So there is no driftwood either. No rusty nails in splintery wood. Seashells are only permitted right by the waterline. And when a rare wind and heavy sea brings in some seaweed, they collect that too.

The young *bagnino* toils away with a pitchfork, gathering seaweed into piles. His girlfriend leans on the shady side of the little van he hoists it into. She watches him. Her costume is a tropical cocktail of colour against cinnamon skin and she has a big synthetic pink flower in her hair. Her boyfriend hoists up heavy piles of seaweed. He keeps the beach clean for us.

As long as you're not expecting a direct encounter with nature (of the variety my mother was after), Pescara is impeccable.

But the real pleasure here, and one you won't imagine till you've experienced it, is this chance to observe the same people at play *every day*, to know where to find them and how to avoid them in this rich warren of shade and light. How would Aschenbach ever have fallen in love with Tadzio if he hadn't been able to watch him on the Lido every day, to know where he would be? In Pescara you have time to get your eye in. People cease to be just shapes, ugly or attractive; you get to know exactly how they move and gesture, what their routine is, the mothers' neuroses and the men's newspapers, the pensioners' scars. You overhear their conversation, which puts colour in bodies and faces quite as much as the sun. You learn how so and so clips her nails, how this man smokes. You find people capable of reading for hours on their backs holding their books up against the sun, others who can never find a position comfortable enough to finish a newspaper article. You see an extraordinary number of folk tackling the pages of the *Settimana enigmistica*, the *Puzzler's Weekly*, forty pages of crosswords and riddles. Even Signora Jukebox does it when she's not got her orange sanding card in her hand, searching for some part of her body to file down. It's a splendid intimacy these sunshades bring.

Unknowingly, between their swims and fights and

sandcastles, the children become engaged in this intense sport of watching each other. On perhaps the third or fourth day, Stefi will be saying, 'Why does that girl follow the *bagnino* round all the time.' Michele will say quite angrily, 'Why doesn't she leave him alone? How is he supposed to save people drowning if she's always falling over him?' They are repeating what they have overheard everybody else saying on the beach and under all the other sunshades. The *bagnino*'s girlfriend is the focus of attention at the Medusa this summer. Everybody pretends to be indignant at the way she never, never leaves him be. She sits beside him at his observation chair at the front. She lies on the back of his little rowing catamaran when he paddles out among the bathers. She follows him on all his rounds of the sunshades. Everybody is waiting for the moment when those two will start touching each other . . .

Il certificato di verginità

I plunge into the water, followed by the children. It's around nine o'clock. The sea is shallow, tepid, motionless. Yet most bathers turn back, or just walk the shallows parallel with the shore: grandmothers with straw hats and sunglasses, fat men deep in conversation. In the first stretch of water, the older boys play games of volleyball or *tamburello*. Almost nobody ventures out of their depth.

I encourage my own children to swim. I have mock fights with them. I persuade them to paddle out to the rocky breakwater and even to dive on the other side, in the open sea, where nobody goes. In doing so I am constantly aware of obeying a different cultural programming, of not being relaxed enough. Other parents just like to stand in the warm shallows, admiring their own brown skins glistening in the sun and water, ignoring their children, enjoying the mill of people near the shore.

And if someone does swim seriously, it is a boy. None of

the girls seem to swim. The girls stand at wading depth and make a gesture I don't remember seeing in England. In up to their thighs, they lift handfuls of water and let it dribble down over their bodies. They repeat the gesture perhaps three or four times. You imagine they're getting acclimatized, ready for the plunge, but just when you think they're going to plunge, they turn round and wade out again. Watching them, realising the motions are habitual, I'm reminded of something I once translated, about a mythical girl called Iphimedeia. She had fallen in love with Poseidon and would often walk along the beach, go down into the sea, raise the water from the waves and let it flow down over her body. It was a gesture of love, of seduction. And it worked. Finally, Poseidon emerged from the water, wrapped himself round her and promptly generated two children. After which Iphimedeia no doubt became just another of the young mothers on the beach. 'Do you want a banana, Benedetta? Come on, you need some fruit after your *pizzetta*. Don't throw sand. Don't bother your little sister. No, you can't go in the water till ten o'clock. You haven't digested yet. And you need some cream on your tummy, you're burning, can't you feel you're burning?'

Iphimedeia, the Medusa, the eternal return, the sharpness of figures against the light, like stark silhouettes on Greek vases, it seems one always has half a sense of myth by the Mediterranean, the land's edge is also the edge of a timeless world of Latin archetypes.

Though I'm always lapsing back into my practical workaday Anglo-Saxon mentality. Having crawled exhausted out of the sea, I'm now toiling over a huge round sandcastle in several tiers with moat and perimeter wall and secret tunnels and dungeons. It's a very English-looking thing. The kids join in. They love it, as I loved to do this with my own father and mother. So do other people's kids. A tiny Patrizia helps Stefi find shells for the battlements. Somebody's little Marcello is running back and forth with a bucket for water for the moat. Eventually, to my surprise a small crowd forms by the water's edge to admire the flying buttresses, the crenellated walls. We've got it up to about three feet now. It's a pretty big castle. People break off their strolls to stand and stare. Endeavour of this magnitude has considerable curiosity value here.

Later, back at the sunshade, we find Aunt Paola. Since we're not in Pescara for long this year, she is letting us share her sunshade, a gesture almost as generous as letting somebody share your bathroom. And given that my father- and mother-in-law are away for a few days, she is eager to help me and, like all the Baldassarre family, to offer advice. After all, it's a generally acknowledged truth in Italy that a man can't be expected to look after children on his own for more than a couple of hours.

Zia Paola is old, white-haired, slightly hunched, discreet, gracious. Her voice is pleasantly low and gravelly. And the first thing she says is not to buy mozzarella on a Monday. It would be a mistake to buy mozzarella on a Monday because they might well have been keeping it in the shop over the weekend, and in this heat . . .

Also, I should be very careful about salad. She can tell me a place where I can get good fresh tomatoes and lettuces at a cheap price.

She speaks for some time and in great detail about shopping and menus. Rather than myself, it is the children who join in, already better at discussing food than I am:

they explain how Mamma dresses the salad, which pasta they like best. Stefi is particularly eager. She always drinks some of Daddy's wine, she says.

Paola promises she will bring me some local wine a friend makes. Then she warns me that I mustn't use the towel after laying it in the sand. One can catch skin irritations in this way. God only knows what funguses there are in the sand. I shall have to wash it now and leave it to dry in direct sunlight. And on second thoughts, perhaps it would be better not to give the children mozzarella at all in this weather, not even if I buy it fresh on Tuesdays or Wednesdays, since in this kind of heat those things tend to ferment in the stomach.

Paola has been so kind I feel I must return the favour somehow, and seeing that she talks so constantly about food, I invite her to a restaurant. Perhaps tomorrow. With her daughter. But she declines the offer. She is too *fastidiosa*, she says. There are too many things she doesn't like or can't eat. Stefi says she feels exactly the same way. The little girl nods very sagely, damp hair falling over her eyes. For example, she doesn't like runner beans, and Michele doesn't like peas . . . 'You never know,' Paola is saying, 'in a restaurant, how long the food has been in the freezer, whether they've washed their hands or not, what they've put in it to make it look nice. Eating out is so unhealthy.' I decide I'd better not tell her that I am about to take the kids up to the terrace bar for their much-loved antipasto of *pizzetta* and Coca Cola.

For this is what the routine now demands: shower, *aperitivo*, antipasto, computer games, home.

I can't recall the presence of showers on English beaches, but in today's anal post-peasant Italy it is unthinkable that one should be in contact with something organic like seawater without then taking a thorough shower to clean off. More practically, there is the problem that salt on the skin can be very unpleasant when the temperature is up in the high thirties.

Here, then, is the only part of my children's beach experience that involves something approaching heroism. As I said, the Medusa's showers are cold, and what's more, powerful. Either they're off or they're full on, drenching you with a pounding delivery of freezing water. Yet everybody seems to love it. People queue up by the four showers between terrace and bathing huts. They stand under the cold water and shriek. The children dance and scream. Then, after only a minute, perhaps even less, of intense cold on burning skin, they're out already, laughing and shivering their way into bathrobes. It's as if all that excitement of contact with the elements, that thrill of endurance, hardship, all those qualities our English parents hoped we would thrive on as children, were condensed here into a few shockingly icy seconds, the better to enjoy the sensual pressure of the sun afterwards, the splendid sense of well-being brought on by bright light and colour and abundant food.

'*Una pizzetta rossa,*' Stefi says, '*e quattro gettoni.*' Four tokens.

We're standing at the bar. I order a *bicicletta,* a bicycle, which actually is nothing more than a mixture of a pink *gingerino,* some kind of bittersweet soda, and a very large glass of white wine, the kind of drink that would look out of place on a Saturday night in the Queen's Head or the Pig and Donkey in Clapham or Stoke Newington, but that winks very colourfully here in the dazzling sun.

The fat boy serving has a T-shirt on that says, I'M A LATIN LOVER. I wish him well. His mother remembers to ask where my wife is and, on hearing the news that she's expecting, expresses amazement at our *coraggio*. Secretly, I know she is imagining that this third child, six years after the second is a mistake. Every Italian adult I have spoken to is convinced of that and will be all the more so if I bother to deny it.

'It's another girl,' I tell her, since we know from the scan.

'Oh well,' she smiles, 'you already have your *maschietto*.'

It's so reassuring to know beforehand what people are going to say.

And the children's boyish and girlish personalities are so evident now! Michele has grabbed his tokens to go and play his computer game at the far end of the terrace. He's anxious to get in there before the crowd arrives. Stefi waits behind at the bar to pick up his pizza and Coca Cola for him. Then she will go and stand by the machine, and she will feed him and water him as he plays. It's touching and somewhat frightening this sweet femininity she has. Obviously, she's terribly impressed by the way he attacks the machine's buttons and toggles, generating improbable martial arts in a figure called The Vigilante, who strides up and down New York subway carriages battering well-equipped crooks. Then the other children who huddle round are impressed because Michele can read the instructions and comments in English. Especially the bit when The Vigilante finally hits the deck and a doctor appears with caricature rimless glasses on his forehead and starts pressing fiercely on his barrel chest, while red letters flash:

'If you want your hero to revive, you have thirty seconds to insert another token.' Michele reads the message to the other boys. He has a way I have never managed to cure him of of slightly over accenting the ends of the words: 'Iff you wanta yourr hero to reviv-ve . . .' so that for a moment it seems the action really is happening in the Bronx. 'You havva thirty . . .' Stefi gets in the second token just in time, then claps when a particularly ugly thug goes down under a hail of spanner blows. Her admiration, her quiet supporting presence, holding her brother's pizza and Coke, isn't so far away from that of the *bagnino*'s girl-friend . . .

All I have to do now, while the children get their daily dose of electronics, is sit and eat my *pizzetta* and drink my *bicicletta*, and wonder what I'm going to make for lunch. I sit. A large crowd of fifteen-year-olds are hanging around the jukebox, putting on favourite songs. By the end of the week I'll know which girls are going to put on which songs. For it's always the girls who put on the songs, though sometimes they may beg the money off a boy. One girl, still a child but with a woman's body and elegance, is dancing, in a bikini that says MORE ENERGY round the waistband and again on a sort of tight sash affair beneath her breasts. She is beautiful. But the boys are perfectly relaxed about it. Like the *bagnino* and his girl perhaps, it's not so much that they're unimpressed as that they haven't really noticed yet. They're eating *pizzetta* and discussing the exams they just finished. Then I realise that more interesting to them than the women are all the fashion accessories they have about them: the silvered sunglasses hung over top pockets, the gold chains round neck and wrist, the Swatches and fluorescent headbands and pin-head earrings and purple money pouches and leather key rings . . .

All of a sudden the whole group decides to move over to the other side of the terrace and the phone, where everybody crowds round the dancing girl with her MORE ENERGY costume. She is about to make an important call. She lifts the receiver and dials. As she speaks, the others mouth encouragement or pull faces. Is she phoning a boyfriend? Is she trying to get her parents to let her stay out? She's struggling not to laugh. The others are clowning wildly. And I think, one of the reasons I've stayed in Italy is that I believe, perhaps erroneously, perhaps sentimentally, perhaps merely in reaction to my own childhood of church halls and rainy weekends – I do believe that kids have a better time here, that adolescence is more fun here. Certainly I never saw a group of people so confident and at ease with themselves and their youth. I wish it for my children.

Then you pick up the paper someone has left and read a story that knocks you out, that prompts revisions. Still licking the pizza grease off my fingertips and sucking the ice block from the *bicicletta*, I've got half an eye on the kids, half on two men complaining about refereeing standards, one with AMO LUCIA tattooed on his shoulder – I love Lucia – when my attention is caught by the fact that it's the very same name as the one in the big headline on the page I've turned. 'LUCIA IMMACOLATA?' it asks.

Lucia . . . *Corriere della Sera* describes her with endearing enthusiasm as a splendid Calabrian blonde, eighteen years old, the most sought after of her neighbourhood . . . The story goes like this. For reasons unspecified, Mother sent

Lucia away to her aunt in Naples for a while at the beginning of summer. Result: everybody in her apartment block and street assumed that she was being quietly removed from the scene to have an abortion, or even to give birth. There's a nice expression in Italian here, '*malelingue*' – evil tongues, gossips – and what these evil tongues were saying was that Lucia was a slut. This distressed the mother, who was afraid that if everybody believed this slander, the girl wouldn't easily be able to get married. She thus went to a gynaecologist at the main hospital in Reggio Calabria to have him examine the girl and give her an official, yes, official, '*Certificato di Verginità*'. With this in her hand she then went round to knock on all the doors of the estate and show it to people. Her daughter was a virgin, she said. She had the proof. The rumours must stop. But this was a mistake. Not only were the *malelingue* not impressed by this, but they immediately began to put it about that the mother must have paid the gynaecologist to produce the document; and given that she was a poor woman and widowed, the only way she could possibly have paid a professional man like that was in kind . . . her daughter's, of course. Lucia went to bed with the gynaecologist to get her certificate of virginity! Understandably, this spicy paradox was all too much for the mother, who was now demonstrating that she did indeed have some savings by taking out legal action against the *malelingue* . . .

Reading this story under the shade of a tamarisk tree, sprawled in this lounge of light and shade, of dazzling colour and domesticated outsideness, I start to think about the whole question of virginity and what it might mean: is it different in different countries? I think of the age people lose it, the age my own children will lose it . . . Do I want to know when they do? No. No, I most certainly don't. And this seems to me the point of the story. That surely we should not know whether Lucia is a virgin or not. It is none of our business. And we most certainly shouldn't ask. A façade of innocence must be maintained while Lucia is allowed to do as she wishes, if she wishes, hopefully with good sense and within limits. Really, *il certificato di verginità*, like so many documents in Italian life (the one indicating the price of my house, for example), is only a rather crude means of shoring up that façade, re-establishing a generous official version that it would be folly to question. There may be elements of hypocrisy, but it does seem to me that this is the most civilised approach, and the most exciting. Lucia is a game lass *and* a virgin . . .

The girls and boys are still round the phone. Another young maiden is calling now. She has a butterfly tattooed just above her breast. Did Iphimedeia have a tattoo? One of the boys is trying to tickle the inside of her legs with a seagull feather. MORE ENERGY meanwhile has bought an ice lolly, which has made her lips swell to bright strawberry. Then the *bagnino*'s girlfriend, amazingly without the *bagnino*, comes up to her and links arms. Ah, so they're friends! And there is such a complicity and craft in their smiles, such female guile, can you really believe that they . . .

But then you see that expression in ten-year-olds sometimes, in six-year-olds even. As now, when my little daughter comes up to me, consciously flouncing her pleated blue dress, and says, 'Papà-a, o Papà-a, wake up, Papà.' She pops the sweetest kiss right on my lips, and immediately I know that she, too, wants an ice lolly. And that Michele has finished his game. Another morning at the beach is over. Now I must get back and make them lunch. Except that I'm overtaken by an extraordinary languor. Has the Medusa turned me to stone? It takes a heroic effort to recover such concepts as responsibility, to deny the children their lollies, to insist on salad and mozzarella back home.

'And it won't ferment in your stomach,' I manage to say, when Stefi objects. 'That's just Zia Paola fussing too much.' I love mozzarella. And it's easy. As we walk past three rocking horses, past the bubble gum machine, past MORE ENERGY examining some unimaginable blemish on the *bagnino*'s girl's shoulder, Michele describes with the most innocent enthusiasm how he just beat more than twenty crooks to death with a crowbar . . .

Lo chalet svizzero, la savana, il carcere . . .

The seafront road under vertical sunshine. The sense of chaos one so often gets in Italy upon leaving the ceremony of bar or restaurant for the no-prisoners anarchy of the street. We stand at the kerb. It's dangerous. I have to point out to Michele that a man on a motorbike who has both hands behind his head to adjust his ponytail (a crash-helmet is strapped to the pillion) is in no position to stop at a zebra crossing. Even if he wanted to. Wait, Michele. Wait, Stefi. Choose the driver you're going to challenge. A fat man in a Mercedes will not want his bumpers bloody . . .

Then back to the Baldassarre property, where one has to shrug off the assaults of an army of people ready to eat the children before they can eat their lunch.

How can I explain this?

The Baldassarre property covers a couple of acres of flat sandy terrain off Via Luigi Cadorna. Around the space are three buildings. One is a fairly noble though dilapidated old house overlooking Via Cadorna itself. The upstairs tenant is a mad lady. Indeed, as we approach, here comes the first thing to avoid. Having parked her ancient Seicento under the balcony, she will come out every half an hour or so and pour buckets of water over it from three metres above to keep it cool in the summer sun. The splashes reach almost across the street. They splatter the windows of the downstairs tenants, a young Persian architect and his Turkish wife, who run a late-night bar in town and hence are just getting up as we return. It's funny how the children don't find it funny, or sad, this business of the scrawny old woman with her plastic washing-up bowl taking aim from above. They merely repeat the indignance they've heard from other sources. They can't grasp the mad poignancy of it.

You enter the property fifty yards of flaking green railings further on. All the way along Via Cadorna little stones set in the flags along the street announce that the pavement is *Proprietà privata*. Householders own the land beyond their fences and paid for the pavement to be laid. Notably, there is no pavement outside Nonno's property, only coarse grass sprouting from long-broken tarmac. He didn't pay. He wasn't around when this group effort was made. On the green railing a big black arrow with yellow lettering announces 'ARIANNA INFORMATICA – 100 mt.' One day, stepping round the fast-evaporating puddles by the Seicento, Michele asks me what it means, Arianna informatica. It must be some kind of computer company, I tell him. And I suggest that since Arianna (Ariadne) helped Theseus find his way through the labyrinth to kill the minotaur, perhaps the company is proposing to offer a similar kind of assistance. Ironically, we have never been able to locate Arianna informatica. We only know that it lies or lay a hundred metres away in that direction. There doesn't even appear to be any labyrinth it could be lost in. The sign is very old.

Likewise very old is the second house that confronts you at the bottom of the path when you get in the gate. This everybody refers to as *lo chalet svizzero* – the Swiss chalet – a one-storey building whose mud and stone walls were planted directly on the sandy soil with only the shallowest foundations. Perhaps two hundred years ago. Its stucco is the colour of milk spilt on a dusty floor. The shutters are bottle green.

Here Antonietta lurks. Either she sits on her chair by the door, scrawny cat in the shade beneath her seat, or she is working at her sink, a huge stone thing of the variety one generally associates with those films of the thirties and forties that sought to evoke a fast-disappearing peasant reality. For the story about the Baldassarre property is that having inherited the place shortly after the war, Nonno and Nonna then lived most of their lives abroad, directing building sites around the world, with the result that, apart from the Persian and the Turk, the tenants are still those installed forty years ago, paying rents that have barely altered since.

Antonietta has turned eighty. She used to babysit Rita and her brothers. She is squat, buxom, frail to the point of tottering on her shabby slippers with black stockings rolled down on unsightly varicosity. Her skirt is black and her shawls are black. It's an old toothless Italy. But she's so eager to be with the new, to have the children, to talk to them, to hear their talk, to caress them, to give them sweets. She is always waiting for us.

Today she is at her sink, powerless wrists rubbing some fabric against the rough stone, for these sinks have a sort of scouring surface built in. Immediately, she smiles, waves, hobbles round to greet us. She has a present for me and for the children. From her windowsill she takes a saucepan covered with a cloth, beneath which slops a minestrone with pasta and beans. For the children there are packets of *ciunga*, a bizarre phonetic derivation of those noble words, chewing gum.

Michele and Stefi aren't sure whether they like Antonietta or not. They are frightened by the flaking skin on her face, the mottled hands. With me, despite all I tell them about respect for our elders, concern for those who are infirm, they refer to her as *la strega*, the witch. Her voice does have that wheedling seduction one associates with being lured into traps. The kids grab their gum and run. I stay to thank the old lady, wondering if I'll be able to persuade them to eat the minestrone, since I know from past experience that Antonietta has a habit of cooking everything to a mush, perhaps forgetting what life was like with solid teeth.

We now cross what Rita calls the savannah to the property's third and last building. Hidden from the street behind the front house. This is a low, two-storey block with a flat roof. Nonno built it himself in the fifties but ran out of enthusiasm, or money, or both, and never put the planned third storey and the slanting roof on. Now, with its cement grey walls and a sort of gloomy utilitarian recalcitrance, it has the air of a bunker built for some forgotten conflict, or for an overspill of unwanted refugees. We call it *il carcere*, the prison house. When a piece of what you thought was dirt darts across the cracks in the wall, that was a lizard . . .

The savannah, on the other hand, is the area of entirely untended grass between the three houses. Fig and plum trees rise above the tall weeds, and the space is split in two by an inexplicable fence whose top wire everybody uses for their washing. All the underwear and hosiery hanging there is immediately recognisable as belonging to old people. For the two top apartments of the prison house are also let out to tenants who have known no other home these forty years and more. To the left are two aging spinster sisters, Clara and Iolanda, who like Antonietta would love to gobble up the children with their eyes and ears, if only the cruel little things would stay still for a moment. When these two old ladies walk along the path through the savannah, it's as if they were leaning on each other. Neither one could make it on her own, you fear, so that if one or the other were to go down, perhaps through a collision with my rumbustious son, racing by on his bicycle, then the other would surely fall, too. But Clara and Iolanda are more educated than Antonietta. They wear more modern clothes: loose trousers and coloured blouses. At some point in the holiday we will have to sit in their suffocating living room and drink sweet coffee amongst doilies and framed photos of the dead and a scatter of religious publications of the kind that show young saints in heaven-lit ecstasy. Iolanda, the older, tells me she hasn't been down to the beach these twenty years and more.

The other top flat, approached by an outside staircase, belongs to a cripple and his wife, but they are rarely seen and far too halfhearted in their attempts to attract the children's attention. The only occasional indication we get of their presence is when the husband decides to use his crutches rather than his wheelchair to move from TV to kitchen. For we are in the flat below his, the other ground-floor flat being where Nonna and Nonno live.

Makeshift wires cross the savannah on makeshift poles. They sag from the house on the street to the prison house, from the prison house to the Swiss chalet. For Nonno has never seen why he should pay the electricity company three separate base rates for three separate buildings.

Does all this sound terribly Gormenghast and unattractive, terribly primitive and grim? I do hope not. For the truth is that Nonno's property has a charm all its own. The tall, waving grasses, the fig trees, the abandoned bric-a-brac, they instill a feeling (reinforced by fifties fittings and piping and furniture and cutlery) that time stopped long ago, that there really isn't and indeed never could be any reason for hurry. I'm pleased that the children can get to know this place. Our world in Verona is so modern and middle-class, so restrictive and clean, with so many things the children mustn't spoil. Whereas here . . .

As we're hanging out the bathing costumes, Zia Maria and Zio Franco appear. The relatives always visit more when Nonno and Nonna are away, and though they chat politely to me and politely marvel at my ability to feed and clothe two children, it's really Michele and Stefi they want to see. Franco has brought them some metal puzzles he's made. Perhaps sixty-five now, Franco took an offer of early retirement from the railways some thirty years ago and has done nothing since. Nothing, that is, if you don't count his memorising all the jokes in every week's *Settimana enigmistica* and his ability to mend fridges and broken water pistols and to invent fascinating little puzzles where you have to work out how to separate three-dimensional shapes like twisted nails or loops of stiff wire and then put them back together again. Franco is always light-hearted, merrily crouching with his arms round Michele and Stefi, his too-young, clean-shaven face inanely bright as he explains what they have to do.

Zia Maria, rotund, jolly, always brightly dressed, always made up, is most notable for her extraordinary knowledge of those sporting events in which Italy has taken part with merit. She knows all the players in the national football side. And all the reserves. She follows both the Tour de France and the Giro d'Italia. She knows the name of every Olympic gold medalist. And if the Italians began to shine at tiddlywinks, she would know the names of all the protagonists, in both the men's and women's teams, and who had a bruised thumbnail and who had been banned for using weighted winks or sniffing cocaine before a game. Zia Maria is a darling and the children love her. 'Just a short visit,' she explains, as most days, 'to see if you need something.' They offer to do my shopping for me. When I decline, I can see they're unhappy about it. They're part of that vast army of Italians who found themselves with nothing to do far too soon and rejoiced, but then are always trying to eat into other people's space. If one could adopt grandchildren, they would.

Having finally shaken everybody off – the sacredness of twelve-thirty makes it easier – I lay a table on a patch of cut grass behind the prison house under a grubby sunshade Nonna once proudly told me she recovered from rubbish in the street. And at last – the metal puzzles confiscated until afterwards – we sit down to our mozzarella and tomatoes and salad and bread. And wine.

But not without interruptions.

I am just trying to explain why Nonno's kiwi plants (to

our left) will never bear any kiwis if he doesn't tend and prune them, and then, even more difficult, to explain why people like Nonno are always starting things but never finishing them (for I should have remarked that a row of vines was once planted, too, and that a half of one wall of the prison house *is* stuccoed, and about ten yards of the main path *is* paved, and in the corner there's a shed under construction as of a decade ago that has posts and a roof but no walls) – yes, I'm just trying to reduce a vast psychological territory to something that will give the impression of sense to two infants at different stages of development, when an urgent clucking and flapping explodes inside the prison house, detonated apparently by a unison shout from Clara and Iolanda, the decaying spinsters.

Two fat brown hens come racing out of the house and rush off into an undergrowth of kiwis, vines, geraniums, bougainvillea, weeds of every variety. For when I said that the fence dividing the savannah in half was inexplicable, I meant that it was so in this: that it was never sufficiently finished to restrict Nonno's hens to one side or the other. These two animals thus have free rein of the whole property, and, not to put too fine a point on it, they shit all over the place. Iolanda comes out to tell me I must remember to keep the outside door to the prison house closed, otherwise those beastly hens go and do it right up the stairs. 'And it's illegal, Signor Tim,' she reminds me. 'It's illegal to keep chickens in an urban area.' As if my knowing this or even Nonno's knowing this, which he obviously does, could make any difference at all when Nonna is determined not only to have her hens and her fresh eggs every day, but to allow them to roam where they will. Then the truth is that Nonno actually takes pleasure in his tenants' outrage. 'With what they're paying,' he says, 'if they don't like it they can go.' He dreams of getting rid of all his ancient tenants and miraculously redeveloping the place, something that would no doubt be started but never finished. Yet whenever one of the old folk is ill, which is often, he is always ready to drive them to hospital, and when Antonietta's husband died and there was no grave for him, Nonno allowed the man to prolong his tenancy in the Baldassarre family grave in the cemetery on the hill. When I took the children up there one day to see the place, I was not surprised to find that Great Grandfather Rocco's tomb was still without a proper headstone.

Iolanda retreats to let us eat in peace. Stefi stands up and despite all my protests picks up one of the hens and starts to stroke and soothe it as if it had been mistreated, while Michele vociferously repeats what he has heard Nonna complain of sometimes, that when she's away for a few days, Antonietta steals all the eggs that are meant for us. Stefi demands that we buy some chickens ourselves and keep them in Via delle Primule. It is wonderful how it doesn't occur to children that people who install remote control gates and sprinkler systems and who are capable of spending hours discussing the exact curve of a flower bed and the varieties of shrubs to put in it would not look kindly on the arrival of a couple of grubbing, dirtying chickens. The two Italys have to be kept far apart.

When I say no, Stefi bursts into tears, hugging the chicken so hard it dashes off in fright.

Michele tells me how cruel I am.

Shamefully, I solve the situation by telling them they can have one of Antonietta's chewing gums.

Siesta

Lunch over, there's the brief farce of attempting, under instructions from Rita, to get the children to have a siesta. For while it is true that in summer, and above all on holiday, most Italians like to have a siesta, it is equally true that children the world over do not.

We lie in the room we're all sharing, roll down old wooden slat shutters (museum pieces) and start to chat. Now, what was the thing you enjoyed most this morning, children? They're kicking each other across their beds. Stefi whines as soon as the game doesn't go her way . . .

Let's play the rhyming game, I suggest. You choose a word and then have to think of all the possible rhymes. Chewing his *ciunga*, Michele immediately begins to think of words that will rhyme with the naughty words he knows: *razzo* (rocket), because then in a few moments he will feel legitimised in proudly announcing *cazzo* (prick), upon which Stefi will go into paroxysms of laughter. Or *mulo* (mule) so that he can then pull out *culo* (arse).

The room is simple. Whitewash and stone tiles. From the wall above me, as Michele swears and Stefi giggles, a heart shaped canvas of the Virgin (but would she ever have got her certificate?) looks on with motherly patience. She's heard all this and worse. And when, some time in the middle of the holiday, discussing the baby Mummy is going to have, I find I have chosen one of these siesta times to sketch out the facts of life, Our Good Lady doesn't attempt to contradict me, as perhaps she might. I give the children the gist, relieved as all parents no doubt are to have found the moment and got it over with. 'So that's how it is,' I tell them. Michele is unimpressed. He half smiles. Am I taking them for a ride? Not one of your better stories, Stefi says, and then informs me that when her friend Francesca had a little baby sister it was because their parents *bought* it for her. This is the euphemism parents use in Italy. 'We've decided to buy you *un bel bambino.*'

'Look, you can't buy a child,' I have to tell her. 'Who would you buy it from? Somebody has to make it.' But Michele is quick to remind me that Stefano and Marta and Beppe have all gone to Brazil this summer, precisely with a purchase in mind. Beppe told him they were paying ten thousand dollars to be able to bring back a child . . .

Well, okay, I decide to leave it at that. The general idea has been fielded anyway. With time things will no doubt fall into place. The kids are laughing and kicking each other, while I'm getting pretty drowsy after all the wine I've drunk. In a last desperate attempt to keep them on their beds, I suggest the association game. Who's going to start?

'*Spiaggia*,' Michele says.

'*Ombrellone*,' I reply.

'*Bello*,' Stefi says.

'No Stefi you can't use adjectives.'

'*Bagnino* . . .'

'*Ragazza* . . .'

'*Stupida* . . .'

'Stefi, I said you can't use adjectives. You have to use words that are things.'

Stefi thinks. 'What was the word?'

'*La ragazza del bagnino*,' Michele repeats.

'*Bambino*,' Stefi announces.

Perhaps something has sunk in after all . . .

'*Mamma*,' Michele picks up, predictably enough.

'*Buona*,' Stefi goes on. Another adjective. But this time I don't intervene. Very vaguely I hear their voices calling Papà! Papà! Your turn! Come on, Papà! and I know that I'm falling asleep, and that I'm damned, begging the Virgin's pardon, if I'm going to wake up for this silly game . . .

In a daze of sun and wine my siesta is a vivid dream of their games, for they get up and sneak off as soon as they realise I am asleep. I fight off a gale of shouts and screams to stay under. Vaguely, I'm aware they've found someone to play with. Samuele, the cripple's grandson. The screams seem to revolve round and round the house. It's as if one were sleeping by the hub of a funfair carousel. Something rattles on the shutters, a squirt from their giant machine-gun water pistol, the Liquidator. And another thing troubling my dreams is a vague sense of guilt, of impropriety. I really shouldn't be letting them swear so much. Michele and Samuele are yelling '*Porco Giuda*' (Pig Judah) about every five seconds, interspersed with *'Dio Cristo'* and even, unless I only dreamed it, *'Porco Dio'*, the worst. Is it the Madonna trying to wake me up to deal with this, to save the old spinsters' ears?

I sleep on, and when I finally wake towards four it may be because of the sudden silence. There's no one around. Ranging out on the savannah to find where the children have got to, disturbing lizards on the path, watching the columns of ants at work on the plum trees, I eventually hear voices from Antonietta's house. In the end the television proved her winning card. They're sitting there in another room full of Sacred Hearts and Pietàs watching a daily summer programme where stunningly undressed compères visit every beach up and down the Adriatic to get fifteen-year-olds to karaoke on a stage set right where the sea laps. Antonietta has tears in her eyes because Michele has been telling her how they visited her husband's grave. How *gentile* of me to take them! What a good husband I am! How wonderful that Rita is having another baby!

Antonietta's blouse is unbuttoned down past her bra. It's suffocatingly hot in the Swiss chalet, though the children don't seem to have noticed. Yes, she hurt her leg when she fell out of bed in the spring, but Signor Adelmo was so kind taking her to hospital. She fans herself with a magazine whose cover purports to reveal the third secret of Fatima. Meanwhile, the nymphette on the television is launching almost naked into 'Sei un mito'. She's a full semitone off the backing. And a further semitone away from Stefi's rendering. When Antonietta opens the fridge to get me a beer, I see her egg rack is full. She knows where those chickens go. The old woman pulls out a bottle of beer whose label invites me to participate in Italy's amazing World Cup adventure. How, it's not clear. Trembling, her mottled knuckles knock the bottleneck against a glass. 'Sit down.' I decide I can perhaps face about half an hour of this, maybe spotting all the bizarre juxtapositions I can and observing the way they never seem to grate against each other.

Azzurro

Another old song they always play on the radio in summertime is, 'Il treno dei desideri', or, as some people know it, 'Azzurro'. *Azzurro* is the colour of all Italian national sports teams who are always known as *Gli azzurri*, the blues. Hence, perhaps, the interest of my beer, Nastro azzuro, Blue Riband, in the World Cup. But most of all *azzurro* is the colour of every summer afternoon in this part of the world, a deep, deep azure. The first line of the song goes: '*Azzurro, il pomeriggio è troppo azzurro e lungo per me . . .*' – Blue, the afternoon is too long and blue for me . . . ('blue', it should be noted, has no negative connotations of the depressing variety clouding the colour of that sky).

It's a love song, naturally enough. How can the singer ever get through such a long blue afternoon without his beloved? Well, with the huge income from the immensely successful disc one suspects. But that's as may be. The song is good because it captures, in exactly the right gently crooned cadences, something every Italian must feel from earliest childhood: just how long, how languid, these afternoons are, and the instinctive way you know that one could never do anything more than mark time on such afternoons as this. They are certainly not made for work, and perhaps not even for love. More for respite from the one, dreams of the other, listening to languid songs . . .

Having escaped from Antonietta, we stretch out the long blue afternoon with a dream of a bike ride. We pedal down to the promenade and then along the seafront, either north to Montesilvano or south towards central Pescara and the port. Northwards, the bathing stations soon lose their lushness, their great awnings and tree-shaded terraces, their leisurely confusion of inside and out. Up here, as the town turns to stony hillside and the beach without breakwaters shrinks to a sliver, the concessions are more like frontier outposts, unhappy settlements on the edge of a luckier world, cracked imitations: a small bar, a few plastic seats that have seen better days, sunshades of the smaller, sadder, threadbare variety (that Nonna might collect for the savannah in Via Cadorna). A swing here is just a tyre hanging from two ropes. A roundabout is old tubular metal chairs bracketed to a big round wooden board. In short, out of town the front begins to take on that sort of weary, resigned, under-all-weathers look that so many British beaches have, though without, it must be said, the touching pretensions to gentility.

Then the bathing stations end and the *pineta* begins. A *pineta* is a thick stand of tall maritime pine on the sandy soil where beach meets land, the kind of pines with dramatically windblown trunks and an umbrella of dusty needles. I explain to the children that this pine wood used to stretch down the whole coast, for hundreds of miles, and that when Mummy was a little girl, she and Nonna and her brothers used to take shade under the *pineta,* not under a sunshade.

We get off our bikes and wander on a carpet of cones and needles. The trees are tall, the air very still and richly scented. A buzz of insects only insists on the stillness, the heat of the afternoon. There's even a snatch of birdsong. But almost immediately the kids begin to come across the kind of things you don't want them to – including the now ubiquitous syringe – and you have to haul them back to their bikes.

The *pineta,* its role in summer holidays, in love affairs and murder mysteries, plays such an enchanting part in the Italian fiction I love best: Morante, Moravia, Cassola, Pavese. It must have been a mysterious spell-casting place in the days when it stretched endlessly up the sun-baked coast: quiet, warm, intimate and alien. But it's almost all gone now. It will mean nothing to my children. Five hundred metres of *pineta,* then the bathing stations start again and you're in Montesilvano, a cheaper satellite version of Pescara – European flags round cement monuments and the like. There are high-rise hotels along the front here, geared to cheap package deals. The children marvel at a man and woman suffering badly from sunburn. 'Papà, Papà, those people know how to speak English!' As if this were our own special preserve, a private family language. 'They're red as *peperoni,*' Stefi says, repeating a favourite expression of Rita's. It sets her off singing another of the little songs children always know:

Ma quando tu prendi, tu prendi il solleone
Sei rossa, spellata, sei come un peperone

But when you lie under the hot, hot sun
You're red, you're peeling, you're like a pepper.

It seems a shame that these bleach-white Brits, he with a soft, young man's beer belly and she still blinking at the brightness of it all, should be herded fifteen hundred miles from Luton or Gatwick to miss the nice part of the place by only a kilometre or two, and then get fiercely burnt into the bargain . . .

But normally we avoid Montesilvano. We go south into central Pescara and beyond to the port. Riding the bike is trickier here. There is, as I say, a broad paved promenade, with people walking along it, mainly for leisure, and then people crossing it in a hurry to get to and from the beach. But there are also hordes of bikes going in both directions, and this without observing any rules of right or left, because this is not a proper road, of course, and then mopeds and scooters and motorbikes looking for somewhere to park, or simply, illegally, cruising . . . An aerial video showing how everybody manages to thread through all this without ever giving way to anybody else, but without ever colliding either, might reveal much about the Italian character.

To the right of the paving, as we cycle south, there's the strip of grass, now cut, the palm trees and all the parked scooters. Michele and I once gave up counting them at a hundred and seventy-something after only a few moments' riding. To our left are the bathing stations, quite endless – Las Vegas, Nettuno, Le Onde, Le Sabbie Dorate – and between them all the recreations each concession sets up at the top of the beach. The light is so intense that four boys playing table-tennis are flattened to silhouette. And there are tennis courts, and six-a-side football pitches and volleyball nets . . . All in all, with the promenade and the games beside, it makes for constant movement everywhere, and an overwhelming presence of flesh. For nobody is dressed, least of all the cyclists, least of all ourselves. I don't know why, but there is something particularly foreign to me about near nakedness on bikes and motor-bikes, that combination of skin and the machine, brilliant bathing costumes on leather pillions and soft calves against pressed metal. But perhaps by foreign I just mean something I never saw in my own childhood.

We press on, the children inevitably playing those games that involve having to ride over every drain or manhole cover, whether to right or left of the track. It's amazing how patient the other thousands of cyclists are, how ready to thread and weave. It's so unlike the behaviour of the cars on the road. After a while I stop yelling at them and settle down to enjoy the rich parade of it all. For the bathing stations grow nobler and grander towards the centre with great potted palm trees and flower displays outside, white tablecloths and polished wine glasses in the shady spaces within. You begin to see uniformed waiters standing smart and straight at the doors, or tending to the provincially elegant about their cocktails. There are even the twisted pillars, red lanterns and general bizarrerie of the Shanghai Chinese restaurant, inevitably emitting some cracked oriental tune. Neither the schlock façade nor the music seems out of place here in Pescara.

Next to the Shanghai is a place that seems to have been built entirely of blue tiles. It is the *carabinieri*'s very own bathing station, where the hard-working boys in uniform can come to relax off duty. Would the English police ever be granted their very own spot on the beach? And in prime space, too! I fear not. The *carabinieri* strut up and down the promenade in their splendid black trousers with the red stripes down the side, that Stefi says are only there to help them find their pockets. They usually go in pairs, as do the young girls here, and sometimes a pair of young girls arm in arm will salute a pair of young *carabinieri* side by side. There's a sunny complacency as they all shake hands, a mood of self-congratulation. Michele and Stefi weave in and out, concentrating on the trajectories between manholes, shouting about all the enemy bases they are destroying, taking entirely for granted this balmy abundance of sun and colour and beauty.

'How many computer games do you think there are along this front?' I ask Michele, playing to his love of number and measure. 'In all these bathing stations here. Come on, guess. And guess how many ice-creams there are in how many freezers.'

His eyes roll, almost causing him to have an accident. A smaller child was dragging a huge, inflated dolphin. But they're already Italian enough to avoid each other, albeit at the cost of Michele having to put a foot down.

So, I'm just getting used to this luxury of shade and light, of canvas and painted wood and cement and vegetation – laurels, geraniums, oleanders – colour everywhere, this wealth of tables and lazy revelling, when all of a sudden . . . nothing . . .

Right in the middle of the town, there's an empty space. Right where you feel there should be another Fellini set teeming with life . . . nothing but parapet, beach, sea. The impression we get, as we cycle past this hole, this vacuum, this anomaly, is that of a piece of desert some army has just retired from. TV images of Kuwait. There is litter everywhere – cans, foil, paper – and a thin sprinkling of bodies between, inert on the dirty sand, sprawled, as if slaughtered and stripped in enemy territory. A couple of dogs sniff about, a single white sunshade suggests surrender.

Why, the children want to know. Papà! Why is this ugly place allowed to exist right in the middle of town?

It's the public beach, I explain, an area where anybody can go and lie down and perhaps even set up their own sunshade without having to rent one. It's there by law, so that no one can say the beach is entirely privatised and denied to the very poor, or to those few so idiosyncratic as not to wish to be part of the group in the homely environment of their own deck chairs . . .

You don't find many Italians on the public beach. Usually the people here are Germans or Scandinavians or British, unused to the idea of paying for beach space. Often there are foreign campers parked at the top. You see sleeping bags, even the circle of a small fire. Looking at all the litter, appreciating how rarely they must clean it, I suspect the place is deliberately made as unattractive as possible so as not to harm the business of the bathing stations, whose rent provides the local government with a steady income. But mostly the public beach shows you how the pleasures of Pescara are at least fifty percent man-made. Even under the splendidly azure sky, beach and sea alone are a wasteland.

Maria,
fulgens maris stella

A kilometre on from the public beach, beyond all the bathing stations, are the river and the port. The road turns right, away from the front, to skirt an oily harbour bristling with scores of fishing boats. We turn left onto the jetty. The children have to get off their bikes here because the paving was broken up for works some years ago and has never been repaired. There was enough money to pay for a striking new monument, though. Indeed, it's been visible for most of our ride: a needle, perhaps fifty feet high, in a combination of travertine and cement conglomerate, scaly and graceless, clumsy in a way you couldn't imagine a needle could be clumsy. On top stands a concrete Madonna, the stiff folds of her gown streamlined to rocket fins, as if she were about to be blasted off into the sky. The monument was erected in the *anno mariano* – Mary's Year –

in 1954, and perhaps the paving was broken to bring in the materials, then never repaired. On the needle at eye level, black metal lettering announces:

Maria
Fulgens maris stella
Piscoriae tuere filios

Mary
Bright star of the sea
Watch over your sons the fishermen

But do the fishermen understand Latin? Cycling up the long jetty, you see the boats going in and out – *Madre Teresa, Padre Mariano, Santa Margherita* – and you wonder how strong these appeals for divine protection can be now that the vessels are big and motorized, some with automatic systems for lowering and raising the nets. *San Pietro Pescatore, Santa Lucia* . . . As they pass, wallowing in the first sea swell, the colour of many of the crewmen suggests a different faith, suggests the immigrants' search for that exhausting work modern Europeans are abandoning. There are black men winding ropes, Moroccans hauling nets. *Santa Rita, Santa Monica* . . . Fleetingly, it crosses my mind that Italians have as yet made none of those concessions to other cultures the British have: turbans on ticket collectors and chadors in the nursery. Life's bric-a-brac here is still solidly Catholic. But the sense of inertia is growing. The immigrants are milling at the train stations, and the Italians are mislaying their rosaries amongst the clutter of their economic success. I can't help feeling that this powerful modern boat thrusting out into the Adriatic with its crew of North Africans was most likely called

Santa Monica not out of devotion, but just because no-one can yet imagine any other way to name a fishing boat.

We ride along the jetty. To our right is the channel of water the boats and ships ply. The children try to read the Slav name of some cargo ship: the *Nikolai* something or other, there's too much rust to read the second part. A hydrofoil that still ferries back and forth from Croatia is tied with bright blue ropes. But to the left things are even more interesting. Along the left side of the jetty piles of huge concrete blocks have been dropped haphazard into the sea to form a breakwater. Perched out on these blocks, encroaching just a yard or two onto the jetty, are a line of what I can only think to call giant shacks. Thrown together with sheets of plywood and corrugated iron, railway sleepers, blue tarpaulin, red sheet-metal, chunks of drift-wood, old fences, road signs, they are almost house-size, a good two storeys high, projecting motley and improvised on drunken stakes out over the rocks. Above them rise poles and masts crisscrossed by an impressive schooner rigging of hawsers and stays supporting long sprits stretching out over the water.

The first time you see these shacks, from a distance, they look like a line of old wrecks come to grief miraculously upright and almost orderly on some sandbank exactly perpendicular to the shore. You expect that at any moment one or all will founder for ever. In fact, they are old concessions, licences granted way back and handed down from father to son giving the exclusive right to fish from a designated stretch of pier. Complex pulley systems raise and lower nets from the sprits out over the water. But what strikes you most – as with the farms on the hills above Verona where barns lean on cherry trees and vines twist themselves along wires stretched between shed and pergola – what really perplexes you here, is the tangle of man and nature, the shamelessly makeshift that somehow lasts forever, perhaps because it has bedded itself in so well, in the rocks, in people's minds.

Sneaking glances through a door nailed together with a jumble of planks, the children spy a dank space crammed with fishing equipment – nets, boots, knives – and then a formica table with three big bottles of wine. Back in Via delle Primule, in the allotments behind the factory at the bottom of the street, the old men have similar set ups, improvised sheds crammed with gardening equipment, boots, knives, canes, and then what look like the very same wine bottles: a couple on a table and the rest in big crates against the wall . . .

'Always such big bottles,' Michele observes.

The jetty is about three hundred metres long, with these shacks all down one side. At the end is a small beacon, then another great pile of the concrete blocks tumbling out into the sea like giant sugar cubes. It's a good place for fishing, and there are about ten people out there, mainly old men with immensely long rods armed with five or six spinners, legal here, presumably. Michele is determined to join them, but after our trips to I Laghetti I am not eager for any more fishing experiences. I try to explain that you need different tackle for the sea, surely he'd been aware of that when he wrote to Santa Lucia. This only makes him eager to possess all the equipment. Maybe sometime . . .

Michele ranges out over the treacherous rocks to get close to the action. The sea slaps in the cracks. The old men ruffle his hair. They're happy to explain all their weights and baits, how and where to cast. After all, they're here, like us, to kill the long, blue afternoon. They wear caps and swimming trunks and sandals, nothing else, and they let Michele hold their rods while they light fierce cigarettes and wave to me not to let the little girl on the rocks. 'Not *la bambina*.' Because Stefi's crazy to get out there, too. She wants to join Michele. 'Come on, Papà.' The men wave their arms: 'No, it's too dangerous for a little girl,' they shout. 'It's too dangerous,' Michele calls complacently. Defiantly, I offer Stefi my hand and head out there.

'If you catch a fish,' the man giving his rod to Michele is saying, 'Italy will win six nil tonight.' Tonight there's a game against Nigeria. The great World Cup adventure. Michele grips the rod harder than ever. He may not have enjoyed kicking the ball around in freezing twilight in Montecchio, but he certainly wants Italy to win. Intently, he winds in the line, giving little tugs as the men explain. But nothing. The men laugh. They don't expect Italy to win six nil . . .

About twenty adolescents arrive and start kissing each other enthusiastically and climbing up and down the ladders on the beacon. The fishing boats roll in and out in a long swell. Apparently it's one crew for the day and one for the night, with the changeover about now; five o'clock. The boats coming in have mainly white men on; the boats going out mainly black. And still no sign of a bite from any of the rods here on the rocks. Michele moves from one pensioner to another. Stefi and I are perched on a great cube of rock that slants rather viciously. To pass the time I encourage her new reading habit by getting her to decipher a spray-painted graffiti on the harbour wall opposite. It says:

Quello che tu vedi non è il mare
Ma il mio amore per te, Amalia!

What you see isn't the sea
But my love for you, Amalia!

Stefi is impressed by this declaration, corresponding as it does to the tone of so many children's stories and her infant preoccupation with princes and princesses (curiously, the Italian expression for 'prince charming' is *principe azzurro* – a sportsman? Hardly Roberto Baggio, one feels). Stefi repeats the words *il mio amore per te;* she savours them like sweets, like still-fresh *ciunga*. But she doesn't seem to connect them in any way with what the adolescents are up to, crawling up over the rocks and each other. Perhaps she's right. What always surprises me, though, is how Italians will go off to pet and canoodle in groups, large groups, occasionally breaking off and shouting jokes to each other. They have none of the trepidation and secrecy that seemed such an inevitable part of the package in my adolescence.

Then Stefi is spelling out something else, the name of another fishing boat rolling through the harbour mouth. At last it seems someone has decided to do without a saint's protection. With all the brashness of the modern, this sleek and powerful boat is simply called, *'Tempo è denaro'*. Time is Money.

Michele and his old men have caught nothing. Despite all their expensive equipment, the men don't seem to be concentrating very hard on the sport in hand. The conversation is all jokes about how badly the *azzurri* are playing, how shameful it was when they lost to Ireland, when they didn't beat Mexico, how the boys are spoilt and overpaid and fragile. The afternoon slips by. The azure deepens, evening approaches. Nothing is caught. Until finally somebody new arrives to show everybody how it's done.

He's a surprisingly city-dressed fellow with carefully groomed white whiskers, gold watch and chic blue-framed sunglasses. He parks his scooter by the beacon, takes his shoulder bag and walks to a pole-and-derrick affair I hadn't noticed before at the very point of the jetty, between the rocks to one side and the harbour entrance to the other. From his bag he pulls out a big net about two metres in diameter, which he rigs up to the pole. That takes about two minutes. Down goes the net with the aid of a pulley system. The time to smoke a cigarette drawn from an elegant silver case, then he hauls up, nonchalantly. Three sparkling fish! Out with them, wham them over the head with a short stick, away in a plastic bag . . .

'Papa! Papa!' Michele comes scrambling over the rocks at great risk to life and limb. 'Papà, he's caught some fish!'

This is exciting. The rods are forgotten. The new arrival smokes his cigarettes, tosses the stubs in the water, raises and lowers his net. The next three casts are in vain. The little crowd that had formed begins to disperse. But at the next attempt out leaps a truly grand fish, perhaps sixty or seventy writhing, wriggling centimetres of silver scales and colour.

'Porco Giuda!' Michele breathes in admiration, and I haven't the heart to correct him. I'm impressed myself. A fearful bash with his stick and the man takes the thing to a little door in the base of the beacon on whose cracking grey paint, it seems, he marks out the size of the biggest fish he catches. This one is just marginally smaller than some fading marks of a while ago. There are cries of awe from the adolescents who have broken off their petting to watch. The older fishermen who just haven't been trying hard enough gaze stonily out to sea.

It's another concession. The city man pays a tiny rent for the right to haul up these fish. Doubtless his father had the licence before him. Nobody else is allowed to rig up their net to this pole, though I bet they do sometimes.

Cycling back, that fish grows bigger and bigger in Michele's mind, the man's skill greater and greater. The way he grabbed the thing from the net! In both hands. How big and powerful it was! How it fought and jumped! By the time we've finished our ritual ice-cream at a bathing station with a stunning red-and-yellow awning that turns our faces burnished gold, the fish is about as long as Michele's arms will spread. My attempts to explain the difference between the sport and skill of the old men and their rods as compared to this leisurely massacre of nets and sticks, fall on stony ground, or rather, sinks into deep, deep water. After all, the old men caught nothing (I feel they let me down somehow; they could have given my son a better education).

'There's nothing wrong with nets,' Michele insists, 'the fishing boats use nets.' 'Yes, but at least they risk their lives,' I say, 'going out to sea all night.' I explain the words on the monument. Maria, *piscoriae tuere filios*. 'They go way out to sea, and if there's a storm maybe they don't come back.' Michele is decidedly unimpressed. As with our experience at I Laghetti, it's the sure catch he dreams of, the certainty of success. Like those thousands of Italian hunters who shoot at pheasants released ten minutes earlier from a farm. Or the old hands at the gravel pits, using forbidden spinners. Or the football experts who rejoice when the other team's star is injured and absent. No

Tom Sawyer, Michele sees little virtue in doing things the hard way . . .

Umidità

'What are you up to now?' We're almost back at the Medusa when we run into Zia Paola and her daughter taking a walk. Still living at home, Fulvia is one of those Italian girls whose boyfriends have been saving up to marry for a decade and more. She is thirty-two, but, arm in arm with her mother, looks twenty-five. The radio will tell you that nearly forty percent of Italian thirty-year-olds still live with their parents.

'A last swim,' I explain. I have the bag and the swimming stuff strapped to the back of the bike.

'You really shouldn't,' she says, kind and worried. And adds, '*Troppa umidità.*'

Too much humidity? To go swimming! Here is one of those wonderful moments where I simply don't understand, while the children do. It's not that I can't grasp the meaning of the words. Nobody could speak more clearly than Zia Paola. It's their applicability that eludes me. How can it be too humid to swim? I don't know. I smile and wish mother and daughter a pleasant *passeggiata*.

Walking down to our sunshade, Stefi explains. 'She means the air is so damp we will catch cold when we come out of the water.'

I hadn't noticed, but the late afternoon, early evening, is not so blue as it was. Six-thirty. The slanting sun has found a grey haze in the sky, the breeze has dropped, the air is indeed slightly moist, limp. But the temperature is definitely still up in the thirties . . .

Is this obsession with imagined hazards just a way of showing love?

From her inevitably supine position at the sunshade two rows behind ours, the jukebox mother is telling her boy and somebody else's child that they can't go in the water because they ate so late. She speaks with her eyes closed but the voice is firm. She told them not to eat late, but they wouldn't hear of it. They kept playing. Well, now they can't go in the water. They would drown.

How late did they eat, I wonder. And how much? And why are they still at the beach if they can't go in the sea? The older child runs around whooping and kicking sand over everybody. The mother ignores him, adjusting a silk scarf drawn tight round her thighs. He is perfectly free to misbehave, but not to risk his health.

Then I notice that my own children are speaking to each other in much the same way. Stefi says, 'Michele, you'll have to take your towel down near the water so you can put it round your shoulders as soon as you get out.' 'Don't forget your flip-flops, Stefi,' Michele replies, 'or you'll hurt your little feet on the shells.' It's asphyxiating. And so endearing.

'Michele, you've forgotten to put your suncream on,' Stefi is saying. At six years old! Having just explained to me about the humidity!

We change. There's the old shout of *Cocco!* and the clanking of a bucket, but we don't buy. Coconut would be heavy on our stomachs before a swim. Wouldn't it? The way to the sea is thick with the back and forth of *tamburello*, and some men in their forties and fifties are playing out tonight's big football match, as I remember doing as a boy. 'Albertini to Signori, Signori to Baggio, beats one, beats two, *gol!!!!!*'

'No, it went over the post,' the tubby white Nigerian keeper objects. The post is a green Benetton sweater with fluorescent document pouch for greater definition. The men argue like children about whether it was a goal or not . . .

In the water, a fashionable mother is taking advantage of that honey-look low light spreads to make photographs of her lovely daughter. The girl, perhaps eight or nine, is on a silly inflatable boat with some kind of pedal-paddling affair at the end. Quite unnecessarily she is wearing a bikini top, and she lounges back on the boat voluptuously, hands behind her curly head in a pose television has taught her. The mother crouches in the water with her automatic focus camera, seeking exactly the right shot to frame for some living room shelf in Milan or Turin. But the current drags the boat away. 'Pedal!' the mother shouts. 'Try and keep it where it is.' The girl complains that turning the pedals brings up the seaweed that drifts and laps about in the shallow water. The seaweed is scummy. She won't touch the seaweed! So mother, who has a la-di-da Milan accent, has to come and drag the boat herself and turn it round to have it in the exact right relation to the sun. Then she fusses about her own shadow falling in the picture. Aim, frame . . . too late. The boat has drifted again. The girl refuses to pedal. She seems to be mocking a mother willing to make so many sacrifices for that photo to show off to friends. Perhaps rightly so. The hell with photographing one's children. And it goes on and on and on until finally the snap is snapped, and mother brings the pink and white boat safely to shore so that the little lady will not have to put her feet in amongst the seaweed. Then with a great sigh she slumps into a deck chair and lights a super-slim cigarette.

Why do I secretly hope that picture won't come out?

We splash towards the rocks, past the sign announcing LIMITE DELLE ACQUE SICURE, into the adventure of three or four feet. The children have invented a game called *bruco marino*, sea caterpillar. This involves Papà lying on his belly on the bottom of the sea while they ride or stamp on his back. As he worms caterpillar-like amongst the crabs, he can just vaguely catch through the tepid water the song they have invented to accompany their ride. *'Il bruco marino, ha perso il codino, ha perso il culino, non riesce a cagar.'* The which, translated, will seem even more mindless than in Italian, lacking rhyme and diminutives: The sea caterpillar has lost his little tail, has lost his little bottom, he can't poo.

I prefer not to speculate on whether, since I am the caterpillar, there isn't some awful Freudian significance behind this, or some reference to the whole problem of Italian anality. I plough on, underwater, allowed up for breath every forty seconds or so, until, emerging much farther out than I had meant, we are all witness to a scene that is conclusion and climax, as it were, to one whole aspect of the holiday. The children's discovery of ... well ...

Or let's put it this way: on this, the last day – for as I said all days are one here, and this the last as much as the first – on this last day of our holiday, the mystery of the *bagnino* and his girl, always together but never quite touching, is finally resolved, and in such a way that seems quite deliberately a show for us, an education for the children.

Moravia would have loved it.

We're in about five feet of water, quite near the big rocks, with the children treading water or swimming or hanging on to me. I am finally allowed up from being a sea caterpillar and we turn back towards the shore. Only to find, no more than ten yards away, the *bagnino*'s *moscone*, his little red catamaran lifeguard's skiff.

The *bagnino* has rowed out from the beach despite the fact that there are very few people in the water (doubtless because of the dangerous humidity). As always, his girl is with him in her tropical cocktail bikini, so fetching against the warm buttered toast of her fifteen-year-old skin. They are not touching. He has his job to think of, his responsibilities. He can't hang around snogging in groups like the lucky lads on the jetty. But now, very suddenly, perhaps a hundred yards out and with the boat facing away from the shore, they both slither into the water off the front. That is, they are now standing in five feet of water between the two prongs of the floats that form the front of the catamaran, perfectly hidden from the shore by the built-up wooden platform and slightly elevated rowing position designed to give a *bagnino* the view he needs over waters where babes may be drowning. She stands with her back to the platform, arms over the floats to anchor the thing, he is turned toward her, and thus able to keep half a wary eye on the beach and his boss, the owner of the bathing station. Then they get down to it. They attack each other quite savagely. But the odd thing is that they do this knowing full well that we, almost the only bathers in this damp late afternoon sea, are only perhaps ten yards away, and in the fullest possible view. And knowing that the children, who they have seen with me every day, are young indeed and that I am a respectable adult client of the bathing station. It's as if, having screened themselves from the shore, from the *bagnino*'s boss and any locals who know the boss, they don't give a damn who sees them. All that not touching, the long hot days in and out, the azure blue afternoons, must be trying indeed.

They devour each other.

This time Stefi says with frank appreciation: '*È l'amore*' – it's love – thus distinguishing it from the kids on the rocks. Is she thinking of that graffiti. Could this actually be Amalia? 'It's not the sea you see . . .' But Michele, in the way little boys have of being sworn enemies of romance right up to the day before they're about it themselves, is outraged. 'How can they do that,' he shouts. 'How can they? When the *bagnino*'s supposed to be watching people in the water. What would happen if someone was drowning now, crying for help?'

Simultaneously, both the children have the same idea. In a gale of giggles, treading water, they both cry, '*Aiuto!!!*' Help! '*Aiu-u-to-o-o!*' waving their arms and trying to get the *bagnino*'s attention. They're laughing so hard they can hardly stay above water. Stefi gasps, goes under, gets a mouthful. An excellent imitation of someone drowning.

But the *bagnino* doesn't even turn, so determinedly are those two making up for lost time. 'Stop, kids, I insist. Stop, that's not fair.' I take them back to the shore, play the whole thing down. 'Quick, we'll have to get dry before getting damp!' But you can see they are impressed by the event. It's this bathing station situation that has done it, the intimacy it generates, the way you feel you know people, the way you watch and speculate. They would hardly have noticed had it been two people we'd never seen before. Now they will talk about it for ages, though I never hear them connect it with what Papà told them about how Mamma's baby came about. We are such strange animals in this sense. We have such ways of knowing and not knowing, communicating and not communicating. This, I suspect, as with the Calabrian girl's debatable virginity, is how it should be.

The beachgoers are gathering their magazines and tanning oils and departing, fussing with their clutter of towels and spades and the inflatable toys they can't bring themselves to deflate, otherwise they'd have to blow them up again tomorrow. The Medusa's cleaning team are setting out, closing and tying the sunshades in case there's a late-night storm, starting up their sieving machine to pick up the cigarette stubs and ring pulls.

We set off. Despite the damp, the children insist on their cold showers. I chicken out. I'm not that crazy. While I wait for them, I read a notice by the cabins headed *Capitaneria di porto* (Port Authority). Every bathing station is obliged to have one. Poster-size but written in print fit for a paperback, it gives an impressive list of rules expressed in exquisitely legal language regarding the duties of bathing stations, the lifeguard service, boating rights, bathing rights, fishing rights, first-aid equipment, safety measures, etc. I'm just checking that the *bagnino* was indeed in flagrant disobedience of these rules when the PA comes on. The *piccola bambina* Marcia Maroni has got lost. Has anybody seen the *piccola bambina* Marcia Maroni, and if so could they please take her at once to her parents, who are anxiously waiting at the office of the Medusa bathing station.

A little child is missing! The awful thought comes to me that someone may indeed be drowning while our *bagnino* is still canoodling. And I feel he just doesn't deserve that. It's not fair. I'm anxious for him. Then the message repeats. *La piccola bambina, Marcia Maroni, di quattordici anni* . . . The little girl, Marcia Maroni, fourteen years old . . . I smile with relief. How flexible that word *bambina* is! More likely Marcia is the *bagnino*'s girl rather than somebody he is supposed to be saving.

The kids come chasing out of the shower, and the first thing Stefi does is run to the path to look down between the sunshades to the sea. Yes, the *moscone* is still there, she cries. They giggle. But now I notice something else, too. On the pole beside the *bagnino*'s chair the red flag is up, to announce, according to the rules of the Capitaneria di porto, a potential bathing hazard. The smart blond boy has covered his ass. So to speak.

Caporetto

Cycling back from the sea, seven-thirtyish, Michele notices the name of the street for the first time: Via Luigi Cadorna; while I observe that someone has come along and painted white circles round the drains. At last they're going to lift the damn things so that they don't lie a treacherous foot below the present level of the tarmac.

'Who was Luigi Cadorna?'

Stefi is cycling round and round one of the painted drains in her little blue dress.

'Luigi Cadorna was a *maresciallo*, commander in chief of the Italian army in the First War.'

Michele wants to know more.

So I have to tell him that Luigi Cadorna was held responsible for Italy's greatest and most costly defeat of the war, Caporetto. It was such a disaster that the name Caporetto has become synonymous with cataclysmic defeat. And when some corrupt politician is voted out of power, or some opera singer is booed out of La Scala, the newspapers will invariably say, that was so and so's Caporetto, that was the end for him.

'Why,' Michele asks innocently, 'did they name a street after this man, if he was responsible for such a defeat?'

This is an excellent question, though looking at what kind of street Via Luigi Cadorna is – the broken paving, the abandoned railway line, the litter, the sunken drains, the often overpowering smell of cats – one can perhaps understand. Instead I tell him that Nonno agrees entirely, with Michele's perplexity that is. Indeed, Nonno has twice written to the town council asking for the name to be changed, objecting to having to live on a street named after someone who was not only incompetent, which is to be expected (my father-in-law does not have a high opinion of the men he fought under in the Second War), but who is *widely perceived to have been so*, which is far worse.

But I'm overdoing it here. Michele can't understand what I'm talking about.

Look, I tell him. Lots of people think the Italian football trainer Arrigo Sacchi is incompetent, *non bravo*. If Italy win, they won't say so. They'll say he's *bravo*. But if Italy lose, especially if they lose tonight against a team like Nigeria, then everybody is always and forever going to say he is incompetent, even if he wasn't.

How almost fateful those words were!

And how speaking of the devil can conjure him up! Not Luigi Cadorna, fortunately, nor Arrigo Sacchi, but Nonno. For when we return we find him sitting under a battered sunshade on the edge of the savannah reading a letter. Nonna is in the deep grass making little jumps at the fig trees. As always their appearance is unannounced and unexpected. They weren't able, they had said, to be back during our holiday.

There are the usual extravagant embraces, expressions of undying affection, of admiration at how wonderful everyone looks, and it occurs to me that, as with the strict routine of almost every aspect of Italian life (and this holiday has been no exception), so this predictable and required theatricality is another way of helping people to live well. Never is it easier to be oneself and relaxed about it than when you know exactly what is expected of you. There is so little that has to be decided here, either in what you do or how you do it: you take the kids to the beach early to get the healthiest of the day, you shout at them and smother them in affection, you have your *pizzetta* and *aperitivo* at 11.30, the shadows move in precise ellipses round the sunshades, you embrace your mother-in-law warmly.

'Oh, Tim,' she lies. 'You're my favourite son.'

Leaving me with a bowl of fresh figs, Nonna takes the kids off through the deep grass to find where the chickens have laid their eggs. She wears a battered straw hat, a wide skirt, a T-shirt. At seventy, there is still something girlish, certainly capricious, about her. The way she walks you'd say she romps. The children romp after her. 'Nonnina, Nonnina!' they cry. She turns and caresses them again and hugs them and ruffles their hair and pinches their golden skin and says how much she'd like to eat them alive – her *nonna* always used to say that, I'll eat you alive – and how sorry she is they couldn't be here during our holiday, but they had to look after – surprise, surprise – a sick relative. Now where has that silly *pìopìo* laid its eggs. Silly chick chocks. Her *nonna* always said chickens could be intelligent, but never when it came to laying their eggs. Where can they have put them? Antonietta, I notice, has retired to the crack between her shutters.

I go and sit with Nonno. He wears khaki shorts and shirt, revealing his fat, freckled legs, his fat, freckled chest. The buttons are straining. A hat, even more battered than his wife's, is tipped back on a round, freckled forehead. He pours liberally from a supermarket carton of table wine, lights a Camel Light. I realise he is upset about something.

What?

'Children. Oh, children, *caro mio*,' he says. 'What else.' He tips back his hat even further. 'You're crazy having another,' he says frankly. 'Crazy.' He shakes his head.

I point out that he had three.

The rotation of the headshake increases and seems all the more impressive since the man has no neck. 'I didn't say I wasn't crazy.'

I wait. The fact is that Nonno loves mysteries. He loves setting you up, then not telling you things. Retaining an area of independent operation is an important principle for the Italian male. Nobody, for example, has ever known the extent of my father-in-law's income or bank balance. No one ever knows where he goes when he goes on a trip. It's not unlike the question of Lucia's virginity.

I decide we will call our next child Lucia, since we know it will be a girl. If Rita agrees. Lucia is a lovely name. She'll have her saint's day when the presents get handed out . . .

When I have the patience not to ask any questions, but just to accept some wine and a cigarette, he finally says: 'In my case though there were mitigating circumstances.'

What is all this about? His short trousers, I notice, round

his huge girth, have a tag proclaiming the brand name: Old Dog.

'In the sense,' he reflects, 'that mine was the first generation this happened to.'

What happened? But I don't ask.

From across the savannah come excited cries in the evening air. They have recovered an egg. An egg! *O bravo piòpiò!*

I remark that the neighbours have been complaining about the hens shitting on the stairs. That cheers the old man up. We laugh together. Another cause for optimism, I tell him, is that they've been painting white circles round the drains on Luigi Cadorna. They must be going to fix them up. His laugh turns to derision. 'No, *caro mio*, what it means is there is a bike race passing through the street. The riders have to be warned about the drains, since if they hit them that would be the end of their race. So they paint circles round them, but they don't fix them.'

'Ah. Perhaps the mad woman will throw a bucket of water over the cyclists.'

Again he laughs, but is not to be brought out of his depression. Not even when I peel a fig and split open its pulpy redness for him. After another silence, scratching lightly, he says the point is that these days, not only do you have to support your kids in their infancy, but throughout their lives as well. *Ecco il problema*, throughout their lives to the bitter end. In the modern world there is never a moment, never a situation, when you're not responsible for your kids, when you don't have to satisfy their enormous appetites. He stubs out his cigarette. Since that wasn't true for him when he was a child, he can be forgiven for not foreseeing the way the world was going. Whereas I should have been wise to the thing.

He begins to list, though clearly this is still not the nub of the problem, all the *sacrifici* he has made for his children: taking them round the world with him on his international assignments, always giving them vitamins and iron and whatever was supposed to make them healthy, always paying for the best medical treatment money could buy, always finding the best schools, supporting them through their university education, paying the rent on their flats, paying while they were unemployed, paying while they were employed but not properly paid (as so often happens in Italy), even paying off their debts, contracted without his knowledge . . .

The list goes on and on, with a mixture of genuine complaint and resigned humour. And is it over? Is it over? No it is not over!

So here we are at last. I wait a little more, and finally he has to tell me. When he returned home, he found two letters waiting for him. He pulls them out of the top pocket of his shirt. He doesn't know which has made him more depressed. 'You want to write about Italian children?' he says. 'So read.'

They are letters from the twins, Rita's younger brothers, the children's beloved uncles, with whom I am on excellent terms. The first is from Renato in Rome. Typed, it expresses itself in somewhat bald terms, which are listed one by one, like the research projects in Michele's school, like the little boy's essay on fishing.

Point one: Nonno's property, if sold for development, would be worth a fortune. Point two: this property belongs to the whole family, not just to Nonno, for the whole family had to make *sacrifici* in order for Nonno not to sell when times were hard (here Renato remembers, apocryphally, Nonno insists, a time when they had to use newspaper to wipe their bottoms). Point three: it is ridiculous that the children should have to wait till Nonno's death to enjoy their inheritance. Taxes would wipe out a great deal of the money and they would be too old to enjoy it. Point four: given all of the above, it is Nonno's *duty* to his children to sell *now*. ('Duty' and 'now' are underlined.) Point five: with some of the money he can buy himself an *appartamentino*, quite big enough for himself and Nonna.

Nonno is shaking his head.

'A veritable Caporetto,' I remark, since I have this on my mind.

'No, two,' he says. 'Two!'

As if after Waterloo there were anything left for another Waterloo!

The other letter is from the twin in Verona, Roberto. He is about to marry and hence needs to buy a house. The *fidanzata*'s parents have offered a sum of money, but only on the condition that his parents make an equal contribution. Since this is a major moment in his life, he feels he has a right to expect that Nonno do his duty and . . .

They don't grow up, the old man protests. They hang on to Papà and Mamma forever. They don't even want to be independent. Half of them are still at home at forty. Still being served hand and foot. They think they're owed everything. They see other parents buying their children houses, so they think I should too. I'm supposed to bleed myself dry for their pleasure. I'm supposed to move out of my own house for their satisfaction. He makes a graphic gesture of one opening his wallet and just emptying the contents all over the ash path.

'Tieni famiglia,' I tell him.

He grunts.

I suggest their behaviour, albeit selfish, is only human. It's true that most parents are buying apartments for their children. It's true of at least half the couples up our street. Not to mention the fact that everybody seems to speak obsessively of duty in this country . . .

Nonno splutters, pours more wine, lights another cigarette, then, in a manner I like so much in him, he suddenly relaxes. He sits back on his chair, lifts his feet to another chair pushed against the bougainvillea, crosses his chubby legs, tips his hat forward over his baldness, grunts, laughs.

'What are you going to do?'

He reaches forward, still from his reclining position, takes the letters and very deliberately tears them up, replacing them in neat piles on the table.

'Niente,' he says. 'Nothing. I forget they wrote, they'll forget they've written.'

If only Luigi Cadorna could have done the same after Caporetto.

Then staring right in my eye from his own twinkling blue, he announces, as if it were the world's greatest truth, *'Gli schiaffi dei figli sono carezze per i genitori.'* It's the ultimate statement of the *sacrifici* principle: 'A child's blows are caresses for the parents.' After a silence of about ten seconds we both burst out laughing.

Nonna returns with two eggs and a tirade against Antonietta, whom I just saw her embracing warmly. The children fire their water pistols at columns of ants climbing the cracked stucco, at lizards soaking up the very last eight o'clock sunrays. Then it's dinner outside: ham and figs and boiled eggs and salad. But even after such a long day, even with the prospect of Italy–Nigeria at ten o'clock, the children are still not satisfied. So Stefi begins a seduction job on Nonno. She sits next to the old man and strokes his hand as he breaks open a *panino*. She snuggles up to him. He asks for a kiss, but she doesn't give it to him. Our holiday has doubtless heightened her sense of the value of her kisses. I've noticed she's been withholding them from me. Or rather, she's been dosing them out. She's applying the *ricatti* principle and knows she can do it more effectively than her older brother, who just bounces about and demands things. Perhaps this is the difference between Rita's relationship with her parents and that of the twins . . .

'Won't you take us to the *patatine*,' Stefi simpers. 'It's our last night, Nonno. Please take us to the *patatine*.'

Patatine are chips. There's a man who parks his van along the front near the Medusa and sells chips and Coca Cola, beer and hamburgers.

'I'll give you a kiss,' she says, 'if you take us to the *patatine*.'

And whereas children hate it when they're being blackmailed, when they have to give something to get something, adults love it. Nonna is most impressed. '*O la ciccinina!*' she laughs. '*O la civetta*, the little flirt!' And she says her grandmother used to say that while everything had its price, a kiss is always priceless. This seems somewhat inappropriate when Stefi has just indicated the tag with such cynical precision: about seven thousand lire for two portions of chips and two Coca Colas. But of course, if I say something to that effect, I will be accused of *la tipica freddezza anglo-sassone*, typical Anglo-Saxon coldness. I know that this is what is said about me among other members of the family . . .

As it turns out, not only has Nonno got the price of a kiss, but actually thinks it's cheap. He stands up, thrusting back a chair held together with rusty bolts, and in all his tubby majesty raises a dramatic arm, as if ordering a charge.

'To the *patatine*!' he cries.

Stefi echoes, 'To the *patatine*!'

Michele shouts: '*Avanti popolo*!' which is how the Red Flag goes . . . He raises his water pistol and aims at one of the chickens grubbing along towards him. Nonna is furious.

So it's back one last time along Luigi Cadorna, by the freshly painted circles for the cyclists to avoid, over the railway line, across the lethal road to the front, where the man in his van has rigged up a portable TV to watch the World Cup and gives a running commentary on something like Switzerland–Spain while forgetting whether we wanted ketchup or not, whether we wanted Coca Cola or not, and how many beers. How many beers? Because Nonna and Nonno and I are all having beers. 'Give me a portion of chips too,' Nonno confuses the man further. 'Me, too,' says Nonna. Once a festive spirit has begun there's no end to it. Michele reaches for his chips, and as he does so, I remember how high up, as a child, how very high up, ice-cream men and hot-dog men always used to look in their vans, and how this somehow gave one the impression that they were bestowing largess, that they were toweringly generous. Whereas the generosity in this case is . . .

'Mine,' Nonno says, going for his wallet. But I'm Italian enough now to know this can't be allowed. This would put me in a very bad light.

'No, I'll pay.'

There follows the usual back and forth, conducted with the usual over-the-top insistence, and always with the implication that the other person is being ridiculous making an offer. 'Oh, come on, don't be silly.' 'Not at all, not at all. It's my invitation.'

Grabbing their chips, the children ignore us. They are asking about who should have the blue plastic fork and who the pink. Did the *patatine* man really give Stefi a pink fork and Michele a blue on purpose? Surely he is too distracted by his game. Someone has scored, or nearly.

'*Porco Giuda!*' Michele shouts.

Nonna laughs indulgently. But she could have killed him for spraying her chickens.

And I pick up the tab, as I always knew I would. It's risen to fifteen thousand lire since the earlier estimate. Extortionate. The price I've had to pay, I somehow can't help thinking, for the kiss Stefi saw in the sea, or all the kisses of all the Marcias and Amalias that appear to have inspired her.

Tengo famiglia.

Tradition has it that you eat your chips sitting on the low seafront wall by the six-a-side football court. One might think that a better place would be the terrace of the Medusa, but as if to show that Italians don't always have good taste, this is lit in the evening by low-slung fluorescent lights, which, like Gorgon's eyes, turn all to stone beneath them, while the lovely trees and all the soft rustling shapes of the place are lost in ink above.

So we sit and eat and drink and watch the floodlit six-a-side teams. They are brilliant. They play with such style, such panache, and so cleanly. You wonder if some of these local boys shouldn't be immediately enlisted among the *azzurri*. Everybody gets excited by the game, and the children want to know who you're rooting for so that they can root for them too, except that mostly Michele wants to root for the team that will win.

'*Evviva i rossi!*' he finally decides when they score a goal.

The crowd is still sauntering back and forth along the front, as it has since eight this morning. The traffic is still booming. People are still in their bathing costumes, perhaps on bicycles weaving in and out, or in each other's arms, or holding the handles of their two-year-olds' tricycles. Only towards the fatal hour of ten, does the crowd suddenly disappear, the evening suddenly grow quiet. It's time for the big game. The *patatine* man is left in peace . . .

And of course, Nigeria score first. And Italy don't score. And the game goes on and on and on, and still Italy don't score. And don't even look like scoring. Until Nonno and Nonna begin to say the same things about the *azzurri* they have just been saying about their children. That they're all spoilt kids. That they've been given too much. Too much money. They think everything's due to them. They don't try. Everybody in Italy has got too rich since the war. They themselves stayed away and travelled the world and didn't get rich at all, and then when they come back, what do they find, they find everybody is rolling in it, everyone's rich and spoilt and the national team can't beat the Africans . . .

Still the *azzurri* don't score. I fear this game bodes ill for the twins and their financial requirements. I try to distract my in-laws with some linguistic reflections. 'Notice how the commentator always says *intervento regolare* – fair tackle – when an Italian makes a dubious tackle that the referees lets by, and then *intervento giudicato regolare* – judged fair – when the others do it. With the obvious subtext . . .

But nobody wants to hear this kind of remark. For still Italy haven't scored. It's nail-biting. It's unbelievable. The *azzurri* are going out. To Nigeria! Michele starts to get quite angry with me because I don't care enough, because I probably want Italy to go out. I'm not Italian. But he is. He's Italian, and he wants Italy to win. He's in tears. I actually feel guilty – it's the first time he's shown any national feeling of this intensity – and I have to insist that I do want Italy to win, though the truth is I find the commentator so unpleasant and smug I'd just love to hear what he'd have to say when . . .

More sensibly, Stefi has lost interest and is trying to stand on her head on the couch, perhaps to show off her pretty pink knickers. About every ten seconds she says, 'Has anybody made a goal? Has anybody made a goal?' Which only gets Michele the more furious.

For still Italy haven't scored. With five minutes to go the commentator has started talking about the team as *them* rather than *us*. This is ominous, indeed. And now he uses the word *Caporetto*! Yes, there it is. Defeat, disaster. Shame. Beaten by the Africans, the immigrants. These exact words are not said, of course, but the sense of imminent humiliation throbs with racism. Nonno and Nonna are silent, staring. The whole of Italy is silent.

Until *GOL! GOL!* Baggio's scored. No, *we* have scored.

Our boys have scored. The *azzurri* have scored. *Bravissimi azzurri*. The TV explodes. The room explodes. The world outside explodes. Half the team cross themselves. And Stefi too, upside down on the couch (is this sacrilegious?). And later, when Italy win the game with a dubious penalty in off the post, it will be horns honking late into the night and fireworks and people getting killed driving their cars too fast or trying to get ten people on a Vespa . . .

In bed, before her goodnight kiss, Stefi says, 'You promised.'

'Promised what?'

'Yes, you did promise,' Michele tells me more seriously. He's radiant, of course. Italy won. But Stefi is averting her face. Then I remember. Tomorrow, June 24th, is San Giovanni Battista, not quite the summer solstice but nearly, and Zia Paola has explained to the children that there's a tradition that on this, the shortest night of the year, one gets up before the dawn to go down to the beach to see the sun rise over the Adriatic. And though it must be *controindicato*, for the air is so humid, some people actually take a swim as well. So Paola told them. Apparently, in some state of semiconsciousness, I have promised.

'Well, if you had gone to bed in decent time . . .'

Can't you just hear your own father's voice sometimes, when you start explaining why a promised treat is impossible? That tone of inexorable reason.

'It's so late now, it's past midnight . . .'

'Per favore, Papà!'

'No!'

Nonno, standing at the door, says, 'I'll take them. I never sleep much.'

Then you feel jealous that someone else is going to give

your children such an experience, and you cave in. 'Okay . . .'

'O Papà!'

The arms now reach up to grab me round the neck. The red lips are going to kiss me on the mouth. I shall have to tell her to be a little less obvious about this kind of behaviour. Two weeks at the beach may have been too much.

Aurora

So here's a real honest to goodness *sacrificio*, a project worthy of my mother's kind of holiday . . . To see the sun rise over the Adriatic in midsummer, you have to get up at about four o'clock. On this particular night that means less than four hours' sleep. If only it was sleep . . . For even when the honking has died down, and the occasional firecracker, and the shouts of youths on Luigi Cadorna, even then the hot night is full of cats moaning and howling and generally giving the impression that love is some sort of infernal punishment. Not a new idea. Nonna's *nonna* apparently used to say that the way to discourage lovemaking cats was to pour a bucket of water over them, and this I once managed to do, back in Verona. It worked well enough, too; only afterwards I felt somewhat mean. So tonight I just get out of bed and walk barefoot into the savannah to shoo them off, remembering again, as I do so, the lovingly anchored catamaran and Michele and Stefi calling help. Coming back into the house, there is a huge frog sitting in moonlight on the doormat. He looks as though he's waiting for something. As if he might turn into Roberto Baggio or something. Roberto bloody Baggio. *Principe azzurro.* I will never be Italian. I will never in my heart of hearts be able to support the Italian national football team. My boy idolises the sullen bugger. Good for him.

And now there's a mosquito in the room. The whine of warm, warm nights. The stickiness of the sheets. But the sheets are your only defence. Then the rumble of a train in the distance, the clonking of the prostatic cripple upstairs crutch-bound for the bathroom, and always, in between, the treble whirr of the crickets, insistent, an acoustic pressure so constant you're not aware of it until for the miracle of a few seconds it stops. Then starts again. I have no difficulty, as it turns out, being up and about before the dawn . . .

My father-in-law has a lovely way of announcing himself when he thinks he's waking you, or surprising you. He appears at a window and says, 'Whey! Whey, Tim! Whey, *ragazzi*!' where 'whey' is as much a whistle as a word, somehow both soothing and urgent. He's got his trilby on to protect his baldness and a light jacket. In his Old Dog shorts he flaunts an air of down-market safari.

Kids in their clothes then and off. They're dead, of course. They barely know what's happening. Outside, the savannah is flopping with frogs. I would never have imagined. Never seen one during the day. Nonno remarks that he made this trip several times when he was a kid. And he took Rita and the boys, too. People used to light bonfires then, up on the hill. Before there were any houses there. Before there were any bathing stations. Though he doesn't know why. He can't imagine what any of it's got to do with Giovanni Battista. So often it's difficult to know whether a celebration was instituted for a saint, or merely became associated with his day. In any event, the important thing is that even after the motive has been forgotten, the celebration goes on.

We walk down Luigi Cadorna, taking advantage of the white circles not to fall into the potholes. There's a puddle round the crazy woman's Seicento. Nonno is concerned that the buckets of water she tosses will cause mould on the stucco. Enjoying a few hours of relative cool, the husky dog sees fit to bark at us. Which finally wakes the children up.

'*Porco Giuda!*' Michele says, rubbing his eyes.

Enough, I tell him severely. Really, that's enough. Say that again and I'll, I'll . . . I can't think of anything.

'You're just jealous because Italia won,' he tells me smugly. He always says Italia even when he's speaking English.

I can already see myself refusing all future requests for loans.

Stefi then asks who Giovanni Battista was. He was the one, Michele announces, who said Jesus was God, only he wasn't really. He wasn't God.

Stefi, despite being glad to skip the *ora di religione*, protests that he was. Still relatively fresh from the *scuola materna*, and stories of Christ's tears collected in phials and crucifixes that protect you from evil, Stefi is a determined believer. They begin a fierce, was–wasn't argument relative to the deity of Christ.

'He was not God. How could a man be God?'

At ten past four in the morning!

I interrupt to remark that Giovanni Battista had his head cut off.

'Betrayed by a dancing woman,' Nonno says, shaking an Old Dog head.

But the children lose interest now when a car roars down the seafront road flying a great tricolour from the window.

'*Alè! Evviva!*' Michele shouts. There's the echo of another *Alè!* '*Grande Italia!*' Michele shouts.

'*Santa patata, Miccko,*' I protest, 'they only beat Nigeria two–one after extra time.'

'*Capperi!*' Nonno says, 'What we need now is a cappuccino and a brioche.'

Capperi (capers) is a word I shall have to get used to using, a nice harmless expletive you can pull out in front of the children, but not as silly as *Santa patata*.

'*Avanti popolo,*' Stefi says when we get to the beach. '*Alla riscossa!*' To arms! As if this were D-Day or something and us approaching from the sea.

We walk down through the Delfino Verde. It's a bit nearer than the Medusa. Four-twenty a.m. Away from the street lights you realise the night is hardly dark at all: there's a soft glow amongst the folded deck chairs, drooping sunshades; the sand is faintly luminous and uncannily cold when it sifts into your sandals. The children feel the awe of a familiar place at an unfamiliar time, they learn that the beach isn't always *la stessa spiaggia*, or not at dawn; as sometimes there is ice on the hot road, fog on the sunny coast, a reverse side to everything. There'll come the day when Roberto Baggio doesn't score at the last minute, when whoever it is stops writing graffiti about Amalia.

Then we almost run into two people in their sleeping bags. The blonde, blonde hair of northerners. I shush the kids. Nonno remarks that he has more respect for these travellers than for his own boys, always off on luxury holidays at their father's expense. Or back to Mamma to be served hand and foot. But I know he loves it when the boys come home.

Here we are then at the sea's edge. The water isn't even lapping. There's just a steady sheen in the growing light and beyond that the etched black of the rocks. Out at sea, the flash of a beacon makes time intermittent, slows it down, stretches it out. On, off. On, off. There isn't a breath of wind. I hope we didn't come too early.

We stand and wait. Far from being the packed scene of Nonno's childhood, there is almost no one on the beach and certainly no bonfires up on the hills. About a hundred yards down from us a family of five have opened the deck chairs in the first row of sunshades and arranged themselves to face the horizon. Further down still, a group of adolescents are sitting in a circle. Probably they never went to bed. They're quiet, talking in whispers. For a moment I'm reminded of those situations where you arrive at a remote bus stop and can't decide from the size of the queue whether the bus is due any minute or not for another hour or so. Perhaps the people are not even waiting for your bus at all. Perhaps the adolescents don't know this is the day you watch the sun rise. They finish all their nights sitting in a circle on the beach. Then there's a clatter from behind us, and it's the woman who runs the Delfino Verde raising the shutter to her bar. Amazingly, the bar is going to open. With relief I reflect that you can rely on a shopkeeper to know when things are going to happen.

Michele has stripped to his bathing costume and is dancing by the water's edge. That never ending dilemma.

Do you deter kids, or let them do as vitality prompts? Do they have to be strictly civilised or are they innately more civilised than us? Understand how the grain of a people curls around this knotty question and you have their culture in one. Am I getting more and more indecisive because I am falling between the stools of two cultures? I'm not English any more, but I still can't worship Baggio . . . Or is it just age?

'Wait till you've seen the sun rise,' I tell him. 'That's what we're here for. Then you can go in for just a minute. But no cold shower.'

'Where's Nonno gone?' Stefi enquires.

Indeed, where has Nonno gone? I swivel round. No sign. Has the sea taken him? Its very stillness gives the water a mysterious feel. But Nonno, as I've said before, is famous for his unannounced arrivals and departures.

Then, in just a few minutes, the dawn. The sky suddenly brightens and lifts itself from the sea. Lines sharpen. Not least the horizon. Colours are found. The prosaic floods in like a tide. Already, I want to slow it down: sand beige, sunshades green-and-yellow, the red *moscone* pulled up on the shore. Same old beach. Without reaching out a single rosy finger to warn us, the sun rims the distance between two breakwaters.

The children are agog at the size of it. It's huge. And the colour. Not unlike that of my eyes right now. '*Il sole*,' Stefi breathes, 'red as a *peperone*!' She gazes. She likes to be mesmerised, likes a moment to be what it should be, as if her determined awe could create a magic in the sun, the way candles in churches make a god, and theatrical embraces a mother-in-law. Further along the beach the adolescents cheer. There is even the sound of an *Ale, ale!*, as if the great red ball now half clear of the water had been kicked there with terrible precision by you know who. Then, more miraculously still, Nonno reappears with a bag full of croissants. '*Bello*,' he says with his mouth full.

Following the example of other spectators, the children rush into the water. For a few moments they bathe in a dazzle of red as the sun rolls a regal carpet across the water. Their bodies shine in the horizontal rays. They have that wonderful enamel you can only mix with young skin and water and bright light. Then already the sun's too bright to look at, and hence in a curious way not there any more, dissolved in an everyday glare that kindles traffic noises along the seafront road and finds an overnight litter of cans and wrappers that the *bagnino* will have to clear. Immediately, the children lose interest and rush out shivering for their croissants. Michele rudely demands to know which is the biggest. Then it's up the beach to the bar for the ceremony of the cappuccino, the more familiar rituals of Italian life.

'Maybe Lucia will be born when we get home,' Michele says. And Stefi immediately replies, 'I can't wait to kiss her.'

'Madness,' Nonno says, thinking of the mouths that have to be fed, the bodies clothed, the coddling and spoiling and pampering, and then again the debts paid, the apartments bought, the enquiries about the will.

'No better place to grow up than Italy,' I tease him.

Spooning foam into his mouth like a big baby, the crumbs of a second brioche on his lips, my father-in-law is quick to correct me: 'No better place,' he says, 'not to grow up!'

[illegible]

[illegible] room into the mouth [illegible]

[illegible] place [illegible] grow up [illegible]